BLACK RECONSTRUCTION
IN AMERICA

BLACK
RECONSTRUCTION
IN AMERICA

W. E. B. Du Bois

WITH AN INTRODUCTION BY
DAVID LEVERING LEWIS

ATHENEUM
New York   1992

MAXWELL MACMILLAN CANADA
Toronto

MAXWELL MACMILLAN INTERNATIONAL
New York   Oxford   Singapore   Sydney

Ad Virginiam Vitae Salvatorem

Atheneum
Macmillan Publishing Company
866 Third Avenue
New York, NY 10022

Maxwell Macmillan Canada, Inc.
1200 Eglinton Avenue East
Suite 200
Don Mills, Ontario M3C 3N1

Macmillan Publishing Company is part of the Maxwell Communication
Group of Companies.

Library of Congress Cataloging-in-Publication Data
DuBois, W. E. B. (William Edward Burghardt), 1868–1963.
    [Black reconstruction]
    Black reconstruction in America / W. E. B. Du Bois: with an
introduction by David Levering Lewis.
        p.   cm.
    Originally published under title: Black reconstruction. New York:
Harcourt, Brace, c1935.
    Includes bibliographical references and index.
    ISBN 0-689-70820-3
    1. Reconstruction.   2. Afro-Americans—History—1863–1877.
3. Afro-Americans—Politics and government.   4. Afro—Americans—
Employment—History—19th century.   I. Lewis, David L.   II. Title.
973'.0496073—dc20   91–42251   CIP

10 9 8 7 6 5 4 3 2

Printed in the United States of America

CONTENTS

INTRODUCTION

Three weeks before the 1909 annual American Historical Association meeting, William Edward Burghardt Du Bois, then a professor at Atlanta University, informed Harvard historian Albert Bushnell Hart that he could not "afford the expense of coming north" to present his paper that December. "I will have to give it up," he regretted. Hart had been Du Bois' dissertation advisor. Holding the then distinctly minority view that Reconstruction had not been an unqualified mistake, the Harvard professor immediately arranged his former student's travel to New York City. On the morning of December 30th, before an audience that included Columbia's William Archibald Dunning, founder of the regnant school of Reconstruction historiography, Du Bois presented "Reconstruction and Its Benefits," the germinal essay for what would ultimately become *Black Reconstruction*, his massive, revisionist 1935 masterpiece. To argue, as the forty-one-year-old Atlanta professor did, that the Reconstruction experiment had given to the defeated South democratic government, free public schools, and progressive social legislation was unprecedented. Du Bois readily conceded that many African-American leaders had been inefficient and corrupt after the Civil War. "Granted then that the Negroes were to some extent venal but to a much larger extent ignorant and deceived," he insisted that the real issue was whether or not the newly emancipated showed "any signs of a disposition to learn better things?" It was the failure of the federal government to create and sustain an effective Freedmen's Bureau that had perpetuated slavery under different forms and locked the South into feudalsim, he concluded—the refusal to "establish for ten, twenty, or forty years with careful distribution of land and capital and a system of education for the children."

Although Hart informed his former student immediately after the AHA presentation that Dunning himself "had spoken . . . of the paper in high terms," "Reconstruction and Its Benefits," despite publication in the July 1910 volume of *The American Historical Review*, had no significant impact upon mainstream Reconstruction scholarship. According to northern, white journalist James S. Pike's lurid, firsthand account of the period in South Carolina, *The Prostrate State* (1878), there had been no benefits from Reconstruction. Beginning with Woodrow Wilson's sermonizing *Division and Reunion, 1829–1889*, published in 1893, and James Ford Rhodes' influential, seven-volume *History of the United States from the Compromise of 1850*, completed in 1906, white historians and political scientists documented, denounced, and derided African-American ignorance,

vii

venality, and exploitation under Reconstruction. The drumbeat of Dunningite dissertations from Columbia rolled on steadily for two decades, beginning with James W. Garner's *Reconstruction in Mississippi* (1901), Walter L. Fleming's rabid *Civil War and Reconstruction in Alabama* (1905), and Thomas S. Staples' moderately bigotted *Reconstruction in Arkansas, 1862–1874* (1923). Not to be outdone, ex-Confederate John W. Burgess of Columbia's political science department struck one of the loudest notes in midcacophony with *Reconstruction and the Constitution* in 1911. Even after the Dunningite school began to recede before the kinder and gentler revisionism inaugurated by historians Francis Butler Simkins and Robert Hilliard Woody (*South Carolina during Reconstruction*, 1932) and the impressively balanced Vernon Lane Wharton (*The Negro in Mississippi*, 1947), the 1929 potboiler by journalist-diplomat Claude Bowers, *The Tragic Era: The Revolution After Lincoln*, congealed racist interpretations of Reconstruction in the popular mind as solidly as had D. W. Griffith's film, *The Birth of a Nation*, fourteen years earlier.

African-American scholars were not silent, only unheard or dismissed by the white academy. In 1913, Du Bois' Crisis Publishing Company printed a useful memoir about Texas politician Norris Wright Cuney by his daughter, Maud Cuney Hare. In that same year, the African-American former speaker of the Mississippi House of Representatives and U.S. Congressman, John R. Lynch, published *Facts of Reconstruction*, a memoir taken seriously by no more than a handful of scholars (principally those subscribing to Carter G. Woodson's new *Journal of Negro History*). In the March 1913 edition of *The Crisis*, Du Bois exposed historian Ulrich B. Phillips' fallacious conclusions about declining per capita output of African-American cotton growers after the Civil War. Returning to the charge eleven years later in "The Reconstruction of Freedom," a large and vigorously argued chapter in his *The Gift of Black Folk*, he propounded the heterodoxies that slavery "was the cause" of the Civil War, that African-American motives for helping to win the war had been "primarily economic," and that enfranchisement of the slaves was the "greatest and most important step toward world democracy of all men of all races ever taken in the modern world." [pp. 186, 217] Mainstream historians had deplored universal manhood suffrage in the South as the greatest folly. "No language has been spared to describe the results of Negro suffrage as the worst imaginable," Du Bois charged in this essay, which anticipated the main arguments he would develop in *Black Reconstruction*. Historian Herbert Aptheker reminds us that the year following this essay, Du Bois' second Harvard history professor, Edward Channing, assailed African-Americans in the latest volume of his *History of the United States*. "In his pure condition undiluted by white or yellow blood, the Negro is essentially a communist and a fatalist," this Back Bay aristocrat declared. Against such headwinds, Alreutheus A. Taylor published two careful monographs on Reconstruction in South Carolina and Virginia in 1924 and 1926, respectively, while David G. Houston, A. E. Perkins, and Mason J. Brewer, among a handful of other African-American scholars, gamely attempted throughout the late 20s and early 30s to redress the historiographical imbalance.

Speaking for the Talented Tenth (the African-American men and women who had rallied to Du Bois in his leadership contest with Booker T. Washington), Anna J. Cooper, principal of the District of Columbia's elite M Street High School, implored Du Bois to answer the Dunnings and Bowers—"adequately, fully, ably, finally & again it seems to me Thou art the Man!" That was precisely what he had already undertaken definitively that year, 1929, in his *Encyclopaedia Britannica* entry, "The Negro in the United States." In the final exchange of letters with its editor, he refused to allow *Britannica* to publish his article unless the following two sentences were included" "White historians have ascribed the faults and failures of Reconstruction to Negro ignorance and corruption. But the Negro insists that it was Negro loyalty and the Negro vote alone that restored the South to the Union; established the new Democracy, both for white and black, and instituted the public schools." Editor F. H. Hooper regretted that he could not "pass the article with this new paragraph" and, therefore, was compelled to reject it. Although incensed, Du Bois could hardly have been astonished. Only two years had elapsed since the first volume of Charles and Mary Beard's epic *Rise of American Civilization*. Like Frederick Jackson Turner, they and other Progressive historians dismissed the African-American as a factor in the sectional conflict. The Beards saw the cause of the Civil War in the machinations of northern capital to destroy the South's veto power over national economic policy.

Goaded by the Bowers volume, *Britannica* censorship, the economic determinism of the Beards, and cheered on by Cooper, James Weldon Johnson, and others, Du Bois embarked on the research and writing of his Reconstruction history, securing a five thousand-dollar grant from the Rosenwald Fund in February 1931 and a supplementary grant from the Carnegie Corporation of one thousand dollars at the beginning of 1934 and another two hundred and fifty dollars in November. A contract with a five hundred-dollar advance had been negotiated with the publishing firm of Harcourt, Brace & Company soon after the Rosenwald grant. By the time the final pages of *Black Reconstruction in America* (the Harcourt, Brace editor's accepted modification of "Black Reconstruction of Democracy in America,") were being written, Du Bois had noisily broken his fourteen-year tie to the NAACP and accepted a professorship in sociology at the recently reorganized Atlanta University. Although his considerable research and writing activities in connection with the ambitious *Encyclopedia of the Negro* project competed with the monograph, Du Bois' Atlanta University professorship allowed for greater flexibility than had his editorial and organizational duties at the NAACP. A publisher's advance and two foundation stipends should have permitted him to make use of unpublished archival records at universities, state repositories, and court houses throughout the South. The Atlanta University professor chose instead to confine himself to government reports, proceedings of state constitutional conventions, unpublished dissertations, and virtually every relevant published monograph. His surprising decision to make only occasional use of newspapers for the period must have been dictated by a determination to complete the manuscript within the projected timeframe.

That Du Bois did not work the archives would constitute one of the gravest criticisms by professional historians of *Black Reconstruction*. Not only was such a charge of little concern to him, for whom the rationale of the book was preeminently one of aggressive reinterpretation rather than original research, but critics have generally chosen to ignore an insuperable research handicap confronting the author. As the experiences of John Hope Franklin, Margaret Rowley, and Helen Edmunds, among many professional African-American historians of the South, attest, before the Civil Rights Era it was rarely possible for them to gain access to such records. When they did, the circumstances were unique and the conditions of access segregated and usually deplorable. It is hard to imagine Du Bois motoring from "white" court house to campus entreating entry of redfaced custodians or even, should he have been admitted, agreeing to remain out of sight in small, windowless back rooms poring over records. On his lunch break, moreover, there would have been no available canteen or even water fountain. One of the goals of *Black Reconstruction* was surely to open up the world of scholarship to that "opportunity for real and new democracy" that had once existed in the immediate aftermath of the Civil War.

The book had grown to enormous size with the first draft in early May 1933, and editor Charles Pearce at Harcourt, Brace was understandably concerned about the author's ambitious revisions, Du Bois having informed him after the second draft in July that *Black Reconstruction* was "not yet a piece of literature. It still resembled, as I am sure you sensed, from the first chapter, a Ph.D. thesis. . . ." [B1Recn-13] As galleys were rushed back and forth between Atlanta and New York in late March 1934, followed by streams of amended page proofs that September, the fall 1934 publication date fell casualty to the eleventh-hour commentaries of young historians at Atlanta and Howard universities assigned by Du Bois to read and research portions of the manuscript. Revision costs mounted to the point that the publisher finally protested a seven hundred-dollar overrun of the contract. Fortunately, the Carnegie subventions defrayed them, while the author rewrote and corrected. "My method of writing is a method of 'after-thoughts,'" he explained to the politely distressed Alfred Harcourt. Still cleaning up last-minute permissions for quotations, Du Bois mailed the final batch of proofs on April 22, 1935.

A certain lore surrounds the book. Because it was ignored by the *American Historical Review* and widely disparaged by mainstream historians during the Cold War Era, the impression persists that *Black Reconstruction* received scant notice at the time or, to the extent that it did, was dismissed as serious scholarship. Although sales were modest (1,984 copies sold by 1938 out of a total first printing of 2,150) and book clubs were uninterested (Bowers' *Tragic Era* had been a Literary Guild selection), the critical reaction to *Black Reconstruction* was exceptional. On the June 13th publication date, a Thursday, *The New York Times, Herald Tribune*, and *World-Telegram* carried lengthy reviews. In the *Tribune*, Lewis Gannett was mesmerized, professing to be unaware of "anything finer [that] has been written in English in recent years." When a scholar like Henry Steele Commager could justify the Black Codes enacted by white southerners immediately after the Civil War, Gannett welcomed Du Bois' "impassioned attack upon slave-minded historians." Rehabilitation of the two *bêtes noires* of Reconstruction critics, Representative Thaddeus Stevens of Pennsylvania and Senator Charles Sumner of Massachusetts, especially gratified Gannett. The daily book reviewer for the *Times*, John Chamberlain, noted that *Black Reconstruction* had "stirred up a rumpus." Chamberlain conceded that Du Bois may not have rebutted the contention of Progressive historians that slavery and abolition were not moral issues but subordinate factors in "a life-and-death struggle between the Northern industrialists and Southern planters." Nevertheless, the *Times'* reviewer judged that the book achieved its purpose in presenting a "stirring, bitterly eloquent brief for the part the American Negro played in the effort to create an egalitarian democracy of black and white alike in the post–Civil War South."

Yale historian William MacDonald was both captivated and critical in the Sunday edition of the *Times*, on June 16. While he, too, had reservations about Du Bois' acerbic criticism of the Beards, wondered why a scholar subventioned by the Rosenwald Fund and the Carnegie Corporation had not made fuller use of primary sources, including twelve of the most important collections in the field, and was dubious about interpretations "shot through with Marxian economics," MacDonald believed that Du Bois was "absolutely justified in his rancorous onslaught on American historians of the Civil War period." He found the global context of proletarian exploitation in which Du Bois situated the emancipatory struggle of African-Americans to be as magnificently depicted as it was suspect. But MacDonald saw the book's "calmer" sections on the Reconstruction governments as substantial refutations of scandalous white historiography. Furthermore, the reviewer could see no validity to the charges he had heard that Du Bois "sometimes errs in the direction of 'black chauvinism.'" MacDonald's summation was both austere and generous:

> One puts down this extraordinary book with mixed feelings. Of the Negroes' part in reconstruction it is beyond question the most painstaking and thorough study ever made. There is no need to accept the author's views about racial equality in order to recognize the imposing contribution which he has made to a critical period in American history, nor need one be a Marxian to perceive that, in treating the Negro experience as a part of the American labor movement in general, he has given that movement an orientation very different from what it has commonly had. Yet there runs through the book a note of challenge which seems to point, in the author's mind at least, to the imminence of an inescapable and deadly racial struggle.

On the previous day, the New York *Post* had printed the hypercritcal review of a white southerner who was both knowledgeable of Du Bois' subject and conflicted about it. "At a thousand points it arouses difficult and complicated questions," Herschel Brickell confessed. He considered the main thesis of *Black Reconstruction* "extremely farfetched," but in conceding that it aroused "a desire to discuss the Civil War and its postlude that could require many columns to satisfy," Brickell unwittingly paid the author a high compliment. In the Nashville *Tennesseean* of the same date, June 16, the review by John R. Selby (syndicated to several major southern newspapers) alerted the region to a bombshell: "There is a feeling of ripeness in the writing as well, and an occasional passage of almost Old Testament grandeur. 'Provocative' is a mild adjective for *Black Reconstruction*" Selby warned. The Sunday *Herald Tribune* reviewer, Henry Raymond Mussey, a northern white history professor at Wellesley College, fully agreed with Selby—"This is a book of controversy." Yet it was "a solid history of the Reconstruction period," even if Mussey thought Du Bois' passionate advocacy was as unenlightened as that of the Negrophobic historians. *Time Magazine*, June 23, printed Du Bois' photograph and vital statistics below the caption "Ax-Grinder," giving the impression more of a Post Office wanted bulletin than a review. The magazine's warning to readers was certainly accurate that most would think they were "in an historical wonderland in which all familiar scenes and landmarks have been changed or swept away."

The southern white historian whose recent scholarship had a signficantly moderating influence upon Reconstruction studies also made a point of emphasizing the book's extreme partisanship. "All the truth is not on one side," said Duke University professor Robert Hilliard Woody in the January 1936 number of the *North Carolina Historical Review*. Given the ideological and professional stakes involved, Woody's admission that, although the book's economic paradigms were highly questionable, its facts were "fairly well buttressed" was remarkable. The South's leading sociologist, Howard Odom, another North Carolinian, ventured similar equivocal judgments in his *Journal of Social Forces*, commending Du Bois' historical insights and moral judgments but sighing that "it was asking too much to expect a single generation to change the powerful folkways of the century." That was also pretty much the resigned view of University of North Carolina history professor Benjamin B. Kendrick in the January *Southern Review*. Kendrick, who had known the white historians arraigned by Du Bois—Dunning, Fleming, Phillips, G. D. R. Hamilton—clubbily denied that they had been as anti-Negro as the author charged. Furthermore, it had not been Du Bois' "black proletariat" that had caused the southern social and political upheaval after the Civil War, Kendrick countered, but rather "the principals in the affair were the capitalists; and their henchmen, the politicans. . . ."

The North Carolina professor closed his lengthy critique with one of the most intelligent observations of the day. In contrast to the many reviews similar to that of University of Chicago historian Avery Craven's in *The American Journal of Sociology*, which sneered that *Black Reconstruction*'s "temper is as bad as the sources" (with an after-thought about Du Bois making "a real contribution by placing this struggle in the larger drive for democracy"), Kendrick understood that the "debate between us cannot be decided by an 'appeal to the sources'. We can both find support there for our respective contentions." Since Pike and Wilson, the story of Reconstruction as told by most white scholars had promoted reunion of white North and white South at the expense of the civil rights and economic opportunity of black people. Du Bois intended *Black Reconstruction* as a *tour de force* of legitimate propaganda for his people, making the point in Carlylean prose early in the first chapter: "It was thus the black worker, as founding stone of a new economic system in the nineteenth century and for the modern world, who brought civil war in America. He was its underlying cause, in spite of every effort to base the strife upon union and national power." Kendrick realized that even if Du Bois had stood hat in hand until the white South eventually made its sources available, the issue would still have been less one of historiography than of ideology, of sources in the service of a social order.

And so it went. The Progressive newspaper magnate, Oswald Garrison Villard, one of the founders of the NAACP, stifled his chronic aversion to Du Bois in a major *Saturday Review* panegyric. African-American historian Rayford Logan, one of Du Bois' protégés, was equally enthusiastic in the *Christian Register*, lamenting America's lost "golden opportunity to found a political and industrial democracy" during Reconstruction. The *Nation's* reviewer (July 24, 1935) was unimpressed and patronizing of "an old man" who had "turned to reading Marx" and, according to labor economist Sterling D. Spero, had produced a book coupling race consciousness to the class struggle, thereby adding "more confusion than light to the understanding of one of the crucial epochs of American history." For Marxists of the day, who had not forgiven Du Bois' espousal in *The Crisis* of an African-American cooperative movement separate from the national economy and mainstream labor ("A Negro Nation Within the Nation"), *Black Reconstruction* was viewed as a dangerous primer for black nationalism. Combining Sorel and Marx with what the more respectful but more critical reviewer in *Living Age* (September 1935) characterized as a "belief that ultimate Negro salvation, both economic and political, may be found only through a more or less complete 'segregation' from all contacts with the white peoples," the book was alleged to promote racial mysticisim. Harold Ward charged that Du Bois was wrongheaded to convert newly freed agrarian laborers into a conscious mass struggling to bring about a socialist economic order in the South.

First had come the General Strike of the slaves to force the collapse of the Confederacy, Du Bois contended. "It was a strike on a wide basis against the conditions of work. It was a general strike," he explained, "that involved directly in the end perhaps a half million people. They wanted to stop the economy of the plantation system, and to do that they left the plantations." In this planned upheaval, however, the book made racial solidarity both the agency of progress and its nemesis. Because southern white labor had succumbed to the racially divisive politics of the planter oligarchy, its common economic interests with the black proletariat had been severed and the establishment of democracy in the region had failed. The *Living Age* commentary gently reproved the distinguished Atlanta professor for failing to comprehend that the class struggle—interracial above all—was the primary force for social change, not racial solidarity. Du Bois had been "too ready to assume" concluded Ward, "that white workers were somehow consistently hostile to Negroes, as workers" in the South.

Criticisms similar to those of the *Nation* and *Living Age* were repeated in various degrees by young African-American scholars who reviewed *Black Reconstruction*: economist Abram Harris in *New Republic* (August 7, 1935); attorney Loren Miller in *New Masses* (October 29, 1935); political scientist Ralph Bunche in the *Journal of Negro Education*, who doubted the author's grasp of Marx but condescendingly observed that Du Bois seemed capable of grasping "the full significance of the struggle of the American Negro laboring mass . . ."); and even historian Charles H. Wesley in the National Urban League's journal, *Opportunity* (August 1935). If Wesley's review betrayed a young man's relish at faulting an icon, it nevertheless, made a number of reasoned objections, to Du Bois' sweeping generalizations, caricaturing of complexities, and tendency to soar into poetry when the facts were dubious. And the book simply had too many quotations *in extenso*, he thought. The premier African-American sociologist of the day, Charles S. Johnson, was also critically careful in his *Survey Graphic* appreciation of *Black Reconstruction* (January 1936). Dubious of what he saw as Marxist reductionism and alert to its narrative license, Johnson managed to engage the mind of the book masterfully: "The major thesis of this book is that the result of the Civil War was an enfranchisement of labor, black and white, but the entrenched bigotries of the 'landed oligarchy' and the ignorant racial prejudices of white labor so weakened the strength of labor as to render it helpless before the forces of industrialism and capitalism."

Pro or con, students of American history were in large agreement that the debate over Reconstruction had been irreversibly transformed. As Buell Gallagher, the white educator and future president of the City College of New York, wrote in *The Collegian*, "no college man can call himself literate on questions of race in America or in American history, until he has read this pioneering study." For all its factual errors and interpretive hyperbole, *Black Reconstruction* was, as its author had predicted to the president of the Carnegie Corporation in late 1934, a work that "can never be ignored." Du Bois scholar Aptheker has found after careful textual examination that the mistaken details are less egregious than hearsay in the profession has led many to suppose. The conceptual flaws are more troubling. The *New Republic* reviewer, who claimed never to have read a "more completely fantastic attempt at applying Marxian dogma to history," spoke for scholars who have continued to find Du Bois' General Strike concept fallacious. Similarly, the splendid chapters on what Du Bois characterized as proletarian dictatorships, valiantly laboring to bring democratic socialism to South Carolina, Mississippi, and Louisiana, are gainsaid by more recent research (Thomas Holt, William C. Harris, David C. Rankin, and Joel Williamson, *inter alia*) disclosing significant class, color, and political divisions among African-American southern leaders.

If these are more than professional quibbles, the influence of *Black Reconstruction*, often unacknowledged, has, nevertheless, been transformative and enduring in the historiography of Reconstruction. Howard K. Beale's 1940, turning-point essay in the *American Historical Review*, "On Rewriting Reconstruction History," was, as Beale himself advised Du Bois, influenced by *Black Reconstruction*, an indebtedness also acknowledged by C. Vann Woodward in an April 3, 1938 letter to Du Bois. The young Woodward had followed the author's work "with interest and profit for a number of years" and stressed his "indebtedness for the insight which your admirable book, *Black Reconstruction*, provided me." When the eighty-five-year-old Du Bois came as a political pariah to Berkeley in spring of 1953 (the regent's infamous Rule 17 barred him from speaking on campus), he was informed by students who came to hear him in a nearby Unitarian church that *Black Reconstruction* was alive and well in their history department. Little more than a decade would pass before Berkeley's Kenneth Stampp published his revisionist *The Era of Reconstruction, 1865–1877* (1965). Four years earlier, John Hope Franklin, then head of the Brooklyn College history department, had offered *Reconstruction after the Civil War* (1961), the first major revisionist study of the period by an African-American since Du Bois.

In the magnificent final chapter of his book, "The Propaganda of History," Du Bois *had* unfurled the manifesto opening the conflict with the Dunningites and their sympathizers:

> I write then in a field devastated by passion and belief. Naturally, as a Negro, I cannot do this writing without believing in the essential humanity of Negroes, in their ability to be educated, to do the work of the modern world. . . .
>
> This chapter, therefore, which in logic should be a survey of books and sources, becomes of sheer necessity an arraignment of American historians and an indictment of their ideals. With a determination unparalleled in science, the mass of American writers have started out so to distort the facts of the greatest critical period of American history as to prove right wrong and wrong right. . . . It simply shows that with sufficient general agreement and determination among the dominant classes, the truth of history may be utterly distorted and contradicted and changed to any convenient fairy tale that the masters of men wish.

When Atheneum reissued *Black Reconstruction* as a paperback in 1969, six years after its author's death in Ghana, the war against racist

Reconstruction historiography had been won. The book had returned the African-American to the drama and, as Du Bois biographer Elliott Rudwick wrote before the appearance of Eric Foner's comprehensive *Reconstruction: America's Unfinished Revolution, 1863–1877* (1988), "it remains to this day the best summary of Negro participation in the governments of the Southern states during Reconstruction."

—DAVID LEVERING LEWIS
Rutgers University

TO THE READER

The story of transplanting millions of Africans to the new world, and of their bondage for four centuries, is a fascinating one. Particularly interesting for students of human culture is the sudden freeing of these black folk in the Nineteenth Century and the attempt, through them, to reconstruct the basis of American democracy from 1860-1880.

This book seeks to tell and interpret these twenty years of fateful history with especial reference to the efforts and experiences of the Negroes themselves.

For the opportunity of making this study, I have to thank the Trustees of the Rosenwald Fund, who made me a grant covering two years; the Directors of the National Association for the Advancement of Colored People, who allowed me time for the writing; the President of Atlanta University, who gave me help and asylum during the completion of the work; and the Trustees of the Carnegie Fund who contributed toward the finishing of the manuscript. I need hardly add that none of these persons are in any way responsible for the views herein expressed.

It would be only fair to the reader to say frankly in advance that the attitude of any person toward this story will be distinctly influenced by his theories of the Negro race. If he believes that the Negro in America and in general is an average and ordinary human being, who under given environment develops like other human beings, then he will read this story and judge it by the facts adduced. If, however, he regards the Negro as a distinctly inferior creation, who can never successfully take part in modern civilization and whose emancipation and enfranchisement were gestures against nature, then he will need something more than the sort of facts that I have set down. But this latter person, I am not trying to convince. I am simply pointing out these two points of view, so obvious to Americans, and then without further ado, I am assuming the truth of the first. In fine, I am going to tell this story as though Negroes were ordinary human beings, realizing that this attitude will from the first seriously curtail my audience.

W. E. BURGHARDT DU BOIS

Atlanta, December, 1934

BLACK RECONSTRUCTION
IN AMERICA

I. THE BLACK WORKER

How black men, coming to America in the sixteenth, seventeenth,
eighteenth and nineteenth centuries, became a central thread in
the history of the United States, at once a challenge to its democracy and always an important part of its economic history and
social development

Easily the most dramatic episode in American history was the sudden move to free four million black slaves in an effort to stop a great
civil war, to end forty years of bitter controversy, and to appease the
moral sense of civilization.

From the day of its birth, the anomaly of slavery plagued a nation
which asserted the equality of all men, and sought to derive powers
of government from the consent of the governed. Within sound of
the voices of those who said this lived more than half a million black
slaves, forming nearly one-fifth of the population of a new nation.

The black population at the time of the first census had risen to
three-quarters of a million, and there were over a million at the beginning of the nineteenth century. Before 1830, the blacks had passed the
two million mark, helped by the increased importations just before
1808, and the illicit smuggling up until 1820. By their own repro-
duction, the Negroes reached 3,638,808 in 1850, and before the Civil
War, stood at 4,441,830. They were 10% of the whole population of
the nation in 1700, 22% in 1750, 18.9% in 1800 and 11.6% in 1900.

These workers were not all black and not all Africans and not all
slaves. In 1860, at least 90% were born in the United States, 13% were
visibly of white as well as Negro descent and actually more than one-
fourth were probably of white, Indian and Negro blood. In 1860, 11%
of these dark folk were free workers.

In origin, the slaves represented everything African, although most
of them originated on or near the West Coast. Yet among them appeared the great Bantu tribes from Sierra Leone to South Africa; the
Sudanese, straight across the center of the continent, from the Atlantic
to the Valley of the Nile; the Nilotic Negroes and the black and
brown Hamites, allied with Egypt; the tribes of the great lakes; the
Pygmies and the Hottentots; and in addition to these, distinct traces
of both Berber and Arab blood. There is no doubt of the presence of
all these various elements in the mass of 10,000,000 or more Negroes

3

transported from Africa to the various Americas, from the fifteenth to the nineteenth centuries.

Most of them that came to the continent went through West Indian tutelage, and thus finally appeared in the United States. They brought with them their religion and rhythmic song, and some traces of their art and tribal customs. And after a lapse of two and one-half centuries, the Negroes became a settled working population, speaking English or French, professing Christianity, and used principally in agricultural toil. Moreover, they so mingled their blood with white and red America that today less than 25% of the Negro Americans are of unmixed African descent.

So long as slavery was a matter of race and color, it made the conscience of the nation uneasy and continually affronted its ideals. The men who wrote the Constitution sought by every evasion, and almost by subterfuge, to keep recognition of slavery out of the basic form of the new government. They founded their hopes on the prohibition of the slave trade, being sure that without continual additions from abroad, this tropical people would not long survive, and thus the problem of slavery would disappear in death. They miscalculated, or did not foresee the changing economic world. It might be more profitable in the West Indies to kill the slaves by overwork and import cheap Africans; but in America without a slave trade, it paid to conserve the slave and let him multiply. When, therefore, manifestly the Negroes were not dying out, there came quite naturally new excuses and explanations. It was a matter of social condition. Gradually these people would be free; but freedom could only come to the bulk as the freed were transplanted to their own land and country, since the living together of black and white in America was unthinkable. So again the nation waited, and its conscience sank to sleep.

But in a rich and eager land, wealth and work multiplied. They twisted new and intricate patterns around the earth. Slowly but mightily these black workers were integrated into modern industry. On free and fertile land Americans raised, not simply sugar as a cheap sweetening, rice for food and tobacco as a new and tickling luxury; but they began to grow a fiber that clothed the masses of a ragged world. Cotton grew so swiftly that the 9,000 bales of cotton which the new nation scarcely noticed in 1791 became 79,000 in 1800; and with this increase, walked economic revolution in a dozen different lines. The cotton crop reached one-half million bales in 1822, a million bales in 1831, two million in 1840, three million in 1852, and in the year of secession, stood at the then enormous total of five million bales.

Such facts and others, coupled with the increase of the slaves to which they were related as both cause and effect, meant a new world; and all the more so because with increase in American cotton and Negro slaves, came both by chance and ingenuity new miracles for manufacturing, and particularly for the spinning and weaving of cloth.

The giant forces of water and of steam were harnessed to do the world's work, and the black workers of America bent at the bottom of a growing pyramid of commerce and industry; and they not only could not be spared, if this new economic organization was to expand, but rather they became the cause of new political demands and alignments, of new dreams of power and visions of empire.

First of all, their work called for widening stretches of new, rich, black soil—in Florida, in Louisiana, in Mexico; even in Kansas. This land, added to cheap labor, and labor easily regulated and distributed, made profits so high that a whole system of culture arose in the South, with a new leisure and social philosophy. Black labor became the foundation stone not only of the Southern social structure, but of Northern manufacture and commerce, of the English factory system, of European commerce, of buying and selling on a world-wide scale; new cities were built on the results of black labor, and a new labor problem, involving all white labor, arose both in Europe and America.

Thus, the old difficulties and paradoxes appeared in new dress. It became easy to say and easier to prove that these black men were not men in the sense that white men were, and could never be, in the same sense, free. Their slavery was a matter of both race and social condition, but the condition was limited and determined by race. They were congenital wards and children, to be well-treated and cared for, but far happier and safer here than in their own land. As the Richmond, Virginia, *Examiner* put it in 1854:

"Let us not bother our brains about what *Providence* intends to do with our Negroes in the distant future, but glory in and profit to the utmost by what He has done for them in transplanting them here, and setting them to work on our plantations. . . . True philanthropy to the Negro, begins, like charity, at home; and if Southern men would act as if the canopy of heaven were inscribed with a covenant, in letters of fire, that *the Negro is here, and here forever; is our property, and ours forever;* . . . they would accomplish more good for the race in five years than they boast the institution itself to have accomplished in two centuries. . . ."

On the other hand, the growing exploitation of white labor in Europe, the rise of the factory system, the increased monopoly of land, and the problem of the distribution of political power, began to send wave after wave of immigrants to America, looking for new freedom, new opportunity and new democracy.

The opportunity for real and new democracy in America was broad. Political power at first was, as usual, confined to property holders and an aristocracy of birth and learning. But it was never securely based on land. Land was free and both land and property were possible to nearly every thrifty worker. Schools began early to multiply and open their doors even to the poor laborer. Birth began to count for less and less and America became to the world a land of economic opportunity. So the world came to America, even before the Revolution, and afterwards during the nineteenth century, nineteen million immigrants entered the United States.

When we compare these figures with the cotton crop and the increase of black workers, we see how the economic problem increased in intricacy. This intricacy is shown by the persons in the drama and their differing and opposing interests. There were the native-born Americans, largely of English descent, who were the property holders and employers; and even so far as they were poor, they looked forward to the time when they would accumulate capital and become, as they put it, economically "independent." Then there were the new immigrants, torn with a certain violence from their older social and economic surroundings; strangers in a new land, with visions of rising in the social and economic world by means of labor. They differed in language and social status, varying from the half-starved Irish peasant to the educated German and English artisan. There were the free Negroes: those of the North free in some cases for many generations, and voters; and in other cases, fugitives, new come from the South, with little skill and small knowledge of life and labor in their new environment. There were the free Negroes of the South, an unstable, harried class, living on sufferance of the law, and the good will of white patrons, and yet rising to be workers and sometimes owners of property and even of slaves, and cultured citizens. There was the great mass of poor whites, disinherited of their economic portion by competition with the slave system, and land monopoly.

In the earlier history of the South, free Negroes had the right to vote. Indeed, so far as the letter of the law was concerned, there was not a single Southern colony in which a black man who owned the requisite amount of property, and complied with other conditions, did not at some period have the legal right to vote.

Negroes voted in Virginia as late as 1723, when the assembly enacted that no free Negro, mulatto or Indian "shall hereafter have any vote at the elections of burgesses or any election whatsoever." In North Carolina, by the Act of 1734, a former discrimination against Negro voters was laid aside and not reënacted until 1835.

A complaint in South Carolina, in 1701, said:

"Several free Negroes were receiv'd, & taken for as good Electors as the best Freeholders in the Province. So that we leave it with Your Lordships to judge whether admitting Aliens, Strangers, Servants, Negroes, &c, as good and qualified Voters, can be thought any ways agreeable to King Charles' Patent to Your Lordships, or the English Constitution of Government." Again in 1716, Jews and Negroes, who had been voting, were expressly excluded. In Georgia, there was at first no color discrimination, although only owners of fifty acres of land could vote. In 1761, voting was expressly confined to white men.[1]

In the states carved out of the Southwest, they were disfranchised as soon as the state came into the Union, although in Kentucky they voted between 1792 and 1799, and Tennessee allowed free Negroes to vote in her constitution of 1796.

In North Carolina, where even disfranchisement, in 1835, did not apply to Negroes who already had the right to vote, it was said that the several hundred Negroes who had been voting before then usually voted prudently and judiciously.

In Delaware and Maryland they voted in the latter part of the eighteenth century. In Louisiana, Negroes who had had the right to vote during territorial status were not disfranchised.

To sum up, in colonial times, the free Negro was excluded from the suffrage only in Georgia, South Carolina and Virginia. In the Border States, Delaware disfranchised the Negro in 1792; Maryland in 1783 and 1810.

In the Southeast, Florida disfranchised Negroes in 1845; and in the Southwest, Louisiana disfranchised them in 1812; Mississippi in 1817; Alabama in 1819; Missouri, 1821; Arkansas in 1836; Texas, 1845. Georgia in her constitution of 1777 confined voters to white males; but this was omitted in the constitutions of 1789 and 1798.

As slavery grew to a system and the Cotton Kingdom began to expand into imperial white domination, a free Negro was a contradiction, a threat and a menace. As a thief and a vagabond, he threatened society; but as an educated property holder, a successful mechanic or even professional man, he more than threatened slavery. He contradicted and undermined it. He must not be. He must be suppressed, enslaved, colonized. And nothing so bad could be said about him that did not easily appear as true to slaveholders.

In the North, Negroes, for the most part, received political enfranchisement with the white laboring classes. In 1778, the Congress of the Confederation twice refused to insert the word "white" in the Articles of Confederation in asserting that free inhabitants in each state should be entitled to all the privileges and immunities of free citizens of the several states. In the law of 1783, free Negroes were recognized as a basis of taxation, and in 1784, they were recognized as voters in the territories. In the Northwest Ordinance of 1787, "free male inhabitants of full age" were recognized as voters.

The few Negroes that were in Maine, New Hampshire and Vermont could vote if they had the property qualifications. In Connecticut they were disfranchised in 1814; in 1865 this restriction was retained, and Negroes did not regain the right until after the Civil War. In New Jersey, they were disfranchised in 1807, but regained the right in 1820 and lost it again in 1847. Negroes voted in New York in the eighteenth century, then were disfranchised, but in 1821 were permitted to vote with a discriminatory property qualification of $250. No property qualification was required of whites. Attempts were made at various times to remove this qualification but it was not removed until 1870. In Rhode Island they were disfranchised in the constitution which followed Dorr's Rebellion, but finally allowed to vote in 1842. In Pennsylvania, they were allowed to vote until 1838 when the "reform" convention restricted the suffrage to whites.

The Western States as territories did not usually restrict the suffrage, but as they were admitted to the Union they disfranchised the Negroes: Ohio in 1803; Indiana in 1816; Illinois in 1818; Michigan in 1837; Iowa in 1846; Wisconsin in 1848; Minnesota in 1858; and Kansas in 1861.

The Northwest Ordinance and even the Louisiana Purchase had made no color discrimination in legal and political rights. But the states admitted from this territory, specifically and from the first, denied free black men the right to vote and passed codes of black laws in Ohio, Indiana and elsewhere, instigated largely by the attitude and fears of the immigrant poor whites from the South. Thus, at first, in Kansas and the West, the problem of the black worker was narrow and specific. Neither the North nor the West asked that black labor in the United States be free and enfranchised. On the contrary, they accepted slave labor as a fact; but they were determined that it should be territorially restricted, and should not compete with free white labor.

What was this industrial system for which the South fought and risked life, reputation and wealth and which a growing element in the North viewed first with hesitating tolerance, then with distaste and finally with economic fear and moral horror? What did it mean to be a slave? It is hard to imagine it today. We think of oppression beyond all conception: cruelty, degradation, whipping and starvation, the absolute negation of human rights; or on the contrary, we may think of the ordinary worker the world over today, slaving ten, twelve, or fourteen hours a day, with not enough to eat, compelled by his physical necessities to do this and not to do that, curtailed in his movements and his possibilities; and we say, here, too, is a slave called a "free worker," and slavery is merely a matter of name.

But there was in 1863 a real meaning to slavery different from that we may apply to the laborer today. It was in part psychological, the enforced personal feeling of inferiority, the calling of another Master; the standing with hat in hand. It was the helplessness. It was the defenselessness of family life. It was the submergence below the arbitrary will of any sort of individual. It was without doubt worse in these vital respects than that which exists today in Europe or America. Its analogue today is the yellow, brown and black laborer in China and India, in Africa, in the forests of the Amazon; and it was this slavery that fell in America.

The slavery of Negroes in the South was not usually a deliberately cruel and oppressive system. It did not mean systematic starvation or murder. On the other hand, it is just as difficult to conceive as quite true the idyllic picture of a patriarchal state with cultured and humane masters under whom slaves were as children, guided and trained in work and play, given even such mental training as was for their good, and for the well-being of the surrounding world.

The victims of Southern slavery were often happy; had usually adequate food for their health, and shelter sufficient for a mild climate. The Southerners could say with some justification that when the mass of their field hands were compared with the worst class of laborers in the slums of New York and Philadelphia, and the factory towns of New England, the black slaves were as well off and in some particulars better off. Slaves lived largely in the country where health conditions were better; they worked in the open air, and their hours were about the current hours for peasants throughout Europe. They received no formal education, and neither did the Irish peasant, the English factory-laborer, nor the German *Bauer;* and in contrast with these free white laborers, the Negroes were protected by a certain primitive sort of old-age pension, job insurance, and sickness insurance; that is, they must be supported in some fashion, when they were too old to work; they must have attention in sickness, for they represented invested capital; and they could never be among the unemployed.

On the other hand, it is just as true that Negro slaves in America represented the worst and lowest conditions among modern laborers. One estimate is that the maintenance of a slave in the South cost the master about $19 a year, which means that they were among the poorest paid laborers in the modern world. They represented in a very real sense the ultimate degradation of man. Indeed, the system was so reactionary, so utterly inconsistent with modern progress, that we simply cannot grasp it today. No matter how degraded the factory hand, he is not real estate. The tragedy of the black slave's position was precisely this; his absolute subjection to the individual will of an owner and to "the cruelty and injustice which are the invariable consequences of the exercise of irresponsible power, especially where authority must be sometimes delegated by the planter to agents of inferior education and coarser feelings."

The proof of this lies clearly written in the slave codes. Slaves were not considered men. They had no right of petition. They were "devisable like any other chattel." They could own nothing; they could make no contracts; they could hold no property, nor traffic in property; they could not hire out; they could not legally marry nor constitute families; they could not control their children; they could not appeal from their master; they could be punished at will. They could not testify in court; they could be imprisoned by their owners, and the criminal offense of assault and battery could not be committed on the person of a slave. The "willful, malicious and deliberate murder" of a slave was punishable by death, but such a crime was practically impossible of proof. The slave owed to his master and all his family a respect "without bounds, and an absolute obedience." This authority could be transmitted to others. A slave could not sue his master; had no right of redemption; no right to education or religion; a promise made to a slave by his master had no force nor validity. Children followed the condition of the slave mother. The slave could have no access to the judiciary. A slave might be condemned to death for striking any white person.

Looking at these accounts, "it is safe to say that the law regards a Negro slave, so far as his civil status is concerned, purely and absolutely property, to be bought and sold and pass and descend as a tract of land, a horse, or an ox." [2]

The whole legal status of slavery was enunciated in the extraordinary statement of a Chief Justice of the United States that Negroes had always been regarded in America "as having no rights which a white man was bound to respect."

It may be said with truth that the law was often harsher than the practice. Nevertheless, these laws and decisions represent the legally permissible possibilities, and the only curb upon the power of the master was his sense of humanity and decency, on the one hand, and the conserving of his investment on the other. Of the humanity of large numbers of Southern masters there can be no doubt. In some cases, they gave their slaves a fatherly care. And yet even in such cases the strain upon their ability to care for large numbers of people and the necessity of entrusting the care of the slaves to other hands than their own, led to much suffering and cruelty.

The matter of his investment in land and slaves greatly curtailed the owner's freedom of action. Under the competition of growing industrial organization, the slave system was indeed the source of immense profits. But for the slave owner and landlord to keep a large or even reasonable share of these profits was increasingly difficult. The price of the slave produce in the open market could be hammered down by merchants and traders acting with knowledge and collusion. And the slave owner was, therefore, continually forced to find his profit not in the high price of cotton and sugar, but in beating even further down the cost of his slave labor. This made the slave owners in early days kill the slave by overwork and renew their working stock; it led to the widely organized interstate slave trade between the Border States and the Cotton Kingdom of the Southern South; it led to neglect and the breaking up of families, and it could not protect the slave against the cruelty, lust and neglect of certain owners.

Thus human slavery in the South pointed and led in two singularly contradictory and paradoxical directions—toward the deliberate commercial breeding and sale of human labor for profit and toward the intermingling of black and white blood. The slaveholders shrank from acknowledging either set of facts but they were clear and undeniable.

In this vital respect, the slave laborer differed from all others of his day: he could be sold; he could, at the will of a single individual, be transferred for life a thousand miles or more. His family, wife and children could be legally and absolutely taken from him. Free laborers today are compelled to wander in search for work and food; their families are deserted for want of wages; but in all this there is no such direct barter in human flesh. It was a sharp accentuation of control over men beyond the modern labor reserve or the contract coolie system.

Negroes could be sold—actually sold as we sell cattle with no reference to calves or bulls, or recognition of family. It was a nasty business. The white South was properly ashamed of it and continually belittled and almost denied it. But it was a stark and bitter fact. Southern papers of the Border States were filled with advertisements:—"I wish to purchase fifty Negroes of both sexes from 6 to 30 years of age for which I will give the highest cash prices."

"Wanted to purchase—Negroes of every description, age and sex."

The consequent disruption of families is proven beyond doubt:

"Fifty Dollars reward.—Ran away from the subscriber, a Negro girl, named Maria. She is of a copper color, between 13 and 14 years of age—bareheaded and barefooted. She is small for her age—very sprightly and very likely. She stated she was *going to see her mother* at Maysville. Sanford Tomson."

"Committed to jail of Madison County, a Negro woman, who calls her name Fanny, and says she belongs to William Miller, of Mobile. She formerly belonged to John Givins, of this county, who now owns *several of her children*. David Shropshire, Jailer."

"Fifty Dollar reward.—Ran away from the subscriber, his Negro man Pauladore, commonly called Paul. I understand Gen. R. Y. Hayne *has purchased his wife and children* from H. L. Pinckney, Esq., and has them on his plantation at Goosecreek, where, no doubt, the fellow is frequently *lurking*. T. Davis." One can see Pauladore "lurking" about his wife and children.[3]

The system of slavery demanded a special police force and such a force was made possible and unusually effective by the presence of the poor whites. This explains the difference between the slave revolts in the West Indies, and the lack of effective revolt in the Southern United States. In the West Indies, the power over the slave was held by the whites and carried out by them and such Negroes as they could trust. In the South, on the other hand, the great planters formed proportionately quite as small a class but they had singularly enough at their command some five million poor whites; that is, there were actually more white people to police the slaves than there were slaves. Considering the economic rivalry of the black and white worker in the North, it would have seemed natural that the poor white would have refused to police the slaves. But two considerations led him in the opposite direction. First of all, it gave him work and some authority as overseer, slave driver, and member of the patrol system. But above and beyond this, it fed his vanity because it associated him with the masters. Slavery bred in the poor white a dislike of Negro toil of all sorts. He never regarded himself as a laborer, or as part of any labor movement. If he had any ambition at all it was to become a planter and to own "niggers." To these Negroes he transferred all the dislike and hatred which he had for the whole slave system. The result was that the system was held stable and intact by the poor white. Even with the late ruin of Haiti before their eyes, the planters, stirred as they were, were nevertheless able to stamp out slave revolt. The dozen revolts of the eighteenth century had dwindled to the plot of Gabriel in 1800, Vesey in 1822, of Nat Turner in 1831 and crews of the *Amistad* and *Creole* in 1839 and 1841. Gradually the whole white South became an armed and commissioned camp to keep Negroes in slavery and to kill the black rebel.

But even the poor white, led by the planter, would not have kept the black slave in nearly so complete control had it not been for what may be called the Safety Valve of Slavery; and that was the chance which a vigorous and determined slave had to run away to freedom.

Under the situation as it developed between 1830 and 1860 there were grave losses to the capital invested in black workers. Encouraged by the idealism of those Northern thinkers who insisted that Negroes were human, the black worker sought freedom by running away from slavery. The physical geography of America with its paths north, by swamp, river and mountain range; the daring of black revolutionists like Henson and Tubman; and the extra-legal efforts of abolitionists made this more and more easy.

One cannot know the real facts concerning the number of fugitives, but despite the fear of advertising the losses, the emphasis put upon fugitive slaves by the South shows that it was an important economic item. It is certain from the bitter effort to increase the efficiency of the fugitive slave law that the losses from runaways were widespread and continuous; and the increase in the interstate slave trade from Border States to the deep South, together with the increase in the price of slaves, showed a growing pressure. At the beginning of the nineteenth century, one bought an average slave for $200; while in 1860 the price ranged from $1,400 to $2,000.

Not only was the fugitive slave important because of the actual loss involved, but for potentialities in the future. These free Negroes were furnishing a leadership for the mass of the black workers, and especially they were furnishing a text for the abolition idealists. Fugitive slaves, like Frederick Douglass and others humbler and less gifted, increased the number of abolitionists by thousands and spelled the doom of slavery.

The true significance of slavery in the United States to the whole social development of America lay in the ultimate relation of slaves to democracy. What were to be the limits of democratic control in the United States? If all labor, black as well as white, became free— were given schools and the right to vote—what control could or should be set to the power and action of these laborers? Was the rule of the mass of Americans to be unlimited, and the right to rule extended to all men regardless of race and color, or if not, what power of dictatorship and control; and how would property and privilege be protected? This was the great and primary question which was in the minds of the men who wrote the Constitution of the United States and continued in the minds of thinkers down through the slavery controversy. It still remains with the world as the problem of democracy expands and touches all races and nations.

And of all human development, ancient and modern, not the least singular and significant is the philosophy of life and action which slavery bred in the souls of black folk. In most respects its expression was stilted and confused; the rolling periods of Hebrew prophecy and biblical legend furnished inaccurate but splendid words. The subtle folk-lore of Africa, with whimsy and parable, veiled wish and wisdom; and above all fell the anointing chrism of the slave music, the only gift of pure art in America.

Beneath the Veil lay right and wrong, vengeance and love, and sometimes throwing aside the veil, a soul of sweet Beauty and Truth stood revealed. Nothing else of art or religion did the slave South give to the world, except the Negro song and story. And even after slavery, down to our day, it has added but little to this gift. One has but to remember as symbol of it all, still unspoiled by petty artisans, the legend of John Henry, the mighty black, who broke his heart working against the machine, and died "with his Hammer in His Hand."

Up from this slavery gradually climbed the Free Negro with clearer, modern expression and more definite aim long before the emancipation of 1863. His greatest effort lay in his coöperation with the Abolition movement. He knew he was not free until all Negroes were free. Individual Negroes became exhibits of the possibilities of the Negro race, if once it was raised above the status of slavery. Even when, as so often, the Negro became Court Jester to the ignorant American mob, he made his plea in his songs and antics.

Thus spoke "the noblest slave that ever God set free," Frederick Douglass in 1852, in his 4th of July oration at Rochester, voicing the frank and fearless criticism of the black worker:

"What, to the American slave, is your 4th of July? I answer: a day that reveals to him, more than all other days in the year, the gross injustice and cruelty to which he is the constant victim. To him your celebration is a sham; your boasted liberty, an unholy license; your national greatness, swelling vanity; your sounds of rejoicing are empty and heartless; your denunciation of tyrants, brass-fronted impudence; your shouts of liberty and equality, hollow mockery; your prayers and hymns, your sermons and thanksgivings, with all your religious parade and solemnity, are, to him, mere bombast, fraud, deception, impiety and hypocrisy—a thin veil to cover up crimes which would disgrace a nation of savages. . . .

"You boast of your love of liberty, your superior civilization, and your pure Christianity, while the whole political power of the nation (as embodied in the two great political parties) is solemnly pledged to support and perpetuate the enslavement of three millions of your countrymen. You hurl your anathemas at the crown-headed tyrants of Russia and Austria and pride yourselves on your democratic institutions, while you yourselves consent to be the mere *tools* and *bodyguards* of the tyrants of Virginia and Carolina. You invite to your shores fugitives of oppression from abroad, honor them with banquets, greet them with ovations, cheer them, toast them, salute them, protect them, and pour out your money to them like water; but the fugitives from your own land you advertise, hunt, arrest, shoot, and kill. You glory in your refinement and your universal education; yet you maintain a system as barbarous and dreadful as ever stained the character of a nation—a system begun in avarice, supported in pride, and perpetuated in cruelty. You shed tears over fallen Hungary, and make the sad story of her wrongs the theme of your poets, statesmen, and orators, till your gallant sons are ready to fly to arms to vindicate her cause against the oppressor; but, in regard to the ten thousand wrongs of the American slave, you would enforce the strictest silence, and would hail him as an enemy of the nation who dares to make those wrongs the subject of public discourse!" [4]

Above all, we must remember the black worker was the ultimate exploited; that he formed that mass of labor which had neither wish nor power to escape from the labor status, in order to directly exploit other laborers, or indirectly, by alliance with capital, to share in their exploitation. To be sure, the black mass, developed again and again, here and there, capitalistic groups in New Orleans, in Charleston and in Philadelphia; groups willing to join white capital in exploiting labor; but they were driven back into the mass by racial prejudice before they had reached a permanent foothold; and thus became all the more bitter against all organization which by means of race prejudice, or the monopoly of wealth, sought to exclude men from making a living.

It was thus the black worker, as founding stone of a new economic system in the nineteenth century and for the modern world, who brought civil war in America. He was its underlying cause, in spite of every effort to base the strife upon union and national power.

That dark and vast sea of human labor in China and India, the South Seas and all Africa; in the West Indies and Central America and in the United States—that great majority of mankind, on whose bent and broken backs rest today the founding stones of modern industry—shares a common destiny; it is despised and rejected by race and color; paid a wage below the level of decent living; driven, beaten, prisoned and enslaved in all but name; spawning the world's raw material and luxury—cotton, wool, coffee, tea, cocoa, palm oil, fibers, spices, rubber, silks, lumber, copper, gold, diamonds, leather—how shall we end the list and where? All these are gathered up at prices lowest of the low, manufactured, transformed and transported at fabulous gain; and the resultant wealth is distributed and displayed and made the basis of world power and universal dominion and armed arrogance in London and Paris, Berlin and Rome, New York and Rio de Janeiro.

Here is the real modern labor problem. Here is the kernel of the problem of Religion and Democracy, of Humanity. Words and futile gestures avail nothing. Out of the exploitation of the dark proletariat comes the Surplus Value filched from human beasts which, in cultured lands, the Machine and harnessed Power veil and conceal. The emancipation of man is the emancipation of labor and the emancipation of labor is the freeing of that basic majority of workers who are yellow, brown and black.

Dark, shackled knights of labor, clinging still
Amidst a universal wreck of faith
To cheerfulness, and foreigners to hate.
These know ye not, these have ye not received,
But these shall speak to you Beatitudes.
Around them surge the tides of all your strife,
Above them rise the august monuments
Of all your outward splendor, but they stand
Unenvious in thought, and bide their time.

LESLIE P. HILL

---

1. Compare A. E. McKinley, *The Suffrage Franchise in the Thirteen English Colonies in America*, p. 137.
2. *A Picture of Slavery Drawn from the Decisions of Southern Courts*, p. 5.
3. Compare Bancroft, *Slave-Trading in the Old South;* Weld, *American Slavery as It Is.*
4. Woodson, *Negro Orators and Their Orations*, pp. 218-19.

II. THE WHITE WORKER

How America became the laborer's Promised Land; and flocking
here from all the world the white workers competed with black
slaves, with new floods of foreigners, and with growing exploitation, until they fought slavery to save democracy and then lost
democracy in a new and vaster slavery

The opportunity for real and new democracy in America was broad.
Political power was at first as usual confined to property holders and
an aristocracy of birth and learning. But it was never securely based
on land. Land was free and both land and property were possible to
nearly every thrifty worker. Schools began early to multiply and open
their doors even to the poor laborer. Birth began to count for less and
less and America became to the world a land of opportunity. So the
world came to America, even before the Revolution, and afterward
during the nineteenth century, nineteen million immigrants entered
the United States.

The new labor that came to the United States, while it was poor,
used to oppression and accustomed to a low standard of living, was
not willing, after it reached America, to regard itself as a permanent
laboring class and it is in the light of this fact that the labor movement among white Americans must be studied. The successful, well-
paid American laboring class formed, because of its property and
ideals, a petty bourgeoisie ready always to join capital in exploiting
common labor, white and black, foreign and native. The more energetic and thrifty among the immigrants caught the prevalent American idea that here labor could become emancipated from the necessity
of continuous toil and that an increasing proportion could join the
class of exploiters, that is of those who made their income chiefly by
profit derived through the hiring of labor.

Abraham Lincoln expressed this idea frankly at Hartford, in March,
1860. He said:

"I am not ashamed to confess that twenty-five years ago I was a
hired laborer, mauling rails, at work on a flat boat—just what might
happen to any poor man's son." Then followed the characteristic philosophy of the time: "I want every man to have his chance—and I believe a black man is entitled to it—in which he can better his condition—when he may look forward and hope to be a hired laborer this

year and the next, work for himself afterward, and finally to hire men to work for him. That is the true system."

He was enunciating the widespread American idea of the son rising to a higher economic level than the father; of the chance for the poor man to accumulate wealth and power, which made the European doctrine of a working class fighting for the elevation of all workers seem not only less desirable but even less possible for average workers than they had formerly considered it.

These workers came to oppose slavery not so much from moral as from the economic fear of being reduced by competition to the level of slaves. They wanted a chance to become capitalists; and they found that chance threatened by the competition of a working class whose status at the bottom of the economic structure seemed permanent and inescapable. At first, black slavery jarred upon them, and as early as the seventeenth century German immigrants to Pennsylvania asked the Quakers innocently if slavery was in accord with the Golden Rule. Then, gradually, as succeeding immigrants were thrown in difficult and exasperating competition with black workers, their attitude changed. These were the very years when the white worker was beginning to understand the early American doctrine of wealth and property; to escape the liability of imprisonment for debt, and even to gain the right of universal suffrage. He found pouring into cities like New York and Philadelphia emancipated Negroes with low standards of living, competing for the jobs which the lower class of unskilled white laborers wanted.

For the immediate available jobs, the Irish particularly competed and the employers because of race antipathy and sympathy with the South did not wish to increase the number of Negro workers, so long as the foreigners worked just as cheaply. The foreigners in turn blamed blacks for the cheap price of labor. The result was race war; riots took place which were at first simply the flaming hostility of groups of laborers fighting for bread and butter; then they turned into race riots. For three days in Cincinnati in 1829, a mob of whites wounded and killed free Negroes and fugitive slaves and destroyed property. Most of the black population, numbering over two thousand, left the city and trekked to Canada. In Philadelphia, 1828-1840, a series of riots took place which thereafter extended until after the Civil War. The riot of 1834 took the dimensions of a pitched battle and lasted for three days. Thirty-one houses and two churches were destroyed. Other riots took place in 1835 and 1838 and a two days' riot in 1842 caused the calling out of the militia with artillery.

In the forties came quite a different class, the English and German workers, who had tried by organization to fight the machine and in the end had to some degree envisaged the Marxian reorganization of industry through trade unions and class struggle. The attitude of these people toward the Negro was varied and contradictory. At first they blurted out their disapprobation of slavery on principle. It was a phase of all wage slavery. Then they began to see a way out for the worker in America through the free land of the West. Here was a solution such as was impossible in Europe: plenty of land, rich land, land coming daily nearer its own markets, to which the worker could retreat and restore the industrial balance ruined in Europe by the expropriation of the worker from the soil. Or in other words, the worker in America saw a chance to increase his wage and regulate his conditions of employment much greater than in Europe. The trade unions could have a material backing that they could not have in Germany, France or England. This thought, curiously enough, instead of increasing the sympathy for the slave turned it directly into rivalry and enmity.

The wisest of the leaders could not clearly envisage just how slave labor in conjunction and competition with free labor tended to reduce all labor toward slavery. For this reason, the union and labor leaders gravitated toward the political party which opposed tariff bounties and welcomed immigrants, quite forgetting that this same Democratic party had as its backbone the planter oligarchy of the South with its slave labor.

The new immigrants in their competition with this group reflected not simply the general attitude of America toward colored people, but particularly they felt a threat of slave competition which these Negroes foreshadowed. The Negroes worked cheaply, partly from custom, partly as their only defense against competition. The white laborers realized that Negroes were part of a group of millions of workers who were slaves by law, and whose competition kept white labor out of the work of the South and threatened its wages and stability in the North. When now the labor question moved West, and became a part of the land question, the competition of black men became of increased importance. Foreign laborers saw more clearly than most Americans the tremendous significance of free land in abundance, such as America possessed, in open contrast to the land monopoly of Europe. But here on this free land, they met not only a few free Negro workers, but the threat of a mass of slaves. The attitude of the West toward Negroes, therefore, became sterner than that of the East. Here was the possibility of direct competition with slaves, and the absorption of Western land into the slave system. This must be resisted at all costs, but beyond this, even free Negroes must be discouraged. On this the Southern poor white immigrants insisted.

In the meantime, the problem of the black worker had not ceased to trouble the conscience and the economic philosophy of America. That the worker should be a bond slave was fundamentally at variance with the American doctrine, and the demand for the abolition of slavery had been continuous since the Revolution. In the North, it had resulted in freeing gradually all of the Negroes. But the comparatively small number of those thus freed was being augmented now by fugitive slaves from the South, and manifestly the ultimate plight of the black worker depended upon the course of Southern slavery. There arose, then, in the thirties, and among thinkers and workers, a demand that slavery in the United States be immediately abolished.

This demand became epitomized in the crusade of William Lloyd Garrison, himself a poor printer, but a man of education, thought and indomitable courage. This movement was not primarily a labor movement or a matter of profit and wage. It simply said that under any condition of life, the reduction of a human being to real estate was a crime against humanity of such enormity that its existence must be immediately ended. After emancipation there would come questions of labor, wage and political power. But now, first, must be demanded that ordinary human freedom and recognition of essential manhood which slavery blasphemously denied. This philosophy of freedom was a logical continuation of the freedom philosophy of the eighteenth century which insisted that Freedom was not an End but an indispensable means to the beginning of human progress and that democracy could function only after the dropping of feudal privileges, monopoly and chains.

The propaganda which made the abolition movement terribly real was the Fugitive Slave—the piece of intelligent humanity who could say: I have been owned like an ox. I stole my own body and now I am hunted by law and lash to be made an ox again. By no conception of justice could such logic be answered. Nevertheless, at the same time white labor, while it attempted no denial but even expressed faint sympathy, saw in this fugitive slave and in the millions of slaves behind him, willing and eager to work for less than current wage, competition for their own jobs. What they failed to comprehend was that the black man enslaved was an even more formidable and fatal competitor than the black man free.

Here, then, were two labor movements: the movement to give the black worker a minimum legal status which would enable him to sell his own labor, and another movement which proposed to increase the wage and better the condition of the working class in America, now largely composed of foreign immigrants, and dispute with the new American capitalism the basis upon which the new wealth was to be divided. Broad philanthropy and a wide knowledge of the elements of human progress would have led these two movements to unite and in their union to become irresistible. It was difficult, almost impossible, for this to be clear to the white labor leaders of the thirties. They had their particularistic grievances and one of these was the competition of free Negro labor. Beyond this they could easily vision a new and tremendous competition of black workers after all the slaves became free. What they did not see nor understand was that this competition was present and would continue and would be emphasized if the Negro continued as a slave worker. On the other hand, the Abolitionists did not realize the plight of the white laborer, especially the semi-skilled and unskilled worker.

While the Evans brothers, who came as labor agitators in 1825, had among their twelve demands "the abolition of chattel slavery," nevertheless, George was soon convinced that freedom without land was of no importance. He wrote to Gerrit Smith, who was giving land to Negroes, and said:

"I was formerly, like yourself, sir, a very warm advocate of the abolition of slavery. This was before I saw that there was *white* slavery. Since I saw this, I have materially changed my views as to the means of abolishing Negro slavery. I now see, clearly, I think, that to give the landless black the privilege of changing masters now possessed by the landless *white* would hardly be a benefit to him in exchange for his surety of support in sickness and old age, although he is in a favorable climate. If the Southern form of slavery existed at the North, I should say the black would be a great loser by such a change."[1]

At the convention of the New England anti-slavery society in 1845, Robert Owen, the great champion of coöperation, said he was opposed to Negro slavery, but that he had seen worse slavery in England than among the Negroes. Horace Greeley said the same year: "If I am less troubled concerning the slavery prevalent in Charleston or New Orleans, it is because I see so much slavery in New York which appears to claim my first efforts."

Thus despite all influences, reform and social uplift veered away from the Negro. Brisbane, Channing, Owen and other leaders called a National Reform Association to meet in New York in May, 1845. In October, Owen's "World Conference" met. But they hardly mentioned slavery. The Abolitionists did join a National Industrial Congress which met around 1845-1846. Other labor leaders were openly hostile toward the abolitionist movement, while the movement for free land increased.

Thus two movements—Labor-Free Soil, and Abolition, exhibited fundamental divergence instead of becoming one great party of free labor and free land. The Free Soilers stressed the difficulties of even the free laborer getting hold of the land and getting work in the great congestion which immigration had brought; and the abolitionists stressed the moral wrong of slavery. These two movements might easily have coöperated and differed only in matters of emphasis; but the trouble was that black and white laborers were competing for the same jobs just of course as all laborers always are. The immediate competition became open and visible because of racial lines and racial philosophy and particularly in Northern states where free Negroes and fugitive slaves had established themselves as workers, while the ultimate and overshadowing competition of free and slave labor was obscured and pushed into the background. This situation, too, made extraordinary reaction, led by the ignorant mob and fomented by authority and privilege; abolitionists were attacked and their meeting places burned; women suffragists were hooted; laws were proposed making the kidnaping of Negroes easier and disfranchising Negro voters in conventions called for purposes of "reform."

The humanitarian reform movement reached its height in 1847-1849 amid falling prices, and trade unionism was at a low ebb. The strikes from 1849-1852 won the support of Horace Greeley, and increased the labor organizations. Labor in eastern cities refused to touch the slavery controversy, and the control which the Democrats had over the labor vote in New York and elsewhere increased this tendency to ignore the Negro, and increased the division between white and colored labor. In 1850, a Congress of Trade Unions was held with 110 delegates. They stressed land reform but said nothing about slavery and the organization eventually was captured by Tammany Hall. After 1850 unions composed of skilled laborers began to separate from common laborers and adopt a policy of closed shops and a minimum wage and excluded farmers and Negroes. Although this movement was killed by the panic of 1857, it eventually became triumphant in the eighties and culminated in the American Federation of Labor which today allows any local or national union to exclude Negroes on any pretext.

Other labor leaders became more explicit and emphasized race rather than class. John Campbell said in 1851: "Will the white race ever agree that blacks shall stand beside us on election day, upon the rostrum, in the ranks of the army, in our places of amusement, in places of public worship, ride in the same coaches, railway cars, or steamships? Never! Never! or is it natural, or just, that this kind of equality should exist? God never intended it; had he so willed it, he would have made all one color." [2]

New labor leaders arrived in the fifties. Hermann Kriege and Wilhelm Weitling left their work in Germany, and their friends Marx and Engels, and came to America, and at the same time came tens of thousands of revolutionary Germans. The Socialist and Communist papers increased. Trade unions increased in power and numbers and held public meetings. Immediately, the question of slavery injected itself, and that of abolition.

Kriege began to preach land reform and free soil in 1846, and by 1850 six hundred American papers were supporting his program. But Kriege went beyond Evans and former leaders and openly repudiated abolition. He declared in 1846:

"That we see in the slavery question a property question which cannot be settled by itself alone. That we should declare ourselves in favor of the abolitionist movement if it were our intention to throw the Republic into a state of anarchy, to extend the competition of 'free workingmen' beyond all measure, and to depress labor itself to the last extremity. That we could not improve the lot of our 'black brothers' by abolition under the conditions prevailing in modern society, but make infinitely worse the lot of our 'white brothers.' That we believe in the peaceable development of society in the United States and do not, therefore, here at least see our only hope in condition of the extremest degradation. That we feel constrained, therefore, to oppose Abolition with all our might, despite all the importunities of sentimental philistines and despite all the poetical effusions of liberty-intoxicated ladies." [3]

Wilhelm Weitling, who came to America the following year, 1847, started much agitation but gave little attention to slavery. He did not openly side with the slaveholder, as Kriege did; nevertheless, there was no condemnation of slavery in his paper. In the first German labor conference in Philadelphia, under Weitling in 1850, a series of resolutions were passed which did not mention slavery. Both Kriege and Weitling joined the Democratic party and numbers of other immigrant Germans did the same thing, and these workers, therefore, became practical defenders of slavery. Doubtless, the "Know-Nothing" movement against the foreign-born forced many workers into the Democratic party, despite slavery.

The year 1853 saw the formation of the Arbeiterbund, under Joseph Weydemeyer, a friend of Karl Marx. This organization advocated Marxian socialism but never got a clear attitude toward slavery. In 1854, it opposed the Kansas-Nebraska bill because "Capitalism and land speculation have again been favored at the expense of the mass of the people," and "This bill withdraws from or makes unavailable in a future homestead bill vast tracts of territory," and "authorizes the further extension of slavery; but we have, do now, and shall continue to protest most emphatically against both white and black slavery."

Nevertheless, when the Arbeiterbund was reorganized in December, 1857, slavery was not mentioned. When its new organ appeared in April, 1858, it said that the question of the present moment was not the abolition of slavery, but the prevention of its further extension and that Negro slavery was firmly rooted in America. One small division of this organization in 1857 called for abolition of the slave trade and colonization of Negroes, but defended the Southern slaveholders.

In 1859, however, a conference of the Arbeiterbund condemned all slavery in whatever form it might appear, and demanded the repeal of the Fugitive Slave Law. The Democratic and pro-slavery New York *Staats-Zeitung* counseled the people to abstain from agitation against the extension of slavery, but all of the German population did not agree.

As the Chartist movement increased in England, the press was filled with attacks against the United States and its institutions, and the Chartists were clear on the matter of slavery. Their chief organ in 1844 said: "That damning stain upon the American escutcheon is one that has caused the Republicans of Europe to weep for very shame and mortification; and the people of the United States have much to answer for at the bar of humanity for this indecent, cruel, revolting and fiendish violation of their boasted principle—that 'All men are born free and equal.'"

The labor movement in England continued to emphasize the importance of attacking slavery; and the agitation, started by the work of Frederick Douglass and others, increased in importance and activity. In 1857, George I. Holyoake sent an anti-slavery address to America, signed by 1,800 English workingmen, whom Karl Marx himself was guiding in England, and this made the black American worker a central text. They pointed out the fact that the black worker was furnishing the raw material which the English capitalist was exploiting together with the English worker. This same year, the United States Supreme Court sent down the Dred Scott decision that Negroes were not citizens.

This English initiative had at first but limited influence in America. The trade unions were willing to admit that the Negroes ought to be free sometime; but at the present, self-preservation called for their slavery; and after all, whites were a different grade of workers from blacks. Even when the Marxian ideas arrived, there was a split; the earlier representatives of the Marxian philosophy in America agreed with the older Union movement in deprecating any entanglement with the abolition controversy. After all, abolition represented capital. The whole movement was based on mawkish sentimentality, and not on the demands of the workers, at least of the white workers. And so the early American Marxists simply gave up the idea of intruding the black worker into the socialist commonwealth at that time.

To this logic the abolitionists were increasingly opposed. It seemed to them that the crucial point was the matter of freedom; that a free laborer in America had an even chance to make his fortune as a worker or a farmer; but, on the other hand, if the laborer was not free, as in the case of the Negro, he had no opportunity, and he inevitably degraded white labor. The abolitionist did not sense the new subordination into which the worker was being forced by organized capital, while the laborers did not realize that the exclusion of four million workers from the labor program was a fatal omission. Wendell Phillips alone suggested a boycott on Southern goods, and said that the great cause of labor was paramount and included mill operatives in New England, peasants in Ireland, and laborers in South America who ought not to be lost sight of in sympathy for the Southern slave.

In the United States shortly before the outbreak of the Civil War there were twenty-six trades with national organizations, including the iron and steel workers, machinists, blacksmiths, etc. The employers formed a national league and planned to import more workmen from foreign countries. The iron molders started a national strike July 5, 1859, and said: "Wealth is power, and practical experience teaches us that it is a power but too often used to oppress and degrade the daily laborer. Year after year the capital of the country becomes more and more concentrated in the hands of a few, and, in proportion as the wealth of the country becomes centralized, its power increases, and the laboring classes are impoverished. It therefore becomes us, as men who have to battle with the stern realities of life, to look this matter fair in the face; there is no dodging the question; let every man give it a fair, full and candid consideration, and then act according to his honest convictions. *What position are we, the mechanics of America, to hold in Society?*"

There was not a word in this address about slavery and one would not dream that the United States was on the verge of the greatest labor revolution it had seen. Other conferences of the molders, machinists and blacksmiths and others were held in the sixties, and a labor mass meeting at Faneuil Hall in Boston in 1861 said: "The truth is that the workingmen care little for the strife of political parties and the intrigues of office-seekers. We regard them with the contempt they deserve. We are weary of this question of slavery; it is a matter which does not concern us; and we wish only to attend to our business,

and leave the South to attend to their own affairs, without any interference from the North."[4]

In all this consideration, we have so far ignored the white workers
of the South and we have done this because the labor movement
ignored them and the abolitionists ignored them; and above all, they
were ignored by Northern capitalists and Southern planters. They
were in many respects almost a forgotten mass of men. Cairnes describes the slave South, the period just before the war:

"It resolves itself into three classes, broadly distinguished from each
other, and connected by no common interest—the slaves on whom
devolves all the regular industry, the slaveholders who reap all its
fruits, and an idle and lawless rabble who live dispersed over vast
plains in a condition little removed from absolute barbarism."

From all that has been written and said about the ante-bellum South,
one almost loses sight of about 5,000,000 white people in 1860 who lived
in the South and held no slaves. Even among the two million slaveholders, an oligarchy of 8,000 really ruled the South, while as an observer said: "For twenty years, I do not recollect ever to have seen or
heard these non-slaveholding whites referred to by the Southern gentleman as constituting any part of what they called the South."[5] They
were largely ignorant and degraded; only 25% could read and write.

The condition of the poor whites has been many times described:

"A wretched log hut or two are the only habitations in sight. Here
reside, or rather take shelter, the miserable cultivators of the ground,
or a still more destitute class who make a precarious living by ped-
dling 'lightwood' in the city. . . .

"These cabins . . . are dens of filth. The bed if there be a bed is a
layer of something in the corner that defies scenting. If the bed is
nasty, what of the floor? What of the whole enclosed space? What of
the creatures themselves? Pough! Water in use as a purifier is unknown. Their faces are bedaubed with the muddy accumulation of
weeks. They just give them a wipe when they see a stranger to take
off the blackest dirt. . . . The poor wretches seem startled when you
address them, and answer your questions cowering like culprits."[6]

Olmsted said: "I saw as much close packing, filth and squalor, in
certain blocks inhabited by laboring whites in Charleston, as I have
witnessed in any Northern town of its size; and greater evidences of
brutality and ruffianly character, than I have ever happened to see,
among an equal population of this class, before."[7]

Two classes of poor whites have been differentiated: the mountain
whites and the poor whites of the lowlands. "Below a dirty and ill-
favored house, down under the bank on the shingle near the river, sits
a family of five people, all ill-clothed and unclean; a blear-eyed old

woman, a younger woman with a mass of tangled red hair hanging about her shoulders, indubitably suckling a baby; a little girl with the same auburn evidence of Scotch ancestry; a boy, and a younger child all gathered about a fire made among some bricks, surrounding a couple of iron saucepans, in which is a dirty mixture looking like mud, but probably warmed-up sorghum syrup, which with a few pieces of corn pone, makes their breakfast.

"Most of them are illiterate and more than correspondingly ignorant. Some of them had Indian ancestors and a few bear evidences of Negro blood. The so-called 'mountain boomer,' says an observer, 'has little self-respect and no self-reliance. . . . So long as his corn pile lasts the "cracker" lives in contentment, feasting on a sort of hoe cake made of grated corn meal mixed with salt and water and baked before the hot coals, with addition of what game the forest furnishes him when he can get up the energy to go out and shoot or trap it. . . . The irregularities of their moral lives cause them no sense of shame. . . . But, notwithstanding these low moral conceptions, they are of an intense religious excitability.' " [8]

Above this lowest mass rose a middle class of poor whites in the making. There were some small farmers who had more than a mere sustenance and yet were not large planters. There were overseers. There was a growing class of merchants who traded with the slaves and free Negroes and became in many cases larger traders, dealing with the planters for the staple crops. Some poor whites rose to the professional class, so that the rift between the planters and the mass of the whites was partially bridged by this smaller intermediate class.

While revolt against the domination of the planters over the poor whites was voiced by men like Helper, who called for a class struggle to destroy the planters, this was nullified by deep-rooted antagonism to the Negro, whether slave or free. If black labor could be expelled from the United States or eventually exterminated, then the fight against the planter could take place. But the poor whites and their leaders could not for a moment contemplate a fight of united white and black labor against the exploiters. Indeed, the natural leaders of the poor whites, the small farmer, the merchant, the professional man, the white mechanic and slave overseer, were bound to the planters and repelled from the slaves and even from the mass of the white laborers in two ways: first, they constituted the police patrol who could ride with planters and now and then exercise unlimited force upon recalcitrant or runaway slaves; and then, too, there was always a chance that they themselves might also become planters by saving money, by investment, by the power of good luck; and the only heaven that attracted them was the life of the great Southern planter.

There were a few weak associations of white mechanics, such as printers and shipwrights and iron molders, in 1850-1860, but practically no labor movement in the South.

Charles Nordhoff states that he was told by a wealthy Alabaman, in 1860, that the planters in his region were determined to discontinue altogether the employment of free mechanics. "On my own place," he said, "I have slave carpenters, slave blacksmiths, and slave wheelwrights, and thus I am independent of free mechanics." And a certain Alfred E. Mathews remarks: "I have seen free white mechanics obliged to stand aside while their families were suffering for the necessaries of life, when the slave mechanics, owned by rich and influential men, could get plenty of work; and I have heard these same white mechanics breathe the most bitter curses against the institution of slavery and the slave aristocracy."

The resultant revolt of the poor whites, just as the revolt of the slaves, came through migration. And their migration, instead of being restricted, was freely encouraged. As a result, the poor whites left the South in large numbers. In 1860, 399,700 Virginians were living out of their native state. From Tennessee, 344,765 emigrated; from North Carolina, 272,606, and from South Carolina, 256,868. The majority of these had come to the Middle West and it is quite possible that the Southern states sent as many settlers to the West as the Northeastern states, and while the Northeast demanded free soil, the Southerners demanded not only free soil but the exclusion of Negroes from work and the franchise. They had a very vivid fear of the Negro as a competitor in labor, whether slave or free.

It was thus the presence of the poor white Southerner in the West that complicated the whole Free Soil movement in its relation to the labor movement. While the Western pioneer was an advocate of extreme democracy and equalitarianism in his political and economic philosophy, his vote and influence did not go to strengthen the abolition-democracy, before, during, or even after the war. On the contrary, it was stopped and inhibited by the doctrine of race, and the West, therefore, long stood against that democracy in industry which might have emancipated labor in the United States, because it did not admit to that democracy the American citizen of Negro descent.

Thus Northern workers were organizing and fighting industrial integration in order to gain higher wage and shorter hours, and more and more they saw economic salvation in the rich land of the West. A Western movement of white workers and pioneers began and was paralleled by a Western movement of planters and black workers in the South. Land and more land became the cry of the Southern political leader, with finally a growing demand for reopening of the African slave trade. Land, more land, became the cry of the peasant farmer in the North. The two forces met in Kansas, and in Kansas civil war began.

The South was fighting for the protection and expansion of its agrarian feudalism. For the sheer existence of slavery, there must be a continual supply of fertile land, cheaper slaves, and such political power as would give the slave status full legal recognition and protection, and annihilate the free Negro. The Louisiana Purchase had furnished slaves and land, but most of the land was in the Northwest. The foray into Mexico had opened an empire, but the availability of this land was partly spoiled by the loss of California to free labor. This suggested a proposed expansion of slavery toward Kansas, where it involved the South in competition with white labor: a competition which endangered the slave status, encouraged slave revolt, and increased the possibility of fugitive slaves.

It was a war to determine how far industry in the United States should be carried on under a system where the capitalist owns not only the nation's raw material, not only the land, but also the laborer himself; or whether the laborer was going to maintain his personal freedom, and enforce it by growing political and economic independence based on widespread ownership of land.

This brings us down to the period of the Civil War. Up to the time that the war actually broke out, American labor simply refused, in the main, to envisage black labor as a part of its problem. Right up to the edge of the war, it was talking about the emancipation of white labor and the organization of stronger unions without saying a word, or apparently giving a thought, to four million black slaves. During the war, labor was resentful. Workers were forced to fight in a strife between capitalists in which they had no interest and they showed their resentment in the peculiarly human way of beating and murdering the innocent victims of it all, the black free Negroes of New York and other Northern cities; while in the South, five million non-slaveholding poor white farmers and laborers sent their manhood by the thousands to fight and die for a system that had degraded them equally with the black slave. Could one imagine anything more paradoxical than this whole situation?

America thus stepped forward in the first blossoming of the modern age and added to the Art of Beauty, gift of the Renaissance, and to Freedom of Belief, gift of Martin Luther and Leo X, a vision of democratic self-government: the domination of political life by the intelligent decision of free and self-sustaining men. What an idea and what an area for its realization—endless land of richest fertility, natural resources such as Earth seldom exhibited before, a population infinite in variety, of universal gift, burned in the fires of poverty and caste, yearning toward the Unknown God; and self-reliant pioneers, unafraid of man or devil. It was the Supreme Adventure, in the last Great Battle of the West, for that human freedom which would release the human spirit from lower lust for mere meat, and set it free to dream and sing.

And then some unjust God leaned, laughing, over the ramparts of heaven and dropped a black man in the midst.

It transformed the world. It turned democracy back to Roman Imperialism and Fascism; it restored caste and oligarchy; it replaced freedom with slavery and withdrew the name of humanity from the vast majority of human beings.

But not without struggle. Not without writhing and rending of spirit and pitiable wail of lost souls. They said: Slavery was wrong but not all wrong; slavery must perish and not simply move; God made black men; God made slavery; the will of God be done; slavery to the glory of God and black men as his servants and ours; slavery as a way to freedom—the freedom of blacks, the freedom of whites; white freedom as the goal of the world and black slavery as the path thereto. Up with the white world, down with the black!

Then came this battle called Civil War, beginning in Kansas in 1854, and ending in the presidential election of 1876—twenty awful years. The slave went free; stood a brief moment in the sun; then moved back again toward slavery. The whole weight of America was thrown to color caste. The colored world went down before England, France, Germany, Russia, Italy and America. A new slavery arose. The upward moving of white labor was betrayed into wars for profit based on color caste. Democracy died save in the hearts of black folk.

Indeed, the plight of the white working class throughout the world today is directly traceable to Negro slavery in America, on which modern commerce and industry was founded, and which persisted to threaten free labor until it was partially overthrown in 1863. The resulting color caste founded and retained by capitalism was adopted, forwarded and approved by white labor, and resulted in subordination of colored labor to white profits the world over. Thus the majority of the world's laborers, by the insistence of white labor, became the basis of a system of industry which ruined democracy and showed its perfect fruit in World War and Depression. And this book seeks to tell that story.

Have ye leisure, comfort, calm,
Shelter, food, love's gentle balm?

Or what is it ye buy so dear
With your pain and with your fear?

The seed ye sow, another reaps;
The wealth ye find, another keeps;
The robes ye weave, another wears;
The arms ye forge, another bears.

PERCY BYSSHE SHELLEY

1. Schlüter, *Lincoln, Labor and Slavery*, p. 66.
2. Campbell, *Negromania*, p. 545.
3. Schlüter, *Lincoln, Labor and Slavery*, pp. 72, 73.
4. Schlüter, *Lincoln, Labor and Slavery*, p. 135.
5. Schlüter, *Lincoln, Labor and Slavery*, p. 86.
6. Simkins and Woody, *South Carolina During Reconstruction*, p. 326.
7. Olmsted, *Seaboard Slave States*, p. 404.
8. Hart, *The Southern South*, pp. 34, 35.

III. THE PLANTER

How seven per cent of a section within a nation ruled five million
white people and owned four million black people and sought to
make agriculture equal to industry through the rule of property
without yielding political power or education to labor

Seven per cent of the total population of the South in 1860 owned
nearly 3 million of the 3,953,696 slaves. There was nearly as great
a concentration of ownership in the best agricultural land. This meant
that in a country predominantly agricultural, the ownership of labor,
land and capital was extraordinarily concentrated. Such peculiar organization of industry would have to be carefully reconciled with the
new industrial and political democracy of the nineteenth century if
it were to survive.

Of the five million whites who owned no slaves some were united
in interest with the slave owners. These were overseers, drivers and
dealers in slaves. Others were hirers of white and black labor, and
still others were merchants and professional men, forming a petty
bourgeois class, and climbing up to the planter class or falling down
from it. The mass of the poor whites, as we have shown, were economic outcasts.

Colonial Virginia declared its belief in natural and inalienable
rights, popular sovereignty, and government for the common good,
even before the Declaration of Independence. But it soon became the
belief of doctrinaires, and not a single other Southern state enacted
these doctrines of equality until after the Civil War. The Reconstruction constitutions incorporated them; but quite logically, South
Carolina repudiated its declaration in 1895.

The domination of property was shown in the qualifications for
office and voting in the South. Southerners and others in the Constitutional Convention asked for property qualifications for the President of the United States, the federal judges, and Senators. Most
Southern state governments required a property qualification for the
Governor, and in South Carolina, he must be worth ten thousand
pounds. Members of the legislature must usually be landholders.

Plural voting was allowed as late as 1832. The requirement of the
ownership of freehold land for officeholders operated to the disadvantage of merchants and mechanics. In North Carolina, a man must

own 50 acres to vote for Senator, and in 1828, out of 250 voters at Wilmington, only 48 had the qualifications to vote for Senator. Toward the time of the Civil War many of these property qualifications disappeared.

Into the hands of the slaveholders the political power of the South was concentrated, by their social prestige, by property ownership and also by their extraordinary rule of the counting of all or at least three-fifths of the Negroes as part of the basis of representation in the legislature. It is singular how this "three-fifths" compromise was used, not only to degrade Negroes in theory, but in practice to disfranchise the white South. Nearly all of the Southern states began with recognizing the white population as a basis of representation; they afterward favored the black belt by direct legislation or by counting three-fifths of the slave population, and then finally by counting the whole black population; or they established, as in Virginia and South Carolina, a "mixed" basis of representation, based on white population and on property; that is, on land and slaves.

In the distribution of seats in the legislature, this manipulation of political power appears. In the older states representatives were assigned arbitrarily to counties, districts and towns, with little regard to population. This was for the purpose of putting the control in the hands of wealthy planters. Variations from this were the basing of representation on the white population in one House, and taxation in the other, or the use of the Federal proportion; that is, free persons and three-fifths of the slaves, or Federal proportion and taxation combined. These were all manipulated so as to favor the wealthy planters. The commercial class secured scant representation as compared with agriculture.

"It is a fact that the political working of the state [of South Carolina] is in the hands of one hundred and fifty to one hundred and eighty men. It has taken me six months to appreciate the *entireness* of the fact, though of course I had heard it stated." *

In all cases, the slaveholder practically voted both for himself and his slaves and it was not until 1850 and particularly after the war that there were signs of self-assertion on the part of the poor whites to break this monopoly of power. Alabama, for instance, in 1850, based representation in the general assembly upon the white inhabitants, after thirty years of counting the whole white and black population. Thus the Southern planters had in their hands from 1820 to the Civil War political power equivalent to one or two million freemen in the North.

They fought bitterly during the early stages of Reconstruction to retain this power for the whites, while at the same time granting no political power to the blacks. Finally and up to this day, by making good their efforts to disfranchise the blacks, the political heirs of the planters still retain for themselves this added political representation as a legacy from slavery, and a power to frustrate all third party movements.

Thus, the planters who owned from fifty to one thousand slaves and from one thousand to ten thousand acres of land came to fill the whole picture in the South, and literature and the propaganda which is usually called history have since exaggerated that picture. The planter certainly dominated politics and social life—he boasted of his education, but on the whole, these Southern leaders were men singularly ignorant of modern conditions and trends and of their historical background. All their ideas of gentility and education went back to the days of European privilege and caste. They cultivated a surface acquaintance with literature and they threw Latin quotations even into Congress. Some few had a cultural education at Princeton and at Yale, and to this day Princeton refuses to receive Negro students, and Yale has admitted a few with reluctance, as a curious legacy from slavery.

Many Southerners traveled abroad and the fashionable European world met almost exclusively Americans from the South and were favorably impressed by their manners which contrasted with the gaucherie of the average Northerner. A Southerner of the upper class could enter a drawing room and carry on a light conversation and eat according to the rules, on tables covered with silver and fine linen. They were "gentlemen" according to the older and more meager connotation of the word.

Southern women of the planter class had little formal education; they were trained in dependence, with a smattering of French and music; they affected the latest European styles; were always described as "beautiful" and of course must do no work for a living except in the organization of their households. In this latter work, they were assisted and even impeded by more servants than they needed. The temptations of this sheltered exotic position called the finer possibilities of womanhood into exercise only in exceptional cases. It was the woman on the edge of the inner circles and those of the struggling poor whites who sought to enter the ranks of the privileged who showed superior character.

Most of the planters, like most Americans, were of humble descent, two or three generations removed. Jefferson Davis was a grandson of a poor Welsh immigrant. Yet the Southerner's assumptions impressed the North and although most of them were descended from the same social classes as the Yankees, yet the Yankees had more recently been reënforced by immigration and were strenuous, hard-working men, ruthlessly pushing themselves into the leadership of the new industry. Such folk not only "love a lord," but even the fair imitation of one.

The leaders of the South had leisure for good breeding and high living, and before them Northern society abased itself and flattered and fawned over them. Perhaps this, more than ethical reasons, or even economic advantage, made the way of the abolitionist hard. In New York, Saratoga, Philadelphia and Cincinnati, a slave baron, with his fine raiment, gorgeous and doll-like women and black flunkies, quite turned the heads of Northern society. Their habits of extravagance impressed the nation for a long period. Much of the waste charged against Reconstruction arose from the attempt of the post-war population, white and black, to imitate the manners of a slave-nurtured gentility, and this brought furious protest from former planters; because while planters spent money filched from the labor of black slaves, the poor white and black leaders of Reconstruction spent taxes drawn from recently impoverished planters.

From an economic point of view, this planter class had interest in consumption rather than production. They exploited labor in order that they themselves should live more grandly and not mainly for increasing production. Their taste went to elaborate households, well-furnished and hospitable; they had much to eat and drink; they consumed large quantities of liquor; they gambled and caroused and kept up the habit of dueling well down into the nineteenth century. Sexually they were lawless, protecting elaborately and flattering the virginity of a small class of women of their social clan, and keeping at command millions of poor women of the two laboring groups of the South.

Sexual chaos was always the possibility of slavery, not always realized but always possible: polygamy through the concubinage of black women to white men; polyandry between black women and selected men on plantations in order to improve the human stock of strong and able workers. The census of 1860 counted 588,352 persons obviously of mixed blood—a figure admittedly below the truth.

"Every man who resides on his plantation may have his harem, and has every inducement of custom, and of pecuniary gain [The law declares that the children of slaves are to follow the fortunes of the mother. Hence the practice of planters selling and bequeathing their own children.], to tempt him to the common practice. Those who, notwithstanding, keep their homes undefiled may be considered as of incorruptible purity." [1]

Mrs. Trollope speaks of the situation of New Orleans' mulattoes:

"Of all the prejudices I have ever witnessed, this appears to us the most violent, and the most inveterate. Quadroon girls, the acknowledged daughters of wealthy American or Creole fathers, educated with all the style and accomplishments which money can procure at New Orleans, and with all the decorum that care and affection can give—exquisitely beautiful, graceful, gentle, and amiable, are not admitted, nay, are not on any terms admissible, into the society of the Creole families of Louisiana. They cannot marry; that is to say, no ceremony can render any union with them legal or binding." [2]

"It is known by almost everybody who has heard of the man, Richard M. Johnson, a Democratic Vice-President of the United States, that he had colored daughters of whom he was proud; and his was not an exceptional case." [3] Several Presidents of the United States have been accused of racial catholicity in sex.

And finally, one cannot forget that bitter word attributed to a sister of a President of the United States: "We Southern ladies are complimented with names of wives; but we are only mistresses of seraglios." [4]

What the planters wanted was income large enough to maintain the level of living which was their ideal. Naturally, only a few of them had enough for this, and the rest, striving toward it, were perpetually in debt and querulously seeking a reason for this indebtedness outside themselves. Since it was beneath the dignity of a "gentleman" to encumber himself with the details of his finances, this lordly excuse enabled the planter to place between himself and the black slave a series of intermediaries through whom bitter pressure and exploitation could be exercised and large crops raised. For the very reason that the planters did not give attention to details, there was wide tendency to commercialize their growing business of supplying raw materials for an expanding modern industry. They were the last to comprehend the revolution through which that industry was passing and their efforts to increase income succeeded only at the cost of raping the land and degrading the laborers.

Theoretically there were many ways of increasing the income of the planter; practically there was but one. The planter might sell his crops at higher prices; he might increase his crop by intensive farming, or he might reduce the cost of handling and transporting his crops; he might increase his crops by making his laborers work harder and giving them smaller wages. In practice, the planter, so far as prices were concerned, was at the mercy of the market. Merchants and manufacturers by intelligence and close combination set the current prices of raw material. Their power thus exercised over agriculture was not unlimited but it was so large, so continuous and so steadily and intelligently exerted that it gradually reduced agriculture to a subsidiary industry whose returns scarcely supported the farmer and his labor.

The Southern planter in the fifties was in a key position to attempt to break and arrest the growth of this domination of all industry by trade and manufacture. But he was too lazy and self-indulgent to do this and he would not apply his intelligence to the problem. His capitalistic rivals of the North were hard-working, simple-living zealots devoting their whole energy and intelligence to building up an industrial system. They quickly monopolized transport and mines and factories and they were more than willing to include the big plantations. But the planter wanted results without effort. He wanted large income without corresponding investment and he insisted furiously upon a system of production which excluded intelligent labor, machinery, and modern methods. He toyed with the idea of local manufactures and ships and railroads. But this entailed too much work and sacrifice.

The result was that Northern and European industry set prices for Southern cotton, tobacco and sugar which left a narrow margin of profit for the planter. He could retaliate only by more ruthlessly exploiting his slave labor so as to get the largest crops at the least expense. He was therefore not deliberately cruel to his slaves, but he had to raise cotton enough to satisfy his pretensions and self-indulgence, even if it brutalized and commercialized his slave labor.

Thus slavery was the economic lag of the 16th century carried over into the 19th century and bringing by contrast and by friction moral lapses and political difficulties. It has been estimated that the Southern states had in 1860 three billion dollars invested in slaves, which meant that slaves and land represented the mass of their capital. Being generally convinced that Negroes could only labor as slaves, it was easy for them to become further persuaded that slaves were better off than white workers and that the South had a better labor system than the North, with extraordinary possibilities in industrial and social development.

The argument went like this: raw material like cotton, tobacco, sugar, rice, together with other foodstuffs formed the real wealth of the United States, and were produced by the Southern states. These crops were sold all over the world and were in such demand that the industry of Europe depended upon them. The trade with Europe must be kept open so that the South might buy at the lowest prices such manufactured goods as she wanted, and she must oppose all Northern attempts to exalt industry at the expense of agriculture.

The North might argue cogently that industry and manufacture could build up in the United States a national economy. Writers on economics began in Germany and America to elaborate and insist upon the advantages of such a system; but the South would have none of it. It meant not only giving the North a new industrial prosperity, but doing this at the expense of England and France; and the Southern planters preferred Europe to Northern America. They not only preferred Europe for social reasons and for economic advantages, but they sensed that the new power of monopolizing and distributing capital through a national banking system, if permitted in the North in an expanding industry, would make the North an even greater financial dictator of the South than it was at the time.

The South voiced for the Southern farmer, in 1850, words almost identical with those of the Western farmer, seventy-five years later. "All industry," declared one Southerner, "is getting legislative support against agriculture, and thus the profits are going to manufacture and trade, and these concentrated in the North stand against the interests of the South."

It could not, perhaps, be proven that the Southern planter, had he been educated in economics and history, and had he known the essential trends of the modern world, could have kept the Industrial Revolution from subordinating agriculture and reducing it to its present vasssalage to manufacturing. But it is certain that an enlightened and far-seeing agrarianism under the peculiar economic circumstances of the United States during the first half of the nineteenth century could have essentially modified the economic trend of the world.

The South with free rich land and cheap labor had the monopoly of cotton, a material in universal demand. If the leaders of the South, while keeping the consumer in mind, had turned more thoughtfully to the problem of the American producer, and had guided the production of cotton and food so as to take every advantage of new machinery and modern methods in agriculture, they might have moved forward with manufacture and been able to secure an approximately large amount of profit. But this would have involved yielding to the demands of modern labor: opportunity for education, legal protection of women and children, regulation of the hours of work, steadily increasing wages and the right to some voice in the administration of the state if not in the conduct of industry.

The South had but one argument against following modern civilization in this yielding to the demand of laboring humanity: it insisted on the efficiency of Negro labor for ordinary toil and on its essential equality in physical condition with the average labor of Europe and America. But in order to maintain its income without sacrifice or exertion, the South fell back on a doctrine of racial differences which it asserted made higher intelligence and increased efficiency impossible for Negro labor. Wishing such an excuse for lazy indulgence, the planter easily found, invented and proved it. His subservient religious leaders reverted to the "Curse of Canaan"; his pseudo-scientists gathered and supplemented all available doctrines of race inferiority; his scattered schools and pedantic periodicals repeated these legends, until for the average planter born after 1840 it was impossible not to believe that all valid laws in psychology, economics and politics stopped with the Negro race.

The espousal of the doctrine of Negro inferiority by the South was primarily because of economic motives and the inter-connected political urge necessary to support slave industry; but to the watching world it sounded like the carefully thought out result of experience and reason; and because of this it was singularly disastrous for modern civilization in science and religion, in art and government, as well as in industry. The South could say that the Negro, even when brought into modern civilization, could not be civilized, and that, therefore, he and the other colored peoples of the world were so far inferior to the whites that the white world had a right to rule mankind for their own selfish interests.

Never in modern times has a large section of a nation so used its combined energies to the degradation of mankind. The hurt to the Negro in this era was not only his treatment in slavery; it was the wound dealt to his reputation as a human being. Nothing was left; nothing was sacred; and while the best and more cultivated and more humane of the planters did not themselves always repeat the calumny, they stood by, consenting by silence, while blatherskites said things about Negroes too cruelly untrue to be the word of civilized men. Not only then in the forties and fifties did the word Negro lose its capital letter, but African history became the tale of degraded animals and sub-human savages, where no vestige of human culture found foothold.

Thus a basis in reason, philanthropy and science was built up for Negro slavery. Judges on the bench declared that Negro servitude was to last, "if the apocalypse be not in error, until the end of time." The Atlanta *Daily Intelligencer* of January 9, 1860, said, "We can't see for the life of us how anyone understanding fully the great principle that underlies our system of involuntary servitude, can discover any monstrosity in subjecting a Negro to slavery of a white man. We contend on the contrary that the monstrosity, or, at least, the un-naturalness in this matter, consists in finding Negroes anywhere in white communities not under the control of the whites. Whenever we see a Negro, we presuppose a master, and if we see him in what is commonly called a 'free state,' we consider him out of his place.

This matter of manumission, or emancipation 'now, thank heaven, less practiced than formerly,' is a species of false philanthropy, which we look upon as a cousin-German to Abolitionism—bad for the master, worse for the slave."

Beneath this educational and social propaganda lay the undoubted evidence of the planter's own expenses. He saw ignorant and sullen labor deliberately reducing his profits. In fact, he always faced the negative attitude of the general strike. Open revolt of slaves—refusal to work—could be met by beating and selling to the harsher methods of the deep South and Southwest as punishment. Running away could be curbed by law and police. But nothing could stop the dogged slave from doing just as little and as poor work as possible. All observers spoke of the fact that the slaves were slow and churlish; that they wasted material and malingered at their work. Of course, they did. This was not racial but economic. It was the answer of any group of laborers forced down to the last ditch. They might be made to work continuously but no power could make them work well.

If the European or Northern laborer did not do his work properly and fast enough, he would lose the job. The black slave could not lose his job. If the Northern laborer got sick or injured, he was discharged, usually without compensation; the black slave could not be discharged and had to be given some care in sicknesses, particularly if he represented a valuable investment. The Northern and English employer could select workers in the prime of life and did not have to pay children too young to work or adults too old. The slave owner had to take care of children and old folk, and while this did not cost much on a farm or entail any great care, it did seriously cut down the proportion of his effective laborers, which could only be balanced by the systematic labor of women and children. The children ran loose with only the most general control, getting their food with the other slaves. The old folk foraged for themselves. Now and then they were found dead of neglect, but usually there was no trouble in their getting at least food enough to live and some rude shelter.

The economic difficulties that thus faced the planter in exploiting the black slave were curious. Contrary to the trend of his age, he could not use higher wage to induce better work or a larger supply of labor. He could not allow his labor to become intelligent, although intelligent labor would greatly increase the production of wealth. He could not depend on voluntary immigration unless the immigrants be slaves, and he must bear the burden of the old and sick and could only balance this by child labor and the labor of women.

The use of slave women as day workers naturally broke up or made impossible the normal Negro home and this and the slave code led to a development of which the South was really ashamed and which it often denied, and yet perfectly evident: the raising of slaves in the Border slave states for systematic sale on the commercialized cotton plantations.

The ability of the slaveholder and landlord to sequester a large share of the profits of slave labor depended upon his exploitation of that labor, rather than upon high prices for his product in the market. In the world market, the merchants and manufacturers had all the advantage of unity, knowledge and purpose, and could hammer down the price of raw material. The slaveholder, therefore, saw Northern merchants and manufacturers enrich themselves from the results of Southern agriculture. He was angry and used all of his great political power to circumvent it. His only effective economic movement, however, could take place against the slave. He was forced, unless willing to take lower profits, continually to beat down the cost of his slave labor.

But there was another motive which more and more strongly as time went on compelled the planter to cling to slavery. His political power was based on slavery. With four million slaves he could balance the votes of 2,400,000 Northern voters, while in the inconceivable event of their becoming free, their votes would outnumber those of his Northern opponents, which was precisely what happened in 1868.

As the economic power of the planter waned, his political power became more and more indispensable to the maintenance of his income and profits. Holding his industrial system secure by this political domination, the planter turned to the more systematic exploitation of his black labor. One method called for more land and the other for more slaves. Both meant not only increased crops but increased political power. It was a temptation that swept greed, religion, military pride and dreams of empire to its defense. There were two possibilities. He might follow the old method of the early West Indian sugar plantations: work his slaves without regard to their physical condition, until they died of over-work or exposure, and then buy new ones. The difficulty of this, however, was that the price of slaves, since the attempt to abolish the slave trade, was gradually rising. This in the deep South led to a strong and gradually increasing demand for the reopening of the African slave trade, just as modern industry demands cheaper and cheaper coolie labor in Asia and half-slave labor in African mines.

The other possibility was to find continual increments of new, rich land upon which ordinary slave labor would bring adequate return. This land the South sought in the Southeast; then beyond the Mississippi in Louisiana and Texas, then in Mexico, and finally, it turned its face in two directions: toward the Northwestern territories of the United States and toward the West Indian islands and South America. The South was drawn toward the West by two motives: first the possibility that slavery in Kansas, Colorado, Utah and Nevada would be at least as profitable as in Missouri, and secondly to prevent the expansion of free labor there and its threat to slavery. This challenge was a counsel of despair in the face of modern industrial development and probably the radical South expected defeat in the West and hoped the consequent resentment among the slaveholders would set the South toward a great slave empire in the Caribbean. Jefferson Davis was ready to reopen the African slave trade to any future acquisition south of the Rio Grande.

This brought the South to war with the farmers and laborers in the North and West, who wanted free soil but did not want to compete with slave labor. The fugitive slave law of 1850 vastly extended Federal power so as to nullify state rights in the North. The Compromise of 1850 permitted the extension of slavery into the territories, and the Kansas-Nebraska Bill, 1854, deprived Congress of the right to prohibit slavery anywhere. This opened the entire West to slavery. War followed in Kansas. Slaveholders went boldly into Kansas, armed and organized:

"The invaders went in such force that the scattered and unorganized citizens could make no resistance and in many places they did not attempt to vote, seeing the polls surrounded by crowds of armed men who they knew came from Missouri to control the election and the leaders of the invaders kept their men under control, being anxious to prevent needless violence, as any serious outbreak would attract the attention of the country. In some districts the actual citizens protested against the election and petitioned the governor to set it aside and order another.

"We can tell the impertinent scoundrels of the *Tribune* that we will continue to lynch and hang, to tar and feather and drown every white-livered Abolitionist who dares to pollute our soil." [5] Shut out from the United States territories by the Free Soil movement, the South determined upon secession with the distinct idea of eventually expanding into the Caribbean.

There was, however, the opposition in the Border States. The employers of labor in the Border States had found a new source of revenue. They did not like to admit it. They surrounded it with a certain secrecy, and it was exceedingly bad taste for any Virginia planter to have it indicated that he was deliberately raising slaves for sale; and yet that was a fact.

In no respect are the peculiar psychological difficulties of the planters better illustrated than with regard to the interstate slave trade. The theory was clear and lofty; slaves were a part of the family—"my people," George Washington called them. Under ordinary circumstances they were never to be alienated, but supported during good behavior and bad, punished and corrected for crime and misdemeanor, rewarded for good conduct. It was the patriarchal clan translated into modern life, with social, religious, economic and even blood ties.

This was the theory; but as a matter of fact, the cotton planters were supplied with laborers by the Border States. A laboring stock was deliberately bred for legal sale. A large number of persons followed the profession of promoting this sale of slaves. There were markets and quotations, and the stream of black labor, moving continuously into the South, reached yearly into the thousands.

Notwithstanding these perfectly clear and authenticated facts, the planter persistently denied them. He denied that there was any considerable interstate sale of slaves; he denied that families were broken up; he insisted that slave auctions were due to death or mischance, and pa·ticularly did he insist that the slave traders were the least of human beings and most despised.

This deliberate contradiction of plain facts constitutes itself a major charge against slavery and shows how the system often so affronted the moral sense of the planters themselves that they tried to hide from it. They could not face the fact of Negro women as brood mares and of black children as puppies.

Indeed, while we speak of the planters as one essentially unvarying group, there is evidence that the necessities of their economic organization were continually changing and deteriorating their morale and pushing forward ruder, noisier, less cultivated elements than characterized the Southern gentleman of earlier days. Certainly, the cursing, brawling, whoring gamblers who largely represented the South in the late fifties, evidenced the inevitable deterioration that overtakes men when their desire for income and extravagance overwhelms their respect for human beings. Thus the interstate slave trade grew and flourished and the demand for the African slave trade was rapidly becoming irresistible in the late fifties.

From fifty to eighty thousand slaves went from the Border States to the lower South in the last decade of slavery. One planter frankly said that he "calculated that the moment a colored baby was born, it was worth to him $300." So far as possible, the planters in selling off their slaves avoided the breaking up of families. But they were facing flat economic facts. The persons who were buying slaves in the cotton belt were not buying families, they were buying workers, and thus by economic demand families were continually and regularly broken up; the father was sold away; the mother and the half-grown children separated, and sometimes smaller children were sold. One of the subsequent tragedies of the system was the frantic efforts, before and after emancipation, of Negroes hunting for their relatives throughout the United States.

A Southerner wrote to Olmsted: "In the states of Maryland, Virginia, North Carolina, Kentucky, Tennessee and Missouri, as much attention is paid to the breeding and growth of Negroes as to that of horses and mules. Further south, we raise them both for use and for market. Planters command their girls and women (married or unmarried) to have children; and I have known a great many Negro girls to be sold off because they did not have children. A breeding woman is worth from one-sixth to one-fourth more than one that does not breed."

Sexual chaos arose from economic motives. The deliberate breeding of a strong, big field-hand stock could be carried out by selecting proper males, and giving them the run of the likeliest females. This in many Border States became a regular policy and fed the slave trade. Child-bearing was a profitable occupation, which received every possible encouragement, and there was not only no bar to illegitimacy, but an actual premium put upon it. Indeed, the word was impossible of meaning under the slave system.

Moncure D. Conway, whose father was a slaveholder near Fredericksburg, Virginia, wrote: "As a general thing, the chief pecuniary resource in the Border States is the breeding of slaves; and I grieve to say that there is too much ground for the charges that general licentiousness among the slaves, for the purpose of a large increase, is compelled by some masters and encouraged by many. The period of maternity is hastened, the average youth of Negro mothers being nearly three years earlier than that of any free race, and an old maid is utterly unknown among the women."

J. E. Cairnes, the English economist, in his passage with Mr. McHenry on this subject, computed from reliable data that Virginia had bred and exported to the cotton states between the years of 1840 and 1850 no less than 100,000 slaves, which at $500 per head would have yielded her $50,000,000.

The law sometimes forbade the breaking up of slave families but:

"Not one of these prohibitions, save those of Louisiana, and they but slightly, in any way referred to or hampered the owner of unencumbered slave property: he might sell or pawn or mortgage or give it away according to profit or whim, regardless of age or kinship.

"Elsewhere in the typical South—in Virginia, North Carolina, South Carolina, Tennessee, Arkansas and Texas—there seems to have been no restriction of any sort against separating mothers and children or husbands and wives or selling children of any age. Slavery was, indeed, a 'peculiar institution.'" [6]

The slave-trading Border States, therefore, in their own economic interest, frantically defended slavery, yet opposed the reopening of the African slave trade to which the Southern South was becoming more and more attracted. This slave trade had curious psychological effects upon the planter. When George Washington sold a slave to the West Indies for one hogshead "of best rum" and molasses and sweetmeats, it was because "this fellow is both a rogue and a runaway." [7]

Thus tradition grew up that the sale of a slave from a gentleman's plantation was for special cause. As time went on and slavery became systematized and commercialized under the Cotton Kingdom, this was absolutely untrue. The "buying or selling of slaves was not viewed as having any taint of 'hated' slave-trading; yet it early became a fully credited tradition, implicitly accepted generation after generation, that 'all traders were hated.'" [8]

The sacrifices necessary for economic advance, Southern planters were on the whole too selfish and too provincial to make. They would not in any degree curtail consumption in order to furnish at least part of the necessary increase of capital and make dependence upon debt to the North and to Europe less necessary. They did not socialize the ownership of the slave on any large scale or educate him in technique; they did not encourage local and auxiliary industry or manufacture, and thus make it possible for their own profit to exploit white labor and give it an economic foothold. This would have involved, to be sure, increased recognition of democracy, and far from yielding to any such inevitable development, the South threw itself into the arms of a reaction at least two centuries out of date. Governor McDuffie of South Carolina called the laboring class, bleached or unbleached, a "dangerous" element in the population.

A curious argument appeared in the *Charleston Mercury* of 1861: "Within ten years past as many as ten thousand slaves have been drawn away from Charleston by the attractive prices of the West, and [white] laborers from abroad have come to take their places. These laborers have every disposition to work above the slave, and if there were opportunity, would be glad to do so; but without such opportunity they come into competition with him; they are necessarily restive to the contact. Already there is disposition to exclude him from the trades, from public works, from drays, and the tables of the hotels; he is even now excluded to a great extent, and . . . when more laborers . . . shall come in greater numbers to the South, they will still more increase the tendency to exclusion; they will question the right of masters to employ their slaves in any work that they may wish for; they will invoke the aid of legislation; they will use the elective franchise to that end; they will acquire the power to determine municipal elections; they will inexorably use it; and thus the town of Charleston, at the very heart of slavery, may become a fortress of democratic power against it."

The planters entirely misconceived the extent to which democracy was spreading in the North. They thought it meant that the laboring class was going to rule the North for labor's own economic interests. Even those who saw the seamy side of slavery were convinced of the rightness of the system because they believed that there were seeds of disaster in the North against which slavery would be their protection; "indications that these are already beginning to be felt or anticipated by prophetic minds, they think they see in the demands for 'Land Limitation,' in the anti-rent troubles, in strikes of workmen, in the distress of emigrants at the eddies of their current, in diseased philanthropy, in radical democracy, and in the progress of socialistic ideas in general. 'The North,' say they, 'has progressed under the high pressure of unlimited competition; as the population grows denser, there will be terrific explosions, disaster, and ruin, while they will ride quietly and safely at the anchor of slavery.' " [9]

Thus the planters of the South walked straight into the face of modern economic progress. The North had yielded to democracy, but only because democracy was curbed by a dictatorship of property and investment which left in the hands of the leaders of industry such economic power as insured their mastery and their profits. Less than this they knew perfectly well they could not yield, and more than this they would not. They remained masters of the economic destiny of America.

In the South, on the other hand, the planters walked in quite the opposite direction, excluding the poor whites from nearly every economic foothold with apparently no conception of the danger of these five million workers who, in time, overthrew the planters and utterly submerged them after the Civil War; and the South was equally determined to regard its four million slaves as a class of submerged workers and to this ideal they and their successors still cling.

Calhoun once said with perfect truth: There has never yet existed "a wealthy and civilized society in which one portion of the community did not, in point of fact, live on the labor of the other." Governor McDuffie of South Carolina said: "God forbid that my descendants, in the remotest generations, should live in any other than a community having the institution of domestic slavery." [10]

The South elected to make its fight through the political power which it possessed because of slavery and the disfranchisement of the poor whites. It had in American history chosen eleven out of sixteen Presidents, seventeen out of twenty-eight Judges of the Supreme Court, fourteen out of nineteen Attorneys-General, twenty-one out of thirty-three Speakers of the House, eighty out of one hundred thirty-four Foreign Ministers. It demanded a fugitive slave law as strong as words could make it and it was offered constitutional guarantees which would have made it impossible for the North to meddle with the organization of the slave empire.

The South was assured of all the territory southwest of Missouri and as far as California. It might even have extended its imperialistic sway toward the Caribbean without effective opposition from the North or Europe. The South had conquered Mexico without help and beyond lay the rest of Mexico, the West Indies and South America, open to Southern imperialistic enterprise. The South dominated the Army and Navy. It argued that a much larger proportion of the population could go to war in the South than in the North. There might, of course, be danger of slave insurrection in a long war with actual invasion, but the possibility of a long war or any war at all Southerners discounted, and they looked confidently forward to being either an independent section of the United States or an independent country with a stable economic foundation which could dictate its terms to the modern world on the basis of a monopoly of cotton, and a large production of other essential raw materials.

The South was too ignorant to know that their only chance to establish such economic dictatorship and place themselves in a key economic position was through a national economy, in a large nation where a home market would absorb a large proportion of the production, and where agriculture, led by men of vision, could demand a fair share of profit from industry.

When, therefore, the planters surrendered this chance and went to war with the machine to establish agricultural independence, they lost because of their internal weakness. Their whole labor class, black and white, went into economic revolt. The breach could only have been healed by making the same concessions to labor that France, England, Germany and the North had made. There was no time for such change in the midst of war. Northern industry must, therefore, after the war, make the adjustment with labor which Southern agriculture refused to make. But the loss which agriculture sustained through the stubbornness of the planters led to the degradation of agriculture throughout the modern world.

Due to the stubbornness of the South and the capitalism of the

West, we have had built up in the world an agriculture with a minimum of machines and new methods, conducted by ignorant labor and producing raw materials used by industry equipped with machines and intelligent labor, and conducted by shrewd business men. The result has been that a disproportionate part of the profit of organized work has gone to industry, while the agricultural laborer has descended toward slavery. The West, instead of becoming a country of peasant proprietors who might have counteracted this result, surrendered itself hand and foot to capitalism and speculation in land.

The abolition of American slavery started the transportation of capital from white to black countries where slavery prevailed, with the same tremendous and awful consequences upon the laboring classes of the world which we see about us today. When raw material could not be raised in a country like the United States, it could be raised in the tropics and semi-tropics under a dictatorship of industry, commerce and manufacture and with no free farming class.

The competition of a slave-directed agriculture in the West Indies and South America, in Africa and Asia, eventually ruined the economic efficiency of agriculture in the United States and in Europe and precipitated the modern economic degradation of the white farmer, while it put into the hands of the owners of the machine such a monopoly of raw material that their domination of white labor was more and more complete.

The crisis came in 1860, not so much because Abraham Lincoln was elected President on a platform which refused further land for the expansion of slavery, but because the cotton crop of 1859 reached the phenomenal height of five million bales as compared with three million in 1850. To this was added the threat of radical abolition as represented by John Brown. The South feared these social upheavals but it was spurred to immediate action by the great cotton crop. Starting with South Carolina, the Southern cotton-raising and slave-consuming states were forced out of the Union.

Their reason for doing this was clearly stated and reiterated. For a generation, belief in slavery was the Southern shibboleth:

"A suspicion of heresy on the subject of the 'peculiar institution' was sufficient to declare the ineligibility of any candidate for office; nay, more, orthodoxy began to depend upon the correct attitude toward the doctrine of 'Squatter Sovereignty' and the extreme view held as to Federal protection of slavery in the territories." [11]

Jefferson Davis said that the North was "impairing the security of property and slaves and reducing those states which held slaves to a condition of inferiority."

Senator Toombs said that property and slaves must be entitled to the same protection from the government as any other property. The South Carolina convention arraigned the North for increasing hostility "to the institution of slavery," and declared for secession because the North had assumed the right of deciding upon the propriety of Southern domestic institutions.

Governor R. C. Wickliffe in his message at the extra session of the legislature of Louisiana expressed his belief that the election was "a deliberate design to pervert the powers of the Government to the immediate injury and ultimate destruction of the peculiar institution of the South." [12]

Slidel's farewell speech in the *Congressional Globe* of February 5, 1861:

"We separate," he said, "because of the hostility of Lincoln to our institutions. . . . If he were inaugurated without our consent there would be slave insurrections in the South." [13]

The Alabama Commissioner to Maryland arraigned the Lincoln government as proposing not "to recognize the right of the Southern citizens to property in the labor of African slaves." The Governor of Alabama arraigned the Republicans for desiring "the destruction of the institution of slavery."

In the Southern Congress, at Montgomery on the 2d of February, 1861, Senator Wigfall, from Texas, said that he was fighting for slavery, and for nothing else. The patent of nobility is in the color of the skin. He wanted to live in no country in which a man who blacked his boots and curried his horse was his equal. Give Negroes muskets and make them soldiers, and the next subject introduced for discussion will be miscegenation. [14] And finally, Alexander H. Stephens, Vice President of the Confederacy, stated fully the philosophy of the new Confederate government: "The new Constitution has put at rest forever all the agitating questions relating to our peculiar institutions—African slavery as it exists among us—the proper status of the Negro in our form of civilization. *This was the immediate cause of the late rupture and present revolution. Jefferson, in his forecast, had anticipated this as the 'rock upon which the old union would split.'* He was right. What was conjecture with him is now a realized fact. But whether he fully comprehended the great truth upon which that rock stood and stands may be doubted. The prevailing ideas entertained by him and most of the leading statesmen at the time of the formation of the old Constitution, were that the enslavement of the African was in violation of the laws of nature; that it was wrong in principle, socially, morally and politically. It was an evil they knew not well how to deal with, but the general opinion of the men of that day was that, somehow or other, in the order of Providence, the institution would be

evanescent and pass away. . . . Those ideas, however, were fundamentally wrong. They rested upon the assumption of the equality of
races. This was an error. It was a sandy foundation, and the idea of a
government built upon it; when the 'storm came and the winds blew,
it fell.'

"Our new government is founded upon exactly the opposite idea,
its foundations are laid, its corner-stone rests upon the great truth
that the Negro is not equal to the white man. That slavery—subordination to the superior race—is his natural and normal condition.
This, our new government, is the first in the history of the world,
based upon this great physical and moral truth. This truth has been
slow in the process of its development, like all other truths in the
various departments of science. It has been so even amongst us. Many
who hear me, perhaps, can recollect well, that this truth was not
generally admitted, even within their day. . . .

"Now they are universally acknowledged. May we not, therefore,
look with confidence to the ultimate universal acknowledgment of
the truths upon which our system rests. It is the first government ever
instituted upon principles of strict conformity to nature, and the
ordination of Providence, in furnishing the materials of human society. Many governments have been founded upon the principle of
certain classes; but the classes thus enslaved, were of the same race,
and in violation of the laws of nature. Our system commits no such
violation of nature's laws. The Negro, by nature, or by the curse
against Canaan, is fitted for that condition which he occupies in our
system. The architect, in the construction of buildings, lays the foundation with the proper materials, the granite; then comes the brick
or the marble. The substratum of our society is made of the material
fitted by nature for it, and by experience we know that it is best, not
only for the superior, but for the inferior race that it should be so.
It is, indeed, in conformity with the ordinance of the Creator. It is not
for us to inquire into the wisdom of His ordinances, or to question
them. For His own purposes He has made one race to differ from
another, as He has had 'one star to differ from another star in
glory.' " [15]

The rift between the Southern South and the Border States was
bridged by omission of all reference to the reopening of the slave trade
and stressing the reality of the Northern attack upon the institution
of slavery itself.

The movement against the slave trade laws in the Southern South
was strong and growing. In 1854, a grand jury in the Williamsburg
district of South Carolina declared: "As our unanimous opinion, that
the Federal law abolishing the African Slave Trade is a public griev-

ance. We hold this trade has been and would be, if reëstablished, a blessing to the American people and a benefit to the African himself."

Two years later, the Governor of the state in his annual message argued for a reopening of the trade and declared: "If we cannot supply the demand for slave labor, then we must expect to be supplied with a species of labor we do not want" (*i.e.*, free white labor). The movement was forwarded by the commercial conventions. In 1855, at New Orleans, a resolution for the repeal of the slave trade laws was introduced but not reported by committee. In 1856, at Savannah, the convention refused to debate the matter of the repeal of the slave trade laws but appointed a committee. At the convention at Knoxville, in 1857, a resolution declaring it inexpedient to reopen the trade was voted down. At Montgomery, in 1858, a committee presented an elaborate majority report declaring it "expedient and proper that the foreign slave trade should be reopened." After debate, it was decided that it was inexpedient for any single state to attempt to reopen the African slave trade while that state is one of the United States of America. Finally, at Vicksburg in 1859, it was voted 40-19, "that all laws, state or Federal, prohibiting the African slave trade, ought to be repealed."

Both the provisional and permanent constitutions of the Confederate states forbade the importation of Negroes from foreign countries, except the "slave-holding states or territories of the United States of America." Nevertheless, the foreign ministers of the Confederate states were assured that while the Confederate government had no power to reopen the slave trade, the states could, if they wanted to, and that the ministers were not to discuss any treaties to prohibit the trade.[16]

Thus the planters led the South into war, carrying the five million poor whites blindly with them and standing upon a creed which opposed the free distribution of government land; which asked for the expansion of slave territory, for restricted functions of the national government, and for the perpetuity of Negro slavery.

What irritated the planter and made him charge the North and liberal Europe with hypocrisy, was the ethical implications of slavery. He was kept explaining a system of work which he insisted was no different in essence from that in vogue in Europe and the North. They and he were all exploiting labor. He did it by individual right; they by state law. They called their labor free, but after all, the laborer was only free to starve, if he did not work on their terms. They called his laborer a slave when his master was responsible for him from birth to death.

The Southern argument had strong backing in the commercial North. Lawyer O'Conner of New York expressed amid applause that calm reasoned estimate of the Negro in 1859, which pervaded the North:

"Now, Gentlemen, nature itself has assigned his condition of servitude to the Negro. He has the strength and is fit to work; but nature, which gave him this strength, denied him both the intelligence to rule and the will to work. Both are denied to him. And the same nature which denied him the will to work, gave him a master, who should enforce this will, and make a useful servant of him in a climate to which he is well adapted for his own benefit and that of the master who rules him. I assert that it is no injustice to leave the Negro in the position into which nature placed him; to put a master over him; and he is not robbed of any right, if he is compelled to labor in return for this, and to supply a just compensation for his master in return for the labor and the talents devoted to ruling him and to making him useful to himself and to society."

What the planter and his Northern apologist did not readily admit was that this exploitation of labor reduced it to a wage so low and a standard of living so pitiable that no modern industry in agriculture or trade or manufacture could build upon it; that it made ignorance compulsory and had to do so in self-defense; and that it automatically was keeping the South from entering the great stream of modern industry where growing intelligence among workers, a rising standard of living among the masses, increased personal freedom and political power, were recognized as absolutely necessary.

The ethical problem here presented was less important than the political and far less than the economic. The Southerners were as little conscious of the hurt they were inflicting on human beings as the Northerners were of their treatment of the insane. It is easy for men to discount and misunderstand the suffering or harm done others. Once accustomed to poverty, to the sight of toil and degradation, it easily seems normal and natural; once it is hidden beneath a different color of skin, a different stature or a different habit of action and speech, and all consciousness of inflicting ill disappears.

The Southern planter suffered, not simply for his economic mistakes—the psychological effect of slavery upon him was fatal. The mere fact that a man could be, under the law, the actual master of the mind and body of human beings had to have disastrous effects. It tended to inflate the ego of most planters beyond all reason; they became arrogant, strutting, quarrelsome kinglets; they issued commands; they made laws; they shouted their orders; they expected deference and self-abasement; they were choleric and easily insulted. Their "honor" became a vast and awful thing, requiring wide and insistent deference. Such of them as were inherently weak and inefficient were all the more easily angered, jealous and resentful; while the few who were superior, physically or mentally, conceived no bounds to their power and personal prestige. As the world had long learned, nothing is so calculated to ruin human nature as absolute power over human beings.

On the other hand, the possession of such power did not and could not lead to its continued tyrannical exercise. The tyrant could be kind and congenial. He could care for his chattels like a father; he could grant indulgence and largess; he could play with power and find tremendous satisfaction in its benevolent use.

Thus, economically and morally, the situation of the planter became intolerable. What was needed was the force of great public opinion to make him see his economic mistakes and the moral debauchery that threatened him. But here again in the planter class no room was made for the reformer, the recalcitrant. The men who dared such thought and act were driven out or suppressed with a virulent tyranny reminiscent of the Inquisition and the Reformation. For these there was the same peculiar way of escape that lay before the slave. The planter who could not stand slavery followed the poor whites who could not stand Negroes, they followed the Negro who also could not stand slavery, into the North; and there, removed from immediate contact with the evils of slavery, the planter often became the "copperhead," and theoretical champion of a system which he could not himself endure.

Frederick Douglass thus summed up the objects of the white planter: "I understand this policy to comprehend five cardinal objects. They are these: 1st, The complete suppression of all anti-slavery discussion. 2d, The expatriation of the entire free people of color from the United States. 3d, The unending perpetuation of slavery in this republic. 4th, The nationalization of slavery to the extent of making slavery respected in every state of the Union. 5th, The extension of slavery over Mexico and the entire South American states." [17]

This whole system and plan of development failed, and failed of its own weakness. Unending effort has gone into painting the claims of the Old South, its idyllic beauty and social charm. But the truth is inexorable. With all its fine men and sacrificing women, its hospitable homes and graceful manners, the South turned the most beautiful section of the nation into a center of poverty and suffering, of drinking, gambling and brawling; an abode of ignorance among black and white more abysmal than in any modern land; and a system of industry so humanly unjust and economically inefficient that if it had not committed suicide in civil war, it would have disintegrated of its own weight.

With the Civil War, the planters died as a class. We still talk as though the dominant social class in the South persisted after the war. But it did not. It disappeared. Just how quickly and in what manner the transformation was made, we do not know. No scientific study of the submergence of the remainder of the planter class into the ranks of the poor whites, and the corresponding rise of a portion of the poor whites into the dominant portion of landholders and capitalists, has been made. Of the names of prominent Southern families in Congress in 1860, only two appear in 1870, five in 1880. Of 90 prominent names in 1870, only four survived in 1880. Men talk today as though the upper class in the white South is descended from the slaveholders; yet we know by plain mathematics that the ancestors of most of the present Southerners never owned a slave nor had any real economic part in slavery. The disaster of war decimated the planters; the bitter disappointment and frustration led to a tremendous mortality after the war, and from 1870 on the planter class merged their blood so completely with the rising poor whites that they disappeared as a separate aristocracy. It is this that explains so many characteristics of the post-war South: its lynching and mob law, its murders and cruelty, its insensibility to the finer things of civilization.

Not spring; from us no agony of birth
Is asked or needed; in a crimson tide
Upon the down-slope of the world
We, the elect, are hurled
In fearful power and brief pride
Burning at last to silence and dark earth.
Not Spring.   JAMES RORTY

* Quoted in speech of Charles Sumner, in the United States Senate, December 20, 1865, from "a private letter which I have received from a government officer." *Congressional Globe,* 39th Congress, 1st Session, p. 93, Column 2.

1. Nevin, *American Social History as Recorded by British Travellers,* p. 209.
2. Trollope, Frances, *Domestic Manners of the Americans,* p. 10.
3. *An Appeal of a Colored Man to His Fellow-Citizens of a Fairer Hue, in the United States,* 1877, pp. 33, 34.
4. Goodell, *American Slave Code,* p. 111.
5. Brewster, *Sketches of Southern Mystery, Treason and Murder,* pp. 48, 51.
6. Bancroft, *Slave-Trading in the Old South,* p. 199.
7. Mazyck, *George Washington and the Negro,* p. 13.
8. Bancroft, *Slave-Trading in the Old South,* p. 381.
9. Olmsted, *A Journey in the Seaboard Slave States,* pp. 183-184.
10. *Studies in Southern History and Politics,* footnote, pp. 329, 346.
11. Ficklen, *History of Reconstruction in Louisiana,* p. 12.
12. Ficklen, *Reconstruction in Louisiana,* p. 15.
13. Ficklen, *Reconstruction in Louisiana,* p. 27.
14. *New Orleans Tribune,* February 15, 1865.
15. Stewart, *The Reward of Patriotism,* pp. 41-43.
16. Compare Du Bois, *Suppression of Slave-Trade,* Chapter XI.
17. Woodson, *Negro Orators and Their Orations,* p. 224.

IV. THE GENERAL STRIKE

*How the Civil War meant emancipation and how the black worker
won the war by a general strike which transferred his labor from
the Confederate planter to the Northern invader, in whose army
lines workers began to be organized as a new labor force*

When Edwin Ruffin, white-haired and mad, fired the first gun at
Fort Sumter, he freed the slaves. It was the last thing he meant to
do but that was because he was so typically a Southern oligarch. He
did not know the real world about him. He was provincial and lived
apart on his plantation with his servants, his books and his thoughts.
Outside of agriculture, he jumped at conclusions instead of testing
them by careful research. He knew, for instance, that the North
would not fight. He knew that Negroes would never revolt.

And so war came. War is murder, force, anarchy and debt. Its
end is evil, despite all incidental good. Neither North nor South had
before 1861 the slightest intention of going to war. The thought was
in many respects ridiculous. They were not prepared for war. The
national army was small, poorly equipped and without experience.
There was no file from which someone might draw plans of subjugation.

When Northern armies entered the South they became armies of
emancipation. It was the last thing they planned to be. The North
did not propose to attack property. It did not propose to free slaves.
This was to be a white man's war to preserve the Union, and the
Union must be preserved.

Nothing that concerned the amelioration of the Negro touched the
heart of the mass of Americans nor could the common run of men
realize the political and economic cost of Negro slavery. When, therefore, the Southern radicals, backed by political oligarchy and economic
dictatorship in the most extreme form in which the world had seen
it for five hundred years, precipitated secession, that part of the North
that opposed the plan had to hunt for a rallying slogan to unite the
majority in the North and in the West, and if possible, bring the
Border States into an opposing phalanx.

Freedom for slaves furnished no such slogan. Not one-tenth of the
Northern white population would have fought for any such purpose.
Free soil was a much stronger motive, but it had no cogency in this

contest because the Free Soilers did not dream of asking free soil in the South, since that involved the competition of slaves, or what seemed worse than that, of free Negroes. On the other hand, the tremendous economic ideal of keeping this great market for goods, the United States, together with all its possibilities of agriculture, manufacture, trade and profit, appealed to both the West and the North; and what was then much more significant, it appealed to the Border States.

> "To the flag we are pledged, all its foes we abhor,
> And we ain't for the nigger, but we are for the war."

The Border States wanted the cotton belt in the Union so that they could sell it their surplus slaves; but they also wanted to be in the same union with the North and West, where the profit of trade was large and increasing. The duty then of saving the Union became the great rallying cry of a war which for a long time made the Border States hesitate and confine secession to the far South. And yet they all knew that the only thing that really threatened the Union was slavery and the only remedy was Abolition.

If, now, the far South had had trained and astute leadership, a compromise could have been made which, so far as slavery was concerned, would have held the abnormal political power of the South intact, made the slave system impregnable for generations, and even given slavery practical rights throughout the nation.

Both North and South ignored in differing degrees the interests of the laboring classes. The North expected patriotism and union to make white labor fight; the South expected all white men to defend the slaveholders' property. Both North and South expected at most a sharp, quick fight and victory; more probably the South expected to secede peaceably, and then outside the Union, to impose terms which would include national recognition of slavery, new slave territory and new cheap slaves. The North expected that after a threat and demonstration to appease its "honor," the South would return with the right of slave property recognized and protected but geographically limited.

Both sections ignored the Negro. To the Northern masses the Negro was a curiosity, a sub-human minstrel, willingly and naturally a slave, and treated as well as he deserved to be. He had not sense enough to revolt and help Northern armies, even if Northern armies were trying to emancipate him, which they were not. The North shrank at the very thought of encouraging servile insurrection against the whites. Above all it did not propose to interfere with property. Negroes on the whole were considered cowards and inferior beings whose very presence in America was unfortunate. The abolitionists, it was true, expected action on the part of the Negro, but how much, they could not say. Only John Brown knew just how revolt had come and would come and he was dead.

Thus the Negro himself was not seriously considered by the majority of men, North or South. And yet from the very beginning, the Negro occupied the center of the stage because of very simple physical reasons: the war was in the South and in the South were 3,953,740 black slaves and 261,918 free Negroes. What was to be the relation of this mass of workers to the war? What did the war mean to the Negroes, and what did the Negroes mean to the war? There are two theories, both rather over-elaborated: the one that the Negro did nothing but faithfully serve his master until emancipation was thrust upon him; the other that the Negro immediately, just as quickly as the presence of Northern soldiers made it possible, left serfdom and took his stand with the army of freedom.

It must be borne in mind that nine-tenths of the four million black slaves could neither read nor write, and that the overwhelming majority of them were isolated on country plantations. Any mass movement under such circumstances must materialize slowly and painfully. What the Negro did was to wait, look and listen and try to see where his interest lay. There was no use in seeking refuge in an army which was not an army of freedom; and there was no sense in revolting against armed masters who were conquering the world. As soon, however, as it became clear that the Union armies would not or could not return fugitive slaves, and that the masters with all their fume and fury were uncertain of victory, the slave entered upon a general strike against slavery by the same methods that he had used during the period of the fugitive slave. He ran away to the first place of safety and offered his services to the Federal Army. So that in this way it was really true that he served his former master and served the emancipating army; and it was also true that this withdrawal and bestowal of his labor decided the war.

The South counted on Negroes as laborers to raise food and money crops for civilians and for the army, and even in a crisis, to be used for military purposes. Slave revolt was an ever-present risk, but there was no reason to think that a short war with the North would greatly increase this danger. Publicly, the South repudiated the thought of its slaves even wanting to be rescued. The New Orleans *Crescent* showed "the absurdity of the assertion of a general stampede of our Negroes." The London *Dispatch* was convinced that Negroes did not want to be free. "As for the slaves themselves, crushed with the wrongs of Dred Scott and Uncle Tom—most provoking—they cannot be brought to 'burn with revenge.' They are spies for their masters. They obstinately refuse to run away to liberty, outrage and starvation. They work in the fields as usual when the planter and overseer are away and only the white women are left at home."

Early in the war, the South had made careful calculation of the military value of slaves. The Alabama *Advertiser* in 1861 discussed the slaves as a "Military Element in the South." It said that "The total white population of the eleven states now comprising the Confederacy is 5,000,000, and, therefore, to fill up the ranks of the proposed army, 600,000, about ten per cent of the entire white population, will be required. In any other country than our own such a draft could not be met, but the Southern states can furnish that number of men, and still not leave the material interest of the country in a suffering condition."

The editor, with fatuous faith, did not for a moment contemplate any mass movement against this program on the part of the slaves. "Those who are incapacitated for bearing arms can oversee the plantations, and the Negroes can go on undisturbed in their usual labors. In the North, the case is different; the men who join the army of subjugation are the laborers, the producers and the factory operatives. Nearly every man from that section, especially those from the rural districts, leaves some branch of industry to suffer during his absence. The institution of slavery in the South alone enables her to place in the field a force much larger in proportion to her white population than the North, or indeed any country which is dependent entirely on free labor. The institution is a tower of strength to the South, particularly at the present crisis, and our enemies will be likely to find that the 'Moral Cancer' about which their orators are so fond of prating, is really one of the most effective weapons employed against the Union by the South." [1]

Soon the South of necessity was moving out beyond this plan. It was no longer simply a question of using the Negroes at home on the plantation to raise food. They could be of even more immediate use, as military labor, to throw up breastworks, transport and prepare food and act as servants in camp. In the Charleston *Courier* of November 22, able-bodied hands were asked to be sent by their masters to work upon the defenses. "They would be fed and properly cared for."

In 1862, in Charleston, after a proclamation of martial law, the governor and counsel authorized the procuring of Negro slaves either by the planter's consent or by impressment "to work on the fortifications and defenses of Charleston harbor."

In Mississippi in 1862, permission was granted the Governor to impress slaves to work in New Iberia for salt, which was becoming the Confederacy's most pressing necessity. In Texas, a thousand Negroes were offered by planters for work on the public defenses.

By 1864, the matter had passed beyond the demand for slaves as military laborers and had come to the place where the South was seriously considering and openly demanding the use of Negroes as soldiers. Distinctly and inevitably, the rigor of the slave system in the South softened as war proceeded. Slavery showed in many if not all respects its best side. The harshness and the cruelty, in part, had to disappear, since there were left on the plantations mainly women and children, with only a few men, and there was a certain feeling and apprehension in the air on the part of the whites which led them to capitalize all the friendship and kindness which had existed between them and the slaves. No race could have responded to this so quickly and thoroughly as the Negroes. They felt pity and responsibility and also a certain new undercurrent of independence. Negroes were still being sold rather ostentatiously in Charleston and New Orleans, but the long lines of Virginia Negroes were not marching to the Southwest. In a certain sense, after the first few months everybody knew that slavery was done with; that no matter who won, the condition of the slave could never be the same after this disaster of war. And it was, perhaps, these considerations, more than anything else, that held the poised arm of the black man; for no one knew better than the South what a Negro crazed with cruelty and oppression and beaten back to the last stand could do to his oppressor.

The Southerners, therefore, were careful. Those who had been kind to their slaves assured them of the bad character of the Yankee and of their own good intentions.

Thus while the Negroes knew there were Abolitionists in the North, they did not know their growth, their power or their intentions and they did hear on every side that the South was overwhelmingly victorious on the battlefield. On the other hand, some of the Negroes sensed what was beginning to happen. The Negroes of the cities, the Negroes who were being hired out, the Negroes of intelligence who could read and write, all began carefully to watch the unfolding of the situation. At the first gun of Sumter, the black mass began not to move but to heave with nervous tension and watchful waiting. Even before war was declared, a movement began across the border. Just before the war large numbers of fugitive slaves and free Negroes rushed into the North. It was estimated that two thousand left North Carolina alone because of rumors of war.

When W. T. Sherman occupied Port Royal in October, 1861, he had no idea that he was beginning emancipation at one of its strategic points. On the contrary, he was very polite and said that he had no idea of interfering with slaves. In the same way, Major General Dix, on seizing two counties of Virginia, was careful to order that slavery was not to be interfered with or slaves to be received into the line. Burnside went further, and as he brought his Rhode Island regiment through Baltimore in June, he courteously returned two Negroes who tried to run away with him. They were "supposed to be slaves," although they may have been free Negroes. On the 4th of July, Colonel Pryor of Ohio delivered an address to the people of Virginia in which he repudiated the accusation that the Northern army were Abolitionists.

"I desire to assure you that the relation of master and servant as recognized in your state shall be respected. Your authority over that species of property shall not in the least be interfered with. To this end, I assure you that those under my command have peremptory orders to take up and hold any Negroes found running about the camp without passes from their masters." [2]

Halleck in Missouri in 1862 refused to let fugitive slaves enter his lines. Burnside, Buell, Hooker, Thomas Williams and McClellan himself, all warned their soldiers against receiving slaves and most of them permitted masters to come and remove slaves found within the lines.

The constant charge of Southern newspapers, Southern politicians and their Northern sympathizers, that the war was an abolition war, met with constant and indignant denial. Loyal newspapers, orators and preachers, with few exceptions, while advocating stringent measures for putting down the Rebellion, carefully disclaimed any intention of disturbing the "peculiar institution" of the South. The Secretary of State informed foreign governments, through our ministers abroad, that this was not our purpose. President Lincoln, in his earlier messages, substantially reiterated the statement. Leading generals, on entering Southern territory, issued proclamations to the same effect. One even promised to put down any slave insurrection "with an iron hand," while others took vigorous measures to send back the fugitives who sought refuge within their lines.

"In the early years of the war, if accounts do not err, during the entire period McClellan commanded the Army of the Potomac, 'John Brown's Body' was a forbidden air among the regimental bands. The Hutchinsons were driven from Union camps for singing abolition songs, and in so far as the Northern army interested itself at all in the slavery question, it was by the use of force to return to their Southern masters fugitives seeking shelter in the Union lines. While the information they possessed, especially respecting the roads and means of communication, should have been of inestimable service to the Federals, they were not to be employed as laborers or armed as soldiers. The North avoided the appearance of a desire to raise the Negroes from the plane of chattels to the rank of human beings." [3]

Here was no bid for the coöperation of either slaves or free Negroes. In the North, Negroes were not allowed to enlist and often refused with indignation. "Thus the weakness of the South temporarily became her strength. Her servile population, repulsed by Northern pro-slavery sentiment, remained at home engaged in agriculture, thus releasing her entire white population for active service in the field; while, on the other hand, the military resources of the North were necessarily diminished by the demands of labor." [4]

It was as Frederick Douglass said in Boston in 1865, that the Civil War was begun "in the interests of slavery on both sides. The South was fighting to take slavery out of the Union, and the North fighting to keep it in the Union; the South fighting to get it beyond the limits of the United States Constitution, and the North fighting for the old guarantees;—both despising the Negro, both insulting the Negro."

It was, therefore, at first by no means clear to most of the four million Negroes in slavery what this war might mean to them. They crouched consciously and moved silently, listening, hoping and hesitating. The watchfulness of the South was redoubled. They spread propaganda: the Yankees were not only not thinking of setting them free, but if they did anything, they would sell them into worse slavery in the West Indies. They would drive them from even the scant comfort of the plantations into the highways and purlieus. Moreover, if they tried to emancipate the slaves, they would fail because they could not do this without conquest of the South. The South was unconquerable.

The South was not slow to spread propaganda and point to the wretched condition of fugitive Negroes in order to keep the loyalty of its indispensable labor force. The Charleston *Daily Courier* said February 18, 1863: "A company of volunteers having left Fayette County for the field of action, Mr. Nance sent two Negro boys along to aid the company. Their imaginations became dazzled with the visions of Elysian fields in Yankeedom and they went to find them. But Paradise was nowhere there, and they again sighed for home. The Yanks, however, detained them and cut off their ears close to their heads. These Negroes finally made their escape and are now at home with Mr. Nance in Pickens. They are violent haters of Yankees and their adventures and experiences are a terror to Negroes of the region, who learned a lesson from their brethren whose ears are left in Lincolndom!"

The Charleston *Mercury*, May 8, 1862, said: "The Yankees are fortifying Fernandina (Florida) and have a large number of Negroes engaged on their works. Whenever the Negroes have an opportunity, they escape from their oppressors. They report that they are worked hard, get little rest and food and no pay."

The Savannah *Daily News* reports in 1862 that many stolen Negroes had been recaptured: "The Yankees had married a number of the women and were taking them home with them. I have seen some who refused to go and others who had been forced off at other times who had returned."

It was a lovely dress parade of Alphonse and Gaston until the Negro spoiled it and in a perfectly logical way. So long as the Union stood still and talked, the Negro kept quiet and worked. The moment the Union army moved into slave territory, the Negro joined it. Despite all argument and calculation and in the face of refusals and commands, wherever the Union armies marched, appeared the fugitive slaves. It made no difference what the obstacles were, or the attitudes of the commanders. It was "like thrusting a walking stick into an ant-hill," says one writer. And yet the army chiefs at first tried to regard it as an exceptional and temporary matter, a thing which they could control, when as a matter of fact it was the meat and kernel of the war.

Thus as the war went on and the invading armies came on, the way suddenly cleared for the onlooking Negro, for his spokesmen in the North, and for his silent listeners in the South. Each step, thereafter, came with curious, logical and inevitable fate. First there were the fugitive slaves. Slaves had always been running away to the North, and when the North grew hostile, on to Canada. It was the safety valve that kept down the chance of insurrection in the South to the lowest point. Suddenly, now, the chance to run away not only increased, but after preliminary repulse and hesitation, there was actual encouragement.

Not that the government planned or foresaw this eventuality; on the contrary, having repeatedly declared the object of the war as the preservation of the Union and that it did not propose to fight for slaves or touch slavery, it faced a stampede of fugitive slaves.

Every step the Northern armies took then meant fugitive slaves. They crossed the Potomac, and the slaves of northern Virginia began to pour into the army and into Washington. They captured Fortress Monroe, and slaves from Virginia and even North Carolina poured into the army. They captured Port Royal, and the masters ran away, leaving droves of black fugitives in the hands of the Northern army. They moved down the Mississippi Valley, and if the slaves did not rush to the army, the army marched to the slaves. They captured New Orleans, and captured a great black city and a state full of slaves.

What was to be done? They tried to send the slaves back, and even used the soldiers for recapturing them. This was all well enough as long as the war was a dress parade. But when it became real war, and slaves were captured or received, they could be used as much-needed laborers and servants by the Northern army.

This but emphasized and made clearer a truth which ought to have been recognized from the very beginning: The Southern worker, black and white, held the key to the war; and of the two groups, the black worker raising food and raw materials held an even more strategic place than the white. This was so clear a fact that both sides should have known it. Fremont in Missouri took the logical action of freeing slaves of the enemy round about him by proclamation, and President Lincoln just as promptly repudiated what he had done. Even before that, General Butler in Virginia, commander of the Union forces at Fortress Monroe, met three slaves walking into his camp from the Confederate fortifications where they had been at work. Butler immediately declared these men "contraband of war" and put them to work in his own camp. More slaves followed, accompanied by their wives and children. The situation here was not quite so logical. Nevertheless, Butler kept the fugitives and freed them and let them do what work they could; and his action was approved by the Secretary of War.

"On May twenty-sixth, only two days after the one slave appeared before Butler, eight Negroes appeared; on the next day, forty-seven, of all ages and both sexes. Each day they continued to come by twenties, thirties and forties until by July 30th the number had reached nine hundred. In a very short while the number ran up into the thousands. The renowned Fortress took the name of the 'freedom fort' to which the blacks came by means of a 'mysterious spiritual telegraph.' " [5]

In December, 1861, the Secretary of the Treasury, Simon Cameron, had written, printed and put into the mails his first report as Secretary of War without consultation with the President. Possibly he knew that his recommendations would not be approved, but "he recommended the general arming of Negroes, declaring that the Federals had as clear a right to employ slaves taken from the enemy as to use captured gunpowder." This report was recalled by the President by telegraph and the statements of the Secretary were modified. The incident aroused some unpleasantness in the cabinet.

The published report finally said:

"Persons held by rebels, under such laws, to service as slaves, may, however, be justly liberated from their constraint, and made more valuable in various employments, through voluntary and compensated service, than if confiscated as subjects of property."

Transforming itself suddenly from a problem of abandoned plantations and slaves captured while being used by the enemy for military purposes, the movement became a general strike against the slave system on the part of all who could find opportunity. The trickling streams of fugitives swelled to a flood. Once begun, the general strike of black and white went madly and relentlessly on like some great saga.

"Imagine, if you will, a slave population, springing from antecedent barbarism, rising up and leaving its ancient bondage, forsaking its local traditions and all the associations and attractions of the old plantation life, coming garbed in rags or in silks, with feet shod or bleeding, individually or in families and larger groups,—an army of slaves and fugitives, pushing its way irresistibly toward an army of fighting men, perpetually on the defensive and perpetually ready to attack. The arrival among us of these hordes was like the oncoming of cities. There was no plan in this exodus, no Moses to lead it. Unlettered reason or the mere inarticulate decision of instinct brought them to us. Often the slaves met prejudices against their color more bitter than any they had left behind. But their own interests were identical, they felt, with the objects of our armies; a blind terror stung them, an equally blind hope allured them, and to us they come." [6]

"Even before the close of 1862, many thousands of blacks of all ages, ragged, with no possessions, except the bundles which they carried, had assembled at Norfolk, Hampton, Alexandria and Washington. Others, landless, homeless, helpless, in families and in multitudes, including a considerable number of wretched white people, flocked North from Tennessee, Kentucky, Arkansas and Missouri. All these were relieved in part by army rations, irregularly issued, and by volunteer societies of the North, which gained their money from churches and individuals in this country and abroad. In the spring of 1863, there were swarming crowds of Negroes and white refugees along the line of defense made between the armies of the North and South and reaching from Maryland to Virginia, along the coast from Norfolk to New Orleans. Soldiers and missionaries told of their virtues and vices, their joy and extreme suffering. The North was moved to an extraordinary degree, and endless bodies of workers and missionaries were organized and collected funds for materials.

"Rude barracks were erected at different points for the temporary shelter of the freedmen; but as soon as possible the colonies thus formed were broken up and the people encouraged to make individual contracts for labor upon neighboring plantations. In connection with the colonies, farms were cultivated which aided to meet the expenses. Hospitals were established at various points for the sick, of whom there were great numbers. The separation of families by the war, and illegitimate birth in consequence of slavery, left a great number of children practically in a state of orphanage." [7]

This was the beginning of the swarming of the slaves, of the quiet but unswerving determination of increasing numbers no longer to work on Confederate plantations, and to seek the freedom of the Northern armies. Wherever the army marched and in spite of all obstacles came the rising tide of slaves seeking freedom. For a long time, their treatment was left largely to the discretion of the department managers; some welcomed them, some drove them away, some organized them for work. Gradually, the fugitives became organized and formed a great labor force for the army. Several thousand were employed as laborers, servants, and spies.

A special war correspondent of the New York *Tribune* writes: "'God bless the Negroes,' say I, with earnest lips. During our entire captivity, and after our escape, they were ever our firm, brave, unflinching friends. We never made an appeal to them they did not answer. They never hesitated to do us a service at the risk even of life, and under the most trying circumstances revealed a devotion and a spirit of self-sacrifice that was heroic. The magic word 'Yankee' opened all their hearts, and elicited the loftiest virtues. They were ignorant, oppressed, enslaved; but they always cherished a simple and a beautiful faith in the cause of the Union and its ultimate triumph, and never abandoned or turned aside from a man who sought food or shelter on his way to Freedom." [8]

This whole move was not dramatic or hysterical, rather it was like the great unbroken swell of the ocean before it dashes on the reefs. The Negroes showed no disposition to strike the one terrible blow which brought black men freedom in Haiti and which in all history has been used by all slaves and justified. There were some plans for insurrection made by Union officers:

"The plan is to induce the blacks to make a simultaneous movement of rising, on the night of the 1st of August next, over the entire States in rebellion, to arm themselves with any and every kind of weapon that may come to hand, and commence operations by burning all the railroad and country bridges, and tear up railroad tracks, and to destroy telegraph lines, etc., and then take to the woods, swamps, or the mountains, where they may emerge as occasion may offer for provisions and for further depredations. No blood is to be shed except in self-defense. The corn will be ripe about the 1st of August and with this and hogs running in the woods, and by foraging upon the plantations by night, they can subsist. This is the plan in substance, and if we can obtain a concerted movement at the time named it will doubtless be successful." [9]

Such plans came to naught for the simple reason that there was an easier way involving freedom with less risk.

The South preened itself on the absence of slave violence. Governor Walker of Florida said in his inaugural in 1865: "Where, in all the records of the past, does history present such an instance of steadfast devotion, unwavering attachment and constancy as was exhibited by the slaves of the South throughout the fearful contest that has just ended? The country invaded, homes desolated, the master absent in the army or forced to seek safety in flight and leave the mistress and her helpless infants unprotected, with every incitement to insubordination and instigation, to rapine and murder, no instance of insurrection, and scarcely one of voluntary desertion has been recorded."

The changes upon this theme have been rung by Southern orators many times since. The statement, of course, is not quite true. Hundreds of thousands of slaves were very evidently leaving their masters' homes and plantations. They did not wreak vengeance on unprotected women. They found an easier, more effective and more decent way to freedom. Men go wild and fight for freedom with bestial ferocity when they must—where there is no other way; but human nature does not deliberately choose blood—at least not black human nature. On the other hand, for every slave that escaped to the Union army, there were ten left on the untouched and inaccessible plantations.

Another step was logical and inevitable. The men who handled a spade for the Northern armies, the men who fed them, and as spies brought in information, could also handle a gun and shoot. Without legal authority and in spite of it, suddenly the Negro became a soldier. Later his services as soldier were not only permitted but were demanded to replace the tired and rebellious white men of the North. But as a soldier, the Negro must be free.

The North started out with the idea of fighting the war without touching slavery. They faced the fact, after severe fighting, that Negroes seemed a valuable asset as laborers, and they therefore declared them "contraband of war." It was but a step from that to attract and induce Negro labor to help the Northern armies. Slaves were urged and invited into the Northern armies; they became military laborers and spies; not simply military laborers, but laborers on the plantations, where the crops went to help the Federal army or were sold North. Thus wherever Northern armies appeared, Negro laborers came, and the North found itself actually freeing slaves before it had the slightest intention of doing so, indeed when it had every intention not to.

The experience of the army with the refugees and the rise of the departments of Negro affairs were a most interesting, but unfortunately little studied, phase of Reconstruction. Yet it contained in a sense the key to the understanding of the whole situation. At first, the rush of the Negroes from the plantations came as a surprise and was variously interpreted. The easiest thing to say was that Negroes were tired of work and wanted to live at the expense of the government; wanted to travel and see things and places. But in contradiction to this was the extent of the movement and the terrible suffering of the refugees. If they were seeking peace and quiet, they were much better off on the plantations than trailing in the footsteps of the army or squatting miserably in the camps. They were mistreated by the soldiers; ridiculed; driven away, and yet they came. They increased with every campaign, and as a final gesture, they marched with Sherman from Atlanta to the sea, and met the refugees and abandoned human property on the Sea Islands and the Carolina Coast.

This was not merely the desire to stop work. It was a strike on a wide basis against the conditions of work. It was a general strike that involved directly in the end perhaps a half million people. They wanted to stop the economy of the plantation system, and to do that they left the plantations. At first, the commanders were disposed to drive them away, or to give them quasi-freedom and let them do as they pleased with the nothing that they possessed. This did not work. Then the commanders organized relief and afterward, work. This came to the attention of the country first in Pierce's "Ten Thousand Clients." Pierce of Boston had worked with the refugees in Virginia under Butler, provided them with food and places to live, and given them jobs and land to cultivate. He was successful. He came from there, and, in conjunction with the Treasury Department, began the work on a vaster scale at Port Royal. Here he found the key to the situation. The Negroes were willing to work and did work, but they wanted land to work, and they wanted to see and own the results of their toil. It was here and in the West and the South that a new vista opened. Here was a chance to establish an agrarian democracy in the South: peasant holders of small properties, eager to work and raise crops, amenable to suggestion and general direction. All they needed was honesty in treatment, and education. Wherever these conditions were fulfilled, the result was little less than phenomenal. This was testified to by Pierce in the Carolinas, by Butler's agents in North Carolina, by the experiment of the Sea Islands, by Grant's department of Negro affairs under Eaton, and by Banks' direction of Negro labor in Louisiana. It is astonishing how this army of striking labor furnished in time 200,000 Federal soldiers whose evident ability to fight decided the war.

General Butler went from Virginia to New Orleans to take charge of the city newly captured in April, 1862. Here was a whole city half-filled with blacks and mulattoes, some of them wealthy free Negroes and soldiers who came over from the Confederate side and joined the Federals.

Perhaps the greatest and most systematic organizing of fugitives took place in New Orleans. At first, Butler had issued orders that no slave: would be received in New Orleans. Many planters were unable to make slaves work or to support them, and sent them back of the Fedral lines, planning to reclaim them after the war was over. Butler mancipated these slaves in spite of the fact that he knew this was gainst Lincoln's policy. As the flood kept coming, he seized abandoned sugar plantations and began to work them with Negro labor for the benefit of the government.

By permission of the War Department, and under the authority of the Confiscation Act, Butler organized colonies of fugitives, and regulated employment. His brother, Colonel Butler, and others worked plantations, hiring the Negro labor. The Negroes stood at Butler's right hand during the trying time of his administration, and particularly the well-to-do free Negro group were his strongest allies. He was entertained at their tables and brought down on himself the wrath and contempt, not simply of the South, but even of the North. He received the black regiment, and kept their black officers, who never forgot him. Whatever else he might have been before the war, or proved to be afterwards, "the colored people of Louisiana under the proper sense of the good you have done to the African race in the United States, beg leave to express to you their gratitude."

From 1862 to 1865, many different systems of caring for the escaped slaves and their families in this area were tried. Butler and his successor, Banks, each sought to provide for the thousands of destitute freedmen with medicine, rations and clothing. When General Banks took command, there was suffering, disease and death among the 50,000 Negroes. On January 30, 1863, he issued a general order making labor on public works and elsewhere compulsory for Negroes who had no means of support.

Just as soon, however, as Banks tried to drive the freedmen back to the plantations and have them work under a half-military slave régime, the plan failed. It failed, not because the Negroes did not want to work, but because they were striking against these particular conditions of work. When, because of wide protest, he began to look into the matter, he saw a clear way. He selected Negroes to go out and look into conditions and to report on what was needed, and they made a faithful survey. He set up a little state with its department of education, with its landholding and organized work, and after experiment it ran itself. More and more here and up the Mississippi Valley, under other commanders and agents, experiments extended and were successful.

Further up the Mississippi, a different system was begun under General Grant. Grant's army in the West occupied Grand Junction, Mississippi, by November, 1862. The usual irregular host of slaves then swarmed in from the surrounding country. They begged for protection against recapture, and they, of course, needed food, clothing and shelter. They could not now be reënslaved through army aid, yet no provision had been made by anybody for their sustenance. A few were employed as teamsters, servants, cooks and scouts, yet it seemed as though the vast majority must be left to freeze and starve, for when the storms came with the winter months, the weather was of great severity.

Grant determined that Negroes should perform many of the camp duties ordinarily done by soldiers; that they should serve as fatigue men in the departments of the surgeon general, quartermaster, and commissary, and that they should help in building roads and earthworks. The women worked in the camp kitchens and as nurses in the hospitals. Grant said, "It was at this point where the first idea of the Freedmen's Bureau took its origin."

Grant selected as head of his Department of Negro Affairs, John Eaton, chaplain of the Twenty-Seventh Ohio Volunteers, who was soon promoted to the colonelcy of a colored regiment, and later for many years was a Commissioner of the United States Bureau of Education. He was then constituted Chief of Negro Affairs for the entire district under Grant's jurisdiction.

"I hope I may never be called on again to witness the horrrible scenes I saw in those first days of the history of the freedmen in the Mississippi Valley. Assistants were hard to get, especially the kind that would do any good in our camps. A detailed soldier in each camp of a thousand people was the best that could be done. His duties were so onerous that he ended by doing nothing. . . . In reviewing the condition of the people at that time, I am not surprised at the marvelous stories told by visitors who caught an occasional glimpse of the misery and wretchedness in these camps. . . . Our efforts to do anything for these people, as they herded together in masses, when founded on any expectation that they would help themselves, often failed; they had become so completely broken down in spirit, through suffering, that it was almost impossible to arouse them.

"Their condition was appalling. There were men, women and children in every stage of disease or decrepitude, often nearly naked, with flesh torn by the terrible experiences of their escapes. Sometimes they were intelligent and eager to help themselves; often they were bewildered or stupid or possessed by the wildest notions of what liberty might mean—expecting to exchange labor, and obedience to the will of another, for idleness and freedom from restraint. Such ignorance and perverted notions produced a veritable moral chaos. Cringing deceit, theft, licentiousness—all the vices which slavery inevitably fosters—were hideous companions of nakedness, famine, and disease. A few had profited by the misfortunes of the master and were jubilant in their unwonted ease and luxury, but these stood in lurid contrast to the grimmer aspects of the tragedy—the women in travail, the helplessness of childhood and of old age, the horrors of sickness and of frequent death. Small wonder that men paused in bewilderment and panic, foreseeing the demoralization and infection of the Union soldier and the downfall of the Union cause." [10]

There were new and strange problems of social contact. The white soldiers, for the most part, were opposed to serving Negroes in any manner, and were even unwilling to guard the camps where they were segregated or protect them against violence. "To undertake any form of work for the contrabands, at that time, was to be forsaken by one's friends and to pass under a cloud." [11]

There was, however, a clear economic basis upon which the whole work of relief and order and subsistence could be placed. All around Grand Junction were large crops of ungathered corn and cotton. These were harvested and sold North and the receipts were placed to the credit of the government. The army of fugitives were soon willing to go to work; men, women and children. Wood was needed by the river steamers and woodcutters were set at work. Eaton fixed the wages for this industry and kept accounts with the workers. He saw to it that all of them had sufficient food and clothing, and rough shelter was built for them. Citizens round about who had not abandoned their plantations were allowed to hire labor on the same terms as the government was using it. Very soon the freedmen became self-sustaining and gave little trouble. They began to build themselves comfortable cabins, and the government constructed hospitals for the sick. In the case of the sick and dependent, a tax was laid on the wages of workers. At first it was thought the laborers would object, but, on the contrary, they were perfectly willing and the imposition of the tax compelled the government to see that wages were promptly paid. The freedmen freely acknowledged that they ought to assist in helping bear the burden of the poor, and were flattered by having the government ask their help. It was the reaction of a new labor group, who, for the first time in their lives, were receiving money in payment for their work. Five thousand dollars was raised by this tax for hospitals, and with this money tools and property were bought. By wholesale purchase, clothes, household goods and other articles were secured by the freedmen at a cost of one-third of what they might have paid the stores. There was a rigid system of accounts and monthly reports through army officials.

In 1864, July 5, Eaton reports: "These freedmen are now disposed of as follows: In military service as soldiers, laundresses, cooks, officers' servants, and laborers in the various staff departments, 41,150; in cities on plantations and in freedmen's villages and cared for, 72,500. Of these 62,300 are entirely self-supporting—the same as any industrial class anywhere else—as planters, mechanics, barbers, hackmen, draymen, etc., conducting enterprises on their own responsibility or working as hired laborers. The remaining 10,200 receive subsistence from the government. 3,000 of them are members of families whose heads are carrying on plantations and have under cultivation 4,000 acres of cotton. They are to pay the government for their sustenance from the first income of the crop. The other 7,200 include the paupers—that is to say, all Negroes over and under the self-supporting age, the crippled and sick in hospital, of the 113,650 and those engaged in their care. Instead of being unproductive, this class has now under cultivation 500 acres of corn, 790 acres of vegetables and 1,500 acres of cotton, besides working at wood-chopping and other industries. There are reported in the aggregate over 100,000 acres of cotton under cultivation. Of these about 7,000 acres are leased and cultivated by blacks. Some Negroes are managing as high as 300 or 400 acres."

The experiment at Davis Bend, Mississippi, was of especial interest. The place was occupied in November and December, 1864, and private interests were displaced and an interesting socialistic effort made with all the property under the control of the government. The Bend was divided into districts with Negro sheriffs and judges who were allowed to exercise authority under the general control of the military officers. Petty theft and idleness were soon reduced to a minimum and "the community distinctly demonstrated the capacity of the Negro to take care of himself and exercise under honest and competent direction the functions of self-government." [12]

When General Butler returned from Louisiana and resumed command in Virginia and North Carolina, he established there a Department of Negro Affairs, with the territory divided into districts under superintendents and assistants. Negroes were encouraged to buy land, build cabins and form settlements, and a system of education was established. In North Carolina, under Chaplain Horace James, the poor, both black and white, were helped; the refugees were grouped in small villages and their work systematized, and enlisted men taught in the schools, followed by women teachers from the North. Outside of New Bern, North Carolina, about two thousand freedmen were settled and 800 houses erected. The department at Port Royal continued. The Negroes showed their capacity to organize labor and even to save and employ a little capital. The government built 21 houses for the people on Edisto Island. The carpenters were Negroes under a Negro foreman. There was another village of improved houses near Hilton Head.

"Next as to the development of manhood: this has been shown in the first place in the prevalent disposition to acquire land. It did not appear upon our first introduction to these people, and they did not seem to understand us when we used to tell them that we wanted them to own land. But it is now an active desire. At the recent tax sales, six out of forty-seven plantations sold were bought by them, comprising two thousand five hundred and ninety-five acres, sold for twenty-one hundred and forty-five dollars. In other cases, the Negroes had authorized the superintendent to bid for them, but the land was reserved by the United States. One of the purchases was that made by Harry, noted above. The other five were made by the Negroes on the plantations, combining the funds they had saved from the sale of their pigs, chickens and eggs, and from the payments made to them for work,—they then dividing off the tract peaceably among themselves. On one of these, where Kit, before mentioned, is the leading spirit, there are twenty-three fieldhands. They have planted and are cultivating sixty-three acres of cotton, fifty of corn, six of potatoes, with as many more to be planted, four and a half of cowpeas, three of peanuts, and one and a half of rice. These facts are most significant." [13]

Under General Saxton in South Carolina, the Negroes began to buy land which was sold for non-payment of taxes. Saxton established regulations for the cultivation of several abandoned Sea Islands and appointed local superintendents.

"By the payment of moderate wages, and just and fair dealing with them, I produced for the government over a half million dollars' worth of cotton, besides a large amount of food beyond the needs of the laborers. These island lands were cultivated in this way for two years, 1862 and 1863, under my supervision, and during that time I had about 15,000 colored freedmen of all ages in my charge. About 9,000 of these were engaged on productive labor which relieved the government of the support of all except newly-arrived refugees from the enemy's lines and the old and infirm who had no relations to depend upon. The increase of industry and thrift of the freedmen was illustrated by their conduct in South Carolina before the organization of the Freedmen's Bureau by the decreasing government expenditure for their support. The expense in the department of the South in 1863 was

$41,544, but the monthly expense of that year was steadily reduced, until in December it was less than $1,000." [14]

Into this fairly successful land and labor control was precipitated a vast and unexpected flood of refugees from previously untouched strongholds of slavery. Sherman made his march to the sea from Atlanta, cutting the cotton kingdom in two as Grant had invaded it along the Mississippi.

"The first intimation given me that many of the freedmen would be brought hither from Savannah came in the form of a request from the General that I would 'call at once to plan the reception of seven hundred who would be at the wharf in an hour.' This was Christmas day, and at 4 P.M., we had seven hundred—mainly women, old men and children before us. A canvass since made shows that half of them had traveled from Macon, Atlanta and even Chattanooga. They were all utterly destitute of blankets, stockings or shoes; and among the seven hundred there were not fifty articles in the shape of pots or kettles, or other utensils for cooking, no axes, very few coverings for many heads, and children wrapped in the only article not worn in some form by the parents." Frantic appeals went out for the mass of Negro refugees who followed him.

A few days after Sherman entered Savannah, Secretary of War Stanton came in person from Washington. He examined the condition of the liberated Negroes found in that city. He assembled twenty of those who were deemed their leaders. Among them were barbers, pilots and sailors, some ministers, and others who had been overseers on cotton and rice plantations. Mr. Stanton and General Sherman gave them a hearing.

As a result of this investigation into the perplexing problems as to what to do with the growing masses of unemployed Negroes and their families, General Sherman issued his epoch-making Sea Island Circular, January 18, 1865. In this paper, the islands from Charleston south, the abandoned rice fields along the rivers for thirty miles back from the sea and the country bordering the St. John's River, Florida, were reserved for the settlement of the Negroes made free by the acts of war and the proclamation of the President.

General Rufus Saxton was appointed Inspector of Settlements and Plantations and was required to make proper allotments and give possessory titles and defend them until Congress should confirm his actions. It was a bold move. Thousands of Negro families were distributed under this circular, and the freed people regarded themselves for more than six months as in permanent possession of these abandoned lands. Taxes on the freedmen furnished most of the funds to run these first experiments. On all plantations, whether owned or leased, where freedmen were employed, a tax of one cent per pound on cotton and a proportional amount on all other products was to be collected as a contribution in support of the helpless among the freed people. A similar tax, varying with the value of the property, was levied by the government upon all leased plantations in lieu of rent.

Saxton testified: "General Sherman's Special Field Order No. 15 ordered their colonization on forty-acre tracts, and in accordance with which it is estimated some forty thousand were provided with homes. Public meetings were held, and every exertion used by those whose duty it was to execute this order to encourage emigration to the Sea Islands, and the faith of the government was solemnly pledged to maintain them in possession. The greatest success attended the experiment, and although the planting season was very far advanced before the transportation to carry the colonists to the Sea Islands could be obtained, and the people were destitute of animals and had but few agricultural implements and the greatest difficulty in procuring seeds, yet they went out, worked with energy and diligence to clear up the ground run to waste by three years' neglect; and thousands of acres were planted and provisions enough were raised for those who were located in season to plant, besides a large amount of sea island cotton for market. The seizure of some 549,000 acres of abandoned land, in accordance with the act of Congress and orders from the head of the bureau for the freedman and refugees, still further strengthened these ignorant people in the conviction that they were to have the lands of their late masters; and, with the other reasons before stated, caused a great unwillingness on the part of the freedmen to make any contracts whatever. But this refusal arises from no desire on their part to avoid labor, but from the causes above stated. . . .

"To test the question of their forethought and prove that some of the race at least thought of the future, I established in October, 1864, a savings bank for the freedmen of Beaufort district and vicinity. More than $240,000 had been deposited in this bank by freedmen since its establishment. I consider that the industrial problem has been satisfactorily solved at Port Royal, and that, in common with other races, the Negro has industry, prudence, forethought, and ability to calculate results. Many of them have managed plantations for themselves, and show an industry and sagacity that will compare favorably in their results—making due allowances—with those of white men."

Eventually, General Saxton settled nearly 30,000 Negroes on the Sea Islands and adjacent plantations and 17,000 were self-supporting within a year. While 12,000 or 13,000 were still receiving rations, it was distinctly understood that they and their farms would be held responsible for the payment. In other such cases, the government had found that such a debt was a "safe and short one."

Negroes worked fewer hours and had more time for self-expression. Exports were less than during slavery. At that time the Negroes were mere machines run with as little loss as possible to the single end of making money for their masters. Now, as it was in the West Indies, emancipation had enlarged the Negro's purchasing power, but instead of producing solely for export, he was producing to consume. His standard of living was rising.

Along with this work of the army, the Treasury Department of the United States Government was bestirring itself. The Secretary of the Treasury, Salmon P. Chase, early in 1862, had his attention called to the accumulation of cotton on the abandoned Sea Islands and plantations, and was sure there was an opportunity to raise more. He, therefore, began the organization of freedmen for cotton raising, and his successor, William Pitt Fessenden, inaugurated more extensive plans for the freedmen in all parts of the South, appointing agents and organizing freedmen's home colonies.

On June 7, 1862, Congress held portions of the states in rebellion responsible for a direct tax upon the lands of the nation, and in addition Congress passed an act authorizing the Secretary of the Treasury to appoint special agents to take charge of captured and abandoned property. Military officers turned over to the Treasury Department such property, and the plantations around Port Royal and Beaufort were disposed of at tax sales. Some were purchased by Negroes, but the greater number went to Northerners. In the same way in North Carolina, some turpentine farms were let to Negroes, who managed them, or to whites who employed Negroes. In 1863, September 11, the whole Southern region was divided by the Treasury Department into five special agencies, each with a supervising agent for the supervision of abandoned property and labor.

Early in 1863, General Lorenzo Thomas, the adjutant general of the army, was organizing colored troops along the Mississippi River. After consulting various treasury agents and department commanders, including General Grant, and having also the approval of Mr. Lincoln, he issued from Milliken's Bend, Louisiana, April 15th, a lengthy series of instruction covering the territory bordering the Mississippi and including all the inhabitants.

He appointed three commissioners, Messrs. Field, Shickle and Livermore, to lease plantations and care for the employees. He sought to encourage private enterprises instead of government colonies; but he fixed the wages of able-bodied men over fifteen years of age at $7 per month, for able-bodied women $5 per month, for children twelve to fifteen years, half price. He laid a tax for revenue of $2 per 400 pounds of cotton, and five cents per bushel on corn and potatoes.

This plan naturally did not work well, for the lessees of plantations proved to be for the most part adventurers and speculators. Of course such men took advantage of the ignorant people. The commissioners themselves seem to have done more for the lessees than for the laborers; and, in fact, the wages were from the beginning so fixed as to benefit and enrich the employer. Two dollars per month was charged against each of the employed, ostensibly for medical attendance, but to most plantations thus leased no physician or medicine ever came, and there were other attendant cruelties which avarice contrived.

On fifteen plantations leased by the Negroes themselves in this region there was notable success, and also a few other instances in which humanity and good sense reigned; the contracts were generally carried out. Here the Negroes were contented and grateful, and were able to lay by small gains. This plantation arrangement along the Mississippi under the commissioners as well as the management of numerous infirmary camps passed, about the close of 1863, from the War to the Treasury Department. A new commission or agency with Mr. W. P. Mellon of the treasury at the head established more careful and complete regulations than those of General Thomas. This time it was done decidedly in the interest of the laborers.

July 2, 1864, an Act of Congress authorized the treasury agents to seize and lease for one year all captured and abandoned estates and to provide for the welfare of former slaves. Property was declared abandoned when the lawful owner was opposed to paying the revenue. The Secretary of the Treasury, Fessenden, therefore issued a new series of regulations relating to freedmen and abandoned property. The rebellious States were divided into seven districts, with a general agent and special agents. Certain tracts of land in each district were set apart for the exclusive use and working of the freedmen. These reservations were called Freedmen Labor Colonies, and were under the direction of the superintendents. Schools were established, both in the Home Colonies and in the labor colonies. This new system went into operation the winter of 1864-1865, and worked well along the Atlantic Coast and Mississippi Valley. In the Department of the Gulf, however, there was discord between the treasury agents and the military authorities, and among the treasury officials themselves. The treasury agents, in many cases, became corrupt, but these regulations remained in force until the Freedmen's Bureau was organized in 1865.

By 1865, there was strong testimony as to the efficiency of the Negro worker. "The question of the freedmen being self-supporting no longer agitated the minds of careful observers."

Carl Schurz felt warranted in 1865 in asserting: "Many freedmen—not single individuals, but whole 'plantation gangs'—are working well; others are not. The difference in their efficiency coincides in a great measure with a certain difference in the conditions under which they live. The conclusion lies near, that if the conditions under which they work well become general, their efficiency as free laborers will become general also, aside from individual exceptions. Certain it is, that by far the larger portion of the work done in the South is done by freedmen!"

Whitelaw Reid said in 1865: "Whoever has read what I have written about the cotton fields of St. Helena will need no assurance that another cardinal sin of the slave, his laziness—'inborn and ineradicable,' as we were always told by his masters—is likewise disappearing under the stimulus of freedom and necessity. Dishonesty and indolence, then, were the creation of slavery, not the necessary and constitutional faults of the Negro character."

"Returning from St. Helena in 1865, Doctor Richard Fuller was asked what he thought of the experiment of free labor, as exhibited among his former slaves, and how it contrasted with the old order of things. 'I never saw St. Helena look so well,' was his instant reply; 'never saw as much land there under cultivation—never saw the same general evidences of prosperity, and never saw Negroes themselves appearing so well or so contented.' Others noticed, however, that the islands about Beaufort were in a better condition than those nearer the encampments of the United States soldiers. Wherever poultry could be profitably peddled in the camps, cotton had not been grown, nor had the Negroes developed, so readily, into industrious and orderly communities." [15] Similar testimony came from the Mississippi Valley and the West, and from Border States like Virginia and North Carolina.

To the aid of the government, and even before the government took definite organized hold, came religious and benevolent organizations. The first was the American Missionary Association, which grew out of the organization for the defense of the Negroes who rebelled and captured the slave ship *Amistad* and brought it into Connecticut in 1837. When this association heard from Butler and Pierce, it responded promptly and had several representatives at Hampton and South Carolina before the end of the year 1861. They extended their work in 1862-1863, establishing missions down the Atlantic Coast, and in Missouri, and along the Mississippi. By 1864, they had reached the Negroes in nearly all the Southern States. The reports of Pierce, Dupont and Sherman aroused the whole North. Churches and missionary societies responded. The Friends contributed. The work of

the Northern benevolent societies began to be felt, and money, clothing and, finally, men and women as helpers and teachers came to the
various centers.

"The scope of our work was greatly enlarged by the arrival of white
refugees—a movement which later assumed very large proportions.
As time went on Cairo (Illinois) became the center of our activities
in this direction. It was the most northerly of any of our camps, and
served as the portal through which thousands of poor whites and
Negroes were sent into the loyal states as fast as opportunities offered
for providing them with homes and employment. Many of these became permanent residents; some were sent home by Union soldiers
to carry on the work in the shop or on the farm which the war had
interrupted. It became necessary to have a superintendent at Cairo
and facilities for organizing the bands of refugees who were sent
North by the army. There was an increasing demand for work." [16]

New organizations arose, and an educational commission was organized in Boston, suggested by the reports of Pierce, and worked
chiefly in South Carolina. Afterward, it became the New England
Freedmen's Aid Society and worked in all the Southern States. February 22, 1862, the National Freedmen's Relief Association was formed
in New York City. During the first year, it worked on the Atlantic
Coast, and then broadened to the whole South. The Port Royal Relief
Committee of Philadelphia, later known as the Pennsylvania Freedmen's Relief Association, the National Freedmen's Relief Association
of the District of Columbia, the Contraband Relief Association of
Cincinnati, afterward called the Western Freedmen's Commission, the
Women's Aid Association of Philadelphia and the Friends' Associations, all arose and worked. The number increased and extended into
the Northwest. The Christian Commission, organized for the benefit
of soldiers, turned its attention to Negroes. In England, at Manchester
and London, were Freedmen's Aid Societies which raised funds; and
funds were received from France and Ireland.

Naturally, there was much rivalry and duplication of work. A
union of effort was suggested in 1862 by the Secretary of the Treasury and accomplished March 22, 1865, when the American Freedmen's Union Commission was incorporated, with branches in the
chief cities. Among its officers were Chief Justice Chase and William
Lloyd Garrison. In 1861, two large voluntary organizations to reduce
suffering and mortality among the freedmen were formed. The
Western Sanitary Commission at St. Louis, and the United States
Sanitary Commission at Washington, with branches in leading cities,
then began to relieve the distress of the freedmen. Hospitals were
improved, supplies distributed, and Yeatman's plan for labor devised.

Destitute white refugees were helped to a large extent. But even then, all of these efforts reached but a small portion of the mass of people freed from slavery.

Late in 1863, President Yeatman of the Western Sanitary Commission visited the freedmen in the Mississippi Valley. He saw the abuses of the leasing system and suggested a plan for organizing free labor and leasing plantations. It provided for a bureau established by the government to take charge of leasing land, to secure justice and freedom to the freedmen; hospital farms and homes for the young and aged were to be established; schools with compulsory attendance were to be opened. Yeatman accompanied Mellon, the agent of the department, to Vicksburg in order to inaugurate the plan and carry it into effect. His plan was adopted by Mellon, and was, on the whole, the most satisfactory.

Thus, confusion and lack of system were the natural result of the general strike. Yet, the Negroes had accomplished their first aim in those parts of the South dominated by the Federal army. They had largely escaped from the plantation discipline, were receiving wages as free laborers, and had protection from violence and justice in some sort of court.

About 20,000 of them were in the District of Columbia; 100,000 in Virginia; 50,000 in North Carolina; 50,000 in South Carolina, and as many more each in Georgia and Louisiana. The Valley of the Mississippi was filled with settlers under the Treasury Department and the army. Here were nearly 500,000 former slaves. But there were 3,500,000 more. These Negroes needed only the assurance that they would be freed and the opportunity of joining the Northern army. In larger and larger numbers, they filtered into the armies of the North. And in just the proportion that the Northern armies became in earnest, and proposed actually to force the South to stay in the Union, and not to make simply a demonstration, in just such proportion the Negroes became valuable as laborers, and doubly valuable as withdrawing labor from the South. After the first foolish year when the South woke up to the fact that there was going to be a real, long war, and the North realized just what war meant in blood and money, the whole relation of the North to the Negro and the Negro to the North changed.

The position of the Negro was strategic. His was the only appeal which would bring sympathy from Europe, despite strong economic bonds with the South, and prevent recognition of a Southern nation built on slavery. The free Negroes in the North, together with the Abolitionists, were clamoring. To them a war against the South simply had to be a war against slavery. Gradually, Abolitionists no longer need fear the mob. Disgruntled leaders of church and state began to talk of freedom. Slowly but surely an economic dispute and a political test of strength took on the aspects of a great moral crusade.

The Negro became in the first year contraband of war; that is, property belonging to the enemy and valuable to the invader. And in addition to that, he became, as the South quickly saw, the key to Southern resistance. Either these four million laborers remained quietly at work to raise food for the fighters, or the fighter starved. Simultaneously, when the dream of the North for man-power produced riots, the only additional troops that the North could depend on were 200,000 Negroes, for without them, as Lincoln said, the North could not have won the war.

But this slow, stubborn mutiny of the Negro slave was not merely a matter of 200,000 black soldiers and perhaps 300,000 other black laborers, servants, spies and helpers. Back of this half million stood 3½ million more. Without their labor the South would starve. With arms in their hands, Negroes would form a fighting force which could replace every single Northern white soldier fighting listlessly and against his will with a black man fighting for freedom.

This action of the slaves was followed by the disaffection of the poor whites. So long as the planters' war seemed successful, "there was little active opposition by the poorer whites; but the conscription and other burdens to support a slaveowners' war became very severe; the whites not interested in that cause became recalcitrant, some went into active opposition; and at last it was more desertion and disunion than anything else that brought about the final overthrow." [17]

Phillips says that white mechanics in 1861 demanded that the permanent Confederate Constitution exclude Negroes from employment "except agricultural domestic service, so as to reserve the trades for white artisans." Beyond this, of course, was a more subtle reason that, as the years went on, very carefully developed and encouraged for a time the racial aspect of slavery. Before the war, there had been intermingling of white and black blood and some white planters openly recognized their colored sons, daughters and cousins and took them under their special protection. As slavery hardened, the racial basis was emphasized; but it was not until war time that it became the fashion to pat the disfranchised poor white man on the back and tell him after all he was white and that he and the planters had a common object in keeping the white man superior. This virus increased bitterness and relentless hatred, and after the war it became a chief ingredient in the division of the working class in the Southern States.

At the same time during the war even the race argument did not keep the Southern fighters from noticing with anger that the big slaveholders were escaping military service; that it was a "rich man's war and the poor man's fight." The exemption of owners of twenty Negroes from military service especially rankled; and the wholesale withdrawal of the slaveholding class from actual fighting which this rule made possible, gave rise to intense and growing dissatisfaction.

It was necessary during these critical times to insist more than usual that slavery was a fine thing for the poor white. Except for slavery, it was said: "'The poor would occupy the position in society that the slaves do—as the poor in the North and in Europe do,' for there must be a menial class in society and in 'every civilized country on the globe, besides the Confederate states, the poor are the inferiors and menials of the rich.' Slavery was a greater blessing to the non-slaveholding poor than to the owners of slaves, and since it gave the poor a start in society that it would take them generations to work out, they should thank God for it and fight and die for it as they would for their 'own liberty and the dearest birthright of freemen.'" [18]

But the poor whites were losing faith. They saw that poverty was fighting the war, not wealth.

"Those who could stay out of the army under color of the law were likely to be advocates of a more numerous and powerful army. . . . Not so with many of those who were not favored with position and wealth. They grudgingly took up arms and condemned the law which had snatched them from their homes. . . . The only difference was the circumstance of position and wealth, and perhaps these were just the things that had caused heartburnings in more peaceful times.

"The sentiments of thousands in the upland countries, who had little interest in the war and who were not accustomed to rigid centralized control, was probably well expressed in the following epistle addressed to President Davis by a conscript. . . .

". . . 'It is with intense and multifariously proud satisfaction that he [the conscript] gazes for the last time upon our holy flag—that symbol and sign of an adored trinity, cotton, niggers and chivalry.'" [19]

This attitude of the poor whites had in it as much fear and jealousy of Negroes as disaffection with slave barons. Economic rivalry with blacks became a new and living threat as the blacks became laborers and soldiers in a conquering Northern army. If the Negro was to be free where would the poor white be? Why should he fight against the blacks and his victorious friends? The poor white not only began to desert and run away; but thousands followed the Negro into the Northern camps.

Meantime, with perplexed and laggard steps, the United States Government followed the footsteps of the black slave. It made no difference how much Abraham Lincoln might protest that this was not a war against slavery, or ask General McDowell "if it would not be well to allow the armies to bring back those fugitive slaves which have crossed the Potomac with our troops" (a communication which was marked "secret"). It was in vain that Lincoln rushed entreaties and then commands to Frémont in Missouri, not to emancipate the slaves of rebels, and then had to hasten similar orders to Hunter in South Carolina. The slave, despite every effort, was becoming the center of war. Lincoln, with his uncanny insight, began to see it. He began to talk about compensation for emancipated slaves, and Congress, following almost too quickly, passed the Confiscation Act in August, 1861, freeing slaves which were actually used in war by the enemy. Lincoln then suggested that provision be made for colonization of such slaves. He simply could not envisage free Negroes in the United States. What would become of them? What would they do? Meantime, the slave kept looming. New Orleans was captured and the whole black population of Louisiana began streaming toward it. When Vicksburg fell, the center of perhaps the vastest Negro population in North America was tapped. They rushed into the Union lines. Still Lincoln held off and watched symptoms. Greeley's "Prayer of Twenty Millions" received the curt answer, less than a year before Emancipation, that the war was not to abolish slavery, and if Lincoln could hold the country together and keep slavery, he would do it.

But he could not, and he had no sooner said this than he began to realize that he could not. In June, 1862, slavery was abolished in the territories. Compensation with possible colonization was planned for the District of Columbia. Representatives and Senators from the Border States were brought together to talk about extending this plan to their states, but they hesitated.

In August, Lincoln faced the truth, front forward; and that truth was not simply that Negroes ought to be free; it was that thousands of them were already free, and that either the power which slaves put into the hands of the South was to be taken from it, or the North could not win the war. Either the Negro was to be allowed to fight, or the draft itself would not bring enough white men into the army to keep up the war.

More than that, unless the North faced the world with the moral strength of declaring openly that they were fighting for the emancipation of slaves, they would probably find that the world would recognize the South as a separate nation; that ports would be opened; that trade would begin, and that despite all the military advantage of the North, the war would be lost.

In August, 1862, Lincoln discussed Emancipation as a military measure; in September, he issued his preliminary proclamation; on

January 1, 1863, he declared that the slaves of all persons in rebellion were "henceforward and forever free."

The guns at Sumter, the marching armies, the fugitive slaves, the fugitives as "contrabands," spies, servants and laborers; the Negro as soldier, as citizen, as voter—these steps came from 1861 to 1868 with regular beat that was almost rhythmic. It was the price of the disaster of war, and it was a price that few Americans at first dreamed of paying or wanted to pay. The North was not Abolitionist. It was overwhelmingly in favor of Negro slavery, so long as this did not interfere with Northern moneymaking. But, on the other hand, there was a minority of the North who hated slavery with perfect hatred; who wanted no union with slaveholders; who fought for freedom and treated Negroes as men. As the Abolition-democracy gained in prestige and in power, they appeared as prophets, and led by statesmen, they began to guide the nation out of the morass into which it had fallen. They and their black friends and the new freedmen became gradually the leaders of a Reconstruction of Democracy in the United States, while marching millions sang the noblest war-song of the ages to the tune of "John Brown's Body":

Mine eyes have seen the glory of the coming of the Lord,
He is trampling out the vintage where the grapes of wrath are stored,
He hath loosed the fateful lightning of his terrible swift sword,
His Truth is marching on!

---

1. *Public Opinion Before and After the Civil War*, p. 4.
2. Williams, *History of the Negro Race in America*, II, p. 244.
3. Oberholtzer, *Abraham Lincoln*, p. 263.
4. *Results of Emancipation in the United States of America* by a Committee of the American Freedman's Union Commission in 1867, p. 6.
5. *Journal of Negro History*, X, p. 134.
6. Eaton, *Grant, Lincoln and the Freedmen*, p. 2.
7. *Results of Emancipation in the United States of America* by a Committee of the American Freedman's Union Commission in 1867, p. 21.
8. Brown, *Four Years in Secessia*, p. 368.
9. Ashe and Tyler, *Secession, Insurrection of the Negroes, and Northern Incendiarism*, p. 12.
10. Eaton, *Grant, Lincoln and the Freedmen*, pp. 2, 3, 19, 22, 134.
11. Eaton, *Grant, Lincoln and the Freedmen*, p. 22.
12. Eaton, *Grant, Lincoln and the Freedmen*, p. 166.
13. Pierce, "Freedmen at Port Royal," *Atlantic Monthly*, XII, p. 310.
14. *Testimony Before Reconstruction Committee*, February 21, 1866, Part II, p. 221.
15. Taylor, *Reconstruction in South Carolina*, pp. 29, 30.
16. Eaton, *Grant, Lincoln and the Freedmen*, pp. 37, 38.
17. Campbell, *Black and White in the Southern States*, p. 165.
18. Moore, *Conscription and Conflict in the Confederacy*, p. 145.
19. Moore, *Conscription and Conflict in the Confederacy*, pp. 18-20.

V. THE COMING OF THE LORD

How the Negro became free because the North could not win
the Civil War if he remained in slavery. And how arms in his
hands, and the prospect of arms in a million more black hands,
brought peace and emancipation to America

Three movements, partly simultaneous and partly successive, are
treated in different chapters. In the last chapter, we chronicled the
swarming of the slaves to meet the approaching Union armies; in
this we consider how these slaves were transformed in part from
laborers to soldiers fighting for their own freedom; and in succeeding chapters, we shall treat the organization of free labor after the war.

In the ears of the world, Abraham Lincoln on the first of January,
1863, declared four million slaves "thenceforward and forever free."
The truth was less than this. The Emancipation Proclamation applied
only to the slaves of those states or parts of states still in rebellion
against the United States government. Hundreds of thousands of such
slaves were already free by their own action and that of the invading
armies, and in their cases, Lincoln's proclamation only added possible
legal sanction to an accomplished fact.

To the majority of slaves still within the Confederate lines, the
proclamation would apply only if they followed the fugitives. And
this Abraham Lincoln determined to induce them to do, and thus
to break the back of the rebellion by depriving the South of its principal labor force.

Emancipation had thus two ulterior objects. It was designed to
make easier the replacement of unwilling Northern white soldiers
with black soldiers; and it sought to put behind the war a new push
toward Northern victory by the mighty impact of a great moral ideal,
both in the North and in Europe.

This national right-about-face had been gradually and carefully accomplished only by the consummate tact of a leader of men who went
no faster than his nation marched but just as fast; and also by the
unwearying will of the Abolitionists, who forced the nation onward.

Wendell Phillips said in Washington in 1862:

"Gentlemen of Washington! You have spent for us two million
dollars per day. You bury two regiments a month, two thousand men
by disease without battle. You rob every laboring man of one-half of

his pay for the next thirty years by your taxes. You place the curse of intolerable taxation on every cradle for the next generation. What do you give us in return? What is the other side of the balance sheet? The North has poured out its blood and money like water; it has leveled every fence of constitutional privilege, and Abraham Lincoln sits today a more unlimited despot than the world knows this side of China. What does he render the North for this unbounded confidence? Show us something; or I tell you that within two years the indignant reaction of the people will hurl the cabinet in contempt from their seats, and the devils that went out from yonder capital, for there has been no sweeping or garnishing, will come back seven times stronger; for I do not believe that Jefferson Davis, driven down to the Gulf, will go down to the waters and perish as certain brutes mentioned in the Gospel did."

Horace Greeley was at Lincoln's heels. He wrote in August, 1862, his editorial, "Prayer of Twenty Millions," which drew Lincoln's well-known reply: "If there be those who would not save the Union unless they could at the same time save slavery, I do not agree with them. If there be those who would not save the Union unless they could at the same time destroy slavery, I do not agree with them. My paramount object in this struggle is to save the Union and is not either to save or to destroy slavery. If I could save the Union without freeing any slaves, I would do it; and if I could save it by freeing all the slaves, I would also do that. What I do about slavery and the colored race, I do because I believe it would help to save the Union. . . ."

"Suppose I do that," said Lincoln to Greeley, discussing general emancipation. "There are now 20,000 of our muskets on the shoulders of Kentuckians who are bravely fighting our battles. Every one of them will be thrown down or carried over to the rebels."

"Let them do it," said Greeley. "The cause of the Union will be stronger if Kentucky should secede with the rest, than it is now."

In September, 1862, Lincoln said to representatives of the Chicago Protestants:

"I admit that slavery is at the root of the rebellion, or at least its sine qua non. . . . I will also concede that Emancipation would help us in Europe. . . . I grant, further, that it would help somewhat at the North, though not so much, I fear, as you and those you represent imagine. . . . And then, unquestionably, it would weaken the Rebels by drawing off their laborers, which is of great importance; but I am not so sure we could do much with the Blacks. If we were to arm them, I fear that in a few weeks the arms would be in the hands of the Rebels. . . .

"What good would a proclamation of Emancipation from me do, especially as we are now situated? I do not want to issue a document that the whole world will see must necessarily be inoperative, like the Pope's bull against the comet. . . ."[1]

Nevertheless, just nine days later, Lincoln issued his preliminary Emancipation Proclamation. What caused the sudden change? Was it the mounting mass of Negroes rushing into Union lines? Was it the fighting of Negro soldiers which showed that weapons given to them were never found in the hands of Confederates, or was it the curious international situation?

The failure or success of the war hung by a thread. If England and France should recognize the Confederacy, there was little doubt that the Union cause would be beaten; and they were disposed to recognize it. Or did Lincoln realize that since a draft law was needed to make unwilling Northern soldiers fight, black soldiers were the last refuge of the Union? The preliminary proclamation came in September, and in October and November mass meetings in New York and Brooklyn denounced the proposal as inexpedient and adopted resolutions against it with jeers. Ministers, like the Reverend Albert Barnes of Philadelphia, preached against emancipation, declaring that the control of slavery ought to be left absolutely and exclusively to the states. The New York *Herald* pointed out that even if the proclamation was effective, slave property would have to be restored or paid for eventually by the United States government. "The *Herald* is correct. The slaves taken from our citizens during the war have to be accounted for at its end, either by restoration or indemnity."[2] The New Orleans *Picayune* pointed out in November that abolition would flood the North with Negroes, and that this would "tend to degrade white labor and to cheapen it."

The final proclamation was issued January 1, 1863, and carried a special admonition to the colored people:

"And I hereby enjoin upon the people so declared to be free to abstain from all violence, unless in necessary self-defense; and I recommend to them that, in all cases when allowed, they labor faithfully for reasonable wages.

"And I further declare and make known that such persons, of suitable condition, will be received into the armed service of the United States to garrison forts, positions, stations, and other places, and to man vessels of all sorts in said service.

"And upon this act, sincerely believed to be an act of justice, warranted by the Constitution upon military necessity, I invoke the considerate judgment of mankind, and the gracious favor of Almighty God."

The Charleston *Courier* jeered:

"The Pope's bull against the comet has been issued, and I suppose Mr. Lincoln now breathes more freely. The wonderful man by a dash of his wonderful pen has set free (on paper) all the slaves of the South, and henceforth this is to be in all its length and breadth the land of liberty! . . .

"Meanwhile, I would invite his own and the attention of all his deluded followers to a paragraph in the late number of the New Orleans *Picayune,* wherein it is stated that inquests had been held upon the bodies of 21 contrabands in one house alone in that city. These poor Negroes had been stolen or enticed away from the comfortable homes of their masters, and left to starve and rot by these philanthropic (?) advocates of liberty for the slave." [3]

The Savannah *Republican* in March declared:

"In our judgment, so far as the Border States are concerned, his proposition will have exactly the opposite effect to that for which it was designed. Those states, who have held on to the Union with the belief that their Southern sisters were hasty and wrong in the belief that they were about to be brought under an abolition government, will now see that they were right and that all their worst apprehensions have been justified by the acts of that government."

Beauregard sent an impudent telegram to Miles at Richmond:

"Has the bill for the execution of abolition prisoners, after January next, been passed? Do it, and England will be stirred into action. It is high time to proclaim the black flag after that period; let the execution be with the garrote."

The reaction to emancipation in the North was unfavorable so far as political results indicated, although many motives influenced the voters. The elections of 1862 in New York, New Jersey, Pennsylvania, Ohio, Indiana and Illinois went Democratic, and in other parts of the West, Lincoln lost support. In the Congress of 1860, there were seventy-eight Republicans and thirty-seven Democrats, and in 1862, the administration had only fifty-seven supporters, with sixty-seven in the opposition.

Only among Negroes and in England was the reaction favorable, and both counted. The Proclamation made four and a half million laborers willing almost in mass to sacrifice their last drop of blood for their new-found country. It sent them into transports of joy and sacrifice. It changed all their pessimism and despair into boundless faith. It was the Coming of the Lord.

The Proclamation had an undoubted and immediate effect upon England. The upper classes were strongly in favor of the Confederacy, and sure that the Yankees were fighting only for a high tariff and hurt vanity. Free-trade England was repelled by this program, and attracted by the free trade which the Confederacy offered. There was strong demand among manufacturers to have the government interfere and recognize the Southern States as an independent nation. The church and universities were in favor of the Confederacy, and all the great periodicals. Even the philanthropists, like Lord Shaftesbury, Carlyle, Buxton and Gladstone, threw their sympathies to the South. Carlyle sneered at people "cutting each other's throats because one-half of them prefer hiring their servants for life, and the other by the hour." [4]

As Henry Adams assures us:

"London was altogether beside itself on one point, in especial; it created a nightmare of its own, and gave it the shape of Abraham Lincoln. Behind this it placed another demon, if possible more devilish, and called it Mr. Seward. In regard to these two men, English society seemed demented. Defense was useless; explanation was vain; one could only let the passion exhaust itself. One's best friends were as unreasonable as enemies, for the belief in poor Mr. Lincoln's brutality and Seward's ferocity became a dogma of popular faith." [5]

Confederate warships were being built and harbored in English ports and in September, 1862, Palmerston, believing that the Confederates were about to capture Washington, suggested intervention to members of his cabinet. Lord John Russell wanted to act immediately, but the rebels were driven back at Antietam the same month, and the preliminary Emancipation Proclamation appeared. Gladstone and Russell still tried to force intervention, but Palmerston hesitated.

There was similar demand in France, but not as strong, because cotton did not play so large a part. Nevertheless, the textile workers in both France and England were hard-pressed by the cotton famine. Napoleon III was in favor of the South, but the mass of the French nation was not. Napoleon was assured by the Confederate government that a Southern alliance with French Mexico and a guaranty of Cuba could be had for the asking, if France would recognize the Confederacy. No danger from the North was anticipated, for Seward was certain to accept Napoleon's assurances of France's neutrality.

Public opinion stood back of the English government and was, on the whole, in favor of the South; but Garrison and Douglass by their visits, and later Harriet Beecher Stowe, had influenced the opinion of the middle and laboring classes. Nevertheless, it was reported in 1862: "We find only here and there among the Englishmen one who does not fanatically side with the slave states." Various meetings in favor of the South were arranged by the workingmen and the General Council of Workingmen's Associations opposed the pro-Southern movement. The war had created a great scarcity of cotton, and in addition to this, there had already been an over-production of the cotton industry in England in 1860, so that the effect of the blockade was not felt until later, so far as the sale of goods was concerned. But the factories closed, and more than half the looms and spindles lay idle. Especially in Lancashire there was great distress among laborers. Fever and prostitution were prevalent in 1865.

Notwithstanding this, the English workers stood up for the abolition of Negro slavery, and protested against the intervention of the English. Up until 1863, it was argued with some show of right that the North was not fighting to free the slaves; but on the contrary, according to Lincoln's own words, "was perfectly willing to settle the war and leave the Negroes in slavery." But as soon as Lincoln issued the Emancipation Proclamation, the workingmen of England held hundreds of meetings all over the country and in all industrial sections, and hailed his action.

Ernest Jones, the leader of the Chartist movement, raised his eloquent voice against slavery. During the winter of 1862-1863, meeting after meeting in favor of emancipation was held. The reaction in England to the Emancipation Proclamation was too enthusiastic for the government to dare take any radical step. Great meetings in London and Manchester stirred the nation, and gave notice to Palmerston that he could not yet take the chance of recognizing the South. In spite of Russell and Gladstone, he began to withdraw, and the imminent danger of recognition of the South by England and France passed.

In the monster meeting of English workingmen at St. James' Hall, London, March 26, 1863, John Bright spoke; and John Stuart Mill declared that: "Higher political and social freedom has been established in the United States." Karl Marx testified that this meeting held in 1863 kept Lord Palmerston from declaring war against the United States. On December 31, 1863, at meetings held simultaneously in London and Manchester, addresses were sent to Lincoln, drafted by Karl Marx. The London address said:

"Sir: We who offer this address are Englishmen and workingmen. We prize as our dearest inheritance, bought for us by the blood of our fathers, the liberty we enjoy—the liberty of free labor on a free soil. We have, therefore, been accustomed to regard with veneration and gratitude the founders of the great republic in which the liberties of the Anglo-Saxon race have been widened beyond all the precedents of the old world, and in which there was nothing to condemn or to lament but the slavery and degradation of men guilty only of a colored skin or an African parentage. We have looked with admiration and sympathy upon the brave, generous and untiring efforts of a large party in the Northern States to deliver the Union from this curse and shame. We rejoiced, sir, in your election to the Presidency, as a splendid proof that the principles of universal freedom and equality were rising to the ascendant. We regarded with abhorrence the conspiracy and rebellion by which it was sought at once to overthrow the supremacy of a government based upon the most popular suffrage in the world, and to perpetuate the hateful inequalities of race." [6]

The Manchester address, adopted by six thousand people, said among other things:

"One thing alone has, in the past, lessened our sympathy with your country and our confidence in it; we mean the ascendancy of politicians who not merely maintained Negro slavery, but desired to extend and root it more deeply. Since we have discerned, however, that the victory of the free North in the war which has so sorely distressed us as well as afflicted you, will shake off the fetters of the slave, you have attracted our warm and earnest sympathy.

"We joyfully honor you, as the President, and the Congress with you, for the many decisive steps towards practically exemplifying your belief in the words of your great founders: 'All men are created free and equal.' . . .

"We assume that you cannot now stop short of a complete uprooting of slavery. It would not become us to dictate any details, but there are broad principles of humanity which must guide you. If complete emancipation in some states be deferred, though only to a predetermined day, still, in the interval, human beings should not be counted chattels. Woman must have rights of chastity and maternity, men the rights of husbands; masters the liberty of manumission. Justice demands for the black, no less than for the white, the protection of the law—that his voice may be heard in your courts. Nor must any such abomination be tolerated as slave-breeding States and a slave market—if you are to earn the high reward of all your sacrifices in the approval of the universal brotherhood and of the Divine Father. It is for your free country to decide whether anything but immediate and total emancipation can secure the most indispensable rights of humanity, against the inveterate wickedness of local laws and local executives.

"We implore you, for your own honor and welfare, not to faint in your providential mission. While your enthusiasm is aflame, and the tide of events runs high, let the work be finished effectually. Leave no root of bitterness to spring up and work fresh misery to your children. It is a mighty task, indeed, to reorganize the industry, not only of four millions of the colored race, but of five millions of whites.

Nevertheless, the vast progress you have made in the short space of twenty months fills us with hope that every stain on your freedom will shortly be removed, and that the erasure of that foul blot upon civilization and Christianity—chattel slavery—during your Presidency, will cause the name of Abraham Lincoln to be honored and revered by posterity." [7]

Lincoln in reply said that he knew the suffering of the working-men in Manchester and Europe in this crisis, and appreciated the action of the English workingmen as an example of "sublime Christian heroism," which "has not been surpassed in any age or in any country." He declared that the Civil War was "the attempt to overthrow this government, which was built upon a foundation of human rights, and to substitute one which should rest exclusively on the basis of human slavery."

In the North, the Emancipation Proclamation meant the Negro soldier, and the Negro soldier meant the end of the war.

"We have come to set you free!" cried the black cavalrymen who rode at the head of the Union Army as it entered Richmond in 1864. These soldiers were in the division of Godfrey Weitzel; when Ben Butler first assigned Negro troops to Weitzel's command in Louisiana, Weitzel resigned. It was a good thing for him that he recalled this resignation, for his black soldiers at Port Hudson wrote his name in history.

Here was indeed revolution. At first, this was to be a white man's war. First, because the North did not want to affront the South, and the war was going to be short, very short; and secondly, if Negroes fought in the war, how could it help being a war for their emancipation? And for this the North would not fight. Yet scarcely a year after hostilities started, the Negroes were fighting, although unrecognized as soldiers; in two years they were free and enrolling in the army.

Private Miles O'Reilly expressed in the newspapers a growing public opinion:

> "Some say it is a burnin' shame
> To make the naygurs fight,
> An' that the thrade o' bein' kilt
> Belongs but to the white;
>
> "But as for me 'upon me sowl'
> So liberal are we here,
> I'll let Sambo be murthered in place o' meself
> On every day in the year."

In December, 1861, Union officers were ordered not to return fugitive slaves on pain of court-martial. In 1862 came Hunter's black regiment in South Carolina.

In the spring of 1862, General Hunter had less than eleven thousand men under his command, and had to hold the whole broken seacoast of Georgia, South Carolina and Florida. He applied often and in vain to the authorities at Washington for reënforcements. All the troops available in the North were less than sufficient for General McClellan's great operations against Richmond, and the reiterated answer of the War Department was: "You must get along as best you can. Not a man from the North can be spared."

"No reënforcements to be had from the North; vast fatigue duties in throwing up earthworks imposed on our insufficient garrison; the enemy continually increasing, both in insolence and numbers; our only success the capture of Fort Pulaski, sealing up Savannah; and this victory offset, if not fully counterbalanced, by many minor gains of the enemy; this was about the condition of affairs as seen from the headquarters fronting Port Royal bay, when General Hunter one morning, 'with twirling glasses, puckered lips and dilated nostrils' [he had just received another "don't-bother-us-for-reënforcements" dispatch from Washington] announced his intention of 'forming a Negro regiment, and compelling every able-bodied black man in the department to fight for the freedom which could not but be the issue of our war.' " [8]

Hunter caused all the necessary orders to be issued, and took upon himself the responsibility for the irregular issue of arms, clothing, equipments and rations involved in collecting and organizing the first experimental Negro regiments.

Reports of the organization of the First South Carolina Infantry were forwarded to headquarters in Washington, and the War Department took no notice. Nothing was said, nor was any authority given to pay the men or furnish them subsistence. But at last a special dispatch steamer plowed her way over the bar with word from the War Department, "requiring immediate answer."

It was a demand for information in regard to the Negro regiment, based on a resolution introduced by Wickliffe of Kentucky. These resolutions had been adopted by Congress. Hunter laughed, but as he was without authority for any of his actions in this case, it seemed to his worried Adjutant-General that the documents in his hands were no laughing matter. But Hunter declared:

"That old fool has just given me the very chance I was growing sick for! The War Department has refused to notice my black regiment; but now, in reply to this resolution, I can lay the matter before the country, and force the authorities either to adopt my Negroes, or to disband them." [9]

So Hunter wrote: "No regiment of 'fugitive slaves' has been, or is being, organized in this department. There is, however, a fine regiment of loyal persons whose late masters are fugitive rebels." He said that he did this under instructions given by the late Secretary of War, and his general authority to employ "all loyal persons offering their service in defense of the Union." He added:

"Neither have I had any specific authority for supplying these persons with shovels, spades, and pickaxes, when employing them as laborers; nor with boats and oars, when using them as lighter-men; but these are not points included in Mr. Wickliffe's resolutions. To me it seemed that liberty to employ men in any particular capacity implied and carried with it liberty, also, to supply them with the necessary tools; and, acting upon this faith, I have clothed, equipped and armed the only loyal regiment yet raised in South Carolina, Georgia or Florida. . . .

"The experiment of arming the blacks, so far as I have made it, has been a complete and even marvelous success. They are sober, docile, attentive, and enthusiastic; displaying great natural capacities in acquiring the duties of the soldier. They are now eager beyond all things to take the field and be led into action; and it is the unanimous opinion of the officers who have had charge of them that, in the peculiarities of this climate and country, they will prove invaluable auxiliaries, fully equal to the similar regiments so long and successfully used by the British authorities in the West India Islands.

"In conclusion, I would say, it is my hope—there appearing no possibility of other reënforcements, owing to the exigencies of the campaign in the Peninsula—to have organized by the end of next fall, and be able to present to the government, from forty-eight to fifty thousand of these hardy and devoted soldiers."

When the reply was read in the House of Representatives: "Its effects were magical. The clerk could scarcely read it with decorum; nor could half his words be heard amidst the universal peals of laughter in which both Democrats and Republicans appeared to vie as to which should be the more noisy. . . . It was the great joke of the day, and coming at a moment of universal gloom in the public mind, was seized upon by the whole loyal press of the country as a kind of politico-military champagne cocktail."

When the Confederate Government heard of this, it issued an order reciting that "as the government of the United States had refused to answer whether it authorized the raising of a black regiment by General Hunter or not," said general, his staff, and all officers under his command who had directly or indirectly participated in the unclean thing, should hereafter be outlaws not covered by the laws of war; but to be executed as felons for the crime of "inciting Negro insurrection wherever caught."

In Louisiana, the colored creoles in many cases hesitated. Some of them had been owners of slaves, and some actually fought in the Confederate Army, but were not registered as Negroes. On November 23, 1861, the Confederate grand parade took place in New Orleans, and one feature of the review was a regiment of free men of color, 1,400 in number. The *Picayune* speaks of a later review on February 9, 1862:

"We must pay deserved compliment to the companies of free men of color, all well-dressed, well-drilled, and comfortably uniformed. Most of these companies have provided themselves with arms unaided by the administration."

When Butler entered the city in 1862, the Confederates fled tumultuously or laid aside their uniforms and stayed. The free Negro regiment did neither, but offered its services to the Federal army. Butler at first was in a quandary.

"The instructions given by General McClellan to General Butler were silent on this most perplexing problem. On leaving Washington, Butler was verbally informed by the President, that the government was not yet prepared to announce a Negro policy. They were anxiously considering the subject, and hoped, ere long, to arrive at conclusions." [10]

Butler found the Negroes of great help to him, but he could not, as in Virginia, call them "contraband," because he had no work for them. He wanted to free them, but on May 9, the news came that Hunter's proclamation in South Carolina had been revoked. Butler, however, abolished the whipping houses, and encouraged the Negroes who called on him. "One consequence was that the general had a spy in every house, behind each rebel's chair, as he sat at table."

General Butler asked for reënforcements all summer on account of the growing strength of Vicksburg and Port Hudson, the condition of Mobile and camps near New Orleans. The answer from Washington was: "We cannot spare you one man; we will send you men when we have them to send. You must hold New Orleans by all means and at all hazards."

Earlier, General Phelps, who commanded the Federal forces about seven miles from New Orleans, had received a number of refugees, some of them in chains and some of them bleeding from wounds. Butler ordered him May 23, 1862, to exclude these from his lines. He replied at length:

"Added to the four millions of the colored race whose disaffection is increasing even more rapidly than their number, there are at least four millions more of the white race whose growing miseries will naturally seek companionship with those of the blacks."

He demanded that the President should abolish slavery, and that the Negroes be armed. Butler forwarded Phelps' reply to Washington. Phelps again demanded the right to arm Negro troops. He was ordered July 1, 1862, to use the Negroes to cut wood. He immediately handed in his resignation, saying:

"I am willing to prepare African regiments for the defense of the government against its assailants. I am not willing to become the mere slave-driver which you propose, having no qualifications in that way." [11]

The use of Negro troops was precipitated by the attack which Breckinridge made August 5, 1862, on Baton Rouge. Butler had to have troops to defend New Orleans, and had applied to Washington, but none could be sent. Therefore, by proclamation, August 22, 1862, Butler "called on Africa," accepted the free Negro regiment which had offered its services, and proceeded to organize other Negro troops. He recited at length the previous action of the Confederate Governor in organizing the Negro regiment, April 23, 1861, and quoted directly from the Confederate Governor's proclamation:

"Now, therefore, the Commanding General, believing that a large portion of this militia force of the State of Louisiana are willing to take service in the volunteer forces of the United States, and be enrolled and organized to 'defend their homes' from 'ruthless invaders'; to protect their wives and children and kindred from wrong and outrage; to shield their property from being seized by bad men; and to defend the flag of their native country, as their fathers did under Jackson at Chalmette against Packenham and his myrmidons, carrying the black flag of 'beauty and booty':

"Appreciating their motives, relying upon their 'well-known loyalty and patriotism,' and with 'praise and respect' for these brave men— it is ordered that all the members of the 'Native Guards' aforesaid, and all other free colored citizens recognized by the first and late governor and authorities of the State of Louisiana, as a portion of the militia of the State, who shall enlist in the volunteer service of the United States, shall be duly organized by the appointment of proper officers, and accepted, paid, equipped, armed and rationed as are other volunteer troops of the United States, subject to the approval of the President of the United States." [12]

Thousands of volunteers under Butler's appeal appeared. In fourteen days, a regiment was organized with colored line officers and white field officers. More than half of the privates were not really free Negroes but fugitive slaves. A second regiment with colored line officers was enlisted, and a third, with colored mess officers.

In the Kansas Home Guard were two regiments of Indians, and among them over four hundred Negroes; and 2,500 Negroes served in the contingent that came from the Indian nations. Many of them enlisted early in 1862.

In the meantime, the war was evidently more than a dress parade or a quick attack upon Richmond. One hundred thousand "three months" soldiers were but a "drop in the bucket." More and more troops must be had. The time of enlistment for many of the white troops was already expiring, and at least Negro troops could be used on fatigue duty in the large stretches of territory held by the Federal armies down the Atlantic Coast, and in the Mississippi Valley, and in the Border States.

Senator Henry Wilson of Massachusetts, Chairman of the Senate Committee on Military Affairs, introduced a bill in July, 1862, which empowered the President to accept Negroes for constructing entrenchments, or any other war service for which they might be found competent. If owned by rebels, such Negroes were to be freed, but nothing was said of their families. Thaddeus Stevens championed the bill in the House, and it was signed by Lincoln, July 17, 1862.

The debate was bitter. Senator Sherman of Ohio said:

"The question rises, whether the people of the United States, struggling for national existence, should not employ these blacks for the maintenance of the Government. The policy heretofore pursued by the officers of the United States has been to repel this class of people from our lines, to refuse their services. They would have made the best spies; and yet they have been driven from our lines."

Fessenden of Maine added: "I tell the generals of our army, they must reverse their practices and their course of proceeding on this subject. . . . I advise it here from my place—treat your enemies as enemies, as the worst of enemies, and avail yourselves like men, of every power which God has placed in your hands, to accomplish your purpose within the rules of civilized warfare." Race, of Minnesota, declared that "not many days can pass before the people of the United States North must decide upon one or two questions: we have either to acknowledge the Southern Confederacy as a free and independent nation, and that speedily; or we have as speedily to resolve to use all the means given us by the Almighty to prosecute this war to a successful termination. The necessity for action has arisen. To hesitate is worse than criminal." The Border States demurred, and Davis of Kentucky was especially bitter with threats.

The bill finally was amended so as to pay the black soldier's bounty to his owner, if he happened to be a slave!

All that was simply permissive legislation, and for a time the War Department did nothing. Some of the commanders in the field, however, began to move. On the other hand, Senator Davis of Kentucky tried in January, 1863, to stop the use of any national appropriations to pay Negro soldiers. This attempt was defeated, and on January 6, 1863, five days after the Emancipation Proclamation, the Secretary of War authorized the Governor of Massachusetts to raise two Negro regiments for three years' service. These were the celebrated 54th and 55th Negro regiments—the first regularly authorized Negro regiments of the war.

The recruiting of the 54th Massachusetts Regiment of colored men was completed by the 13th of May. It had been planned to have the regiment pass through New York, but the Chief of Police warned that it would be subject to insult, so that it went by sea to South Carolina.

In October, the Adjutant-General of the United States issued a general order permitting the military employment of Negroes. The Union League Club of New York appointed a committee to raise Negro troops, and after some difficulty with Governor Seymour, they received from Washington authority to raise a regiment. One thousand Negroes responded within two weeks, and by January 27, 1864, a second regiment was raised. No bounty was offered them, and no protection promised their families. One of the regiments marched through the city.

"The scene of yesterday," says a New York paper, "was one which marks an era of progress in the political and social history of New York. A thousand men with black skins and clad and equipped with the uniforms and arms of the United States Government, marched from their camp through the most aristocratic and busy streets, received a grand ovation at the hands of the wealthiest and most respectable ladies and gentlemen of New York, and then moved down Broadway to the steamer which bears them to their destination—all amid the enthusiastic cheers, the encouraging plaudits, the waving handkerchiefs, the showering bouquets and other approving manifestations of a hundred thousand of the most loyal of our people." [18]

Pennsylvania was especially prominent in recruiting Negro troops. A committee was appointed, which raised $33,388, with which they proposed to raise three regiments. The committee founded Camp William Penn at Shelton Hill, and the first squad went into camp June 26, 1863. The first regiment, known as the Third United States, was full July 24, 1863. The third regiment, known as the Eighth United

States, was full December 4, 1863. Two more regiments were full
January 6 and February 3. The regiments went South, August 13,
October 14, 1863, and January 16, 1864.

In the Department of the Cumberland, the Secretary of War authorized George L. Stearns of Massachusetts to recruit Negroes. Stearns
was a friend of John Brown, and a prominent Abolitionist. He took up
headquarters at Nashville, and raised a number of regiments. In the
Department of the Gulf, General Banks, May 1, 1863, proposed an
army corps to be known as the Corps d'Afrique. It was to consist of
eighteen regiments, infantry, artillery and calvary, and to be organized
in three divisions of three brigades each, with engineers and hospitals,
etc. He said in his order:

"The Government makes use of mules, horses, uneducated and educated white men, in the defense of its institutions. Why should not
the Negro contribute whatever is in his power for the cause in which
he is as deeply interested as other men? We may properly demand
from him whatever service he can render."

In March, 1863, the Secretary of War sent the Adjutant-General,
Lorenzo Thomas, into the South on a tour of inspection. Stanton's
orders said:

"The President desires that you should confer freely with Major-
General Grant, and the officers with whom you may have communication, and explain to them the importance attached by the Government to the use of the colored population emancipated by the President's Proclamation, and particularly for the organization of their
labor and military strength. . . .

"You are authorized in this connection, to issue in the name of this
department, letters of appointment for field and company officers,
and to organize such troops for military service to the utmost extent
to which they can be obtained in accordance with the rules and regulations of the service." [14]

Thomas spoke to the army officers in Louisiana, and expressed
himself clearly.

"You know full well—for you have been over this country—that
the Rebels have sent into the fields all their available fighting men—
every man capable of bearing arms; and you know they have kept
at home all their slaves for the raising of subsistence for their armies
in the field. In this way they can bring to bear against us all the
strength of their so-called Confederate States; while we at the North
can only send a portion of our fighting force, being compelled to leave
behind another portion to cultivate our fields and supply the wants
of an immense army. THE ADMINISTRATION HAS DETERMINED TO TAKE
FROM THE REBELS THIS SOURCE OF SUPPLY—TO TAKE THEIR NEGROES AND

COMPEL THEM TO SEND BACK A PORTION OF THEIR WHITES TO CULTIVATE THEIR DESERTED PLANTATIONS—AND VERY POOR PERSONS THEY WOULD BE TO FILL THE PLACE OF THE DARK-HUED LABORER. THEY MUST DO THIS, OR THEIR ARMIES WILL STARVE. . . .

"All of you will some day be on picket duty; and I charge you all, if any of this unfortunate race come within your lines, that you do not turn them away, but receive them kindly and cordially. They are to be encouraged to come to us; they are to be received with open arms; they are to be fed and clothed; they are to be armed." [15]

It would not have been American, however, not to have maintained some color discrimination, however petty. First, there was the matter of pay. The pay of soldiers at the beginning of the war was $13 a month. Negro soldiers enlisted under the same law. In the instructions to General Saxton, August 25, 1862, it was stated that the pay should be the same as that of the other troops. Soon, however, this was changed, and Negro soldiers were allowed but $10 a month, and $3 of this was deducted for clothing. Many of the regiments refused to receive the reduced pay. The 54th Massachusetts Infantry refused pay for a whole year until the regiment was treated as other regiments. The State of Massachusetts made up the difference to disabled and discharged soldiers until June 15, 1864, when the law was changed. In the Department of the Gulf, white troops who did provost duties about the city were paid $16 a month, while the Negro regiments were paid $7. At one time, this came near causing a mutiny.

But the Negroes did not waver. John M. Langston in a speech in Ohio in August, 1862, said:

"Pay or no pay, let us volunteer. The good results of such a course are manifold. But this one alone is all that needs to be mentioned in this connection. I refer to thorough organization. This is the great need of the colored Americans."

With regard to officers, the people of Pennsylvania secured from the Secretary of War permission to establish a free military school for the education of candidates for commissioned officers among the colored troops. The school was established, and within less than six months, examined over 1,000 applicants and passed 560. In the Department of the Gulf, Butler was in favor of colored officers, because in the First Colored Regiment there were a number of well-trained and intelligent Negro officers. But Banks was very much against colored officers, and would not use them. There was at first a very great distaste on the part of white men for serving in colored regiments. Hunter found this difficulty with his first regiment, but he quickly cured it by offering commissions to competent non-commissioned officers. Later, when the black troops made their reputation in battle, the chance to command them was eagerly sought.

Congress finally freed the wives and children of enlisted soldiers; a measure which Davis of Kentucky quickly opposed on the ground that "The government had no power to take private property except for public use, and without just compensation to the owner."

Abraham Lincoln, under a fire of criticism, warmly defended the enlistment of Negro troops. "The slightest knowledge of arithmetic will prove to any man that the rebel armies cannot be destroyed with Democratic strategy. It would sacrifice all the white men of the North to do it. There are now in the service of the United States near two hundred thousand able-bodied colored men, most of them under arms, defending and acquiring Union territory. . . .

"ABANDON ALL THE POSTS NOW GARRISONED BY BLACK MEN; TAKE TWO HUNDRED THOUSAND MEN FROM OUR SIDE AND PUT THEM IN THE BATTLE-FIELD OR CORNFIELD AGAINST US, AND WE WOULD BE COMPELLED TO ABANDON THE WAR IN THREE WEEKS. . . .

"My enemies pretend I am now carrying on this war for the sole purpose of abolition. So long as I am President, it shall be carried on for the sole purpose of restoring the Union. But no human power can subdue this rebellion without the use of the emancipation policy, and every other policy calculated to weaken the moral and physical forces of the rebellion. Freedom has given us two hundred thousand men raised on Southern soil. It will give us more yet. Just so much it has subtracted from the enemy." [16]

The question as to whether Negroes should enlist in the Federal army was not nearly as clear in 1863 as it seems today. The South still refused to believe that the Civil War would end in the emancipation of slaves. There not only were strong declarations to the contrary in the North, but there was still the determined opposition of the Border States. The Confederates industriously spread propaganda among slaves, alleging that Northerners mistreated the Negroes, and were selling them to the West Indies into harsher slavery. Even in the North, among the more intelligent free Negroes, there was some hesitancy.

Frederick Douglass spoke for the free and educated black man, clear-headed and undeceived: "Now, what is the attitude of the Washington government towards the colored race? What reasons have we to desire its triumph in the present contest? Mind, I do not ask what was its attitude towards us before this bloody rebellion broke out. I do not ask what was its disposition, when it was controlled by the very men who are now fighting to destroy it, when they could no longer control it. I do not even ask what it was two years ago, when McClellan shamelessly gave out that in a war between loyal slaves and disloyal masters, he would take the side of the masters against the slaves—when he openly proclaimed his purpose to put down slave insurrections with an iron hand—when glorious Ben Butler, now stunned into a conversion to anti-slavery principles (which I have every reason to believe sincere), proffered his services to the Governor of Maryland, to suppress a slave insurrection, while treason ran riot in that State, and the warm, red blood of Massachusetts soldiers still stained the pavements of Baltimore.

"I do not ask what was the attitude of this government when many of the officers and men who had undertaken to defend it openly threatened to throw down their arms and leave the service if men of color should step forward to defend it, and be invested with the dignity of soldiers. Moreover, I do not ask what was the position of this government when our loyal camps were made slave-hunting grounds, and United States officers performed the disgusting duty of slave dogs to hunt down slaves for rebel masters. These were all the dark and terrible days for the republic. I do not ask you about the dead past. I bring you to the living present.

"Events more mighty than men, eternal Providence, all-wise and all-controlling, have placed us in new relations to the government and the government to us. What that government is to us today, and what it will be tomorrow, is made evident by a very few facts. Look at them, colored men. Slavery in the District of Columbia is abolished forever; slavery in all the territories of the United States is abolished forever; the foreign slave trade, with its ten thousand revolting abominations, is rendered impossible; slavery in ten States of the Union is abolished forever; slavery in the five remaining States is as certain to follow the same fate as the night is to follow the day. The independence of Haiti is recognized; her Minister sits beside our Prime Minister, Mr. Seward, and dines at his table in Washington, while colored men are excluded from the cars in Philadelphia; showing that a black man's complexion in Washington, in the presence of the Federal Government, is less offensive than in the city of brotherly love. Citizenship is no longer denied us under this government.

"Under the interpretation of our rights by Attorney General Bates, we are American citizens. We can import goods, own and sail ships and travel in foreign countries, with American passports in our pockets; and now, so far from there being any opposition, so far from excluding us from the army as soldiers, the President at Washington, the Cabinet and the Congress, the generals commanding and the whole army of the nation unite in giving us one thunderous welcome to share with them in the honor and glory of suppressing treason and upholding the star-spangled banner. The revolution is tremendous, and it becomes us as wise men to recognize the change, and to shape our action accordingly.

"I hold that the Federal Government was never, in its essence, anything but an antislavery government. Abolish slavery tomorrow, and not a sentence or syllable of the Constitution need be altered. It was purposely so framed as to give no claim, no sanction to the claim of property in man. If in its origin slavery had any relation to the government, it was only as the scaffolding to the magnificent structure, to be removed as soon as the building was completed. There is in the Constitution no East, no West, no North, no South, no black, no white, no slave, no slaveholder, but all are citizens who are of American birth.

"Such is the government, fellow-citizens, you are now called upon to uphold with your arms. Such is the government, that you are called upon to coöperate with in burying rebellion and slavery in a common grave. Never since the world began was a better chance offered to a long enslaved and oppressed people. The opportunity is given us to be men. With one courageous resolution we may blot out the handwriting of ages against us. Once let the black man get upon his person the brass letters U. S.; let him get an eagle on his button, and a musket on his shoulder, and bullets in his pocket, and there is no power on the earth or under the earth which can deny that he has earned the right of citizenship in the United States." [17]

In the meantime, two fateful occurrences took place. First, the white workers of New York declared in effect that the Negroes were the cause of the war, and that they were tired of the discrimination that made workers fighters for the rich. They, therefore, killed all the Negroes that they could lay their hands on. On the other hand, in Louisiana and South Carolina, Negro soldiers were successfully used in pitched battle.

The opposition to the war in the North took various forms. There was the open sedition, led by Vallandingham and ending in the mass opposition of the working classes. This Copperhead movement was pro-slavery and pro-Southern, and was met in part by closer understanding and alliance between the Abolitionists and the Republican administration. But the working class movement was deeper and more difficult. It was the protest of the poor against being compelled to fight the battles of the rich in which they could conceive no interest of theirs. If the workers had been inspired by the sentiment against slavery which animated the English workers, results might have been different. But the Copperheads of the North, and the commercial interests of New York, in particular, were enabled to turn the just indignation of the workers against the Negro laborers, rather than against the capitalists; and against any war, even for emancipation.

When the draft law was passed in 1863, it meant that the war could no longer be carried on with volunteers; that soldiers were going to be compelled to fight, and these soldiers were going to be poor men who could not buy exemption. The result throughout the country was widespread disaffection that went often as far as rioting. More than 2,500 deserters from the Union army were returned to the ranks from Indianapolis alone during a single month in 1862; the total desertions in the North must have been several hundred thousands.

It was easy to transfer class hatred so that it fell upon the black worker. The end of war seemed far off, and the attempt to enforce the draft led particularly to disturbances in New York City, where a powerful part of the city press was not only against the draft, but against the war, and in favor of the South and Negro slavery.

The establishment of the draft undertaken July 13 in New York City met everywhere with resistance. Workingmen engaged in tearing down buildings were requested to give their names for the draft; they refused, and drove away the officers. The movement spread over the whole city. Mobs visited workshops and compelled the men to stop work. Firemen were prevented from putting out fires, telegraph wires were cut, and then at last the whole force of the riot turned against the Negroes. They were the cause of the war, and hence the cause of the draft. They were bidding for the same jobs as white men. They were underbidding white workers in order to keep themselves from starving. They were disliked especially by the Irish because of direct economic competition and difference in religion.

The Democratic press had advised the people that they were to be called upon to fight the battles of "niggers and Abolitionists"; Governor Seymour politely "requested" the rioters to await the return of his Adjutant-General, whom he had dispatched to Washington to ask the President to suspend the draft.

The report of the Merchants' Committee on the Draft Riot says of the Negroes: "Driven by the fear of death at the hands of the mob, who the week previous had, as you remember, brutally murdered by hanging on trees and lamp posts, several of their number, and cruelly beaten and robbed many others, burning and sacking their houses, and driving nearly all from the streets, alleys and docks upon which they had previously obtained an honest though humble living —these people had been forced to take refuge on Blackwell's Island, at police stations, on the outskirts of the city, in the swamps and woods back of Bergen, New Jersey, at Weeksville, and in the barns and out-houses of the farmers of Long Island and Morrisania. At these places were scattered some 5,000 homeless men, women and children." [18]

The whole demonstration became anti-Union and pro-slavery. Attacks were made on the residence of Horace Greeley, and cheers were heard for Jefferson Davis. The police fought it at first only half-heartedly and with sympathy, and finally, with brutality. Soldiers were summoned from Fort Hamilton, West Point and elsewhere.

The property loss was put at $1,200,000, and it was estimated that between four hundred and a thousand people were killed. When a thousand troops under General Wool took charge of the city, thirteen rioters were killed, eighteen wounded, and twenty-four made prisoners. Four days the riot lasted, and the city appropriated $2,500,000 to indemnify the victims.

In many other places, riots took place, although they did not become so specifically race riots. They did, however, show the North that unless they could replace unwilling white soldiers with black soldiers, who had a vital stake in the outcome of the war, the war could not be won.

It had been a commonplace thing in the North to declare that Negroes would not fight. Even the black man's friends were skeptical about the possibility of using him as a soldier, and far from its being to the credit of black men, or any men, that they did not want to kill, the ability and willingness to take human life has always been, even in the minds of liberal men, a proof of manhood. It took in many respects a finer type of courage for the Negro to work quietly and faithfully as a slave while the world was fighting over his destiny, than it did to seize a bayonet and rush mad with fury or inflamed with drink, and plunge it into the bowels of a stranger. Yet this was the proof of manhood required of the Negro. He might plead his cause with the tongue of Frederick Douglass, and the nation listened almost unmoved. He might labor for the nation's wealth, and the nation took the results without thanks, and handed him as near nothing in return as would keep him alive. He was called a coward and a fool when he protected the women and children of his master. But when he rose and fought and killed, the whole nation with one voice proclaimed him a man and brother. Nothing else made emancipation possible in the United States. Nothing else made Negro citizenship conceivable, but the record of the Negro soldier as a fighter.

The military aid of the Negroes began as laborers and as spies. A soldier said: "This war has been full of records of Negro agency in our behalf. Negro guides have piloted our forces; Negro sympathy cared for our prisoners escaping from the enemy; Negro hands have made for us naval captures; Negro spies brought us valuable information. The Negroes of the South have been in sympathy with us from the beginning, and have always hailed the approach of our flag with the wildest demonstrations of joy." [19]

All through the war and after, Negroes were indispensable as informers, as is well known. The Southern papers had repeated notices of the work of Negro spies. In Richmond, a white woman with dispatches for the Confederate army was arrested in 1863 on information given by a Negro. At the Battle of Manassas, the house of a free Negro was used as a refuge for the dead and wounded Union men. Negro pilots repeatedly guided Federal boats in Southern waters, and there were several celebrated cases of whole boats being seized by Negro pilots. A typical instance of this type was the action of William F. Tillman, a colored steward on board the brig *S. J. Waring,* which carried a cargo valued at $100,000. He had succeeded, by leading a revolt, in freeing the vessel from the Confederates who had seized it, and with the aid of a German and a Canadian had brought the vessel into port at New York. This action brought up the question of whether a Negro could be master of a vessel. In the Official Opinions of the Attorney-General for 1862, it was declared that a free colored man if born in the United States was a citizen of the United States and that he was competent to be master of a vessel engaged in the coasting trade.

The case of Smalls and the *Planter* at Charleston, South Carolina, became almost classic. "While at the wheel of the *Planter* as Pilot in the rebel service, it occurred to me that I could not only secure my own freedom, but that of numbers of my comrades in bonds, and moreover, I thought the *Planter* might be of some use to Uncle Abe. . . .

"I reported my plans for rescuing the *Planter* from the rebel captain to the crew (all colored), and secured their secrecy and coöperation.

"On May 13, 1862, we took on board several large guns at the Atlantic Dock. At evening of that day, the Captain went home, leaving the boat in my care, with instruction to send for him in case he should be wanted. . . . At half-past three o'clock on the morning of the 14th of May, I left the Atlantic Dock with the *Planter,* went to the *Ettaoue;* took on board my family; and several other families, then proceeded down Charleston River slowly. When opposite . . . Fort Sumter at 4 A.M., I gave the signal, which was answered from the Fort, thereby giving permission to pass. I then made speed for the Blockading Fleet. When entirely out of range of Sumter's guns, I hoisted a white flag, and at 5 A.M., reached a U. S. blockading vessel, commanded by Capt. Nicholas, to whom I turned over the *Planter*." [20]

After Lincoln was assassinated, General Hancock appealed to Negroes for help in capturing his murderers:

"Your President has been murdered! He has fallen by the assassin and without a moment's warning, simply and solely because he was your friend and the friend of our country. Had he been unfaithful to you and to the great cause of human freedom he might have lived. The pistol from which he met his death, though held by Booth, was held by the hands of treason and slavery. Think of this and remember how long and how anxiously this good man labored to break your chains and make you happy. I now appeal to you, by every consideration which can move loyal and grateful hearts, to aid in discovering and arresting his murderer." [21]

This was issued on the 24th of April. On the next day, the cavalry and police force, having crossed the Potomac, received information from a colored woman that the fugitives had been seen there. They were followed toward Bowling Green, and then toward Port Royal. There an old colored man reported that four individuals, in company with a rebel Captain, had crossed the river to Bowling Green. This information brought the police to Garrett's house, where Booth was found.

Negro military labor had been indispensable to the Union armies. "Negroes built most of the fortifications and earth-works for General Grant in front of Vicksburg. The works in and about Nashville were cast up by the strong arm and willing hand of the loyal Blacks. Dutch Gap was dug by Negroes, and miles of earth-works, fortifications, and corduroy-roads were made by Negroes. They did fatigue duty in every department of the Union army. Wherever a Negro appeared with a shovel in his hand, a white soldier took his gun and returned to the ranks. There were 200,000 Negroes in the camps and employ of the Union armies, as servants, teamsters, cooks, and laborers." [22]

The South was for a long time convinced that the Negro could not and would not fight. "The idea of their doing any serious fighting against white men is simply ridiculous," said an editorial in the Savannah *Republican*, March 25, 1863.

Of the actual fighting of Negroes, a Union general, Morgan, afterward interested in Negro education, says:

"History has not yet done justice to the share borne by colored soldiers in the war for the Union. Their conduct during that eventful period, has been a silent, but most potent factor in influencing public sentiment, shaping legislation, and fixing the status of colored people in America. If the records of their achievements could be put into shape that they could be accessible to the thousands of colored youth in the South, they would kindle in their young minds an enthusiastic devotion to manhood and liberty." [23]

Black men were repeatedly and deliberately used as shock troops, when there was little or no hope of success. In February, 1863, Colonel Thomas Wentworth Higginson led black troops into Florida, and declared: "It would have been madness to attempt with the bravest white troops what successfully accomplished with black ones." [24]

In April, there were three white companies from Maine and seven Negro companies on Ship Island, the key to New Orleans. The black troops with black officers were attacked by Confederates who outnumbered them five to one. The Negroes retreated so as to give the Federal gunboat *Jackson* a chance to shell their pursuers. But the white crew disliked the Negro soldiers, and opened fire directly upon the black troops while they were fighting the Confederates. Major Dumas, the Negro officer in command, rescued the black men; repulsed the Confederates, and brought the men out safely. The commander called attention to these colored officers: "they were constantly in the thickest of the fight, and by their unflinching bravery, and admirable handling of their commands, contributed to the success of the attack, and reflected great honor upon the flag." [25]

The first battle with numbers of Negro troops followed soon after. Banks laid siege to Port Hudson with all his forces, including two black regiments. On May 23, 1863, the assault was ordered, but the various coöperating organizations did not advance simultaneously. The Negro regiments, on the North, made three desperate charges, losing heavily, but maintained the advance over a field covered with recently felled trees. Confederate batteries opened fire upon them. Michigan, New York and Massachusetts white troops were hurled back, but the works had to be taken. Two Negro regiments were ordered to go forward, through a direct and cross fire.

"The deeds of heroism performed by these colored men were such as the proudest white men might emulate. Their colors are torn to pieces by shot, and literally bespattered by blood and brains. The color-sergeant of the 1st Louisiana, on being mortally wounded, hugged the colors to his breast, when a struggle ensued between the two color-corporals on each side of him, as to who should have the honor of bearing the sacred standard, and during this generous contention, one was seriously wounded. One black lieutenant actually mounted the enemy's works three or four times, and in one charge the assaulting party came within fifty paces of them. Indeed, if only ordinarily supported by artillery and reserve, no one can convince us that they would not have opened a passage through the enemy's works.

"Captain Callioux of the 1st Louisiana, a man so black that he actually prided himself upon his blackness, died the death of a hero, leading on his men in the thickest of the fight." [26]

"Colonel Bassett being driven back, Colonel Finnegas took his place, and his men being similarly cut to pieces, Lieutenant-Colonel Bassett reformed and recommenced; and thus these brave people went on, from morning until 3:30 P.M., under the most hideous carnage that men ever had to withstand, and that very few white ones would have had nerve to encounter, even if ordered to. During this time, they rallied, and *were ordered to make six distinct charges,* losing thirty-seven killed, and one hundred and fifty-five wounded, and one hundred and sixteen missing,—the majority, if not all, of these being in all probability, now lying dead on the gory field, and without the rites of sepulture; for when, by flag of truce, our forces in other direction were permitted to reclaim their dead, the benefit, through some neglect, was not extended to these black regiments!" [27]

In June, came the battle of Milliken's Bend. Grant, in order to capture Vicksburg, had drawn nearly all his troops from Milliken's Bend, except three Negro regiments, and a small force of white cavalry. This force was surprised by the Confederates, who drove the white cavalry to the very breastworks of the fort. Here the Confederates rested, expecting to take the fortifications in the morning. At three o'clock, they rushed over with drawn bayonets, but the Negroes drove them out of the forts and held them until the gunboats came up. One officer describes the fight:

"Before the colonel was ready, the men were in line, ready for action. As before stated, the rebels drove our force toward the gunboats, taking colored men prisoners and murdering them. This so enraged them that they rallied, and charged the enemy more heroically and desperately than has been recorded during the war. It was a genuine bayonet charge, a hand-to-hand fight, that has never occurred to any extent during this prolonged conflict. Upon both sides men were killed with the butts of muskets. White and black men were lying side by side, pierced by bayonets, and in some instances transfixed to the earth. In one instance, two men, one white and the other black, were found dead, side by side, each having the other's bayonet through his body. If facts prove to be what they are now represented, this engagement of Sunday morning will be recorded as the most desperate of this war. Broken limbs, broken heads, the mangling of bodies, all prove that it was a contest between enraged men: on the one side from hatred to a race; and on the other, desire for self-preservation, revenge for past grievances and the inhuman murder of their comrades." [28]

The month of July, 1863, was memorable. General Meade had driven Lee from Gettysburg, Grant had captured Vicksburg, Banks had captured Port Hudson, and Gilmore had begun his operations on Morris Island. On the 13th of July, the draft riot broke out in New York City, and before it was over, a Negro regiment in South Carolina, the 54th Massachusetts, was preparing to lead the assault on Fort Wagner. It was a desperate, impossible venture, which failed, but can never be forgotten.

The black Fifty-Fourth Massachusetts regiment was to lead the assault. "Wagner loomed, black, grim and silent. There was no glimmer of light. Nevertheless, in the fort, down below the level of the tide, and under roofs made by huge trunks of trees, lay two thousand Confederate soldiers hidden. Our troops advanced toward the fort, while our mortars in the rear tossed bombs over their heads. Behind the 54th came five regiments from Connecticut, New York, New Hampshire, Pennsylvania and Maine. The mass went quickly and silently in the night. Then, suddenly, the walls of the fort burst with a blinding sheet of vivid light. Shot, shells of iron and bullets crushed through the dense masses of the attacking force. I shall never forget, the terrible sound of that awful blast of death which swept down, battered or dead, a thousand of our men. Not a shot had missed its aim. Every bolt of iron and lead tasted of human blood.

"The column wavered and recovered itself. They reached the ditch before the fort. They climbed on the ramparts and swarmed over the walls. It looked as though the fort was captured. Then there came another blinding blaze from concealed guns in the rear of the fort, and the men went down by scores. The rebels rallied, and were reënforced by thousands of others, who had landed on the beach in the darkness unseen by the fleet. They hurled themselves upon the attacking force. The struggle was terrific. The supporting units hurried up to aid their comrades, but as they raised the ramparts, they fired a volley which struck down many of their own men. Our men rallied again, but were forced back to the edge of the ditch. Colonel Shaw, with scores of his black fighters, went down struggling desperately. Resistance was vain. The assailants were forced back to the beach, and the rebels drilled their recovered cannons anew on the remaining survivors."

When a request was made for Colonel Shaw's body, a Confederate Major said: "We have buried him with his niggers." [29]

In December, 1863, Morgan led Negro troops in the battle of Nashville. He declared a new chapter in the history of liberty had been written. "It had been shown that marching under a flag of freedom, animated by a love of liberty, even the slave becomes a man and a hero." Between eight and ten thousand Negro troops took part in the battles around Nashville, all of them from slave states.

When General Thomas rode over the battlefield, and saw the bodies of colored men side by side with the foremost on the very works of the enemy, he turned to his staff, saying: "Gentlemen, the question is settled: Negroes will fight."

How extraordinary, and what a tribute to ignorance and religious hypocrisy, is the fact that in the minds of most people, even those of liberals, only murder makes men. The slave pleaded; he was humble; he protected the women of the South, and the world ignored him. The slave killed white men; and behold, he was a man!

The New York *Times* said conservatively, in 1863:

"Negro soldiers have now been in battle at Port Hudson and at Milliken's Bend in Louisiana, at Helena in Arkansas, at Morris Island in South Carolina, and at or near Fort Gibson in the Indian territory. In two of these instances they assaulted fortified positions, and led the assault; in two, they fought on the defensive, and in one, they attacked rebel infantry. In all of them, they acted in conjunction with white troops, and under command of white officers. In some instances, they acted with distinguished bravery, and in all, they acted as well as could be expected of raw troops."

Even the New York *Herald* wrote in May, 1864:

"The conduct of the colored troops, by the way, in the actions of the last few days, is described as superb. An Ohio soldier said to me today, 'I never saw men fight with such desperate gallantry as those Negroes did. They advanced as grim and stern as death, and when within reach of the enemy struck about them with pitiless vigor, that was almost fearful.' Another soldier said to me: 'These Negroes never shrink, nor hold back, no matter what the order. Through scorching heat and pelting storms, if the order comes, they march with prompt, ready feet.' Such praise is great praise, and it is deserved."

And there was a significant dispatch in the New York *Tribune* July 26th:

"In speaking of the soldierly qualities of our colored troops, I do not refer especially to their noble action in the perilous edge of the battle; that is settled, but to their docility and their patience of labor and suffering in the camp and on the march."

Grant was made Lieutenant-General in 1864, and began to reorganize the armies. When he came East, he found that few Negro troops had been used in Virginia. He therefore transferred nearly twenty thousand Negroes from the Southern and Western armies to the army of Virginia. They fought in nearly all the battles around Petersburg and Richmond, and officers on the field reported:

"The problem is solved. The Negro is a man, a soldier, a hero. Knowing of your laudable interest in the colored troops, but particularly those raised under the immediate auspices of the Supervisory Committee, I have thought it proper that I should let you know how they acquitted themselves in the late actions in front of Petersburg, of which you have already received newspaper accounts. If you remember, in my conversations upon the character of these troops, I carefully avoided saying anything about their fighting qualities till I could have an opportunity of trying them." [30]

When the siege of Petersburg began, there were desperate battles the 16th, 17th and 18th of June. The presence of Negro soldiers rendered the enemy especially spiteful, and there were continual scrimmages and sharp shooting. Burnside's 9th Corps had a brigade of black troops, who advanced within fifty yards of the enemy works. There was a small projecting fort which it was decided to mine and destroy. The colored troops were to charge after the mine was set off. An inspecting officer reported that the "black corps was fittest for the perilous services," but Meade objected to colored troops leading the assault. Burnside insisted. The matter was referred to Grant, and he agreed with Meade. A white division led the assault and failed. The battle of the Crater followed. Captain McCabe says: "It was now eight o'clock in the morning. The rest of Potter's (Federal) division moved out slowly, when Ferrero's Negro division, the men beyond question, inflamed with drink [There are many officers and men, myself among the number, who will testify to this], burst from the advanced lines, cheering vehemently, passed at a double quick over a crest under a heavy fire, and rushed with scarcely a check over the heads of the white troops in the crater, spread to their right, and captured more than two hundred prisoners and one stand of colors."

General Grant afterward said: "General Burnside wanted to put his colored troops in front. I believe if he had done so, it would have been a success." [31]

The following spring, April 3rd, the Federal troops entered Richmond. Weitzel was leading, with a black regiment in his command —a long blue line with gun-barrels gleaming, and bands playing: "John Brown's body lies a-moldering in the grave but his soul goes marching on."

President Lincoln visited the city after the surrender, and the Connecticut colored troops, known as the 29th Colored Regiment, witnessed his entry. One member of this unit said:

"When the President landed, there was no carriage near, neither did he wait for one, but leading his son, they walked over a mile to General Weitzel's headquarters at Jeff Davis' mansion, a colored man acting as guide. . . . What a spectacle! I never witnessed such rejoicing in all my life. As the President passed along the street, the colored people waved their handkerchiefs, hats and bonnets, and expressed their gratitude by shouting repeatedly, 'Thank God for His goodness; we have seen His salvation.' . . .

"No wonder tears came to his eyes, when he looked on the poor colored people who were once slaves, and heard the blessings uttered from thankful hearts and thanksgiving to God and Jesus. . . . After visiting Jefferson Davis' mansion, he proceeded to the rebel capitol, and from the steps delivered a short speech, and spoke to the colored people, as follows:

"'In reference to you, colored people, let me say God has made you free. Although you have been deprived of your God-given rights by your so-called masters, you are now as free as I am, and if those that claim to be your superiors do not know that you are free, take the sword and bayonet and teach them that you are—for God created all men free, giving to each the same rights of life, liberty and the pursuit of happiness.'"[32]

The recruiting of Negro soldiers was hastened after the battle of Fort Wagner, until finally no less than 154 regiments, designated as United States Negro troops, were enlisted. They included 140 infantry regiments, seven cavalry regiments, 13 artillery regiments, and 11 separate companies and batteries.[33] The whole number enlisted will never be accurately known, since in the Department of the Gulf and elsewhere, there was a practice of putting a living Negro soldier in a dead one's place under the same name.

Official figures say that there were in all 186,017 Negro troops, of whom 123,156 were still in service, July 16, 1865; and that the losses during the war were 68,178. They took part in 198 battles and skirmishes. Without doubt, including servants, laborers and spies, between three and four hundred thousand Negroes helped as regular soldiers or laborers in winning the Civil War.

The world knows that noble inscription on St. Gaudens' Shaw Monument in Boston Common written by President Eliot:

THE WHITE OFFICERS

Taking Life and Honor in their Hands—Cast their lot with Men of a Despised Race Unproved in War—and Risked Death as Inciters of a Servile Insurrection if Taken Prisoners, Besides Encountering all the Common Perils of Camp, March, and Battle.

THE BLACK RANK AND FILE

Volunteered when Disaster Clouded the Union Cause—Served without Pay for Eighteen Months till Given that of White Troops—Faced Threatened Enslavement if Captured—Were Brave in Action—Patient under Dangerous and Heavy Labors and Cheerful amid Hardships and Privations.

TOGETHER

They Gave to the Nation Undying Proof that Americans of African Descent Possess the Pride, Courage, and Devotion of the Patriot Soldier—One Hundred and Eighty Thousand Such Americans Enlisted under the Union Flag in MDCCCLXIII-MDCCCLXV.

Not only did Negroes fight in the ranks, but also about 75 served as commissioned officers, and a large number as subalterns. Major F. E. Dumas of Louisiana was a free Negro, and a gentleman of education, ability and property. He organized a whole company of his own slaves, and was promoted to the rank of Major. Many of the other Louisiana officers were well-educated. Among these officers were 1 Major, 27 Captains and 38 Lieutenants, and nearly 100 non-commissioned officers. In the other colored regiments, most of the officers were whites; but Massachusetts commissioned 10 Negro officers, and Kansas 3. There were, outside Louisiana, 1 Lieutenant-Colonel, 1 Major, 2 Captains, 2 Surgeons, and 4 Lieutenants, whose records are known. There were a number of mulattoes who served as officers in white regiments; one was on the staff of a Major-General of Volunteers.[34] Medals of honor were bestowed by the United States government for heroic conduct on the field of battle upon 14 Negroes.

The Confederates furiously denounced the arming of Negroes. The Savannah *Republican* called Hunter "the cold-blooded Abolition miscreant, who from his headquarters at Hilton Head, is engaged in executing the bloody and savage behests of the imperial gorilla, who from his throne of human bones at Washington, rules, reigns and riots over the destinies of the brutish and degraded North." The officers in command of black troops were branded as outlaws. If captured, they were to be treated as common felons. To be killed by a Negro was a shameful death. To be shot by the Irish and Germans from Northern city slums was humiliating, but for masters to face armed bodies of their former slaves was inconceivable. When, therefore, black men were enrolled in Northern armies, the Confederates tried to pillory the government internationally on the ground that this was arming barbarians for servile war.

In a message to the Confederate Congress, Jefferson Davis asked "our fellowmen of all countries to pass judgment on a measure by which several millions of human beings of an inferior race—peaceful and contented laborers in their sphere—are doomed to extermination, while at the same time they are encouraged to a general assassination of their masters by the insidious recommendation to abstain from violence unless in necessary defense. Our own detestation of those who have attempted the most execrable measures recorded in the history of guilty men is tempered by profound contempt for the impotent rage which it discloses. So far as regards the action of this government on such criminals as may attempt its execution, I confine myself to informing you that I shall—unless in your wisdom you deem some other course expedient—deliver to the several State authorities all commissioned officers of the United States that may hereafter be captured by our forces in any of the States embraced in the Proclamation, that they may be dealt with in accordance with the laws of those States providing for the punishment of criminals engaged in exciting servile insurrection." [35]

In December, 1862, he issued a proclamation, "that all Negro slaves captured in arms be at once delivered over to the executive authorities, of the respective States to which they belonged and to be dealt with according to the law of the said States," which, of course, meant death. The same month, the Confederate Congress passed resolutions confirming in the main the President's Proclamation ordering that commissioned officers commanding Negro troops be put to death by the Confederate government, while the Negroes be turned over to the states.

The fire of the Confederates was always concentrated upon the black troops, and Negroes captured suffered indignities and cruelties. Frederick Douglass, who visited the White House in the President's carriage "to take tea," appealed in behalf of his fellow blacks. If they served in Federal uniform, he said that they should receive the treatment of prisoners of war. This treatment of Negro soldiers brought rebuke from Abraham Lincoln; but worse than that, it brought fearful retaliation upon the field of battle.

The most terrible case of Confederate cruelty was the massacre at Fort Pillow. When Major Booth refused to surrender the fort the Confederate General Forrest gave a signal, and his troops made a fierce charge. In ten minutes, they had swept in. Federal troops surrendered; but an indiscriminate massacre followed. The black troops were shot down in their tracks; pinioned to the ground with bayonets and saber. Some were clubbed to death while dying of wounds; others were made to get down upon their knees, in which condition they were shot to death. Some were burned alive, having been fastened inside the buildings, while still others were nailed against the houses, tortured, and then burned to a crisp.

The dilemma of the South in the matter of Negro troops grew more perplexing. Negroes made good soldiers; that, the Northern experiment had proven beyond peradventure. The prospect of freedom was leading an increasing stream of black troops into the Federal army. This stream could be diverted into the Southern army, if the lure of freedom were offered by the Confederacy. But this would be an astonishing ending for a war in defense of slavery!

In the first year of the war large numbers of Negroes were in the service of the Confederates as laborers. In January, at Mobile, numbers of Negroes from the plantations of Alabama were at work on the redoubts. These were very substantially made, and strengthened by sand-bags and sheet-iron. Elsewhere in the South Negroes were employed in building fortifications, as teamsters and helpers in army service. In 1862, the Florida Legislature conferred authority upon the Governor to impress slaves for military purposes, if so authorized by the Confederate Government. The Confederate Congress provided by law in February, 1864, for the impressment of 20,000 slaves for menial service in the Confederate army. President Davis was so satisfied with their labor that he suggested, in his annual message, November, 1864, that this number should be increased to 40,000, with the promise of emancipation at the end of their service.[36]

In Louisiana, the Adjutant-General's Office of the Militia stated that "the Governor and the Commander-in-Chief relying implicitly upon the loyalty of the free colored population of the city and state, for the protection of their homes, their property and for Southern rights, from the pollution of a ruthless invader, and believing that the military organization which existed prior to February 15, 1862, and elicited praise and respect for the patriotic motives which prompted it, should exist for and during the war, calls upon them to maintain their organization and hold themselves prepared for such orders as may be transmitted to them."

These "Native Guards" joined the Confederate forces but they did not leave the city with these troops. When General Butler learned of this organization, he sent for several of the prominent colored men and asked why they had accepted service under the Confederate government. They replied that they dared not refuse, and hoped by serving the Confederates to advance nearer to equality with the whites.

In Charleston on January 2, 150 free colored men offered their services to hasten the work of throwing up redoubts along the coast. At Nashville, Tennessee, April, 1861, a company of free Negroes offered their services to the Confederates, and at Memphis a recruiting office was opened. The Legislature of Tennessee authorized Governor Harris, on June 28, 1861, to receive into military service all male persons of color between the ages of fifteen and fifty. A procession of several hundred colored men marched under the command of Confederate officers and carried shovels, axes, and blankets. The observer adds, "they were brimful of patriotism, shouting for Jeff Davis and singing war songs." A paper in Lynchburg, Virginia, commenting on the enlistment of 70 free Negroes to fight for the defense of the State, concluded with "three cheers for the patriotic Negroes of Lynchburg."

After the firing on Fort Sumter, several companies of Negro volunteers passed through Augusta on their way to Virginia. They consisted of sixteen companies of volunteers and one Negro company from Nashville. In November of the same year, twenty-eight thousand troops passed before Governor Moore, General Lowell and General Ruggles at New Orleans. The line of march was over seven miles, and one regiment comprised 1,400 free colored men. The Baltimore *Traveler* commenting on arming Negroes at Richmond, said: "Contrabands who have recently come within the Federal lines at Williamsport, report that all the able-bodied men in that vicinity are being taken to Richmond, formed into regiments, and armed for the defense of that city."

In February, 1862, the Confederate Legislature of Virginia considered a bill to enroll all free Negroes in the State for service with the Confederate forces.

While then the Negroes helped the Confederates as forced laborers and in a few instances as soldiers, the Confederates feared to trust them far, and hated the idea of depending for victory and defense on these very persons for whose slavery they were fighting. But in the last days of the struggle, no straw could be overlooked. In December, 1863, Major-General Patrick R. Cleburne, who commanded a division in Hardee's Corps of the Confederate Army of the Tennessee, sent in a paper in which the employment of the slaves as soldiers of the South was vigorously advocated. Cleburne urged that "freedom within a reasonable time" be granted to every slave remaining true to the Confederacy, and was moved to this action by the valor of the Fifty-Fourth Massachusetts, saying: "If they [the Negroes] can be made to face and fight bravely against their former masters, how much more probable is it that with the allurement of a higher reward, and led by those masters, they would submit to discipline and face dangers?"

President Davis was not convinced, and endorsed Cleburne's plea with the statement: "I deem it inexpedient at this time to give publicity to this paper, and request that it be suppressed."

In September, 1864, Governor Allen of Louisiana wrote to J. A. Seddon, Secretary of War in the Confederate government: "The time has come to put into the army every able-bodied Negro as a soldier. The Negro knows he cannot escape conscription if he goes to the enemy. He must play an important part in the war. He caused the fight, and he will have his portion of the burden to bear. . . . I would free all able to bear arms, and put them in the field at once." In that year, 1864, 100,000 poor whites deserted the Confederate armies. In November, 1864, Jefferson Davis in his message to the Confederate Congress recognized that slaves might be needed in the Confederate army. He said: "The subject is to be viewed by us, therefore, solely in the light of policy and our social economy. When so regarded, I must dissent from those who advise a general levy and arming of slaves for the duty of soldiers. Until our white population shall prove insufficient for the armies we require and can afford to keep the field, to employ as a soldier the Negro, who has merely been trained to labor, and as a laborer under the white man accustomed from his youth to the use of firearms, would scarcely be deemed wise or advantageous by any; and this is the question before us. But should the alternative ever be presented of subjugation or of the employment of the slave as a soldier, there seems no reason to doubt what should be our decision."

In response to an inquiry from the Confederate Secretary of War, as to arming slaves, Howell Cobb of Georgia opposed the measure to arm the Negroes. "I think that the proposition to make soldiers of our slaves is the most pernicious idea that has been suggested since the war began . . . you cannot make soldiers of slaves or slaves of soldiers. The moment you resort to Negro soldiers, your white soldiers will be lost to you, and one secret of the favor with which the proposition is received in portions of the army is the hope when Negroes go into the army, they [the whites] will be permitted to retire. It is simply a proposition to fight the balance of the war with Negro troops. You can't keep white and black troops together and you can't trust Negroes by themselves. . . . Use all the Negroes you can get for all purposes for which you need them but don't arm them. The day you make soldiers of them is the beginning of the end of the revolution."

J. P. Benjamin, Secretary of State, on the other hand, declared that the slaves would be made to fight against the South, if Southerners failed to arm them for their own defense. He advocated emancipation for such black soldiers at a large meeting at Richmond: "We have 680,000 blacks capable of bearing arms, and who ought now to be in the field. Let us now say to every Negro who wishes to go into the ranks on condition of being free, go and fight—you are free." [37]

In a letter to President Davis, another correspondent added: "I would not make a soldier of the Negro if it could be helped, but we are reduced to this last resort." Sam Clayton of Georgia wrote: "The recruits should come from our Negroes, nowhere else. We should away with pride of opinion, away with false pride, and promptly take hold of all the means God has placed without our reach to help us through this struggle—a war for the right of self-government. Some people say that Negroes will not fight. I say they will fight. They fought at Ocean Pond [Olustee, Florida], Honey Hill and other places. The enemy fights us with Negroes, and they will do very well to fight the Yankees."

In January, 1865, General Lee sent his celebrated statement to Andrew Hunter:

"We should not expect slaves to fight for prospective freedom when they can secure it at once by going to the enemy, in whose service they will incur no greater risk than in ours. The reasons that induce me to recommend the employment of Negro troops at all render the effect of the measures I have suggested upon slavery immaterial, and in my opinion the best means of securing the efficiency and fidelity of this auxiliary force would be to accompany the measure with a well-digested plan of gradual and general emancipation. As that will be the result of the continuance of the war, and will certainly occur if the enemy succeeds, it seems to me most advisable to do it at once, and thereby obtain all the benefits that will accrue to our cause. [38]

This letter was discussed by the Confederates, and February 8, Senator Brown of Mississippi, introduced into the Confederate Congress a resolution which would have freed 200,000 Negroes and enrolled them in the army. This was voted down.

Jefferson Davis in a letter to John Forsythe, February, 1865, said that "all arguments as to the positive advantage or disadvantage of employing them are beside the question, which is simply one of relative advantage between having their fighting element in our ranks or in those of the enemy."

On February 11, another bill to enroll 200,000 Negro soldiers was introduced, and for a while it looked as though it would pass. General Lee again wrote, declaring the measure not only expedient but necessary, and that "under proper circumstances, the Negroes will make efficient soldiers."

The Richmond *Whig* of February 20, 1865, declared "that the proposition to put Negroes in the army has gained rapidly of late, and promises in some form or other to be adopted. . . . The enemy has taught us a lesson to which we ought not to shut our eyes. He has caused him to fight as well, if not better, than have his white troops of the same length of service."

Jefferson Davis discussed the matter with the Governor of Virginia, and said that he had been in conference with the Secretary of War and the Adjutant-General. He declared that the aid of recruiting officers for the purpose of enlisting Negroes would be freely accepted. March 17, it was said: "We shall have a Negro army. Letters are pouring into the departments from men of military skill and character asking authority to raise companies, battalions, and regiments of Negro troops." [39]

Thus on recommendation from General Lee and Governor Smith of Virginia, and with the approval of President Davis, an act was passed by the Confederate Congress, March 13, 1865, enrolling slaves in the Confederate army. Each State was to furnish a quota of the total 300,000. The preamble of the act reads as follows:

"An Act to increase the Military Force of the Confederate States: The Congress of the Confederate States of America so enact, that, in order to provide additional forces to repel invasion, maintain the rightful possession of the Confederate States, secure their independence and preserve their institutions, the President be, and he is hereby authorized to ask for and accept from the owners of slaves, the services of such number of able-bodied Negro men as he may deem expedient, for and during the war, to perform military service in whatever capacity he may direct. . . ." The language used implied that volunteering was to be rewarded by freedom.

General Lee coöperated with the War Department in hastening the recruiting of Negro troops. Recruiting officers were appointed in nearly all Southern States. Lieutenant John L. Cowardin, Adjutant, 19th Battalion, Virginia Artillery, was ordered April 1, 1865, to recruit Negro troops according to the act. On March 30, 1865, Captain Edward Bostick was ordered to raise four companies in South Carolina. Other officers were ordered to raise companies in Alabama, Florida, and Virginia. "It was the opinion of President Davis, on learning of the passage of the act, that not so much was accomplished as would have been, if the act had been passed earlier so that during the winter the slaves could have been drilled and made ready for the spring campaign of 1865."

It was too late now, and on April 9, 1865, Lee surrendered.

Negroes well within the Confederate lines were not insensible of what was going on. A colored newspaper said:

"Secret associations were at once organized in Richmond, which rapidly spread throughout Virginia, where the venerable patriarchs of the oppressed people prayerfully assembled together to deliberate upon the proposition of taking up arms in defense of the South. There was but one opinion as to the rebellion and its object; but the question which puzzled them most was, how were they to act the part about to be assigned to them in this martial drama? After a cordial interchange of opinions, it was decided with great unanimity, and finally ratified by all the auxiliary associations everywhere, that black men should promptly respond to the call of the Rebel chiefs, whenever it should be made, for them to take up arms.

"A question arose as to what position they would likely occupy in an engagement, which occasioned no little solicitude; from which all minds were relieved by agreeing that if they were placed in front as soon as the battle began the Negroes were to raise a shout about Abraham Lincoln and the Union, and, satisfied there would be plenty of supports from the Federal force, they were to turn like uncaged tigers upon the rebel hordes. Should they be placed in the rear, it was also understood, that as soon as firing began, they were to charge furiously upon the chivalry, which would place them between two fires; which would disastrously defeat the army of Lee, if not accomplish its entire annihilation." [40]

Of the effect of Negro soldiers in the Northern army, there can be no doubt. John C. Underwood, resident of Virginia for twenty years, said before the Committee on Reconstruction:

"I had a conversation with one of the leading men in that city, and he said to me that the enlistment of Negro troops by the United States was the turning-point of the rebellion; that it was the heaviest blow they ever received. He remarked that when the Negroes deserted their masters, and showed a general disposition to do so and join the forces of the United States, intelligent men everywhere saw that the matter was ended. I have often heard a similar expression of opinion from others, and I am satisfied that the origin of this bitterness towards the Negro is this belief among the leading men that their weight thrown into the scale decided the contest against them. However the fact may be, I think that such is a pretty well settled conclusion among leading Rebels in Virginia." [41]

A Union general said: "The American Civil War of 1861-1865 marks an epoch not only in the history of the United States, but in that of democracy, and of civilization. Its issue has vitally affected the course of human progress. To the student of history it ranks along with the conquests of Alexander; the incursions of the Barbarians; the Crusades; the discovery of America, and the American Revolution. It settled the question of our National unity with all the consequences attaching thereto. It exhibited in a very striking manner the power of a free people to preserve their form of government against its most dangerous foe, Civil War. It not only enfranchised four millions of American slaves of African descent, but made slavery forever impossible in the great Republic, and gave a new impulse to the cause of human freedom." [42]

It was not the Abolitionist alone who freed the slaves. The Abolitionists never had a real majority of the people of the United States back of them. Freedom for the slave was the logical result of a crazy attempt to wage war in the midst of four million black slaves, and trying the while sublimely to ignore the interests of those slaves in the outcome of the fighting. Yet, these slaves had enormous power in their hands. Simply by stopping work, they could threaten the Confederacy with starvation. By walking into the Federal camps, they showed to doubting Northerners the easy possibility of using them as workers and as servants, as farmers, and as spies, and finally, as fighting soldiers. And not only using them thus, but by the same gesture, depriving their enemies of their use in just these fields. It was the fugitive slave who made the slaveholders face the alternative of surrendering to the North, or to the Negroes.

It was this plain alternative that brought Lee's sudden surrender. Either the South must make terms with its slaves, free them, use them to fight the North, and thereafter no longer treat them as bondsmen; or they could surrender to the North with the assumption that the North, after the war, must help them to defend slavery, as it had before. It was then that Abolition came in as a determining factor, and itself was transformed to a new democratic movement.

So in blood and servile war, freedom came to America. What did it mean to men? The paradox of a democracy founded on slavery had at last been done away with. But it became more and more customary as time went on, to linger on and emphasize the freedom which emancipation brought to the masters, and later to the poor whites. On the other hand, strangely enough, not as much has been said of what freedom meant to the freed; of the sudden wave of glory that rose and burst above four million people, and of the echoing shout that brought joy to four hundred thousand fellows of African blood in the North. Can we imagine this spectacular revolution? Not, of course, unless we think of these people as human beings like ourselves. Not unless, assuming this common humanity, we conceive ourselves in a position where we are chattels and real estate, and then suddenly in a night become "thenceforward and forever free." Unless we can do this, there is, of course, no point in thinking of this central figure in emancipation. But assuming the common humanity of these people, conceive of what happened: before the war, the slave was curiously isolated; this was the policy, and the effective policy of the slave system, which made the plantation the center of a black group with a network of white folk around and about, who kept the slaves from contact with each other. Of course, clandestine contact there always was; the passing of Negroes to and fro on errands; particularly the semi-freedom and mingling in cities; and yet, the mass of slaves were curiously provincial and kept out of the currents of information.

There came the slow looming of emancipation. Crowds and armies of the unknown, inscrutable, unfathomable Yankees; cruelty behind and before; rumors of a new slave trade; but slowly, continuously, the wild truth, the bitter truth, the magic truth, came surging through.

There was to be a new freedom! And a black nation went tramping after the armies no matter what it suffered; no matter how it was treated, no matter how it died. First, without masters, without food, without shelter; then with new masters, food that was free, and improvised shelters, cabins, homes; and at last, land. They prayed; they worked; they danced and sang; they studied to learn; they wanted to wander. Some for the first time in their lives saw Town; some left the plantation and walked out into the world; some handled actual money, and some with arms in their hands, actually fought for freedom. An unlettered leader of fugitive slaves pictured it: "And then we saw the lightning—that was the guns! and then we heard the thunder—that was the big guns; and then we heard the rain falling, and that was the drops of blood falling; and when we came to git in the craps it was dead men that we reaped."

The mass of slaves, even the more intelligent ones, and certainly the great group of field hands, were in religious and hysterical fervor. This was the coming of the Lord. This was the fulfillment of prophecy and legend. It was the Golden Dawn, after chains of a thousand years. It was everything miraculous and perfect and promising. For the first time in their life, they could travel; they could see; they could change the dead level of their labor; they could talk to friends and sit at sundown and in moonlight, listening and imparting wonder-tales. They could hunt in the swamps, and fish in the rivers. And above all, they could stand up and assert themselves. They need not fear the patrol; they need not even cringe before a white face, and touch their hats.

To the small group of literate and intelligent black folk, North and South, this was a sudden beginning of an entirely new era. They were at last to be recognized as men; and if they were given the proper social and political power, their future as American citizens was assured. They had, therefore, to talk and agitate for their civil and political rights. With these, in thought and object, stood some of the intelligent slaves of the South.

On the other hand, the house servants and mechanics among the freed slaves faced difficulties. The bonds which held them to their former masters were not merely sentiment. The masters had stood between them and a world in which they had no legal protection except the master. The masters were their source of information. The question, then, was how far they could forsake the power of the masters, even when it was partially overthrown? For whom would the slave mechanic work, and how could he collect his wages? What would be his status in court? What protection would he have against the competing mechanic?

Back of this, through it all, combining their own intuitive sense with what friends and leaders taught them, these black folk wanted two things—first, land which they could own and work for their own crops. This was the natural outcome of slavery. Some of them had been given by their masters little plots to work on, and raise their own food. Sometimes they raised hogs and chickens, in addition. This faint beginning of industrial freedom now pictured to them economic freedom. They wanted little farms which would make them independent.

Then, in addition to that, they wanted to know; they wanted to be able to interpret the cabalistic letters and figures which were the key to more. They were consumed with curiosity at the meaning of the world. First and foremost, just what was this that had recently happened about them—this upturning of the universe and revolution of the whole social fabric? And what was its relation to their own dimly remembered past of the West Indies and Africa, Virginia and Kentucky?

They were consumed with desire for schools. The uprising of the black man, and the pouring of himself into organized effort for education, in those years between 1861 and 1871, was one of the marvelous occurrences of the modern world; almost without parallel in the history of civilization. The movement that was started was irresistible. It planted the free common school in a part of the nation, and in a part of the world, where it had never been known, and never been recognized before. Free, then, with a desire for land and a frenzy for schools, the Negro lurched into the new day.

Suppose on some gray day, as you plod down Wall Street, you should see God sitting on the Treasury steps, in His Glory, with the thunders curved about him? Suppose on Michigan Avenue, between the lakes and hills of stone, and in the midst of hastening automobiles and jostling crowds, suddenly you see living and walking toward you, the Christ, with sorrow and sunshine in his face?

Foolish talk, all of this, you say, of course; and that is because no American now believes in his religion. Its facts are mere symbolism; its revelation vague generalities; its ethics a matter of carefully balanced gain. But to most of the four million black folk emancipated by civil war, God was real. They knew Him. They had met Him personally in many a wild orgy of religious frenzy, or in the black stillness of the night. His plan for them was clear; they were to suffer and be degraded, and then afterwards by Divine edict, raised to manhood and power; and so on January 1, 1863, He made them free.

It was all foolish, bizarre, and tawdry. Gangs of dirty Negroes howling and dancing; poverty-stricken ignorant laborers mistaking war, destruction and revolution for the mystery of the free human soul; and yet to these black folk it was the Apocalypse. The magnificent trumpet tones of Hebrew Scripture, transmuted and oddly changed, became a strange new gospel. All that was Beauty, all that was Love, all that was Truth, stood on the top of these mad mornings and sang with the stars. A great human sob shrieked in the wind, and tossed its tears upon the sea,—free, free, free.

———

There was joy in the South. It rose like perfume—like a prayer. Men stood quivering. Slim dark girls, wild and beautiful with wrinkled hair, wept silently; young women, black, tawny, white and golden, lifted shivering hands, and old and broken mothers, black and gray, raised great voices and shouted to God across the fields, and up to the rocks and the mountains.

A great song arose, the loveliest thing born this side the seas. It was a new song. It did not come from Africa, though the dark throb and beat of that Ancient of Days was in it and through it. It did not come from white America—never from so pale and hard and thin a thing, however deep these vulgar and surrounding tones had driven. Not the Indies nor the hot South, the cold East or heavy West made that music. It was a new song and its deep and plaintive beauty, its great cadences and wild appeal wailed, throbbed and thundered on the world's ears with a message seldom voiced by man. It swelled and blossomed like incense, improvised and born anew out of an age long past, and weaving into its texture the old and new melodies in word and in thought.

They sneered at it—those white Southerners who heard it and never understood. They raped and defiled it—those white Northerners who listened without ears. Yet it lived and grew; always it grew and swelled and lived, and it sits today at the right hand of God, as America's one real gift to beauty; as slavery's one redemption, distilled from the dross of its dung.

The world at first neither saw nor understood. Of all that most Americans wanted, this freeing of slaves was the last. Everything black was hideous. Everything Negroes did was wrong. If they fought for freedom, they were beasts; if they did not fight, they were born slaves. If they cowered on the plantations, they loved slavery; if they ran away, they were lazy loafers. If they sang, they were silly; if they scowled, they were impudent.

The bites and blows of a nation fell on them. All hatred that the whites after the Civil War had for each other gradually concentrated itself on them. They caused the war—they, its victims. They were guilty of all the thefts of those who stole. They were the cause of wasted property and small crops. They had impoverished the South, and plunged the North into endless debt. And they were funny, funny —ridiculous baboons, aping man.

Southerners who had suckled food from black breasts vied with each other in fornication with black women, and even in beastly incest. They took the name of their fathers in vain to seduce their own sisters. Nothing—nothing that black folk did or said or thought or sang was sacred. For seventy years few Americans had dared say a fair word about a Negro.

There was no one kind of Negro who was freed from slavery. The freedmen were not an undifferentiated group; there were those among them who were cowed and altogether bitter. There were the cowed who were humble; there were those openly bitter and defiant, but whipped into submission, or ready to run away. There were the debauched and the furtive, petty thieves and licentious scoundrels. There were the few who could read and write, and some even educated beyond that. There were the children and grandchildren of white masters; there were the house servants, trained in manners, and in servile respect for the upper classes. There were the ambitious, who sought by means of slavery to gain favor or even freedom; there were the artisans, who had a certain modicum of freedom in their work, were often hired out, and worked practically as free laborers. The impact of legal freedom upon these various classes differed in all sorts of ways.

And yet emancipation came not simply to black folk in 1863; to white Americans came slowly a new vision and a new uplift, a sudden freeing of hateful mental shadows. At last democracy was to be justified of its own children. The nation was to be purged of continual sin not indeed all of its own doing—due partly to its inheritance; and yet a sin, a negation that gave the world the right to sneer at the pretensions of this republic. At last there could really be a free commonwealth of freemen.

Thus, amid enthusiasm and philanthropy, and religious fervor that surged over the whole country, the black man became in word "henceforward and forever free."

"Fondly do we hope and fervently do we pray, that this mighty scourge of war may speedily pass away. Yet, if God wills that it continue until all the wealth piled up by the bondman's two hundred and fifty years of unrequited toil shall be sunk, and until every drop of blood drawn by the lash shall be paid by another drawn with the sword, as was said three thousand years ago, so still it must be said, 'the judgments of the Lord are true and righteous altogether.'" Thus spake Father Abraham, "the Imperial Gorilla of Washington," Lord of armies vaster than any the Caesars ever saw, over a barnyard reeking with offal, and a land dripping with tears and blood. Suddenly, there was Reason in all this mad orgy. Suddenly the world knew why this blundering horror of civil war had to be. God had come to America, and the land, fire-drunk, howled the hymn of joy:

> Freude, schöner Götterfunken,
> Tochter aus Elysium,
> Wir betreten feuertrunken,
> Himmlische, dein Heiligtum.
> Deine Zauber binden wieder,
> Was die Mode streng geteilt,
> Alle Menschen werden Brüder,
> Wo dein sanfter Flügel weilt.
> Seid umschlungen, Millionen!
>
> Alle Menschen . . .
> Alle Menschen . . .
>
> JOHANN SCHILLER

---

1. Williams, *History of the Negro Race in America*, II, pp. 265-266.
2. Charleston *Daily Courier*, January 8, 1863.
3. Charleston *Daily Courier*, February 16, 1863.
4. Jordon and Pratt, *Europe and the American Civil War*, p. 73.
5. *Education of Henry Adams*, pp. 130-131.
6. Schlüter, *Lincoln, Labor and Slavery*, p. 158.
7. Schlüter, *Lincoln, Labor and Slavery*, pp. 161, 162, 163.
8. Wilson, *History of the Black Phalanx*, pp. 146, 147.
9. Wilson, *History of the Black Phalanx*, pp. 151-154.
10. Parton, *Butler in New Orleans*, pp. 491, 493.

11. Wilson, *History of the Black Phalanx*, p. 192.
12. Wilson, *History of the Black Phalanx*, p. 195.
13. Williams, *History of the Negro Race in America*, II, pp. 292, 293.
14. Wilson, *History of the Black Phalanx*, p. 120.
15. Williams, *History of the Negro Race in America*, pp. 289, 290. (Italics ours.)
16. Herz, *Abraham Lincoln*, II, pp. 931-932. (Italics ours.)
17. Woodson, *Negro Orators*, pp. 249, 251.
18. *Report of the Merchants Committee*, p. 7.
19. Wilson, *History of the Black Phalanx*, p. 394.
20. Story told by Smalls to the A. M. E. General Conference, Philadelphia, May, 1864.
21. *New Orleans Tribune*, May 4, 1865.
22. Williams, *History of the Negro Race in America*, II, p. 262.
23. Wilson, *History of the Black Phalanx*, p. 305.
24. Williams, *History of the Negro Race in America*, II, p. 314.
25. Wilson, *History of the Black Phalanx*, p. 211.
26. Williams, *History of the Negro Race in America*, II, p. 321.
27. Williams, *History of the Negro Race in America*, II, pp. 320, 321.
28. Williams, *History of the Negro Race in America*, II, p. 327.
29. Wilson, *History of the Black Phalanx*, p. 256.
30. Williams, *History of the Negro Race in America*, II, pp. 338, 339.
31. *Testimony Before Congressional Committee;* cited in Wilson, p. 428.
32. Hill, *Sketch of the 29th Regiment of Connecticut Colored Troops*, pp. 26, 27.
33. Nicolay and Hay give 149 regiments. VI, p. 468.
34. *Cf.* Wilson, *History of the Black Phalanx*, Chapter IV; and Williams, *History of the Negro Race in America*, II, pp. 299-301.
35. Wilson, *History of the Black Phalanx*, pp. 316, 317.
36. The following account is mainly from Charles Wesley's article, *Journal of Negro History*, IV, pp. 242-243.
37. Wilson, *History of the Black Phalanx*, pp. 491, 492.
38. Wilson, *History of the Black Phalanx*, p. 490.
39. Wilson, *History of the Black Phalanx*, p. 494.
40. New Orleans *Tribune*, February 25, 1865.
41. *Report of the Joint Committee on Reconstruction*, 1866, p. 8.
42. General T. J. Morgan, in Wilson, *Black Phalanx*, p. 289.

VI. LOOKING BACKWARD

How the planters, having lost the war for slavery, sought to begin
again where they left off in 1860, merely substituting for the individual ownership of slaves, a new state serfdom of black folk

The young Southern fanatic who murdered **Abraham** Lincoln said,
according to the New York *Times*, April 21, 1865:

". . This country was formed for the white, not the black man;
and looking upon African slavery from the same standpoint held by
the noble framers of our Constitution, I, for one, have ever considered
it of the greatest blessings (both for themselves and us) that God ever
bestowed upon a favored nation. Witness heretofore our wealth and
power ; witness their elevation and enlightenment above their race elsewhere. I have lived among it most of my life and have seen *less* harsh
treatment from master to man than I have beheld in the North from
father to son. Yet Heaven knows, *no one* would be willing to do *more*
for the Negro race than I, could I but see a way to still better their
condition. But Lincoln's policy is only preparing the way for their
total annihilation."

The South had risked war to protect this system of labor and to
expand it into a triumphant empire; and even if all of the Southerners did not agree with this broader program, even these had risked war
in order to ward off the disaster of a free labor class, either white or
black.

Yet, they had failed. After a whirlwind of battles, in which the
South had put energy, courage and skill, and most of their money; in
the face of inner bickerings and divided councils, jealousy of leaders,
indifference of poor whites and the general strike of black labor,
they had failed in their supreme effort, and now found themselves
with much of their wealth gone, their land widely devastated, and
some of it confiscated, their slaves declared free, and their country
occupied by a hostile army. "The South faced all sorts of difficulties.
The hostilities, military and naval, had practically destroyed the whole
commercial system of the South, and reduced the people to a pitiable
primitive, almost barbaric level. . . .

"It has been said that the ruining of the planting class in the South
through war was more complete than the destruction of the nobility

and clergy in the French Revolution. The very foundations of the system were shattered." [1]

There was at the end of the war no civil authority with power in North and South Carolina, Georgia, Florida, Alabama, Mississippi and Texas; and in the other states, authority was only functioning in part under Congress or the President. "The Northern soldiers were transported home with provisions for their comfort, and often with royal welcomes, while the Southern soldiers walked home in poverty and disillusioned."

Lands had deteriorated because of the failure to use fertilizers. The marketing of the crops was difficult and the titles to land and crops disputed. Government officials seized much of the produce and the cotton tax of 3 cents a pound bore hard upon the planters. The mortality of the whites was so great in the decade following 1865, as to be "a matter of common remark." [2]

When a right and just cause loses, men suffer. But men also suffer when a wrong cause loses. Suffering thus in itself does not prove the justice or injustice of a cause. It always, however, points a grave moral. Certainly after the war, no one could restrain his sorrow at the destruction and havoc brought upon the whites; least of all were the Negroes unsympathetic. Perhaps never in the history of the world have victims given so much of help and sympathy to their former oppressors. Yet the most pitiable victims of the war were not the rich planters, but the poor workers; not the white race, but the black.

Naturally, the mass of the planters were bitterly opposed to the abolition of slavery. First, they based their opposition upon a life-long conviction that free Negro labor could not be made profitable. The New Orleans *Picayune* said, July 8, 1862:

"In sober earnest, we say, and we believe all who know anything from observation or experience will corroborate our assertion, that this is an absolute impossibility. There could be no full crop produced under that system. The earlier processes might be performed in a manner and to some extent; but the later and more arduous, those upon the prompt performance of which depends the production of any crop at all, would be slighted, if not indeed entirely lost. The thriftless, thoughtless Negro would jingle his last month's wages in the planter's face and tell him to do the rest of the work himself. Look at Jamaica, Barbadoes, Antigua, and the other British West Indies where this experiment is having a most suggestive trial."

The Texas *Republican,* a weekly newspaper, said: "The ruinous effects of freeing four millions of ignorant and helpless blacks would not be confined to the South, but the blight would be communicated to the North, and the time would come when the people of that section would be glad to witness a return to a system attended with more philanthropy and happiness to the black race than the one they seem determined to establish; for they will find that compulsory labor affords larger crops and a richer market for Yankee manufacturers." The masters were advised, therefore, not to turn their slaves loose to become demoralized, but to maintain a kind and protecting care over them.

In addition to this, it was said that even if free Negro labor miraculously proved profitable, Negroes themselves were impossible as freemen, neighbors and citizens. They could not be educated and really civilized. And beyond that if a free, educated black citizen and voter could be brought upon the stage this would in itself be the worst conceivable thing on earth; worse than shiftless, unprofitable labor; worse than ignorance, worse than crime. It would lead inevitably to a mulatto South and the eventual ruin of all civilization.

This was a natural reaction for a country educated as the South had been; and that the mass of the planters passionately believed it is beyond question, despite difficulties of internal logic. Even the fact that some thought free Negro labor practicable, and many knew perfectly well that at least some Negroes were capable of education and even of culture, these stood like a rock wall against anything further: against Negro citizens, against Negro voters, against any social recognition in politics, religion or culture.

The poor whites, on the other hand, were absolutely at sea. The Negro was to become apparently their fellow laborer. But were the whites to be bound to the black laborer by economic condition and destiny, or rather to the white planter by community of blood? Almost unanimously, following the reaction of such leaders as Andrew Johnson and Hinton Helper, the poor white clung frantically to the planter and his ideals; and although ignorant and impoverished, maimed and discouraged, victims of a war fought largely by the poor white for the benefit of the rich planter, they sought redress by demanding unity of white against black, and not unity of poor against rich, or of worker against exploiter.

This brought singular schism in the South. The white planter endeavored to keep the Negro at work for his own profit on terms that amounted to slavery and which were hardly distinguishable from it. This was the plain voice of the slave codes. On the other hand, the only conceivable ambition of a poor white was to become a planter. Meantime the poor white did not want the Negro put to profitable work. He wanted the Negro beneath the feet of the white worker.

Right here had lain the seat of the trouble before the war. All the regular and profitable jobs went to Negroes, and the poor whites were excluded. It seemed after the war immaterial to the poor white that profit from the exploitation of black labor continued to go to the planter. He regarded the process as the exploitation of black folk by white, not of labor by capital. When, then, he faced the possibility of being himself compelled to compete with a Negro wage worker, while both were the hirelings of a white planter, his whole soul revolted. He turned, therefore, from war service to guerrilla warfare, particularly against Negroes. He joined eagerly secret organizations, like the Ku Klux Klan, which fed his vanity by making him co-worker with the white planter, and gave him a chance to maintain his race superiority by killing and intimidating "niggers"; and even in secret forays of his own, he could drive away the planter's black help, leaving the land open to white labor. Or he could murder too successful freedmen.

It was only when they saw the Negro with a vote in his hand, backed by the power and money of the nation, that the poor whites who followed some of the planters into the ranks of the "scalawags" began to conceive of an economic solidarity between white and black workers. In this interval they received at the hands of the black voter and his allies a more general right to vote, to hold office and to receive education, privileges which the planter had always denied them. But before all this was so established as to be intelligently recognized, armed revolt in the South became organized by the planters with the coöperation of the mass of poor whites. Taking advantage of an industrial crisis which throttled both democracy and industry in the North, this combination drove the Negro back toward slavery. Finally the poor whites joined the sons of the planters and disfranchised the black laborer, thus nullifying the labor movement in the South for a half century and more.

As the Civil War staggered toward its end, the country began to realize that it was not only at the end of an era, but it was facing the beginning of a vaster and more important cycle. The emancipation of four million slaves might end slavery, but would it not also be the end of its four million victims? To be sure there were many prophets, South and North, who foretold this fate of Negro extinction, but they were wrong. It was the beginning of Negro development, and what was this development going to be?

Back of all the enthusiasm and fervor of victory in the North came a wave of reflection that represented the sober after-thought of the nation. It harked back to a time when not one person in ten believed in Negroes, or in emancipation, or in any attempt to conquer the South. This feeling began to arise before the war closed, and after it ended it rose higher and higher into something like dismay. From before the time of Washington and Jefferson down to the Civil War, the nation had asked if it were possible for free Negroes to become American citizens in the full sense of the word.

The answers to this problem, historically, had taken these forms:

1. Negroes, after conversion to Christianity, were in the same position as other colonial subjects of the British King. This attitude disappeared early in colonial history.

2. When the slave trade was stopped, Negroes would die out. Therefore, the attack upon slavery must begin with the abolition of the slave trade and after that the race problem would settle itself. This attitude was back of the slave trade laws, 1808-20.

3. If Negroes did not die out, and if gradually by emancipation and the economic failure of slavery they became free, they must be systematically deported out of the country, back to Africa or elsewhere, where they would develop into an independent people or die from laziness or disease. This represented the attitude of liberal America from the end of the War of 1812 down to the beginning of the Cotton Kingdom.

4. Negroes were destined to be perpetual slaves in a new economy which recognized a caste of slave workers. And this caste system might eventually displace the white worker. At any rate, it was destined to wider expansion toward the tropics. This was the attitude of the Confederacy.

It is clear that from the time of Washington and Jefferson down to the Civil War, when the nation was asked if it was possible for free Negroes to become American citizens in the full sense of the word, it answered by a stern and determined "No!" The persons who conceived of the Negroes as free and remaining in the United States were a small minority before 1861, and confined to educated free Negroes and some of the Abolitionists.

This basic thought of the American nation now began gradually to be changed. It bore the face of fear. It showed a certain dismay at the thought of what the nation was facing after the war and under hypnotism of a philanthropic idea. The very joy in the shout of emancipated Negroes was a threat. Who were these people? Were we not loosing a sort of gorilla into American freedom? Negroes were lazy, poor and ignorant. Moreover their ignorance was more than the ignorance of whites. It was a biological, fundamental and ineradicable ignorance based on pronounced and eternal racial differences. The democracy and freedom open and possible to white men of English stock, and even to Continental Europeans, were unthinkable in the case of Africans. We were moving slowly in an absolutely impossible direction

Meantime, there was anarchy in the South and the triumph of brute physical force over large areas. The classic report on conditions in the South directly after the war is that of Carl Schurz. Carl Schurz was of the finest type of immigrant Americans. A German of education and training, he had fought for liberal thought and government in his country, and when driven out by the failure of the revolution of 1848, had come to the United States, where he fought for freedom. No man was better prepared dispassionately to judge conditions in the South than Schurz. He was to be sure an idealist and doctrinaire, but surely the hard-headed and the practical had made mess enough with America. This was a time for thought and plan. Schurz's reports on his journey remain today with every internal evidence of truth and reliability.

His mission came about in this way: he had written Johnson on his North Carolina effort at Reconstruction and Johnson invited him to call.

"President Johnson received me with the assurance that he had read my letters with great interest and appreciation, and that he was earnestly considering the views I had presented in them. But in one respect, he said, I had entirely mistaken his intentions. His North Carolina proclamation was not to be understood as laying down a general rule for the reconstruction of all 'the states lately in rebellion.' It was to be regarded as merely experimental, and he thought that the condition of things in North Carolina was especially favorable for the making of such an experiment. As to the Gulf States, he was very doubtful and even anxious. He wished to see those states restored to their constitutional relations with the general government as quickly as possible, but he did not know whether it could be done with safety to the Union men and to the emancipated slaves. He therefore requested me to visit those states for the purpose of reporting to him whatever information I could gather as to the existing condition of things, and of suggesting to him such measures as my observations might lead me to believe advisable." [3]

In his report, Schurz differentiated four classes in the South:

"1. Those who, although having yielded submission to the national government only when obliged to do so, have a clear perception of the irreversible changes produced by the war, and honestly endeavor to accommodate themselves to the new order of things.

"2. Those whose principal object is to have the states without delay restored to their position and influence in the Union and the people of the states to the absolute control of their home concerns. They are ready in order to attain that object to make any ostensible concession that will not prevent them from arranging things to suit their taste as soon as that object is attained.

"3. The incorrigibles, who still indulge in the swagger which was so customary before and during the war, and still hope for a time when the Southern confederacy will achieve its independence.

"4. The multitude of people who have no definite ideas about the circumstances under which they live and about the course they have to follow; whose intellects are weak, but whose prejudices and impulses are strong, and who are apt to be carried along by those who know how to appeal to the latter." [4]

He thus describes the movements immediately following the war:

"When the war came to a close, the labor system of the South was already much disturbed. During the progress of military operations large numbers of slaves had left their masters and followed the columns of our armies; others had taken refuge in our camps; many thousands had enlisted in the service of the national government. Extensive settlements of Negroes had been formed along the seaboard and the banks of the Mississippi, under the supervision of army officers and treasury agents, and the government was feeding the colored refugees who could not be advantageously employed in the so-called contraband camps.

"Many slaves had also been removed by their masters, as our armies penetrated the country, either to Texas or to the interior of Georgia and Alabama. Thus a considerable portion of the laboring force had been withdrawn from its former employments. But a majority of the slaves remained on the plantations to which they belonged, especially in those parts of the country which were not touched by the war, and where, consequently, the emancipation proclamation was not enforced by the military power. Although not ignorant of the stake they had in the result of the contest, the patient bondmen waited quietly for the development of things.

"But as soon as the struggle was finally decided, and our forces were scattered about in detachments to occupy the country, the so far unmoved masses began to stir. The report went among them that their liberation was no longer a mere contingency, but a fixed fact. Large numbers of colored people left the plantations; many flocked to our military posts and camps to obtain the certainty of their freedom, and others walked away merely for the purpose of leaving the places on which they had been held in slavery, and because they could now go with impunity. Still others, and their number was by no means inconsiderable, remained with their former masters and continued their work on the field, but under new and as yet unsettled conditions, and under the agitating influence of a feeling of restlessness.

"In some localities, however, where our troops had not yet penetrated and where no military post was within reac¹, planters endeavored and partially succeeded in maintaining between themselves and the Negroes the relation of master and slave partly by concealing from them the great changes that had taken place, and partly by terrorizing them into submission to their behests. But aside from these exceptions, the country found itself thrown into that confusion which is naturally inseparable from a change so great and so sudden. The white people were afraid of the Negroes, and the Negroes did not trust the white people; the military power of the national government stood there, and was looked up to, as the protector of both. . . .

"Some of the planters with whom I had occasion to converse expressed their determination to adopt the course which best accords with the spirit of free labor, to make the Negro work by offering him fair inducements, to stimulate his ambition, and to extend to him those means of intellectual and moral improvement which are best calculated to make him an intelligent, reliable and efficient free laborer and a good and useful citizen. . . .

"I regret to say that views and intentions so reasonable I found confined to a small minority. Aside from the assumption that the Negro will not work without physical compulsion, there appears to be another popular notion prevalent in the South which stands as no less serious an obstacle in the way of a successful solution of the problem. It is that the Negro exists for the special object of raising cotton, rice and sugar for the whites, and that it is illegitimate for him to indulge, like other people, in the pursuit of his own happiness in his own way. . . .

"I made it a special point in most of the conversations I had with Southern men to inquire into their views with regard to this subject. I found, indeed, some gentlemen of thought and liberal ideas who readily acknowledged the necessity of providing for the education of the colored people, and who declared themselves willing to cooperate to that end to the extent of their influence. Some planters thought of establishing schools on their estates, and others would have been glad to see measures taken to that effect by the people of the neighborhoods in which they lived. But whenever I asked the question whether it might be hoped that the legislatures of their states or their county authorities would make provisions for Negro education, I never received an affirmative, and only in two or three instances feebly encouraging answers. At last I was forced to the conclusion that, aside from a small number of honorable exceptions, the popular prejudice is almost as bitterly set against the Negro's having the advantage of education as it was when the Negro was a slave.

There may be an improvement in that respect, but it would prove only how universal the prejudice was in former days. Hundreds of times I heard the old assertion repeated, that 'learning will spoil the nigger for work,' and that 'Negro education will be the ruin of the South.' Another most singular notion still holds a potent sway over the minds of the masses—it is, that the elevation of the blacks will be the degradation of the whites. . . .

"The emancipation of the slaves is submitted to only in so far as chattel slavery in the old form could not be kept up. But although the freedman is no longer considered the property of the individual master, he is considered the slave of society, and all independent state legislation will share the tendency to make him such. The ordinances abolishing slavery passed by the conventions under the pressure of circumstances will not be looked upon as barring the establishment of a new form of servitude."

Carl Schurz summed the matter up:

"Wherever I go—the street, the shop, the house, the hotel, or the steamboat—I hear the people talk in such a way as to indicate that they are yet unable to conceive of the Negro as possessing any rights at all. Men who are honorable in their dealings with their white neighbors, will cheat a Negro without feeling a single twinge of their honor. To kill a Negro, they do not deem murder; to debauch a Negro woman, they do not think fornication; to take the property away from a Negro, they do not consider robbery. The people boast that when they get freedmen's affairs in their own hands, to use their own expression, 'the niggers will catch hell.'

"The reason of all this is simple and manifest. The whites esteem the blacks their property by natural right, and however much they admit that the individual relations of masters and slaves have been destroyed by the war and by the President's emancipation proclamation, they still have an ingrained feeling that the blacks at large belong to the whites at large."

Corroboration of the main points in the thesis of Schurz came from many sources.[5] From Virginia:

"Before the abolition of slavery, and before the war, it was the policy of slaveholders to make a free Negro as despicable a creature and as uncomfortable as possible. They did not want a free Negro about at all. They considered it an injury to the slave, as it undoubtedly was, creating discontent among the slaves. The consequences were that there was always an intense prejudice against the free Negro. Now, very suddenly, all have become free Negroes; and that was not calculated to allay that prejudice."

A colored man testified:

"There was a distinct tendency toward compulsion, toward re-established slavery under another name. Negroes coming into York-town from regions of Virginia and thereabout, said that they had worked all year and received no pay and were driven off the first of January. The owners sold their crops and told them they had no further use for them and that they might go to the Yankees, or the slaveholders offered to take them back but refused to pay any wages. A few offered a dollar a month and clothing and food. They were not willing to pay anything for work."

The courts aided the subjection of Negroes. George S. Smith of Virginia, resident since 1848, said that he had been in the Provost Marshal's department and "have had great opportunities of seeing the cases that are brought before him. Although I am prejudiced against the Negro myself, still I must tell the truth, and must acknowl-edge that he has rights. In more than nine cases out of ten that have come up in General Patrick's office, the Negro has been right and the white man has been wrong, and I think that that will be found to be the case if you examine the different provost marshals."

It was common for Virginians in 1865 and 1866 to advocate whole-sale expulsion of the Negroes. This attitude arose from the slave trade:

"The slave system in Virginia has been such as to exhaust very largely the able-bodied laborers; I have been informed that twenty-thousand of that class were annually sold from Virginia; consequently, a very large portion of the colored population there is composed of the aged, infirm, women and children, and the being freed from the necessity of supporting them is really a great relief in the present pov-erty of the people—a relief to their former owners."

Of course, those who wanted Negro labor immediately and were pushed on by the current high prices for products, were willing to compromise in some respects.

"The more intelligent people there, those who have landed estates, need their labor. Being dependent upon them for labor, they see the necessity of employing them, and are disposed to get along with them. All of the people, however, are extremely reluctant to grant the Negro his civil rights—those privileges that pertain to freedom, the protection of life, liberty and property before the laws, the right to testify in the courts, etc. They are all very reluctant to concede that; and if it is ever done, it will be because they are forced to do it. They are re-luctant even to consider and treat the Negro as a free man."

Lieutenant Sanderson, who was in North Carolina for three years, said that as soon as the Southerners came in in full control, they in-tended to put in force laws "not allowing a contraband to stay in any section over such a length of time without work; if he does, to seize him and sell him. In fact, that is done now in the county of Gates, North Carolina. The county police, organized under orders from headquarters, did enforce that.

"Mr. Parker told me that he had hired his people for the season: that directly after the surrender of General Lee, he called them up and told them they were free; that he was better used to them than to others, and would prefer hiring them; that he would give them board and two suits of clothing to stay with him till the 1st day of January, 1866, and one Sunday suit at the end of that time; that they consented willingly—in fact, preferred to remain with him, etc. But from his people I learned that though he did call them up, as stated, yet when one of them demurred at the offer, his son James flew at him and cuffed and kicked him; that after that they were all 'perfectly willing to stay'; they were watched night and day; that Bob, one of the men, had been kept chained nights; that they were actually afraid to try to get away."

Sometimes the resentment at the new state of affairs was funny. A county judge near Goldsboro, who had never been addressed by a Negro unbidden, came to the quarters of Lieutenant Sanderson:

" 'Lieutenant, what am I to stand from these freed people? I suppose you call them free. What insults am I obliged to suffer? I am in a perfect fever.' I told him I saw he was, and asked him what he complained of? If there was anything wrong I would right it. 'Well,' said he, 'one of these infernal niggers came along as I sat on my piazza this morning and bowed to me, and said good morning;—one of your soldiers!' "

From Alabama it was reported:

"The planters hate the Negro, and the latter class distrust the former, and while this state of things continues, there cannot be harmonious action in developing the resources of the country. Besides, a good many men are unwilling yet to believe that the 'peculiar institution' of the South has been actually abolished, and still have the lingering hope that slavery, though not in name, will yet in some form practically exist. And hence the great anxiety to get back into the Union, which being accomplished, they will then, as I have heard it expressed, 'fix the Negro!' . . .

"It is the simple fact, capable of indefinite proof, that the black man does not receive the faintest shadow of justice. I aver that in nine cases out of ten within my own observation, where a white man has provoked an affray with a black and savagely misused him, the black man has been fined for insolent language because he did not receive the chastisement in submissive silence, while the white man has gone free." [6]

The New York *Herald* says of Georgia:

"Springing naturally out of this disordered state of affairs is an organization of 'regulators,' so called. Their numbers include many ex-Confederate cavaliers of the country, and their mission is to visit summary justice upon any offenders against the public peace. It is needless to say that their attention is largely directed to maintaining quiet and submission among the blacks. *The shooting or stringing up of some obstreperous 'nigger' by the 'regulators' is so common an occurrence as to excite little remark. Nor is the work of proscription confined to the freedmen only.* The 'regulators' go to the bottom of the matter, and strive to make it uncomfortably warm for any new settler with demoralizing innovations of wages for 'niggers.' " [7]

A committee of the Florida legislature reported in 1865 that it was true that one of the results of the war was the abolition of African slavery.

"But it will hardly be seriously argued that the simple act of emancipation of itself worked any change in the social, legal or political status of such of the African race as were already free. Nor will it be insisted, we presume, that the emancipated slave technically denominated a 'freedman' occupied any higher position in the scale of rights and privileges than did the 'free Negro.' If these inferences be correct, then it results as a logical conclusion, that all the arguments going to sustain the authority of the General Assembly to discriminate in the case of 'free Negroes' equally apply to that of 'freedmen,' or emancipated slaves.

"But it is insisted by a certain class of radical theorists that the act of emancipation did not stop in its effect in merely severing the relation of master and slave, but that it extended further, and so operated as to exalt the entire race and placed them upon terms of perfect equality with the white man. These fanatics may be very sincere and honest in their convictions, but the result of the recent elections in Connecticut and Wisconsin shows very conclusively that such is not the sentiment of the majority of the so-called Free States."

Some Southerners saw in emancipation nothing but extermination for the Negro race. The Provisional Governor of Florida became almost tearful over the impending fate of the Negroes and the guilt of the North.

"This unfortunate class of our population, but recently constituting the happiest and best provided for laboring population in the world, by no act of theirs or voluntary concurrence of ours; with no prior training to prepare them for their new responsibilities, have been suddenly deprived of the fostering care and protection of their old masters and are now to become, like so many children gamboling upon the brink of the yawning precipice, careless of the future and intent only on revelling in the present unrestrained enjoyment of the newly found bauble of freedom. . . ."[8]

Judge Humphrey of Alabama said:

"I believe in case of a return to the Union, we would receive political coöperation so as to secure the management of that labor by those who were slaves. There is really no difference, in my opinion, whether we hold them as absolute slaves or obtain their labor by some other method. Of course, we prefer the old method. But that question is not now before us!"

A twelve-year resident of Alabama said:

"There is a kind of innate feeling, a lingering hope among many in the South that slavery will be regalvanized in some shape or other. They tried by their laws to make a worse slavery than there was before, for the freedman has not now the protection which the master from interest gave him before."[9]

'Every day, the press of the South testifies to the outrages that are being perpetrated upon unoffending colored people by the state militia. These outrages are particularly flagrant in the states of Alabama and Mississippi, and are of such character as to demand most imperatively the interposition of the national Executive. These men are rapidly inaugurating a condition of things—a feeling—among the freedmen that will, if not checked, ultimate in insurrection. The freedmen are peaceable and inoffensive; yet if the whites continue to make it all their lives are worth to go through the country, as free people have a right to do, they will goad them to that point at which submission and patience cease to be a virtue.

"I call your attention to this matter after reading and hearing from the most authentic sources—officers and others—for weeks, of the continuance of the militia robbing the colored people of their property —arms—shooting them in the public highways if they refuse to halt when so commanded, and lodging them in jail if found from home without passes, and ask, as a matter of simple justice to an unoffending and downtrodden people that you use your influence to induce the President to issue an order or proclamation forbidding the organization of state militia."[10]

In Mississippi:

"In respectful earnestness I must say that if at the end of all the blood that has been shed and the treasure expended, the unfortunate Negro is to be left in the hands of his infuriated and disappointed former owners to legislate and fix his *status,* God help him, for his cup of bitterness will overflow indeed. Was ever such a policy conceived in the brain of men before?"

Sumner quotes "an authority of peculiar value"—a gentleman writing from Mississippi:

"I regret to state that under the civil power deemed by all the inhabitants of Mississippi to be paramount, the condition of the freedmen in many portions of the country has become deplorable and painful in the extreme. *I must give it as my deliberate opinion that the freedmen are today, in the vicinity where I am now writing, worse off in most respects than when they were held slaves.* If matters are permitted to continue on as they now seem likely to be, it needs no prophet to predict a rising on the part of the colored population, and a terrible scene of bloodshed and desolation. Nor can anyone blame the Negroes if this proves to be the result. *I have heard since my arrival here, of numberless atrocities that have been perpetrated upon the freedmen.* It is sufficient to state that the old overseers are in power again. . . . The object of the Southerners appears to be to make good their often-repeated assertions, to the effect that the Negroes would die if they were freed. To make it so, they seem determined to goad them to desperation, in order to have an excuse to turn upon and annihilate them."

General Fisk early in 1866 said:

"I have today received the statement of two very respectable colored men who went into northern Mississippi from Nashville and rented plantations. Both of them were men of means, and one a reputed son of Isham G. Harris, a former Governor of Tennessee. Both were very intelligent colored men. They have been driven out and warned not to put their feet within the state again. Their written statements and affidavits I have, and will cheerfully place them in the hands of the committee if they desire it. They are reliable men; I know them both."

A former Mississippi slaveholder wrote:

"As a man who has been deprived of a large number of persons he once claimed as slaves, I protest against such a course. If it is intended to follow up the abolition of slavery by a liberal and enlightened policy, by which I mean bestowing upon them the full rights of other citizens, then I can give this movement my heart and hand. But if the Negro is to be left in a helpless condition, far more miserable than that of slavery, I would ask what was the object of taking him from those who claimed his services.

"General Chetlain tells us that while he was in command, for two months, of the Jackson District, containing nine counties, there was an average of one black man killed every day, and that in moving out forty miles on an expedition he found seven Negroes wantonly butchered. Colonel Thomas, assistant commissioner of the [Freedmen's] bureau for this state, tells us that there is now a daily average of two or three black men killed in Mississippi; the sable patriots in blue as they return, are the objects of especial spite."

Governor Sharkey of Mississippi said:

"My expectation concerning them is that they are destined to extinction, beyond all doubt. We must judge of the future by the past. I could tell you a great many circumstances to that effect; I am sorry I did not come prepared with means to state the percentage of deaths among them. It is alarming, appalling, I think they will gradually die out."

General Fisk received a letter from a rich planter living in DeSoto County, Mississippi. "He had on his plantation a little girl, and wrote me a long letter in relation to it, which closed up by saying: 'As to recognizing the rights of freedmen to their children, I will say there is not one man or woman in all the South who believes they are free, but we consider them as stolen property—stolen by the bayonets of the damnable United States government. Yours truly, T. Yancey.'

"There is one thing that must be taken into account, and that is there will exist a very strong disposition among the masters to control these people and keep them as a subordinate and subjected class. Undoubtedly they intend to do that. I think the tendency to establish a system of serfdom is the great danger to be guarded against. I talked with a planter in the La Fourche district, near Tebadouville; he said he was not in favor of secession; he avowed his hope and expectation that slavery would be restored there in some form. I said: 'If we went away and left these people now, do you suppose you could reduce them to slavery?' He laughed to scorn the idea that they could not. 'What!' said I. 'These men who have had arms in their hands?' 'Yes,' he said; 'we should take the arms away from them, of course.'"

There was no inconsiderable number of Southerners who stoutly maintained that Negroes were not free. The Planters' Party of Louisiana in 1864 proposed to revive the Constitution of 1852 with all its slavery features. They believed that Lincoln had emancipated the slaves in the rebellious parts of the country as a war measure. Slavery remained intact within the Federal lines except as to the return of fugitives, and might be reinstated everywhere at the close of hostilities; or, in any case, compensation might be obtained by loyal citizens through the decision of the Supreme Court.

The situation in Texas was peculiar. During the war, Texan produce had been sent to Europe by the way of Mexico, and a steady stream of cash came in which made slavery all the more valuable. At the end of the war slavery was essentially unimpaired. When the Federal soldiers approached, some of the planters set their Negroes free and some Negroes ran away, but most of the Negroes were kept on the plantations to await Federal action, and there was widespread belief that slavery was an institution and would continue in some form.

The Houston, Texas, *Telegraph* was of the opinion that emancipation was certain to take place but that compulsory labor would replace slavery. Since the Negro was to be freed by the Federal Government solely with a view to the safety of the Union, his condition would be modified only so far as to insure this, but not so far as materially to weaken the agricultural resources of the country. Therefore, the Negroes would be compelled to work under police regulations of a stringent character.

Mr. Sumner reported in 1866 a special slave trade from the South to the West Indies and South America.

"Another big trade is going on; that of running Negroes to Cuba and Brazil. They are running through the country dressed in Yankee clothes, hiring men, giving them any price they ask, to make turpentine on the bay, sometimes on the rivers, sometimes to make sugar. They get them on the cars. Of course the Negro don't know where he is going. They get him to the bay and tell him to go on the steamer to go around the coast, and away goes poor Cuffee to slavery again. They are just cleaning out this section of the country of the likeliest men and women in it. Federal officers are mixed up in it, too."

So much for the attitude of the owning class, the former slave-owners. But the great mass of the Southerners were not slaveholders; they were white peasant-farmers, artisans, with a few merchants and professional men. Large numbers of these were fed by the Federal government and formed a considerable proportion of the fugitives after the war.

General Hatch reported in 1866: "The poorer classes of the white people have an intense dislike" toward Negroes in Mississippi. Five-sixths of the soldiers in the Confederate Army were not slave-owners, and had fought against the competition of Negroes, and for their continued slavery.

"The most discouraging feature was the utter helplessness of the white community in the face of the terrible problem. Almost any thoughtful traveler could see that the majority of the whites were parasites, idlers and semi-vagabonds. According to Sidney Andrews, 'The Negro, as bad as his condition is,' said he, 'seems to me, on the whole, to accommodate himself more easily than the whites to the changed situation. I should say that the question at issue in the South is not 'What shall be done with the Negro?' but 'What shall be done with the whites?' The blacks manage to live comfortably for the most part and help each other; but the whites, accustomed to having all their affairs managed by an aristocracy which was then ruined, seemed powerless. They chose committees and reported cases of suffering, but any organized action on a large scale could not be expected. It was hoped that aid for the whites would come from the North, for fearful distress from hunger was inevitable."

General Turner said of the conditions in Virginia:

"Among the lower classes of the whites there is a spirit of aggression against the Negro. . . . And a great many of the Negroes are inclined to take the thing in their own hands; they are not disposed to be imposed upon by those people, if they can have half a show to defend themselves. . . .

"With the lower classes—I speak now more particularly of the city of Richmond—probably the feeling does not exist to such an extent in the rural districts—there is an impulsive feeling of aggression—a desire to get the Negro out of the way. They do not think of his rights; they do not appear to know what it means; only they feel that the Negro has something."

General Fisk spoke of Tennessee:

"It is a melancholy fact that among the bitterest opponents of the Negro in Tennessee are the intensely radical loyalists of the mountain district—the men who have been in our armies. . . ."

"The poorer classes of the white people have an intense dislike toward them," said General Hatch. He especially emphasized the situation in Tennessee and spoke of the aid that was being given the white fugitives. He said that the Negro knew that without legal rights he was not safe from the poor whites, and that they had not issued to the Negroes one-tenth of the rations that they had given the poor whites.

"The hatred toward the Negro as a freeman is intense among the low and brutal, who are the vast majority. Murders, shootings, whippings, robbing and brutal treatment of every kind are daily inflicted upon them, and I am sorry to say in most cases they can get no redress. They don't know where to complain or how to seek justice after they have been abused and cheated. The habitual deference toward the white man makes them fearful of his anger and revenge."

The Union members of the Tennessee legislature said:

"That long before the war common laborers had learned to curse the Yankees and Abolitionists and to talk about Negro equality and his rights in the territories. With all this went a great degree of personal violence. Leaving out for the moment the group violence, the organized fight against the Negro which was continuous, the personal physical opposition was continually in existence."

A candidate for Congress in Virginia in 1865 said:

"I am opposed to the Southern states being taxed at all for the redemption of this national debt, either directly or indirectly; and *I will vote to repeal all laws that have heretofore been passed for that purpose;* and, in doing so, I do not consider that I violate any obligations to which the South was a party. *We have never plighted our faith for the redemption of the war debt.* The people will be borne down with taxes for years to come; even if the war debt is repudiated, it will be the duty of the government to support the maimed and disabled soldiers, and this will be a great expense; and if the United States Government requires the South to be taxed for the support of Union soldiers, we should insist that all disabled soldiers should be maintained by the United States Government *without regard to the side they had taken in the war.*

"The national debt doubtless seems to you beyond the reach of any hand. Yet I regard it as very probable that one or two or all of three things will be attempted within three years after the Southern members of Congress are admitted to seats—the repudiation of the national debt, the assumption of the Confederate debt, or the payment of several hundred million dollars to the South for property destroyed and slaves emancipated."

A leader from South Carolina, James H. Campbell, said:

"I believe that when our votes are admitted into that Congress, if we are tolerably wise, governed by a moderate share of common sense, we will have our own way. I am speaking now not to be reported. We will have our own way yet, if we are true to ourselves. We know the past, we know not what is to be our future. Are we not in a condition to accept what we cannot help? Are we not in a condition where it is the part of wisdom to wait and give what we cannot avoid giving? I believe as surely as we are a people, so surely, if we are guided by wisdom, we will by the beginning of the next presidential election which is all that is known of the Constitution—for when you talk of the Constitution of the United States it means the presidential election and the share of the spoils—I believe then we may hold the balance of power."

Thus gradually, the South conceived a picture. It deliberately looked backward towards slavery in a day when two Southern poor whites were Presidents of the United States.

Although he was the Emancipator, Abraham Lincoln, too, in many respects, was looking backward toward the past. Lincoln's solution for the Negro problem was colonization. In this respect he went back to the early nineteenth century when the American Colonization Society was formed, with what proved to be two antagonistic objects: The first was the philanthropic object of removing the Negro to Africa and starting him on the road to an independent culture in his own fatherland. The second and more influential object was to get rid of the free Negro in the United States so as to make color caste the permanent foundation of American Negro slavery. The contradiction of these two objects was the real cause of the failure of colonization, since it early incurred the bitter opposition of both Abolitionists and Negro leaders. The result of the movement was the establishment of Liberia in an inhospitable land and without adequate capital and leadership. The survival of that little country to our day is one of the miracles of Negro effort, despite all of the propaganda of criticism that has been leveled against that country.

When the Negro question became prominent before the war, the project of colonization was revived, and Abraham Lincoln believed in it "as one means of solving the great race problem involved in the existence of slavery in the United States. . . . Without being an enthusiast, Lincoln was a firm believer in colonization." [11]

In the Lincoln-Douglas debates, Lincoln said at Peoria, Illinois:

"If all earthly power were given me, I should not know what to do as to the existing institution. My first impulse would be to free all the slaves and send them to Liberia—to their own native land. But a moment's reflection would convince me that, whatever of high hope (as I think there is) there may be in this, in the long run its sudden execution is impossible. If they were all landed there in a day, they would all perish in the next ten days; and there are not surplus shipping and surplus money enough in the world to carry them there in many times ten days. What then? Free them all and keep them among us as underlings? Is it quite certain that this betters their condition? I think that I would not hold one in slavery at any rate, yet the point is not clear enough for me to denounce people upon. What next? Free them and make them politically and socially our equals? My own feelings will not admit of this, and if mine would, we well know that those of the great mass of whites will not." [12]

Later, speaking at Springfield, Illinois, Lincoln declared: "That the separation of races is the only perfect preventive of amalgamation."

Several prominent Republicans espoused deportation in 1859. F. B. Blair of Missouri wrote to Senator Doolittle of Minnesota:

"I am delighted that you are pressing the colonization scheme in your campaign speeches. I touched upon it three or four times in my addresses in Minnesota and if I am any judge of effect it is the finest theme with which to get at the hearts of the people and [it] can be defended with success at all points. . . . I made it the culminating point and inevitable result of Republican doctrine." [13]

When the general strike of slaves began during the war, and the black fugitives began to pour into the Federal lines, Lincoln again brought forward his proposal of colonization, not simply for the freedmen, but for such free Negroes as should wish to emigrate. He suggested an appropriation for acquiring suitable territory and for other expenses.

By an act of April 16, 1862, which abolished slavery in the District of Columbia, Congress made an appropriation of $100,000 for voluntary Negro emigrants at an expense of $100 each; and later, July 16, an additional appropriation of $500,000 was made at Lincoln's request. The President was authorized "to make provision for transportation, colonization, and settlement, in some tropical country beyond the limits of the United States, of such persons of the African race, made free by the provisions of this act, as may be willing to emigrate, having first obtained the consent of the government of said country to their protection and settlement within the same, with all the rights and privileges of freemen." [14]

By an act of July 17, 1862, the President was authorized to colonize Negroes made free by the confiscation acts. Proceeds from confiscated property were to replace monies appropriated for colonization.

Charles Sumner vigorously attacked these plans. He said colonization was unwise: "Because, besides its intrinsic and fatal injustice, you will deprive the country of what it most needs, which is labor. Those freedmen on the spot are better than mineral wealth. Each is a mine, out of which riches can be drawn, provided you let him share the product, and through him that general industry will be established which is better than anything but virtue, and is, indeed, a form of virtue." [15]

In several cases, President Lincoln interviewed delegations on the subject. He believed that a good colonization scheme would greatly encourage voluntary emancipation in the Border States. He spoke to the Border State representatives and said that room in South America for Negro colonization could be obtained cheaply. He received in August, 1862, a committee of colored men, headed by E. M. Thomas, and urged colonization on account of the difference of race.

"Should the people of your race be colonized and where? Why should they leave this country? You and we are different races. We have between us a broader difference than exists between almost any other two races. Whether it is right or wrong I need not discuss, but this physical difference is a great disadvantage to us both, as I think. Your race suffers very greatly, many of them, by living among us, while ours suffers from your presence. In a word, we suffer on each side. If this is admitted it affords a reason why we should be separated. If we deal with those who are not free at the beginning and whose intellects are clouded by slavery, we have very poor material to start with. If intelligent colored men, such as are before me, would move in this matter much might be accomplished." [16]

A bill was introduced into the House in 1862 appropriating $200,-000,000—$20,000,000 to colonize and the rest to purchase 600,000 slaves of Unionist owners in Border States. The bill was not passed but the committee made an elaborate report on colonization July 16, 1862, declaring:

· "The most formidable difficulty which lies in the way of emancipation in most if not in all the slave states is the belief which obtains especially among those who own no slaves that if the Negroes shall become free they must still continue in our midst, and . . . in some measure be made equal to the Anglo-Saxon race. . . . The belief [in the inferiority of the Negro race] . . . is indelibly fixed upon the public mind. The differences of the races separate them as with a wall of fire; there is no instance in history where liberated slaves have lived in harmony with their former masters when denied equal rights—but the Anglo-Saxon will never give his consent to Negro equality, and the recollections of the former relation of master and slave will be perpetuated by the changeless color of the Ethiop's skin. Emancipation therefore without colonization could offer little to the Negro race. A revolution of the blacks might result, but only to their undoing. To appreciate and understand this difficulty it is only necessary for one to observe that in proportion as the legal barriers established by slavery have been removed by emancipation the prejudice of caste becomes stronger and public opinion more intolerant to the Negro race." [17]

In his second annual message, December 1, 1862, the President referred to communications from colored men who favored emigration, and to protests from several South American countries against receiving Negroes. He requested further appropriations for colonizing free Negroes with their own consent, but showed a deviation from his former philosophy:

"I cannot make it better known than it already is, that I strongly favor colonization; and yet I wish to say there is an objection urged against free colored persons remaining in the country, which is largely imaginary, if not sometimes malicious. It is insisted that their presence would injure and displace white labor more by being free than by remaining slaves. If they stay in their old places they jostle no white laborers; if they leave their old places, they leave them open to white laborers. Logically then there is neither more nor less of it. Emancipation, even without deportation, would probably enhance the wages of white labor and very surely would not reduce them. Reduce the supply of black labor by colonizing the black laborer out of the country and by precisely so much you increase the demand for and wages of white labor."

Several negotiations were begun with foreign countries that owned colonies in the West Indies, and with South American countries. The Cabinet discussed the matter. Bates wanted compulsory deportation, but the President objected to this. Finally, he settled on two projects: one, in Panama, and the other in the West Indies, where an island was ceded by Haiti. An adventurer, named Kock, undertook to carry five thousand colored emigrants to the island, but the result was a fiasco and a large number of the four hundred actually sent died of disease and neglect, and were finally brought back to the United States on a war vessel.

As late as April, 1865, President Lincoln said to General Butler:

" 'But what shall we do with the Negroes after they are free?' inquired Lincoln. 'I can hardly believe that the South and North can live in peace unless we get rid of the Negroes. Certainly they cannot, if we don't get rid of the Negroes whom we have armed and disciplined and who have fought with us, to the amount, I believe, of some 150,000 men. I believe that it would be better to export them all to some fertile country with a good climate, which they could have to themselves. You have been a staunch friend of the race from the time you first advised me to enlist them at New Orleans. You have had a great deal of experience in moving bodies of men by water—your movement up the James was a magnificent one. Now we shall have no use for our very large navy. What then are our difficulties in sending the blacks away? . . .

" 'I wish you would examine the question and give me your views upon it and go into the figures as you did before in some degree so as to show whether the Negroes can be exported.' Butler replied: 'I will go over this matter with all diligence and tell you my conclusions as soon as I can.' The second day after that Butler called early in the morning and said: 'Mr. President, I have gone very carefully over my calculations as to the power of the country to export the Negroes of the South and I assure you that, using all your naval vessels and all the merchant marine fit to cross the seas with safety, it will be impossible for you to transport to the nearest place that can be found fit for them—and that is the Island of San Domingo, half as fast as Negro children will be born here.' " [18]

The Secretary of the Interior in December, 1863, reported that the Negroes were no longer willing to leave the United States and that they were needed in the army. For these reasons, he thought that they should not be forcibly deported. On July 2, 1864, all laws relating to Negro colonization were repealed.

Lincoln was impressed by the loss of capital invested in slaves, but curiously never seemed seriously to consider the correlative loss of wage and opportunity of slave workers, the tangible results of whose exploitation had gone into the planters' pockets for two centuries.

A. K. McClure says: "Some time in August, 1864, I spent an hour or more with him alone at the White House, and I, then, for the first time spoke with frankness on the subject of restoring the Insurgent States. . . . He startled me by his proposition that he had carefully written out in his own hand on a sheet of note paper, proposing to pay the South $400,000,000 for the loss of their slaves. He was then a candidate for reëlection, and grave doubts were entertained, until after Sherman's capture of Atlanta and Sheridan's victories in the valley, as to the result of the contest between Lincoln and McClellan; and he well knew that if public announcement had been made of his willingness to pay the South $400,000,000 for emancipation it would have defeated him overwhelmingly." [19]

This project of compensation for lost capital invested in slaves was permanently dropped and Lincoln had to turn to the question of the relation of the seceded states to the Union once the war was ended. The situation was absolutely unique. It was impossible to appeal to constitutional precedence, for the Constitution never contemplated anything like the things that had happened between 1861 and 1865.

The grave question of the future relation of the seceded states to the Union could not be settled by Lincoln's pragmatic procedure. It must be visioned as a whole and put into law and logic. Toward this, Lincoln was moving slowly and tentatively seeking a formula that would work and yet be just to all men of all colors, and consistent with the legal fabric of the nation.

Charles Sumner first laid down a comprehensive formula February 11, 1862:

"I. RESOLVED, That any vote of secession, or other act, by a state hostile to the supremacy of the Constitution within its territory, *is inoperative and void against the Constitution,* and, when sustained by *force,* becomes a practical abdication by the State of all rights under the Constitution, while the treason it involves works instant forfeiture of all functions and powers essential to the continued existence of the State as a body politic; so that from such time forward the territory falls under the exclusive jurisdiction of Congress, as other territory, and the State becomes, according to the language of the law, felo-de-se." [20]

This plan was too radical for Lincoln, but that spring he proceeded to appoint military governors in Tennessee, North Carolina, Arkansas and Louisiana, where the Union Army held parts of the states. During the summer, he corresponded with Southern friends in Louisiana, and in December, due to his pressure, two members of Congress were elected in Louisiana from New Orleans and its suburbs, which was the only part under the control of the Union Army.

The Confederate legislature which was meeting simultaneously at Shreveport declared:

"(1) Every citizen [Negroes were not citizens] should vote who had not forfeited his citizenship by electing to adhere to the government of the United States.

"(2) Five hundred thousand dollars were voted to pay for slaves lost by death or otherwise, while impressed on the public works.

"(3) Any slave bearing arms against the inhabitants of the state or the Confederate States, or who should engage in any revolt or rebellion or insurrection should suffer death." [21]

The two Louisiana Congressmen were admitted to Congress with some hesitation, and Lincoln was encouraged to make further experiment along this line. In his message of December 8, 1863, therefore, he outlined a general plan of Reconstruction.

He regarded the states as still existing, even during the war, and that the rebellion was a combination of disloyal persons in the states. Reconstruction was an executive problem which consisted in creating a loyal class in the states and supporting that class by military power until it organized and operated the state government. The loyal class was to swear allegiance to the United States and to the Acts of Congress unless they were held void or changed, and all persons could take this oath unless they were civil officials of the Confederate Government, or military officers above the rank of Colonel or Lieutenant in the navy; or unless they had resigned from Congress or the United States Courts, or from army and navy, in order to aid the rebellion; or unless they had not treated colored soldiers or the leaders of colored soldiers as prisoners of war.

Such a loyal class he was prepared to recognize in Arkansas, Texas, Louisiana, Mississippi, Tennessee, Alabama, Georgia, Florida, South Carolina and North Carolina, when they formed not less than one-tenth of the votes cast in their state at the presidential election of 1860. Lincoln was careful to say that whether members who went to Congress from any of these states should be admitted or not rested exclusively with the Houses of Congress and not with the President.

Virginia was not included because Lincoln had already recognized the government at Alexandria as the true government of Virginia during the war, and, therefore, assumed that Virginia needed no Reconstruction, but was to be treated like Kentucky and Missouri. Of course, the support of a government consisting of only one-tenth of its voters had to come from the outside; that is, from the Federal army. In his accompanying proclamation of the same date, the President also engaged by this proclamation not to object to any provision which might be adopted by such state governments in relation to the freed people of the states which should recognize and declare their permanent freedom and provide for present condition "as a laboring, landless, and homeless class."

Here emerged a clear feature of the Lincoln plan which has not been emphasized. On this matter of the freedom of the Negroes, and a real, not a nominal freedom, Abraham Lincoln was adamant. In December, 1863, his "message contained an unusually forcible and luminous expression of the principles embraced in the proclamation. The President referred to the dark and doubtful days which followed the announcement of the policy of emancipation and of the employment of black soldiers; the gradual justification of those acts by the successes which the national arms had since achieved; of the change of the public spirit of the Border States in favor of emancipation; the enlistment of black soldiers, and their efficient and creditable behavior in arms; the absence of any tendency to servile insurrection or to violence and cruelty among the Negroes; the sensible improvement in the public opinion of Europe and of America.

"In justification of his requiring, in the oath of amnesty, a submission to and support of the anti-slavery laws and proclamations, he said: 'Those laws and proclamations were enacted and put forth for the purpose of aiding in the suppression of the rebellion. To give them their fullest effect, there had to be a pledge for their maintenance. In my judgment they have aided and will further aid the cause for which they were intended. To now abandon them would be not only to relinquish a lever of power, but would also be a cruel and an astounding breach of faith.'"

The reception of Lincoln's message to Congress in December, 1863, was enthusiastic:

"Men acted as though the millennium had come. Chandler was delighted, Sumner was joyous, apparently forgetting for the moment his doctrine of state suicide; while at the other political pole, Dixon and Reverdy Johnson said the message was 'highly satisfactory.' Henry Wilson said to the President's secretary: 'He has struck another great blow. Tell him for me, God bless him.' The effect was similar in the House of Representatives. George S. Boutwell, who represented the extreme anti-slavery element of New England, said: 'It is a very able and shrewd paper. It has great points of popularity, and it is right.' Owen Lovejoy, the leading abolitionist of the West, seemed to see on the mountain the feet of one bringing good tidings. 'I shall live,' he said, 'to see slavery ended in America.' . . . Francis W. Kellogg of Michigan went shouting about the lobby: 'The President is the only man. There is none like him in the world. He sees more widely and more clearly than any of us.' Henry T. Blow, the radical member from St. Louis (who was six months later denouncing Mr. Lincoln as a traitor to freedom) said: 'God bless old Abe! I am one of the Radicals who have always believed in him.' Horace Greeley, who was on the floor of the House, went so far as to say the message was 'devilish good.' " [22]

The causes of this jubilation were, however, dangerously diverse; the Abolitionists saw mainly the determination of Lincoln utterly to abolish slavery. This had not been clear before. Lincoln had never been an Abolitionist; he had never believed in full Negro citizenship; he had tried desperately to win the war without Negro soldiers, and he had emancipated the slaves only on account of military necessity. On the other hand, Lincoln learned; he stood now for abolishing slavery forever; he gave full credit and praise to Negro soldiers; and he was soon to face the problem of Negro citizenship.

Northern capital and Southern sympathizers in the North hailed the message because it carried no note of revenge or punishment, and contemplated speedy restoration of political independence in the South and normal industry.

Now came the very pertinent question as to just how this freedom of Negroes was to be enforced and maintained. Lincoln, working at this problem in Louisiana, in his correspondence with Banks, who was now in command, and Shepley, Military Governor, encouraged preparations for a reconstructed state government. Banks arranged to elect state officials and accepted as the basis of voting the provisions of the Louisiana Constitution of 1852 which, of course, allowed no Negroes to vote.

Accordingly, he declared the electors to be:

"Every free white male, 21 years of age, who had been resident in the state 12 months, and in the parish 6 months, who shall be a citizen of the United States and shall have taken the oath prescribed by the President in December, 1863." The total vote on February 22, 1864, was 11,355, of which Hahn received 6,171, Fellows, 2,959, and Flanders, 2,225, giving a majority to Hahn for Governor. [23]

If this experiment in Reconstruction had been attempted anywhere but in Louisiana, it is possible that the whole question of Negro suffrage would not have been raised then or perhaps for many years after. But by peculiar fate, it happened that a problem of Negro voting was immediately raised in Louisiana by the election of 1864, which simply could not be ignored. Usually, the argument concerning Negro suffrage after the war was met by an expression of astonishment that anybody could for a moment consider the admission of ignorant, brutish field hands to the ballot-box in the South. But that was not the problem which faced General Banks and Abraham Lincoln in 1864.

In Louisiana, where the question of Negro suffrage first arose as a problem, there existed a group of free Negroes. Their fathers had been free when Louisiana was annexed to the United States. Their numbers had increased from 7,585 in 1810 to 25,505 in 1840, and then declined to 18,647 in 1860, by emigration and by passing over into the white race on the part of their octoroon and lighter members.

Negroes in Louisiana in 1860 owned fifteen million dollars' worth of property. The Ricaud family alone in 1859 owned 4,000 acres of land and 350 slaves, at a total value of $250,000. The development of this mulatto group was extraordinary. Beginning under the French and Spanish, they played a remarkable part in the history of the state. The Spanish government while in possession of Louisiana had raised among them two companies of militia, "composed of all the mechanics which the city possessed."

This group of Negroes took part in the Battle of New Orleans in 1815, and was extravagantly praised by Andrew Jackson. They were the cause of an extraordinary blossoming of artistic life, which made New Orleans in the early part of the nineteenth century the most picturesque city of America. Negro musicians and artists arose. Eugene Warburg, a colored man, went from New Orleans to become a sculptor in France. Dubuclet became a musician in France, and the Seven Lamberts taught and composed in North and South America and Europe. Sidney was decorated for his work by the King of Portugal, and Edmund Dede became a director of a leading orchestra in France.

Alexandre Pickhil was a painter, who died between 1840 and 1850. Joseph Abeillard was an architect and planned many New Orleans buildings before the war. Norbert Rillieux invented the vacuum-pan used in producing sugar; as an engineer and contractor Rillieux had no rivals in Louisiana. The general periodicals in New Orleans praised him but seldom alluded to his Negro descent.

In 1843-1845, New Orleans colored folk issued a magazine and seventeen of the young mulatto poets collected an anthology called *Les Cenelles,* which they published as a small volume. They were all men educated either in France, or in private schools in Louisiana, and were in contact with some of the best writers and literature of the day. It is doubtful if anywhere else in the United States a literary group of equal culture could have been found at the time. In 1850, four-fifths of the free Negroes living in New Orleans could read and write, and they had over a thousand children in school. Among them were carpenters, tailors, shoemakers and printers, besides teachers, planters and professional men.

James Derham, a colored man in New Orleans in 1800, had a medical practice of $3,000 a year. He was especially commended by Dr. Benjamin Rush. Below the professional level were numbers of Negroes of ability. There was the celebrated sorceress, Marie Laveau, who, about 1835, exercised an extraordinary influence throughout the city. In 1850, Louisiana had a colored architect, 6 physicians, 4 engineers, and over 20 teachers in schools and in music. As early as 1803, free colored men were admitted to the police force to patrol outside the city limits, to catch runaway slaves and stop looting and crime.

There was systematic common law marriage between whites and mulattoes. The connections formed with the quadroons and octoroons were often permanent enough for the rearing of large families, some of whom obtained their freedom through the affection of their father-master, and received the education he would have bestowed upon legitimate offspring.

When Butler came to New Orleans, it was one of these colored creoles who entertained him at a banquet of seven courses served on silver.

"The secret, darling desire of this class is to rank as human beings in their native city; or, as the giver of the grand banquet expressed it, 'No matter where I fight; I only wish to spend what I have, and fight as long as I can, if only my boy may stand in the street equal to a white boy when the war is over.'" [24]

"The best blood of the South flowed in their veins, and a great deal of it; for 'the darkest of them,' said General Butler, 'were about of the complexion of the late Mr. Webster.'" [25]

This was the history of the free Negroes of New Orleans, and to this must be added their labor, coöperation and enlistment as soldiers. Could the government of the United States allow Confederate soldiers to vote simply because they were white, and exclude Union soldiers simply because they were yellow or black? Even if the Negroes had been quiescent and willing to be ignored at this critical time, their rights were indisputable. But they were not quiet.

The Negroes themselves made strong statements. In November, 1863, the free men of color held a meeting in New Orleans and drew up an appeal to Governor Shepley "asking to be allowed to register and vote." They reviewed their services under Jackson, who called them "my fellow citizens" just after the battle of New Orleans, and they declared their present loyalty to the Union. "For forty-nine years," the petition ran, "they have never ceased to be peaceable citizens, paying their taxes on assessments of more than nine million dollars."

But, however strongly this petition appealed to Shepley, it was manifestly impossible to grant it at this time. The decisive reason was that if Negroes had been allowed to vote in this election they would have formed the majority of the voting population of Union Louisiana!

So far as is known, Shepley returned no answer to the appeal; for in the following January, the colored Union Radical Association sent a committee to call on Shepley requesting him to recognize the "rights" of the free colored population to the franchise. Shepley, unwilling and unable to assume such responsibility, referred the committee to General Banks, but the latter gave them no definite reply. He explained later:

"I thought it unwise to give them the suffrage, as it would have created a Negro constituency. The whites might give suffrage to the Negroes, but if the Negroes gave suffrage to the whites, it would result in the Negro losing it. My idea was to get a decision from Judge Durell declaring a man with a major part of white blood should possess all the rights of a white man; but I had a great deal to do, and a few men who wanted to break the bundle of sticks without loosening the band defeated it." [26]

Accordingly, the colored committee sent P. M. Tourné to Washington to advocate their claims before the President. The President sent a man named McKee to New Orleans to study conditions among the colored people. Lincoln was impressed but characteristically reticent and slow in action.

General Banks next issued a call for a constitutional convention to be held March 28, 1864, to amend the Constitution of 1852. Contrary to this Constitution, he based representation in the new government on the white population alone, so as to reduce the power of the great landholders; and Negroes were not allowed to vote. The total vote for this convention was only 6,400.

When asked to direct the Louisiana Constitutional Convention of 1864, Lincoln refused and wrote: "While I very well know what I would be glad for Louisiana to do, it is quite a difficult thing for me to assume direction in the matter. I would be glad for her to make a new Constitution recognizing the Emancipation Proclamation, and adopting emancipation in those parts of the state to which the Proclamation does not apply. And while she is at it, I think it would not be objectionable for her to adopt some practical system by which the two races could gradually lift themselves out of their old relation to each other, and both come out better prepared for the new. Education for young blacks should be included in the plan. After all, the power or element of 'contract' may be sufficient for this probationary period, and by its simplicity and flexibility be better.

"As an anti-slavery man, I have a motive to desire emancipation which pro-slavery men do not have; but even they have strong enough reasons to thus place themselves again under the shield of the Union, and to thus perpetually hedge against the recurrence of the scenes through which we are now passing. . . .

"For my own part, I think I shall not, in any event, retract the Emancipation Proclamation; nor, as executive, ever return to slavery any person who is free by the terms of that Proclamation, or by any of the acts of Congress. If Louisiana shall send members to Congress, their admission will depend, as you know, upon the respective Houses and not upon the President." [27]

Here again was the same insistence that Negro freedom must be real and guaranteed and again the puzzling question, how could this be accomplished? Abraham Lincoln took a forward step and by his letter of March 13 to the newly elected Governor Hahn, he made the first tentative suggestion for a Negro suffrage in the South. Evidently, the persistent agitation of colored New Orleans inspired this:

"Executive Mansion,
"Washington, March 13, 1864.
"HON. MICHAEL HAHN:

"My dear Sir: In congratulating you on having fixed your name in history as the first Free State Governor of Louisiana, now you are about to have a convention, which, among other things, will probably define the elective franchise, I barely suggest, for your private consideration, whether some of the colored people may not be let in, as, for instance, the very intelligent, and especially those who have fought gallantly in our ranks. They would probably help in some trying time in the future to keep the jewel of Liberty in the family of freedom. But this is only suggestion, not to the public, but to you alone.

"Truly yours,
"A. LINCOLN." [28]

This was a characteristic Lincoln gesture. He did not demand or order; he suggested, and incidentally adduced logical arguments of tremendous strength. This letter of Lincoln's, says Blaine, was "of deep and almost prophetic significance. It was perhaps the earliest proposition from any authentic source to endow the Negro with the right of suffrage." [29]

Thus, with his unflinching honesty of logic, Lincoln faced the problem of Negro voters. It was unthinkable that Negroes who had fought to preserve the Union or that Negroes of education and property should be excluded from the right to vote by the very nation whose life they had saved. On the other hand, unless a state saw this clearly, he did not see how it could be forced to see it. He made the suggestion, therefore, quietly and secretly, and he knew that he had a slowly growing public opinion in the North behind him.

"To keep the jewel of Liberty in the family of freedom," was a splendid and pregnant phrase and it had back of it unassailable facts.

The delegates met April 6, 1864, and sat for 78 days. The convention was divided on the question of compensation for loyal slaveholders, the education of the freedmen at the expense of the state, and Negro suffrage. Slavery was abolished by a vote of 72-13. An appeal was made to Congress for compensation for slaves; and on May 10, the convention adopted a resolution declaring that the legislature should never pass any act authorizing free Negroes to vote. Banks and Hahn, however, brought pressure to bear and some forty votes were changed, so that June 23, Gorlinsky moved that "The legislature shall have power to pass laws extending the right of suffrage to such persons, citizens of the United States, as by military service, by taxation to support the government, or by intellectual fitness, may be deemed entitled thereto." Many members did not understand this, but Sullivan of New Orleans denounced it as "A nigger resolution," and moved to lay it on the table. Without discussion, it was adopted 48-32.

Before the assembling of the convention, Banks on his own responsibility had appointed a Board of Education, of three members, for the freedmen's schools and given it power to establish schools in every school district, and to levy a tax to support the system. This order was discussed in the convention, and finally approved by a vote of 72-9. Also, by a vote of 53-27, general taxation for the support of free public schools for all was approved. The convention discussed a proposition of recognizing all persons as white who had less than one-fourth of Negro blood. But this involved too intricate inquiries into ancestry, a matter which often in Louisiana led to duels and murder. It was, therefore, voted down.

The expense of this white convention amounted to more than $1,000 a day and included liquor, cigars, carriage hire, stationery and furniture. It illustrated the extravagant habits of the time, and was quite as bad as any similar waste in South Carolina when Negroes were part of the legislature. The New Orleans *Times* described some of the proceedings of the convention as "sickening and disgusting" and said that the president was "drunk and a damned fool," and that "pandemonium" had reigned.[80]

The Constitution was finally adopted, 67-16, and the convention adjourned in August with a provision that it could be reconvoked by the president for further amending the Constitution. The Constitution was adopted by a vote of 6,836 to 1,566.

On September 5, 1864, a legislature was elected according to the new Constitution. There were 9,838 votes cast, and it was alleged that many colored persons were allowed to register and vote. The new legislature met October 3, 1864. This legislature is said by some authorities to have refused by a large majority to grant the suffrage to the Negro. Ficklin, on the other hand, says that no final vote was actually taken. Certainly the legislature was against Negro suffrage. And when a petition was introduced from five thousand Negroes, "many if not the majority" of whom had been in the Federal army, asking for the suffrage, no action was taken. One member, apparently expressing the general sentiment, said: "It will be time enough to grant this petition when all the other free states grant it and set us the example. When this state grants it, I shall go to China." [31]

Governor Hahn made no suggestion, and when he resigned from office, said that universal suffrage would be granted "whenever it is deemed wise and timely. Louisiana has already done more than three-fourths of the Northern states."

The Legislature refused to permit marriages between blacks and whites, and there was one attempt to refer the question of Negro suffrage to the people. The Thirteenth Amendment was adopted and United States Senators were elected, including Governor Hahn for the term beginning in 1865.

Meantime, the whole problem of Reconstruction in Louisiana came up in Congress and met the opposition represented by the Wade-Davis Bill.

In Arkansas, in a similar way, by white suffrage, an anti-slavery Constitution was adopted, and Senators and Representatives elected in the spring of 1864.

Yet, after all, this was general and preliminary, and certain details must be settled before Representatives and Senators from these states could be received in Congress; especially the question loomed as to how far Reconstruction was going to be an automatic executive function and how far a matter of Congressional supervision.

Congress, thereupon, decided to lay down a fundamental plan. The part of the President's message on Reconstruction was referred in the House to a select committee, of which Henry Winter Davis was chairman. The result was a congressional scheme of Reconstruction.

The Wade-Davis Bill, passed July 4, 1864, provided that the eleven states which had seceded were to be treated as rebellious communities, over each of which the President would appoint a Provisional Governor. This Governor should exercise all powers of government until the state was recognized by Congress as restored. Whenever the Governor regarded the rebellion in his state as suppressed, he was to direct the United States Marshal to enroll all resident white male citizens, and give them an opportunity to swear allegiance to the United States. When a majority of these citizens had taken the oath, they could elect delegates to a convention and the convention would establish a state government. Persons who had held any office under the Confederate government could not vote for delegates, or be elected as delegates to the convention. The Convention was to adopt a state constitution which must abolish slavery, repudiate Confederate and state debts incurred by the Confederates, and disqualify Confederate officials from voting, or being elected Governor or a member of the Legislature. When this Constitution was ratified by a majority of the voters, the President, with the consent of Congress, would proclaim the state government as established. After that, Representatives, Senators, and presidential electors could be chosen. The bill also abolished slavery in the rebellious states during the process of Reconstruction.

Thus Congress followed Charles Sumner's "State Suicide" theory and formulated Reconstruction measures which regarded the seceding states as territories and administered them as such by civil government until they were re-admitted.

This bill did not differ radically from the President's plan. It was quite as liberal to the Confederates and wiser in requiring a majority of voters, instead of only one-tenth, for Reconstruction. It was more methodical and complete because Lincoln had been leaving the matter vague until he could sense more clearly the possibilities.

Both the Wade-Davis plan and the Lincoln plan excluded the Negro from the right of suffrage. In the House there was a motion to strike out the word "white," but this was cut off by the previous question. Boutwell regretted, May 4, that this limitation of the right to vote seemed required by the present judgment of the House and of the country. When the bill came to the Senate July 1, Wade, as Chairman, reported it to the Committee with an amendment striking out the word "white." This amendment received only five votes, including that of Charles Sumner. Sumner, however, finally voted for the bill because of its provisions against slavery. He had already introduced, May 27, 1864, another resolution anticipating the Committee of Fifteen in the 39th Congress, and declaring that no representatives from Confederate states should be admitted without a vote of both Houses. Lincoln, however, became more and more obdurate. He wrote: "Some single mind must be master," and he wished strongly to carry through Reconstruction without too much interference.

When the Wade-Davis Bill came to the President July 4, 1864, he laid it aside and refused to sign it, explaining his position July 8, 1864, in a proclamation: "While I am—as I was in December last, when by proclamation I propounded a plan of restoration—unprepared by formal approval of this bill to be inflexibly committed to any single plan of restoration; and while I am also unprepared to declare that the free State constitutions and governments, already adopted and installed in Arkansas and Louisiana, shall be set aside and held for naught, thereby repealing and discouraging the loyal citizens who have set up the same as to further effort, or to declare a constitutional competency in Congress to abolish slavery in states; but am at the same time sincerely hoping and expecting that a constitutional amendment abolishing slavery throughout the nation may be adopted, nevertheless, I am fully satisfied with the system for restoration contained in the bill as one very proper plan for the loyal people of any state choosing to adopt it; and I am, and at all times shall be, prepared to give the executive aid and assistance to any such people, so soon as military resistance to the United States shall have been suppressed in any such state, and the people thereof shall have sufficiently returned to their obedience to the Constitution and the laws of the United States, in which cases military governors will be appointed, with directions to proceed according to the bill."

Senator Wade and Representative Davis took their contentions to the country in the summer of 1864.

"We have read without surprise, but not without indignation, the proclamation of the President of the 8th of July, 1864. The supporters of the Administration are responsible to the country for its conduct; and it is their right and duty to check the encroachments of the Executive on the authority of Congress, and to require it to confine itself to its proper sphere."

They denounced Lincoln's Reconstruction plan and emphasized the distinction between Executive and Legislative power in Reconstruction. Despite the manifesto and opposition on other grounds, Lincoln was reëlected; but the issue remained to be fought out between Congress and Johnson.

Again in his message of December, 1864, Lincoln returned even more emphatically to the matter of the freedom of the slaves. One cannot be in much doubt as to what Abraham Lincoln's reaction would have been to the black codes of South Carolina and Mississippi. Certainly no state with such laws concerning the black laborer would have been admitted to the Union with Abraham Lincoln's consent:

"While I remain in my present position I shall not attempt to retract or modify the Emancipation Proclamation. Nor shall I return to slavery any person who is free by the terms of that Proclamation, or by any of the Acts of Congress. *If the people should, by whatever mode or means, make it an Executive duty to reënslave such persons, another, and not I, must be their instrument to perform it."* [32]

The Trumbull Resolution of February 18, 1865, recognizing the restored Louisiana government, revealed a disposition in the Senate to yield to Lincoln. But the rising Abolition-democracy protested. Wendell Phillips spoke in Faneuil Hall.

"Gentlemen, you know very well that this nation called 4,000,000 of Negroes into citizenship to save itself. (Applause.) It never called them for their own sakes. It called them to save itself. (Cries of 'Hear, Hear.') And today this resolution offered in Faneuil Hall would take from the President of such a nation the power to protect the millions you have just lifted into danger. (Cries of 'Played out,' 'Sit down,' etc.) You won't let him protect them. (Cries of 'No.') What more contemptible object than a nation which for its own selfish purpose summons four millions of Negroes to such a position of peril, and then leaves them defenseless."

In the Senate, Sumner was adamant in his demand that all men, irrespective of color, should be equal as citizens in the reconstructed states. He believed that a first false step in this matter would be fatal. The debate began February 23, 1865, and Sumner fought every step. He moved a substitute which received only eight votes. He tried to displace the resolution, and filibustered. When asked to give up, he replied, "That is not my habit."

Sumner sent in a second substitute declaring that the cause of human rights and of the Union needed the ballots as well as the muskets of colored men. He offered another amendment imposing equal suffrage as the fundamental condition for the admission of the seceded states. A night session was called which lasted until nearly Sunday morning. Sumner was rebuked for his arrogance and assumed superiority and the Senate finally adjourned, half an hour before midnight.

Only five days of the session remained. Wade now entered the debate and denounced the Louisiana government as a mockery and compared it to the Lecompton Constitution of Kansas. Sumner again bitterly arraigned the proposed Louisiana state government as "a mere seven months' abortion, begotten by the bayonet, in criminal conjunction with the spirit of caste, and born before its time, rickety, unformed, unfinished, whose continued existence will be a burden, a reproach, and a wrong." [33]

The bill finally failed. It was Sumner's greatest parliamentary contest and with his triumph, the cause of Negro suffrage was won. Wendell Phillips, Frederick Douglass, Parker Pillsbury and others wrote to congratulate Sumner. Douglass said:

"The friends of freedom all over the country have looked to you and confided in you, of all men in the United States Senate, during all this terrible war. They will look to you all the more now that peace dawns, and the final settlement of our national troubles is at hand. God grant you strength equal to your day and your duties, is my prayer and that of millions!"

Ashley's Reconstruction bill came before the House of Representatives January 16, February 21, and February 22, 1865. Each draft confined suffrage to white male citizens, except one, in which colored soldiers were admitted to the suffrage. Ashley opposed this discrimination, but his committee overruled him.

In his last public speech, April 11, 1865, Lincoln returned to the subject of Reconstruction. "The new Constitution of Louisiana, declaring Emancipation for the whole State, practically applies the proclamation to the part previously excepted. It does not adopt apprenticeship for freed people, and it is silent, as it could not well be otherwise, about the admission of members to Congress. So that, as it applies to Louisiana, every member of the Cabinet fully approved the plan. The message went to Congress, and I received many commendations of the plan, written and verbal, and not a single objection to it from any professed emancipationist came to my knowledge until after the news reached Washington that the people of Louisiana had begun to move in accordance with it. From about July, 1862, I had corresponded with different persons supposed to be interested [in] seeking a reconstruction of a State government for Louisiana. When the message of 1863, with the plan before mentioned, reached New Orleans, General Banks wrote me that he was confident that the people, with his military cooperation, would reconstruct substantially on that plan. I wrote to him and some of them to try it. They tried it, and the result is known. Such only has been my agency in setting up the Louisiana government. . . .

"We all agree that the seceded States, so-called, are out of their proper practical relation with the Union, and that the sole object of the Government, civil and military, in regard to those States, is to again get them into that proper practical relation. I believe that it is not only possible, but in fact easier, to do this without deciding or even considering whether these States have ever been out of the Union, than with it. Finding themselves safely at home, it would be utterly immaterial whether they had ever been abroad. Let us all join in doing the acts necessary to restoring the proper practical relations between these States and the Union, and each forever after innocently indulge his own opinion whether in doing the acts he brought the States from without into the Union, or only gave them proper assistance, they never having been out of it. The amount of constituency, so to speak, on which the new Louisiana government rests, would be more satisfactory to all if it contained 50,000, or 30,000, or even 20,000, instead of only about 12,000, as it does. It is also unsatisfactory to some that the elective franchise is not given to the colored man. I would myself prefer that it were now conferred on the very intelligent, and on those who serve our cause as soldiers.

"Still, the question is not whether the Louisiana government, as it stands, is quite all that is desirable. The question is, will it be wiser to take it as it is and help to improve it, or to reject and disperse it? Can Louisiana be brought into proper practical relation with the Union sooner by sustaining or by discarding her new State government? Some twelve thousand voters in the heretofore slave State of Louisiana have sworn allegiance to the Union, assumed the rightful political power of the state, held elections, organized a State government, adopted a free State constitution, giving the benefit of public schools equally to black and white, and empowered the Legislature to confer the elective franchise upon the colored man. Their Legislature has already voted to ratify the constitutional amendment, recently passed by Congress, abolishing slavery throughout the nation. These twelve thousand persons are thus fully committed to the Union and to perpetual freedom in the State—committed to the very things, and nearly all the things, the nation wants—and they ask the nation's recognition and its assistance to make good their committal.

"Now, if we reject and spurn them, we do our utmost to disorganize and disperse them. We, in effect, say to the white man: You are worthless or worse; we will neither help you, nor be helped by you. To the blacks we say: This cup of liberty which these, your old masters, hold to you. lips, we will dash from you, and leave you to the chances of gathering the spilled and scattered contents in some vague and undefined when, where, and how. If this course, discouraging and paralyzing both white and black, has any tendency to bring Louisiana into proper practical relations with the Union, I have so far been unable to perceive it. If, on the contrary, we recognize and sustain the new government of Louisiana, the converse of all this is made true. We encourage the hearts and nerve the arms of the twelve thousand to adhere to their work, and argue for it, and proselyte for it, and fight for it, and feed it, and grow it, and ripen it to a complete success. The colored man, too, in seeing all united for him, is inspired with vigilance and energy and daring to the same end. Grant that he desires the elective franchise, will he not attain it sooner by saving the already advanced steps towards it than by running backward over them? Concede that the new government of Louisiana is only to what it should be as the egg is to the fowl, we shall sooner have the fowl by hatching the egg than by smashing it." [34]

The tragic death of Lincoln has given currency to the theory that the Lincoln policy of Reconstruction would have been far better and more successful than the policy afterward pursued. If it is meant by this that Lincoln would have more carefully followed public opinion and worked to adjust differences, this is true. But Abraham Lincoln himself could not have settled the question of Emancipation, Negro citizenship and the vote, without tremendous difficulty.

First of all he was bitterly hated by the overwhelming mass of Southerners. Mark Pomeroy, a Northern Copperhead, voiced the extreme Southern opinion when he wrote:

"It is you Republicans who set up at the head of the nation a hideous clown . . . who became a shameless tyrant, a tyrant justly felled by an avenging hand, and who now rots in his tomb while his poisonous soul is consumed by the eternal flames of hell." [35]

Even conservative Southern papers continually referred to Lincoln as a "gorilla" or a "clown." And when we consider the fact that Lincoln was determined upon real freedom for the Negro, upon his education, and at least a restricted right to vote, it is difficult to see how the South could have been brought to agreement with him.

In the South there was absence of any leadership corresponding in breadth and courage to that of Abraham Lincoln. Here comes the penalty which a land pays when it stifles free speech and free discussion and turns itself over entirely to propaganda. It does not make any difference if at the time the things advocated are absolutely right, the nation, nevertheless, becomes morally emasculated and mentally hogtied, and cannot evolve that healthy difference of opinion which leads to the discovery of truth under changing conditions.

Suppose, for instance, there had been in the South in 1863 a small but determined and clear-thinking group of men who said: "The Negro is free and to make his freedom real, he must have land and education. He must be guided in his work and development but guided toward freedom and the right to vote. Such complete freedom and the bestowal of suffrage must be a matter of some years, but at present we do not propose to take advantage of this and retain political power based on the non-voting parts of our population. We, therefore, accept the constitutional amendment against slavery; we accept any other amendment which will base representation on voting, or other proposals which will equalize the voting power of North and South. We admit the right of the government to exercise a judicious guardianship over the slaves so long as we have reasonable voice in this guardianship, and that the interests of the employer as well as the employee shall be kept in mind. And in anticipation of this development, we propose to pass a reasonable code of laws recognizing the new status of the Negro."

If there had been in the white South at this time far-seeing leadership or even some common sense, the subsequent history of Reconstruction and of the Negro in the United States would have been profoundly changed. Suppose a single state like Louisiana had allowed the Negro to vote, with a high property qualification, or the ability to read and write, or service in the army, or all these? Charles Sumner and Thaddeus Stevens would not have been wholly satisfied, but certainly their demands would have been greatly modified. Both of them were perfectly willing to wait for Negro suffrage until the Negro had education and had begun his economic advance. But they did insist that he must have the chance to advance.

There cannot be the slightest doubt that such a program would have gathered enough support in the North to have made the history of Reconstruction not easy and without difficulty, but far less difficult than it proved to be. There were in the South in 1865 men who saw this truth plainly and said so. But true effective leadership was denied them; just as before the war public opinion in the South was hammered into idolatrous worship of slavery, so after the war, even more bitterly and cruelly, public opinion demanded a new unyielding conformity.

Here was a land of poignant beauty, streaked with hate and blood and shame, where God was worshiped wildly, where human beings were bought and sold, and where even in the twentieth century men are burned alive. The situation here in 1865 was fatal, and fatal because of the attitude of men's minds rather than because of material loss and disorganization. The human mind, its will and emotions, congealed to one set pattern, until here were people who knew they knew one thing above all others, just as certainly as they knew that the sun rose and set; and that was, that a Negro would not work without compulsion, and that slavery was his natural condition. If by force and law the Negro was free, his only chance to remain free was transportation immediately to Africa or some outlying district of the world, where he would soon die of starvation or disease. Such colonization was impracticable, and Southern slavery, as it existed before the war, was the best possible system for the Negro; and this the vast majority of Southerners were forced to believe as firmly in 1865 as they did in 1860.

The whole proof of what the South proposed to do to the emancipated Negro, unless restrained by the nation, was shown in the Black Codes passed after Johnson's accession, but representing the logical result of attitudes of mind existing when Lincoln still lived. Some of

these were passed and enforced. Some were passed and afterward repealed or modified when the reaction of the North was realized. In
other cases, as for instance, in Louisiana, it is not clear just which laws
were retained and which were repealed. In Alabama, the Governor
induced the legislature not to enact some parts of the proposed code
which they overwhelmingly favored.

The original codes favored by the Southern legislatures were an
astonishing affront to emancipation and dealt with vagrancy, apprenticeship, labor contracts, migration, civil and legal rights. In all cases,
there was plain and indisputable attempt on the part of the Southern
states to make Negroes slaves in everything but name. They were
given certain civil rights: the right to hold property, to sue and be
sued. The family relations for the first time were legally recognized.
Negroes were no longer real estate.

Yet, in the face of this, the Black Codes were deliberately designed
to take advantage of every misfortune of the Negro. Negroes were
liable to a slave trade under the guise of vagrancy and apprenticeship
laws; to make the best labor contracts, Negroes must leave the old
plantations and seek better terms; but if caught wandering in search
of work, and thus unemployed and without a home, this was vagrancy,
and the victim could be whipped and sold into slavery. In the turmoil
of war, children were separated from parents, or parents unable to
support them properly. These children could be sold into slavery, and
"the former owner of said minors shall have the preference." Negroes
could come into court as witnesses only in cases in which Negroes
were involved. And even then, they must make their appeal to a jury
and judge who would believe the word of any white man in preference to that of any Negro on pain of losing office and caste.

The Negro's access to the land was hindered and limited; his right
to work was curtailed; his right of self-defense was taken away, when
his right to bear arms was stopped; and his employment was virtually
reduced to contract labor with penal servitude as a punishment for
leaving his job. And in all cases, the judges of the Negro's guilt or
innocence, rights and obligations were men who believed firmly, for
the most part, that he had "no rights which a white man was bound to
respect."

Making every allowance for the excitement and turmoil of war, and
the mentality of a defeated people, the Black Codes were infamous
pieces of legislation.

Let us examine these codes in detail.[86] They covered, naturally, a
wide range of subjects. First, there was the question of allowing Negroes to come into the state. In South Carolina the constitution of
1865 permitted the Legislature to regulate immigration, and the con-

sequent law declared "that no person of color shall migrate into and reside in this State, unless, within twenty days after his arrival within the same, he shall enter into a bond, with two freeholders as sureties . . . in a penalty of one thousand dollars, conditioned for his good behavior, and for his support."

Especially in the matter of work was the Negro narrowly restricted. In South Carolina, he must be especially licensed if he was to follow on his own account any employment, except that of farmer or servant. Those licensed must not only prove their fitness, but pay an annual tax ranging from $10-$100. Under no circumstances could they manufacture or sell liquor. Licenses for work were to be granted by a judge and were revocable on complaint. The penalty was a fine double the amount of the license, one-half of which went to the informer.

Mississippi provided that "every freedman, free Negro, and mulatto shall on the second Monday of January, one thousand eight hundred and sixty-six, and annually thereafter, have a lawful home or employment, and shall have written evidence thereof . . . from the Mayor . . . or from a member of the board of police . . . which licenses may be revoked for cause at any time by the authority granting the same."

Detailed regulation of labor was provided for in nearly all these states.

Louisiana passed an elaborate law in 1865, to "regulate labor contracts for agricultural pursuits." Later, it was denied that this legislation was actually enacted; but the law was published at the time and the constitutional convention of 1868 certainly regarded this statute as law, for they formally repealed it. The law required all agricultural laborers to make labor contracts for the next year within the first ten days of January, the contracts to be in writing, to be with heads of families, to embrace the labor of all the members, and to be "binding on all minors thereof." Each laborer, after choosing his employer, "shall not be allowed to leave his place of employment until the fulfillment of his contract, unless by consent of his employer, or on account of harsh treatment, or breach of contract on the part of the employer; and if they do so leave, without cause or permission, they shall forfeit all wages earned to the time of abandonment. . . .

"In case of sickness of the laborer, wages for the time lost shall be deducted, and where the sickness is feigned for purposes of idleness, . . . and also should refusal to work be continued beyond three days, the offender shall be reported to a justice of the peace, and shall be forced to labor on roads, levees, and other public works, without pay, until the offender consents to return to his labor. . . .

"When in health, the laborer shall work ten hours during the day in summer, and nine hours during the day in winter, unless otherwise stipulated in the labor contract; he shall obey all proper orders of his employer or his agent; take proper care of his work mules, horses, oxen, stock; also of all agricultural implements; and employers shall have the right to make a reasonable deduction from the laborer's wages for injuries done to animals or agricultural implements committed to his care, or for bad or negligent work. Bad work shall not be allowed. Failing to obey reasonable orders, neglect of duty and leaving home without permission, will be deemed disobedience. . . . For any disobedience a fine of one dollar shall be imposed on the offender. For all lost time from work hours, unless in case of sickness, the laborer shall be fined twenty-five cents per hour. For all absence from home without leave, the laborer will be fined at the rate of two dollars per day. Laborers will not be required to labor on the Sabbath except to take the necessary care of stock and other property on plantations and do the necessary cooking and household duties, unless by special contract. For all thefts of the laborers from the employer of agricultural products, hogs, sheep, poultry or any other property of the employer, or willful destruction of property or injury, the laborer shall pay the employer double the amount of the value of the property stolen, destroyed or injured, one half to be paid to the employer, and the other half to be placed in the general fund provided for in this section. No live stock shall be allowed to laborers without the permission of the employer. Laborers shall not receive visitors during work hours. All difficulties arising between the employers and laborers, under this section, shall be settled, and all fines be imposed, by the former; if not satisfactory to the laborers, an appeal may be had to the nearest justice of the peace and two freeholders, citizens, one of said citizens to be selected by the employer and the other by the laborer; and all fines imposed and collected under this section shall be deducted from the wages due, and shall be placed in a common fund, to be divided among the other laborers employed on the plantation at the time when their full wages fall due, except as provided for above."

Similar detailed regulations of work were in the South Carolina law. Elaborate provision was made for contracting colored "servants" to white "masters." Their masters were given the right to whip "moderately" servants under eighteen. Others were to be whipped on authority of judicial officers. These officers were given authority to return runaway servants to their masters. The servants, on the other hand, were given certain rights. Their wages and period of service must be specified in writing, and they were protected against "unreasonable" tasks, Sunday and night work, unauthorized attacks on their persons, and inadequate food.

Contracting Negroes were to be known as "servants" and contractors as "masters." Wages were to be fixed by the judge, unless stipulated. Negroes of ten years of age or more without a parent living in the district might make a valid contract for a year or less. Failure to make written contracts was a misdemeanor, punishable by a fine of $5 to $50; farm labor to be from sunrise to sunset, with intervals for meals; servants to rise at dawn, to be careful of master's property and answerable for property lost or injured. Lost time was to be deducted from wages. Food and clothes might be deducted. Servants were to be quiet and orderly and to go to bed at reasonable hours. No night work or outdoor work in bad weather was to be asked, except in cases of necessity, visitors not allowed without the master's consent. Servants leaving employment without good reason must forfeit wages. Masters might discharge servants for disobedience, drunkenness, disease, absence, etc. Enticing away the services of a servant was punishable by a fine of $20 to $100. A master could command a servant to aid him in defense of his own person, family or property. House servants at all hours of the day and night, and at all days of the week, "must answer promptly all calls and execute all lawful orders."

The right to sell farm products "without written evidence from employer" was forbidden in South Carolina, and some other states. "A person of color who is in the employment of a master, engaged in husbandry, shall not have the right to sell any corn, rice, peas, wheat, or other grain, any flour, cotton, fodder, hay, bacon, fresh meat of any kind, poultry of any kind, animals of any kind, or any other product of a farm, without having written evidence from such master, or some person authorized by him, or from the district judge or a magistrate, that he has the right to sell such product."

There were elaborate laws covering the matter of contracts for work. A contract must be in writing and usually, as in South Carolina, white witnesses must attest it and a judge approve it. In Florida, contracts were to be in writing and failure to keep the contracts by disobedience or impudence was to be treated as vagrancy. In Kentucky, contracts were to be in writing and attested by a white person. In Mississippi, contracts were to be in writing attested by a white person, and if the laborer stopped work, his wages were to be forfeited for a year. He could be arrested, and the fee for his arrest must be paid by the employer and taken out of his wages.

There were careful provisions to protect the contracting employer from losing his labor. In Alabama, "When any laborer or servant, having contracted as provided in the first section of this act, shall afterward be found, before the termination of said contract, in the service or employment of another, that fact shall be *prima facie* evidence that such person is guilty of violation of this act, if he fail and refuse to forthwith discharge the said laborer or servant, after being notified and informed of such former contract and employment."

Mississippi provided "that every civil officer shall, and every person may, arrest and carry back to his or her legal employer any freedman, free Negro, or mulatto who shall have quit the service of his or her employer before the expiration of his or her term of service without good cause; and said officer and person shall be entitled to receive for arresting and carrying back every deserting employee aforesaid the sum of five dollars, and ten cents per mile from the place of arrest to the place of delivery, and the same shall be paid by the employer and held as a set-off for so much against the wages of said deserting employee."

It was provided in some states, like South Carolina, that any white man, whether an officer or not, could arrest a Negro. "Upon view of a misdemeanor committed by a person of color, any person present may arrest the offender and take him before a magistrate, to be dealt with as the case may require. In case of a misdemeanor committed by a white person toward a person of color, any person may complain to a magistrate, who shall cause the offender to be arrested, and, according to the nature of the case, to be brought before himself, or be taken for trial in the district court."

On the other hand, in Mississippi, it was dangerous for a Negro to try to bring a white person to court on any charge. "In every case where any white person has been arrested and brought to trial, by virtue of the provisions of the tenth section of the above recited act, in any court in this State, upon sufficient proof being made to the court or jury, upon the trial before said court, that any freedman, free Negro or mulatto has falsely and maliciously caused the arrest and trial of said white person or persons, the court shall render up a judgment against said freedman, free Negro or mulatto for all costs of the case, and impose a fine not to exceed fifty dollars, and imprisonment in the county jail not to exceed twenty days; and for a failure of said freedman, free Negro or mulatto to pay, or cause to be paid, all costs, fines and jail fees, the sheriff of the county is hereby authorized and required, after giving ten days' public notice, to proceed to hire out at public outcry, at the court-house of the county, said freedman, free Negro or mulatto, for the shortest time to raise the amount necessary to discharge said freedman, free Negro or mulatto from all costs, fines, and jail fees aforesaid."

Mississippi declared that: "Any freedman, free Negro, or mulatto, committing riots, routs, affrays, trespasses, malicious mischief and cruel treatment to animals, seditious speeches, insulting gestures, language or acts, or assaults on any person, disturbance of the peace, exercising the functions of a minister of the gospel without a license from some regularly organized church, vending spirituous or intoxicating liquors, or committing any other misdemeanor, the punishment of which is not specifically provided for by law, shall, upon conviction thereof, in the county court, be fined not less than ten dollars, and not more than one hundred dollars, and may be imprisoned, at the discretion of the court, not exceeding thirty days."

As to other civil rights, the marriage of Negroes was for the first time recognized in the Southern states and slave marriages legalized. South Carolina said in general: "That the statutes and regulations concerning slaves are now inapplicable to persons of color; and although such persons are not entitled to social or political equality with white persons, they shall have the right to acquire, own, and dispose of property, to make contracts, to enjoy the fruits of their labor, to sue and be sued, and to receive protection under the law in their persons and property."

Florida forbade "colored and white persons respectively from intruding upon each other's public assemblies, religious or other, or public vehicle set apart for their exclusive use, under punishment of pillory or stripes, or both."

Very generally Negroes were prohibited or limited in their ownership of firearms. In Florida, for instance, it was "unlawful for any Negro, mulatto, or person of color to own, use, or keep in possession or under control any bowie-knife, dirk, sword, firearms, or ammunition of any kind, unless by license of the county judge of probate, under a penalty of forfeiting them to the informer, and of standing in the pillory one hour, or be whipped not exceeding thirty-nine stripes, or both, at the discretion of the jury."

Alabama had a similar law making it illegal to sell, give or rent firearms or ammunition of any description "to any freedman, free Negro or mulatto."

Mississippi refused arms to Negroes. "No freedman, free Negro, or mulatto, not in the military service of the United States Government, and not licensed to do so by the board of police of his or her county, shall keep or carry firearms of any kind, or any ammunition, dirk, or bowie-knife; and on conviction thereof, in the county court, shall be punished by fine, not exceeding ten dollars, and pay the costs of such proceedings, and all such arms or ammunition shall be forfeited to the informer."

A South Carolina Negro could only keep firearms on permission in writing from the District Judge. "Persons of color constitute no part of the militia of the State, and no one of them shall, without permission in writing from the district judge or magistrate, be allowed to keep a firearm, sword, or other military weapon, except that one of them, who is the owner of a farm, may keep a shot-gun or rifle, such as is ordinarily used in hunting, but not a pistol, musket, or other firearm or weapon appropriate for purposes of war . . . and in case of conviction, shall be punished by a fine equal to twice the value of the weapon so unlawfully kept, and if that be not immediately paid, by corporal punishment."

The right of buying and selling property was usually granted but sometimes limited as to land. Mississippi declared: "That all freedmen, free Negroes and mulattoes may sue and be sued, implead and be impleaded in all the courts of law and equity of this State, and may acquire personal property and choses in action by descent or purchase, and may dispose of the same in the same manner and to the same extent that white persons may: *Provided,* that the provisions of this section shall not be so construed as to allow any freedman, free Negro or mulatto to rent or lease any lands or tenements, except in incorporated towns or cities, in which places the corporate authorities shall control the same."

The most important and oppressive laws were those with regard to vagrancy and apprenticeship. Sometimes they especially applied to Negroes; in other cases, they were drawn in general terms but evidently designed to fit the Negro's condition and to be enforced particularly with regard to Negroes.

The Virginia Vagrant Act enacted that "any justice of the peace, upon the complaint of any one of certain officers therein named, may issue his warrant for the apprehension of any person alleged to be a vagrant and cause such person to be apprehended and brought before him; and that if upon due examination said justice of the peace shall find that such person is a vagrant within the definition of vagrancy contained in said statute, he shall issue his warrant, directing such person to be employed for a term not exceeding three months, and by any constable of the county wherein the proceedings are had, be hired out for the best wages which can be procured, his wages to be applied to the support of himself and his family. The said statute further provides, that in case any vagrant so hired shall, during his term of service, run away from his employer without sufficient cause, he shall be apprehended on the warrant of a justice of the peace and returned to the custody of his employer, who shall then have, free from any other hire, the services of such vagrant for one month in addition to the original term of hiring, and that the employer shall then have power, if authorized by a justice of the peace, to work such vagrant with ball and chain. The said statute specified the persons who shall be considered vagrants and liable to the penalties imposed by it. Among those declared to be vagrants are all persons who, not having the wherewith to support their families, live idly and without employment, and refuse to work for the usual and common wages given to other laborers in the like work in the place where they are."

In Florida, January 12, 1866: "It is provided that when any person of color shall enter into a contract as aforesaid, to serve as a laborer for a year, or any other specified term, on any farm or plantation in this State, if he shall refuse or neglect to perform the stipulations of his contract by willful disobedience of orders, wanton impudence or disrespect to his employer, or his authorized agent, failure or refusal to perform the work assigned to him, idleness, or abandonment of the premises or the employment of the party with whom the contract was made, he or she shall be liable, upon the complaint of his employer or his agent, made under oath before any justice of the peace of the county, to be arrested and tried before the criminal court of the county, and upon conviction shall be subject to all the pains and penalties prescribed for the punishment of vagrancy."

In Georgia, it was ruled that "All persons wandering or strolling about in idleness, who are able to work, and who have no property to support them; all persons leading an idle, immoral, or profligate life, who have no property to support them and are able to work and do not work; all persons able to work having no visible and known means of a fair, honest, and respectable livelihood; all persons having a fixed abode, who have no visible property to support them, and who live by stealing or by trading in, bartering for, or buying stolen property; and all professional gamblers living in idleness, shall be deemed and considered vagrants, and shall be indicted as such, and it shall be lawful for any person to arrest said vagrants and have them bound over for trial to the next term of the county court, and upon conviction, they shall be fined and imprisoned or sentenced to work on the public works, for not longer than a year, or shall, in the discretion of the court, be bound over for trial to the next term of the county court, and upon conviction, they shall be fined and imprisoned or sentenced to work on the public works, for not longer than a year, or shall, in the discretion of the court, be bound out to some person for a time not longer than one year, upon such valuable consideration as the court may prescribe."

Mississippi provided "That all freedmen, free Negroes, and mulattoes in this state over the age of eighteen years, found on the second Monday in January, 1866, or thereafter, with no lawful employment or business, or found unlawfully assembling themselves together, either in the day or night time, and all white persons so assembling with freedmen, free Negroes or mulattoes, or usually associating with freedmen, free Negroes or mulattoes on terms of equality, or living in adultery or fornication with a freedwoman, free Negro or mulatto, shall be deemed vagrants, and on conviction thereof shall be fined in the sum of not exceeding, in the case of a freedman, free Negro or mulatto, fifty dollars, and a white man two hundred dollars and imprisoned, at the discretion of the court, the free Negro not exceeding ten days, and the white men not exceeding six months."

Sec. 5 provides that "all fines and forfeitures collected under the provisions of this act shall be paid into the county treasury for general county purposes, and in case any freedman, free Negro or mulatto, shall fail for five days after the imposition of any fine or forfeiture upon him or her, for violation of any of the provisions of this act to pay the same, that it shall be, and is hereby made, the duty of the Sheriff of the proper county to hire out said freedman, free Negro or mulatto, to any person who will, for the shortest period of service, pay said fine or forfeiture and all costs; *Provided,* a preference shall be given to the employer, if there be one, in which case the employer shall be entitled to deduct and retain the amount so paid from the wages of such freedman, free Negro or mulatto, then due or to become due; and in case such freedman, free Negro or mulatto cannot be hired out, he or she may be dealt with as a pauper."

South Carolina declared to be vagrants all persons without fixed and known places of abode and lawful employment, all prostitutes and all persons wandering from place to place and selling without a license; all gamblers; idle and disobedient persons; persons without sufficient means of support; persons giving plays or entertainments without license; fortune-tellers, beggars, drunkards and hunters. If a person of color is unable to earn his support, his near relatives must contribute. Pauper funds were composed of fines paid by Negroes and taxes on Negroes. On the other hand, former slaves who were helpless and had been on plantations six months previous to November 10, 1865, could not be evicted before January 1, 1867.

In Alabama, the "former owner" was to have preference in the apprenticing of a child. This was true in Kentucky and Mississippi.

Mississippi "provides that it shall be the duty of all sheriffs, justices of the peace, and other civil officers of the several counties in this state to report to the probate courts of their respective counties semi-annually, at the January and July terms of said courts, all freedmen, free Negroes and mulattoes, under the age of eighteen, within their respective counties, beats, or districts, who are orphans, or whose parent or parents have not the means, or who refuse to provide for and support said minors, and thereupon it shall be the duty of said probate court to order the clerk of said court to apprentice said minors to some competent and suitable person, on such terms as the court may direct, having a particular care to the interest of said minors; *Provided,* that the former owner of said minors shall have the preference when, in the opinion of the court, he or she shall be a suitable person for that purpose."

South Carolina established special courts for colored people, to be created in each district to administer the law in respect to persons of colo.. The petit juries of these courts were to consist of only six men. The local magistrate "shall be specially charged with the supervision of persons of color in his neighborhood, their protection, and the prevention of their misconduct." Public order was to be secured by the organization of forty-five or more militia regiments.

"Capital punishment was provided for colored persons guilty of willful homicide, assault upon a white woman, impersonating her husband for carnal purposes, raising an insurrection, stealing a horse, a mule, or baled cotton, and house-breaking. For crimes not demanding death, Negroes might be confined at hard labor, whipped, or transported; 'but punishments more degrading than imprisonment shall not be imposed upon a white person for a crime not infamous.' " [37]

In most states Negroes were allowed to testify in courts but the testimony was usually confined to cases where colored persons were involved, although in some states, by consent of the parties, they could testify in cases where only white people were involved. In Alabama "all freedmen, free Negroes and mulattoes, shall have the right to sue and be sued, plead and be impleaded in all the different and various courts of this State, to the same extent that white persons now have by law. And they shall be competent to testify only in open court, and only in cases in which freedmen, free Negroes, and mulattoes are parties, either plaintiff or defendant, and in civil or criminal cases, for injuries in the persons and property of freedmen, free Negroes and mulattoes, and in all cases, civil or criminal, in which a freedman, free Negro, or mulatto, is a witness against a white person, or a white person against a freedman, free Negro or mulatto, the parties shall be competent witnesses."

North Carolina, March 10, 1866, "gives them all the privileges of white persons before the courts in the mode of prosecuting, defending, continuing, removing, and transferring their suits at law in equity," and makes them eligible as witnesses, when not otherwise incompetent, in "all controversies at law and in equity where the rights of persons or property of persons of color shall be put in issue, and would be concluded by the judgment or decree of courts; and also in pleas of the State, where the violence, fraud, or injury alleged shall be charged to have been done by or to persons of color. In all other civil and criminal cases such evidence shall be deemed inadmissible, unless by consent of the parties of record."

Mississippi simply reenacted her slave code and made it operative so far as punishments were concerned. "That all the penal and criminal laws now in force in this State, defining offenses, and prescribing the mode of punishment for crimes and misdemeanors committed by slaves, free Negroes or mulattoes, be and the same are hereby reenacted, and declared to be in full force and effect, against freedmen, free Negroes, and mulattoes, except so far as the mode and manner of trial and punishment have been changed or altered by law."

North Carolina, on the other hand, abolished her slave code, making difference of punishment only in the case of Negroes convicted of rape. Georgia placed the fines and costs of a servant upon the master. "Where such cases shall go against the servant, the judgment for costs upon written notice to the master shall operate as a garnishment against him, and he shall retain a sufficient amount for the payment thereof, out of any wages due to said servant, or to become due during the period of service, and may be cited at any time by the collecting officer to make answer thereto."

The celebrated ordinance of Opelousas, Louisiana, shows the local ordinances regulating Negroes. "No Negro or freedman shall be allowed to come within the limits of the town of Opelousas without special permission from his employer, specifying the object of his visit and the time necessary for the accomplishment of the same.

"Every Negro freedman who shall be found on the streets of Opelousas after ten o'clock at night without a written pass or permit from his employer, shall be imprisoned and compelled to work five days on the public streets, or pay a fine of five dollars.

"No Negro or freedman shall be permitted to rent or keep a house within the limits of the town under any circumstances, and anyone thus offending shall be ejected, and compelled to find an employer or leave the town within twenty-four hours.

"No Negro or freedman shall reside within the limits of the town of Opelousas who is not in the regular service of some white person or former owner, who shall be held responsible for the conduct of said freedman.

"No Negro or freedman shall be permitted to preach, exhort, or otherwise declaim to congregations of colored people without a special permission from the Mayor or President of the Board of Police, under the penalty of a fine of ten dollars or twenty days' work on the public streets.

"No freedman who is not in the military service shall be allowed to carry firearms, or any kind of weapons within the limits of the town of Opelousas without the special permission of his employer, in writing, and approved by the Mayor or President of the Board.

"Any freedman not residing in Opelousas, who shall be found within its corporate limits after the hour of 3 o'clock, on Sunday, without a special permission from his employer or the Mayor, shall be arrested and imprisoned and made to work two days on the public streets, or pay two dollars in lieu of said work." [38]

Of Louisiana, Thomas Conway testified February 22, 1866: "Some of the leading officers of the state down there—men who do much to form and control the opinions of the masses—instead of doing as they promised, and quietly submitting to the authority of the government, engaged in issuing slave codes and in promulgating them to their subordinates, ordering them to carry them into execution, and this to the knowledge of state officials of a higher character, the governor and others. And the men who issued them were not punished except as the military authorities punished them. The governor inflicted no punishment on them while I was there, and I don't know that, up to this day, he has ever punished one of them. These codes were simply the old black code of the state, with the word 'slave' expunged, and 'Negro' substituted. The most odious features of slavery were preserved in them. They were issued in three or four localities in the state, not a hundred miles from New Orleans, months after the surrender of the Confederate forces, and years after the issuance of the Emancipation Proclamation.

"I have had delegations to frequently come and see me—delegations composed of men who, to my face, denied that the proclamation issued by President Lincoln was a valid instrument, declaring that the Supreme Court would pronounce it invalid. Consequently they have claimed that their Negroes were slaves and would again be restored to them. In the city of New Orleans last summer, under the orders of the acting mayor of the city, Hugh Kennedy, the police of that city conducted themselves towards the freedmen, in respect to violence and ill usage, in every way equal to the old days of slavery; arresting them on the streets as vagrants, without any form of law whatever, and simply because they did not have in their pockets certificates of employment from their former owners or other white citizens.

"I have gone to the jails and released large numbers of them, men who were industrious and who had regular employment; yet because they had not the certificates of white men in their pockets they were locked up in jail to be sent out to plantations; locked up, too, without my knowledge, and done speedily and secretly before I had information of it. Some members of the Seventy-Fourth United States Colored

Infantry, a regiment which was mustered out but one day, were arrested the next because they did not have these certificates of employment. This was done to these men after having served in the United States army three years. They were arrested by the police under the order of the acting mayor, Mr. Hugh Kennedy. . . ." [39]

The aim and object of these laws cannot be mistaken. "In many cases the restraints imposed went to the length of a veritable 'involuntary servitude.' " [40]

Professor Burgess says: "Almost every act, word or gesture of the Negro, not consonant with good taste and good manners as well as good morals, was made a crime or misdemeanor, for which he could first be fined by the magistrates and then consigned to a condition of almost slavery for an indefinite time, if he could not pay the bill." [41]

Dunning admits that "The legislation of the reorganized governments, under cover of police regulations and vagrancy laws, had enacted severe discriminations against the freedmen in all the common civil rights." [42]

A recent study says of South Carolina:

"The interests of both races would have been better served had there never been a 'black code.' This would be true even if there had been no Northern sentiment to take into account. Economically, the laws were impracticable, since they tried to place the Negro in a position inferior to that which competition or his labor would have given him." [43]

"But it is monotonous iteration to review the early legislation of the reconstructed governments established under the proclamation of the President. In most of the states the laws established a condition but little better than that of slavery, and in one important respect far worse; for in place of the property interest, which would induce the owner to preserve and care for his slave, there was substituted the guardianship of penal statutes; and the ignorant black man, innocent of any intention to commit a wrong, could be bandied about from one temporary owner to another who would have no other interest than to wring out of him, without regard to his ultimate condition, all that was possible during the limited term of his thraldom." [44]

These slave laws have been defended in various ways. They were passed in the midst of bitterness and fear and with great haste; they were worded somewhat like similar vagrancy laws in Northern States; they would have been modified in time; they said more than they really meant. All of this may be partly true, but it remains perfectly evident that the black codes looked backward toward slavery.

This legislation profoundly stirred the North. Not the North of industry and the new manufactures, but the ordinary everyday people of the North, who, uplifted by the tremendous afflatus of war, had seen a vision of something fine and just, and who, without any personal affection for the Negro or real knowledge of him, nevertheless were convinced that Negroes were human, and that Negro slavery was wrong; and that whatever freedom might mean, it certainly did not mean reënslavement under another name.

Here, then, was the dominant thought of that South with which Reconstruction must deal. Arising with aching head and palsied hands it deliberately looked backward. There came to the presidential chair, with vast power, a man who was Southern born; with him came inconceivable fears that the North proposed to make these Negroes really free; to give them a sufficient status even for voting, to give them the right to hold office; that there was even a possibility that these slaves might out-vote their former masters; that they might accumulate wealth, achieve education, and finally, they might even aspire to marry white women and mingle their blood with the blood of their masters.

It was fantastic. It called for revolt. It called in extremity for the renewal of war. The Negro must be kept in his place by hunger, whipping and murder. As W. P. Calhoun of Greenville, South Carolina, said as late as 1901: "Character, wealth, learning, good behavior, and all that makes up or constitutes good citizenship in the black man is positively of no avail whatever. Merit cannot win in this case." [45]

The cry of the bewildered freeman rose, but it was drowned by the Rebel yell.

———

> I am a Southerner;
> I love the South; I dared for her
> To fight from Lookout to the sea,
> With her proud banner over me.
> But from my lips thanksgiving broke,
> As God in battle-thunder spoke,
> And that Black Idol, breeding drouth
> And dearth of human sympathy
> Throughout the sweet and sensuous South,
>   Was, with its chains and human yoke,
> Blown hellward from the cannon's mouth,
>   While Freedom cheered behind the smoke!
>   MAURICE THOMPSON

———

1. Compare Dunning, *Reconstruction, Political and Economic*, pp. 11-13; Beard, *American Civilization*, II, p. 99.
2. Herbert, "The Conditions of the Reconstruction Problems," *Atlantic Monthly*, LXXXVII, p. 146.

3. *The Reminiscences of Carl Schurz*, III, pp. 157-158.
4. 39th Congress, 1st Session, Senate Executive Document Number 2, *Report of Carl Schurz.*
5. *Report of the Joint Committee on Reconstruction*, 1866, Part II.
6. *Congressional Globe*, 39th Congress, 1st Session, Part I, p. 94.
7. *Congressional Globe*, 39th Congress, 1st Session, Part I, p. 94.
8. Wallace, *Carpetbag Rule in Florida*, pp. 34-35.
9. Quotations of testimony are from *Report of the Joint Committee on Reconstruction*, 1866, Parts II, III, and IV.
10. *Congressional Globe*, 39th Congress, 1st Session, Part I, p. 94.
11. Nicolay-Hay, *Abraham Lincoln*, VI, pp. 354-355.
12. Wesley, "Lincoln's Plan for Colonizing the Emancipated Negro," *Journal of Negro History*, IV, p. 9.
13. Fleming, *Deportation and Colonization: Studies in Southern History and Politics*, p. 10.
14. Nicolay-Hay, *Abraham Lincoln*, VI, p. 357.
15. Quoted: *Journal of Negro History*, IV, pp. 11-12.
16. Wesley, "Lincoln's Plan for Colonizing the Emancipated Negro," *Journal of Negro History*, IV, pp. 12-13.
17. Fleming, *Deportation and Colonization: Studies in Southern History and Politics*, p. 13.
18. Wesley, "Lincoln's Plan for Colonizing the Emancipated Negro," *Journal of Negro History*, IV, p. 20.
19. McClure, A. K., *Recollections.*
20. Sumner, Charles, *Complete Works*, VI, p. 302.
21. Ficklen, *History of Reconstruction in Louisiana*, John Hopkins Studies, 28th Series, pp. 65, 66.
22. Nicolay-Hay, *Abraham Lincoln*, IX, pp. 105-110.
23. Compare Ficklen, *History of Reconstruction in Louisiana*, p. 62.
24. Parton, *General Butler in New Orleans*, pp. 489-490.
25. Parton, *General Butler in New Orleans*, p. 517.
26. Ficklen, *History of Reconstruction in Louisiana*, p. 65.
27. Compare Ficklen.
28. McPherson, *History of United States During Reconstruction*, p. 20.
29. Blaine, *Twenty Years of Congress*, II, p. 40.
30. Ficklen, *History of Reconstruction in Louisiana*, pp. 74-77.
31. Ficklen, *History of Reconstruction in Louisiana*, p. 89.
32. Italics ours.
33. Pierce, *Memoirs and Letters of Charles Sumner*, IV, p. 226.
34. Nicolay-Hay, *Abraham Lincoln*, IX, pp. 459-462.
35. Clemenceau, *American Reconstruction, 1865-1870*, p. 232.
36. Quotations from McPherson, *History of United States During Reconstruction*, pp. 29-44.
37. Simkins and Woody, *South Carolina During Reconstruction*, pp. 49, 50.
38. Warmoth, *War, Politics and Reconstruction*, p. 274.
39. *Report of the Joint Committee on Reconstruction*, 1866, Part IV, pp. 78-79.
40. *Atlantic Monthly*, LXXXVII, January, 1910, p. 6.
41. Du Bois, *Reconstruction and Its Benefits*, p. 784.
42. Dunning, *Essays on the Civil War and Reconstruction*, p. 92.
43. Simkins and Woody, *Reconstruction in South Carolina*, p. 51.
44. Morse, *Thaddeus Stevens*, American Statesmen, pp. 253-254.
45. Brewster, *Sketches of Southern Mystery*, p. 275.

VII. LOOKING FORWARD

How two theories of the future of America clashed and blended just after the Civil War: the one was abolition-democracy based on freedom, intelligence and power for all men; the other was industry for private profit directed by an autocracy determined at any price to amass wealth and power. The uncomprehending resistance of the South, and the pressure of black folk, made these two thoughts uneasy and temporary allies

A printer and a carpenter, a rail-splitter and a tailor—Garrison, Christ, Lincoln and Johnson, were the tools of the greatest moral awakening America ever knew, chosen to challenge capital invested in the bodies of men and annul the private profit of slavery.

This done, two quite distinct but persistently undifferentiated visions of the future dominated the triumphant North after the war. One was the prolongation of Puritan idealism, transformed by the frontier into a theory of universal democracy, and now expressed by Abolitionists like Wendell Phillips, students of civilization like Charles Sumner, and leaders of the common people like Thaddeus Stephens, together with some of the leaders of the new labor movement. The other trend was entirely different and is confused with the democratic ideal because the two ideals lay confused in so many individual minds. This was the development of industry in America and of a new industrial philosophy.

The new industry had a vision not of work but of wealth; not of planned accomplishment, but of power. It became the most conscienceless, unmoral system of industry which the world has experienced. It went with ruthless indifference towards waste, death, ugliness and disaster, and yet reared the most stupendous machine for the efficient organization of work which the world has ever seen.

Thus the end of the Civil War was the beginning of vast economic development in the industrial expansion of the East, in the agricultural growth of the Middle West, in the new cattle industry of the plains, in the mining enterprises of the Rockies, in the development of the Pacific Coast, and in the reconstruction of the Southern market.

Behind this extraordinary industrial development, as justification in the minds of men, lay what we may call the great American Assumption, which up to the time of the Civil War, was held more or less explicitly by practically all Americans. The American Assumption was that wealth is mainly the result of its owner's effort and that any average worker can by thrift become a capitalist. The curious thing about this assumption was that while it was not true, it was undoubtedly more nearly true in America from 1820 to 1860 than in any other contemporary land. It was not true and not recognized as true during Colonial times; but with the opening of the West and the expanding industry of the twenties, and coincident with the rise of the Cotton Kingdom, it was a fact that often a poor white man in America by thrift and saving could obtain land and capital; and by intelligence and good luck he could become a small capitalist and even a rich man; and conversely a careless spendthrift though rich might become a pauper, since hereditary safeguards for property had little legal sanction.

Thus arose the philosophy of "shirt-sleeves to shirt-sleeves," on which the American theory of compensated democracy was built. It asked simply, in eighteenth century accents, freedom from government interference with individual ventures, and a voice in the selection of government officials. The continued freedom of economic opportunity and ever possible increase of industrial income, it took for granted. This attitude was back of the adoption of universal suffrage, the disappearance of compulsory military service and imprisonment for debt, which characterized Jacksonian democracy. The American Assumption was contemporary with the Cotton Kingdom, which was its most sinister contradiction. The new captains of industry in the North were largely risen from the laboring class and thus living proof of the ease of capitalistic accumulation. The validity of the American Assumption ceased with the Civil War, but its tradition lasted down to the day of the Great Depression, when it died with a great wail of despair, not so much from bread lines and soup kitchens, as from poor and thrifty bank depositors and small investors.

The American labor movement, founded in the spirit that regarded America as a refuge from oppression and free for individual development according to conscience and ability, grew and expanded in America, basing itself frankly upon the American Assumption. Its object was rule by the people, the wide education of people so that they could rule intelligently, and economic opportunity of wealth free for thrift. It found itself hindered by slavery in the South: directly, because of the growing belief of the influential planter class in oligarchy and the degradation of labor; and indirectly by the competition of slave labor and the spread of the slave psychology. It became, therefore, at first more and more opposed to slavery as ethically wrong, politically dangerous, and economically unprofitable.

Capital, on the other hand, accepted widespread suffrage as a fact forced on the world by revolution and the growing intelligence of the working class. But since the new industry called for intelligence in its workers, capitalists not only accepted universal suffrage but early discovered that high wages in America made even higher profits possible; and that this high standard of living was itself a protection for capital in that it made the more intelligent and best paid of workers allies of capital and left its ultimate dictatorship undisturbed. Nevertheless, industry took pains to protect itself wherever possible. It excluded illiterate foreign voters from the ballot and advocated a reservoir of non-voting common labor; and it stood ready at any time by direct bribery or the use of its power to hire and discharge labor, to manipulate the labor vote.

The true significance of slavery in the United States to the whole social development of America, lay in the ultimate relation of slaves to democracy. What were to be the limits of democratic control in the United States? If all labor, black as well as white, became free, were given schools and the right to vote, what control could or should be set to the power and action of these laborers? Was the rule of the mass of Americans to be unlimited, and the right to rule extended to all men, regardless of race and color, or if not, what power of dictatorship would rule, and how would property and privilege be protected? This was the great and primary question which was in the minds of the men who wrote the Constitution of the United States and continued in the minds of thinkers down through the slavery controversy. It still remains with the world as the problem of democracy expands and touches all races and nations.

The abolition-democracy was the liberal movement among both laborers and small capitalists, who united in the American Assumption, but saw the danger of slavery to both capital and labor. It began its moral fight against slavery in the thirties and forties and, gradually transformed by economic elements, concluded it during the war. The object and only real object of the Civil War in its eyes was the abolition of slavery, and it was convinced that this could be thoroughly accomplished only if the emancipated Negroes became free citizens and voters.

The abolition-democracy saw clearly the difficulties of this step, due to the ignorance and poverty of the freedmen. For the first time in the classic democracy in the United States, it was made aware that the American Assumption was not and could not be universally true. Some of the leaders of the labor movement even came to see that it was not true in the case of the mass of white labor. But that

thought came to the Abolitionists afterwards and in the minds of only
a few clear-sighted men like Wendell Phillips.

At the time of the Civil War, it was, however, perfectly clear to
Sumner and Stevens that freedom in order to be free required a
minimum of capital in addition to political rights and that this could
be insured against the natural resentment of the planters only by some
sort of dictatorship. Thus abolition-democracy was pushed towards
the conception of a dictatorship of labor, although few of its advocates
wholly grasped the fact that this necessarily involved dictatorship by
labor over capital and industry.

On the other hand, industrialists after the war expected the South
to seize upon the opportunity to make increased profit by a more intelligent exploitation of labor than was possible under the slave system. They looked upon free Negro labor as a source of profit, and
considered freedom, that is, a legal doing away with individual physical control, all that the Negroes or their friends could ask. They did
not want for Negro labor any special protection or political power or
capital, any more than they wanted this for Irish, German or Scan-
dinavian labor in the North. They expected some popular education
and a gradual granting of the right to vote, which would be straitly
curtailed in its power for mischief by the far larger power of capital.

The South, however, persisted in its pre-war conception of these
two tendencies in the North. It sought to reëstablish slavery by force,
because it had no comprehension of the means by which modern
industry could secure the advantages of slave labor without its responsibilities. The South, therefore, opposed Negro education, opposed
land and capital for Negroes, and violently and bitterly opposed any
political power. It fought every conception inch by inch: no real
emancipation, limited civil rights, no Negro schools, no votes for
Negroes.

In the face of such intransigence, Northern industry was, on the
whole, willing to yield, since none of these concessions really obstructed
the expansion of industry and capital in the nation. When, however,
the South went beyond reason and truculently demanded not simply
its old political power but increased political power based on disfranchised Negroes, which it openly threatened to use for the revision of
the tariff, for the repudiation of the national debt, for disestablishing
the national banks, and for putting the new corporate form of industry
under strict state regulation and rule, Northern industry was frightened and began to move towards the stand which abolition-democracy
had already taken; namely, temporary dictatorship, endowed Negro
education, legal civil rights, and eventually even votes for Negroes to
offset the Southern threat of economic attack.

The abolition-democracy was not deceived. It at once feared and dared. It wanted no revenge on the South and held no hatred. It did want to train Negroes in intelligence, experience and labor, the ownership of land and capital, and the exercise of civil rights and the use of political power. In the advocacy of these things it reached the highest level of self-sacrificing statesmanship ever attained in America; and two of the greatest leaders of the ideal, Stevens and Sumner, voluntarily laid down their lives on the altar of democracy and were eventually paid, as they must have anticipated they would be paid, by the widespread contempt of America.

Even to this day, the grandsons of Abolitionists, ashamed of their fathers' faith in black men, are salving their conscience with a theory that democratic government by intelligent men of character is impossible, when, in fact, nothing else is possible; and the grandsons of the planters and of the poor whites who displaced them are excusing their apostasy to civilization by charging the Negro with all the evil caused by war, destruction and greed, and by the deeds of white men, Northern and Southern.

The abolition-democracy advocated Federal control to guide and direct the rise of the Negro, but they desired this control to be civil rather than military, like the strict government of territories until new states should develop. They had to help them in the furtherance of this plan a degree of enthusiasm, humility and hard work on the part of the depressed Negro which is not paralleled in modern history. When now they were offered alliance with Northern industry, temporary military control instead of civil government, and then immediate citizenship and the right to vote for Negroes, instead of a period of guardianship, they accepted because they could not refuse; because they knew that this was their only chance and that nothing else would be offered. Their theory of democracy led them to risk all, even in the absence of that economic and educational minimum which they knew was next to indispensable. When Sumner saw his failure here, he went home and wept. But the belief in the self-resurrection of democracy was strong in these men and lent unconscious power to the American Assumption. They expected that both Northern industry and the South, in sheer self-defense, would have to educate Negro intelligence and depend on Negro political power.

The South was too astonished for belief, when it saw industry and democracy in the North united for a policy of coercion. In the past, the South had always been able by mere gesture of concession to bring Northern industry to its knees begging. It did not realize how strong Industry had grown and how conscious its power; and how boundless its plans. It did not realize that the basis of the

South's own power had literally been swept away. Even the West, on which the South had long counted in theory, although sympathy had seldom led to effective action, while it fought industrial monopoly, the national debt and the money power, yet when it had to choose between a continuation of Southern oligarchy and a great democratic movement, swung inevitably towards democracy. Northern capital went South and vied with the planters for the direction of the Negro vote. The poor whites scurried to cover, now here, now there, and a dictatorship of labor ensued, with a new democratic Constitution, new social legislation, public schools and public improvements. But of that we shall speak more in detail in later chapters.

On the other hand, Northern industry seemed at last free and untrammeled. It began in 1876 an exploitation which was built on much the same sort of slavery which it helped to overthrow in 1863. It murdered democracy in the United States so completely that the world does not recognize its corpse. It established as dominant in industry a monarchical system which killed the idea of democracy.

The basis of the argument for Negro suffrage has usually been interpreted as a gesture of vengeance. But it was much deeper than this. It was phrased, first by Abraham Lincoln himself, as a method of retaining "the Jewel of Liberty in the Family of Freedom"; this was echoed, however unwillingly, by Andrew Johnson as a sop to the Radicals; but it gradually came in the thought of the nation to be an inescapable thing. Votes for Negroes were in truth a final compromise between business and abolition and were forced on abolition by business as the only method of realizing the basic principles of abolition-democracy.

All of the selfishness, cunning and power that were back of the new industry of the North have been looked upon as simply the other side of abolition-democracy; and the reason for this was that in several cases, the two ideas were mingled in individuals' minds. One can see that in the sermons of Henry Ward Beecher, who was a great advocate of votes for Negroes, but nevertheless instinctively capitalistic; standing on the side of the exploiter, he had scant sympathy for the exploited. There was something of this, although not nearly as much, in the case of Thaddeus Stevens, who was at heart the greatest and most uncompromising of abolitionist-democrats, but who advocated not only universal suffrage and free schools, but protection for Pennsylvania iron; yet in that protection he had just as distinctly in mind the welfare of the laborer as the profit of the employer.

What, then, was the strength of the democratic movement which succeeded the war? In many respects it was emotional. It swept the land with its music and poetry. A war, which to the intense dissatisfaction of the Abolitionists had begun with the distinct object, even on the part of the great Emancipator, to save and protect slavery, and in no way to disturb it, except to keep it out of competition with the free peasant of the West, had resulted in Emancipation. Men like William Lloyd Garrison, who had no sympathy with the platform of the Republicans in 1860, became suddenly the center of the stage of the new dispensation. Thus, a legal-metaphysical dispute, involving the right of slave states to expand into the territories, was rapidly changed, first to a question of freedom for slaves, and then to a struggle for inaugurating a new form of national government in the United States.

When the physical war ended, then the real practical problems presented themselves. How was slavery to be effectively abolished? And what was to be the status of the Negroes? What was the condition and power of the states which had rebelled? The legal solution of these questions was easy. The states that had attempted to rebel had failed. They must now resume their relations to the government. Slavery had been abolished as a war measure. This should be confirmed and extended by a constitutional amendment. Some control of the Negro population must be devised in the place of slavery, so as to introduce the Negro into his new freedom. The power of the national government had been greatly expanded by war. This expansion must be consolidated so that in the future secession would be impossible and slavery never reëstablished.

The difficulty with this legalistic formula was that it did not cling to facts. Slavery was not abolished even after the Thirteenth Amendment. There were four million freedmen and most of them on the same plantation, doing the same work that they did before emancipation, except as their work had been interrupted and changed by the upheaval of war. Moreover, they were getting about the same wages and apparently were going to be subject to slave codes modified only in name. There were among them thousands of fugitives in the camps of the soldiers or on the streets of the cities, homeless, sick and impoverished. They had been freed practically with no land nor money, and, save in exceptional cases, without legal status, and without protection.

Negroes deserved not only the pity of the world but the gratitude of both South and North. Under extraordinary provocation they had acted like decent human beings; they had protected their masters' families, when their masters were away fighting for black slavery. They did this naturally because they were not sure that the North was fighting for freedom, and because they did not know which side would win. But, at any rate, they did it. And even when they understood that the North, willing or unwilling, was bound towards freedom, and that they could fight for their own freedom, they were neither vindictive nor cruel towards their former masters, although they were quite naturally widely accused of "laziness" and "impudence," which are the only weapons of offense which a rising social class can easily use.

These black men wanted freedom; they wanted education; they wanted protection. They had been of great help to the Union armies and that help had been given under great stress. Black soldiers had been outlawed, and in many cases ruthlessly murdered by the enemy who refused to regard them as soldiers or as human. They took chances every time they put on a uniform. Yet after the war they were still not free; they were still practically slaves, and how was their freedom to be made a fact? It could be done in only one way. They must have the protection of law; and back of law must stand physical force. They must have land; they must have education. How was all this to be done?

Lincoln tried hard in the Border States, long before the end of the war, to get voluntary emancipation and pay for the slaves, so that a new system of labor under favorable circumstances could be arranged. The Border States would have none of it. The war ended in anarchy as war always ends. The cost had been so great that there could be no thought of pay for the slaves, even on the part of the South, after the first flush of Reconstruction. There was no possibility of paying for capital destroyed in other ways, or of quickly restoring the neglected land and tools.

Thus by the sheer logic of facts, there arose in the United States a clear and definite program for the freedom and uplift of the Negro, and for the extension of the realization of democracy. Some of the men who had this vision were identified with the new industry, but saw no incongruity or opposition between their ideas or between the rise and expansion of tariff-protected corporations and their equally sincere beliefs in democratic methods. Others were not identified with industry at all. They were, some of them, rich men, supported by incomes derived from industry; most of them were poor men earning a salary. Some of them were laborers. These men started from the Abolitionist's point of view. Slavery was wrong because it reduced human beings to the level of animals. The abolition of slavery meant not simply abolition of legal ownership of the slave; it meant the uplift of slaves and their eventual incorporation into the body civil, politic, and social, of the United States. There was, of course, much difference as to the exact extent of this incorporation, but less and less desire to limit it in any way by law.

The Negro must have civil rights as a citizen; he must eventually have political rights like every other citizen of the United States. And while social rights could not be a matter of legislation, they, on the other hand, must not be denied through legislation, but remain a matter of free individual choice. This outlook and theory of the Abolitionists received tremendous impetus from the war. Those who had been classed as fanatics, who had been left out of the society of the respected, and mobbed, North, East and West, suddenly became the moral justification by which the North marched on to victory.

All of the great literature of the Civil War was based mainly upon human freedom, and in so far as it stressed union, it had to make it "liberty" and union. The war songs, the war stories, the war afflatus, were based on the freedom of the slaves, just as in the World War we mobilized the mass of mankind in a war to end war and to promote the freedom and union of nations.

Moreover, the new abolition-democracy that came after the war had a tremendous and unexpected source and method of propaganda, and that lay in the crusade of the New England schoolmarm. "The annals of this Ninth Crusade are yet to be written—the tale of a mission that seemed to our age far more quixotic than the quest of St. Louis seemed to his. Behind the mist of ruin and rapine waved the calico dresses of women who dared, and after the hoarse mouthings of the field guns rang the rhythm of the alphabet. Rich and poor they were, serious and curious. Bereaved now of a father, now of a brother, now of more than these, they came seeking a life work in planting the New England schoolhouse among the white and black of the South. They did their work well. In that first year they taught one hundred thousand souls, and more." [1]

Here for the first time there was established between the white and black of this country a contact on terms of essential social equality and mutual respect. There had been contact between Negroes and white people in the old South; and in some cases contact of beautiful friendship, and even warm love and affection. But this was spasmodic and exceptional and had to be partially concealed; and always it was spoiled by the sense of inferiority on the part of the Negro, and the will to rule on the part of the whites.

But in a thousand schools of the South after the war were brought together the most eager of the emancipated blacks and that part of the North which believed in democracy; and this social contact of human beings became a matter of course. The results were of all sorts. Sometimes the teachers became disgusted; sometimes the students became sullen and impudent; but, on the whole, the result was one of the most astonishing successes in new and sudden human contacts. We must also remember that the population of the sixties was divided into church congregations, and the great majority of these Methodist,

Baptist, Congregational, Presbyterian and Quaker congregations in the North were represented directly or indirectly in the South, after the war, by one of their members who reported the work that she (and it was usually *she*) was doing with colored people. This work, to an unusual degree, was so successful and so helpful that her words carried widespread conviction.

At the beginning of the war probably not one white American in a hundred believed that Negroes could become an integral part of American democracy. They were slaves and cowards, ignorant by nature and not by lack of teaching. Even if they were going to be freed, they must be got rid of or rid the land of themselves. During the war came the first real revulsion of feeling when it was found that Negroes could and would fight; were apt subjects for military discipline, and indispensable in the conduct of the war. Beyond that came the change in feeling when the rise of schools over all the South showed that the Negro would and could learn. There might be continued doubt as to the extent of the learning and the height to which the race could rise; but nobody in that day of widespread immigration from Europe could doubt that the Negro was capable of at least as much education as the ordinary Northern laborer.

Present America has no conception of the cogency of this argument. In 1865, the right of all free Americans to be voters was unquestioned, and had not been questioned since the time of Andrew Jackson, except in the case of women, where it interfered with sex-ownership. The burden of the proof lay on the man who said there could be in the United States four or five million Americans without the right to vote. What would they be? What status would they hold? Would they not inevitably be slaves, in spite of the fact that they were called free? There were, to be sure, Northern states which would not allow Negroes to vote; but many of the Northern states did; and most of those that did not had comparatively few Negroes. The whole argument against Negro suffrage, even in those states, had been based on the status of the slave in the South. When the slave became free, a new problem was staged for such Northern states.

Two men stand in the forefront of this new attempt to expand and implement democracy: Charles Sumner and Thaddeus Stevens.

Sumner had been fighting steadily not simply against slavery, but for the manhood rights of the free Negro, ever since he entered Congress. By amending the Act of March 3, 1863, he stopped discrimination on street cars between Washington and Alexandria and by the Act of March 3, 1865, extended this to all the railways of the District. June 25, 1864, by amending an appropriation bill, he stopped discrimination in the United States courts, a result which he called "The most important of all in establishing the manhood and citizenship of the colored people. . . . For this result, I have labored two years."

He fought for equal pay to Negro soldiers and finally secured a favorable decision of the Attorney-General. In 1863-1864, he fought unsuccessfully against "white" suffrage in the new territory of Montana; he tried to include colored citizens among the voters of the city of Washington, but lost again.

"At this moment of revolution, when our country needs the blessing of Almighty God and the strong arms of all her children, this is not the time for us solemnly to enact injustice. In duty to our country and in duty to God, I plead against any such thing. We must be against slavery in its original shape, and in all its brood of prejudice and error." [2]

Four years later, Senator Doolittle said that Sumner had "always been in favor of pushing Negro suffrage; he was the originator of that notion; he is the master of that new school of Reconstruction."

In December, 1864, Sumner sketched an anti-slavery amendment. This was adopted by the American Anti-Slavery Society and early in the session was moved by Ashley of Ohio and Wilson of Iowa in the House, and Henderson of Missouri in the Senate. Sumner yielded to Trumbull, who adopted the formula of the Ordinance of 1787, which finally became the Thirteenth Amendment in 1865. Sumner secured a special committee on slavery and freedmen in the Senate in January, 1864, and became the Chairman. He introduced a bill to repeal all fugitive slave laws and the Committee reported it. It was opposed by both Democratic and Republican Senators. It was amended so as to save the law of 1793, and the Committee dropped it. Two months later, a House bill reached the Senate, and Sumner reported it. Saulsbury of Delaware wanted "one day without the nigger." The bill was finally passed, 27-12, and Lincoln signed it June 28, 1864.

Sumner indeed assumed a mighty task, and one realized it as he stood February 5, 1866, before the Senate of the United States, before all the Representatives that could crowd into the hall, before an audience including the whole nation and in some degree the whole world. He spoke four hours on two successive days. Public interest was intense; the galleries of the Senate were crowded, and there were a number of colored people, including Frederick Douglass and Henry Highland Garnett.

The voice of the speaker was solemn and earnest. His style and presence held the audience to every word.[3] "Rarely, if ever did he make a deeper impression in the Senate or awaken wider interest in the country." Thomas Wentworth Higginson found nothing in contemporary statesmanship, here or abroad, to equal the speech, and when Sumner sat down, the audience broke into applause. Charles Sumner was at the time fifty-five years of age, handsome, but heavy of carriage, a scholar and gentleman, no leader of men but a leader of thought, and one of the finest examples of New England culture and American courage. His speech laid down a Magna Charta of democracy in America.

"I begin by expressing a heart-felt aspiration that the day may soon come when the states lately in rebellion may be received again into the copartnership of political power and the full fellowship of the Union. But I see too well that it is vain to expect this day, which is so much longed for, until we have obtained that security for the future, which is found only in the Equal Rights of All, whether in the court-room or at the ballot-box. This is the Great Guarantee, without which all other guarantees will fail. This is the sole solution of our present troubles and anxieties. This is the only sufficient assurance of peace and reconciliation. . . .

"Our fathers solemnly announced the Equal Rights of all men, and that Government had no just foundation except in the consent of the governed; and to the support of the Declaration, heralding these self-evident truths, they pledged their lives, their fortunes, and their sacred honor. . . . And now the moment has come when these vows must be fulfilled to the letter. In securing the Equal Rights of the freedman, and his participation in the Government, which he is taxed to support, we shall perform those early promises of the Fathers, and at the same time the supplementary promises only recently made to the freedman as the condition of alliance and aid against the Rebellion. A failure to perform these promises is moral and political bankruptcy. . . .

"Twice already, since rebel slavery rose . . . [necessity] has spoken to us, insisting: first, that the slaves should be declared free; and secondly, that muskets should be put into their hands for the common defense. Yielding to necessity, these two things were done. Reason, humanity, justice were powerless in this behalf; but necessity was irresistible. And the result testifies how wisely the Republic acted. Without emancipation, followed by the arming of the slaves, rebel slavery would not have been overcome. With these the victory was easy.

"At last the same necessity which insisted first upon emancipation and then upon the arming of the slaves, insists with the same unanswerable force upon the admission of the freedman to complete Equality before the law, so that there shall be no ban of color in court-room or at the ballot-box, and government shall be fixed on its only rightful foundation—the consent of the governed. Reason, humanity, and justice, all of which are clear for this admission of the freedman, may fail to move you; but you must yield to necessity, which now requires that these promises shall be performed. . . .

"The freedman must be protected. To this you are specially pledged by the Proclamation of President Lincoln, which, after declaring him 'free,' promises to *maintain* this freedom, not for any limited period, but for all time. But this cannot be done so long as you deny him the shield of impartial *laws.* Let him be heard in court and let him vote. Let these rights be guarded sacredly. Beyond even the shield of *impartial* laws, he will then have that protection which comes from the consciousness of manhood. Clad in the full panoply of citizenship he will feel at last that he is a man. At present he is only a recent chattel, awaiting your justice to be transmuted into manhood. If you would have him respected in his rights, you must begin by respecting him in your laws. If you would maintain him in his freedom, you must begin by maintaining him in the equal rights of citizenship.

"Foremost is the equality of all men. Of course, in a declaration of rights, no such supreme folly was intended as that all men are created equal in form or capacity, bodily or mental; but simply that they are created equal in rights. This is the first of the self-evident truths that are announced, leading and governing all the rest. Life, liberty, and the pursuit of happiness are among inalienable rights; but they are all held in subordination to that primal truth. Here is the starting-point of the whole, and the end is like the starting-point. In announcing that governments derive their just powers from the consent of the governed, the Declaration repeats again the same proclamation of Equal Rights. Thus is Equality the Alpha and the Omega, in which all other rights are embraced. Men may not have a natural right to certain things, but most clearly they have a natural right to *impartial* laws, by which they shall be secured in Equal Rights. Equality in rights is the first of rights. . . .

"Taking the sum total of the population in the eleven states, we find 5,447,222 whites to 3,666,110 colored persons; and you are now to decide, whether in the discharge of your duties under the Constitution, and bound to guaranty a republican form of government, you will disfranchise this mighty mass, shutting them out from those Equal Rights promised by our fathers, and from all voice in the government of their country. They surpass in numbers by at least a million the whole population of the colonies at the time our fathers raised the cry, 'Taxation without Representation is Tyranny'; and now you are to decide whether you will strip them of representation while you subject them to a grinding taxation by tariff and excise, acting directly and indirectly, which dwarfs into insignificance everything attempted by the British Parliament. . .

"Let me be understood. What I especially ask is impartial suffrage, which is, of course, embraced in universal suffrage. What is universal is necessarily impartial. For the present, I simply insist that all shall be equal before the law, so that, in the enjoyment of this right, there shall be no restriction which is not equally applicable to all. Any further question, in the nature of 'qualification,' belongs to another stage of debate. And yet I have no hesitation in saying that universal suffrage is a universal right, subject only to such regulations as the safety of society may require. These may concern (1) age, (2) character, (3) registration, (4) residence. Nobody doubts that minors may be excluded, and so, also, persons of infamous life. Registration and residence are both prudential requirements for the safeguard of the ballot-box against the Nomads and Bohemians of politics, and to compel the exercise of this franchise where a person is known among his neighbors and friends. Education also may, under certain circumstances, be a requirement of prudence, especially valuable in a Republic where so much depends on the intelligence of the people. These temporary restrictions do not in any way interfere with the rights of suffrage, for they leave it *absolutely accessible to all*. . . .

"The ballot is a *schoolmaster*. Reading and writing are of inestimable value, but the ballot teaches what these cannot teach. It teaches manhood. Especially is it important to a race whose manhood has been denied. The work of redemption cannot be complete if the ballot is left in doubt. The freedman already knows his friends by the unerring instinct of the heart. Give him the ballot, and he will be educated into the principles of the government. Deny him the ballot, and he will continue an alien in knowledge as in rights. His claim is exceptional, as your injustice is exceptional. For generations you have shut him out from all education, making it a crime to teach him to read for himself the Book of Life. Let not the tyranny of the past be an apology for any further exclusion. . . .

"Having pleaded for the freedman, I now plead for the Republic; for to each alike the ballot is a *necessity*. It is idle to expect any true peace while the freedman is robbed of this transcendent light and left a prey to that vengeance which is ready to wreak upon him the disappointment of defeat. The country, sympathetic with him, will be in a position of perpetual unrest. With him it will suffer and with him alone can it cease to suffer. Only through him can you redress the balance of our political system and assure the safety of patriot citizens. Only through him can you save the national debt from the inevitable repudiation which awaits it when recent rebels in conjunction with Northern allies once more bear sway. His is our best guarantee. Use him. He was once your fellow-soldier; he has always been your fellow-man. . . .

"I speak today hoping to do something for my country, and especially for that unhappy portion which has been arrayed in arms against us. The people there are my fellow-citizens, and gladly would I hail them, if they would permit it, as no longer a 'section,' no longer 'the South,' but an integral part of the Republic—under a Constitution which knows no North and no South and cannot tolerate any 'sectional' pretensions. Gladly do I offer my best efforts in all sincerity for their welfare. But I see clearly that there is nothing in the compass of mortal power so important to them in every respect, morally, politically, and economically—that there is nothing with such certain promise to them of beneficent results—there is nothing so sure to make their land smile with industry and fertility as the decree of Equal Rights which I now invoke. Let the decree go forth to cover them with blessings, sure to descend upon their children in successive generations. They have given us war; we give them peace. They have raged against us in the name of Slavery. We send them back the benediction of Justice for all. They menace hate; we offer in return all the sacred charities of country together with oblivion of the past. This is our 'Measure for Measure.' This is our retaliation. This is our only revenge. . . .

"In the fearful tragedy now drawing to a close there is a destiny, stern and irresistible as that of the Greek Drama, which seems to master all that is done, hurrying on the death of Slavery and its whole brood of sin. There is also a Christian Providence which watches this battle for right, caring especially for the poor and downtrodden who have no helper. The freedman still writhing under cruel oppression now lifts his voice to God the avenger. It is for us to save ourselves from righteous judgment. Never with impunity can you outrage human nature. Our country which is guilty still, is paying still the grievous penalty. Therefore by every motive of self-preservation we are summoned to be just. And thus is the cause associated indissolubly with the national life. . . .

"Strike at the Black Code, as you have already struck at the Slave Code. There is nothing to choose between them. Strike at once; strike hard. You have already proclaimed Emancipation; proclaim Enfranchisement also. And do not stultify yourselves by setting at naught the practical principle of the Fathers, that all just government stands only on the consent of the governed, and its inseparable corollary, that *taxation without representation is tyranny*. What was once true is true forever, although we may for a time lose sight of it, and this is the case with those imperishable truths to which you have been, alas! so indifferent. Thus far the work is only *half done*. . . .

"According to the best testimony now, the population of the earth—embracing Caucasians, Mongolians, Malays, Africans, and Americans—is about thirteen hundred millions, of whom only three hundred and seventy-five millions are 'white men,' or little less than one-fourth, so that, in claiming exclusive rights for 'white men,' you degrade nearly three-quarters of the Human Family, made in the 'image of God' and declared to be of 'one blood,' while you sanction a Caste offensive to religion, an Oligarchy inconsistent with Republican Government, and a Monopoly which has the whole world as its footstool.

"Against this assumption I protest with mind, soul, and heart. It is false in religion, false in statesmanship, and false in economy. It is an extravagance, which, if enforced, is foolish tyranny. Show me a creature with erect countenance looking to heaven, made in the image of God, and I show you a MAN who, of whatever country or race, whether darkened by equatorial sun or blanched by northern cold, is with you a child of the heavenly father, and equal with you in title to all the rights of human nature."

The second seer of democracy was Thaddeus Stevens. He was a man different entirely in method, education and thought from Charles Sumner. We know Stevens best when he was old and sick, and when with grim and awful courage he made the American Congress take the last step which it has ever taken towards democracy. Yet in one respect Stevens in his thought was even more realistic than Charles Sumner, although Sumner later followed him; from the first, Stevens knew that beneath all theoretical freedom and political right must lie the economic foundation. He said at Lancaster, Pennsylvania, September 7, 1865:

"The whole fabric of Southern society must be changed, and it never can be done if this opportunity is lost. . . . How can republican institutions, free schools, free churches, free social intercourse, exist in a mingled community of nabobs and serfs; of the owners of twenty thousand acre manors with lordly palaces and the occupants of narrow huts inhabited by 'low white trash'? If the South is ever to be made a safe republic let her lands be cultivated by the toil of the owners or the free labor of intelligent citizens. This must be done even though it drives her nobility into exile! If they go, all the better. It will be hard to persuade the owner of ten thousand acres of land, who drives a coach and four, that he is not degraded by sitting at the same table or in the same pew, with the embrowned and hard-handed farmer who has himself cultivated his own thriving homestead of 150 acres. The country would be well rid of the proud, bloated and defiant rebels. . . . The foundations of their institutions . . . must be broken up and relaid, or all our blood and treasure have been spent in vain." [4]

"He figured that there were in the rebel states four hundred sixty-five million acres of land. Of this three hundred ninety-four million acres were owned by 70,000 persons, each of whom possessed more than two hundred acres. He argued that these three hundred ninety four million acres ought to be confiscated by the government. To each adult freedman should be given forty acres which approximately would dispose of about forty million acres. The remaining three hundred fifty-four million acres, he would divide into suitable farms and sell to the highest bidder. Including city property it should bring an average price of ten dollars an acre, making a total of three billion five hundred forty million in six per cent bonds, the income of which should go towards the payment of pensions to the deserving veterans, and the widows and orphans of soldiers and sailors who had been killed in the war. Two hundred million dollars should be appropriated to reimburse loyal men in both North and South whose property had been destroyed or damaged during the war. With the remaining three billion, forty million dollars he would pay the national debt. Stevens argued that since all this property which has to be confiscated was owned by 70,000 persons, the vast majority of the people in the South would not be affected by this policy. These 70,000 were the arch-traitors and since they had caused an unjust war they should be made to suffer the consequences." [5]

Sumner, thinking along these lines, had hesitated. He said in June, 1862, when confiscation first was broached:

"I confess frankly that I look with more hope and confidence to liberation than to confiscation. To give freedom is nobler than to take property. . . . There is in confiscation, unless when directed against the criminal authors of the rebellion, a harshness inconsistent with that mercy which it is always a sacred duty to cultivate. . . . But liberation is not harsh; and it is certain, if properly conducted, to carry with it the smiles of a benignant Providence." [6]

Later, however, he began to see the economic demands of emancipation and he wrote to John Bright, March 13, 1865: "Can emancipation be carried out without using the lands of the slave-masters? We must see that the freedmen are established on the soil, and that they may become proprietors. From the beginning I have regarded confiscation only as ancillary to emancipation. The great plantations, which have been so many nurseries of the rebellion, must be broken up, and the freedmen must have the pieces. It looks as if we were on the eve of another agitation. I insist that the rebel states shall not come back except on the footing of the Declaration of Independence, with all persons equal before the law, and government founded on the consent of the governed. In other words, there shall be no discrimination on account of color. If all whites vote, then must all blacks; but there shall be no limitation of suffrage for one more than for the other. It is sometimes said 'What! let the freedman, yesterday a slave, vote?' I am inclined to think that there is more harm in refusing than in conceding the franchise. It is said that they are as intelligent as the Irish just arrived; but the question has become immensely practical in this respect: Without their votes we cannot establish stable governments in the Rebel States. Their votes are as necessary as their muskets; of this I am satisfied. Without them, the old enemy will reappear, and under the forms of law take possession of the governments, choose magistrates and officers, and in alliance with the Northern Democracy, put us all in peril again, postpone the day of tranquillity, and menace the national credit by assailing the national debt. To my mind, the nation is now bound by self-interest—ay, self-defense—to be thoroughly just. The Declaration of Independence has pledges which have never been redeemed. We must redeem them, at least as regards the rebel states which have fallen under our jurisdiction. Mr. Lincoln is slow in accepting truths. I have reminded him that if he would say the word we might settle this question promptly and rightly. He hesitates. Meanwhile I feel it my duty to oppose his scheme of government in Louisiana, which for the present is defeated in Congress." [7]

Stevens' declaration found few echoes. Senator Wade of Ohio was the only one who blazed a further path toward industrial democracy. He "declared in public meetings that after the abolition of slavery, a radical change in the relations of capital and of property in land is next upon the order of the day." And Wade added frankly that this democratic movement of freedom and power for men was easily confused in men's minds with the older slogans of freedom for trade and industry.

"There is no doubt," he also remarked, "that if by an insurrection [the colored people] could contrive to slay one half their oppressors, the other half would hold them in the highest respect and no doubt treat them with justice."

All of this simply increased Industry's fear of Western radicalism and was regarded as advocacy of industrial revolution. These were the demands of the extreme leaders of abolition-democracy; leaders like Phillips and Douglass agreed with the demand for the ballot. Wendell Phillips said at the annual meeting of the Massachusetts Anti-Slavery Society in 1865:

"Our philosophy of government since the Fourth day of July, 1776, is that no class is safe, no freedom is real, no emancipation is effectual which does not place in the hands of the man himself the power to protect his own rights. That is the genius of American Institutions.

"The Negro must be given the franchise because we have no other timber to build states with, and unless we build with him, we must postpone reconstruction for so many years, that the very patronage of territorial government would swamp republican institutions. Keep them territories, let the democracy come in eight years or four, with the money power of this bank system in one hand and territorial government in the other, and republican government will be almost a failure."

At a Tremont Temple meeting in Boston, it was "Resolved, That since the denial of rights to black men was the cause of the disruption of the Union, their enfranchisement and free equality before the law must be the cornerstone of the Reconstruction."

Douglass said, "I am for the 'immediate, unconditional and universal' enfranchisement of the black man, in every state in the Union. Without this his liberty is a mockery; without this, you might as well almost retain the old name of slavery for his condition; for, in fact, if he is not the slave of the industrial master, he is the slave of society, and holds his liberty as a privilege, not as a right. He is at the mercy of the mob, and has no means of protecting himself."

Not all Abolitionists agreed, however; Garrison in the *Liberator* refused to demand immediate enfranchisement. He said, in 1864, in reply to an English critic, "When was it ever known that liberation from bondage was accompanied by a recognition of political equality? Chattels personal may be instantly translated from the auction-block into freemen; but when were they ever taken at the same time to the ballot-box, and invested with all political rights and immunities? According to the laws of development and progress, it is not practicable. To denounce or complain of President Lincoln for not disregarding public sentiment, and not flying in the face of these laws, is hardly just. Besides, I doubt whether he has the constitutional right to decide this matter. Ever since this government was organized, the right of suffrage has been determined by each state in the Union for itself, so that there is no uniformity in regard to it. In some free states, colored citizens are allowed to vote; in others, they are not. It is always a state, never a national matter.

"Nor, if the freed blacks were admitted to the polls by Presidential fiat, do I see any permanent advantage likely to be secured by it; for, submitted to as a necessity at the outset, as soon as the state was organized and left to manage its own affairs, the white population, with their superior intelligence, wealth, and power, would unquestionably alter the franchise in accordance with their prejudices, and exclude

those thus summarily brought to the polls. Coercion would gain nothing. In other words—as in your own country—universal suffrage will
be hard to win and to hold without general preparation of feeling and
sentiment. But it will come, both at the South and with you; yet only
by a struggle *on the part of the disfranchised,* and a growing conviction of its justice, 'in the good time coming.' With the abolition of
slavery in the South, prejudice or 'colorphobia,' the natural product of
the system, will gradually disappear—as in the case of your West Indian colonies—and black men will win their way to wealth, distinction, eminence, and official station. I ask only a charitable judgment of
President Lincoln respecting this matter, whether in Louisiana or any
other state." [8]

Here was sound political argument but unsound economics based
on the American Assumption of wealth through thrift, applied to
slaves, where Thaddeus Stevens alone knew it could not be applied.
Nevertheless the demand for Negro suffrage grew, chiefly because of
the necessity of implementing emancipation and making Negro freedom real. The New York *Times* said in April, 1865:

"Nobody, we believe, wishes to keep any Southern state under disabilities simply as punishment. Mr. Sumner, himself, probably does
not want to transform the Southern states into territories for any such
object. The real concern herein is whether the Southern states, if restored at once to their full state rights, would not abuse them by an
oppression of the black race. This race has rendered an assistance to
the government in times of danger that entitles them to its benign care.
The government cannot, without the worst dishonor, permit the bondage of the black man to be continued in any form. It is bound by every
moral principle, as well as every prudential consideration, not to remit
him to the tender mercies of an enemy. But it is to be hoped that the
Southern people will understand that the interests of both races require a just relation between them and that they will secure this by a
prompt change of their state constitution and laws."

The New York *Tribune* laid down seven points in May, 1865:

"1. Everyone must realize that the blacks will not emigrate but stay
in America.

"2. The blacks may not be spared, for their labor makes land valuable, and the land may not be spared.

"3. Fair pay for fair work is a sine qua non.

"4. Education for freedmen.

"5. With education comes self-elevation, and the desire to deny him
the vote will disappear.

"6. However, white men who are ignorant and vicious, vote. Suffrage for blacks regardless of this ignorance.

"7. Fidelity to the political creed of the nation to secure the happiness of all."

Later, Horace Greeley said: "We would consent to submit to the suffrage only those who could read and write or those who pay taxes or are engaged in some trade. Any standard which could limit the voting privilege to the competent and deserving would be agreeable to us." He adds, "The Abolitionists are most anxious that political rights, and especially the right of self-protection by suffrage, shall be accorded to the freedmen of the South; and waiving all questions of power, they would gladly prefer that such extension of suffrage be accorded by, rather than imposed on, Southern whites. They cannot realize that hanging some of the late insurgents as rebels and traitors will dispose the survivors toward according the elective franchise even to the most capable of emancipated blacks. In fact the obstacles to such extension of suffrage are many and formidable—they are not to be surmounted (though many act as though they could) by a mere order from the War Department, nor even by an act of Congress."

The most popular argument for Negro suffrage was that of Carl Schurz:

"It would seem that the interference of the national authority in the home concerns of the Southern states would be rendered less necessary, and the whole problem of political and social reconstruction be made simplified, if, while the masses lately arrayed against the government are permitted to vote, the large majority of those who were always loyal, and are naturally anxious to see the free labor problem successfully solved, were not excluded from all influence upon legislation. In all questions concerning the Union, the national debt, and the future social organization of the South, the feelings of the colored man are naturally in sympathy with the views and aims of the national government. And while the Southern whites fought against the Union, the Negro did all he could to aid it; while the Southern white sees in the national government his conqueror, the Negro sees in it his protector; while the white owes to the national debt his defeat, the Negro owes to it his deliverance; while the white considers himself robbed and ruined by the emancipation of the slaves, the Negro finds in it the assurance of future prosperity and happiness. In all the important issues the Negro would be led by natural impulse to forward the ends of the government, and by making his influence, as part of the voting body, tell upon the legislation of the states, render the interference of the national authority less necessary.

"As the most difficult of the pending questions are intimately connected with the status of the Negro in Southern society, it is obvious that a correct solution can be more easily obtained if he has a voice in the matter. In the right to vote, he would find the best permanent protection against oppressive class-legislation, as well as against individual persecution. The relations between the white and black races even if improved by the gradual wearing off of the present animosities, are likely to remain long under the troubling influence of prejudice.

"It is a notorious fact that the rights of a man of some political power are far less exposed to violations than those of one who is, in matters of public interest, completely subject to the will of others. A voter is a man of influence; small as that influence may be in the single individual, it becomes larger when that individual belongs to a numerous class of voters who are ready to make common cause with him for the protection of his rights. Such an individual is an object of interest to the political parties that desire to have the benefits of his ballot. It is true, the bringing face to face at the ballot box of the white and the black races may here and there lead to an outbreak of feeling, and the first trials ought certainly to be made while the national power is still there to prevent or repress disturbances; but the practice once successfully inaugurated under the protection of that power, it would probably be more apt than anything else to obliterate old antagonisms, especially if the colored people—which is probable, as soon as their own rights are sufficiently secured—divide their votes between the different political parties.

"The effect of the extension of the franchise to the colored people upon the development of free labor and upon the security of human rights in the South being the principal object in view, the objections raised on the ground of the ignorance of the freedman become unimportant. Practical liberty is a good school, and, besides, if any qualification can be found, applicable to both races, which does not interfere with the attainment of the main object, such qualification would in that respect be unobjectionable. But it is idle to say that it will be time to speak of Negro suffrage when the whole colored race will be educated, for the ballot may be necessary to him to secure his education. It is also idle to say that ignorance is the principal ground upon which Southern men object to Negro suffrage, for if it were, that numerous class of colored people in Louisiana who are as highly educated, as intelligent and as wealthy as any corresponding class of whites, would have been enfranchised long ago.

"It has been asserted that the Negro would be but a voting machine in the hand of his employer. On this point opinions seem to differ. I have heard it said in the South that the freedmen are more likely to be influenced by their schoolmasters and preachers. But even if we suppose the employer to control to a certain extent the Negro laborer's vote, two things are to be taken into consideration: 1. The class of employers or landed proprietors will in a few years be very different from what it was heretofore; in consequence of the general breaking up, a great many of the old slaveholders will be obliged to give up their lands and new men will step into their places; and 2. The employer will hardly control the vote of the Negro laborer so far as to make him vote against his own liberty. The beneficial effect of an extension of suffrage does not always depend upon the intelligence with which the newly admitted voters exercise their right, but sometimes upon the circumstances in which they are placed; and the circumstances in which the freedmen of the South are placed are such that when they only vote for their own liberty and rights, they vote for the rights of free labor, for the success of an immediate important reform, for the prosperity of the country, and for the general interests of mankind. If, therefore, in order to control the colored voter, the employer or whoever he may be, is first obliged to concede to the freedman the great point of his own rights as a man and a free laborer, the great social reform is completed, the most difficult problem is solved, and all other questions it will be comparatively easy to settle.

"In discussing the matter of Negro suffrage, I deemed it my duty to confine myself strictly to the practical aspects of the subject. I have, therefore, not touched its moral merits nor discussed the question whether the national government is competent to enlarge the elective franchise in the states lately in rebellion by its own act.

"I deem it proper, however, to offer a few remarks on the assertion frequently put forth that the franchise is likely to be extended to the colored man by the voluntary action of the Southern whites themselves. My observation leads me to a contrary opinion. Aside from a very few enlightened men, I found but one class of people in favor of the enfranchisement of the blacks: it was the class of Unionists who found themselves politically ostracized and looked upon the enfranchisement of the loyal Negroes as the salvation of the whole loyal element. But their numbers and influence are sadly insufficient to secure such a result. The masses are strongly opposed to colored suffrage; anybody that dares to advocate it is stigmatized as a dangerous fanatic; nor do I deem it probable that in the ordinary course of things, prejudices will wear off to such an extent as to make it a popular measure. Outside of Louisiana, only one gentleman who occupied a prominent political position in the South expressed to me an opinion favorable to it. He declared himself ready to vote for an amendment to the constitution of his state bestowing the right of suffrage upon all male citizens without distinction of color, who could furnish evidence of their ability to read and write, without, however, disfranchising those who are now voters and are not able to fulfill that condition. This gentleman is now a member of one of the state conventions, but I presume he will not risk his political standing in the South by moving such an amendment in that body.

"The only manner in which, in my opinion, the Southern people can be induced to grant to the freedman some measure of self-protecting power in the form of suffrage is to make it a condition precedent to 'readmission.'

"Practical attempts on the part of the Southern people to deprive the Negro of his rights as a freeman may result in bloody collisions, and will certainly plunge Southern society into restless fluctuations and anarchical confusion. Such evils can be prevented only by continuing the control of the national government in the states lately in rebellion, until free labor is fully developed and firmly established, and the advantages and blessings of the new order of things have disclosed themselves. This desirable result will be hastened by a firm declaration on the part of the government that national control in the South will not cease until such results are secured. Only in this way can that security be established in the South which will render numerous immigration possible, and such immigration would materially aid a favorable development of things.

"The solution of the problem would be very much facilitated by enabling all the loyal and free-labor elements in the South to exercise a healthy influence upon legislation. It will hardly be possible to secure the freedman against oppressive class legislation and private persecution unless he be endowed with a certain measure of political power.

"As to the future peace and harmony of the Union, it is of the highest importance that the people lately in rebellion be not permitted to build up another 'peculiar institution' whose spirit is in conflict with the fundamental principles of our political system; for as long as they cherish interests peculiar to them in preference to those they have in common with the rest of the American people, their loyalty to the Union will always be uncertain.

"I desire not to be understood as saying that there are no well-meaning men among those who were comprised in the rebellion. There are many, but none of these in number nor in influence are strong enough to control the manifest tendency of the popular spirit. There are great reasons for hope that a determined policy on the part of the national government will produce innumerable and valuable conversions. This consideration counsels leniency as to persons, such as is demanded by the human and enlightened spirit of our times, and vigor and firmness in the carrying out of principles such as are demanded by the national sense of justice and the exigencies of our situation." [10]

The inevitable result of the Civil War eventually had to be the enfranchisement of the laboring class, black and white, in the South. It could not, as the South clamored to make it, result in the mere legalistic freeing of the slaves. On the other hand, it would not go as far as economic emancipation for which Stevens and the freedmen clamored, because the industrial North instinctively recoiled from this and the Northern white working man himself had not achieved such economic emancipation. The politically enfranchised slave was accused, as every laboring class has been, of ignorance and bad manners, of poverty and crime. And when he tried to go to school and tried to imitate the manners of his brothers, and demanded real economic emancipation through ownership of land and right to use capital, there arose the bitter shriek of property, and the charge of corruption and theft was added to that of ignorance and poverty, just as we have seen in our day in the case of Russia.

Democracy, that inevitable end of all government, faces eternal paradox. In all ages, the vast majority of men have been ignorant and poor, and any attempt to arm such classes with political power brings the question: Can Ignorance and Poverty rule? If they try to rule, their success in the nature of things must be halting and spasmodic, if not absolutely nil; and it must incur the criticism and raillery of the wise and the well-to-do. On the other hand, if the poor, unlettered toilers are given no political power, and are kept by exploitation in poverty, they will remain submerged unless rescued by revolution; and a philosophy will prevail, teaching that the submergence of the mass is inevitable and is on the whole best, not only for them, but for the ruling classes.

In all this argument there is seldom a consideration of the possibility that the great mass of people may become intelligent, with incomes that insure a decent standard of living. In such case, no one could deny the right and inevitableness of democracy. And in the meantime, in bridging the road from ignorance and poverty to intelligence and an income sufficient for civilization, the real power must be in someone's hands. Shall this power be a dictatorship for the benefit of the rich, the cultured and the fortunate? This is the basic problem of democracy and it was discussed before the people of the United States in unusual form directly after the Civil War. It was a test of the nation's real belief in democratic institutions. And the fact that the ideal of abolition-democracy carried the nation as far as it did in the matter of Negro suffrage must always be a source of intense gratification for those who believe in humanity and justice.

"In a republic the people precede their government. Throughout the war the people demanded more stringent and more energetic measures than the administration was prepared to adopt. They called for emancipation before it was proclaimed; for a Freedmen's Bureau before it was organized; for a Civil Rights bill before it was passed; and for impartial suffrage before it was finally, by act of Congress, secured. In the history of emancipation the voluntary activities of a portion of the people in benevolent, philanthropic and Christian effort preceded, prepared for, and helped to produce that governmental action which has largely contributed to the present condition and well-grounded hopes of the colored people." [11]

The reports on conditions in the South gained wide currency and had great influence. Salmon P. Chase, Whitelaw Reid, Carl Schurz, all supported with views and logic the prevailing trend of abolition-democracy. In the South itself, long before there was any unanimity in the North on the subject of Negro suffrage or signs of pressure, the question of votes for Negroes came to the front. It was first precipitated by the proposed Thirteenth Amendment abolishing slavery. December 14, 1863, Ashley of Ohio had introduced into the House an amendment prohibiting slavery, and Wilson of Iowa introduced a similar amendment. Both were referred, but not discussed until five months after their introduction. Four other similar amendments were introduced in the House during the season.

In the Senate, January 11, 1864, Henderson of Missouri introduced an amendment to abolish slavery, which was referred. A few days later, Charles Sumner submitted a joint resolution against slavery. The committee preferred Henderson's resolution. The Border State men were especially opposed and Garrett Davis of Kentucky made long and fiery speeches and offered eight amendments. Senator Powell of Kentucky also offered various amendments.

A proposed Thirteenth Amendment finally passed the Senate April 8, 1863, by a vote of 36-6. It was considered in the House the last day of May. On June 15, it was approved by a vote of 95-66, but this was less than the necessary two-thirds majority.

Meantime, Lincoln had been reëlected, receiving 2,216,067 out of 4,011,413 votes; Maryland had abolished slavery, and there was a movement for abolition throughout the Border States. At the second session of the 38th Congress, the President urged the passage of the Thirteenth Amendment. On January 31, 1865, Ashley called the proposed Thirteenth Amendment for reconsideration. Eleven Democrats deserted their leader and enabled the resolution to pass, on January 31, 1865.

Blaine said: "When the announcement was made, the Speaker became powerless to preserve order. The members upon the Republican side sprang upon their seats cheering, shouting, and waving hands, hats, and canes, while the spectators upon the floor and in the galleries joined heartily in the demonstrations. Upon the restoration of order, Mr. Ingersoll of Illinois rose and said, 'Mr. Speaker, in honor of this immortal and sublime event, I move that this House do now adjourn.' " [12] This amendment was signed by the President and submitted to the states. On December 18, 1865, it was declared adopted by the Secretary of State.

The Amendment carried an unusual provision in Section II which asserted: "Congress shall have power to enforce this article by appropriate legislation." Charles Sumner and others declared that this gave Congress power to enfranchise Negroes if such a step was necessary to their freedom. The South took cognizance of this argument. Of the states which seceded, Virginia and Louisiana ratified the Thirteenth Amendment in February, 1865, and Arkansas in April. All of these states were at the time in the control of minorities supported by the Union armies, and strong pressure was exerted on them by the administration in Washington.

In November, 1865, South Carolina ratified with this proviso:

"That any attempt by Congress towards legislating upon the political status of former slaves, or their civil relations, would be contrary to the Constitution of the United States as it now is, or as it would be altered by the proposed amendment; is in conflict with the policy of the President, declared in his amnesty proclamation, and with the restoration of that harmony upon which depend the vital interests of the American Union." [13]

Alabama ratified the Amendment the same month with this proviso:

"That this amendment to the Constitution of the United States is adopted by the Legislature of Alabama with the understanding that it does not confer upon Congress the power to legislate upon the political status of freedmen in this State." [14]

North Carolina and Georgia ratified in December just before the amendment was proclaimed. Mississippi refused ratification until after the Amendment was in force. Florida ratified it with the Alabama reservations. Texas did not ratify until 1870. It is difficult to see in these proceedings any indication that the South was willing to abolish slavery and certainly there was not the slightest indication of granting any Negro political rights.

In South Carolina, "the assembly shunned all suggestions that suffrage be given the Negro in any form." When a number of Charleston Negroes prepared a memorial on this, the convention refused to hear it. "It cannot but be the earnest desire of all members," said the Charleston *Daily Courier,* "that the matter be ignored *in toto* during the session. . . . The white democracy, especially that of the up-country, felt that a restricted suffrage which took no account of racial discriminations would disfranchise a large portion of the white vote and give the large landowners an unfair influence through their control of Negro votes. . . ." "It may safely be said," wrote the Columbia correspondent of the Charleston *Daily Courier,* "that the views and opinions of Sumner, Thad Stevens, Wilson, and some other Northern Radicals have been considered too unworthy to be seriously commented upon by the members of the convention. It is well known that the sentiments of those gentlemen are extremely unpopular in the North." [15]

Universally, the South was reported as adamant on the subject of Negroes voting. "That is not a question they even allow themselves to debate. They consider it too monstrous a proposition even to debate. That is one of the things they imagine they will never submit to. They will suffer confiscation and everything before they will endure the degradation." [16]

Governor Walker of Florida said in his inaugural speech: "Each one of us knows that we could not give either an honest or conscientious assent to Negro suffrage. There is not one of us that would not feel that he was doing wrong, and bartering his self-respect, his conscience and his duty to his country and to the Union itself, for the benefits he might hope to obtain by getting back into the Union. Much as I worship the Union, and much as I would rejoice to see my State once more recognized as a member thereof, yet it is better, a thousand times better, that she should remain out of the Union, even as one of her subjugated provinces, than go back, 'eviscerated of her manhood,' despoiled of her honor, recreant of her duty, without her self-respect, and of course without the respect of the balance of mankind—a miserable thing, with seeds of moral and political death in herself, soon to be communicated to all her associates." [17]

Judge Underwood of Virginia reports a candid gentleman of Alexandria talking to him in friendly conversation:

" 'Sooner than see the colored people raised to a legal and political equality, the Southern people would prefer their total annihilation.' I had regarded him as well informed and almost as candid a man as we have among the Rebels." [18] Grattan, a native of Virginia, said February 10, 1866:

"I believe that if the blacks are left to themselves, if all foreign influence were taken away, the whites would control their votes. It is not in that the difficulty lies, but it is in the repugnance which the white race would feel to that sort of political equality. It is the same sort of repugnance which a man feels toward a snake. He does not feel any animosity to the snake, but there is a natural shrinking from it." [19] He thought that any attempt to give the Negroes a vote would lead to their extermination.

In all this reported opposition to Negro suffrage, the grounds given were racial and social animosity, and never the determination of land and capital to restrict the political power of labor. Yet this last reason was the fundamental one.

While the South was in suspense, and the abolition-democracy was slowly debating and crystallizing opinion, industry in the North was forging forward with furious intensity; and this movement was foremost and predominant in the mind and vision of living persons in that day. During the war, business prospered. There were few failures and the inflated currency increased prices and favored business profits; while, on the other hand, it decreased real wages and the income of farmers. Wealth became concentrated among the manufacturers, merchants, the financiers and the speculators. There was, consequently, a large accumulation of capital for investment in new business enterprises; industrial development was hastened. Inventions and technical improvements increased. Plants became larger and more efficient; steel manufacture became the basis of modern industry and developed rapidly because of the demands of war. The metal industry, thus expanded, turned to the production of peace goods. The war itself called for more efficiency and larger plants and consolidation of plants.

The freeing of the nation from the strangling hands of oligarchy in the South freed not only black men but white men, not only human spirit, but business enterprise all over the land. This happened in surprising ways. Quite naturally, and logically, under the stress of war, national and local taxes rose and rose and rose yet again, forcing the whole community and nation to pay for things formerly paid for by individuals. First, necessary money was provided by taxing imports; then, to encourage local manufacturers of goods that must be had for war; thus by imperceptible transition, the nation was taxed to support manufacturers. The South had forced down the tariff until in 1857 there was practically free trade. Northern manufacturers during the war pressed for higher tariff rates. Taxes on imported goods were the easiest method of raising money. The tariff acts of 1862-1864 raised the average rates of taxation to 37.2% and 47%. And since then the tariff rates have been raised higher and higher so as to foster industrial monopoly.

The industrialists were not without scientific support. Henry Carey,

the American economist, published his "Principles of Social Science"
in 1858-1859. He attacked free trade and joined the German Liszt in
a demand for a self-contained national economy. Carey sought to show
the beneficial effects that the proximity of protected industry would
have upon agriculture. Thus in the name of the new national spirit,
came "America for Americans" as a great and self-sufficing farming
and manufacturing country.

We emerged, therefore, from the war with a tremendous industry,
over-organized, but efficient in many directions through the exigencies
and demands of war. Two things beckoned further; first, the discovery and realization of the extraordinary natural resources of America,
its iron, coal and oil, its forests, and of course raw materials like wool,
sugar and cotton; secondly, a unified and wonderful system of transportation. The nation borrowed three billion dollars for war and paid
heavy interest because of the price of gold. The money borrowed by
the government had to be spent and spent quickly without deliberation, without careful decision. Contractors and managers, therefore,
who furnished goods to the government could make, legally and il-
legally, fabulous sums. The prosperity which thus came to them had to
be passed on in part to the workers, who received higher wages, and
who, despite the increased cost of living, had money to spend freely.
Boom times were on. There was plenty of money for investment and
plenty of chances for investment. Speculation ran riot. The whole
moral fabric of the country was changed, not simply by the blood and
cruelty, hate and destruction, of war, but by the prospects of a golden
future. We are told that when the Secretary of the Treasury visited
New York early in 1864, he found business men interested not in the
blood of battle but in the stock market. Workers and foreigners caught
the fever and naturally enough held the South to blame for the past.
Had not the South held up the distribution of the Western lands since
1845 against the protest of Northern farmers and new immigrants;
against Southern poor whites led by Andrew Johnson, and with sympathy on the part of the managers and hirers of labor of the North?
Early in the war, the Homestead Law was passed and threw open the
Western lands to settlers on easy terms. The new farmers and the new
immigrant laborers were scarcely aware when this land was given
mostly to railroads to help finance them, and then sold to farmers at
prices which made profitable farming increasingly difficult. They saw
agricultural prices rising; they expected them, of course, to continue
to rise.

Railways in the United States increased from three miles in 1828 to
23,476 miles in 1860, 30,283 miles in 1870, and over 50,000 miles in
1880. The railroads had been financed by selling bonds abroad before

the war and after the war by large increases in domestic capital invested. Gifts of public lands were showered upon the railway builders, amounting to half the farm area opened by the Homestead Act. Great railway systems began to be consolidated, and through them population drifted to the cities.

Especially did industry begin to fear the unrest in the West after the war. The West was uneasy. It became more uneasy on account of the land distribution to the railroads, the high and discriminatory railroad rates, the whole money situation, and the taxation. Finance and industry, therefore, after the war, while it looked forward confidently to tremendous industrial development, was wary. It proposed to protect itself. There was going to be no new free trade, no agricultural bloc, no drives for cheap money, no state intervention in industry. The new national development, protected from foreign competition, must be protected from state intervention. Otherwise state control of railroads and industries, state taxation and regulation, would reduce the United States to a series of small exclusive industrial territories instead of one vast market.

All this thought and development went on with little attention to the social or political results of the war. But soon attention had to be given to these matters. Although industry was now in control of the national government, the Republican party which represented it was a minority party; and Northern and Southern Democrats, especially Southern Democrats with increased power by counting the full Negro population, together with Western malcontents, could easily oust the Republicans. It was because of this thought that Northern industry made its great alliance with abolition-democracy. The consummation of this alliance came slowly and reluctantly and after vain effort toward understanding with the South which was unsuccessful until 1876.

When Lincoln first laid down his general proclamation concerning Reconstruction, industry paid little attention to it: let the South come back; let it come back quickly, and let us go to work and make money and repair the losses of the war by increased business; and then let the nation go far beyond this through domination of the American market, and perhaps even of the markets of the world.

However, right here the dreams of the industrialists were quickly shadowed by unwelcome reflections. In the harsh voices of certain leading citizens of the South, who were about to return to Congress, there was something of that same arrogance that had cowed the North in days gone by. What these voices said concerning Negroes and, indeed, concerning slavery, was of little importance to industry; but if they proposed to come back with increased political power, would this mean a drive for free trade? Would it mean a drive against the national banks? Would it mean an attempt to readjust and tax the immense profit made in the rise of the national debt? Beyond this, could it be that the new South was set upon some move to make the whole country assume all or part of the Confederate debt and pay for emancipated slaves? Perhaps not, but this was something to watch. State economic rights must be curbed. Southern opposition to finance and the tariff must be kept in bounds. Very soon, then, the party which represented sound money—that is, the payment of interest on depreciated currency at the same rate as though it had been gold—and who wanted Federal control of industry, began to see the necessity of consolidating their political power.

This point of view of industry began to be expressed frankly. Brewer of Newport wrote Sumner: "In a selfish point of view free suffrage to the blacks is desirable. Without their support, Southerners will certainly again unite, and there is too much reason to fear successfully, with the Democrats of the North, and the long train of evils sure to follow their rule is fearful to contemplate . . . a great reduction of the tariff doing away with its protective feature—perhaps free trade to culminate with repudiation . . . and how sweet and complete will be the revenge of the former if they can ruin the North by free trade and repudiation."

The most selfish argument was made by Elizur Wright of Boston in 1865. He said that it would take years of military subjugation to educate the white South out of its rebel propensities so that a majority of it could be relied on for loyal state government. In the meantime two things would happen: "1st. The public debt would accumulate, for a military occupation never pays as it goes. 2nd. The blacks are largely trained to arms, for they are the cheapest and best troops we can have under the circumstances. Hence, when we arrive at the period when loyal state governments—that will go alone—can be set up, the blacks must be enfranchised or they will be ready and willing to fight for a government of their own; and here is more war, and more public debt, and more taxation.

"If the Southern states are brought back in too soon the North would either have to pay the rebel debt or borrow the rebel theory and secede from the very Union that had been restored by conquering the rebels.

"There is only one way to avoid this and make our victory immediately fruitful. In two states, a decided majority of the population is black, and, by necessity, loyal. In five others, the black element is more than one-third; and it is strong enough to make an effective balance of power in every state where the rebellious element is of any serious magnitude. Again, the particular chivalry which got up and engineered the rebellion has such an honor of sharing political power with its former chattels that when the enfranchisement of the blacks is determined on as the sine qua non of Reconstruction, and its own military power is overthrown, it will emigrate to a more congenial political atmosphere. We have then nothing to do but convert whites enough to make a majority when added to the enfranchised blacks, to have state governments that can be trusted to stand alone. I think I could easily convince any man, who does not allow his prejudices to stand in the way of his interests, that it will probably make a difference of at least $1,000,000,000 in the development of the national debt, whether we reconstruct on the basis of loyal white and black votes, or on white votes exclusively, and that he can better afford to give the government at least one-quarter of his estate than have it try the latter experiment.

"I am not disputing about tastes. A Negro's ballot may be more vulgar than his bullet. Being already in for it, the question with me is, how the one or the other can be made to protect my property from taxation; and I am sure I would rather give away half the little I have, than to have the victories of 1865 thrown away, as I am sure they will be, if, endeavoring to keep the South in subjugation by black armies, the government allows 4,000,000 of black population to continue disfranchised."

Thus industry between 1860-1870 was in control of the government but was insecure. The Republican party which represented it was a minority party, and if Northern and Southern Democrats had been able to unite with the disaffected West, the Republicans would have been swept out of power. But the Republican party, united with abolition-democracy and using their tremendous moral power and popularity, their appeal to freedom, democracy and the uplift of mankind, might buttress the threatened fortress of the new industry. And finally in extremity, votes for Negroes would save the day. Thus a movement, which began primarily and sincerely to abolish slavery and insure the Negroes' rights, became coupled with a struggle of capitalism to retain control of the government as against Northern labor and Southern and Western agriculture.

The union of these two points of view is seen in an Ohio pamphlet then current. "What is to be done with six millions of rebels? What shall be done with four million blacks?

"1. Loyal white men only shall vote.

"2. Loyal white men and rebels, except certain classes, shall vote.

"3. Loyal men, white and black, shall vote.

"4. Loyal men, white and black, and as many of the rebels as can be controlled by loyal voters, shall vote.

"5. Educational standards.

"6. Segregation of whites and blacks. The blacks to be in one territory with full rights to vote.

"7. Rebel states to be held by military power until the rebels have purged themselves.

"In the first plan, 1,200,000 voters in the rebel states will have as much voting power as two million voters in the North. Under the second plan before the Rebellion, the South, with six million whites, boasted as much political power as 8,400,000 of the North. By this second plan, 6,000,000 would possess the power of 10,000,000 of the North. By the third plan, one voter in the South would have more voting power than two voters in the North. Under the fourth plan, the uneducated blacks are almost the only friends of the government, while the educated whites are all wrong. This illustrates the folly of an educational standard. Under the sixth plan, the whites forced the mixing of the races of the country, and those men who have been raised on Negro milk, and some of them who have children by Negro mothers, should not talk about separation."

Slowly the rank and file of the nation began to respond to the combined argument of industrialists and Abolitionists, especially as their seeming unity of purpose increased. A correspondent of the New York *Tribune* writes in 1865 from the South:

"The freed people are truly and unreservedly our friends, and they are almost the *only* ones. They are more intelligent as a class, and more available as a trustworthy material for citizenship, than I expected to find them. The poor whites whom I saw are decidedly inferior to the average of the slave population. If there is to be for the future a stable basis for loyal states in the South, it must be made up largely of the freed people. It will not do at present to trust the ballot in the hands of the white men who have been rebels, and still are such under the guise of Union men. I believe this to be true whether the blacks be allowed to vote or not. There should be a long intermediate probationary state prescribed before they are again allowed to approach the ballot-box." [20]

The abolition-democracy found support in the West. The German and Scandinavians, who had settled in the Northwest, were naturally democratic. Before the war, they had stood against Southern pretensions, and in their midst, the Republican party was born. They disliked aristocracy and they disliked the South because the South was against foreigners and immigration. Among the Germans were many labor leaders and doctrinaires, so that the Northwest could be counted on for democracy. But at the same time, it could be counted on for opposition to the new industrial organization with which the Northeastern Abolitionists were making alliance. However, the union of industrialists and the Abolitionists became closer, and since it was unanswered by any move towards democracy in the South or any sympathy for democracy by Johnson, the West followed the Abolitionists, until later they were seduced by the *kulak* psychology of land ownership.

In the displacement of Southern feudal agriculture by Northern industry, where did the proletariat, the worker, stand? The proletariat is usually envisaged as united, but their real interests were represented in America by four sets of people: the freed Negro, the Southern poor white, and the Northern skilled and common laborer. These groups never came to see their common interests, and the financiers and capitalists easily kept the upper hand. On the other hand, the West and South bore peculiar relations to the new industry. The South clung to the ideal of aristocracy and had no thought of the real democratic movement. Even the poor whites thought of emancipation as giving them a better chance to become rich planters, landowners and employers of Negro labor, and never until the twentieth century envisaged themselves as a labor class. The Western farmers in the same way vacillated between the ideal of speculative landholders and peasant farmers. They harked back to the opportunism of the frontier and wanted freedom to exploit as well as to vote. In New York, Negroes had replaced workers who were on strike, and the two parties fought on the docks of the Morgan Line. In Ohio there were various outbreaks; in Cincinnati and in Pennsylvania, New Jersey, Chicago, Cleveland, Detroit, Buffalo and Albany, race riots occurred during the war. In 1862, Negro longshoremen were assaulted, and colored working men employed in a Brooklyn tobacco factory were mobbed in August. In July, 1862, there were disturbances in New York City, and finally, in 1863, July 13, came the terrible draft riot. As Abraham Lincoln said, March 21, 1864, "None are so deeply interested to resist the present rebellion as the working people. Let them beware of prejudice, working division and hostility among themselves. The most notable feature of a disturbance in your city last summer was the hanging of some working people by other working people. It should never be so. The strongest bond of human sympathy, outside of the family relation, should be one uniting all working people, of all nations, and tongues, and kindreds."

When Lincoln died a year later, Irish organizations refused to march with Negroes, and the common council of New York City refused to allow Negroes in the Lincoln funeral procession; but the New York *Tribune* announced that through the intervention of the Police Commissioner, "a place in the procession had been assigned to the colored societies and other personages, and the police will see that they occupy it without hindrance from any quarter." Meantime, the common council declined to revoke their order.

When the war closed, a million men were returning to the labor market. Gold was at its height, prices were high, and unemployment spread. Strikes took place, soldiers were used to put them down, and laws were introduced to prevent strikes.

The labor movement comprehended, therefore, chiefly Northern skilled laborers. Among them organization was growing. Recovering from the oppressions of war, there were 79 craft unions at the end of 1863, and they had grown to 270 in 1864. Ten national unions were formed between 1863 and 1866, and by 1870 there were 32 national unions. But almost none of these unions mentioned the Negro, or considered him or welcomed him. A "National Assembly of North America" was held at Louisville, Kentucky, in 1864, and passed resolutions concerning working men and labor conditions; but it said nothing of the greatest revolution in labor that had happened in America for a hundred years—the emancipation of slaves.

Meantime, a new flood of cheap immigrant labor was brought into the country to work on the railroads and in the new industries. Northern mill owners who had feared free farms because they might decrease the number of laborers and raise their wages, were appeased by the promotion of alien immigration. It was interesting to hear the Union Party, as the Republicans called themselves in 1864, say, in their platform: "Foreign immigration which in the past had added so much to the wealth and development of resources and the increase of power to this nation—the aspirations of the oppressed of all nations—should be fostered and encouraged by a liberal and just policy." That year the Bureau of Immigration was created, and it was authorized to import workers bound for a term of service. The letter of the law was afterwards changed, but the practice continued for a long time.

In 1860, immigrants were coming in at the rate of 130,000 a year. The outbreak of the war brought the number down, but the new homestead laws began to attract them so that after the war immigration quickly rose from 200,000 to 350,000 a year, and in 1873, had reached 460,000 annually.

It was all too true, as Senator Wilson of Massachusetts said in the 38th Congress, but it was a truth that white laborers did not yet realize: "We have advocated the rights of the black man, because the black man was the most oppressed type of toiling man of this country. I tell you, sir, that the man who is the enemy of the black laboring man is the enemy of the white laboring man the world over. The same influences that go to keep down and crush the rights of the poor black man bear down and oppress the poor white laboring man."

The First International Workingmen's Association formed by Karl Marx in London in 1864 wrote Lincoln after his second election and said: "From the commencement of the titanic American strife, the workingmen of Europe felt distinctly that the Star-Spangled Banner carried the destiny of their class. The contest for the territories which opened the epoch, was it not to decide whether the virgin soil of immense tracts should be wedded to the labor of the immigrant or be prostituted by the tramp of the slave driver?

"When an oligarchy of 300,000 slaveholders dared to inscribe for the first time in the annals of the world 'Slavery' on the banner of armed revolt, when on the very spots where hardly a century ago the idea of one great Democratic Republic had first sprung up, whence the first declaration of the rights of man was issued, and the first impulse given to the European Revolution of the eighteenth century, when on those very spots counter-revolution, with systematic thoroughness, gloried in rescinding 'the ideas entertained at the time of the formation of the old Constitution' and maintained 'slavery to be a beneficial institution,' indeed, the only solution of the great problem of the 'relation of capital to labor,' and cynically proclaimed property in man 'the cornerstone of the new edifice'—then the working classes of Europe understood at once, even before the fanatic partisanship of the upper classes, for the Confederate gentry had given its dismal warnings, that the slaveholders' rebellion was to sound the tocsin for a general holy war of property against labor, and that for the men of labor, with their hopes for the future, even their past conquests were at stake in that tremendous conflict on the other side of the Atlantic. Everywhere they bore therefore patiently the hardships imposed upon them by the cotton crisis, opposed enthusiastically the pro-slavery intervention importunities of their betters, and from most parts of Europe contributed their quota of blood to the good of the cause.

"While the workingmen, the true political power of the North, allowed slavery to defile their own republic, while before the Negro, mastered and sold without his concurrence, they boasted it the highest prerogative of the white-skinned laborer to sell himself and choose his own master, they were unable to attain the true freedom of labor, or to support their European brethren in their struggle for emancipation; but this barrier to progress has been swept off by the red sea of civil war.

"The workingmen of Europe felt sure that as the American War of Independence initiated a new era of ascendency for the Middle Class, so the American Anti-Slavery war will do for the working classes.

They consider it an earnest sign of the epoch to come that it fell to the lot of Abraham Lincoln, the single-minded son of the working class, to lead his country through the matchless struggles for the rescue of the enchained race and the Reconstruction of a social world." [21]

The first fruit of the growing understanding between industrial expansion and abolition-democracy was the Freedmen's Bureau. While industry in the North was dividing the labor movement and establishing a far more effective dictatorship of capital over labor than it had ever had before, it was compelled in the South to institute another dictatorship, designedly and expressly for the protection of emancipated Negro labor. In the Freedmen's Bureau, the United States started upon a dictatorship by which the landowner and the capitalist were to be openly and deliberately curbed and which directed its efforts in the interest of a black and white labor class. If and when universal suffrage came to reënforce this point of view, an entirely different development of American industry and American civilization must ensue. The Freedmen's Bureau was the most extraordinary and far-reaching institution of social uplift that America has ever attempted. It had to do, not simply with emancipated slaves and poor whites, but also with the property of Southern planters. It was a government guardianship for the relief and guidance of white and black labor from a feudal agrarianism to modern farming and industry. For this work there was and had to be a full-fledged government of men. "It made laws, executed them and interpreted them; it laid and collected taxes, defined and punished crimes, maintained and used military force, and dictated such measures as it thought necessary and proper for the accomplishment of its varied ends. Naturally, all these powers were not exercised continuously nor to their fullest extent; and yet, as General Howard has said, 'scarcely any subject that has to be legislated upon in civil society failed, at one time or another, to demand the action of this singular Bureau.'" [22] Thus the Freedmen's Bureau, which rose automatically as a result of the slaves' general strike during the war, and came directly out of the consolidation of the various army departments of Negro affairs, now loomed as the greatest plan of reasoned emancipation yet proposed. For this reason, the bill for its establishment met covert and open opposition. It was opposed by all advocates of slavery, and all persons North and South who did not propose that emancipation should really free the slaves; it was advocated by every element that wanted to achieve this vast social revolution by reasoned leadership, money and sacrifice. It was finally emasculated and abolished by those in the North who grudged its inevitable cost, and by that Southern sentiment which passed the black codes.

A bill to establish a Bureau in the War Department for the care of refugees and freedmen was passed March 3, 1865. It had been proposed as early as 1863, when a number of petitions for a bureau of emancipation were presented to Congress. In January, 1863, less than a month after the Emancipation Proclamation, T. D. Eliot introduced into the House the first bill. But the committee did not report it, and the Freedmen's Aid Societies renewed their petitions.

At the opening of the new session in December, 1863, Eliot introduced another bill. This bill was objected to in the House because of its cost, its charitable features, and the possible corruption of its employees. Eliot defended the bill vigorously. The Negroes had been freed by proclamation, law, and force, and their freedom must be maintained. They were freed through selfish motives, to weaken the enemy. It would be the depth of meanness to let them now grope their way without guidance or protection. The President, by proclamation, had pledged the maintenance of Negro freedom, and Congress had recognized its obligation to secure employment and support of Negroes on abandoned lands. Negroes were now oppressed by Southerners and Northern harpies. Further legislation was imperatively demanded. In the ensuing debates, the bill was defended as encouraging the enlistment of colored soldiers, and as calculated to bring order out of the present chaos. It would form a new class of consumers for Northern products. On the other hand, opponents insisted that the Bureau would open a vast field for corruption, and that it was a revolutionary effort on the part of a government of limited powers. Brooks of New York denounced it because it would put black labor under Northern taskmasters in competition with white labor and capitalists in the North. It was passed March 1, 1864, by the close vote of 69-67.

In the Senate it was referred to the Committee on Slavery and Freedom, of which Charles Sumner was chairman. Here it was transformed from a temporary makeshift and war expedient and began to take the form of a great measure of social uplift and reform. The Bureau was attached to the Treasury Department. Sumner pressed the bill, arguing that private benevolence could not cope with the problem and that a bureau was necessary; that the Treasury was already in charge of abandoned property and had special agents in the field. The bill passed the Senate, June 28, by a vote of 21-9. The House refused to concur and the whole subject went over to the next session. Renewed arguments and petitions came in favor of the bill. In July, seven Freedmen's Aid associations of the West met in Indianapolis. They drew up a memorial complaining of the current methods of dealing with the freedmen and asking for a supervising agent, because of the failure of Congress to establish a bureau.

December 20, 1864, the matter was taken up again in the House and a conference committee appointed with Sumner and Eliot. This committee reported February 2, 1865, and recommended an independent Department of Freedmen and Abandoned Lands. In the debates, there was great diversity of opinion. Some feared that the freedman would be too strictly controlled and that this would curtail his "initiative" and "self-reliance." Others urged the necessity of the bill to rescue these wards from ignorance and pauperism, and guide them into confidence and self-control. The bill passed that House by another close vote of 64-62.

However, there appeared at the same time another bill for the relief of both white refugees and freedmen and the temporary use of abandoned property. It was a short and temporary measure. Both these bills went to the Senate. Sumner stoutly defended the comprehensive measure agreed upon in conference. But the opposition of both Democrats and Republicans was too strong and the conference report was rejected. A second conference was held and a new bill presented, creating a Bureau of Refugees, Freedmen and Abandoned Lands in the War Department.

All these proposals meant that there was a question as to whether this bureau was to be a temporary war measure, or a permanent institution for abolishing slavery and inducting Negroes gradually into economic and political freedom. If it were attached to the War Department, it would end with the war. In the Treasury, it would serve to settle problems of taxation, crops and finance, but presumably end when war finance yielded to peace. In the Interior Department or as a separate department, the Freedmen's Bureau would be permanent, with regular revenues and a wide and comprehensive program of work.

The debate on the final bill was limited, and without a vote the report of the Conference Committee was accepted March 3rd. Abraham Lincoln immediately signed the bill. This bill provided for a Bureau to last "during the present War of Rebellion, and for one year thereafter." It had at its head a commissioner appointed by the President with the consent of the Senate, and assistant commissioners might be appointed for each of the ten states in rebellion. Army officers could be used as assistant commissioners. The Secretary of War was to issue necessary provisions, clothing, and fuel, and under the direction of the President, the Commissioner could set aside for freedmen and refugees tracts of land of not more than forty acres to be leased to tenants; the lessees were to be protected in the use of the land for three years at a low rent. At the end of the term, the tenant could purchase the land at an appraised value.

Some Congressmen, like Conness, could not conceive of a Freedmen's Bureau conducted for the benefit of labor. "Where will the freedman get the capital to buy his horse or his oxen and other agricultural implements, to put his crop of cotton or corn in the ground? All these require capital far beyond the ability of the freedman to command, and renders the scheme impractical so far as it professed to be of benefit to the freedman.

"The inevitable result will be that the freedman will lease no land. He will not be able to lease and cultivate land. He will not be able to purchase equipment of horse and agricultural implements that will be necessary for its cultivation. Then he must fall into general line and become simply a laborer to be hired to some man with whom they are secretly in partnership, with whom they share the profits and the produce of the freedman's labor from these abandoned lands." [23] The inevitable corollary that under the especial circumstances of emancipated slave labor, the state must furnish capital, was inconceivable to men like Conness. He, like Lane of Indiana, made the old American Assumption of economic independence open to all. "I am opposed to the whole theory of the Freedmen's Bureau. I would make them free under the law. I would protect them in the courts of justice; if necessary, I would give them the right of suffrage, and let loyal slaves vote their rebel masters down and reconstruct the seceded states; but I wish to have no system of guardianship and pupilage and overseership over these Negroes."

There was in the debate, inside and outside of Congress, distinct evidence that industry, rather than pay the cost of social uplift on the scale which an efficient Freedmen's Bureau evidently demanded, would accept immediate Negro suffrage as a preferable panacea. Just as the refuge of those who opposed the right to vote was work for the freedman and regular habits of labor; so on the other hand, those who opposed systematic organization of such work, found refuge in the ballot. Pomeroy had seen thousands of colored and white refugees "coming into my state and I say here distinctly that the colored people are able to take care of themselves and find their places and adapt themselves to their new conditions easier and quicker than the poor white refugees who are driven out of the Border States.

"I desire that those who advocate this bill will stop here and spend their time and talent in demanding for the Negro race all the rights and privileges of freedom. Do this and no Freedmen's Bureau at all is necessary.

"Sir, I am for all races of men. I do not believe that it is necessary to secure the property of one race that another shall be destroyed . . .

"Let us refuse admittance to every rebel state unless the privilege of the elective franchise is granted to the colored man. I believe the future permanency of this government depends upon this, and I believe those who have fought this war have no safety or security without it."

Here was a logical resting place; no funds or permanency for a Freedmen's Bureau, and Negro suffrage to defend Northern industry; and no element fought harder and more determinedly to make this possible than the white South. With the possibility of a government guardianship to conduct the Negro in freedom by industry, land, and education at the expense of the nation, the South deliberately and bitterly fought and maligned the Bureau at every turn, and in the end it received the Reconstruction bills as its just reward.

For the stupendous work which the Freedmen's Bureau must attempt, it had every disadvantage except one. It was so limited in time that it had small chance for efficient and comprehensive planning. It had at first no appropriated funds, but was supposed to depend on the chance accumulations of war time, unclaimed bounties of Negro soldiers, confiscated land and property formerly belonging to the Confederate Government, and rations. Further than this it had to use a rough military machine for administrating delicate social reform. The qualities which make a good soldier do not necessarily make a good social reformer. And while in many instances the Bureau was fortunate in its personnel, in others it was just as unfortunate, and had to put in administrative positions military martinets, men disillusioned and cynical after a terrible war, or careless and greedy and in no way suited for farsighted social building.

The most fortunate thing that Lincoln gave the Bureau was its head, Oliver Howard. Howard was neither a great administrator nor a great man, but he was a good man. He was sympathetic and humane, and tried with endless application and desperate sacrifice to do a hard, thankless duty. "His high reputation as a Christian gentleman gave him the esteem of the humane and benevolent portion of the public, upon whose confidence and coöperation his success was largely to depend." [24]

The task that Howard had was of the gravest, because there were three things that the conquered South fought with bitter determination:

1. Any Federal interference with labor.
2. Arms in the hands of Negroes.
3. Votes for Negroes.

This opposition did not arise primarily from any failure of the Bureau in the performance of its duty, or because its work functioned imperfectly. Even if it had been a perfect and well-planned machine for its mission, the planters in the main were determined to try to coerce both black labor and white, without outside interference of any sort. They proposed to enact and enforce the black codes. They were going to replace legal slavery by customary serfdom and caste. And they were going to do all this because they could not conceive of civilization in the South with free Negro workers, or Negro soldiers or voters.

Howard, therefore, had a battle on his hands from the start. His bureau was limited by temporarily extended and incomplete laws until its main work was practically done in 1869, although some of its functions extended until June 30, 1872. Under these circumstances, the astonishing thing is that the Bureau was able to accomplish any definite and worth-while results; yet it did and the testimony in support of this comes from its friends and enemies.

Howard says: "The law establishing the Bureau committed to it the control of all subjects relating to refugees and freedmen under such regulations as might be prescribed by the head of the Bureau and approved by the President. This almost unlimited authority gave me great scope and liberty of action, but at the same time it imposed upon me very perplexing and responsible duties. Legislative, judicial and executive powers were combined in my commission, reaching all the interests of four millions of people, scattered over a vast territory, living in the midst of another people claiming to be superior, and known to be not altogether friendly. . . ." The conditions facing the Bureau were chaotic. "In every state many thousands were found without employment, without homes, without means of subsistence, crowding into towns and about military posts, where they hoped to find protection and supplies. The sudden collapse of the rebellion, making emancipation an actual, universal fact, was like an earthquake. It shook and shattered the whole previously existing social system. It broke up the old industries and threatened a reign of anarchy. Even well-disposed and humane landowners were at a loss what to do, or how to begin the work of reorganizing society and of rebuilding their ruined fortunes. Very few had any knowledge of free labor, or any hope that their former slaves would serve them faithfully for wages. On the other hand, the freed people were in a state of great excitement and uncertainty. They could hardly believe that the liberty proclaimed was real and permanent. Many were afraid to remain on the same soil that they had tilled as slaves lest by some trick they might find themselves again in bondage. Others supposed that the Government would either take the entire supervision of their labor and support, or divide among them the lands of the conquered owners, and furnish them with all that might be necessary to begin life as an independent farmer." [25]

Twelve labors of Hercules faced the Freedmen's Bureau: to make as rapidly as possible a general survey of conditions and needs in every state and locality; to relieve immediate hunger and distress; to appoint state commissioners and upwards of 900 bureau officials; to put the laborers to work at regular wage; to transport laborers, teachers and officials; to furnish land for the peasant; to open schools; to pay bounties to black soldiers and their families; to establish hospitals and guard health; to administer justice between man and former master; to answer continuous and persistent criticism, North and South, black and white; to find funds to pay for all this.

In four years the Bureau issued over twenty-one million rations to the hungry and unemployed—fifteen and a half million to blacks and five and a half million to whites. The number rose to five million in 1866, and then fell from three and one-half to two and one-half million in 1867-1868. The total cost of food and clothing, 1865-1871, was set down at $3,168,325.

In the eyes of a nation dedicated to profitable industry, as well as in the eyes of bureau officials, the first major problem was to set the Negroes to work under a wage contract. "To secure fairness and to inspire confidence on both sides, the system of written contracts was adopted. No compulsion was used, but all were advised to enter into written agreements and submit them to an officer of the Bureau for approval. The nature and obligations of these contracts were carefully explained to the freedmen, and a copy filed in the office of the agent approving it; this was for their use in case any difficulty arose between them and their employers. The labor imposed upon my officers and agents by this system was very great, as evinced by the fact that in a single state not less than fifty thousand (50,000) such contracts were drawn in duplicate and filled up with the names of all the parties."

The purely economic results of this effort were unusually satisfactory. There was cheating by employers, and malingering by laborers, and widespread disorder; yet "in spite of all disorders that have prevailed and the misfortunes that have fallen upon many parts of the South, a good degree of prosperity and success has already been attained. To the oft-repeated slander that the Negroes will not work, and are incapable of taking care of themselves, it is a sufficient answer that their voluntary labor has produced nearly all the food that supported the whole people, besides a large amount of rice, sugar and tobacco for export, and two millions of bales of cotton each year, on which was paid into the United States treasury during the years 1866 and 1867 a tax of more than forty millions of dollars ($40,000,000). It is not claimed that this result is wholly due to the care and oversight of this Bureau, but it is safe to say, as it has been said repeatedly by intelligent Southern white men, that without the bureau or some similar agency, the material interests of the country would have greatly suffered, and the government would have lost a far greater amount than has been expended in its maintenance. . . ." Three-quarters of a million of dollars was spent in transporting laborers to homes and to work, and teachers and agents to their fields of duty.

The insistent demand of the Negro, aided by army officers and Northern churches and philanthropic organizations, began the systematic teaching of Negroes and poor whites. This beginning the Freedmen's Bureau raised to a widespread system of Negro public schools. The Bureau furnished day and night schools, industrial schools, Sunday schools and colleges. Between June 1, 1865, and September 1, 1871, $5,262,511.26 was spent on schools from Bureau funds, and in 1870 there were in day and night schools 3,300 teachers and 149,581 pupils. Nearly all the present Negro universities and colleges like Howard, Fisk, and Atlanta, were founded or substantially aided in their earliest days by the Freedmen's Bureau.

There were systematic plans to care for the sick. In the summer of 1865 there were detailed in the several states fourteen surgeons and three assistant surgeons, who took care of white and black people in distress, and engaged local surgeons to help them. By September, 1867, there were forty-six hospitals with 5,292 beds. The hospitals were distributed in fourteen different states, and the annual appropriation for medical purposes was nearly $500,000 in 1866 and 1867; the total expenditure for the Medical Department has been estimated to have been $2,000,000. With this money, 452,419 cases were treated, and perhaps an equal number unrecorded. In all, nearly a million persons were given medical aid. The death rate among the freedmen was reduced from 30% to 13% in 1865, and to 2.03% in 1869. Something was done in providing physicians in large towns, inspecting sanitation, and treating lame, blind, deaf and dumb and aged persons and orphans. Temporary care was given the insane.

The judicial work of the Bureau consisted in protecting the Negro from violence and outrage, from serfdom, and in defending his right to hold property and enforce his contracts. It was to see that Negroes had fair trials and that their testimony was received, and their family relations respected. The Commissioner laid down general rules for the administration of justice by bureau officials. Freedmen's courts and boards of arbitration were organized when needed, and while an attempt was made to secure uniformity in these courts, they presented much variety in composition and procedure. Sometimes the Assistant Commissioner constituted the court; sometimes it consisted of an agent appointed by him, and a representative of the freedmen and one of the whites. They acted only in cases where one or both parties were Negroes, and they imposed fines and enforced their judgments.

The financial support of the Bureau was haphazard. No appropriations were made under the original Freedmen's Bureau Bill, but funds were supplied from many departments of Negro affairs and from the handling of abandoned property and from taxes and fees. Nearly eight hundred thousand acres of farming land and about five thousand pieces of town property were transferred to the bureau by military and treasury officers, or taken up by assistant commissioners. Of this enough was leased to produce a revenue of nearly four hundred thousand dollars. Some farms were set aside as homes for the destitute and helpless, and a portion was cultivated by freedmen prior to its restoration. The necessary task of settling the Negroes on their own homesteads was begun by the bureau but soon rendered impossible by lack of land and funds and deliberately hostile executive action. Through the agency of the bureau, the government paid out eight thousand dollars in bounties to over five thousand Negro soldiers and their heirs, and thus helped furnish some capital to the new laborers.

Under the second Freedmen's Bureau Bill, passed in 1866, these sources were being exhausted so that the Army Appropriation bill included $594,450 for the Bureau. Succeeding appropriations brought the total to $12,961,395. Adding the cost of various army supplies used, Howard estimated "the total expenses of our Government for refugees and freedmen to August 31, 1869, have been $13,579,816.82." [26] If we add to this the increase in the army payroll caused by the Bureau, and other items, Pierce estimates that the total expenditure for the Bureau was between $17,000,000 and $18,000,000.

This does not prove that the Freedmen's Bureau was a complete success, for it was not; from the nature of the organization and its limitations it could not be. The white South made it the object of its bitterest attacks. It accused the agents of every crime and mistake and planned for its removal. This was natural; for, in its essence, the bureau was a dictatorship of the army over property for the benefit of labor. It was aimed at the worst methods of exploitation; it sought to give the Negro some standing at law; it compelled the keeping of contracts; and while the testimony as to the net results varies it seems true, as Pierce says: [27] "Notwithstanding abuses and extravagances, the bureau did a great, an indispensable work of mercy and relief, at a time when no other organization or body was in a position to do that work.

"To the Negro was imparted a conception—inadequate and distorted though it may have been—of his civil rights as a freeman. In a land long dominated by slavery, when freedom had just been decreed, when neither black nor white well understood the value of free labor, and before the law of supply and demand could readjust labor relations, the bureau set up a tentative scale of wages. . . . When under the direction of broad, temperate, capable agents, the labor division unquestionably accomplished much of the larger purpose for which it was ordained and which its friends maintain that it fulfilled. All things considered in this branch of the work, more marked success was achieved than a calm study of the perplexing situation would lead the thoughtful man of today to think that such an abnormal and short-lived institution could have attained."

A white citizen of Louisiana adds: "The best influence in settling the state of things in Louisiana, would be to maintain there for some years a rigid administration of the Freedmen's Bureau to protect the blacks and their rights, as well as to see that they complied with reasonable and proper contracts they might make. I consider that such an establishment would stand as a barrier to the encroachments of one class upon the rights of the other." [28]

Other critics are worth hearing. A Virginian, J. M. Botts, said: "I have heard of a great many difficulties and outrages which have proceeded, in some instances, if the truth has been represented to me, from the ignorance and fanaticism of persons connected with the Freedmen's Bureau. . . . On the other hand, there are many of the persons connected with the Freedmen's Bureau who have conducted themselves with great propriety; and where that has been so, there has been no difficulty between the whites and blacks." [29] Judge Hill writes, "Like all other efforts of humanity, the results of the Freedmen's Bureau depended very much upon those appointed to carry it out and give it the aid intended. Where the agent was a man of good sense and free from prejudice to either party or race, good results were attained; but, in many instances, the agents were deficient in these necessary qualifications, and the results were, not only a failure to accomplish the purpose of the bureau, but a decided evil." [30]

Wallace bitterly arraigns the bureau officials in Florida:

"The Freedmen's Bureau, an institution devised by Congress under the influence of the very best people of the Northern States, and intended as a means of protection of the freedmen, and preparing them for the new responsibilities and privileges conferred, in the hands of bad men proved, instead of a blessing, to be the worst curse of the race, as under it he was misled, debased and betrayed." [31]

The various investigations of the bureau brought out damaging facts as to the handling of funds and careless administration and yet "the peculiar difficulties of the bureau's financial problems must not be lost sight of. The amount involved was large. It was impossible to avoid errors in identifying the hordes of nameless, irresponsible claimants to public money entrusted to the bureau. The thousands of agents scattered over a vast area were beyond the close personal supervision of higher officials, and much of the irregularity and fraud was clearly traceable to unscrupulous local agents. There is no reason to believe that the commissioner was guilty of embezzlement, fraud, or personal dishonesty; but he certainly was not a strict constructionist. Doubtless his liberal interpretation of statutes was designed to benefit the freedmen and refugees to whose protection and welfare his efforts were directed. Often such interpretation was due to the delay of Congress in making appropriations demanded by the exigencies of the hour." [32]

Grant brought forward some hearsay criticism during the first year. President Johnson sent two generals South who uncovered cases of fraud and maladministration, but commended Howard and believed the Bureau had done much to preserve order and to organize free labor. A final court of inquiry was commenced by act of Congress in 1874, and sat for forty days.

The committee gave in its majority report its judgment of this extraordinary experiment. "The general effect of the policy pursued by this people towards the freedmen and the general results of the administration of the Freedmen's Bureau by General Howard are matters of history. Without civil convulsion, without any manifestation of violence or hate towards those who had subjected him and his ancestors to the accumulated wrongs of generations of servitude, the enfranchised Negro at once and quietly entered upon new relations of freeman and citizen. During the five years since the bureau has been established, General Howard has directed the expenditure of twelve million nine hundred and sixty-five thousand, three hundred and ninety-five dollars and forty cents; has exercised oversight and care for the freedmen and refugees in seventeen States and the District of Columbia, a territory of 350,000 square miles, and coöperated with benevolent societies, aiding in the education of hundreds of thousands of pupils, and in the relief of vast numbers of destitute and homeless persons of all ages and both sexes. . . .

"The world can point to nothing like it in all the history of emancipation. No thirteen millions of dollars were ever more wisely spent; yet, from the beginning this scheme has encountered the bitterest opposition and the most unrelenting hate. Scoffed at like a thing of shame, often struck and wounded, sometimes in the house of its friends, apologized for rather than defended; yet, with God on its side, the Freedmen's Bureau has triumphed; civilization has received a new impulse, and the friends of humanity may well rejoice. The

Bureau work is being rapidly brought to a close, and its accomplishments will enter into history, while the unfounded accusations brought against it will be forgotten." [33]

This is perhaps an overstatement. The Freedmen's Bureau did an extraordinary piece of work but it was but a small and imperfect part of what it might have done if it had been made a permanent institution, given ample funds for operating schools and purchasing land, and if it had been gradually manned by trained civilian administrators. All this was clear when Andrew Johnson vetoed the Freedmen's Bureau bill in 1866.

For the first time in history the people of the United States listened not only to the voices of the Negroes' friends, but to the Negro himself. He was becoming more and more articulate, in the South as well as in the North.

Also the actions of the Negroes were telling on public opinion, and were given for the first time intelligent and sympathetic publicity. Black soldiers paraded; black petitions, some illiterate, some like that from the District of Columbia, in excellent and logical form, were published. Black men began to enter public movements and there was a subsidence of ridicule and caricature. The meetings and petitions of Southern Negroes were significant and cannot be discounted. Many were doubtless instigated by white friends, but not all; and even these had significant internal evidence of genuine thought and action.

In May, 1864, the Negroes at Port Royal, South Carolina, participated in a meeting which elected delegates to the National Convention at Baltimore in June. Robert Smalls and three other Negroes were among the sixteen delegates, but were denied seats. "On the seventh of August last [1865] a convention of colored men was held in this city [Nashville]. . . . It was resolved that the colored people of the State of Tennessee respectfully and solemnly protest against the congressional delegation from this State being admitted to seats in your honorable bodies until the Legislature of this State enact such laws as shall secure to us our rights as freemen.

"We cannot believe that the General Government will allow us to be left without such protection after knowing, as you do, what services we have rendered to the cause of the preservation of the Union and the maintenance of the laws. We have respectfully petitioned our Legislature upon the subject, and have failed to get them to do anything for us, saying that it was premature to legislate for the protection of our rights." [34] September 3, 1865, a Negro convention was held in Raleigh, North Carolina, and adopted resolutions for proper wages, education, protection for their families, and repeal of unjust discrimination. October 7, 1865, the colored citizens of Mississippi protested

against the reactionary policy of the state and expressed the fear that
they were to be reënslaved. "They set forth that, owing to the prejudice existing there, they have not been able to assemble in convention,
but that they have done as well as they could, through a few of their
number to set forth their grievances. They represent four hundred and
thirty-seven thousand four hundred and four citizens of the United
States, being a majority of nearly one hundred thousand in that State.
These people, in a very brief petition, asked Congress to grant them
the right of suffrage, that 'we may,' they say, 'the more effectually prove
our fidelity to the United States; as we have fought in favor of liberty,
justice, and humanity, we wish to vote in favor of it and give our
influence to the permanent establishment of pure republican institutions in these United States; and also that we may be in a position in
a legal and peaceable way to protect ourselves in the enjoyment of
those sacred rights which were pledged to us by the emancipation
proclamation.' " [85]

A colored people's convention met in Zion Church, Charleston,
S. C., in November, 1865, to protest against the work of the convention
and legislature. This began concerted political action by the Negroes
of the state. Robert C. DeLarge, A. J. Ransier, J. J. Wright, Beverly
Nash, Francis L. Cardozo, M. R. Delany, and Richard H. Cain, were
there. They declared that this was "an extraordinary meeting, unknown in the history of South Carolina, when it is considered *who*
composed it and for what *purposes* it was *allowed* to assemble." Complaint was lodged against the state authoriues in depriving Negroes
"of the rights of the meanest profligate in the country"; Congress was
asked to throw "the strong arm of the law over the entire population
of the state," and grant "equal suffrage," and abolish the "black
code." [86]

The petition of this meeting, signed by people of South Carolina,
was presented to the Senate in December. "They respectfully asked
Congress, in consideration of their unquestioned loyalty, exhibited by
them alike as bond or free, as soldier or laborer, in the Union lines
under the protection of the Government, or within the rebel lines
under the domination of the rebellion, that in the exercise of our high
authority over the reëstablishment of civil government in South Carolina their equal right before the law may be respected; that in the
formation and adoption of the fundamental law of the State, they may
have an equal voice with all loyal citizens, and that Congress will not
sanction any State constitution which does not secure the exercise of
the right of the elective franchise to all loyal citizens otherwise qualified in the common course of American law, without distinction of
color." [87]

The colored people of Alabama, in convention at Mobile, in 1866, called upon Congress to provide some means of making their freedom secure. "They say that in the city where they were assembled in convention several of their churches had been already burned to the ground by the torch of the incendiary, and threats are frequently made to continue the destruction of their property; the means of education for their children are secured to them only by the strong arm of the United States Government against the marked opposition of their white fellow-citizens, while throughout the whole State the right to participate in the franchises of freemen is denied as insulting to white men; and a respectful appeal addressed by some of their people to the late State convention was scornfully laid upon the table, some of the members even refusing to hear its reading. They also state that many of their people daily suffer almost every form of outrage and violence at the hands of whites; that in many parts of the state their people cannot safely leave the vicinity of their homes; they are knocked down and beaten by their white fellow-citizens without having offered any injury or insult as a cause; they are arrested and imprisoned upon false accusations; their money is extorted for their release, or they are condemned to imprisonment at hard labor; that many of their people are now in a condition of practical slavery, being compelled to serve their former owners without pay and to call them 'master.' They express a hope that Congress may be led to give them an opportunity to verify these statements by suitable testimony, and also further hope that Congress will grant them the protection they need." [38]

In 1866, January 10, a Negro convention at Augusta, Georgia, appealed to the Georgia legislature. The freedmen declared that during the period of the war the majority of them had remained silently at their homes, although they had known their power to rise, and to "fire your houses, burn your homes and railroads, and discommode you in a thousand ways." During the war, they had been forced into war service by the South. They had been compelled to throw up breastwork forts and fortifications and do the work of prisoners under the guns of the enemy, where, said they, "many of us in common with yourselves were killed." But now, they declared that they could no longer remain indifferent when the state was passing laws which would bind them in future years. Against these laws, they would protest firmly and openly. Another address in the same year called attention to the treatment which the Negroes were receiving in all walks of life throughout the state. On the railroads they paid equal fare with others, but they did not "get half the accommodation." They were "cursed and kicked by the conductors"—their wives and sisters were "blackguarded and insulted by the scrapings of the earth"—and if they spoke of their treatment they were "frowned upon with contempt and replied to in bitter epithets." [39]

Major Martin R. Delaney, the most distinguished Northern Negro in South Carolina, declared in a letter to President Johnson, "What becomes necessary to secure and perpetuate the Union is simply the *enfranchisement* and recognition of *political equality* of the power that saved the nation from destruction—a recognition of the political equality of the blacks with the whites in all their relations as American citizens. . . ." [40]

"A correspondent of the Charleston *Daily Courier* writing from Sumter, South Carolina, reported November 4, 1866, an organized movement among Negroes to better their condition. They held a large assembly to deal with the problems of the hour, this being a meeting on a larger scale than that of many other such which had been held for that purpose in that section. During the four hours of this meeting the correspondent reported that there was not uttered a word about Negro suffrage and other political questions. The keynote of the meeting was to secure 'a fair and remunerative reward for labor.' The contract system had proved to be unequal and unjust and they were advised to resort to the share system."

The black West protested to the admission of Colorado with white suffrage. On January 24, 1866, Senator Brown of Missouri said: "I present a petition of certain citizens of Denver, in the Territory of Colorado, showing that the State Constitution, framed by a citizens' convention, and adopted by an almost insignificant majority of the legal voters of Colorado, preparatory to admission as a State, excludes all colored citizens of the Territory of Colorado from the right of suffrage by the incorporation in that instrument of the words 'all white male citizens.' The petitioners, therefore, beseech your honorable body not to admit the Territory as a State until the word 'all white' be erased from her constitution." [41]

The most significant meeting took place in the North where a National Convention met in Syracuse, New York, in October, 1864. Besides Frederick Douglass, it was attended by George L. Ruffin, who afterwards became the first Negro to sit on the bench of Massachusetts, George T. Downing of Rhode Island, Robert Hamilton of New York, William Howard Day of New Jersey, Jonathan C. Gibbs, who later became Secretary of State and Superintendent of Education in Florida; Peter H. Clark of Ohio, Henry Highland Garnet, the Negro preacher, Dr. Peter W. Ray of Brooklyn, and many other leaders of the free Negroes. The resolution said: "The weakness of our friends is strength to our foes. When the *Anti-Slavery Standard,* representing the American Anti-Slavery Society, denies that the society asks for the enfranchisement of colored men, and the *Liberator* apologizes for excluding the colored men of Louisiana from the ballot-box, they injure us more vitally than all the ribald jests of the whole pro-slavery press . . .

"In the ranks of the Democratic party, all the worst elements of American society fraternize; and we need not expect a single voice from that quarter for justice, mercy, or even decency. To it we are nothing; the slave-holders everything. . . .

"How stands the case with the great Republican party in question? We have already alluded to it as being largely under the influence of the prevailing contempt for the character and rights of the colored race. This is seen by the slowness of our Government to employ the strong arm of the black man in the work of putting down the rebellion; and in its unwillingness, after thus employing him, to invest him with the same incitements to deeds of daring, as white soldiers; neither giving him the same pay, rations, and protection, nor any hope of rising in the service by meritorious conduct. It is also seen in the fact, that in neither of the plans emanating from this party for reconstructing the institutions of the Southern States, are colored men, not even those who had *fought* for the country, recognized as having any political existence or rights whatever. . . .

"Do you, then, ask us to state, in plain terms, just what we want of you, and just what we think we ought to receive at your hands? We answer: First of all, the complete abolition of the slavery of our race in the United States. We shall not stop to argue. We feel the terrible sting of this stupendous wrong, and that we cannot be free while our brothers are slaves. . . .

"We want the elective franchise in all the states now in the Union, and the same in all such states as may come into the Union hereafter. We believe that the highest welfare of this great country will be found in erasing from its statute-books all enactments discriminating in favor or against any class of its people, and by establishing one law for the white and colored people alike. Whatever prejudice and taste may be innocently allowed to do or to dictate in social and domestic relations, it is plain, that in the matter of government, the object of which is the protection and security of human rights, prejudice should be allowed no voice whatever. . . .

"Your fathers laid down the principle, long ago, that universal suffrage is the best foundation of Government. We believe as your fathers believed, and as they practiced; for, in eleven States out of the original thirteen, colored men exercised the right to vote at the time of the adoption of the Federal Constitution. . . .

"Fellow-citizens, let us entreat you, have faith in your own prin-

ciples. If freedom is good for any, it is good for all. If you need the
elective franchise, we need it even more. You are strong, we are weak;
you are many, we are few; you are protected, we are exposed. Clothe
us with this safeguard of our liberty, and give us an interest in the
country to which, in common with you, we have given our lives and
poured out our best blood. You cannot need special protection. Our
degradation is not essential to your elevation, nor our peril essential
to your safety. You are not likely to be outstripped in the race of improvement by persons of African descent; and hence you have no need
of superior advantage, nor to burden them with disabilities of any
kind. . . .

"We may conquer Southern armies by the sword; but it is another
thing to conquer Southern hate. Now what is the natural counterpoise
against this Southern malign hostility? This it is: give the elective
franchise to every colored man of the South who is of sane mind, and
has arrived at the age of twenty-one years, and you have at once four
millions of friends who will guard with their vigilance, and if need
be, defend with their arms, the ark of Federal Liberty from the treason
and pollution of her enemies. You are sure of enmity of the masters,—
make sure of the friendship of the slaves; for, depend upon it, your
Government cannot afford to encounter the enmity of both." [42]

And so at first Abraham Lincoln looked back towards some stable
place in the relation of blacks and whites in the South on which men
could begin to build a new edifice for freedom, and he gave only one
word that had in it a ring of harshness. He was willing to accept
almost any overture on the part of the South except that he would not
return the Negroes to slavery, and if any law compelled the executive
to do this, that executive would not be Abraham Lincoln. There can
be no doubt that Abraham Lincoln never would have accepted the
Black Codes. He began by looking backward and then turned with
this forward-looking word.

On the other hand, Andrew Johnson started looking forward, towards free land, and the interests of the suppressed laborers in the
South; and then realizing that one-half this laboring class was black,
he turned his face towards reaction. He accepted the Black Codes, and
thus he faced in the winter of 1865 the representatives of the people of
the United States in the 39th Congress assembled.

> Symbolic mother, we thy myriad sons,
> Pounding our stubborn hearts on Freedom's bars,
> Clutching our birthright, fight with faces set,
> Still visioning the stars!
> JESSIE FAUSET.

1. Du Bois, *Souls of Black Folk*, p. 25.
2. Pierce, *Memoirs and Letters of Charles Sumner*, IV, pp. 181, 183.
3. *Congressional Globe*, Sumner's Speech, 39th Congress, 1st Session, Part I, pp. 674, 675, 680, 683, 685, 686, 687.
4. Harberg, *The Heritage of the Civil War*, pp. 11, 12.
5. Compare Woodburn, *Life of Thaddeus Stevens*, Chapter XX.
6. Pierce, *Memoirs and Letters of Charles Sumner*, IV, p. 76.
7. Pierce, *Memoirs and Letters of Charles Sumner*, IV, p. 229.
8. Garrison, *Life of Garrison*, IV, 1861-1879, pp. 123, 124.
9. New York *Tribune*, May 8, 1865.
0. Carl Schurz, *Senate Documents*, No. 2, 39th Congress, 1st Session, 1865-1866, pp. 42-45.
11. *Results of Emancipation*, p. 13.
12. Blaine, *Twenty Years of Congress*, I, p. 538.
13. McPherson, *History of Reconstruction*, p. 23.
14. McPherson, *History of Reconstruction*, p. 21.
15. Simkins and Woody, *South Carolina During Reconstruction*, pp. 41, 42.
16. Testimony of Frederick H. Bruce, *Report of the Joint Committee on Reconstruction*, 1866, Part 2, p. 154.
17. Wallace, *Carpetbag Rule in Florida*, pp. 24, 25.
18. Testimony of Judge J. C. Underwood, *Report of the Joint Committee on Reconstruction*, 1866, Part II, p. 7.
9. *Report of the Joint Committee on Reconstruction*, 1866, Part II, p. 163.
0. New York *Tribune*, April 22, 1865.
21. Schlüter, *Lincoln, Labor and Slavery*, pp. 188-197.
22. Du Bois, *Souls of Black Folk*, p. 27.
23. *Congressional Globe*, 39th Congress, 1st Session.
24. *Howard Investigation*, p. 5.
25. *Atlanta University Studies*, No. 12, pp. 39, 40, 41.
26. Du Bois, *Atlanta University Studies*, II, p. 42.
27. Pierce, *The Freedmen's Bureau*, pp. 104, 160.
28. Testimony of Heinstadt, *Report of the Joint Committee on Reconstruction*, 1866, January 27, Part III, p. 25.
29. *Report of the Joint Committee on Reconstruction*, 1866, Part II, p. 123.
30. Pierce, *The Freedmen's Bureau*, p. 157.
31. Wallace, *Carpetbag Rule in Florida*, p. 40.
32. Pierce, *The Freedmen's Bureau*, pp. 127, 128.
33. *Howard Investigation*, p. 20.
34. *Congressional Globe*, 39th Congress, 1st Session, Part I, p. 107.
35. *Congressional Globe*, 39th Congress, 1st Session, Part I, p. 128.
36. Simkins and Woody, *South Carolina During Reconstruction*, p. 55.
37. *Congressional Globe*, 39th Congress, 1st Session, Part I, pp. 107-108.
38. *Congressional Globe*, 39th Congress, 1st Session, Part I, p. 127.
39. Wesley, *Negro Labor in the United States*, pp. 122, 123.
40. Simkins and Woody, *South Carolina During Reconstruction*, p. 54.
41. *Congressional Globe*, 39th Congress, 1st Session, Part I, p. 390.
42. *Proceedings of the National Convention of Colored Men Held in Syracuse, New York, October 4-7, 1864*, pp. 48-61.

VIII. TRANSUBSTANTIATION OF A POOR WHITE

How Andrew Johnson, unexpectedly raised to the Presidency, was suddenly set between a democracy which included poor whites and black men, and an autocracy that included Big Business and slave barons; and how torn between impossible allegiances, he ended in forcing a hesitant nation to choose between the increased political power of a restored Southern oligarchy and votes for Negroes

Like Nemesis of Greek tragedy, the central problem of America after the Civil War, as before, was the black man: those four million souls whom the nation had used and degraded, and on whom the South had built an oligarchy similar to the colonial imperialism of today, erected on cheap colored labor and raising raw material for manufacture. If Northern industry before the war had secured a monopoly of the raw material raised in the South for its new manufactures; and if Northern and Western labor could have maintained their wage scale against slave competition, the North would not have touched the slave system. But this the South had frustrated. It had threatened labor with nation-wide slave competition and had sent its cotton abroad to buy cheap manufactures, and had resisted the protective tariff demanded by the North.

It was this specific situation that had given the voice of freedom a chance to be heard: freedom for new-come peasants who feared the competition of slave labor; peasants from Europe, New England and the poor white South; freedom for all men black and white through that dream of democracy in which the best of the nation still believed.

The result was war because of the moral wrong, the economic disaster and the democratic contradiction of making human labor real estate; war, because the South was determined to make free white labor compete with black slaves, monopolize land and raw material in the hands of a political aristocracy, and extend the scope of that power; war, because the industrial North refused to surrender its raw material and one of its chief markets to Europe; war, because white American labor, while it refused to recognize black labor as equal and human, had to fight to maintain its own humanity and ideal of equality.

The result of the war left four million human beings just as valuable for the production of cotton and sugar as they had been before the war—but during the war, as laborers and soldiers, these Negroes had made it possible for the North to win, and without their actual and possible aid, the South would never have surrendered; and not least, these four million free men formed in the end the only possible moral justification for an otherwise sordid and selfish orgy of murder, arson and theft.

Now, early in 1865, the war is over. The North does not especially want free Negroes; it wants trade and wealth. The South does not want a particular interpretation of the Constitution. It wants cheap Negro labor and the political and social power based on it. Had there been no Negroes, there would have been no war. Had no Negroes survived the war, peace would have been difficult because of hatred, loss and bitter grief. But its logical path would have been straight.

The South would have returned to its place in Congress with less than its former representation because of the growing North and West. These areas of growing manufacture and agriculture, railroad building and corporations, would have held the political power over the South until the South united with the new insurgency of the West or the old Eastern democratic ideals. Industrialization might even have brought a third party representing labor and raised the proletariat to dominance.

Of this, in 1865 there were only vague signs, and in any case, the former Southern aristocracy would not easily have allied itself with immigrant labor, while the Southern poor whites would have needed long experience and teaching. Thus, the North in the absence of the Negro would have had a vast debt, a problem of charity, distress and relief, such reasonable amnesty as would prevent the old Southern leaders from returning immediately to power, the recognition of the reorganized states, and then work and forgetting.

"Let us have peace." But there was the black man looming like a dark ghost on the horizon. He was the child of force and greed, and the father of wealth and war. His labor was indispensable, and the loss of it would have cost many times the cost of the war. If the Negro had been silent, his very presence would have announced his plight. He was not silent. He was in unusual evidence. He was writing petitions, making speeches, parading with returned soldiers, reciting his adventures as slave and freeman. Even dumb and still, he must be noticed. His poverty had to be relieved, and emancipation in his case had to mean poverty. If he had to work, he had to have land and tools. If his labor was in reality to be free labor, he had to have legal freedom and civil rights. His ignorance could only be removed by that very education which the law of the South had long denied him

and the custom of the North had made exceedingly difficult. Thus
civil status and legal freedom, food, clothes and tools, access to land
and help to education, were the minimum demands of four million
laborers, and these demands no man could ignore, Northerner or
Southerner, Abolitionist or Copperhead, laborer or captain of industry.
How did the nation face this paradox and dilemma?

Led by Abraham Lincoln, the nation had looked back to the status
before the war in order to find a path to which the new nation and
the new condition of the freedmen could be guided. Only one forward
step President Lincoln insisted upon and that was the real continued
freedom of the emancipated slave; but the abolition-democracy went
beyond this because it was convinced that here was no logical stopping
place; and it looked forward to civil and political rights, education and
land, as the only complete guarantee of freedom, in the face of a
dominant South which hoped from the first, to abolish slavery only
in name.

In the North, a new and tremendous dictatorship of capital was
arising. There was only one way to curb and direct what promised to
become the greatest plutocratic government which the world had ever
known. This way was first to implement public opinion by the weapon
of universal suffrage—a weapon which the nation already had in part,
but which had been virtually impotent in the South because of slavery,
and which was at least weakened in the North by the disfranchisement
of an unending mass of foreign-born laborers. Once universal suffrage
was achieved, the next step was to use it with such intelligence and
power that it would function in the interest of the mass of working
men.

To accomplish this end there should have been in the country and
represented in Congress a union between the champions of universal
suffrage and the rights of the freedmen, together with the leaders of
labor, the small landholders of the West, and logically, the poor whites
of the South. Against these would have been arrayed the Northern
industrial oligarchy, and eventually, when they were re-admitted to
Congress, the representatives of the former Southern oligarchy.

This union of democratic forces never took place. On the contrary,
they were torn apart by artificial lines of division. The old anti-Negro
labor rivalry between white and black workers kept the labor elements after the war from ever really uniting in a demand to increase
labor power by Negro suffrage and Negro economic stability. The
West was seduced from a vision of peasant-proprietors, recruited from
a laboring class, into a vision of labor-exploiting farmers and land
speculation which tended to transform the Western farmers into a petty
bourgeoisie fighting not to overcome but to share spoils with the large

land speculators, the monopolists of transportation, and the financiers. Wherever a liberal and democratic party started to differentiate itself from this group, the only alliance offered was the broken oligarchy of the South, with its determination to reenslave Negro labor.

The effective combination which ensued was both curious and contradictory. The masters of industry, the financiers and monopolists, had in self-defense to join with abolition-democracy in forcing universal suffrage on the South, or submit to the reassertion of the old land-slave feudalism with increased political power.

Such a situation demanded an economic guardianship of freedmen, and the first step to this meant at least the beginning of a dictatorship by labor. This, however, had to be but temporary union and was bound to break up before long. The break was begun by the extraordinary corruption, graft and theft that became more and more evident in the country from 1868 on, as a result of the wild idea that industry and progress for the people of the United States were compatible with the selfish sequestration of profit for private individuals and powerful corporations.

But those who revolted from the party of exploitation and high finance did not see allies in the dictatorship of labor in the South. Rather they were entirely misled by the complaint of property from the Southern oligarchy. They failed to become a real party of economic reform and became a reaction of small property-holders against corporations; of a petty bourgeoisie against a new economic monarchy. They immediately joined Big Business in coming to an understanding with the South in 1876, so that by force and fraud the South overthrew the dictatorship of the workers.

But this was only the immediate cause. If there had been no widespread political corruption, North and South, there would still have arisen an absolute difference between those who were trying to conduct the new Southern state governments in the interest of the mass of laborers, black and white, and those North and South who were determined to exploit labor, both in agriculture and industry, for the benefit of an oligarchy. Such an oligarchy was in effect back of the military dictatorship which supported these very Southern labor governments, and which had to support them either as laborers or by developing among them a capitalist class. But as soon as there was understanding between the Southern exploiter of labor and the Northern exploiter, this military support would be withdrawn; and the labor governments, in spite of what they had accomplished for the education of the masses, and in spite of the movements against waste and graft which they had inaugurated, would fail. Under such circumstances, they had to fail, and in a large sense the immediate hope of American democracy failed with them.

Let us now follow this development more in detail. In 1863 and 1864, Abraham Lincoln had made his tentative proposals for reconstructing the South. He had left many things unsaid. The loyal-minded, consisting of as few as one-tenth of the voters whom Lincoln proposed to regard as a state, must naturally, to survive, be supported by the United States Army, until a majority of the inhabitants acquiesced in the new arrangements. It was Lincoln's fond hope that this acquiescence might be swift and clear, but no one knew better than he that it might not.

He was careful to say that Congress would certainly have voice as to the terms on which they would recognize the newly elected Senators and Representatives. This proposal met the general approval of the country, but Congress saw danger and enacted the Wade-Davis Bill. This did not recognize Negro suffrage, and was not radically different from the Lincoln plan, except that the final power and assent of Congress were more prominently set forth.

Lincoln did not oppose it. He simply did not want his hands permanently tied. The bill failed, leaving Lincoln making a careful study of the situation, and promising another statement. He was going forward carefully, hoping for some liberal movement to show itself in the South, and delicately urging it. In the election of 1864, the country stood squarely back of him. The Northern democracy carried only New Jersey, Delaware and Kentucky. But he died, and Andrew Johnson took his place.

Thus, suddenly, April 15, 1865, Andrew Johnson found himself President of the United States, six days after Lee's surrender, and a month and a half after the 38th Congress had adjourned, March 3.

It was the drear destiny of the Poor White South that, deserting its economic class and itself, it became the instrument by which democracy in the nation was done to death, race provincialism deified, and the world delivered to plutocracy. The man who led the way with unconscious paradox and contradiction was Andrew Johnson.

Lately the early life and character of Andrew Johnson have been abundantly studied. He was a fanatical hater of aristocracy. "Through every public act of his runs one consistent, unifying thread of purpose—the advancement of the power, prosperity and liberty of the masses at the expense of intrenched privilege. The slaveholding aristocracy he hated with a bitter, enduring hatred born of envy and ambition. 'If Johnson were a snake,' said his rival, the well-born Isham G. Harris, 'he would lie in the grass to bite the heels of the rich men's children.' The very thought of an aristocrat caused him to emit venom and lash about him in fury." [1]

His political methods were those of the barn-storming demagogue. "Johnson's speeches were tissues of misstatement, misrepresentation, and insulting personalities, directed to the passions and unreasoning impulses of the ignorant voters; assaults upon aristocrats combined with vaunting of his own low origin and the dignity of manual labor." [2] Yet a biographer says that Johnson was "the only President who practiced what he preached, drawing no distinction between rich and poor, or high and low. . . .

"Do not these facts furnish an explanation of Johnson's life? Do they not show why he had the courage to go up against caste and cheap aristocracy, why he dared to stand for the under-dog, whether Catholic, Hebrew, foreigner, mechanic, or child; and to cling like death to the old flag and the Union? . . .

" 'Gladly I would lay down my life,' he wrote, 'if I could so engraft democracy into our general government that it would be permanent.' " [3]

To all this there is one great qualification. Andrew Johnson could not include Negroes in any conceivable democracy. He tried to, but as a poor white, steeped in the limitations, prejudices, and ambitions of his social class, he could not; and this is the key to his career.

Johnson sat in Congress from 1843 to 1853, and was Senator from 1857 to 1862. He favored the annexation of Texas as a gateway for Negro emigration. He was against a high tariff, championed free Western lands for white labor, and favored the annexation of Cuba for black slave labor.

McConnell introduced a homestead bill into Congress in January, 1846. Johnson's bill came in March. He returned to Tennessee as Governor, but induced the legislature to instruct members of Congress to vote for his bill. The bill finally passed the House but was defeated in the Senate, and this was repeated for several sessions. Meantime, Johnson found himself in curious company. He was linked on the one hand to the Free Soilers, and in 1851 went to New York to address a Land Reform Association. On the other hand, the South called him socialistic and Wigfall of Texas dubbed him: "The vilest of Republicans, the reddest of Reds, a sans-culotte, for four years past he has been trying to please the North with his Homestead and other bills." [4] The Abolitionists meanwhile looked askance because Johnson favored the bill for annexing Cuba.

He voted against the Pacific railroad, owned eight slaves and said at one time: "You won't get rid of the Negro except by holding him in slavery." [5] In the midst of such vacillation and contradiction, small wonder that Lane referred to Johnson's "triumphant ignorance and exulting stupidity." Yet Johnson hewed doggedly to certain lines. In 1860, he was advocating his homestead bill again. It finally passed both House and Senate, but Buchanan vetoed it as unconstitutional. Johnson called the message "monstrous and absurd." At last, in June, 1862, after the South had withdrawn from Congress, Johnson's bill was passed and Lincoln signed it.

Yet it was this same Johnson who said in the 36th Congress that if the Abolitionists freed the slaves and let them loose on the South, "the non-slaveholder would join with the slave-owner and extirpate them," and "if one should be more ready to join than another it would be myself."

Johnson early became a follower of Hinton Helper and used his figures. *The Impending Crisis* was "Andrew Johnson's vade mecum —his arsenal of facts." [6]

Johnson made two violent speeches against secession in 1860-61, with bitter personalities against Jefferson Davis, Judah Benjamin and their fellows. He called them rebels and traitors; the galleries yelled and the presiding officers threatened to clear them. Johnson shouted: "I would have them arrested, and if convicted, within the meaning and scope of the Constitution, by the Eternal God, I would execute them; Sir, treason must be punished; its enormity and the extent and depth of the offense must be made known!"

Clingman of North Carolina said that Johnson's speech brought on the Civil War. Alexander Stephens said that it solidified the North. Letters came in to congratulate and to encourage "the only Union Senator from the South." Labor rallied to him. A Baltimore laborer wrote that "the poor working man will no doubt be called on to fight the battles of the rich." From Memphis another wrote: "It was labor that achieved our independence and the laborers are ready to maintain it." The New York Working Man's Association passed a resolution of thanks. [7]

Lincoln set about winning Tennessee, and as a step toward it, asked Andrew Johnson to go and act as Military Governor, and restore the state. Johnson resigned from the Senate and went to Tennessee early in March, 1862. He arrived in Nashville March 12, and took possession of the State House. His courage and sacrifice eventually redeemed the state and restored it to the Union.

Several times Johnson spoke on slavery and the Negro. When he asked that plantations be divided in the South and lands opened in the West, he had in mind white men, who would thus become rich or at least richer. But for Negroes, he had nothing of the sort in mind, except the bare possibility that, if given freedom, they might continue to exist and not die out.

Johnson said in January, 1864, at Nashville in reply to a question as to whether he was in favor of emancipation:

"As for the Negro I am for setting him free but at the same time I assert that this is a white man's government. . . . If whites and blacks can't get along together arrangements must be made to colonize the blacks. . . . In 1843, when I was candidate for Governor, it was said, 'That fellow Johnson is a demagogue, is an Abolitionist.' . . . Because I advocated a white basis for representation—apportioning members of Congress according to the number of qualified voters, instead of embracing Negroes, they called me an Abolitionist. . . . What do we find today? Right goes forward; truth triumphs; justice is supreme; and slavery goes down.

"In fact, the Negroes are emancipated in Tennessee today, and the only remaining question for us to settle, as prudent and wise men, is in assigning the Negro his new relation. Now, what will that be? The Negro will be thrown upon society, governed by the same laws that govern communities, and be compelled to fall back upon his own resources, as all other human beings are. . . . Political freedom means liberty to work, and at the same time enjoy the products of one's labor. . . . If he can rise by his own energies, in the name of God, let him rise. In saying this, I do not argue that the Negro race is equal to the Anglo-Saxon. . . . If the Negro is better fitted for the inferior condition of society, the laws of nature will assign him there!" [8]

As a reward for Johnson's services and to unite the sections Lincoln chose Johnson as his running mate in 1864. Before the campaign June 10, from the St. Cloud Hotel, Johnson gave his philosophy of Reconstruction:

"One of the chief elements of this rebellion is the opposition of the slave aristocracy to being ruled by men who have risen from the ranks of the people. This aristocracy hated Mr. Lincoln because he was of humble origin, a rail-splitter in early life. One of them, the private secretary of Howell Cobb, said to me one day, after a long conversation, 'We people of the South will not submit to be governed by a man who has come up from the ranks of the common people, as Abe Lincoln has.' He uttered the essential feeling and spirit of this Southern rebellion. Now it has just occurred to me, if this aristocracy is so violently opposed to being governed by Mr. Lincoln, what in the name of conscience will it do with Lincoln and Johnson? . . .

"I am for emancipation for two reasons: First, because it is right in itself; and second, because in the emancipation of the slaves, we break down an odious and dangerous aristocracy; I think that we are freeing more whites than blacks in Tennessee.

"I want to see slavery broken up, and when its barriers are torn down, I want to see industrious, thrifty immigrants pouring in from all parts of the country. Come on! we need your labor, your skill, your capital. . . .

"Ah, these Rebel leaders have a strong personal reason for holding out—to save their necks from the halter. And these leaders must feel the power of the government. Treason must be made odious, and the traitor must be punished and impoverished. Their great plantations must be seized and divided into small farms, and sold to honest, industrious men. The day for protecting the lands and Negroes of these authors of rebellion is past. It is high time it was."[*]

During the campaign he addressed a torchlight procession of thousands of Negroes and whites. He said, October, 1864:

"Who has not heard of the great estates of Mack Cockrill, situated near this city, estates whose acres are numbered by the thousand, whose slaves were once counted by the score? And of Mack Cockrill, their possessor, the great slave-owner and, of course, the leading rebel, who lives in the very wantonness of wealth, wrung from the sweat and toil and stolen wages of others, and who gave fabulous sums to aid Jeff Davis in overturning this Government? . . .

"Who has not heard of the princely estates of General W. D. Harding, who, by means of his property alone, outweighed in influence any other man in Tennessee, no matter what were that other's worth, or wisdom, or ability. Harding, too, early espoused the cause of treason and made it his boast that he had contributed, and directly induced others to contribute, millions of dollars in aid of that unholy cause. . . . It is wrong that Mack Cockrill and W. D. Harding, by means of forced and unpaid labor, should have monopolized so large a share of the lands and wealth of Tennessee; and I say if their immense plantations were divided up and parceled out amongst a number of free, industrious, and honest farmers, it would give more good citizens to the Commonwealth, increase the wages of our mechanics, enrich the markets of our city, enliven all the arteries of trade, improve society, and conduce to the greatness and glory of the State.

"The representatives of this corrupt, and if you will permit me almost to swear a little, this damnable aristocracy, taunt us with our desire to see justice done, and charge us with favoring Negro equality. Of all living men they should be the last to mouth that phrase; and, even when uttered in their hearing, it should cause their cheeks to tinge and burn with shame. Negro equality, indeed! Why, pass any day along the sidewalks of High Street where these aristocrats more particularly dwell—these aristocrats, whose sons are now in the bands of guerillas and cut-throats who prowl and rob and murder around our city—pass by their dwellings, I say, and you will see as many mulatto as Negro children, the former bearing an unmistakable resemblance to their aristocratic owners. . . . Thank God, the war has ended all this . . . a war that has freed more whites than blacks. . . . Suppose the Negro is set free and we have less cotton, we will raise more wool, hemp, flax and silk. . . . It is all an idea that the world can't get along without cotton. And, as is suggested by my friend behind me, whether we attain perfection in the raising of cotton or not, I think we ought to stimulate the cultivation of hemp (great and renewed laughter); for we ought to have more of it and a far better material, a stronger fiber, with which to make a stronger rope. For, not to be malicious or malignant, I am free to say that I believe many who were driven into this Rebellion, are repentant; but I say of the leaders, the instigators, the conscious, intelligent traitors, they ought to be hung." [10]

" 'Looking at this vast crowd of colored people,' continued the Governor, 'and reflecting through what a storm of persecution and obloquy they are compelled to pass, I am almost induced to wish that, as in the days of old, a Moses might arise who should lead them safely to their promised land of freedom and happiness.'

" 'You are our Moses,' shouted several voices, and the exclamation was caught up and cheered until the Capitol rung again. . . .

" 'Well, then,' replied the speaker, 'humble and unworthy as I am, if no other better shall be found, I will indeed be your Moses, and lead you through the Red Sea of war and bondage to a fairer future of liberty and peace. I speak now as one who feels the world his country, and all who love equal rights his friends. I speak, too, as a citizen of Tennessee. I am here on my own soil; and here I mean to stay and fight this great battle of truth and justice to a triumphant end. Rebellion and slavery shall, by God's good help, no longer pollute our State. Loyal men, whether white or black, shall alone control her destinies; and when this strife in which we are all engaged is past, I trust, I know, we shall have a better state of things, and shall all rejoice that honest labor reaps the fruit of its own industry, and that every man has a fair chance in the race of life.' " [11]

Winston interpreted the latter part of this speech as directed to the whites, when clearly he was speaking directly to the colored people; but he was afterward unwilling to live up to its promises. As a matter of fact, he favored emancipation "in order to save the Union and to free the white man and no further. 'Damn the Negroes,' he once said when charged with race equality. 'I am fighting those traitorous aristocrats, their masters.' " [12]

Johnson appeared to take the oath of office as Vice-President so drunk he was taken into prolonged seclusion after a maudlin speech; his resignation was discussed. He was not a habitual drunkard, although he drank "three or four glasses of Robertson's Canada Whiskey" some days. In 1848 Johnson writes that he had been "on a kind of bust—not a big drunk." [13] Both of Johnson's sons became drunkards and were cut off before they reached middle life. Yet Lincoln was right:

"Oh, well, don't you bother about Andy Johnson's drinking. He made a bad slip the other day, but I have known Andy a great many years, and he ain't no drunkard." Johnson was deeply humiliated by the inauguration episode and perhaps here began his alienation from those who might have influenced him best.

Charles A. Dana, Assistant Secretary of War, says that he met Vice-President Johnson in Richmond. "He took me aside and spoke with great earnestness about the necessity of not taking the Confederates back without some conditions or without some punishment. He insisted that their sins had been enormous, and that if they were let back into the Union without any punishment the effect would be very bad. He said they might be very dangerous in the future. The Vice-President talked to me in this strain for fully twenty minutes, I should think—an impassioned, earnest speech on the subject of punishing rebels." [14]

His sudden induction as President was marked by modesty and genuine feeling. Carl Schurz says that the inaugural speech of Andrew Johnson, in 1865, was very pleasing to the liberals of the North, and made them believe that he was going to allow the Negro to have some part in the reconstruction of the states.

For a month after coming to the Presidency, Johnson indulged in speech-making, and his words were still so severe that the anti-slavery people became uneasy, feeling that Johnson would give his attention primarily to punishing the whites rather than protecting the Negroes. April 21, 1865, he said in an interview with some citizens of Indiana:

"They [the Rebel leaders] must not only be punished, but their social power must be destroyed. . . . And I say that, after making treason odious, every Union man and the government should be remunerated out of the pockets of those who have inflicted this great suffering upon the country." This was exactly the thesis of Thaddeus Stevens enunciated in September of the same year.

A number of Virginians visited Johnson in July and complained that they were seeking credits in the North and West, but could get no consideration while they remained under the ban of the government. The President replied: " 'It was the wealthy men who dragooned the people into secession; I know how this thing was done. You rich men used the press and bullied your little men to force the state into secession.' He spoke as a poor white for poor whites and the planters left in gloom."

He kept on insisting upon punishment for the South, and not only personal punishment but economic punishment, so that many conservatives were afraid that they had elected to the Presidency a radical who would seriously attack the South.

This would have been true but for one thing: the Southern poor white had his attitude toward property and income seriously modified by the presence of the Negro. Even Abraham Lincoln was unable for a long time to conceive of free, poor, black citizens as voters in the United States. The problem of the Negroes, as he faced it, worried him, and he made repeated efforts to see if in some way they could not be sent off to Africa or to foreign lands. Johnson had no such broad outlook. Negroes to him were just Negroes, and even as he expressed his radical ideas of helping the poor Southerners, he seldom envisaged Negroes as a part of the poor.

Lincoln came to know Negroes personally. He came to recognize their manhood. He praised them generously as soldiers, and suggested that they be admitted to the ballot. Johnson, on the contrary, could never regard Negroes as men. "He has all the narrowness and ignorance of a certain class of whites who have always looked upon the colored race as out of the pale of humanity." [15]

The Northern press had been quite satisfied with Lincoln's attitude. He had served liberty and America well. "Lincoln," said Senator Doolittle, representing industry in the West, "would have dealt with the Rebels as an indulgent father deals with his erring children. Johnson would deal with them more like a stern and incorruptible judge. Thus in a moment has the scepter of power passed from the hand of flesh to the hand of iron."

At a cabinet meeting with Mr. Lincoln on the last day of his life, Friday, April 14, Stanton submitted the draft of a plan for the restoration of governments in the South. The draft applied expressly to two states, but was intended as a model for others. The President suggested a revision, and the subject was postponed until Tuesday the 18th.

Andrew Johnson became President, and on Sunday, April 16, Stanton read his draft to Sumner and other gentlemen. Sumner interrupted the reading with the inquiry: " 'Whether any provision was made for enfranchising the colored men,' saying, also, that 'unless the black man

is given the right to vote his freedom is a mockery.' Stanton deprecated the agitation of the subject . . . but Sumner insisted that the
black man's right to vote was 'the essence—the great essential.' Stanton's draft, now confined to North Carolina, was considered in the
Cabinet May 9, when it appeared with a provision for suffrage in the
election of members of a constitutional convention for the State. It
included 'the loyal citizens of the United States.' This paragraph, it
appears, Stanton had accepted April 16, as an amendment from Sumner and Colfax. . . . He admitted that it was intended to include
Negroes as well as white men." [16]

Stanton invited an expression of opinion; several members of the
Cabinet were absent. Stanton, Dennison and Speed favored the inclusion; McCulloch, Welles and Usher were against it. The President
expressed no opinion, but Sumner was certain of the President's decision in favor of Negro suffrage.

Sumner sought to keep close to Johnson. He and Chase had an interview with him a week after he had taken the oath of office. Johnson
was reserved but sympathetic and they left light-hearted. A few days
later, when the President and Senator Sumner were alone together,
the President said: " 'On this question [that of suffrage] there is no
difference between us; you and I are alike.' Sumner expressed his joy
and gratitude that the President had taken this position, and that as a
consequence there would thus be no division in the Union party; and
the President replied, 'I mean to keep you all together.' As he walked
away that evening, Sumner felt that the battle of his own life was
ended." [17]

He wrote to Bright, May 1, 1865, encouragingly: "Last evening, I
had a long conversation with him [Johnson], mainly on the rebel
states and how they shall be tranquillized. Of course my theme is
justice to the colored race. He accepted this idea completely, and indeed went so far as to say 'that there is no difference between us.' You
understand that the question whether rebel states shall be treated as
military provinces or territories is simply one of form, with a view to
the great result. It is the result that I aim at! and I shall never stickle
on any intermediate question if that is secured. He deprecates haste;
is unwilling that states should be precipitated back; thinks there must
be a period of probation, but that meanwhile all loyal people, without
distinction of color, must be treated as citizens, and must take part in
any proceedings for reorganization. He doubts at present the expediency of announcing this from Washington lest it should give a handle
to party, but is willing it should be made known to the people in the
rebel states. The Chief Justice started yesterday on a visit to North
Carolina, South Carolina, Florida and New Orleans, and will on his

way touch the necessary strings, so far as he can. I anticipate much from this journey. His opinions are fixed, and he is well informed with regard to those of the President. I would not be too sanguine, but I should not be surprised if we had this great question settled before the next meeting of Congress—I mean by this that we had such expression of opinion and acts as will forever conclude it. My confidence is founded in part upon the essential justice of our aims and the necessity of the case. With the President as well disposed as he shows himself, and the Chief Justice as positive, we must prevail. Will not all this sanctify our war beyond any in history?"

The next day writing to Lieber, Sumner quoted Johnson as saying that "colored persons are to have the right to suffrage; that no state can be precipitated into the Union; that rebel states must go through a term of probation. All this he had said to me before. Ten days ago, the Chief Justice and myself visited him in the evening to speak of these things. I was charmed by his sympathy, which was entirely different from his predecessor's. The Chief Justice is authorized to say wherever he is what the President desires, and to do everything he can to promote organization without distinction of color. The President desires that the movement should appear to proceed from the people. This is in conformity with his general ideas; but he thinks it will disarm the party at home. I told him that while I doubted if the work could be effectively done without federal authority, I regarded the *modus operandi* as an inferior question; and that I should be content, provided equality before the law was secured for all without distinction of color. I said during this winter that the rebel states could not come back, except on the footing of the Declaration of Independence, and the complete recognition of human rights. I feel more than ever confident that all this will be fulfilled. And then what a regenerated land! I had looked for a bitter contest on this question; but with the President on our side, it will be carried by simple avoirdupois."

Chase wrote Johnson from South Carolina the same month: "Suffrage to loyal blacks; I find that readiness and even desire for it is in proportion to the loyalty of those who express opinions. Nobody dissents, vehemently; while those who have suffered from rebellion and rejoice with their whole hearts in the restoration of the National Authority, are fast coming to the conclusion they will find their own surest safety in the proposed extension. . . .

"All seem embarrassed about first steps. I do not entertain the slightest doubt that they would all welcome some simple recommendation from yourself, and would adopt readily any plan which you would suggest. . . .

"I am anxious that *you* should have the lead in this work. It is my deliberate judgment that nothing will so strengthen you with the people or bring so much honor to your name throughout the world as some such short address as I suggested before leaving Washington. Just say to the people: 'Reorganize your state governments. I will aid you in the enrollment of the loyal citizens; you will not expect me to discriminate among men equally loyal; once enrolled, vote for delegates to the Convention to reform your State Constitution. I will aid you in collecting and declaring their suffrages. Your convention and yourselves must do the rest; but you may count on the support of the National Government in all things constitutionally expedient.' " [18]

In April and May of 1866, Tennessee had confined the right to vote to whites. The Tennessee Senate refused a suffrage bill which allowed all blacks and whites of legal age to vote, but excluded after 1875 all who could not read. Sumner wanted Johnson to insist on Negro suffrage in Tennessee, but Johnson explained that if he were in Tennessee he would take a stand, but that he could not in Washington.

Sumner remained in Washington half through May and saw the President almost daily, always seizing opportunity to present his views on Reconstruction, and insisting on suffrage for Negroes.

Just before leaving Washington, Sumner had a final interview with the President. He found him cordial and apparently unchanged. Sumner apologized for repeating his views expressed before. Johnson said, with a smile, "Have I not always listened to you?" Sumner, as he left, "assured his friends and correspondents that the cause he had at heart was safe" with Andrew Johnson.[19]

Disturbing signs, however, began to occur. Carl Schurz wrote in May concerning the plans of Southern leaders in Mississippi, Georgia and North Carolina. Thaddeus Stevens was alarmed at the President's recognition of the Pierpont government of Virginia. A caucus was, therefore, called at the National Hotel at Washington, May 12, to prevent the administration from going completely astray. Wade and Sumner said the President was in no danger, and that he was in favor of Negro suffrage.

Sumner may have been over-sanguine and read into Johnson's words more than Johnson intended, but it is certain that Sumner received a definite understanding that President Johnson stood for real emancipation and Negro suffrage.

Here then was Andrew Johnson in 1865, born at the bottom of society, and during his early life a radical defender of the poor, the landless and the exploited. In the heyday of his early political career, he railed against land monopoly in the South, and after the Civil War, wanted the land of the monopolists divided among peasant proprietors.

Suddenly, by the weird magic of history, he becomes military dictator of a nation. He becomes the man by whom the greatest moral and economic revolution that ever took place in the United States, and perhaps in modern times, was to be put into effect. He becomes the real emancipator of four millions of black slaves, who have suffered more than anything that he had experienced in his earlier days. They not only have no lands; they have not owned even their bodies, nor their clothes, nor their tools. They have been exploited down to the ownership of their own families; they have been poor by law, and ignorant by force. What more splendid opportunity could the champion of labor and the exploited have had to start a nation towards freedom?

Johnson took over Lincoln's cabinet with an Anti-Abolitionist Whig, a Pro-Slavery Democrat, and a liberal student of industry, among others. This cabinet lasted a little over a year when early in July, 1866, three members, Dennison, Harlan and Speed, resigned, being unwilling to oppose Congress.

In all their logical sequence, the Reconstruction policies now associated with Johnson's name were laid down by Seward, and his logic overwhelmed Johnson. As Stevens explained: "Seward entered into him, and ever since they have been running down steep places into the sea."

The Cabinet met at Seward's house May 9, and on May 29, Johnson issued a Proclamation of Amnesty which showed the Seward influence. Indeed, nothing was left, apparently, of Johnson's liberalism, except the exclusion from amnesty, not simply of the leaders of the Confederacy, but of the rich—those worth $20,000 or more. Seward opposed this, but it was the only thing that he yielded to Johnson's liberalism. He early convinced Johnson that Reconstruction was a matter for the President to settle and especially he opened the door to his thorough conversion when the power of further pardons was put into Johnson's hand.

"Seward, who had remained secretary after Lincoln's death, had used all the powers of his persuasive eloquence to satisfy President Johnson that all now to be done was simply to restore the Union by at once readmitting the 'States lately in rebellion' to their full constitutional functions as regular States of the Union, and that then, being encouraged by this mark of confidence, the late master class in the South could be trusted with the recognition and protection of the emancipated slaves. That Mr. Seward urged such advice upon the President, there is good reason for believing. Not only was it common report, but it accorded also strikingly with Mr. Seward's singular turn of mind concerning the slavery question. As after the outbreak of the secession movement he peremptorily relegated the slavery question to the background in spite of its evident importance in the Civil War and of the influence it would inevitably exercise upon the opinion and attitude of foreign nations, so he may have been forgetful of the national duty of honor to secure the rights of the freedmen and the safety of the Southern Union men in his impatient desire to 'restore the Union' in point of form." [20]

Johnson was transformed. From the champion of peasant labor, he saw himself as the restorer of national unity, and the benefactor and almsgiver to those very elements in the South which had formerly despised him. Of his real rôle as emancipator, and the one who was to give effective freedom to Negroes, he still had not the slightest idea. He could not conceive of Negroes as men. And equally, he had no adequate idea of the industrial transformation that was going on in the North. There were, of course, the inevitable scars of the war: the loss of a million men and twelve billion dollars in property; eventual pensions and indirect losses; the revolution in Southern agriculture; the universal lowering of ethical standards which always follows war. The West was uneasy on account of taxes, debt and the money situation. In New York and Boston, men engaged in foreign commerce wanted speedy restoration of the South and a reduction in the tariff to increase their business. These complicated threads varied and changed as time went on. But when the 39th Congress met, the war business boom was still on; failures had disappeared; prices had increased. Wealth was being concentrated among the manufacturers, merchants, financiers and speculators. There were great amounts of waiting capital and all of these interests wanted the war stopped, and the South restored.

Sumner had not left Washington ten days before his hopes for a just reconstruction on the basis of Negro suffrage were killed by the President's proclamation.

Johnson's plan of reconstruction included the abolition of slavery, the repudiation of war debts, the nullification of secession ordinances, and the appointment of provisional governors to help in the reconstruction of civil government. Only those white folks who could take the loyal oath would take part in this reconstruction. In other words, this was practically Lincoln's plan and it was also the Wade-Davis plan, save that there was no open or expressed recognition of any power or function of Congress except as judging the legality of elections. Johnson did not eventually even admit, as Lincoln apparently had agreed, that Congress was final judge as to whether these states could hold legal elections.

Congress had adjourned before Lee's surrender, and it was widely believed that had Lincoln lived, a special session would have been summoned. The Seward-Johnson compromise proposed not to call Congress. In one way, the decision was shrewd. It gave the administration nine months to carry out its policy, and if the policy was successful, Congress would, when it met, be faced by a *fait accompli,* a nation at peace, a South restored with slavery abolished. What more could the nation want?

On the other hand, the attempt was full of risk. Already the power of the Executive had gone far beyond the dreams of living men. It must be curbed sooner or later. The military dictatorship which had carried on the war must, as soon as possible after the war, be tempered by democracy. The attempt to do even what the nation wanted without this was foolish. An attempt to override the will of the nation was suicidal, and yet that was precisely what Seward and Johnson eventually attempted. May 29, the Declaration of Amnesty was issued; and that same month, Provisional Governors were appointed for North Carolina and Mississippi. In June, Georgia, Texas, Alabama and South Carolina were given Governors, and in July, Florida. Thus, three months after the assassination of Lincoln, Reconstruction was in operation; the Union party divided in opinion; the Northern Democrats encouraged, and the South particularly encouraged.

The South thereupon turned its attention on Johnson and brought to bear a second influence next in power to Seward's and in the end exceeding it. Southern leaders descended upon the President; not simply the former slave barons but new representatives of the poor whites. In less than nine months after the Proclamation of Amnesty, 14,000 prominent persons are said to have received pardons from the President.

No wonder the attitude of Johnson towards the South and the leaders of the rebellion was transformed. The very inferiority complex which made him hate the white planter concealed a secret admiration for his arrogance and address. Carl Schurz was coldly received when he returned from the Southern trip which Johnson had urged upon him.

"Arrived at Washington, I reported myself at once at the White House. The President's private secretary, who seemed surprised to see me, announced me to the President, who sent out word that he was busy. When would it please the President to receive me? The private secretary could not tell, as the President's time was much occupied by urgent business. I left the ante-room, but called again the next morning. The President was still busy. I asked the private secretary to submit to the President that I had returned from a three months' journey made at the President's personal request, that I thought it my duty respectfully to report myself back, and that I should be obliged to the

President if he would let me know whether, and, if so, when, he would receive me to that end. The private secretary went in again and brought out the answer that the President would see me in an hour or so. At the appointed time, I was admitted.

"The President received me without a smile of welcome. His mien was sullen. I said that I had returned from the journey which I had made in obedience to his demand and was ready to give him, in addition to the communications I had already sent him, such further information as was in my possession. A moment's silence followed. Then he inquired about my health. I thanked him for the inquiry and hoped the President's health was good. He said it was. Another pause, which I brought to an end by saying that I wished to supplement the letters I had written to him from the South with an elaborate report giving my experiences and conclusions in a connected shape. The President looked up and said that I need not go to the trouble of writing out such a general report on his account. I replied that it would be no trouble at all, but I considered it a duty. The President did not answer. The silence became awkward and I bowed myself out.

"President Johnson evidently wished to suppress my testimony as to the condition of things in the South. I resolved not to let him do so. I had conscientiously endeavored to see Southern conditions as they were. I had not permitted any political considerations or any preconceived opinions on my part, to obscure my perception and discernment in the slightest degree. I had told the truth as I learned it and understood it, with the severest accuracy, and I thought it due to the country that the truth be known.

"Among my friends in Washington there were different opinions as to how the striking change in President Johnson's attitude had been brought about. Some told me that during the summer the White House had been fairly besieged by Southern men and women of high social standing who had told the President that the only element of trouble in the South consisted in a lot of fanatical abolitionists who excited the Negroes with all sorts of dangerous notions, and that all would be well if he would only restore the Southern State governments as quickly as possible, according to his own plan as laid down in his North Carolina proclamation, and that he was a great man to whom they looked up as their savior. Now it was thought that Mr. Johnson, the plebeian who before the war had been treated with undisguised contempt by the slave-holding aristocracy, could not withstand the subtle flattery of the same aristocracy when they flocked around him as humble suppliants cajoling his vanity." [21]

In fact, personally, Johnson liked the slave-holders. He admired their manners; he enjoyed their carriage and clothes. They were quite naturally his ideal of what a gentleman should be. He could not help being tremendously flattered when they noticed him and actually sued for his favor. As compared with Northerners, he found them free, natural and expansive, rather than cold, formal and hypocritical.

Johnson's change of mind during the last ten days of May, 1865, was probably due to the flatteries of Southern leaders; to the notice taken of his intoxication in the Senate by Sumner and others; to the counsels of Preston King and the Blairs who sheltered him after that unfortunate exhibition; and above all to Seward. Johnson's program swung swiftly into its stride.

Already May 9, the laws of the United States had been put in operation in Virginia and the Alexandria government thus recognized. Johnson recognized the reconstruction already accomplished in Louisiana, Arkansas and Tennessee. So that by mid-summer all the seceded states had been reconstructed under the Johnson plan except Texas. During the autumn, summer and winter of 1865, elections for delegates to constitutional conventions were ordered in Mississippi, Alabama, South Carolina, North Carolina, Georgia and Florida, on the basis of white suffrage. Before Congress met, these conventions had all passed ordinances repealing the secession ordinances, or pronouncing them null and void. All except Mississippi and South Carolina had repudiated the Confederate debt. All had amended their constitutions abolishing slavery or recognizing its disappearance. State officers and representatives in Congress had been elected. Senators had also been chosen, except in Florida. All the states had adopted the Thirteenth Amendment, except Florida and Mississippi; North Carolina had adopted the amendment with reservations; Florida adopted the amendment with reservations December 18, and elected Senators.

Against this suddenly marshaled and quickly executed plan of Johnson and his advisers, there was at the time no organized opposition. Congress was unquestionably determined to have the last word in the matter but not decided as to what the word would be. The Abolitionists wanted the freedom of the slaves guaranteed, and some of them saw Negro suffrage as the only method of accomplishing it, while still fewer recognized that a minimum of land and capital was absolutely necessary even to make the ballot effective. The majority of Northerners simply wanted to get rid of the question as quickly as possible. They were disposed to agree in the main with Johnson, but they were afraid that he was moving too fast, and that the South was returning to the Union without guarantees, either so far as the freedmen were concerned, or with regard to the problem of debt, the tariff, and national finance.

Charles Sumner, representing the abolition-democracy, agitated the question all summer. He brought up the matter on the streets, at dinner, and in society. He wrote his views for the *Atlantic Monthly* and had it and his speeches distributed widely. On June 21, 1865, there was a public meeting in Philadelphia, on Negro suffrage, at which reports were read of reaction in the South. Sumner wrote to the members of Johnson's cabinet and urged them to change their course of action and not to follow the advice of Seward. But, although four members of the cabinet were sympathetic, they took no action, and Sumner wrote to Lieber on August 11: "They were all courtiers, as if they were councilors of the King."

Stevens, Davis and Wade were in despair against an executive who had both military power and the power of patronage and was as yet unmoved by any unity of opinion in the North. Moreover, it did not seem wise to make as yet a fight on the basis of Negro suffrage. Too few Northern people agreed with it. Most public men and journalists gave no support to Sumner's demand for Negro suffrage. The Governor of Indiana denounced it; the Governor of Massachusetts was sure of the President's honesty of purpose; the editor of the New York *Evening Post* advised against any coercive action by Congress in the matter of suffrage, and the New York *Times* stood absolutely against it.

"Is there no way to arrest the insane course of the President in reorganization?" asked Stevens, in the summer of 1865. "If something is not done," wrote Sumner, "the President will be crowned King before Congress meets."

The abolitionists opened a campaign to convert the North to Negro suffrage, carrying on a propaganda with the money of industry and the logic of abolition-democracy. The speeches of Sumner, Kelley, Phillips and Douglass on Negro suffrage were printed and sent broadcast. Stearns wrote: "I am distributing 10,000 copies to anti-slavery men in all the free states; but desiring to increase the number to 100,000 or more, invite you to aid in its circulation." [22] He raised $50,000 in the fall of 1865 to send out 100,000 newspapers and 50,000 pamphlets a week, and himself printed between 20,000 and 40,000 copies of Sumner's Worcester speech, October 12, 1865. Later the Schurz report and his newspaper articles formed strong documents.

Yet the conversion of public opinion in the United States to Negro citizenship and suffrage was long and difficult. There were harassing questions that presented themselves to the majority of people in the North: Could a government, by united and determined effort, raise the Negroes to full American citizenship? Of course it could, if they were men; but were they men? Even if they were men, was it good policy thus to raise a great new working, voting class? On this point there was less open argument; but it lay in the minds of business men, and influenced their outlook and action.

Johnson sensed the trend toward Negro suffrage and taking a leaf from Lincoln's book, sought to stem it. But Johnson's mind was not like Lincoln's. Lincoln moved forward to Negro suffrage; Johnson, alarmed, retreated to it. August 15, he had wired to his nominee, Sharkey, Provisional Governor of Mississippi:

"If you could extend the elective franchise to all persons of color who can read the Constitution of the United States in English and write their names, and to all persons of color who own real estate valued at not less than two hundred and fifty dollars, and pay taxes thereon, you would completely disarm the adversary and set an example the other states will follow. This you can do with perfect safety, and you thus place the Southern States, in reference to free persons of color, upon the same basis with the free States. I hope and trust your convention will do this, and, as a consequence, the Radicals, who are wild upon Negro franchise, will be completely foiled in their attempt to keep the Southern States from renewing their relations to the Union by not accepting their senators and representatives." [23]

Blaine says that this advice was sent to other provisional governors, but nothing came of it, chiefly because Johnson did not insist and his heart was not in the suggestion.

Sumner's words showed that union between Northern industrialists and abolition-democracy had been growing during the summer. After the autumn elections, Sumner sent a long telegram to President Johnson. On the Saturday evening before Congress met, he was with him two hours. He found him "changed in temper and purpose . . . no longer sympathetic, or even kindly," but "harsh, petulant and unreasonable." Near the end of the interview, there was a colloquy, in which the President reminded the Senator of murders in Massachusetts and assaults in Boston as an offset to outrages in the South visited on Negroes and white Union men, under the inspiration of political or race animosity. The two parted that evening not to meet again—the senator leaving "with the painful conviction that the President's whole soul was set as a flint against the good cause, and that by assassination of Abraham Lincoln, the rebellion had vaulted into the Presidential chair." [24]

Meantime, the Massachusetts Republican convention approved Negro suffrage as a condition of Reconstruction, and they were followed by Vermont, Iowa, and Minnesota. The other Republican conventions were not explicit, but the conviction grew in the North that state governments in the South, which would curb the political power of ex-Confederates and insure the freedom of Negroes, could not be established without Negro suffrage.

Sumner led in spreading this opinion, stressing naturally the rights of Negroes. He wrote to Mr. Bright, November 14:

"The President's 'experiment' appears to be breaking down; but at what fearful cost! The Rebels have once more been put on their legs; the freedmen and the Unionists are down. This is very sad. I cannot be otherwise than unhappy as I think of it. Our session is uncertain. Nobody can tell certainly what pressure the President will bring to bear on Congress, and how Congress can stand it. I think that Congress will insist upon time—this will be our first demand, and then generally upon adequate guarantees. There are unpleasant stories from Washington; but we must persevere to the end." [25]

In October, Johnson began openly to argue against Negro suffrage. In an interview with George L. Stearns of Massachusetts, he reminded him that Negro suffrage could not have been argued in the North seven years before and that the South must have time to understand its new position.

"If I interfered with the vote in the rebel states, to dictate that no Negro shall vote, I might do the same for my own purpose in Pennsylvania. Our only safety lies in allowing each state to control the right of voting by its own laws, and we have the power to control the rebel states if they go wrong. . . .

"My position here is different from what it would be if I were in Tennessee. There I should try to introduce Negro suffrage gradually; first, those who had served in the army; those who could read and write; and perhaps a property qualification for others, say $200 or $250. It would not do to let the Negro have universal suffrage now; it would breed a war of races." [26]

He went on to develop this thesis which was a favorite one with him: that Negroes and poor whites naturally hated each other; and that the outrages in the South were chiefly of poor whites on Negroes, and Negroes on poor whites; and if suffrage was given the Negro, he would vote with the master and thus precipitate a race war in the South. That there was truth in this fear, the subsequent history of Reconstruction proved; but it did not turn out as Andrew Johnson anticipated.

Johnson had little knowledge of Negroes; although he had owned a few slaves, he accepted most of the current Southern patterns. He believed that the Negro was lazy and could not survive freedom. He was afraid he might be tempted to lawlessness and insurrection. He spoke to certain colored folk May 11, 1865, according to the Philadelphia Press of May 20, and stated that he had to "deplore the existence of an idea among them that they have nothing to do but to fall back upon the government for support in order that they may be taken care of in idleness and debauchery." October 10, 1865, he talked to the First Colored Regiment of the District of Columbia troops who had recently returned from the South. He congratulated them on serving with patience and endurance and exhorted them to be tranquil and peaceful now that the war was ended:

"Freedom is not a mere idea. . . . Freedom is not simply the principle to live in idleness. Liberty does not mean merely to resort to the low saloons and other places of disreputable character. Freedom and liberty does not mean that people ought to live in licentiousness; but liberty means simply to be industrious and to be virtuous, to be upright in all our deals and relations with men. . . . You must give evidence that you are competent for the rights that the government has guaranteed you. . . .

"The institution of slavery is overthrown. But another part remains to be solved, and that is, can four millions of people, reared as they have been, with all the prejudices of the whites—can they take their places in the community, and be made to work harmoniously and congruously in our system? This is a problem to be considered. Are the digestive powers of the American government sufficient to receive this element in a new shape, and digest it and make it work healthfully upon the system that has incorporated it?"

He then hinted at colonization of the Negro population:

"If it should be so that the two races cannot agree and live in peace and prosperity, and the laws of Providence require that they should be separated—in that event, looking to the far distant future, and trusting in God that it may never come—if it should come, Providence, that works mysteriously, but unerringly and certainly, will point out the way, and the mode, and the manner by which these people are to be separated, and they are to be taken to their land of inheritance and promise, for such a one is before them. Hence we are making the experiment." [27]

Congress met in December, 1865, with the determination to control the reconstruction of the Union. And in this there is no question but that Congress was right. If the nation was going backward to the same status in which it was before the war, it was conceivable that this might be done by executive action. But there were two tremendous changes that made this unthinkable: one was the abolition of slavery, and the other was the new political power which the emancipation of these slaves would confer upon the South. Moreover, there appeared from the South, demanding seats at the opening of Congress, the Vice-President of the Confederacy, four Confederate generals, five Confederate colonels, six Confederate cabinet officers, and fifty-eight Confederate Congressmen, none of whom was able to take the oath of allegiance. "The case of Alex H. Stephens, late Vice-president of the Confederacy, was especially aggravating. Four months before he had been a prisoner at Fort Warren. Pardoned by the President, he waited not a moment to repent and returned to Georgia, was elected to the United States Senate, and was now asking admission—asking to govern the country he had been trying to destroy." [28] Moreover one of the worst of the new black codes was passed in Mississippi in November.

Thaddeus Stevens took immediate lead. He called in caucus twenty or thirty of his followers, December 1; on December 2, the Republican caucus met, and Stevens submitted his plan:

1. To claim the whole question of Reconstruction as the exclusive business of Congress.

2. To regard the steps taken by the President as only provisional.

3. Each House to postpone consideration of the admission of members from Southern states.

4. And that a Joint Committee of Fifteen be appointed to inquire into the condition of the former Confederate states.

Without waiting even for the reception of the President's message, Stevens proposed in the House a resolution for a Joint Committee of Fifteen members of the House and Senate to "inquire into the condition of the states which formed the so-called Confederate States of America, and report whether they or any of them are entitled to be represented in either House of Congress, with leave to report at any time by bill or otherwise; and until such report shall have been made and finally acted upon by Congress, no member shall be received into either House from any of the said so-called Confederate States; and all papers relating to the representation of the said states shall be referred to the said committee without debate." [29]

By vote of 129-35 with 18 not voting, the rules were suspended and this resolution passed. This was the first test of political strength in the new Congress.

The Senate did not take up the matter until December 12. The joint resolution was changed to a concurrent resolution in order to make the approval of the President unnecessary. The section of the resolution concerning the reception of members and reference of all papers was objected to and the resolution was amended so as to direct the committee "to inquire into the condition of the States which formed the so-called Confederate States of America, and report whether they, or any of them, are entitled to be represented in either House of Congress, with leave to report at any time by bill or otherwise." [30]

This amended form the House concurred in, but passed another

House resolution to admit no Southern members, and to refer all motions and papers. Eventually, Stevens had his way, and after Johnson's speech of February 22, the Senate assented to excluding representatives from the South until both Houses agreed.

Industry was uneasy at the Stevens plan. The New York *Herald* claimed it created lack of business confidence North and South. Such a lack of confidence, of course, would hinder economic development in the South, and to that extent limit New York's commercial prosperity. Commerce was especially alarmed lest Thaddeus Stevens should use his machine for carrying out his scheme of confiscation of Southern lands. Such wholesale confiscation, capital could not contemplate. Local harmony, law and order, the development of the vast industrial resources of the South, seemed wisest in New York.

Johnson, in his message of December 4, began an extraordinary series of state papers which he could never have written all by himself.

"Johnson's state papers, including vetoes, were uniformly in good temper, conservative, historical and well considered. In the preparation of them he made use of every person on whom he could lay his hands. Bancroft wrote the first message to Congress; Jerre Black, the hero of *Ex Parte Milligan*, wrote the Reconstruction veto; Seward, the precise scholar, supervised much that the President wrote; Stanton, the practical lawyer, wrote the bill to admit North Carolina and other states into the Union in 1865; the Attorney-General, Welles, Secretary of the Navy, and other members of the cabinet he frequently used." [31]

In his first message, he forecast the adoption of the Thirteenth Amendment, which, in fact, occurred December 18th. He explained that because of this anticipated abolition of slavery, he had proceeded to begin reorganization of the states and admission to their full rights in the Union. He knew that this policy was attended with some risk but the risk must be taken:

"The relations of the General Government towards the four millions of inhabitants whom the war has called into freedom has engaged my most serious consideration. On the propriety of attempting to make the freedmen electors by the proclamation of the Executive, I took for my counsel the Constitution itself, the interpretation of that instrument by its authors and their contemporaries, and recent legislation by Congress. When, at the first movement towards independence, the Congress of the United States instructed the several States to institute governments of their own, they left each State to decide for itself the conditions for the enjoyment of the elective franchise. . . . Moreover, a concession of the elective franchise to the freedmen, by act of the President of the United States, must have been extended to all colored men, wherever found, and so must have established a change of suffrage in the Northern, Middle, and Western States, not less than in the Southern and Southwestern. Such an act would have created a new class of voters, and would have been an assumption of power by the President which nothing in the Constitution or laws of the United States would have warranted.

"On the other hand, every danger of conflict is avoided when the settlement of the question is referred to the several States. They can, each for itself, decide on the measure, and whether it is to be adopted at once and absolutely, or introduced gradually and with conditions. In my judgment, the freedmen, if they show patience and manly virtues, will sooner obtain a participation in the elective franchise through the States than through the General Government, even if it had power to intervene. When the tumult of emotions that have been raised by the suddenness of the social change shall have subsided, it may prove that they will receive the kindliest usage from some of those on whom they have heretofore most closely depended.

"But while I have no doubt that now, after the close of the war, it is not competent for the General Government to extend the elective franchise in the several States, it is equally clear that good faith requires the security of the freedmen in their liberty and in their property, their right to labor, and their right to claim the just return of their labor. I cannot too strongly urge a dispassionate treatment of this subject, which should be carefully kept aloof from all party strife. We must equally avoid hasty assumptions of any natural impossibility for the two races to live side by side, in a state of mutual benefit and good will. The experiment involves us in no inconsistency; let us, then, go on and make that experiment in good faith, and not be too easily disheartened. The country is in need of labor, and the freedmen are in need of work, culture, and protection."

And then came a characteristic turn of thought: "While their right of voluntary migration and expatriation is not to be questioned, I would not advise their forced removal and colonization."

Here President Johnson was clearly envisaging the extinction or voluntary removal of four million laborers in the South, and the settlement of the problem of their presence in the United States by replacing them with white labor. On the other hand, he seemed anxious to have them protected in their present new status and it was understood, both from the message and from other sources, that the President was in favor of continuing the Freedmen's Bureau.

The temper of Congress was firm. What should be done in Reconstruction was a matter for deliberation, thought and care. It could not be settled by the Southern leaders who brought on the crisis, working alone in conjunction with the President and his cabinet. On the other hand, what the nation wanted was by no means clear. There was among its millions no one mind. There was among its various groups no unanimity.

The mind of Thaddeus Stevens evolved a course of action. This plan was to set up at least temporarily a cabinet form of responsible government in the United States: to put in power a camarilla of representatives of the various sections, groups and parties, who, by deliberation and inquiry, would find out what action could command a majority in the House and in the Senate. This in itself was the beginning of a momentous change in our government, a change unfortunately never carried completely through; and the failure to carry it through has hampered the United States government ever since.

The original idea of the Congress was a small, deliberative assembly in two Houses which should think and argue matters through, and then have their decisions enforced by the Executive, and coördinated and clarified by a Supreme Court. But Congress grew to unwieldy size; the Executive grew in prestige and power, until during the Civil War, he became a dictator, while the Supreme Court was destined to assume powers which would at times threaten to stop the progress of the nation, almost without appeal.

Moreover, the contingency of an Executive, who far from being the servant of a congressional majority was antagonistic and even a contradictory source of authority and action, never occurred to the fathers. They did not intend to have the President a mere mouthpiece of Congress, and, for this reason, they gave him the *message* and the *veto;* but on the other hand, they never conceived that he should be in himself both executive and lawgiver and yet this he practically was during and after the Civil War; he exemplified at the time of Andrew Johnson a new and extraordinary situation in which the President of the United States in vital particulars was opposed to the overwhelming majority of the party in Congress which had elected him, and refused in effect to do their will.

This had to be remedied, and for this, the Committee of Fifteen, on the motion of Thaddeus Stevens, came into being in the 39th Congress. It was government on the English parliamentary model with two modifications: it was responsible to two Houses instead of to one, which enormously delayed and complicated its functioning; and it contained representatives of the opposition party—although this representation was often nullified through caucuses and sub-committees.

It was the business of the Committee of Fifteen to see how the government of the United States was to be changed after the war, from its form before the war; and this involved, first, some change in the basis of popular representation; secondly, a clarification of the status of the Negro; and finally it brought a modification of the relation of the national government to state government, not simply in civil rights but even more in industry and labor. It was through the first and second that the majority, which eventually dominated the 39th Congress, gained its moral power. It was through the third that the moral power was implemented.

Stevens was too astute a politician to stress first the moral foundation of his argument. In his first speech, as leader of the 39th Congress, he placed his main argument on representation, because he knew that that would appeal to the men sitting in front of him, and representing national wealth and industry.

In December, 1865, when the Thirteenth Amendment was adopted, a curious result followed: twenty-nine Representatives were added to the South. Since the adoption of the Constitution, the basis of congressional representation had been the free population, including free Negroes and three-fifths of the slaves. Stevens said that with this basis of representation unchanged, "The eighty-three Southern members, with the Democrats, that will in the best times be elected from the North, will always give them a majority in Congress and in the Electoral College. They will at the very first election take possession of the White House and the halls of Congress. I need not depict the ruin that would follow. Assumption of the rebel debt or repudiation of the Federal debt would be sure to follow. The oppression of the freedmen; the reamendment of their State constitutions, and the reëstablishment of slavery would be the inevitable result. That they would scorn and disregard their present constitutions, forced upon them in the midst of martial law, would be both natural and just. No one who has any regard for freedom of elections can look upon those governments, forced upon them in duress, with any favor."

This was the cogent, clear argument of Thaddeus Stevens, the politician. But Thaddeus Stevens was never a mere politician. He cared nothing for constitutional subtleties nor even for political power. He was a stern believer in democracy, both in politics and in industry, and he made his second argument turn on the economic freedom of the slave.

"We have turned, or are about to turn, loose four million slaves without a hut to shelter them or a cent in their pockets. The infernal laws of slavery have prevented them from acquiring an education, understanding the commonest laws of contract, or of managing the ordinary business life. This Congress is bound to provide for them until they can take care of themselves. If we do not furnish them with homesteads, and hedge them around with protective laws; if we leave them to the legislation of their late masters, we had better have left them in bondage."

He then resolutely went further in a defense of pure democracy, although he knew that in this argument he was venturing far beyond the practical beliefs of his auditors:

"Governor Perry of South Carolina and other provisional governors and orators proclaim that 'this is the white man's government.' . . . Demagogues of all parties, even some high in authority, gravely shout, 'this is the white man's government.' What is implied by this? That one race of men are to have the exclusive rights forever to rule this nation, and to exercise all acts of sovereignty, while all other races and nations and colors are to be their subjects, and have no voice in making the laws and choosing the rulers by whom they are to be governed. . . .

"Our fathers repudiated the whole doctrine of the legal superiority of families or races, and proclaimed the equality of men before the law. Upon that they created a revolution and built the Republic. They were prevented by slavery from perfecting the superstructure whose foundation they had thus broadly laid. For the sake of the Union they consented to wait, but never relinquished the idea of its final completion.

"The time to which they looked forward with anxiety has come. It is our duty to complete their work. If this Republic is not now made to stand on their great principles, it has no honest foundation, and the Father of all men will still shake it to its center. If we have not yet been sufficiently scourged for our national sin to teach us to do justice to all God's creatures, without distinction of race or color, we must expect the still more heavy vengeance of an offended Father. . . .

"This is not a white man's Government, in the exclusive sense in which it is used. To say so is political blasphemy, for it violates the fundamental principles of our gospel of liberty. This is Man's Government, the Government of all men alike; not that all men will have equal power and sway within it. Accidental circumstances, natural and acquired endowment and ability, will vary their fortunes. But equal rights to all the privileges of the Government is innate in every immortal being, no matter what the shape or color of the tabernacle which it inhabits. . . .

"Sir, this doctrine of a white man's Government is as atrocious as the infamous sentiment that damned the late Chief Justice to everlasting fame; and, I fear, to everlasting fire." [32]

The ensuing debate in the House and Senate flamed over all creation, but it started with a note of moral triumph. The newly elected Speaker declared: "The fires of civil war have broken every fetter in the land and proved the funeral pyre of slavery." The chaplain of the Senate increased this moral afflatus with religious fervor, thankful that "the statue of Freedom now looks down from our capital upon an entire nation of free men, and that we are permitted by the dispensation of Thy Providence, and the way being prepared, to give liberty to the captive, the opening of the prison to them that are bound, and to proclaim the acceptable year of our God."

The chaplain of the House said: "O God, we stand today on the soil of a nation which is, not alone by inference or report, but by the solemn announcement of the constituted authorities, declared free in every part and parcel of its territory. Blessed be Thy name, O God, for Thy wonderful ending of this terrible conflict!"

Congressional amendments of every sort poured into Congress concerning the national and Confederate debt, the civil rights of freedmen, the establishment of republican government, the basis of representation, payment for slaves and the future powers of Federal government and the states. Argument swirled in a maelstrom of logic. No matter where it started, and how far afield in legal metaphysics it strayed, always it returned and had to return to two focal points: Shall the South be rewarded for unsuccessful secession by increased political power; ånd: Can the freed Negro be a part of American democracy?

Thither all argument again and again returned; but it tried desperately to crowd out these real points by appealing to higher constitutional metaphysics. This constitutional argument was astonishing. Around and around it went in dizzy, silly dialectics. Here were grown, sensible men arguing about a written form of government adopted ninety years before, when men did not believe that slavery could outlive their generation in this country, or that civil war could possibly be its result; when no man foresaw the Industrial Revolution or the rise of the Cotton Kingdom; and yet now, with incantation and abracadabra, the leaders of a nation tried to peer back into the magic crystal, and out of a bit of paper called the Constitution, find eternal and immutable law laid down for their guidance forever and ever, Amen!

They knew perfectly well that no such omniscient law existed or ever had existed. Yet, in order to conceal the fact, they twisted and distorted and argued: these states are dead; but states can never die. These states have gone out of the Union; but states can never go out of the Union, and to prevent this we fought and won a war; but while we were fighting, these states were certainly not in the Union, else why did we fight? And how now may they come back? They are already back because they were never really out. Then what were we fighting for? For union. But we had union and we have got union, only these constituent states are dead and we must bring them to life. But states never die. Then they have forfeited statehood and become territories. But statehood cannot be forfeited; conspirators within the states interfered, and now the interference has stopped. But as long as the interference lasted, there was surely no union. Oh, yes, only it did not function; we need not now provide for its functioning again, for the Constitution already provides for that.

Where was the Constitution during the war? But the war is ended; and now the Constitution prevails; unless the Constitution prevails, this is no nation, there is no President; we have no real Congress, since it does not represent the nation. But who represented the nation during the war? And by that token, who saved the nation and killed slavery? Shall the nation that saved the nation now surrender its power to rebels who fought to preserve slavery? There are no rebels! The South is loyal and slavery is dead. How can the loyalty of the South be guaranteed, and has the black slave been made really free? Freedom is a matter of state right. So was secession. Must we fight that battle over again? Yes, if you try to make monkeys equal to men. What caused the war but your own insistence that men were at once monkeys and real estate? Gentlemen, gentlemen, and fellow Americans, let us have peace! But what is peace? Is it slavery of all poor men, and increased political power for the slaveholders? Do you want to wreak vengeance on the conquered and the unfortunate? Do you want to reward rebellion by increased power to rebels?

And so on, around and around, and up and down, day after day, week after week, with only here and there a keen, straight mind to cut the cobwebs and to say in effect with Seward through Johnson: Damn the Nigger; let us settle down to work and trade! Or to declare with Stevens and Sumner: Make the slaves free with land, education and the ballot, and then let the South return to its place. Or to say with Blaine and Conkling and Bingham, not in words but in action: Guard property and industry; when their position is impregnable, let the South return; we will then hold it with black votes, until we capture it with white capital.

After all this blather, the nation and its Congress found itself back to the two plain problems: The basis of representation in Congress and the status of the Negro. When it came to the Negro, the old dogmatism leaped to the fore and would not down. Chandler of New York regarded Farnsworth's demand for Negro equality as not only an attack on foreigners but "an insult to white citizens." When the Constitution said "people," it meant "white people." And he stood for "the purity of the white race." Fink declared that Ohio would never let Negroes vote with his consent. This is "and of right ought to be a white man's government," said Boyer of Pennsylvania, and he declared that eighteen of the twenty-five states now represented in Congress would not let the Negro vote.

Yet the argument for freedom and democracy loomed high and clear. "Slavery, but a short time ago received as a God-given condition of men, has fallen under the banner of a purer morality, and come down with the curses of a Christian world. With the fall of slavery must also fall the things pertaining thereto. The master who yesterday had his heel upon the neck of his slave, today meets that slave upon the level of common equality. . . . The Negro should be carefully considered in this question of Reconstruction, for after all we are our brother's keeper and we must see that even-handed justice is meted out to the black man if possible."

Woodbridge of Vermont declared: "New social and political relations have been established. Four million people have been born in a day. The shackles have been stricken from four million chattels, and they have become in an hour living, thinking, moving, responsible beings, and citizens of these United States. And if Congress does not do something to provide for these people, if they do not prove equal to their duty, and come up to their work like men, the condition of the people will be worse than before."

The South represented by the Border States had to confine itself to constitutional metaphysics, or else blurt out, as some of its spokesmen did, a new defense of the old slavery. The West, on the other hand, had a real and disturbing argument and it was voiced by Voorhees in his dramatic attempt to drive a wedge between Johnson and the Republicans. He said, January 6, 1866:

"How long can the inequalities of our present revenue system be borne? How long will the poor and laborious pay tribute to the rich and the idle? We have two great interests in this country, one of which has prostrated the other. The past four years of suffering and war has been the opportune harvest of the manufacturer. The looms and machine shops of New England and the iron furnaces of Pennsylvania have been more prolific of wealth to their owners than the most dazzling gold mines of the earth. . . .

"They are the results of class legislation, of a monopoly of trade established by law. It may be said that they indicate prosperity. Most certainly they do; but it is the prosperity of one who obtains the property of his neighbor without any equivalent in return. The present law of tariff is being rapidly understood. It is no longer a deception, but rather a well-defined and clearly-recognized outrage. The agricultural labor of the land is driven to the counters of the most gigantic monopoly ever before sanctioned by law. From its exorbitant demands there is no escape. The European manufacturer is forbidden our ports of trade for fear he might sell his goods at cheaper rates and thus relieve the burden of the consumer. We have declared by law that there is but one market in which our citizens shall go to make their purchases, and we have left it to the owners of the markets to fix their own prices." [33]

This was another unanswerable argument. But, having made it, what was Voorhees' remedy? His logical remedy would have been to unite the industrial democracy of the West with the abolition-democracy of the East in order to fight oligarchy in Northern industry and the attempt to reëstablish agricultural oligarchy in the South. Yet this was farthest from his intention. His immediate effort was to embarrass and split the Republicans by forcing them to endorse or repudiate their own President and leader; his ultimate program, if he had one, was to seek with Andrew Johnson to restore oligarchy in the South with a dominant planter class and serfdom for the emancipated Negroes. This was unthinkable, and it deprived the radical West of all moral sympathy and voting power which its economic revolt deserved.

What was it the nation wanted? Charles Sumner told the nation what it ought to want, but there was no doubt but that it did not yet want this. Thaddeus Stevens knew what the nation ought to want, but as a practical politician his business was to see how much of this he could get enacted into actual law.

There came before the 39th Congress some 140 different proposals to change the Constitution of the United States, including 45 on apportionment, 31 on civil and political rights, and 13 forbidding payment for slaves. Over half of these affected the status of the freedmen. Before the Committee of Fifteen could sift these and settle to its larger task of fixing the future basis of representation and the degree of national guardianship which Negro freedmen called for, there seemed to be two measures upon which public opinion in the North was so far crystallized that legislation might safely be attempted. These were: a permanent Freedmen's Bureau, and a bill to protect the civil rights of Negroes. On the first day of business of the 39th Congress, there were introduced into the Senate two bills on these subjects.

The Civil Rights Bill was taken up December 13, but Sherman of Ohio reminded the Senate that there was scarcely a state in the Union that did not make distinctions on account of color, and wished, therefore, to postpone action until the Thirteenth Amendment had been adopted. Saulsbury of Maryland called it "an insane effort to elevate the African race to the dignity of the white race," and claimed that the Thirteenth Amendment would carry no such power as Sherman assumed.

Trumbull of Illinois, on the contrary, declared that the second section of the Thirteenth Amendment as reported by his committee was drawn "for the very purpose of conferring upon Congress authority to see that the first section was carried out in good faith, and for none other; and I hold that under that second section Congress will have the authority, when the constitutional amendment is adopted, not only to pass the bill of the Senator from Massachusetts, but a bill that will be much more efficient to protect the freedman in his rights. We may, if deemed advisable, continue the Freedmen's Bureau, clothe it with additional powers, and if necessary back it up with a military force, to see that the rights of the men made free by the first clause of the constitutional amendment are protected. And, sir, when the constitutional amendment shall have been adopted, if the information from the South be that the men whose liberties are secured by it are deprived of the privilege to go and come when they please, to buy and sell when they please, to make contracts and enforce contracts, I give notice that, if no one else does, I shall introduce a bill and urge its passage through Congress that will secure to those men every one of these rights: they would not be freemen without them." [34]

Congress asked the President for the specific facts concerning the situation in the South. The President replied with the report of General Grant, containing the superficial results of a hasty, five-day trip, and disingenuously tried to suppress the report of Carl Schurz, undoubtedly the most thorough-going and careful inquiry into the situation just after the war that had been made. Sumner expressed his indignation and the evident need of a civil rights bill.

"When I think of what occurred yesterday in this Chamber; when I call to mind the attempt to whitewash the unhappy condition of the rebel States, and to throw the mantle of official oblivion over sickening and heart-rending outrages, where Human Rights are sacrificed and rebel Barbarism receives a new letter of license, I feel that I ought to speak of nothing else. I stood here years ago, in the days of Kansas, when a small community was surrendered to the machinations of slavemasters. I now stand here again, when, alas! an immense region, with millions of people, has been surrendered to the machinations of slavemasters. Sir, it is the duty of Congress to stress this fatal fury. Congress must dare to be brave; it must dare to be just." [35]

He claimed that the Civil Rights Bill aimed "simply to carry out and maintain the Proclamation of Emancipation, by which this republic is solemnly pledged to *maintain* the emancipated slave in his freedom. Such is our pledge: 'and the Executive Government of the United States, including the military and naval authority thereof, will recognize and *maintain the freedom of such persons.*' This pledge is without any limitation in space or time. It is as extended and as immortal as the Republic itself. Does anybody call it vain words? I trust not. To that pledge we are solemnly bound. Wherever our flag floats as long as time endures we must see that it is sacredly observed.

"But the performance of that pledge cannot be entrusted to another; least of all, can it be entrusted to the old slave-masters, embittered against their slaves. It must be performed by the National Government. The power that gave freedom must see that this freedom is maintained. This is according to reason. It is also according to the examples of history. In the British West Indies we find this teaching. Three of England's greatest orators and statesmen, Burke, Canning, and Brougham, at successive periods, united in declaring, from the experience in the British West Indies, that whatever the slave-masters undertook to do for their slaves was always 'arrant trifling,' and that, whatever might be its plausible form, it always wanted 'the executive principle.' More recently the Emperor of Russia, when ordering Emancipation, declared that all efforts of his predecessors in this direction had failed because they had been left to 'the spontaneous initiative of the proprietors.' I might say much more on this head but this is enough. I assume that no such blunder will be made on our part; that we shall not leave to the old proprietors the maintenance of that freedom to which we are pledged, and thus break our own promises and sacrifice a race."

But Congress was not yet ready for this high ground and Sumner's scheme was widely criticized. Whitelaw Reid, in a letter to the Cincinnati *Gazette,* March 3, 1868, recalled the profound surprise and bitterness of feeling with which Sumner's remarks were received by Senators. Republican journals and leaders within the inner circles of the party were hostile.[36]

The Republicans were, especially, afraid of any split with the President lest this bring the Democrats into power; Forney of the Philadelphia *Press* begged Sumner to yield for the sake of harmony within the great political army in which he had been "a conscientious and courageous leader."

Protests against President Johnson's policy were therefore slow in expression. The nation was weary of war and objected to military administration in the South. Capitalists wanted pacification of the Southern territory to open a market closed for four years. They wanted any method which would bring the quickest results. Moreover, Republicans held some of the largest states of the North by narrow majorities. Any unpopular step might put the Democrats in power. Office-holders did not want to break with Johnson and candidates for office were timid.

Congress made in effect the first overture to the South and instead of forcing civil and possibly political rights, turned to take up the bill which proposed government guardianship and tutelage for the blacks. The Civil Rights Bill was postponed and the Freedmen's Bureau Bill, which Johnson's message seemed to accept, was substituted. This was introduced as an amendment to the act of March 3, 1865, and contained the following propositions: (1) That the bureau should continue in force until abolished by law; (2) That it should embrace the whole country wherever there were freedmen and refugees; (3) That bureau officials should have annual salaries of $500 to $1,200; (4) That the President should set apart for the use of freedmen and loyal refugees unoccupied lands in the South, to be allotted in parcels not exceeding forty acres each; (5) That the titles granted in pursuance of General Sherman's orders of January 16, 1865, be made valid; (6) That the commissioner procure land and erect suitable buildings as asylums and schools for dependent freedmen and refugees; (7) That it be the duty of the President to extend military protection and jurisdiction over all cases where any of the civil rights or immunities belonging to white persons, including the rights to make and enforce contracts, to give evidence, to inherit, buy, sell and hold property, etc., are refused or denied by local law, prejudice on account of race, color or previous condition of servitude; or where different punishments or penalties are inflicted than are prescribed for white persons committing like offenses; (8) That it be made a misdemeanor, punishable by a fine of $1,000 or imprisonment for one year or both, for anyone depriving another of the above rights on account of race, color or previous condition of servitude. These last sections were to apply to those states or districts where ordinary judicial proceedings had been interfered with by war.[87]

The bill was opposed as establishing a permanent bureau instead of a war-time emergency institution. Its great power was criticized and it was declared that its expense would be enormous. There were special objections to the validation of land titles under Sherman's orders and to the section on civil rights. It was defended as being not necessarily permanent; as in accordance with our Indian policy; and as not being expensive, since it was manned by army officers. It passed the Senate in January, 1866, by a vote of 37-10.

In the House, Thaddeus Stevens tried to strengthen the bill by the most thorough-going provisions for government guardianship yet proposed. These provisions directed that food, clothes, medical atten-

tion and transportation be furnished white refugees and black freedmen and their families; that public land be set aside in Florida, Mississippi, Alabama, Louisiana and Arkansas, and also from forfeited
estates, to the extent of three million acres of good land; and that
this should be parceled out to loyal white refugees and black freedmen at a rental not to exceed ten cents an acre; and that at the end
of a certain period this land be sold to the applicants at a price not
to exceed two dollars an acre. The occupants of land, under Sherman's
order, were confirmed in their possession, unless the former owner
proved his title, and in that case, other land at the rate of forty acres
a farm should be given to the applicant. The bureau was to erect buildings for asylums and schools, and provide a common school education
for all white refugees and freedmen who applied. This thorough-
going substitute unhappily was lost.

The bill which finally passed the House, February 6, extended the
power of the Freedmen's Bureau to freedmen throughout the whole
United States and provided for food and clothing for the destitute, a
distribution of public lands among freedmen and white refugees in
parcels not exceeding forty acres each at a nominal rent and with an
eventual chance of purchasing. The land assigned by Sherman was
to be held for three years and then, if restored, other lands secured
by rent or purchase. School buildings and asylums were to be erected
when Congress appropriated the money. Full civil rights were to be
enforced, and punishment was provided for those thwarting the civil
rights of Negroes.

This bill encountered strong opposition, especially from the Border
States. Saulsbury of Delaware deliberately reiterated his contention
that Congress had no right to abolish slavery, even if three-fourths
of the states assented! With minor changes the bill was accepted by
the Senate, February 9, and thus the first great measure of Reconstruction went to the President. Southern slavery had now been definitely abolished by constitutional amendment, and government guardianship of the Negro with land and court protection was assured by a
permanent Freedmen's Bureau.

What was the answer of the South to this? Where were Southern
brains and leadership? Why did so many hide, like Toombs? Why
did the South have to trust its guidance to a half-educated, poor white
President and a New York corporation lawyer? Suppose a Southern
leader had appeared at that time and had said frankly: "We propose
to make the Negro actually free in his right to work, his legal status,
and his personal safety. We are going to allow him to get, on easy
terms, homesteads, so as gradually to replace the plantation system
with peasant proprietors; and we are going to provide him and our

poor whites with elementary schools. And when in time, he is able to read and write and accumulate a minimum of property, then, and not until then, he can cast a vote and be represented in Congress."

What was there so wild and revolutionary, so unthinkable, about a manly declaration of this sort? But a native of Alabama knew that this attitude was entirely lacking: "I do not think that Congress should wait for the people of the South to make regulations by which, at some future time, the Negroes will be provided with homes, have their rights as freemen acknowledged, be given a participation in civil rights, and be made a part of the framework of the country. They will not do that; you need not wait for it. If Congress can constitutionally commence a system of educating and elevating the Negroes, let them do it, and not wait for the people of the South to do it." [38]

It is nonsense to say that the South knew nothing about the capabilities of the Negro race. Southerners knew Negroes far better than Northerners. There was not a single Negro slave owner who did not know dozens of Negroes just as capable of learning and efficiency as the mass of poor white people around and about, and some quite as capable as the average slaveholder. They had continually in the course of the history of slavery recognized such men. Here and there teachers and preachers to white folks as well as colored folks had arisen. Artisans and even artists had been recognized. Some of these colored folks were blood relatives of the white slaveholders: brothers and sisters, sons and daughters. They had sometimes been given land, transported to the North or to Europe, freed and encouraged.

Of course, the Southerners believed such persons to be exceptional, but all that was asked of them at this time was to recognize the possibility of exceptions. To such a reasonable offer the nation could and would have responded. It could have paid for the Negro's land and education. It could have contributed to relief and restoration of the South. Instead of that came a determination to reëstablish slavery, murder, arson and flogging; a dogmatic opposition to Negro education and decent legal status; determination to have political power based on voteless Negroes, and no vote to any Negro under any circumstances.

This showed the utter absence of common sense in the leadership of the South. Their attitude was expressed best, however, not by a Southerner but by William H. Seward, and it came in the shape of a veto to the Freedmen's Bureau Bill. If this veto had applied to a civil rights bill or to a bill providing for Negro suffrage, it would have been much more logical; but to veto a bill for the guardianship of Negroes, even though that bill carried and had to carry a defense of civil rights, was reactionary to the last degree. The veto was a shrewd document, as was every argument written by that master of subtle logic. The President was made to say:

"I share with Congress the strongest desire to secure to the freedmen the full enjoyment of their freedom and property and their entire independence and equality in making contracts for their labor." But he objected to the bill because it was "unconstitutional"; because the bureau was permanent; because it did for the colored people what had never been done for white people; because it confiscated land, and because its cost would be prodigious. It was unconstitutional, because it extended jurisdiction all over the United States, and gave the Bureau judicial power in that jurisdiction. It was made permanent in spite of the fact that slavery had been abolished. Conceive a President, born a poor white laborer, saying:

"Congress has never felt itself authorized to spend public money for renting homes for white people honestly toiling day and night, and it was never intended that freedmen should be fed, clothed, educated and sheltered by the United States. The idea upon which slaves were assisted to freedom was that they become a self-sustaining population."

The bureau, he said, would be costly. During war times, we had already spent $5,876,272 for the relief of Negroes, and $2,047,297 for the relief of whites. For 1866, the present bureau needed $11,745,000. Now we are planning to spend money for land and education which will double this sum. The bill proposes to take away land from former owners without due process of law. Finally, comes this extraordinary economic philosophy for serfs:

"Undoubtedly, the freedman should be protected, but he should be protected by the civil authorities, especially by the exercise of all constitutional powers of the courts of the United States and of the states." His condition is not so bad. His labor is in demand, and he can change his dwelling place if one community or state does not please him. The laws that regulate supply and demand will regulate his wages. The freedmen can protect themselves, and being free, they could be self-sustaining, capable of selecting their own employment, insisting on proper wages, and establishing and maintaining their own asylums and schools.

"It is earnestly hoped that, instead of wasting away, they will, by their own efforts, establish for themselves a condition of responsibility and prosperity. It is certain that they can attain that condition only through their own merits and exertions."

This was the answer of Andrew Johnson and William H. Seward to the Freedmen's Bureau Bill. Practically, it said that the Negroes do not need protection. They are free. Let them go to work, earn wages, and support their own schools. Their civil rights and political rights must depend entirely upon their former masters, and the United States has no constitutional authority to interfere to help them. As Stevens said later, the President himself favored confiscation of Southern land for the poor when he was "clothed and in his right mind." [39]

It was an astonishing pronouncement. It was the American Assumption, of the possibility of labor's achieving wealth, applied with a vengeance to landless slaves under caste conditions. The very strength of its logic was the weakness of its common sense.

Yet, Andrew Johnson was the President of the United States. He was the leader of the Republican party which had just won the war. He declared in the face of an astounding array of testimony to the contrary, that the South was peaceful and loyal, and the slaves really free. Congress did not believe the President or agree with him, but some were not yet prepared to break with him. Six Republicans deserted their party and voted to uphold the veto. The result was that by a vote of 30-18, the attempt to over-ride the President's veto failed. The rift made in the Republican party was wide. On the one side stood abolition-democracy in curious alliance with triumphant Northern industry, both united in self-defense against Johnson and the South. This Northern unity, Johnson and Seward intended to disrupt, and did so in part when the veto of the Freedmen's Bureau Bill was sustained. Seward followed this by an appeal for the quick resumption of peace and industry, and Johnson made an appeal to labor unrest and Western radicals. But here again, there was no natural union and this Seward knew. His defense, therefore, of Johnson's plan was intended to soothe both industry and abolition without stressing radicalism.

Washington's Birthday had been fixed upon by the President's friends for a grand demonstration. The New York Aldermen endorsed the President's "conservative, liberal, enlightened, and Christian policy," with "one hundred guns salute on February 21 and one hundred on February 22." Johnson was declared "greater than 'Old Hickory.'" "He was on the highest pinnacle of the mount of fame"; "his feet were planted on the Constitution of his country"; "he was a modern edition of Andrew Jackson bound in calf." "Indeed, it was said by the Radicals in reply to the Democratic fireworks that 'more powder was burned in honor of the veto by the Copperheads than they consumed during the four years of war.'" [40]

Seward said at Cooper Union:

"This, I think, is the difference between the President, who is a man of nerve, in the Executive chair at Washington, and the nervous men who are in the House of Representatives. Both have got the Union restored not with slavery, but without it; not with secession, flagrant or latent, but without it; not with compromise, but without it; not with disloyal states, or representatives, but with loyal states and representatives; not with Rebel debts, but without them; not with exemption from our own debts for suppressing the rebellion, but with equal liabilities upon the Rebels and the loyal men; not with freedmen and refugees abandoned to suffering and persecution, but with freedmen employed in productive, self-sustaining industry, with refugees under the protection of law and order. The man of nerve sees that it has come out right at last, and he accepts the situation.

"He does not forget that in this troublesome world of ours, the most to be secured by anybody is to have things come out right. Nobody can ever expect to have them brought out altogether in his own way. The nervous men, on the other hand, hesitate, delay, debate and agonize—not because it has not come out right, but because they have not individually had their own way in bringing it to a happy termination."

As to the Freedmen's Bureau Bill, he said: "I have not given prominence in these remarks to the conflict of opinion between the President and Congress in reference to the bureau for the Relief of Freedmen and Refugees. That conflict is, in its consequences, comparatively unimportant; it would excite little interest and produce little division if it stood alone. It is because it has become the occasion for revealing the difference that I have already described that it has attained the importance which seems to surround it."

He proceeded to point out that the present Freedmen's Bureau Bill had not expired and might not expire for another year and that, therefore, during the next year Congress might still prolong its existence. "Ought the President of the United States to be denounced in the house of his friends, for refusing in the absence of any necessity, to occupy or retain, and to exercise power greater than those which are exercised by any imperial magistrate in the world? Judge ye! I trust that this fault of declining imperial powers, too hastily tendered by a too confiding Congress, may be forgiven by a generous people." [41]

This was an adroit defense, but Johnson could not let well enough alone. He was deprived of his mentor and assuming his vivid rôle of stump speaker, possibly with a few stimulants, he felt called upon this same Washington's Birthday to reply to a committee which had waited upon him with resolutions. He was speaking after the Fourteenth Amendment in its first form had been reported to the House of Representatives and sent back to the Committee of Fifteen. With that as well as the vetoed Freedmen's Bureau Bill and the pending Civil Rights Bill in mind, he recited again his services to the Union during the war; he reminded his auditors that when rebellion manifested itself in the South, he stood by the government. He was for the Union with slavery; he was for the Union without slavery. In either alternative, he was for the government and the Constitution. Then he went on with the classic argument:

"You have been struggling for four years to put down a rebellion. You contended at the beginning of that struggle that a state had not a right to go out. . . . And when you determine by the executive, by the military and by the public judgment, that these States cannot have any right to go out, this committee turns around and assumes that they are out, and that they shall not come in. . . . I say that when the states that attempted to secede comply with the Constitution, and give sufficient evidence of loyalty, I shall extend to them the right hand of fellowship, and let peace and union be restored. I am opposed to the Davises, and Toombses, the Slidells, and the long list of such. But when I perceive, on the other hand, men . . . still opposed to the Union, I am free to say to you that I am still with the people. . . . Suppose I should name to you those whom I look upon as being opposed to the fundamental principles of this Government, and now laboring to destroy them. I say Thaddeus Stevens of Pennsylvania; I say Charles Sumner of Massachusetts; I say Wendell Phillips of Massachusetts."

Finally, Johnson became melodramatic: "Are they not satisfied with one martyr? Does not the blood of Lincoln appease the vengeance and wrath of the opponents of this Government? Is their thirst still unslaked? Do they want more blood? Have they not honor and courage enough to effect the removal of the Presidential obstacle otherwise than through the hands of the assassin? I am not afraid of assassins," etc., etc.[42]

Small wonder that the New York *Tribune* and the Philadelphia *Press* reported that Johnson was drunk when he made his speech; but the main cause of his drunkenness was not necessarily whiskey, it was constitutional inability to understand men and movements. This was not time to straddle on the slavery question; that question has been settled. The crucial question now was, what will the South do when it comes back to Congress; what will it do to Negroes, and even more important in the minds of many, what will it do to the new industry? The latter question struck deepest, but the former voiced itself loudest.

"The masses of the loyal people must be as agreed to arise against this veto of a measure, intended as a bulwark against slavery and treason, as they were on the night when the flag of the Union was first hauled down from Fort Sumter," said the Chicago *Tribune*.[43]

Congress immediately hit back with a concurrent resolution not to admit Southern Congressmen to either House until the status of the Southern states was settled. This had passed the House of Representatives after dilatory tactics February 20, but was not considered in the Senate until February 23, after Johnson's speech. It was passed after debate March 2, and thus Stevens' original resolution of December 4 was finally confirmed.

Here evidently there was small ground for compromise. Either Johnson must bow to the will of the majority of his party in Congress, or, led by him, the South would be in the saddle in 1866. Many who had criticized Sumner in December, now were on his side.

The President and the South, on the other hand, were greatly encouraged: despite the majority which the Republicans had in Congress, they could not override a Presidential veto; with the reaction that Johnson and the South expected at the next election, the Republicans would lose power and the South, united with Northern and Western Democracy, would rule. The Southerners resumed their drive to complete their black codes and their program of reducing the Negro to a servile caste.

The President, drunk with his new feeling of power, showed his entire misapprehension of the nature of the forces working against him. Congress girded itself for battle, not mainly because the virtual reënslavement of the Negro aroused them, but because this was the symptom of a reassertion of power on the part of the South which might affect the debt, the tariff and the national banking system.

The President and his supporters were going to insist upon the full political power of the South, unhampered by a Freedmen's Bureau or by Negro civil rights. Had it not been for the presence of the Negro, this attitude of the South could not have arisen. Never before in modern history has a conquered people treated their conqueror with such consummate arrogance. The South hid behind the darkness of the colored men and thumbed their noses at the nation.

For the Negro, Andrew Johnson did less than nothing, when once he realized that the chief beneficiary of labor and economic reform in the South would be freedmen. His inability to picture Negroes as men made him oppose efforts to give them land; oppose national efforts to educate them; and above all things, oppose their rights to vote. He even went so far as to change plans which he had thought out and announced before he faced the Negro problem. He once said that representation ought to be based on voters; but no sooner did he learn that Thaddeus Stevens advocated the same thing, than he became dumb on the subject, and had no advice to offer. He had advocated the confiscation of the land of the rich Southerners and penalties on wealth gained through slavery. When he realized that Negroes would be beneficiaries of any such action, he said not another word. He was a thick-and-thin advocate of universal suffrage in the hands of the laborer and common man, until he realized that some people actually thought that Negroes were men. He opposed monopoly on the New Jersey railroads, until Charles Sumner joined him.

The Civil Rights Bill which was taken up next made Negroes citizens of the United States and punished any person who deprived them of civil rights under any state law: "They shall have the same right in every State and Territory in the United States to make and enforce contracts; to sue, be parties and give evidence; to inherit, purchase, lease, sell, hold, and convey real and personal property; and to full and equal benefit of all laws and proceedings for the security of person and property as is enjoyed by the white citizens, and shall be subject to like punishment, pains, and penalties, and to none other, any law, statute, ordinance, regulation, or custom, to the contrary notwithstanding."

It gave to the District Courts of the United States jurisdiction in crimes and offenses against the act, gave the power of arrest to United States marshals and District Attorneys, and provided fines and penalties.

David Bingham, of Ohio, brought up a difficulty. He reminded Congress that the first eight amendments to the Constitution could not be enforced by the Federal Government since they were held to be limitations upon the Federal power, and that, therefore, the power to punish offenses against life, liberty and property was one of the reserved powers of the state. He, therefore, suggested a constitutional amendment which would punish all violations of the bill of rights by state officers. He reminded the House that even when property had been taken by the states without due process of the law, there was no remedy in the Federal Courts, and that this had been affirmed in a recent case in Maryland. His proposal went to the Committee of Fifteen.

The Civil Rights Bill passed the Senate, was amended in the House, and was agreed to by both Houses, March 14, 1866. The debate on the Civil Rights Bill and the Freedmen's Bureau Bill made it clear that the emancipation of the slaves meant increased representation in Congress and in the Electoral College, whenever the Southern states were readmitted, and that this increase in power would take place whether the Negroes were enfranchised or not.

Moreover, the Civil Rights Act might be repealed; the United States might be made to pay all or a part of the Confederate debt, and Congress might repudiate the debt. The debate, therefore, on the Civil Rights Bill made the necessity of a constitutional amendment clear.

On March 27, President Johnson vetoed the Civil Rights Bill with curious logic. He feared that under this bill Chinese, Indians and Gypsies, as well as Negroes, might be made citizens. He declared that a citizen of the United States would not necessarily be a citizen of a state. He again questioned whether it was good policy to act on citizenship of Negroes, since eleven of the thirty-six states were unrepresented.

"Four million of them have just emerged from slavery into freedom. Can it be reasonably supposed that they possess the requisite qualifications to entitle them to all the privileges and equalities of citizens of the United States?"

One wonders what Andrew Johnson expected the Negroes to be. They were not to be citizens; they were not to be voters; and yet he repeatedly assured them that they were free. He went on with another strange argument, declaring that the bill discriminated "against large numbers of intelligent, worthy and patriotic foreigners, and in favor of the Negro, to whom, after long years of bondage, the avenues of freedom and opportunity have just now been suddenly opened." Thus, he thought Negroes less familiar with the character of American institutions than foreigners. And yet foreigners must wait "five years" for naturalization and be "of good moral character."

He said that if Congress could give the equal civil rights enumerated to Negroes, it could also give them the right to vote and the right to hold office. He objected to state officers being liable to arrest for discriminating against Negroes. He objected to the interference of Congress with the judiciary, and assuming jurisdiction of subjects which had always been treated by state courts.

Again, he returned to his astonishing economics:

"The white race and the black race of the South have hitherto lived together under the relation of master and slave—capital owning labor. Now, suddenly, that relation is changed, and, as to ownership, capital and labor are divorced. They stand now each master of itself. In this new relation, one being necessary to the other, there will be a new adjustment, which both are deeply interested in making harmonious. Each has equal power in settling the terms, and, if left to the laws that regulate capital and labor, it is confidently believed that they will satisfactorily work out the problem. Capital, it is true, has more intelligence, but labor is never so ignorant as not to understand its own interests, not to know its own value, and not to see that capital must pay that value.

"This bill frustrates this adjustment. It intervenes between capital and labor, and attempts to settle questions of political economy through the agency of numerous officials, whose interest it will be to foment discord between the two races; for as the breach widens their employment will continue, and when it is closed their occupation will terminate."

He declared that this law establishes "for the security of the colored race safeguards which go infinitely beyond any that the General Government have ever provided for the white race," and, therefore, discriminates against the white race.

He declared the bill a step toward concentrating all legislative power in the national government. "A perfect equality of the white and colored races is attempted to be fixed by Federal law in every State of the Union, over the vast field of state jurisdiction covered by the enumerated rights. In no one of these can any State ever exercise any power of discrimination between the different races."

He then fetched up his heavy artillery of "Social Equality" to stampede the prejudiced.

"In the exercise of State policy over matters exclusively affecting the people of each State, it has frequently been thought expedient to discriminate between the two races. By the statutes of some of the States, Northern as well as Southern, it is enacted, for instance, that white persons shall not intermarry with a Negro or a mulatto." While he did not believe that this particular bill would annul state laws in regard to marriage, nevertheless, if Congress had the power to provide that there should be no discrimination in the matters enumerated in the bill, then it could pass a law repealing the laws of the states in regard to marriage!

He continued: "Hitherto, every subject embraced in the enumeration of rights contained in this bill has been considered as exclusively belonging to the States. They all relate to the internal police and economy of the respective States. . . . If it be granted that Congress can repeal all State laws discriminating between whites and blacks in the subjects covered by this bill, why, it may be asked, may not Congress repeal, in the same way, all state laws discriminating between the two races, on the subject of suffrage and office?"

Speaking of the general effect of the bill, he declared it interfered "with the municipal legislation of the states, with the relations existing exclusively between a State and its citizens, or between inhabitants of the same State—an absorption and assumption of power by the General Government which, if acquiesced in, must sap and destroy our federative system of limited powers, and break down the barriers which preserve the rights of the States. It is another step, or rather stride, toward centralization, and the concentration of all legislative powers in the national government."

The President's veto of the Civil Rights Bill offended the nation. Senator Stewart declared that the President had promised not to veto this bill and for that reason the Senator had voted to sustain the veto of the Freedmen's Bureau Bill. Senator Trumbull had publicly announced that the President would not veto the Civil Rights Bill. Henry Ward Beecher had urged him to sign it.

Even in the President's cabinet, none of the members, except Seward and Wells, agreed with Johnson. Sumner wrote: "Nobody can yet see the end. Congress will not yield. The President is angry and brutal. Seward is the marplot. In the cabinet, on the question of the last veto, there were four against it to three for it; so even there, among his immediate advisers, the President is left in a minority. Stanton reviewed at length the bill, section by section, in the Cabinet, and pronounced it an excellent and safe bill every way from beginning to end. But the veto message was already prepared, and an hour later was sent to Congress." [44]

The time for the final test between Johnson and Congress had come. There ensued some sharp political maneuvering. Morgan, Wiley and Stewart were won over to the majority and Stockton, a Johnson man from New Jersey, was unseated on a technicality. Thus on April 6 and 9 Congress overrode the veto. The Civil Rights Bill became law, and Johnson faced a Congress able to work its will.

There was one other matter, besides amending the Constitution, on which Congress might take significant action. According to the current American creed, full protection of a citizen could only be accomplished by possession of the right to vote. This was not wholly true, even in the North, and with the ballot in the hands of white men. Nevertheless, it still retained a great element of truth, for only with universal suffrage could the mass of workers begin that economic revolution which would eventually emancipate them. They would have to use their ballot at first in conjunction with the petty bourgeois; that is, in conjunction with the small property holder, who was being hard-pressed by the new concentrated capital of industry; in conjunction with the small Western farmer, who was pushed to the wall by the railway and land monopoly. But armed with the ballot, this preliminary fight against the power of capital would clear the way for the final fight which would make democracy real among the workers.

While the Committee of Fifteen was groping its way to action, there was a chance for Congress to express its real feeling on the ballot. There might be a question in the minds of constitutional hair-splitters as to how far Congress could coerce states in defining the right of suffrage. But Congress ruled directly the District of Columbia. Congress had the right to decide as to the political franchise in territories. Would it not be the first step toward a logical and consistent end for Congress to establish Negro suffrage in the District, and in all territories which were set up? Thus, among the first bills introduced in the 39th Congress were bills to give the Negro the right to vote in the District of Columbia, and this demand was supported by petitions and speeches, and especially well-written petitions from the educated Negroes of the District.

In January, 1866, there came a notable petition from the colored people signed by John F. Cook, a wealthy octoroon of a free Negro family, and twenty-five other citizens. It did not come from freedmen or laborers, but from property holders of Negro descent, many of whom had been born free. Kelley of Pennsylvania read it in part to the House:

"We are intelligent enough to be industrious, to have accumulated property, to build and sustain churches and institutions of learning. We are and have been educating our children without the aid of any school fund, and until recently had for many years been furnishing, unjustly as we deem, a portion of the means for the education of the white children of the District.

"We are intelligent enough to be amenable to the same laws and punishable alike with others for the infraction of said laws. We sustain as fair a character on the records of crime and statistics of pauperism as any other class in the community, while unequal laws are continually barring our way in the effort to reach and possess ourselves of the blessings attendant upon a life of industry and self-denial and of virtuous citizenship.

"Experience likewise teaches that that debasement is most humane which is most complete. The possession of only a partial liberty makes us more keenly sensible of the injustice of withholding those other rights which belong to a perfect manhood. Without the right of suffrage, we are without protection, and liable to combinations of outrage. Petty officers of the law, respecting the source of power, will naturally defer to the one having a vote, and the partiality thus shown will work much to the disadvantage of the colored citizens." [45]

However, there were some special reasons for avoiding this ticklish subject. After all, Washington was the capital of the nation. It had long been a center of Southern society. To give the Negroes political freedom and partial control there, was a long step and a decisive one.

The people of the District hastily organized a counter-stroke, and presented to the Senate a communication from the Mayor in which he asserted that a special vote had been taken December 21, "to ascertain the opinion of the people of Washington on the question of Negro suffrage." He meant, of course, the white people, and the vote was overwhelming: 6,591 against Negro suffrage and 35 for it. The communication proceeded, in a fine climax of Southern rhetoric, to say that "This unparalleled unanimity of sentiment which pervades all classes of this community in opposition to the extension of the right of suffrage to that class, engenders an earnest hope that Congress, in according to this expression of their wishes the respect and consideration they would as individual members yield to those whom they immediately represent, would abstain from the exercise of its absolute power, and so avert an impending future apparently so objectionable to those over whom, by the fundamental law of the land, they have exclusive jurisdiction."

A long argument ensued, which showed that Congress was not ready to declare itself on Negro suffrage; further action was postponed for another year, and a bill for Negro suffrage in the District of Columbia did not pass Congress until December, 1866; it became a law in January, 1867.

Meantime, the Committee of Fifteen had met first December 26, 1865. Charles Sumner was considered too radical on the Negro question to be a member of it, and so the committee was headed by a Conservative, Fessenden of Maine, who wished to stand by President Johnson, and was strongly, sometimes even bitterly, opposed to the radicalism of Sumner. Stevens, the great protagonist of curbing the political power of the South and completely emancipating the Negro, was the prime figure in the committee. Then, there were Bingham of Ohio, the more or less conscious defender of property; Conkling of New York, the sophisticated, exquisite corporation lawyer; and Boutwell of Massachusetts. There were three Democrats, of whom the most distinguished was Johnson of Maryland, the strongest Border State representative in Congress, handicapped by a legal mind; and the narrow-minded Rogers of New Jersey.

A sub-committee of the Committee of Fifteen courteously waited on President Johnson, and he consented to do nothing more toward Reconstruction for the present, in order to secure harmony of action. On December 26, at the first meeting of the Committee, Stevens brought forward his proposal to base representation on voters. And singularly enough, later in this same month, Johnson in an interview with Senator Dixon of Connecticut said that if, however, amendments are to be made to the Constitution, changing the basis of representation and taxation (and he did not deem them at all necessary to the present time), he knew of none better than a simple proposition, embraced in a few lines, making in each state the number of qualified voters the basis of representation, and the value of property the basis of direct taxation. Such a proposition could be embraced in the following terms:

"'Representatives shall be apportioned among the several states which may be included within this Union according to the number of qualified voters in each state.' . . .

"Such amendment, the President also suggested, would remove from Congress all issues in reference to the political equality of the races. It would leave the States to determine absolutely the qualifications of their own voters with regard to color; and thus the number of Representatives to which they would be entitled in Congress would depend upon the number upon whom they conferred the right of suffrage.

"The President, in this connection, expressed the opinion that the agitation of the Negro franchise question in the District of Columbia at this time was a mere entering-wedge to the agitation of the question throughout the States, and was ill-timed, uncalled-for, and calculated to do great harm. He believed that it would engender enmity, contention and strife between the two races, and lead to a war between them, which would result in great injury to both, and the certain extermination of the Negro population. Precedence, he thought, should be given to more important and urgent matters, legislation upon which was essential to the restoration of the Union, the peace of the country, and the prosperity of the people." [46]

Here, surely, was logic and understanding in plain sight. But not only did the President eventually drop this proposal, but even in committee, opposition appeared. Boutwell suggested at the third meeting of the Committee, January 9, that he preferred to retain population as the basis of apportionment, with the provision that no state should make "any distinctions in the exercise of the elective franchise on account of race or color." Boutwell was from Massachusetts, and New England, through Blaine, had protested vigorously against the Stevens proposition in the House the day before, January 8. It was a curious situation, which Blaine explained in part; and in part, he did not.

New England had lost a good proportion of its male population by migration to the West, and it did not allow women to vote. New England, moreover, had a large immigrant population which she was using in her mills, and on which a part of her representation in Congress was based. She proposed to make this population still larger. She proposed, also, to reduce the voting power of this laboring population, not only by confining the vote to the native-born and naturalized, but also by a literacy qualification. Through Blaine, therefore, spoke the exploiting manufacturer, and voiced an idea as different from Sumner's as one could well imagine. To base population on voters was, in the eyes of industry, to keep down the representation of the South, to be sure; but also to transfer the balance of political power from the East to the West, and in the West industry was not so sure of its dictatorship. Consequently, the Committee of Fifteen was compelled to take steps in another direction.

On January 12, Bingham introduced a proposal to the committee for a constitutional amendment guaranteeing civil rights. It said: "The Congress shall have the power to make all laws necessary and proper to secure to all persons in every state within this Union, equal protection in their rights of life, liberty and property." [47] This proposition, destined to become part of Section 1 of the Fourteenth Amendment, had been introduced early in December in the House of Representatives.

The Committee of Fifteen referred the Bingham proposal to a sub-committee, consisting wholly of Republicans. At the same time, the committee insisted that the basis of representation provided for in the Constitution should be changed. Johnson of Maryland adhered to the Stevens proposal of making voters the basis. New England and New York objected, and this matter was left to the consideration of the same sub-committee. Meantime, three other propositions were submitted:

1. Representation should be based on population, but if colored people were disfranchised, they should not be counted in the apportionment. (Morill.)

2. Representatives should be apportioned according to population, except that Negroes, Indians, Chinese and other colored persons, if they were not allowed to vote, should not be counted in the apportionment. (Williams.)

3. Representatives were to be apportioned among the states according to the whole number of citizens of the United States; provided that whenever in any State, civil or political rights or privileges should be denied or abridged, on account of race or color, all persons of such race or color should be excluded from the basis of representation or taxation. (Conkling.)

On January 16, a proposed Fourteenth Amendment was considered in two parts; the first part had alternative propositions:

A. Apportioning representation according to the number of citizens and making "inoperative and void" any laws "whereby any distinction is made in political or civil rights or privileges on account of race, creed or color."

B. The alternative proposition was the Conkling proposal.

The second part of the amendment was Bingham's proposal that:

"Congress shall have power to make all laws necessary and proper to secure to all citizens of the United States the same equal protection in the enjoyment of life, liberty and property."

These propositions went to sub-committees and were reported back

January 20. The Civil Rights section of Bingham appeared in the strongest and most specific form which it ever took: "Congress shall have power to make all laws necessary and proper to secure to all citizens of the United States, in every State, the same political rights and privileges; and to all persons in every State equal protection in the enjoyment of life, liberty and property."

It was voted 10-4 to consider this proposition of Bingham's separately; and by a vote of 11-3, the second resolution on apportionment was chosen as a proposed Fourteenth Amendment. This excluded from representation Negroes who were denied the right to vote. Stevens wished to amend this by declaring who were citizens. Conkling, however, moved to strike out the phrase "citizens of the United States," and insert "persons in every state, excluding Indians not taxed." This was a move to insure the counting of the foreign-born as a part of the basis of apportionment, and was in accordance with the New England idea. Stevens, Fessenden and Bingham were against it, but it passed 11-3.

On January 22, this section on apportionment was reported to Congress as a Fourteenth Amendment, and was the first effort of the Committee of Fifteen to prepare for Reconstruction by constitutional amendment. This was before the Freedmen's Bureau Bill or the Civil Rights Bill had passed Congress, and the bill for suffrage in the District of Columbia, while it had passed the House, had not been considered in the Senate, and was not destined to be for several months. This fact is a sufficient answer to the accusation that the Committee of Fifteen purposely delayed action on the problems of Reconstruction. Within less than a month after it began work, it laid its first proposition before Congress.

Stevens reported this first form of the Fourteenth Amendment to the House and asked rather peremptorily that it pass before sundown. His reason was that there were numbers of state legislatures in session and that they could consider it immediately. But he was disappointed. There was too much opposition in his own group. Conkling elaborated and made specific the argument which Stevens had first brought forward:

The four million people who had suddenly been released from slavery, while falling within the category of "free persons," were not yet political persons. "This emancipated multitude has no political *status*. Emancipation vitalizes only natural rights, not political rights. Enfranchisement alone carries with it political rights, and these emancipated millions are no more enfranchised now than when they were slaves. They never had political power. Their masters had a fraction of power as masters." But since the relationship of master and slave was destroyed, this fraction of power could no longer survive in the masters. There was only one place where it could logically go, and that was to the Negroes; but since it was said that "they are unfit to have it . . . it is a power astray, without a rightful owner. It should be resumed by the whole nation at once. . . . If a black man counts at all now, he counts as five-fifths of a man, not as three-fifths. . . . Four millions, therefore, and not three-fifths of four millions, are to be reckoned in here now," and in eleven states most of these four millions were presumed to be "unfit for political existence." Since the framers of the Constitution did not foresee such contingency, and expected that emancipation would come gradually and be accompanied by education and enfranchisement, they provided for no situation whereby eleven states might claim twenty-eight (or twenty-nine) representatives besides their just proportion.

"Twenty-eight votes to be cast here and in the Electoral College for those held not fit to sit as jurors, not fit to testify in the court, not fit to be plaintiff in a suit, not fit to approach the ballot box. Twenty-eight votes, to be more or less controlled by those who once betrayed the Government, and for those so destitute, we are assured, of intelligent instinct as not to be fit for free agency.

"Shall this be? Shall four million beings count four million, in managing the affairs of the nation, who are pronounced by their fellow beings unfit to participate in administering government in the states where they live . . . who are pronounced unworthy of the least and most paltry part in the political affairs? Shall one hundred and twenty-seven thousand white people in New York cast but one vote in this House and have but one voice here, while the same number of white people in Mississippi have three votes and three voices? Shall the death of slavery add two fifths to the entire power which slavery had when slavery was living? Shall one white man have as much share in the Government as three other white men merely because he lives where blacks out-number whites two to one? Shall this inequality exist, and exist only in favor of those . . . who did the foulest and guiltiest act which crimsons the annals of recorded time? No, sir; not if I can help it.

"This proposition," he continued, "rests upon a principle already imbedded in the Constitution, and as old as free government itself," a principle "that representation does not belong to those who have no political existence, but to those who have. The object of the amendment is to enforce this truth. . . . Every State will be left free to extend or withhold the elective franchise on such terms as it pleases, and this without losing anything in representation if the terms are impartial as to all. . . ." If, however, there is found "a race so vile or worthless that to belong to it is alone cause of exclusion from political action, the race is not to be counted here in the Congress." [48]

Thus spoke New York in cold contrast to Thaddeus Stevens but with quite as merciless logic. This argument made it clear that the basis of representation must be changed in some way, unless the South was coming back with increased political power. What change should be made? The West wanted Stevens' original proposition which had early been introduced in Congress by Stevens himself and also separately by two Ohio representatives, and which based representation on voters; but this proposition would have increased the power of the Middle and Western states at the expense of New England, and New England had had her warning from Voorhees. While, then, a majority of Republicans undoubtedly favored this, the proposition could not pass Congress without the support of New England, and the West yielded.

Eliot of Massachusetts submitted an amendment, which was practically the Fifteenth Amendment, but it was agreed that this could not pass Congress. And so, finally, the report was sent back to the Committee of Fifteen.

Meantime, on January 22, the Bingham Amendment on Civil Rights was considered in the Committee of Fifteen and referred to a sub-committee, after Boutwell had tried to make its wording milder, by saying that "Congress shall have power to abolish any distinction in the exercise of the elective franchise."

On January 27, this section was reported from the sub-committee with modifications, and appeared now in the following words: "Congress shall have power to make all laws which shall be necessary and proper to secure to all persons in every state full protection in the enjoyment of life, liberty and property; and to all citizens of the United States the same immunities and also equal political rights and privileges."

It was postponed; Bingham explained in 1871 that, after postponement, he had introduced this section of the amendment in the Committee of Fifteen in the words in which it now stands in the Constitution. He had changed the form in the hope that the amendment might be so framed that "in all the hereafter it might be accepted by the historian of the American Constitution like Magna Charta as the keystone of American legislation." The decision of Marshall *vs.* the City Council of Baltimore, a celebrated case, had induced him to take counsel with Marshall. Thus, curiously enough, constitutional restraints designated to protect persons were changed into a form which eventually made the Federal Government the protector of property against state enactments:

"The Congress shall have power to make all laws which shall be necessary and proper to secure to the citizens of every state all privileges and immunities of citizens in the several states." [49]

This substitute, which Bingham reported to the committee February 3, was adopted in the Committee of Fifteen and on February 10, by a vote of 9-5, it was referred to Congress. It came up before the House of Representatives, February 13, as a proposed constitutional amendment and was debated at length February 27-28, when the House refused to table it, but postponed it until April.

When the Committee of Fifteen received the amendment on apportionment back from the House, it made the minor change of taking out the reference to direct taxes, which was irrelevant and of little importance. So that, again, January 31, the proposition came back to the House of Representatives.

Stevens was unequivocal:

"I do not want them [the Southern states] to have representation— I say it plainly—I do not want them to have the right of suffrage before this Congress has done the great work of regenerating the Constitution and laws of this country according to the principles of the Declaration of Independence." [50] Again, Schenck of Ohio tried to base representation on voters, but this was defeated. Stevens said that he favored it, but that it could not pass Congress. The House passed this form of the Fourteenth Amendment, January 3, 1866, and sent it to the Senate.

In the meantime, the whole aspect of the political situation changed. The Freedmen's Bureau Bill had passed Congress, and, to the astonishment of the country, had been vetoed. The Civil Rights Bill had passed the Senate, and Johnson had made his speech of February 22, definitely aligning himself now with the South and their Northern Democratic allies, and against his own party. Black Codes had been passed in Mississippi, Alabama, South Carolina, Florida, Virginia and Louisiana.

On the other hand, Northern business was afraid.

"Viewed as a practical matter," asked the *Nation*, "what would be the effect upon Government securities of the immediate admission to Congress of 58 Southern Representatives and 22 Senators, nearly all of whom could be counted on as determined repudiationists? . . . It would hardly be a safe thing for the national credit to have such a body of men in Congress, reënforced as they would probably be, by a considerable number of Northern men ready to go for at least qualified repudiation." [51]

Seward, himself, it is said, was greatly disappointed and embarrassed by the Black Codes of the South. He found that the South was getting stronger in Johnson's confidence. Nemesis again dogged Seward's steps, as when before he was defeated for the Presidential nomination by the anti-slavery men to whom he had given a slogan. It was then that Toombs had sneered: "Actæon had been devoured by his dogs." The dogs were at it again. Blaine says that, "When Congress reassembled after the holidays, there was a great change in its attitude. Many feared that the President and the Democrats together would win.

"The leading commercial men, who had become weary of war, contemplated with positive dread the reopening of a controversy which might prove as disturbing to the business of the country as the struggle of arms had been, and without the quickening impulses to trade which active war always imparts. The bankers of the great cities, whose capital and whose deposits all rested upon the credit of the country and were invested in its paper, believed that the speedy settlement of all dissension, and the harmonious coöperation of all departments of the government, were needed to maintain the financial honor of the nation and to reinstate confidence among the people. Against obstacles so menacing, against resistance so ominous, against an array of power so imposing, it seemed to be an act of boundless temerity to challenge the President to a contest, to array public opinion against him, to denounce him, to deride him, to defy him." [52]

The Committee of Fifteen paused to get its bearings. In the first place, what was the attitude of the country toward Negro suffrage? In 1865, Wisconsin had rejected a proposal to let Negroes vote. Minnesota, the same year, had defeated a constitutional amendment giving Negroes the suffrage. Connecticut, also, in 1865 gave a majority of 6,272 against Negro suffrage. Later, in 1867, Ohio defeated Negro suffrage by 50,629. In Michigan, 1868, a new Constitution, omitting the word "white," was defeated by a majority of 38,849. In the Nebraska Constitution of 1866, only whites were allowed the suffrage. In New York and some other states, there was special legislation on the voting of Negroes, which was not changed. Evidently, the country was not ready for Negro suffrage.

Moreover, the pinch of economic difficulties following the war, was beginning to be felt. The price of gold which was at 170 in 1864, rose to 284 in 1865. The income tax had been increased in 1865. The United States was paying out vast sums of interest on its annual debt. Cotton was high, selling at forty-three cents a pound in 1865; it dropped to thirty cents only in 1866, with a crop of 1,900,000 bales, as compared with that marvelous crop that precipitated the Civil War, 5,740,000 bales in 1861. The price of agricultural products had increased, but not nearly as much as the prices of manufactured goods, and the farmers were feeling the difference. Gambling and speculation were wide-spread.

The United States Treasury was trying to reduce the circulation of the depreciated greenbacks, and under the Act of 1866, retired some $75,000,000; but early in 1868, the contraction of the currency was prohibited and the West began to cry for inflation. A Western editor wrote Senator Trumbull of Illinois: "You all in Washington must remember that the excitement of the great contest is dying out, and that commercial and industrial enterprises and pursuits are engaging a large part of public attention. The times are hard; money is close; taxes are heavy; all forms of industry here in the West are heavily burdened; and in the struggle to pay debts and live, people are more mindful of themselves than of any of the fine philanthropic schemes that look to making Sambo a voter, juror and office holder." [53]

Johnson knew nothing of finance, and left the Treasury entirely to McCulloch, who was struggling, October 31, 1865, with a national debt that stood at $2,800,000,000. There was still doubt of the legal tender constitutionality of the greenbacks. Taxation was enormous and applied to almost every available subject. There faced the country a tremendous problem of reorganizing the debt, reëstablishing the currency and reducing the revenue.

Stevens had rushed the Committee of Fifteen as fast as or faster than his majority wished. The first draft of the Fourteenth Amendment reached the Senate and was attacked by Charles Sumner. There was no greater proof of his courage, and his learning and keenness of mind were unquestioned. From the day of his great speech on Kansas to his unswerving advocacy of civil rights for Negroes and their political enfranchisement, he towered above his contemporaries. He was unwilling to compromise like Stevens, and for that reason was not made head of the great Committee of Fifteen. But there was no question about his integrity and his idealism.

Sumner had no sympathy with an amendment which made the disfranchisement of Negroes possible and regarded it as "another compromise with human rights" and a discrimination on account of race and color which hitherto had been kept out of the Constitution. Thus the first proposition which Northern industry made, met the direct opposition of abolition-democracy. Charles Sumner, in a tremendous speech February 6, 1865, laid down the thesis that under no circumstances should it be possible to disfranchise a man simply on account of race or color; that here for the first time we had a chance to realize the democracy which the fathers of the Republic foresaw, and he spoke prophetic words on future disfranchisement.

"I am not insensible to the responsibility which I assume in setting myself against a proposition already adopted in the other House, and having the recommendation of a committee to which the country looks with such just expectations, and to which, let me say, I look with so much trust. But after careful reflection, I do not feel that I can do otherwise. . . .

"There are among us, four millions of citizens now robbed of all share in the government of their country, while at the same time they are taxed according to their means, directly and indirectly, for the support of the Government. Nobody can question this statement. And this bare-faced tyranny of taxation without representation it is now proposed to recognize as not inconsistent with fundamental right and the guarantee of a republican government. Instead of blasting it you go forward to embrace it as an element of political power.

"If, by this, you expect to induce the recent slave-master to confer the right of suffrage without distinction of color, you will find the proposition a delusion and a snare. He will do no such thing. Even the bribe you offer will not tempt him. If, on the other hand, you expect to accomplish a reduction of his political power, it is more than doubtful if you will succeed, while the means you employ are unworthy of our country.

"There are tricks and evasions possible, and the cunning slave-master will drive his coach and six through your amendment stuffed with all his representatives. Should he cheat you in this matter, it will only be a proper return for the endeavor on your part to circumvent him at the expense of fellow-citizens to whom you are bound by every obligation of public faith." [54]

Seldom has a great political prophecy been so strikingly fulfilled!

Stevens in the House had, by his diplomacy, ranged back of his policy the industrial leaders of the North who feared that a return of the South would mean attack upon the tariff, the national banks, the debt, and the whole new post-war economic structure. Sumner in the Senate, on the other hand, took little account of the political game. He set his strategy on the high ground of democracy, and democracy for all men, and it was his opposition that killed the first draft of the Fourteenth Amendment which permitted the disfranchisement of Negroes on penalty of reduced representation. Stevens with infinite pains had gotten this much through the Committee of Fifteen and the House of Representatives. Sumner spoke his convictions despite the desertion of friends and party. Senator Williams of Oregon expressed admiration, but could not follow him. "The echoes of his lofty and majestic periods will linger and repeat themselves among the corridors of history."

There was wide discussion throughout the country. Garrison was converted, and to him Sumner's speech seemed unanswerable. To Whittier, it was irresistible; Phillips' voice was filled with enthusiasm, while Henry Ward Beecher said that the speech rose far above the occasion, "covering a ground which will abide after all contemporary questions of special legislation have passed away."

The proposed amendment went down to defeat on March 9, receiving only 25 votes against 22, instead of the necessary two-thirds majority. Sumner's wide influence, while it did not command the full sympathy of Republicans or Democrats, nevertheless, was enough to block compromise between Northern industry and the abolition-democracy. Fessenden was bitter and Stevens furious. No man demanded more for Negroes than Stevens, or was more thoroughly an advocate of complete democracy. But, as he said, "The control of republics depends on the number, not the quality, of the voters. This is not a government of saints. It has a large sprinkling of sinners."

As the head of the Committee of Fifteen, he was trying to get a proposition for which a two-thirds majority of Congress would vote, and start the country as far on the road towards democracy and abolition of caste as was possible under the circumstances. He complained that his proposition had "been slaughtered by a puerile and pedantic criticism."

Andrew Johnson was deeply incensed by Sumner's speech and sneered at it next day. "I am free to say to you that I do not like to be arraigned by someone who can get up handsomely-rounded periods and deal in rhetoric, and talk about abstract ideas of liberty, who never periled life, liberty, or property. This kind of theoretical, hollow, unpractical friendship amounts to but very little."

He was receiving a group of Negroes who were trying by direct appeal either to get his sympathy or to probe his animus against the race. The Freedmen's Bureau Bill had passed, but Johnson had not yet indicated what action he would take. The Civil Rights Bill and the first draft of the Fourteenth Amendment were before the Senate. Perhaps the delegation hoped to influence him.

Douglass had seen Johnson on inauguration day in 1865 when President Lincoln had pointed Douglass out to him. "The first expression which came to his face, and which I think was the true index of his heart, was one of bitter contempt and aversion. Seeing that I observed him, he tried to assume a more friendly appearance, but it was too late." [55]

In the interview with President Johnson, February 7, 1866, there were present George T. Downing of Rhode Island, William E. Mathews of New York, John Jones of Philadelphia, John F. Cook of Washington, Joseph E. Otis, A. W. Ross, William Whipper, John M. Brown, Alexander Dunlap, Frederick Douglass and his son Lewis.

"What was said on the occasion brought the whole question virtually before the American people. Until that interview the country was not fully aware of the intentions and policy of President Johnson on the subject of reconstruction, especially in respect to the newly emancipated class of the South. After having heard the brief addresses made by him to Mr. Downing and myself, he occupied at least three quarters of an hour in what seemed a set speech, and refused to listen to any reply on our part, although solicited to grant a few moments for that purpose." [56]

The President shook hands with the colored men and then George T. Downing, a leading Negro from Newport, Rhode Island, opened the discussion. He said to the President: "We desire for you to know that we come feeling that we are friends meeting a friend." He said that they represented colored people from the "States of Illinois, Wisconsin, Alabama, Mississippi, Florida, South Carolina, North Carolina, Virginia, Maryland, Pennsylvania, New York, the New England states, and the District of Columbia." They were not satisfied with an amendment prohibiting slavery but wanted it enforced by appropriate legislation.

"We are Americans, native-born Americans; we are citizens. . . . We see no recognition of color or race in the organic law of the land. . . . It has been shown in the present war that the government may justly reach its strong arm into the States and demand from those who owe it allegiance, their assistance and support. May it not reach out a like arm to secure and protect its subjects upon whom it has a claim?"

Then Frederick Douglass came forward and said: "Your noble and humane predecessor placed in our hands the sword to assist in saving the nation, and we do hope that you, his able successor, will favorably regard the placing in our hands, the ballot with which to save ourselves."

The President was evidently embarrassed and floundered. He was not going to make a speech; he had jeopardized life, liberty and property, not only for the colored people, but for the great mass of people. He was a friend of the colored man, but "I do not want to adopt a policy that I believe will end in a contest between races, which if persisted in will result in the extermination of one or the other."

He remembered his speech to Nashville Negroes before the election and repeated his willingness to be a "Moses to lead him from bondage to freedom," but not into a war of races. He said that one can talk about the ballot-box and justice and Declaration of Independence, but "suppose by some magic touch you can say to everyone, 'You shall vote tomorrow.' How much would that ameliorate their condition at this time?"

Then the President approached Douglass and said, "Now let us get closer up to this subject." He said he opposed slavery because it was a monopoly and gave profit and power to an aristocracy. By getting clear of the monopoly, they had abolished slavery.

Douglass started to interrupt, but the President was not through. He went on to show the position of the poor white in relation to the slave owners, and how the slaves despised the poor whites. Douglass denied this personally, but the President insisted that anyway, most colored people did, and this made the poor white man opposed both to the slave and his master; and that, therefore, there was enmity between the colored man and the poor white. Already the colored man had gained his freedom during the war, and if he and the poor white came into competition at the ballot-box, a "war of races" would result.

· Moreover, was it proper to put on a people, without their consent, Negro suffrage? "Do you deny that first great principle of the right of the people to govern themselves?" Here Downing interrupted. "Apply what you have said, Mr. President, to South Carolina, for instance, where a majority of the inhabitants are colored." The President twisted uncomfortably and said that the matter to which he referred "comes up when a government is undergoing a fundamental change" and he preferred to instance Ohio rather than South Carolina. Was it right to force Ohio to make a change in the elective franchise against its will?

He could not touch the question as to whether it was right to prevent a majority in South Carolina from ruling because, to his mind, no number of Negroes could outweigh the will of whites. He stumbled on without mentioning this suppressed minor premise and said, "It is a fundamental tenet of my creed that the will of the people must be obeyed. Is there anything wrong or unfair in that?"

Douglass smiled, still thinking of South Carolina: "A great deal that is wrong, Mr. President, with all respect." But the President insisted: "It is the people of the states that must for themselves determine this thing. I do not want to be engaged in a work that will commence a war of races." Then he indicated that the interview was at an end; he was glad to have met them, and thanked them for the compliment paid him.

Douglass returned the thanks, and said that they had not come to argue but if the President would grant permission, "We would endeavor to controvert some of the positions you have assumed." Mr. Downing, too, suggested persuasively that the President, by his kind explanation, "must have contemplated some reply to the views which he has advanced."

Douglass continued, "I would like to say one or two words in reply: You enfranchise your enemies and disfranchise your friends. . . . My own impression is that the very thing that your Excellency would avoid in the Southern states can only be avoided by the very measure that we proposed. . . . I would like to say a word or so in regard to that matter of the enfranchisement of the blacks as a means of preventing the very thing which your Excellency seems to apprehend—that is a conflict of races."

The President naturally did not want to give publicity to views of Negroes antagonistic to his own, and said shortly that there were other places besides the South for the Negro to live. "But," said Douglass, "the masters have the making of the laws and we cannot get away from the plantation." "What prevents you?" asked Johnson. Douglass replied that, "His master then decides for him where he shall go, where he shall work, how much he shall work. . . . He is absolutely in the hands of those men."

The President replied, "If the master now controls him or his actions, would he not control him in his vote?" Douglass answered: "Let the Negro once understand that he has an organic right to vote, and he will raise up a party in the Southern states among the poor, who will rally with him. There is this conflict that you speak of between the wealthy slave owner and the poor man." The President replied eagerly: "You touch right upon the point there. There is this conflict, and hence, I suggest emigration."

The President then bowed his dark visitors out, saying they were all desirous of accomplishing the same ends but proposed to do so by following different roads. Douglass, turning to leave, said:

"The President sends us to the people and we go to the people." "Yes, sir," answered the President, "I have great faith in the people. I believe they will do what is right." [57]

Afterwards the colored delegation published a reply to various points brought up by the President, and especially stressed the matter of enmity between the Negroes and the poor whites:

"The first point to which we feel especially bound to take exception is your attempt to found a policy opposed to our enfranchisement, upon the alleged ground of an existing hostility on the part of the former slaves towards the poor white people of the South. We admit the existence of this hostility, and hold that it is entirely reciprocal; but you obviously commit an error by drawing an argument from an incident of slavery, and making it a basis for a policy adapted to a state of freedom. The hostility between the white and blacks of the South is easily explained. It has its root and sap in the relation of slavery, and was incited on both sides by the cunning of the slave masters. Those masters secured their ascendency over both the poor whites and blacks by putting enmity between them.

"They divided both to conquer each. There was no earthly reason why the blacks should not hate and dread the poor whites when in a state of slavery, for it was from this class that their masters received their slave catchers, slave-drivers and overseers. They were the men called in upon all occasions by the masters whenever any fiendish outrage was to be committed upon the slave. Now, sir, you cannot but perceive, that the cause of this hatred removed, the effect must be removed also. Slavery is abolished. The cause of this antagonism is removed, and you must see that it is altogether illogical (and putting 'new wine into old bottles') to legislate from slaveholding premises for a people whom you have repeatedly declared it your purpose to maintain in freedom.

"Besides, even if it were true, as you allege, that the hostility of the blacks towards the poor whites must necessarily project itself into a state of freedom, and that this enmity between the two races is even more intense in a state of freedom than in a state of slavery, in the name of heaven, we reverently ask, how can you, in view of your professed desire to promote the welfare of the black man, deprive him of all means of defense and clothe him whom you regard as his enemy in the panoply of political power? Can it be that you recommend a policy which would arm the strong and cast down the defenseless? Can you, by any possibility of reasoning, regard this as just, fair, or wise? Experience proves that those are most abused who can be abused with the greatest impunity. . . .

"On the colonization theory you were pleased to broach, very much could be said. It is impossible to suppose, in view of the usefulness of the black man in times of peace as a laborer in the South, and in time of war as a soldier in the North, and the growing respect for his rights among the people and his increasing adaptation to a high state of civilization in his native land, that there can ever come a time when he can be removed from this country without a terrible shock to its prosperity and peace." [58]

The Committee of Fifteen began its work again. The indomitable Stevens never gave up, never despaired; if he could not get all he wanted, he stood fast and took what he could. He said sadly June 13, 1866, in the House of Representatives, referring to the proposed Fourteenth Amendment with its permission to disfranchise the Negro: "In my youth, in my manhood, in my old age, I had fondly dreamed that when any fortunate chance should have broken up for a while the foundation of our institutions, and released us from obligations the most tyranical that ever man imposed in the name of freedom, that the intelligent, pure and just men of this Republic, true to their professions and their consciences, would have so remodeled all our institutions as to have freed them from every vestige of human oppression, of inequality of rights, of the recognized degradation of the poor, and the superior caste of the rich. In short, that no distinction would be tolerated in this purified Republic but what arose from merit and conduct. This bright dream has vanished 'like the baseless fabric of a vision.' I find that we shall be obliged to be content with patching up the worst portions of the ancient edifice, and leaving it, in many of its parts, to be swept through by the tempests, frosts and the storms of despotism.

"Do you inquire why, holding these views and possessing some will of my own, I accept so imperfect a proposition? I answer, because I live among men and not among angels; among men as intelligent, as determined and as independent as myself, who, not agreeing with me, do not choose to yield up their opinions to mine. Mutual concessions is our only resort, or mutual hostilities." [59]

The Committee of Fifteen now tried to find out by actual inquiry just what the situation in the South was with regard to the Negro. It did this, not so much because anyone was in doubt, as because the situation of the Negro was the most appealing thing that could be used to bring a majority to vote for the industrial North. It would increase the tremendous moral afflatus which made the war more and more symbolic in the minds of the people of the United States of a great triumph of human freedom. Sub-committees of the main committee took testimony for months all over the South and eventually issued an unanswerable array of evidence.

April 20, Robert Dale Owen brought a proposal for a Fourteenth Amendment to Stevens in the Committee of Fifteen. "Stevens picked up my manuscript, looked it carefully over, and then, in his impulsive way, said: 'I'll be plain with you, Owen. We've had nothing before us that comes anywhere near being as good as this, or as complete. It would be likely to pass, too; that's the best of it. We haven't a majority, either in our committee or in Congress, for immediate suffrage; and I don't believe the states have yet advanced so far that they would be willing to ratify it. I'll lay that amendment of yours before our committee tomorrow, if you say so; and I'll do my best to put it through.' " [60]

Previous to this time, the thought was to bring in several separate amendments, but now the attitude was to unite the whole matter in one comprehensive amendment, so that the proposition of April 21 was presented as follows:

"Section 1. No discrimination shall be made by any state, nor by the United States, as to the civil rights of persons because of race, color, or previous condition of servitude.

"Section 2. From and after the fourth day of July, in the year one thousand eight hundred and seventy-six, no discrimination shall be made by any state, nor by the United States, as to the enjoyment of classes of persons of the right of suffrage, because of race, color, or previous condition of servitude.

"Section 3. Until the fourth day of July, one thousand eight hundred and seventy-six, no class of persons, as to the right of any of whom to suffrage discrimination shall be made by any state, because of race, color, or previous condition of servitude, shall be included in the basis of representation.

"Section 4. Debts incurred in aid of insurrection or of war against the Union, and claims of compensation for loss of involuntary service or labor, shall not be paid by any state nor by the United States."

Bingham moved a fifth section to the amendment, along the lines of his previous efforts:

"Section 5. No state shall make or enforce any law which shall abridge the privileges or immunities of citizens of the United States; nor shall any state deprive any person of life, liberty or property without due process of law, nor deny to any person within its jurisdiction the equal protection of the laws."

The Bingham proposal was first adopted and then struck out by the committee. It was voted 7 to 6 to report the first three sections to Congress. Bingham tried in vain to bring in his proposal as a separate amendment.

Thus Owen's proposition was ordered sent to Congress and had a good chance of being adopted; but Fessenden, the chairman, was sick with varioloid and it was decided to delay final report until he was better. Stevens told Owens the sequel:

"Our action on your amendment [said Stevens] had, it seems, gotten noised abroad. In the course of last week the members from New York, from Illinois, and from your state too, Owen—from Indiana—held, each separately, a caucus to consider whether equality of suffrage, present or prospective, ought to form a part of the Republican program for the coming canvass.

"They were afraid, so some of them told us, that if there was a 'nigger in the wood-pile' at all (that was the phrase), it would be used against them as an electioneering handle; and some of them—hang their cowardice!—might lose their elections. By inconsiderable majorities each of these caucuses decided that Negro suffrage in any shape, ought to be excluded from the platform; and they communicated these decisions to us.

"Our committee hadn't backbone enough to maintain its ground. Yesterday, the vote on your plan was reconsidered, your amendment was laid on the table, and in the course of the next three hours we contrived to patch together—well, what you've read this morning." [61]

The sections were changed so as simply to exclude disfranchised Negroes from being made the basis of apportionment. Williams then presented a new section which allowed the Negroes gradually to be enfranchised, and thus gradually to become a basis of representation.

"Representatives shall be apportioned among several states which may be included within this Union according to their respective numbers, counting the whole number of persons in each State excluding Indians not taxed. But whenever in any State the elective franchise shall be denied to any portion of its male citizens, not less than twenty-one years of age, or in any way abridged, except for participation in rebellion or other crime, the basis of representation in such State shall be reduced in the proportion which the number of such male citizens shall bear to the whole number of male citizens not less than twenty-one years of age." This was adopted as Section II of the final amendment.

Finally, on this same date, the Committee reinserted, by a vote of 10-3, Bingham's proposition on civil rights as Section I. Afterward, Conkling, before the Supreme Court, explained this action.

"At the time the Fourteenth Amendment was ratified, individuals and joint stock companies were appealing for congressional and administrative protection against the invidious and discriminating state and local taxes. One instance was that of an express company, whose stock was owned largely by citizens of the State of New York, who came with petitions and bills seeking acts of Congress to aid them in resisting what they deemed oppressive taxation in two states, and oppressive and ruinous rules of damages applied under state laws. That complaints of oppression in respect of property and other rights, made by citizens of Northern states who took up residence in the South, were rife, in and out of Congress."

The Committee then considered Section III. Mr. Harris moved to insert the following:

"Until the 4th day of July, in the year 1870, all persons who voluntarily adhered to the late insurrection, giving it aid and comfort, shall be excluded from the right to vote for Representatives in Congress and for electors for President and Vice President of the United States." [62]

This was finally adopted by a vote of 8-7. The Committee then discussed the readmission of the Southern states with the Fourteenth Amendment as a condition. Finally, the Joint Resolution and the bill concerning the readmission of the Southern states were adopted by a vote of 12-3. This proposed amendment and bill were reported to the House April 30, debated May 8, 9, and 10, and passed May 10. Stevens defended it May 8 and May 10.

"Our fathers had been compelled to postpone the principles of their great Declaration, and wait for their full establishment until a more propitious time. That time ought to be present now. But the public mind has been educated in error for a century. How difficult in a day to unlearn it. In rebuilding, it is necessary to clear away the rotten and defective portions of the old foundations, and to sink deep and found the unrepaired edifice upon the firm foundation of eternal justice. If, perchance, the accumulated quick-sands render it impossible to reach in every part so firm a basis, then it becomes our duty to drive deep and solid the substituted piles on which to build. It would not be wise to prevent the raising of the structure because some corner of it might be founded upon materials subject to the inevitable laws of mortal decay. It were better to shelter the household and trust to the advancing progress of a higher morality and a purer and more intelligent principle to underpin the defective corner. . . .

"This proposition is not all that the committee desired. It falls far short of my wishes, but it fulfills my hopes. I believe it is all that can be obtained in the present state of public opinion. Not only Congress but several States are to be consulted. Upon a careful survey of the whole ground, we did not believe that nineteen of the loyal States could be induced to ratify any proposition more stringent than this. I say nineteen, for I utterly repudiate and scorn the idea that any State not acting in the Union is to be counted on the question of ratification. It is absurd to suppose that any more than three-fourths of the States that propose the Amendment are required to make it valid; that States not here are to be counted as present. Believing then that this is the best proposition that can be made effectual, I accept it. I shall not be driven by clamor or denunciation to throw away a great cause because it is not perfect. I will take all I can get in the cause of humanity and leave it to be perfected by better men in better times. It may be that that time will not come while I am here to enjoy the glorious triumph; but that it will come is as certain as that there is a just God. . . ."

Stevens then referred to the previous draft of the amendment.

"After having received the careful examination and approbation of the committee, and having received the united Republican vote of one hundred and twenty Representatives of the people, it was denounced as 'utterly reprehensible,' and 'unpardonable'; 'to be encountered as a public enemy'; 'positively endangering the peace of the country, and covering its name with dishonor.' 'A wickedness on a larger scale than the crime against Kansas or the fugitive slave law; gross, foul, outrageous; an incredible injustice against the whole African race'; with every other vulgar epithet which polished cultivation could command. . . . I confess my mortification at its defeat. I grieved especially be-

cause it almost closed the door of hope for the amelioration of the condition of the freedmen. But men in pursuit of justice must never
despair. Let us again try and see whether we cannot devise some way
to overcome the united forces of self-righteous Republicans and un-
righteous copperheads. It will not do for those who for thirty years
have fought the beasts at Ephesus to be frightened by the fangs of
modern catamounts." [63]

Thaddeus Stevens continued his speech, May 10: "Let not these
friends of secession sing to me their siren song of peace and good will
until they can stop my ears to the screams and groans of the dying
victims at Memphis. I hold in my hand an elaborate account from a
man whom I know to be of the highest respectability in the country,
every word of which I believe. This account of that foul transaction
only reached me last night. It is more horrible in its atrocity, although
not to the same extent, than the massacre at Jamaica. Tell me Tennessee or any other State is loyal of whom such things are proved! . . .

"Ah, sir, it was but six years ago when they were here, just before
they went out to join the armies of Cataline, just before they left this
Hall. Those of you who were here then will remember the scene in
which every Southern member, encouraged by their allies, came forth
in one yelling body, because a speech for freedom was being made
here; when weapons were drawn, and Barksdale's bowie-knife
gleamed before our eyes. Would you have these men back again so
soon to reënact those scenes? Wait until I am gone, I pray you. I want
not to go through it again. It will be but a short time for my colleagues to wait. . . .

"Now, sir, if the gentlemen had remembered the scenes twenty
years ago, when no man dared to speak without risking his life, when
but a few men did do it—for there were cowards in those days, as
there are in these—you would not have found them asking to bring
these men in, and I only wonder that my friend from Ohio [Mr.
Bingham] should intimate a desire to bring them here."

The announcement of the vote, May 10, was 128 to 37, 19 not voting. It was received with applause on the floor and in the galleries.
Mr. Elridge of Wisconsin rose angrily to a question of order. "I want
to know if it is understood that the proceedings of this House are to
be interrupted by those who come here and occupy the galleries."

"The gentleman from Wisconsin," replied the speaker, "makes the
point of order that expressions of approbation or disapprobation from
persons occupying the galleries are not in order. The chair sustains the
point of order." But Mr. Elridge was still angry.

"I do not want our proceedings to be interrupted by the 'niggerheads'
in the galleries."

The galleries hissed and Stevens asked, "Is it in order for members on the floor to disturb those in the galleries?"

"Members upon the floor should not insult the spectators in the galleries," said the speaker.[64]

The Fourteenth Amendment came up in the Senate April 30, but Fessenden was still ill and no action was taken for two weeks. Finally, May 23, Howard of Michigan began the debate. He declared that the object of the Fourteenth Amendment was primarily to give Congress the power to enforce the guarantees of freedom in the first eight amendments to the Constitution. The West, led by Sherman, Doolittle and others, tried to reintroduce voters as the basis of representation. New England, through Senator Wilson of Massachusetts, was opposed to striking from the basis of representation 2,100,000 unnaturalized foreigners who gave the North 17 representatives. Sherman did not agree. "If it is right to exclude four millions of blacks in the Southern states who are denied representation, is it not also right to exclude all other classes in every other state who are denied political power?"[65]

The question of Negro citizenship was discussed, and Julian of Indiana opposed the conservative stand; to follow conservatism we would recognize the revolting states as still in the Union; it opposes the protection of the millions of loyal colored people of the South through the agency of the Freedmen's Bureau; it opposes the Civil Rights Bill; it opposes, with all bitterness, the policy of giving the freedmen the ballot. On the other hand, radicalism would hold treason a crime; it would base representation on the actual voters; it favors the protection of the colored people of the South through the Freedmen's Bureau and the Civil Rights Bill; it demands the ballot as the right of every colored citizen.

Evidently the breach between the East and West was growing, and coupled with Sumner's attitude, it looked as though the Fourteenth Amendment was again doomed. The Republican party fell back upon the caucus. From May 24 to May 28, the Senate was in session but a few hours, which gave the Republicans time to discuss the whole matter in party caucus. The party at that time showed clear division into conservative, industrial elements, like Fessenden, Trumbull and Morgan; and the abolition-democracy, led by Sumner, Wade and Yates. The opposition of Sumner and the abolition-democracy was finally overcome by the plain facts of the case: this was the utmost that could be got from Congress in defense of democracy. Was it not worth taking? What could be hoped for in further delay?

As a result of the caucuses, certain amendments were made. The second section was amended to strike out the word "citizen" and insert "inhabitants being citizens of the United States." A new first section was inserted: "That all persons born or naturalized in the United States and subject to the jurisdiction thereof, are citizens of the United States and of states wherein they reside."

The Senate's changes thus consisted in defining who were citizens, and in substituting for disfranchisement of all participants in secession until 1870, the ineligibility of certain high officials; it opened the elective franchise to such persons as the states may choose to admit, and adopted the third section in its present form.

We have thus followed, as well as records let us, the inner history of the Reconstruction measures of Congress in the Committee of Fifteen and other sources. Now let us look at the proceedings of Congress, as negotiations on these matters rose among the leaders, here and there and now and then, in a sea of struggling unorganized action.

In the matter of *civil rights,* the final draft of the Fourteenth Amendment said:

"All persons born or naturalized in the United States, and subject to the jurisdiction thereof, are citizens of the United States and of the State wherein they reside. No State shall make or enforce any law which shall abridge the privileges or immunities of citizens of the United States; nor shall any State deprive any person of life, liberty, or property, without due process of law, nor deny to any person within its jurisdiction the equal protection of the laws."

The first proposition on civil rights was introduced into the House by Mr. Stevens, December 5, 1865. On December 6, Bingham of Ohio offered an amendment. Both these resolutions went to the Committee on the Judiciary. Two other propositions were introduced December 11. February 1, 1866, a motion was passed directing the Committee of Fifteen to inquire into this matter. Williams suggested an amendment, February 5, empowering Congress to enforce "all obligations, prohibitions or disabilities imposed by the Constitution on the several states." [66] February 13, 1866, the Committee of Fifteen, as we have noted, reported to both Houses a proposed amendment by Mr. Bingham in the House and by Mr. Fessenden in the Senate. Both motions were indefinitely postponed, and there was a strong desire to get the whole final report of the Committee of Fifteen.

On March 9, 1866, while the Senate was discussing the apportionment of representatives, Senator Yates of Illinois moved an amendment for civil and political rights, but it secured only seven votes. Two other and similar propositions were made in the Senate but received small support. The first section of the resolution reported to the House April 30, 1866, became eventually the civil rights section of the Fourteenth Amendment passed by the House, but the Senate, as we have seen, did not adopt it. Several attempts were made to amend it in the

Senate: Mr. Wade offered a substitute for the entire resolution, but the whole proposition failed. When the second proposition came before the Senate, May 30, Howard of Michigan, in behalf of Senate members of the Joint Committee, presented a series of resolutions which had been adopted by the Republican caucus as a substitute for the House Amendment. The substitute was accepted. The first change was to prefix these words to the first clause of the amendment: "All persons born in the United States and subject to the jurisdiction thereof, are citizens of the United States and of the state wherein they reside."

Later, Fessenden of Maine secured the inclusion of "naturalized persons." Senator Johnson of Maryland tried unsuccessfully to strike out the guarantee that states should not make or enforce any law to abridge the privileges of immunity of citizens.

Disability for participation in secession was covered by Section III:

"No person shall be a senator or representative in Congress, or elector of President and Vice-President, or hold any office, civil or military, under the United States, or under any State, who, having previously taken an oath, as a member of Congress, or as an officer of the United States, or as a member of any State legislature, or as an executive or judicial officer of any State, to support the Constitution of the United States, shall have engaged in insurrection or rebellion against the same, or given aid or comfort to the enemies thereof. But Congress may, by a vote of two-thirds of each house, remove such disability."

Four amendments on disabilities for participation in the rebellion were introduced in 1866. In the report of the Committee of Fifteen April 30, 1866, there was included a third section by which all persons who voluntarily adhered to the late insurrection were excluded from the right to vote until July 4, 1870. Attempts were made to amend this in the House. When the resolution reached the Senate there were 15 attempts to alter this section. On May 30, Senator Howard of Michigan in behalf of the Senate members of the Joint Committee on Reconstruction presented a new draft in which he proposed in place of the third section, the provision which now appears in the Fourteenth Amendment. Many efforts were made to amend it. The Democratic Senators seemed to prefer the Howard substitute to the House amendment. This section passed.

The question of *suffrage* for Negroes was covered by Section II:

"Representatives shall be apportioned among the several States according to their respective numbers, counting the whole number of persons in each State, excluding Indians not taxed. But when the right to vote at any election for the choice of electors for President and Vice-President of the United States, Representatives in Congress, the executive or judicial officers of a State, or the members of the legislature thereof, is denied to any of the male inhabitants of such State, being twenty-one years of age and citizens of the United States, or in any way abridged except for participation in rebellion or other crime, the basis of representation therein shall be reduced in the proportion which the number of such male citizens shall bear to the whole number of male citizens twenty-one years of age in such State."

This question of Negro suffrage gave rise to five proposed amendments just before the Civil War. All these excluded persons of Negro descent from the right to vote, and most of them excluded from them the right to hold office.

In the opening days of the 39th Congress, there were six propositions to guarantee the right to vote to Negroes. Two proposed an educational standard in voting for Federal officials. Boutwell proposed an amendment making unlawful any distinction in the elective franchise on account of race or color. Another amendment proposed to give Congress power to define the qualifications of voters, and members of Congress, and of Presidential electors. Henderson, January 23, 1866, proposed an amendment denying the state the right to discriminate against voters on account of race or color. January 22, 1866, the proposal on the apportionment of Representatives and abridgment of Representatives was presented by the Committee of Fifteen to the House. It was recommitted January 29, and reported again January 31. It passed January 31.

In the Senate, there were five attempts to amend this resolution. Sumner presented a resolution making color discrimination impossible in the courtroom or ballot-box. This was rejected, 39 to 8. Howard proposed to admit to the franchise Negroes in the army and navy, or those able to read and write, or those who had property to the value of $250. This was not acted on. Sumner again attempted to amend the resolution by making illegal discrimination on account of race and color. It was lost, 39-8. A similar proposal by Yates of Illinois was rejected.

Three other propositions to amend the Constitution, relative to the suffrage, were introduced before the close of this Congress. One was a proposition by Stewart of Nevada on March 16; this foreshadowed the subsequent "Grandfather Clause." It admitted the Southern states on several conditions, one of which was: "The extension of the elective franchise to all persons upon the same terms and conditions, making no discrimination on account of race, color or previous condition of servitude; provided that those who were qualified to vote in the year 1860 by the laws of their respective states shall not be disfranchised by reason of any new tests or conditions which have been or may be pre-scribed since that year.

"That when the aforementioned condition shall have been complied with and ratified by a majority of the present voting population, a general amnesty shall be proclaimed.

"That all the loyal states be respectfully requested to incorporate in their constitutions an amendment corresponding to the one above de-scribed.

"That it is not intended to assert a coercive power on the part of Congress, in regard to the regulation of the suffrage in the different states, but only to make an appeal to their own good sense and love of country, with a view to the prevention of serious evils now threatened."

Seward said in 1870, "When the Reconstruction question arose about the Fourteenth Amendment, I proposed that all persons born in the United States after the date of Mr. Lincoln's proclamation abolishing slavery should be entitled to vote on arriving at the age of twenty-one years, and this should enter into Reconstruction." [67]

The resolution for the new Fourteenth Amendment passed the Sen-ate June 8, 1866, by a vote of 33-11; five members not voting. The amended resolution was brought before the House and was called up June 13. After a limited debate, the amendments made by the Senate were concurred in by a vote of 120-32, thirty-two not voting. Thus the Fourteenth Amendment was sent to the states for approval.

After the President's veto of the Freedmen's Bureau Bill, many members wanted the question immediately reconsidered, and the day after the President's speech of February 22, Senator Wilson introduced a bill which was not reported. The legislatures of several states ap-proved of a bill, by petitions which urged maintaining the Bureau. The President tried to counteract this by sending two agents, Generals Steedman and Fullerton, to investigate the Bureau. They were both in sympathy with his policy and made a tour of four months. They com-mended Howard and believed that the Bureau had done much to pre-serve order and organize free labor, but that it had sometimes been dishonestly and injudiciously administered, and that it was time for it to come to an end.

This report was widely circulated and discussed. The charges were investigated and public confidence in the Bureau was shaken. Never-theless, May 22, a bill to continue the Bureau was introduced. It dif-fered from the bill of February 9, in limiting the Bureau to two years. Land held under Sherman's orders was to be restored to former own-ers and other land furnished the dispossessed freedmen. Army officers were retained in the service of the Bureau, and commissioners were authorized to coöperate with agents of benevolent associations; property was to be appropriated for the education of the freedmen, and military protection of their civil rights guaranteed.

After discussion, the bill passed the House May 29, by vote of 96-32. In the Senate, the bill was amended and a conference was held. The conference agreed that the questions arising out of Sherman's orders should be left entirely with the President for settlement. On June 16, the President vetoed the bill and called the Freedmen's Bureau a proposition to transfer four million slaves from their original owners to a new set of taskmasters. By a severe exercise of party discipline, according to Blaine, the necessary two-thirds vote was procured in each House, and the bill passed over the President's veto on the same day that it was received. Thus government guardianship of freedmen was given a temporary extension under a grudging and partly inimical administration. The disposition of Congress to yield in part to the President was manifest.

On June 6, the Committee of Fifteen was reappointed. Sub-committees had been taking testimony all over the South.

The final report of the Committee of Fifteen was made June 18. It made an eight hundred page book and 100,000 copies were distributed. Its majority and minority sections summed up the strongest arguments available for and against the proposed methods of Reconstruction. The part of the majority report that touched the Negro said:

"Slavery had been abolished by constitutional amendment. A large proportion of the population had become, instead of mere chattels, free men and citizens. Through all the past struggle these had remained true and loyal, and had, in large numbers, fought on the side of the Union. It was impossible to abandon them without securing them their rights as free men and citizens. The whole civilized world would have cried out against such base ingratitude, and the bare idea is offensive to all right-thinking men. Hence, it became important to inquire what could be done to secure their rights, civil and political. It was evident to your committee that adequate security could only be found in appropriate constitutional provisions. . . . The increase of representation necessarily resulting from the abolition of slavery was considered the most important element in the questions arising out of the changed condition of affairs, and the necessity for some fundamental action in this regard seemed imperative.

"It appeared to your committee that the rights of these persons by whom the basis of representation had been thus increased should be recognized by the General Government. While slaves, they were not considered as having any rights, civil or political. It did not seem just or proper that all the political advantages derived from their becoming free should be confined to their former masters, who had fought against the Union, and withheld from themselves, who had always been loyal. . . .

"Doubts were entertained whether Congress had power, even under the amended Constitution, to prescribe the qualifications of voters in a state, or could act directly on the subject. It was doubtful, in the opinion of your committee, whether the states would consent to surrender a power they had always exercised, and to which they were attached. As the best, if not the only, method of surmounting the difficulty, and as eminently just and proper in itself, your committee came to the conclusion that political power should be possessed in all the states exactly in proportion as the right of suffrage should be granted, without distinction of color or race. . . .

"It appears quite clear that the anti-slavery amendments, both to the state and Federal Constitutions, were adopted in the South with reluctancy by the bodies which did adopt them, while in some states they have been either passed by in silence or rejected. The language of all the provisions and ordinances of these states on the subject amounts to nothing more than an unwilling admission of an unwelcome truth. . . .

"Looking still further at the evidence taken by your committee, it is found to be clearly shown, by witnesses of the highest character, and having the best means of observation, that the Freedmen's Bureau, instituted for the relief and protection of freedmen and refugees, is almost universally opposed by the mass of the population, and exists in an efficient condition only under military protection, while the Union men of the South are earnest in its defense, declaring with one voice that without its protection the colored people would not be permitted to labor at fair prices, and could hardly live in safety. They also testify that without the protection of United States troops Union men, whether of Northern or Southern origin, would be obliged to abandon their homes. The feeling in many portions of the country towards the emancipated slaves, especially among the uneducated and ignorant, is one of vindictive and malicious hatred. This deep-seated prejudice against color is assiduously cultivated by the public journals, and leads to acts of cruelty, oppression, and murder, which the local authorities are at no pains to prevent or punish. There is no general disposition to place the colored race, constituting at least two-fifths of the population, upon terms even of civil equality. While many instances may be found where large planters and men of the better class accept the situation, and honestly strive to bring about a better order of things by employing the freedmen at fair wages and treating them kindly, the general feeling and disposition among all classes are yet totally averse to the toleration of any class of people friendly to the Union, be they white or black; and this aversion is not infrequently manifested in an insulting and offensive manner. . . ." [68]

This part of the report was signed by twelve members of the Committee. The other three members submitted a Minority Report. It was in the main, the old metaphysical argument, signed by Johnson, the constitutional lawyer from Maryland, Rogers, the extreme advocate of Southern rights from New Jersey, and Grider.

"They are asked to disfranchise a numerous class of their citizens, and also to agree to diminish their representation in Congress, and of course in the electoral college, or to admit to the right of suffrage their colored males of twenty-one years of age and upwards (a class now in a condition of almost utter ignorance), thus placing them on the same political footing with white citizens of that age. For reasons so obvious that the dullest may discover them, the right is not directly asserted of granting suffrage to the Negro. That would be obnoxious to most of the Northern and Western states, so much so that their consent was not to be anticipated; but as the plan adopted, because of the limited number of Negroes in such States, will have no effect on their representation, it is thought it may be adopted, while in the Southern States it will materially lessen their number.

"That these latter States will assent to the measure can hardly be expected. The effect, then, if not the purpose, of the measure is forever to deny representatives to such States, or, if they consent to the condition, to weaken their representative power, and thus, probably, secure a continuance of such a party in power as now controls the legislation of the government. The measure, in its terms and its effect, whether designed or not, is to degrade the Southern States. To consent to it will be to consent to their own dishonor."

Neither Sumner nor Stevens was satisfied with the Fourteenth Amendment. On the last day of the session, July 28, 1866, Thaddeus Stevens made his last defense of Negro suffrage. He was at the time worn out; his health was precarious; he was seventy-three years of age, and he hardly expected to return to his seat in the House. With deep solemnity, he sought " 'to make one more—perhaps an expiring—effort to do something which shall be useful to my fellow men; something to elevate and enlighten the poor, the oppressed, and the ignorant in this great crisis of human affairs.' The black man, he declared, must have the ballot or he would continue to be a slave. There was some alleviation to the lot of a bondman, but 'a freeman deprived of every human right, is the most degraded of human beings.' Without the protection of the ballot-box the freedmen were 'the mere serfs,' and would become 'the victims of their former masters.' He declared that what he had done he had done for humanity. 'I know it is easy,' he said, 'to protect the interests of the rich and powerful; but it is a great labor to guard the rights of the poor and downtrodden—it is the eternal labor of Sisyphus, forever to be renewed. In this, perhaps my final action on this great question, I can see nothing in my political course, especially in regard to human freedom, which I could wish to have expunged or changed. I believe that we must all account here-after for deeds done in the body, and that political deeds will be among those accounts. I desire to take to the bar of that final settlement the record which I shall this day make on the great question of human rights. While I am sure it will not make atonement for half my errors, I hope it will be some palliation. Are there any who will venture to take the list with their negative seal upon it, and who will dare to un-roll it before that stern judge who is the Father of the immortal beings whom they have been trampling under foot, and whose souls they have been crushing out?" [69]

This was not, in fact, his last speech, but it had the tone of a final message. Congress adjourned before a congressional plan of recon-struction reached its final form, but its general outline was clear, and no further compromise between the congressional majority and John-son was possible.

Already, the President's attitude on the Fourteenth Amendment and Reconstruction had led to two suicides, the resignation of three mem-bers of the Cabinet; and although Stanton remained, his retention caused the impeachment of Andrew Johnson. Sumner, much against his will, had remained silent when the Senate, by party caucus, had de-cided upon the Fourteenth Amendment. On the last day of Congress, he wrote the Duchess of Argyll:

"The suffering at the South is great, through the misconduct of the President. His course has kept the rebel spirit alive, and depressed the loyal, white and black. It makes me very sad to see this. Considering the difficulties of their position, the blacks have done wonderfully well. They should have had a Moses as a President; but they had found a Pharaoh." [70]

Particularly had the situation in Louisiana become tense. The New Orleans riot of July 30, 1866, confirmed the Abolitionists in their opin-ion that the reconstructed states were in the power of the rebels, and that they were using their power to put the Negro back into slavery; and that no man, white or black, who was friendly to the Union, was safe in the South. There were reported a thousand murders in the South, with few of the criminals brought to justice. And the country was convinced that the President had disrupted the Union party, and was conspiring with Democrats, North and South, to drive out the Republicans.

In the election of 1866, there was on the side of Congress, a Union party with a center bloc of Republicans; a left wing of radical Abolitionists, and a right wing of reactionary War Democrats. Andrew Johnson tried to unite the Western Radicals and the War Democrats into a new third party, to be reënforced eventually by the returned Secessionists. But between extreme democracy and reaction there was no common ground. He only succeeded in getting the support of a few of the War Democrats, and the copperheads, who were either Southerners living North, or Northern men with Southern principles.

State and national conventions met. Johnson and his friends started out August 14 to form a Johnson Party. The National Union Convention met in Philadelphia with states North and South represented. A special wigwam, two stories high, was erected on Girard Avenue, seating ten thousand people. The interior was decorated with flags. Horace Greeley called it a bread and butter convention, composed of 99% of rebels and copperheads. Thomas Nast ridiculed the convention in his cartoons in *Harper's Weekly*.

Their declaration of principles, accepted unanimously, declared the war had maintained the Constitution and the Union unaltered, and that neither Congress nor the general Government had any authority to deny the constitutional right of congressional representation to any state. They urged the election of Congressmen who would admit all "loyal" representatives from the South. They affirmed the inability of a state either to secede or exclude any other state from the Union, and the constitutional right of each state to decide for itself the qualifications for voting, within its borders. They insisted that the Constitution could not be legally amended, except with all the states voting in Congress, and action by all the legislatures. They denied any desire in the Southern states to restore slavery. They proclaimed the invalidity of the rebel debts, the inviolability of the Federal debt, and the right of freedmen to the same protection of persons and property as afforded to whites. They urged government aid for Federal soldiers and their families. Finally, they expressed whole-hearted endorsement of Andrew Johnson.

The weakness of this meeting was that, first, it contained in fact few Republicans, most of the delegates being well-known Democrats who had opposed Lincoln. It was dubbed the conference of "copperheads," and among the delegates were Vallandigham and Fernando Wood. Secondly, the meeting was not followed up with careful organization.

No sooner had this convention adjourned than Southern Loyalists met in Philadelphia on September 3, to confer with Northern Republicans, including Horace Greeley, John Jacob Astor, Carl Schurz,

Frederick Douglass, Brownlow, Thomas E. Benton, Morton, Cameron, and Gerry. This conference met in two parts, one Northern and one Southern.

Frederick Douglass was elected delegate from Rochester to attend the convention. It was a great honor for a black man in a white city. On the train, he met Southern and Western delegates, including Governor Oliver P. Morton of Indiana. After consultation, a committee waited on him, and through a Louisiana spokesman, insisted on their high respect for him, but also on their fear that it was inexpedient for him to attend the convention, on account of the cry of social and political equality which would be raised against the Republican party. Douglass replied: "Gentlemen, with all respect, you might as well ask me to put a loaded pistol to my head and blow my brains out, as to ask me to keep out of this convention, to which I have been duly elected." [71]

He pointed out that the fact of his election was widely known, and his failure to attend would be inexplicable. Later, he was warned against walking in the procession, and for a while it looked as if he would have to walk alone, until Theodore Tilton of New York offered to walk with him. In that parade, he met a daughter of his former owner!

During the convention, Speed, who had just resigned from the Cabinet, called the President a tyrant, and the Southern Loyalists attacked Johnson, but split on Negro suffrage. A part of the convention finally adopted this declaration: ". . . The Government by national and appropriate legislation, enforced by national authority, shall confer on every citizen in the States we represent, the American birthright of impartial suffrage and equality before the law. This is the one all-sufficient remedy. This is our great and pressing necessity." [72]

Governor Brownlow of Tennessee, in discussing Negro suffrage at this same convention on September 3, 1866, said:

"Some gentlemen, from a mistaken view of my character, said they were afraid of Negro Suffrage, and wanted to dodge it. I have never dodged any subject, nor have I ever been found on both sides of any subject. While I am satisfied with everything done here, I would go further. I am an advocate of Negro suffrage, and impartial suffrage. I would rather associate with loyal Negroes than with disloyal white men. I would rather be buried in a Negro graveyard than in a rebel graveyard; and after death I would sooner go to a Negro heaven than a white rebel's hell." [73]

There followed in September two military conventions, one in Cleveland, September 18, by friends of Johnson, which did not mention Negro suffrage. It denounced the Abolitionists and said that they were trying to force another war. It contained many Democrats and a few conservative Republicans. Confederate officers at Memphis, including General Forrest of Fort Pillow fame, sent sympathy by telegram, which was unfortunate publicity. In answer to this a National Convention of "Citizens, Soldiers and Sailors" was held at Pittsburgh, September 25 and 26. There were many volunteer officers of high rank and Johnson was denounced and the Fourteenth Amendment advocated. This convention had great influence on public opinion and popularized the Fourteenth Amendment.

The issue in the election of the fall of 1866, turned on whether Congress should recognize Southern states as reconstructed by Johnson. It was not a presidential year, but congressmen and state legislatures were to be elected.

The real campaign began in August, with the fourteenth of August convention in Philadelphia. This convention greatly encouraged Johnson, and he wrote it, attacking Congress for preventing the restoration of peace and union, and denying that it was really a legal Congress. "If I had wanted authority, or if I had wished to perpetuate my own power, how easily could I have held and wielded that which was placed in my hands by the measure called Freedmen's Bureau Bill." [74]

On July 4, he had issued another proclamation of general amnesty, and on August 20, he declared the Civil War at an end. Already, in the spring, he had promised to lay the cornerstone of a monument to Stephen A. Douglas in Chicago, and he left Washington, August 28, on a great campaign tour, which was to sweep the country. He took General Grant with him and members of his Cabinet, and Seward joined him in New York. Johnson stopped at Philadelphia, New York, Albany, and then went West by way of Cleveland, Chicago and St. Louis.

It was an extraordinary and increasingly painful effort, by which Johnson definitely defeated himself and his own political policies. He showed genius for saying the wrong thing. In New York, for instance, he asked, "Are we prepared, after the cost of war, to continue the disrupted condition of the country? Why are we afraid of the representatives of the South? Some have grown fat, some have grown rich by the aggression and destruction of others."

In Philadelphia, he declared that God was a tailor, like himself. At Cleveland his audience became a mob while the President himself increased the hubbub. The city authorities had made preparations for a polite reception, but as he proceeded with his harangue, the mob took complete possession of the crowd. Someone cried, "Why not hang Thad Stevens and Wendell Phillips?" "Yes," yelled Johnson, "why not hang them?" [75]

Some towns hung out blacks flags and banners, "No welcome to traitors." Bands played the death march; Johnson shouted in defiance. His egotism was ridiculed. He was charged with being drunk, a traitor and a demagogue. On he reeled. As Burgess said, "The trip degraded the presidential office." The New York *Tribune* watched it with a "feeling of national shame," and called it "the stumbling tour of an inebriated demagogue." The New York *World* excused him by asking: "Who of all presidents had been lower than Lincoln in personal bearing?" The *Herald* put the blame on Seward's shoulders, "the Mephistopheles of the administration." Lowell called the journey "an indecent orgy"; Rhodes says he was "intoxicated" at Cleveland, while Schouler declares he was sober. The culmination came in St. Louis, where Johnson declared that the blood of the New Orleans riot was on Congress, and decried the "diabolical and nefarious policies of Stevens, Phillips and Sumner."

The most charitable thing that the defenders of Andrew Johnson can say of him is that occasionally he got drunk; for too much liquor alone would excuse such extraordinary conduct and performances as his Vice-Presidential inauguration, his speech of February 22, 1866, his exhibition at Cleveland, and his St. Louis debauch. If he was not an occasional drunkard, he was God's own fool.

"He returned to Washington," as Schurz says, "an utterly discomfited and disgraced man, having gone out to win popular support, and having earned only public disgust."

The rôle of Seward during this episode was pathetic. One of the wits of the time spoke of Seward's new office of bear-leader. "Unfortunately he was very unsuccessful even in this task, for he could do little more than apologize for Johnson, and in a few commonplace sentences call upon the audience to support the President in opposition to Congress. At Niagara, he told the crowd that Lincoln had been traduced when alive, but after his assassination all hearts inclined to the deepest sorrow; and it would be the same if Johnson should be taken off. To the citizens of Buffalo he stated the issue as follows: 'The question is between the President and the Congress. Of all that has been done to bring us so near the consummation [of Reconstruction] you see that nothing has been done that was not done through the direction, agency, activity, perseverance and patriotism of Andrew Johnson, President of the United States. Will you stand by Congress? Or will you stand by the President?'"

The Republicans took every advantage of the situation. They saw in Johnson the instinct of the poor white cropping out. "He cannot shake off the boot-licking proclivity, born and bred in him, towards the aristocracy of the South. Miserable fool!"

Stevens made but one speech in the campaign of 1866. He said that he had been directed by his physician neither to think, speak nor read until the next session of Congress; that he had followed the orders not to read almost literally. "It is true, I have amused myself with a little light, frivolous reading. For instance, there was a serial account from day to day of a very remarkable circus that traveled through the country, from Washington to Chicago and St. Louis, and from Louisville back to Washington. I read that with some interest, expecting to see in so celebrated an establishment,—one which from its heralding was to beat Dan Rice and all the old circuses that ever went forth,—I expected great wit from the celebrated character of its clowns." [76]

As the campaign of 1866 progressed, the agitation in favor of granting suffrage to the Negro as a necessary protection of his freedom became marked. First of all, Industry and Trade were convinced that they could not trust the white South. Therefore, the more extreme ideas which Stevens had advocated, were allowed to be broadcast. Their logic was strong and their methods popular. People had faith in laws and wanted some great enactment in keeping with the greatness of the war. It was a ripe time for amending the Constitution and inaugurating final reforms. These reforms might be in advance at the time, but they were worth trying, and there appeared to be no middle path.

Thus, as the campaign went on, Negro suffrage occupied a more and more important position. Stevens, Wade, Sumner, Chase, Schurz and Chandler were in favor of it. To many Northerners it had been at first unthinkable, but more and more they became convinced. The *Nation* urged full Negro suffrage and Negro civil rights, but opposed the exclusion of white leaders from office.

"The doctrine that 'this is a white man's government and intended for white men only,' is, as the Perrys profess it, as monstrous a doctrine as was ever concocted." To allow the states to reorganize on this basis, the *Nation* added, "will make the very name of American democracy a hissing and a byword among the nations of the earth. . . . To have this theory of the nature of our government boldly thrust in our faces now, after the events of the last four years, by men who have come red-handed from the battlefield, and to whose garments the blood of our brothers and sons still clings; and to know that the President, who owes in part at least his ability to be President to the valor and blood of colored troops, concurs with them in this scandalous repudiation of democratic principles, are things which the country, we trust, will find it hard to bear." [77]

For a brief period—for the seven mystic years that stretched between Johnson's "Swing round the Circle" to the Panic of 1873, the majority of thinking Americans of the North believed in the equal manhood of Negroes. They acted accordingly with a thoroughness and clean-cut decision that no age which does not share that faith can in the slightest comprehend. They did not free draft animals, nor enfranchise gorillas, nor welcome morons to Congress. They simply recognized black folk as men. "The South called for war," said James Russell Lowell, "and we have given it to her. We will fix the terms of peace ourselves and we will teach the South that Christ is disguised in a dusky race." [78]

Then came in 1873-76 sudden and complete disillusion not at Negroes but at the world—at business, at work, at religion, at art. A bitter protest of Southern property reënforced Northern reaction; and while after long years the American world recovered in most matters, it has never yet quite understood why it could ever have thought that black men were altogether human.

There were men in the South and former slaveholders who knew the truth and spoke it. They knew that there could be no salvation for the South in time or eternity, until the former slave went forth as a man. But the intrenched intolerance of the South, coupled with the awful grief at the death of the flower of Southern manhood, let such prophets speak but few words. They spoke here and there in nearly every Southern state, but they were soon threatened into silence; and there prevailed a bitter hatred and cry for vengeance from people who could not brook defeat because they had been used to victory, and had the slave-born habit of arrogance. For their grief, none had greater sympathy than the bulk of their former slaves. They served and even succored their former masters; and yet, upon these and their fellows, was eventually placed the whole wrath of the South which it could not turn toward the North. And especially it fell upon those freedmen who felt their freedom; who were uplifted by new ambition; who showed the gathered resentment of two hundred years of whipping, kicks and cuffs; in fine, on them who had rolling in their ears God's great. "Deposuit potentes—"

> "He hath put down the Mighty
> From their seats
> And hath exalted them
> Of low degree!"

After the final elections of 1866, the Republicans had 143 members in the House, and the Democrats 49. All states gave strong majorities to the Republican party, except the Border States of Maryland, Delaware and Kentucky. In the South, Democratic candidates were universally successful. Not counting the South, the Republicans in the Senate had a two-thirds majority, and nearly a three-fourths majority in the House.

Through the winter of 1866-1867, notwithstanding the results of the elections of 1866, the South rejected the Fourteenth Amendment. Virginia gave one vote in favor; North Carolina, 11 out of 148; South Carolina, 1 vote; Georgia, 2 out of 169; Alabama, 10 out of 106; Texas, 5, and Arkansas, 3; Florida, Mississippi and Louisiana were unanimously against it.

Thus the South defied Congress, and demanded that the disfranchised Negro should be counted as basis of representation. The South was encouraged in this stand by the President. The Governor of Alabama telegraphed him that the rejection of the Fourteenth Amendment could be reconsidered by his state, but Johnson discouraged him. This increased the strength of the Republicans in the North.

The President's message of December 4, 1866, with all the earmarks of Seward, was calm and skillful. He said that the war was ended, and that the nation should now proceed as a free, prosperous and united nation. He had already informed Congress of his efforts for the gradual restoration of the States. All that remained now was the admission to Congress of loyal Senators and Representatives. While Congress had been considering this, the President had appointed various public officials, and the Thirteenth Amendment had been passed. Yet Congress hesitated to admit the Southern states to representation, and after eight months, only Tennessee had been admitted. He wished to leave the whole matter of suffrage to the States and he was significantly silent on the Black Codes.

The second session of the 39th Congress began December 3. The Senate asked for a report on the condition of the Southern states, since the President had said practically nothing about it. The President replied, December 19, 1866:

"As a result of the measures instituted by the Executive, with the view of inducing a resumption of the functions of the States comprehended in the inquiry of the Senate, the people of North Carolina, South Carolina, Georgia, Alabama, Mississippi, Louisiana, Arkansas, and Tennessee, have reorganized their respective State governments, and are yielding obedience to the laws and government of the United States with more willingness and greater promptitude than under the circumstances could reasonably have been anticipated. The proposed amendment to the Constitution, providing for the abolition of slavery forever within the limits of the country, has been ratified by each one of those states, with the exception of Mississippi, from which no official information has yet been received; and in nearly all of them measures have been adopted or are now pending, to confer upon freedmen rights and privileges which are essential to their comfort, protection, and security. In Florida and Texas, the people are making commendable progress in restoring their State governments, and no doubt it is entertained that they will, at an early period be in a condition to resume all of their practical relations to the Federal Government.

"It is true that in some of the States the demoralizing effects of the war are to be seen in occasional disorders; but these are local in character, not frequent in occurrence, and are rapidly disappearing as the authority of civil law is extended and sustained. Perplexing questions were naturally to be expected from the great and sudden change in the relations between the two races; but systems are gradually developing themselves under which the freedman will receive the protection to which he is justly entitled, and by means of his labor make himself a useful and independent member of the community in which he has his home."

The transubstantiation of Andrew Johnson was complete. He had begun as the champion of the poor laborer, demanding that the land monopoly of the Southern oligarchy be broken up, so as to give access to the soil, South and West, to the free laborer. He had demanded the punishment of those Southerners who by slavery and war had made such an economic program impossible. Suddenly thrust into the Presidency, he had retreated from this attitude. He had not only given up extravagant ideas of punishment, but he dropped his demand for dividing up plantations when he realized that Negroes would largely be beneficiaries. Because he could not conceive of Negroes as men, he refused to advocate universal democracy, of which, in his young manhood, he had been the fiercest advocate, and made strong alliance with those who would restore slavery under another name.

This change did not come by deliberate thought or conscious desire to hurt—it was rather the tragedy of American prejudice made flesh; so that the man born to narrow circumstances, a rebel against economic privilege, died with the conventional ambition of a poor white to be the associate and benefactor of monopolists, planters and slave drivers. In some respects, Andrew Johnson is the most pitiful figure of American history. A man who, despite great power and great ideas, became a puppet, played upon by mighty fingers and selfish, subtle minds; groping, self-made, unlettered and alone; drunk, not so much with liquor, as with the heady wine of sudden and accidental success.

My wild soul waited on as falcons hover.
I beat the reedy fens as I trampled past.
  I heard the mournful loon
  In the marsh beneath the moon
And then, with feathery thunder, the bird of my desire
    Broke from the cover
    Flashing silver fire.
High up among the stars I saw his pinions spire.
    The pale clouds gazed aghast
As my falcon dropped upon him, and gript and held him fast.
                    WILLIAM ROSE BENÉT

1. Hall, C. A., *Andrew Johnson*, p. 22.
2. Hall, C. A., *Andrew Johnson*, p. 21.
3. Winston, *Andrew Johnson*, pp. xiv, xvi, 24, 25.
4. Winston, *Andrew Johnson*, p. 172; *Congressional Globe*, 36th Congress, 2nd Session, p. 1354.
5. Winston, *Andrew Johnson*, p. 118.
6. Winston, *Andrew Johnson*, p. 108.
7. Hall, *Andrew Johnson*, p. 27; Moore, *Speeches of Andrew Johnson*, p. 294.
8. Hall, *Andrew Johnson*, p. 117; Winston, *Andrew Johnson*, p. 252
9. McPherson, *History of United States During Reconstruction*, pp. 46, 47.
10. Winston, *Andrew Johnson*, pp. 228, 229.
11. Moore, *Speeches of Andrew Johnson*, p. xli.
12. Winston, *Andrew Johnson*, pp. 260, 261.
13. Winston, *Andrew Johnson*, p. 515.
14. Warmoth, *War, Politics and Reconstruction*, p. 26.
15. Pierce, *Memoirs and Letters of Charles Sumner*, IV, p. 276.
16. Pierce, *Memoirs and Letters of Charles Sumner*, IV, p. 244.
17. Pierce, *Memoirs and Letters of Charles Sumner*, IV, pp. 242-243, 245.
18. Fleming, *Documentary History of Reconstruction* (Chase to Johnson), Vol. I, pp. 142, 143.
19. Pierce, *Memoirs and Letters of Charles Sumner*, IV, p. 246.
20. Schurz, *Reminiscences*, III, pp. 202, 203.
21. Schurz, *Reminiscences*, III, pp. 201-204.
22. Beale, *The Critical Year*, p. 68. Footnote.
23. McPherson, *History of United States During Reconstruction*, pp. 19, 20.
24. Pierce, *Memoirs and Letters of Charles Sumner*, IV, pp. 267-268.
25. Pierce, *Memoirs and Letters of Charles Sumner*, IV, pp. 258-259.
26. McPherson, *History of United States During Reconstruction*, p. 49.
27. McPherson, *History of United States During Reconstruction*, pp. 50, 51.
28. Winston, *Andrew Johnson*, p. 314.
29. *Congressional Globe*, 39th Congress, 1st Session, Part I, p. 6.
30. *Congressional Globe*, 39th Congress, 1st Session, Part I, p. 30.
31. Winston, *Andrew Johnson*, p. 381.
32. *Congressional Globe*, 39th Congress, 1st Session, Part I, pp. 74, 75.
33. *Congressional Globe*, 39th Congress, 1st Session, Part I, p. 154.
34. *Congressional Globe*, 39th Congress, 1st Session, Part I, p. 43.
35. *Congressional Globe*, 39th Congress, 1st Session, Part I, pp. 90, 91.
36. Cf. Pierce, *Charles Sumner*, IV. Note at bottom, p. 272.
37. Pierce, *Freedmen's Bureau*, p. 59 (for Sections I-VI); Flack, *The Adoption of the Fourteenth Amendment*, p. 13 (Johns Hopkins University Studies, XXVI).

38. *Report of Committee on Reconstruction*, Part III, pp. 65, 66 (Judge Humphreys).
39. Speech of March 19, 1867.
40. Winston, *Andrew Johnson*, p. 343.
41. Seward, *Works*, VII, p. 532.
42. McPherson, *History of U. S. During Reconstruction*, pp. 60, 61.
43. Cf. Oberholtzer, *A History of the U. S. Since the Civil War*, I, p. 171.
44. Pierce, *Charles Sumner*, IV, p. 276.
45. *Congressional Globe*, 39th Congress, 1st Session, Part I, p. 183.
46. McPherson, *History of United States During Reconstruction*, pp. 51, 52.
47. This account of the Committee of Fifteen mainly follows Kendrick, *Journal of the Joint Committee of Fifteen on Reconstruction.*
48. *Congressional Globe*, 39th Congress, 1st Session, Part I, pp. 356-358.
49. Article 4, Section 2, of the Constitution.
50. *Congressional Globe*, 39th Congress, 1st Session, Part I, p. 536.
51. New York *Nation*, Jan. 11, 1866.
52. Blaine, *Twenty Years of Congress*, Vol. II, pp. 146-147.
53. Beale, *The Critical Year*, p. 229.
54. *Congressional Globe*, 39th Congress, 1st Session, Part I, p. 673.
55. *Life and Times of Frederick Douglass*, p. 442.
56. *Life and Times of Frederick Douglass*, p. 467.
57. McPherson, *History of United States During Reconstruction*, pp. 52-55.
58. *Life and Times of Frederick Douglass*, pp. 467-468.
59. *Congressional Globe*, 39th Congress, 1st Session, Part IV, p. 3148.
60. Kendrick, *Journal of the Joint Committee of Fifteen on Reconstruction*, p. 300.
61. Kendrick, *Journal of the Joint Committee of Fifteen on Reconstruction*, p. 302.
62. Flack, *Adoption of the Fourteenth Amendment* (Johns Hopkins University Studies, XXVI, p. 128).
63. *Congressional Globe*, 39th Congress, 1st Session, Part III, pp. 2459, 2544-2545.
64. *Congressional Globe*, 39th Congress, 1st Session, Part III, p. 2545.
65. *Congressional Globe*, 39th Congress, 1st Session, Part IV, p. 2987.
66. Ames, *Amendments to the Constitution*, p. 220.
67. Seward, *Works*, III, p. 24.
68. McPherson, *History of United States During Reconstruction*, pp. 88-93.
69. McCall, *Thaddeus Stevens*, p. 275-76.
70. Pierce, *Charles Sumner*, p. 359.
71. *Life and Times of Frederick Douglass*, p. 474.
72. McPherson, *History of United States During Reconstruction*, p. 242.
73. Warmoth, *War Politics and Reconstruction*, p. 50.
74. McPherson, *History of United States During Reconstruction*, pp. 129, 133, 137.
75. Oberholtzer, *History of U. S. After the Civil War*, Vol. I, pp. 405, 406.
76. Morse, *Thaddeus Stevens*, pp. 282, 283.
77. New York *Nation*, Sept. 28, 1865. Cf. New York *Herald*, Sept. 20, 1865.
78. *North American Review*, Vol. 102, p. 520.

IX. THE PRICE OF DISASTER

*The price of the disaster of slavery and civil war was the necessity
of quickly assimilating into American democracy a mass of ignorant laborers in whose hands alone for the moment lay the power
of preserving the ideals of popular government; of overthrowing a
slave economy and establishing upon it an industry primarily for
the profit of the workers. It was this price which in the end
America refused to pay and today suffers for that refusal*

The year 1867 comes. The election of 1866 has sent to the 40th
Congress a Republican majority of 42 against 11 in the Senate and
143 against 49 in the House. The decisive battle of Reconstruction
looms. Abolition-democracy demands for Negroes physical freedom,
civil rights, economic opportunity and education and the right to vote,
as a matter of sheer human justice and right. Industry demands profits
and is willing to use for this end Negro freedom or Negro slavery,
votes for Negroes or Black Codes.

The South, beaten in war, and socially and economically disorganized, was knocking at the doors of Congress with increased political
power and with a determination to restore land monopoly, and to reorganize its agrarian industry, and to attempt to restore its capital by
reducing public taxation to the lowest point. Moreover, it had not
given up the idea that the capital which it had lost through the legal
abolition of slavery, should and might be reimbursed from the Federal
Treasury. Especially it was determined to use for its own ends the
increased political power based on voteless Negroes. Finally, there was
the West, beginning to fear the grip of land and transportation
monopoly, rebelling against the power of Eastern industry, and staggering under the weight of public debt and public taxation.

In the midst of these elements stood Andrew Johnson, with the tremendous power which lay in his hands as commander-in-chief of the
Army, with the large patronage which arose through the expansion
of governmental functions during the war, and with a stubborn will
and a resourceful and astute Secretary of State. Logically, Andrew
Johnson as an early leader of land reform, and of democracy in industry for the peasant-farmer and the laboring class, was in position
to lead the democracy of the West. But perversely, he had been induced by flattery, by his Southern birth, and his dislike of New Eng-

325

land puritanism, to place himself at the head of the Southerners. Between the program of the South and that of the West, then, there was absolutely no point of alliance. The South represented the extreme of reactionary capitalism based upon land and on the ownership of labor. It showed no sign of any more sympathy with the labor movement in the North or the extension of democratic methods than it had before the war. There was not a single labor voice raised in the Southern post-war clamor. Yet Johnson could not see this. He continued to flirt with Western liberalism at the very time he was surrendering completely to Southern reaction and ultra-conservatism.

In his advice to the South, he no longer contemplated Negro suffrage in any form, and he said nothing of poor whites. In 1867, Negro votes were refused in the municipal elections in Virginia. Judge Moore asked President Johnson concerning the right of freedmen to participate in these elections, but Johnson gave no answer. On the other hand, in an interview with Charles Halpine, March 5, he sought again to make alliance with the Western unrest. He said: "To the people the national debt is a thing of debt to be paid; but to the aristocracy of bonds and national securities it is a property of more than $2,500,000,000, from which a revenue of $180,000,000 a year is to be received into their pockets. So we now find that an aristocracy of the South, based on $3,000,000,000 in Negroes, who were a productive class, has disappeared, and their place in political control of the country is assumed by an aristocracy based on nearly $3,000,000,000 of national debt—a thing which is not producing anything, but which goes on steadily every year, and must go on for all time until the debt is paid, absorbing and taxing at the rate of six or seven per cent a year for every $100 bond that is represented in its aggregation.

"The war of finance is the next war we have to fight; and every blow struck against my efforts to uphold a strict construction of the laws and the Constitution is in reality a blow in favor of repudiating the national debt. The manufacturers and men of capital in the eastern States and the States along the Atlantic seaboard—a mere strip or fringe on the broad mantle of our country, if you will examine the map—these are in favor of high protective, and, in fact, prohibitory tariffs, and also favor a contraction of the currency. But against both measures the interests and votes of the great producing and non-manufacturing States of the West stand irrevocably arrayed, and a glance at the map and the census statistics of the last twenty years will tell every one who is open to conviction how that war must end." [1]

This was a maladroit argument. It placed the national debt against the loss of slave property as equally sinister phenomena. It suggested partial repudiation and thus frightened and antagonized investors.

It rightly protested against the extravagance of war-time finance, but this protest came from a man who was now the acknowledged leader of property and reaction in the South. What basis of alliance could there be between those determined to control and exploit freed labor in the South and those who wished to fight exploitation and monopoly in the West?

Moreover, in his effort to conciliate and lead the West, Johnson attacked the most powerful enemy before him. That enemy was not abolition-democracy, as he falsely conceived. It was a tremendous, new, and rising power of organized wealth and capitalist industry in the North. Monopoly profits from investments were increasing, and destined to increase, and their increase depended upon a high protective tariff, the validity of the public debt, and the control of the national banks and currency. All of these things were threatened by the South and by Andrew Johnson as leader of the South. On the other hand, humanitarian radicalism, so far as the Negro was concerned, was not only completely harnessed to capital and property in the North, but its program for votes for Negroes more and more became manifestly the only protection upon which Northern industry could depend. The Abolitionists were not enemies of capital.

"The American Abolitionists were typical bourgeois-democratic revolutionists under specific American conditions. They felt their movement linked up with the great humanitarian causes of the day (the 'labor question,' the 'peace question,' the emancipation of women, temperance, philanthropy) and with the bourgeois revolutionary movement in Europe. 'He hailed the revolution (of 1848) in France,' Moorfield Storey tells of Sumner, 'and similar outbreaks in other countries as parts of the great movement for freedom, of which the anti-slavery agitation in America was another part.'" [2]

But the former Abolitionists were gradually developing. Under the leadership of Stevens and Sumner, they were beginning to realize the economic foundation of the revolution necessary in the South. They saw that the Negro needed land and education and that his vote would only be valuable to him as it opened the doors to a firm economic foundation and real intelligence. If now they could get the industrial North, not simply to give the Negro the vote, but to give him land and give him schools, the battle would be won. Here, however, they were only partially successful. Stevens could not get them to listen to his plan of land distribution, and Sumner failed in his effort to provide for a national system of Negro schools. But they could and did get the aid of industry, commerce, and labor for Negro suffrage, and this vast step forward they gladly took. Public opinion followed philanthropy, but it was guided by Big Business.

In the meantime, the nation was in the midst of the transition period. Nothing could be settled until the fate of the Fourteenth Amendment was known, and during this time of waiting, from July 16, 1866, until July 20, 1868, the status of the South and its relation to the Union was unsettled. Slowly, the nation voted on the Fourteenth Amendment, destined to curb the political power of the South. Most of New England and two Western states ratified it in the summer and fall of 1866. Before January, seven Southern states rejected it almost unanimously, and in the first three months of 1867, the whole South and the Border States had pronounced against it. They said, in effect, no Negro citizens nor voters; no guaranty of civil rights to Negroes; and all political power based on the counting of the full Negro population. The North, by 1868, had ratified the Fourteenth Amendment unanimously, although New Jersey, Ohio and Oregon made attempts to reverse their decision, when Democrats gained power in those states.

There was not only the vast final problem of economics and government—there was an immediate transition problem. In the interval during which the nation was awaiting the fate of the Fourteenth Amendment to the Constitution, what was to be the status of the South? The South was in the midst of industrial, civil and political anarchy. Crime, force, and murder, disorganized and wandering laborers, unorganized industry, were widely in evidence. The United States as a sovereign nation could declare the Southern states, where rebellion had occurred, unorganized territory, and could rule them by civil government, backed by Federal police. By those who regarded the Constitution as a fetich, this might be pronounced sacrilegious, but to ordinary human beings it was by far the best and sanest thing that the nation could have done, and it would have saved the United States and the whole world untold injury, retrogression and world war.

This was the plan of both Stevens and Sumner, and constitutional lawyers have pronounced it reasonable. With some reluctance, the nation refused to do this while the South and its friends howled in opposition. It was, one would have thought, an unhallowed attempt to rock the foundations of the universe and overthrow the kingdom of Almighty God. The refusal of the nation was chiefly because the new industry, the money-making financiers and organizers of a vast economic empire, hesitated at a government guardianship of labor and control of industry on a scale that might embarrass future freedom of exploitation, and certainly would increase present taxation.

Many advocates of abolition-democracy were also doubtful. They were still under the "freedom" cry of the eighteenth century and obsessed by the American Assumption of the nineteenth. They were still, on the whole, afraid of the full logic of democracy and the ability of the state to secure servants as honest and efficient as private industry. Only their most courageous leaders dared all.

The easiest way out, then, was to prolong the military rule already established as a necessity of the war. This was cheapest and easiest; but also it was of necessity temporary. It must be a step toward civil rule and it must inaugurate civil rule. The law of March 2, 1867, was enacted. It provided for Negro suffrage. What else could it have provided for? If it had confined the vote to whites, not only would the anti-Negro legislation be confirmed, but the gift of additional political power to the South to be used against Northern industry and against democracy would be outright and irrevocable. Johnson vetoed the bill, and when it was passed over his veto, had recourse to executive action which would nullify it. Eventually it was this that led to the attempt to impeach him.

Let us now, more in detail, study the facts of this development. The second session of the 39th Congress assembled in December, 1866, with a distinct mandate from the people. This mandate called for the reorganization of the Southern states on the basis of the Fourteenth Amendment, and for the definiteness of this mandate the South had only itself and Andrew Johnson to blame.

From 1864 to 1868, by a succession of elections, with wide publicity on both sides, and unusually full discussion, national public opinion had come to these decisions by a large majority.

1. The emancipated slave must be protected because he had helped save the Union which slavery had disrupted.

2. The first protection for the slave was a legal status of freedom. This the South opposed in the fifteen former slave states, including the Border States. Four flatly refused to accept the Thirteenth Amendment. Three others accepted but only on condition that freedom should not imply full civil and political rights. Eight states accepted the Thirteenth Amendment, but five of these and the three which accepted on condition, acted under pressure from Johnson, and their action expressed the opinion of a minority of the former voting population, and for this reason these states feared to refer their action to popular approval.

3. A legal status of freedom without actual civil rights would mean almost nothing. The answer of the South to a proposal of civil rights was the Black Codes, which established a new status of slavery with a modified slave trade.

4. The Freedmen's Bureau and the Civil Rights Bill represented an attempt at Federal intervention to enforce freedom by Federal law.

The South bitterly opposed these attempts on the part of the national government and declared with Johnson that such attempts were unconstitutional.

5. To set this point at rest, the Fourteenth Amendment was proposed which made Negroes citizens, guaranteed them civil rights by national law, and political rights, if they were counted as a basis of representation in Congress. The South promptly rejected this overture unanimously, except in Tennessee, and there the majority of white voters had to be disfranchised before the acceptance was carried through.

But behind all this, and explaining this interest in the Negro on the part of most Northerners, was a growing conviction that an arrogant South was returning to Congress with increased political power; that its leaders were essentially the same men who had disrupted the Union and precipitated a costly and bloody war; that there was no reason to suppose that these men had changed their convictions in the slightest or surrendered for a moment their determination to dominate the country, and fight monopoly in industry with monopoly in agriculture.

In the face of their fatal failure, Southerners were demanding increased political power, and that political power could and in all probability would be used for everything disadvantageous to the majority of the nation: it would be used against the spread of democratic ideals; it would be used for further increasing the political power of the South; it would be used against industry, property, and capital as buttressed by the tariff, the national banks, and the public debt.

It was in vain that before, during and since the war, the North had offered to compromise with this unyielding bloc. There was only one defense against the power of the South and while that was revolutionary and hitherto undreamed of, it was the only way, and it could not be stopped by the stubbornness of one narrow-minded man. That was Negro suffrage.

Senator Sherman of Ohio said March 11, 1867: "A year ago I was not in favor of extending enforced Negro suffrage upon the Southern states." [3] But the rejection of the Fourteenth Amendment led him to give his support.

There was evidently an understanding among the Republican Senators and Representatives that if the legislatures of the Southern states organized under Johnson's scheme of Reconstruction accepted the Fourteenth Amendment and thus would say that either they would allow the Negro to vote or, in case they did not allow him, would forego representation based upon his numbers; then these states would be recognized and admitted to Congress. This was more than fair to the South. Charles Sumner to be sure would not consent to it and Stevens did not like it; but the industrial North was willing to throw the Negro over on these terms.[4]

However, with the exception of Tennessee, the Southern states rejected the Fourteenth Amendment almost unanimously and insisted upon the Black Codes, and accompanied their demand by widespread violence.

Meantime in minor measures the sentiment for Negro suffrage was seen to be crystallizing. Colorado had sought admission in 1866 and had less than 100 Negroes. Sumner opposed the application because of the small population and chiefly because the suffrage was confined to white males. He spoke March 12 and 13, April 17, 19 and 24 on the subject. The bill passed the Senate despite Sumner. In the House, the attempt to strike out the word "white" as a qualification for voters was defeated. The President vetoed the bill on account of insufficient population.

Next session, Sumner's amendment prevailed, but the President again vetoed the bill. Sumner made at the close of the session an unsuccessful attempt to make the same condition in the bill to admit Nebraska but failed; the President did not sign that bill. At the next session, the bill with Negro suffrage was passed over the President's veto. Sumner opposed the admission of Tennessee because Negroes were denied the right to vote. He failed to influence public sentiment but made his opponents apologetic.[5]

Sumner wrote to F. W. Bird, January 10, 1867: "I think you will be satisfied with the result on Nebraska and Colorado. The declaration that there shall be no exclusion from the elective franchise on account of color is not in the form which I preferred; but you have the declaration, which to my mind is a great gain. Is it not? And thus ends a long contest, where at first I was alone. Mr. Stewart of Nevada, who is sitting near me, says that 'it cannot be said now that the Republican party is not committed to Negro suffrage.' You have (1) The District Bill; (2) The Nebraska Bill; (3) The Colorado Bill; and (4) The Territorial Bill passed today, declaring that in the territories there shall be no exclusion from the suffrage on account of color."[6]

In February, 1867, from the Committee of Fifteen, Stevens presented the leading Reconstruction measure. This measure declared that life and property were not safe in the former Confederate states, and that good order had to be enforced until loyal governments could be legally established. It divided the Confederate states into five military divisions: one, Virginia; two, North and South Carolina; three, Georgia, Alabama and Florida; four, Mississippi and Arkansas; five,

Louisiana and Texas. A general with sufficient forces was to be assigned to each of these districts. These generals might use the United State civil courts to enforce the laws, but if these were not effective, they might govern through military commissions. The sentences of commissions must be approved by the commanding officers. United States courts should issue no writs of habeas corpus against the acts of these commissions.

T iis bill established martial law, after the President had declared the war was ended. It put the appointing of the district military masters in . ie hands of the General of the Army instead of the President, and suspended the writ of habeas corpus. Congress hesitated at these tho. ough-going terms. Blaine suggested an Amendment which would pro\ide a way of escape from martial rule by promising admission wh n a state adopted the Fourteenth Amendment and provided for Ne ro suffrage. Stevens refused to accept this and the bill was passed February 13.

The Senate began to consider the bill February 15, and stayed in ses ion until three o'clock in the morning. Resort was had to a party caucus, the Republican Senators meeting at 11 A.M., February 16. Sherman, Sumner, Fessenden and four others were put on a sub-committee to revise the House bill, and remained in session a greater part of the afternoon. The bill was changed so as to restore the appointment of heads of the military districts, and adopt the Blaine amendment. The House had already passed Eliot's bill admitting Louisiana with Negro suffrage and Sumner wished that taken as a model. Sumner asked for Negro suffrage but only one of his committee supported him. At 5 P.M the caucus met and Sumner renewed his proposition, excluding discrimination as to race and color for the basis of suffrage. It was carried in the caucus, 15 to 13 or 14. This action committed the Republican to the requirement of suffrage irrespective of race or color in the ele tion of delegates to the Reconstruction conventions, and as the basis of suffrage for the constitutions of the rebel states. Senator Wilsor of Massachusetts said that "then and there in that small room, in that caucus, was decided the greatest pending question of the No th American continent." [6] It was accepted by the caucus, although Fessenden was greatly displeased. He left the caucus and sought to defeat it by personal appeals. This led to an acrimonious debate in Congress, February 19, but the bill passed after a night's session at 6:22 Sunday morning, February 17.

Congress had a difficult time passing this Reconstruction bill. The House rejected the Senate bill and time was flying. Finally agreement was reached February 20 and Congress expired by limitation on March 4. The essential parts of the bill on Negro suffrage remained.

The President by taking the full time allowed by law in returning his veto would leave only two days for Congress to pass the bill over his veto. Johnson and Seward immediately saw this and the veto was held up to the last moment, reaching the House on the afternoon of March 2. The President said that the bill placed the people of ten states under the complete domination of military rulers; these states had made provisions for the preservation of order, yet it was proposed to put them under military law; "the Negroes have not asked for the privilege of voting, and the vast majority of them have no idea of what it means"; we carried on a four years' war to punish the "crime of defying a constitution; if we now ourselves defy the constitution we prove that they were in fact fighting for Negro liberty."

Stevens demanded immediate consideration of the veto but allowed short statements from Democratic members who declared this bill a death knell of republican liberty.

One opponent declared that the bill should not pass unless he was "overpowered from physical exhaustion, or restrained by the rules of the House." Stevens, in closing the debate, said that he had listened to the gentlemen, because he appreciated "the melancholy feelings with which they are approaching this funeral of the nation," but as he desired the passage of the bill he asked Mr. Blaine to move a suspension of the rules. Mr. Blaine accordingly made the motion, and after an ineffectual attempt at filibustering, the bill was passed over the veto by a vote of 135 yeas to 48 nays. The Senate speedily took similar action, and the Reconstruction bill became a law.

As finally passed, the bill set up the five districts, declaring that no adequate protection for life and property existed there. The President instead of the General of the Army was to assign an army officer to each of these districts. These commanders might rule by martial law, but sentence of death had to be approved by the President. To escape from this régime, there must be universal suffrage without regard to race or color, and the framing of a state constitution with a convention composed of delegates not disqualified by participation in rebellion. The constitution so adopted must provide for universal suffrage, and this constitution must be ratified by a majority of the voters. The constitution must also be approved by Congress. The state could not be admitted until the Fourteenth Amendment had been approved by three-fourths of the states of the United States. Thus Congress avoided making the admission of the states conditional upon their individual acceptance of the Fourteenth Amendment.

Still Andrew Johnson was not beaten; as commander-in-chief of the army he could execute the Reconstruction legislation and he could throw its interpretation into the courts with a good chance of favorable decision; just as the faltering attempt of Congress to give the Negroes land was at last utterly nullified by Johnson's edicts of restoration, so there was equal chance to frustrate Congress in restoring states' functions.

Congress tried to tie Johnson's hands with the Tenure of Office Bill. It was introduced in December, 1866. The Constitution gave the President no express power to dismiss persons from office. But custom and logic had allowed it. The Republicans feared that by dismissal from office Johnson would gain control of the entire executive division of the government at a time of crisis. The bill proposed that all officers appointed with the consent of the Senate could be removed only with the consent of the Senate, except in the case of cabinet officers. The House insisted on including cabinet officers and finally the bill was passed providing that cabinet officers should hold their offices during the term of the President by whom they were appointed and one month thereafter; during that time they could be removed only with the consent of the Senate. This measure went to the President on the 20th of February, together with the Reconstruction bill, and was vetoed March 2. The veto argued, from statutes and uniform practice, that Congress had no power to force the President to retain in office against his judgment subordinates whom he had appointed.

Johnson said with curious logic: "Whenever administration fails, or seems to fail, in securing any of the great ends for which republican government is established, the proper course seems to be to renew the original spirit and forms of the Constitution itself." Who was to be the judge of the "original spirit"—Andrew Johnson or the Congress? Which was to yield? Congress must yield to one stubborn, narrow-minded man or it was forced by the necessity of controlling the Executive, to adopt this revolutionary measure.

Sumner said in December, 1866:

"It is possible that the President may be impeached. If we go forward and supersede the sham governments set up in the rebel states, we encounter the appointing power of the President, who would put in office men who sympathize with him. It is this consideration which makes ardent representatives say that he must be removed. Should this be attempted, a new question will be presented." [7]

Through fear of Johnson's actions, the 40th Congress assembled in special session immediately after adjournment of the 39th, so that Congress was practically in continuous session and there was no interregnum during which Johnson could exercise his uncurbed power.

The new Congress immediately passed a supplementary Reconstruction bill to implement the main measure. This bill laid down a plan of registration for all male citizens, twenty-one years of age and over, who could take the oath of loyalty, and made it the duty of the commanding generals to order elections and choose delegates for constitutional conventions. If the voters favored such conventions, constitutions were to be formed and if adopted transmitted to Congress. The whole machinery of election was placed in the hands of the commanding generals.

The veto of this supplemental bill came immediately. The President in effect declared that the rise of the masses of black labor to political power was "an untried experiment" which "threatened" the whites with "even worse wrongs" than disfranchisement for attempted rebellion, and made "their condition the most deplorable to which any people can be reduced." And this from the life-long man of the people and champion of the rights of the poor!

It was bad enough when Johnson confined himself to speeches, as at Antietam, but when he came to action, Congress was further aroused. First, June 20, he issued liberal instructions concerning the loyal oath and the duty of commanding generals. He decided on advice of his Attorney General, Stanbery, that those taking the oath of loyalty were judges of their own honesty and could not be questioned by the Board of Registration; that actual disfranchisement for rebellion could only be made valid by law or court decision. Disloyal sentiments alone did not involve disfranchisement.

Moreover, in appointing generals, Johnson evidently proposed to appoint, as far as possible, generals who were sympathetic with the South. In July he removed Sheridan from Louisiana and Texas and appointed first General Thomas, a Virginia Democrat, in his place, and finally General Hancock, a loyal follower of Johnson. The removal of Sheridan caused great excitement. The Loyal Legion held a great meeting asking for the immediate summoning of Congress and the deposition of the President. He replaced General Sickles in the Carolinas with General Canby. Sheridan and Sickles were given posts in the North.

These instructions were published June 20 and Congress replied by the Act of July 19, 1867. This act specifically included Virginia, North Carolina, Louisiana and Arkansas in the states to be reconstructed; it provided that all the so-called governments in the South should be subject to the orders of the District Commanders and the General of the army and not of the President. The bill made the Boards of Registration judges of fact in regard to persons seeking to take the oath of loyalty and it extended the time limit for registration of voters.

The bill passed the Houses July 13, and was vetoed July 19. Johnson protested against the attempt of the Federal Government to carry on state governments, and especially against the invasion of the constitutional powers of the President. His words were bitter: "Whilst I hold the chief executive authority of the United States, whilst the obligation rests upon me to see that all the laws are faithfully executed, I can never willingly surrender that trust or the powers given for its execution. I can never give my assent to be made responsible for the faithful execution of laws, and at the same time surrender that trust and the powers which accompany it to any other executive officer, high or low, or to any number of executive officers." The bill was passed over the veto by both Houses by overwhelming majorities, and talk of impeachment started anew.

The discussion which has raged round the Reconstruction legislation is of the same metaphysical stripe characterizing all fetich-worship of the Constitution. If one means by "constitutional" something provided for in that instrument or foreseen by its authors or reasonably implicit in its words, then the Reconstruction Acts were undoubtedly unconstitutional; and so, for that matter, was the Civil War. In fact, the main measures of government during 1861-1870 were "unconstitutional." The only action possibly contemplated by the authors of the Constitution was secession; that action, the constitutional fathers feared and deprecated, but their instrument did not forbid it and distinctly implied the legality of a state withdrawing from the "more perfect union."

Certainly no one could argue that the founders contemplated civil war to preserve the Union or that the Constitution was a pro-slavery document. Yet, unconstitutionally, the South made it a pro-slavery document and unconstitutionally the North prevented the destruction of the Union on account of slavery; and after the war revolutionary measures rebuilt what revolution had disrupted, and formed a new United States on a basis broader than the old Constitution and different from its original conception.

And why not? No more idiotic program could be laid down than to require a people to follow a written rule of government 90 years old, if that rule had been definitely broken in order to preserve the unity of the government and to destroy an economic anachronism. In such a crisis legalists may insist that consistency with precedent is more important than firm and far-sighted rebuilding. But manifestly, it is not. Rule-following, legal precedence, and political consistency are not more important than right, justice and plain commonsense. Through the cobwebs of such political subtlety, Stevens crashed and said that military rule must continue in the South until order was restored, democracy established, and the political power built on slavery smashed. Further than this, both he and Sumner knew that land and education for black and white labor was necessary.

On the first day of the second session of the Thirty-Ninth Congress, Sumner was on hand with his bill for establishing universal suffrage in the District of Columbia. He had accepted a place on the Committee of the District of Columbia, in addition to his other duties, to secure Negro suffrage. The Committee reported a bill in December, 1866. Reading and writing as a qualification was moved as an amendment but was rejected by a vote of 15-19. Sumner voted "No." The bill did not reach a final vote but came up again December 10, 1867, when it passed after four days' debate by a vote of 32-13. The next day it passed the House, and went to the President.

Johnson and Seward, in the veto, kept hammering at the old thesis. Northern states will not allow Negro suffrage to be forced upon them against their will. The Negro population of the District has recently been greatly increased by migration. Their rights can be protected in the District without the right of suffrage, just as much as in Pennsylvania, Ohio and Indiana, which refuse Negroes the right to vote. Because of slavery, the Negro is not as well fitted to vote as the intelligent foreigner. And yet five years' residence and a knowledge of our government are required of the latter.

The bill was re-passed over the President's veto, January 7, and after it came the first proposal to impeach the President. "A great step along the path to universal suffrage without color distinctions has just been taken in the House of Representatives, in its session of the 18th. The bill giving the right to vote to the blacks in the District of Columbia passed with a majority of 114 to 54. An anxious crowd, of whites and blacks mixed, filled the galleries of the House and all the approaches to the Capitol, and the passage of the bill was hailed with a great outburst of frenzied applause." [8]

Three days after the 40th Congress opened, Sumner offered a series of resolutions to provide homes and schools for freedmen. This supplemented the Freedmen's Bureau law and provided a permanent policy of national aid to education and economic redress of the robbery of slavery. The resolutions did not come to a vote; Sumner then tried to amend the Reconstruction Acts of March 22 and July 19 by provisions for free schools in the South without discrimination as to race. A tie vote defeated this effort, although a majority of the Republicans stood by him. He tried again and failed July 11 and July 13. "His disappointment at his failure in 1867 to secure schools and homes for the freedmen was so keen that he left the Senate chamber, and when he reached his house, his grief found vent in tears." [9]

Charles Sumner, frustrated in these demands, continued to direct the line of attack which he had initiated during the Civil War. He had in mind relief for free Negroes in the North as well as freedmen in the South, and he was determined that petty race prejudice in the North should not escape attention because of the fight against slavery and its aftermath in the South.

Early in the spring of 1867, March 11, Stevens introduced a set of resolutions for the enforcement of the Confiscation Act of July 17, 1862, with preamble as follows: "Whereas it is due to justice, as an example to future times, that some proper pain should be inflicted on the people who constituted the 'Confederate States of America,' both because they declared an unjust war against the United States for the purpose of destroying republican liberty and permanently establishing slavery, as well as for the cruel and barbarous manner in which they conducted said war, in violation of all rules of civilized warfare, and also to compel them to make compensation for the damage and expense caused by said war, therefore: Be it enacted that all public lands belonging to the ten states that formed the so-called 'Confederate States of America,' shall be forfeited by said states and become vested forthwith in the United States." The measure further provided as follows: "Section 2, that the President should proceed at once to condemn the property forfeited under the aforesaid Act of July 17, 1862; section 3, that a commission of appraisers be appointed to appraise said property; section 4, that the land so seized and condemned should be distributed among the slaves who had been made free by the war and constitutional amendments, and who were residing on said land on the 4th of March, 1861, or since: to each head of a family 40 acres; to each adult male whether head of a family or not, 40 acres; to each widow, head of a family, 40 acres; to be held by them in fee simple, but to be inalienable for ten years after they should become so seized thereof. Section 5 provided for the raising of the sum of fifty dollars for each homesteader, to be used for the erection of a building on his homestead; and that the further sum of five hundred million dollars be raised for the purpose of pensioning the veterans of the Union army." The bill contained several other sections dealing with the subject in connection with the main features as above set forth.

Stevens called up this measure for consideration by the House on March 19, when he made one of his characteristic speeches, brilliant and pungent; age seems never to have had any effect upon his mental vigor nor any tendency to modify his sharp invectives. Said he: "I am about to discuss the question of pain of belligerent traitors. . . . The pain of traitors has been wholly ignored by a treacherous executive and a sluggish Congress. . . . I wish to make an issue before the American people and see whether they will sanction the perfect impunity of a murderous belligerent and consent that loyal men of this nation who have been despoiled of their property shall remain without remuneration, either by rebel property or the property of the nation. To this issue, I desire to devote the small remainder of my life. . . . No committee or party is responsible for this bill. Whatever merit it possesses is due to Andrew Johnson and myself."

Andrew Johnson did not falter and began to pin his faith on the fall elections of 1867. On September 7, 1867, Johnson extended full pardon to Confederates. His former proclamation, according to the *Tribune,* had "left about one hundred thousand citizens outside the amnesty, but this one leaves out one or two thousand."

Undoubtedly at this time Johnson was being urged toward stronger counter-revolutionary measures. He entertained the idea of ordering the military governors of the five Southern districts to enroll as voters the former Confederates whom he had included in his last Proclamation of Amnesty. Clemenceau said that when some of his Southern friends called on him, he admitted frankly that only the fear of being deposed prevented him from acting and he advised them to take the matter into court.

To court the South flew. Johnson's provisional governor of Mississippi tried in the name of his state to enjoin the President from executing the Reconstruction laws. The Supreme Court found in April, 1867, that its interference would be improper. Thereupon Governor Jackson of Georgia sought to enjoin the Secretary of War, the General of the Army, and the District Commander in Georgia; but the court decided it had no jurisdiction. A second time Georgia went to the Supreme Court and failed. Finally, late in 1867, W. H. McCardle of Mississippi, arrested by military authority under the Reconstruction acts, appealed from the Circuit to the Supreme Court, but Congress over the President's veto repealed the statute which allowed such an appeal, and by this revolutionary procedure made good its supreme power in Reconstruction over court and President.

Radical newspapers published in October a statement that the President had told certain friends in Tennessee that he would resist by force if Congress attempted to impeach him. Johnson denied that he had said anything of the sort, but Republicans made much of the fact that Johnson had ordered cannon furnished to Swann, Governor of Maryland, who like Johnson had been elected by the Republicans and had gone over to the Democrats. Swann asked the government to furnish him with cannon. Johnson gave Stanton the order to deliver the weapons needed. Stanton flatly refused. When General Grant took his place as Secretary of War, the Governor of Maryland renewed his request, which was again granted by Johnson and again refused by Grant. Finally, Swann made up his mind to buy the cannon. Most of the officers serving in Swann's militia were former Confederates.

During the fall campaign of 1867, there was fear of panic in the air on account of the vast circulation of greenbacks and bank notes to the extent of a billion dollars. With money fluctuating in value, trade became a lottery. Higher protection was put on steel and woolen goods. But curiously enough, the Democrats in general avoided the tariff issue. They did not follow Johnson's attack on finance because they saw its inconsistency with the reaction of property in the South. Leaving the economic argument, they embraced with avidity race prejudice and concentrated their campaign on this.

Clemenceau said, "The best point of attack for the Democrats is the Negroes. Any Democrat who did not manage to hint in his speech that the Negro is a degenerate gorilla, would be considered lacking in enthusiasm. The idea of giving political power to a lot of wild men, incapable of civilization, whose intelligence is no higher than that of the animal! That is the theme of all Democratic speeches." [10] With this, of course, went fetich worship of the Constitution.

Johnson looked forward with hope. October elections took place in Ohio and Pennsylvania and showed reaction toward the Democrats.

In Ohio, R. B. Hayes, afterward president, ran against Allan G. Thurman, and Negro suffrage played a large part. Hayes denied the assertion that the government was a white man's government. "It is not the Government of any class or sect or nationality or race. . . . It is not the Government of the native born or of the foreign born, of the rich man or of the poor man, of the white man or of the colored man—it is the Government of the freeman." The "monstrous inconsistency and injustice of excluding one-seventh of our population from all participation in a Government founded on the consent of the governed" was held to be impossible. There was no necessary antagonism between the two races which could not be broken down by justice and equality. [11]

Hayes won by less than 3,000 votes, as compared with a Republican majority of 42,000 in 1866. Also, at the same time, the voters rejected the Negro suffrage amendment by 38,000 votes, and elected a Democratic legislature. There were, however, certain other elements. The Republicans had sought to disfranchise deserters from the army, and Ben Wade had aroused the bitter hostility of Southern elements in southern Ohio.

Ohio expressed itself against the high tariff "to fill the pockets of Eastern monopolists," and in favor of agricultural labor, showing the peculiar contradiction in the minds of the voters. Johnson telegraphed Ohio: "Ohio has done its duty and done it in time. God bless Ohio."

Pennsylvania lost nearly the whole of its Republican majority of thirty thousand. In New York cannon were kept firing for two days.

Most of the state elections came in November, and showed some reaction toward the Democrats but not so great as in October. The Republicans won in Massachusetts, Michigan, Wisconsin, Kansas, Minnesota, Missouri and Illinois, but were completely defeated in New York, New Jersey and Maryland.

New Jersey refused to strike out the word "white" from the requirements for suffrage; in New York, the Republicans did not dare to submit to popular vote the proposal to drop the property discrimination against Negro voters. Maryland adopted a new registry law which gave the vote to whites only.

On the other hand, during 1867, Iowa and Dakota admitted Negroes to the ballot, and Minnesota in 1868. In this latter year Negroes were voting in all the New England states except Connecticut, in Iowa, Minnesota and Dakota—a total of 8 Northern states. The South and its friends had a right to charge that 8 other Northern states refused to enfranchise a class to which they were forcing the South to give the vote.

In the third annual message of Andrew Johnson, December 3, 1867, all masking of the Negro problem is removed. He is no longer evasive as to the relation of the black worker to the white worker and his whole economic argument is drowned in race hate. There is no suggestion that Negro soldiers or Negro property owners or Negroes who can read and write should have any political rights. He bases his whole argument flatly on the inferiority of the Negro race.

"It is the glory of white men," he proclaims magniloquently, "to know that they have had these qualities in sufficient measure to build upon this continent a great political fabric and to preserve its stability for more than ninety years, while in every other part of the world all similar experiments have failed. But if anything can be proved by known facts, if all reasoning upon evidence is not abandoned, it must be acknowledged that in the progress of nations, Negroes have shown less capacity for government than any other race of people. No independent government of any form has ever been successful in their hands. On the contrary, wherever they have been left to their own devices they have shown a constant tendency to relapse into barbarism. In the Southern States, however, Congress has undertaken to confer upon them the privilege of the ballot. Just released from slavery, it may be doubted whether as a class they know more than their ancestors how to organize and regulate civil society. Indeed, it is admitted that the blacks of the South are not only regardless of the rights of property, but so utterly ignorant of public affairs that their voting can consist in nothing more than carrying a ballot to the place where they are directed to deposit it.

"The great difference between the two races in physical, mental and moral characteristics will prevent an amalgamation or fusion of them together in one homogeneous mass. If the inferior obtains the ascendency over the other, it will govern with reference only to its own interests—for it will recognize no common interest—and create such a tyranny as this continent has never yet witnessed. Already the Negroes are influenced by promises of confiscation and plunder. They are taught to regard as an enemy every white man who has any respect for the rights of his own race. If this continues it must become worse and worse, until all order will be subverted, all industry cease, and the fertile fields of the South grow up into a wilderness. Of all the dangers which our nation has yet encountered, none are equal to those which must result from the success of the effort now making to Africanize the half of our country."

It is easy to believe now that the idea that Andrew Johnson and the South planned a coup d'état was fanciful. The point is that sane and thoughtful men at the time widely believed it. No matter how incredible it may seem to us, we must remember that this was a generation to which it had seemed incredible that the South should secede. They had seen the incredible happen at fearful cost. It might happen again. The Republicans, therefore, refused to be frightened by the elections of 1867. Carl Schurz said that "I think that I do not exaggerate that an overwhelming majority of the loyal Union men, North and South, saw in President Johnson a traitor bent upon turning over the national government to the rebels again, and ardently wishing to see him utterly stripped of power, not so much for what he had done, but for what, as they thought, he was capable of doing and likely to do."

Impeachment proceedings now hurried forward. They had begun in December, 1866. On February 28, 1867, the Committee on Judiciary had refused to recommend impeachment of the President but asked for further investigation. March 2, the Reconstruction Act passed, and March 7, impeachment was moved for the second time in the House. Johnson had notified the Senate of the suspension of Secretary Stanton in December, 1867. Early the next year, the Senate refused to concur, Grant gave up the office, and Stanton resumed his duties. Stanton was dismissed again in February, 1868, and the impeachment of Johnson was determined upon in March.

The beginning of the attempt to impeach President Johnson was a memorable scene. Thaddeus Stevens made his speech February 16, 1868. He was hopelessly broken in health, and a hushed and expectant audience listened to every word. He spoke with force and solemnity. "I doubt," said Charles Sumner, "if words were ever delivered to more effect." [12] He was a dying man and this was his last word.

Who in 1867 represented the considered will of the people of the United States? Certainly not Andrew Johnson, backed by Northern copperheads and the supporters of a futile attempt at secession. Just as certainly two-thirds of the members of Congress, with the South excluded as it had been excluded for six terrible years, had a clear right to express the repeatedly registered popular will.

The problem was a difficult one. When can a ruler rule in the United States? The nation by overwhelming majority had declared for union, for emancipation to preserve the Union, for no increase in the political power of the white South, and for Negro suffrage to prevent this increased political power and reward Negro loyalty.

This clear will of the majority of the people, represented in Congress, was frustrated by a President who repeatedly refused to obey the plain mandate of the party which elected him. Johnson virtually declared Congress illegal because the South was unrepresented. Congress denied that a criminal could be his own judge. Who could settle this dispute? By the whole theory of party government, a President must be at least in general accord with his party. His utmost power should not go beyond a suspensory veto compelling a plebiscite. Yet no president in the history of the United States up to this time had used the veto power like Andrew Johnson to oppose the expressed will of the nation. In twenty-three cases, he opposed his will to the will of Congress, while Andrew Jackson, his closest competitor, made only eleven vetoes and pocket vetoes. Party responsibility in government was absolutely blocked at a time of crisis. Under any, even partial, theory of such responsibility, Johnson would have been compelled to resign; but the antiquated constitutional requirements of a system of laws built for another age and for entirely different circumstances were now being applied to unforeseen conditions.

The Constitution made the removal of the President contingent upon his committing "high crimes and misdemeanors." Here then came a plain question of definition: was it a crime, in the judgment of the people of the United States in 1867, for a President to block the overwhelming will of a successful majority of voters during a period of nearly three years? Stevens and those who followed him said that it was. They did not all pretend that Johnson was personally a criminal with treasonable designs, although some believed even that; on the other hand it was clear even to many of Johnson's friends that he was "an unfit person to be President of the United States." [13] They all did assert that he had broken the rules by which responsible government could be carried on.

The trial started March 30, 1868, and ended May 6. Over two-thirds of the members of the United States House of Representatives, 35 out of 54 Senators, and the great majority of the voters of the nation, outside the former slave states, agreed that Johnson should be removed from office. Whether they were right or wrong, the failure legally to convict Johnson has remained to frustrate responsible government in the United States ever since. But no President since Johnson has attempted indefinitely to rule in defiance of Congress.

The leaders of abolition-democracy still pressed on. Sumner was especially active and destined for several more years of active work.

Thaddeus Stevens was near death, but to the very end he fought on. He wished to ask Congress to declare by law that no state had the right to forbid citizens of the United States from taking part in the national elections.

Thaddeus Stevens died August 11, 1868, three weeks after the ratification of the Fourteenth Amendment was announced, and in his last breath and even after death, stood true to his principles. "Two colored clergymen called, and asked leave to see Stevens and pray with him. He ordered them to be admitted; and when they had come to his bedside, he turned and held out his hand to one of them. They sang a hymn and prayed. . . . It was then within ten minutes of midnight, and the end was to come before the beginning of the new day. He lay motionless for a few minutes, then opened his eyes, took one look, placidly closed them, and, without a struggle, the great commoner had ceased to breathe." [14]

Thaddeus Stevens was buried in a colored graveyard. Upon the monument there is the following inscription, prepared by himself: "I repose in this quiet and secluded spot, not from any natural preference for solitude, but finding other cemeteries limited as to race by charter rules, I have chosen this, that I might illustrate in my death the principles which I advocated through a long life, [the] Equality of Man before his Creator."

A Charles Sumner said: "Already he takes his place among illustrious names, which are the common property of mankind. I see him now as I have so often seen him during life. His venerable form moves slowly and with uncertain steps; but the gathered strength of years is in his countenance and the light of victory on his path. Politician calculator, time-server, stand aside! a hero statesman passes to his reward!" [15]

As a result of the legislation of the 39th and 40th Congresses, the United States in 1867 took a portentous forward step in democracy.

For the mass of the nation, it was a step taken under compulsion of fear, without deep forethought and with a rather didactic following out of certain conventional principles which made universal suffrage seem natural and inevitable. To the South, it was the price of that disaster of slavery and war which spelled its history from 1830 to 1865; and it was the only price adequate to that fatal mistake.

To those men who were guiding American industry toward a new and fateful path, the Southern experiment was simply a political move by which they silenced and held in check the tremendous political power built on slavery, which in many ways and for a generation had threatened the nation and checked its economic development.

To a few far-seeing leaders of democracy this experiment appeared in its truer light. It was a test of the whole theory of American government. It was a dictatorship backed by the military arm of the United States by which the governments of the Southern states were to be coerced into accepting a new form of administration, in which the freedmen and the poor whites were to hold the overwhelming balance of political power. As soon as political power was successfully delivered into the hands of these elements, the Federal government was to withdraw and full democracy ensue.

The difficulty with this theory was the failure to realize that such dictatorship must last long enough really to put the mass of workers in power; that this would be in fact a dictatorship of the proletariat which must endure until the proletariat or at least a leading united group, with clear objects and effective method, had education and experience and had taken firm control of the economic organization of the South. Unfortunately, the power set to begin this dictatorship was the military arm of a government which more and more was falling into the hands of organized wealth, and of wealth organized on a scale never before seen in modern civilization.

The new organization of Northern wealth was not comparable to the petty bourgeoisie which seized power after the overthrow of European feudalism. It was a new rule of associated and federated monarchs of industry and finance wielding a vaster and more despotic power than European kings and nobles ever held. It was destined to subdue not simply Southern agrarianism but even individual wealth and brains in the North which were creating a new petty bourgeoisie of small merchants and skilled artisans.

It was inconceivable, therefore, that the masters of Northern industry through their growing control of American government, were going to allow the laborers of the South any more real control of wealth and industry than was necessary to curb the political power of the planters and their successors. As soon as the Southern landholders and merchants yielded to the Northern demands of a plutocracy, at that moment the military dictatorship should be withdrawn and a dictatorship of capital allowed unhampered sway.

We see this more clearly today than the nation of 1868, or any of its leaders, could possibly envisage it; but even then, Northern industry knew that universal suffrage in the South, in the hands of Negroes just freed from slavery, and of white people still enslaved by poverty, could not stand against organized industry. They promptly calculated that the same method of controlling the labor vote would come in vogue in the South as they were already using in the North, and that the industry which used these methods must in the meantime coöperate with Northern industry; that it could not move the foundation stones upon which Northern industry was consolidating its power; that is, the tariff, the money system, the debt, and national in place of state control of industry. This would seem to be what the masters of exploitation were counting upon and it certainly came true in the bargain of 1876.

Thus by singular coincidence and for a moment, for the few years of an eternal second in a cycle of a thousand years, the orbits of two widely and utterly dissimilar economic systems coincided and the result was a revolution so vast and portentous that few minds ever fully conceived it; for the systems were these: first, that of a democracy which should by universal suffrage establish a dictatorship of the proletariat ending in industrial democracy; and the other, a system by which a little knot of masterful men would so organize capitalism as to bring under their control the natural resources, wealth and industry of a vast and rich country and through that, of the world. For a second, for a pulse of time, these orbits crossed and coincided, but their central suns were a thousand light-years apart, even though the blind and ignorant fury of the South and the complacent Philistinism of the North saw them as one.

Reconstruction was an economic revolution on a mighty scale and with world-wide reverberation. Reconstruction was not simply a fight between the white and black races in the South or between master and ex-slave. It was much more subtle; it involved more than this. There have been repeated and continued attempts to paint this era as an interlude of petty politics or nightmare of race hate instead of viewing it slowly and broadly as a tremendous series of efforts to earn a living in new and untried ways, to achieve economic security and to restore fatal losses of capital and investment. It was a vast labor movement of ignorant, earnest, and bewildered black men whose faces had been ground in the mud by their three awful centuries of degradation and who now staggered forward blindly in blood and tears amid petty division, hate and hurt, and surrounded by every disaster of war and industrial upheaval. Reconstruction was a vast labor movement of ignorant, muddled and bewildered white men who had been disinherited of land and labor and fought a long battle with sheer subsistence, hanging on the edge of poverty, eating clay and chasing slaves and now lurching up to manhood. Reconstruction was the turn of white Northern migration southward to new and sudden economic opportunity which followed the disaster and dislocation of war, and an attempt to organize capital and labor on a new pattern and build a new economy. Finally Reconstruction was a desperate effort of a dislodged, maimed, impoverished and ruined oligarchy and monopoly to restore an anachronism in economic organization by force, fraud and slander, in defiance of law and order, and in the face of a great labor movement of white and black, and in bitter strife with a new capitalism and a new political framework.

All these contending and antagonistic groups spoke different and unknown tongues; to the Negro "Freedom" was God; to the poor white "Freedom" was nothing—he had more than he had use for; to the planter "Freedom" for the poor was laziness and for the rich, control of the poor worker; for the Northern business man "Freedom" was opportunity to get rich.

Yet, with interpretation, agreement was possible here; North and South agreed that laborers must produce profit; the poor white and the Negro wanted to get the profit arising from the laborers' toil and not to divide it with the employers and landowners. When Northern and Southern employers agreed that profit was most important and the method of getting it second, the path to understanding was clear. When white laborers were convinced that the degradation of Negro labor was more fundamental than the uplift of white labor, the end was in sight.

Not only did all those factors becloud this extraordinary series of movements so that the truth of the matter in itself was baffling to observers and interpreters—but over all has spread, to this day, a cloud of lying and slander which leaves historians and philosophers aghast and has resulted in a current theory of interpretation which pictures all participants as scoundrels, idiots and heroes—a combination humanly improbable and demonstrably untrue.

One cannot study Reconstruction without first frankly facing the facts of universal lying; of deliberate and unbounded attempts to prove a case and win a dispute and preserve economic mastery and political domination by besmirching the character, motives, and commonsense, of every single person who dared disagree with the dominant philosophy of the white South.

The campaign of slander against "carpetbaggers" rose to a climax which included every Northern person who defended the Negro, and every Northern person in the South who was connected with the army or Freedmen's Bureau or with the institutions of learning, or who admitted the right of the Negro to vote or defended him in any way. It was the general, almost universal, belief that practically without exception these people were liars, jailbirds, criminals and thieves, and the hatred of them rose to a crescendo of curses and filth. Later, this universal attack upon the carpetbaggers was modified considerably, and it was admitted that there were among them some decent and high-minded men, although most of them still were regarded as selfish stealers of public funds.

On the other hand, so far as the Negro was concerned, almost no exceptions were admitted. It was easier to traduce him because everyone was ready to believe the worst and no reply was, for the moment, listened to. There was not a single great black leader of Reconstruction against whom almost unprintable allegations were not repeatedly and definitely made without any attempt to investigate the reliability of sources of information.

For the first time in national history interstate migration became a crime. Hundreds of thousands of Southerners had gone North and West and had been welcomed and integrated into the various states despite their divergent ideas and alien heredity. But when there came a comparatively small number of Northerners into the South, they were reviled unless they conformed absolutely in thought and action with a dead past.

The Northern whites were of many classes: former soldiers and officers, lingering in the South in connection with the army or the Freedmen's Bureau, or as investors and farmers. They were reënforced by an army of men who came South with small capital and in many cases succeeded in making their fortune. Most of these had no especial love for the Negroes. They had come into a white man's war, and now that the Negro was free, they were perfectly free to use him and to organize his industrial and political power for their own advantage.

Many of these were agents for capital and went down from the North with something of the psychology of modern investment in conquered or colonial territory: that is, they brought the capital; they invested it; they remained in charge to oversee the profits; and they acquired political power in order to protect these profits.

On the other hand, there were teachers who came down from the North, army chaplains, social workers and others, who whole-heartedly went into the new democracy to the limit. Extraordinary persons stood forth in this rôle, like General Fisk and Erastus Cravath at Nashville,

Edmund Ware at Atlanta, General Armstrong at Hampton, and dozens of others. They were crusaders in a great cause and meticulously honest. Naturally, their numbers were comparatively small. They reached primarily students, teachers and preachers among the Negroes and only incidentally the class of field hands.

It was a battle between oligarchy whose wealth and power had been based on land and slaves on the one hand; and on the other, oligarchy built on machines and hired labor. The newly organized industry of the North was not only triumphant in the North but began pressing in upon the South; its advance guard was represented by those small Northern capitalists and officeholders who sought to make quick money in raising cotton and taking advantage of the low-priced labor and high cotton prices due to the war famine.

The labor on the market, instead of being owned like the slaves or excluded from competition like the poor whites, suddenly found itself bid for and offered not only money wages, but political power and social status. The bidders had no realization at first how high their labor bids were in Southern custom; they were offering something below the current price of labor in all civilized lands; the Northern United States, England, France, most of Germany and parts of Italy were giving labor some voice in governing and a money wage contract.

To the plantation planters such a wage contract was economic heresy and social revolution. It was blasphemy and eternal damnation to them, and they fought by every conceivable weapon—political power, social influence, murder, assassination and systematic lying.

The mass of poor whites were in an anomalous position. Those of them who were intelligent or had during slavery accumulated any capital or achieved any position, had always attached themselves in sympathy and interest to the planter class. This meant that the mass of ignorant poor white labor had practically no intelligent leadership. Only here and there were there men, like Hinton Helper, who were actual leaders of the poor whites against the planters. The poor white was in a quandary with regard to emancipation. He had viewed slavery as the cause of his own degradation, but he now viewed the free Negro as a threat to his very existence. Suppose that freedom for the Negro meant that Negroes might rise to be landholders, planters and employers? The poor whites thus might lose the last shred of respectability. They had been used to seeing certain classes of the black slaves above them in economic prosperity and social power. But after all, they were still Negroes and slaves. Now that freedom had come, poor whites were faced by the dilemma of recognizing the Negroes as equals or of bending every effort to still keep them beneath the white mass in income and social power.

Here and there certain leaders appeared among the planters, among the more intelligent of the poor whites, and even among the masses, who looked toward political combination and economic alliance with the Negro. Such persons, the Southerners called "scalawags," but they were in fact that part of the white South who saw a vision of democracy across racial lines, and who were willing to build up a labor party in opposition to capitalists and landholders. They were, therefore, especially to be feared and were endlessly reviled. They were forced into certain extreme positions as compared with the carpetbagger and the planter. Men like Hunnicutt of Virginia asked not only political rights, but full social equality for the Negroes, and taunted planters and the carpetbaggers when they did not dare advocate this.

When Andrew Johnson said in his veto of the Reconstruction bill, March 2, 1867: "The Negroes have not asked for the privilege of voting; the vast majority of them have no idea what it means," he was exaggerating. Negroes had certainly voted, not only in the North but in South Carolina in the eighteenth century and in North Carolina, Louisiana and Tennessee in the nineteenth. They had asked to vote in the South repeatedly since Emancipation. The difference that now came was that an indefinitely larger number of Negroes than ever before was enfranchised suddenly, and 99% of them belonged to the laboring class, whereas by law the Negroes who voted in the early history of the country were for the most part property holders, and prospective if not actual constituents of a petty bourgeoisie.

When freedom came, this mass of Negro labor was not without intelligent leadership, and a leadership which because of former race prejudice and the present Color Line, could not be divorced from the laboring mass, as had been the case with the poor whites. The group of intelligent, free Negroes in Washington, Richmond, Charleston and especially New Orleans, had accumulated some wealth and some knowledge of group coöperation and initiative. Almost without exception, they accepted the new responsibility of leading the emancipated slaves, unselfishly and effectively. Free Negroes from the North, most of whom had been born in the South and knew conditions, came back in considerable numbers during Reconstruction, and took their place as leaders. The result was that the Negroes were not, as they are sometimes painted, simply a mass of densely ignorant toilers. The rank and file of black labor had a notable leadership of intelligence during Reconstruction times.

It was, however, a leadership which was not at all clear in its economic thought. On the whole, it believed in the accumulation of wealth and the exploitation of labor as the normal method of economic development. But it also believed in the right to vote as the basis and defense of economic life, and gradually but surely it was forced by the demand of the mass of Negro laborers to face the problem of land. Thus the Negro leaders gradually but certainly turned toward emphasis on economic emancipation. They wanted the Negro to have the right to work at a decent rate of wages, and they expected that the right to vote would come when he had sufficient education and perhaps a certain minimum of property to deserve it. It was this among other things that was the cause of the tremendous push toward education which the Negroes exhibited.

On the other hand, their desire for economic enfranchisement, for real abolition of slavery, had been affronted by the Black Codes. They were scared and hampered in the very beginning of their freedom by these enactments and by the way in which these and other laws were executed.

The government replied before the death of Abraham Lincoln with government guardianship in the shape of the Freedmen's Bureau. This bureau never had a real chance to organize and function properly. It was hastily organized. It had to use the persons at hand and on the ground largely for its personnel. It had at first no government appropriations and in the end only limited appropriations and it was always faced by the probability of quick dissolution. It was surrounded from the beginning by the spirit which enacted the Black Codes. Southerners were desperately opposed to it because it stood between them and the exploitation of labor toward which they were impelled by their losses and the high price of cotton. If they had been allowed to exploit and drive black labor after the war, many Southerners despite their losses could have partially recouped their fortunes. But here came an organization which demanded money wages of employers who had no money, and demanded the modern treatment of labor from former slave drivers.

Beside the Freedmen's Bureau and before it, there was the chance for the Negroes to seek the advice of their former masters and in many cases this was willingly and wisely given, particularly in the case of masters ready to assist a new economic régime; but it was hindered by several considerations. First, any new union between former masters and Negroes was rekindling the old enmity and jealousy of the poor whites against any combination of the white employer and the black laborer which would again exclude the poor white. The planter, therefore, had to be careful of any open sympathy or coöperation with the black laborer. Already his ranks had been decimated by war and his social status threatened by poverty. Then, too, insofar as the black laborer was guided by the Freedmen's Bureau, by Northern philanthropy and by Northern capital, he brought upon himself the bitter enmity of the former master; so that on the whole, while there was considerable advice and help from the former master, in the long run it did not and could not amount to much.

Then, too, we must remember that these former slaveholders did not believe that Negroes could advance in freedom. They knew, of course, that some could, but even if these could, how could white men and masters coöperate with them? The whole trend of teaching had been that this was utterly impossible. If Negroes succeeded and insofar as they did, it would lead straight to social equality and amalgamation; and if they did not succeed it would lead to deterioration in culture and civilization.

The real economic battle, then, lay finally in a series of attempted compromises between planters, carpetbaggers, scalawags, poor white laborers and Negroes. First, the planters moved toward the political control of Negroes to fix their economic control. This the poor whites had of course feared and their fears were voiced repeatedly by Andrew Johnson. Many people in the North looked upon this as a possible and threatening answer to the enfranchisement of the blacks. The combination was frustrated because the carpetbaggers offered the Negroes better terms; offered them the right to vote and to hold office and some economic freedom. When this economic freedom looked toward landholding and higher wages, it could be accomplished only at the expense of the employing class, and so far as Negro labor accepted, as it had to accept the offer of the carpetbaggers and scalawags, it alienated the planters, and not only that, but it frightened the poor whites.

Here again, as in the case of slavery, there was a combination in which the poor whites seemed excluded, unless they made common cause with the blacks. This union of black and white labor never got a real start. First, because black leadership still tended toward the ideals of the petty bourgeois, and white leadership tended distinctly toward strengthening capitalism. The final move which rearranged all these combinations and led to the catastrophe of 1876, was a combination of planters and poor whites in defiance of their economic interests; and with the use of lawless murder and open intimidation. It was a combination that could only have been stopped by government force; and the army which was the agent of the Federal Government was sustained in the South by the organized capital of the North. All that was necessary, then, was to satisfy Northern industry that the new combination in the South was essentially a combination which aimed at capitalistic exploitation on conventional terms. The result was the withdrawal of military support and the revolutionary suppression not only of Negro suffrage but of the economic development of Negro and white labor.

It was not until after the period which this book treats that white labor in the South began to realize that they had lost a great opportunity, that when they united to disfranchise the black laborer they had cut the voting power of the laboring class in two. White labor in the Populist movement of the eighties tried to realign the economic warfare in the South and bring workers of all colors into united opposition to the employer. But they found that the power which they had put in the hands of the employers in 1876 so dominated political life that free and honest expression of public will at the ballot-box was impossible in the South, even for white men. They realized that it was not simply the Negro who had been disfranchised in 1876, it was the white laborer as well. The South had since become one of the greatest centers for exploitation of labor in the world, and labor suffered not only in the South but throughout the country and the world over.

Curious and contradictory has been the criticism and comment accompanying this great controversy and revolution of 1866-1876. Floods of tears and sentiment have been expended on the suffering and disillusionment of the slave baron, while the equally great losses of Northern and Southern labor have been forgotten. And above all, the plight of the most helpless victims of the situation, the black freedmen, has been treated with callous and hardened judgments, cemented with hate. The Northern business man has justly been accused of being motivated, during this period, chiefly by greed and profit. But the profit and greed of the slaveholder which caused the whole catastrophe, and of the planter who forced an unjust and still dangerous solution, has been sicklied o'er with sentiment.

In all this, one sees the old snobbery of class judgment in new form —tears and sentiment for Marie Antoinette on the scaffold, but no sign of grief for the gutters of Paris and the fields of France, where the victims of exploitation and ignorance lay rotting in piles.

The South, after the war, presented the greatest opportunity for a real national labor movement which the nation ever saw or is likely to see for many decades. Yet the labor movement, with but few exceptions, never realized the situation. It never had the intelligence or knowledge, as a whole, to see in black slavery and Reconstruction, the kernel and meaning of the labor movement in the United States.

After Lincoln's assassination, the General Council of the International Workingmen's Association, under Karl Marx, sent an address to Andrew Johnson:

"After a gigantic Civil War, which if we consider its colossal extension and its vast scenes of action, seems in comparison with the Hundred Years' War and the Thirty Years' War and the Twenty-three Years' War of the Old World scarcely to have lasted ninety days, the task, Sir, devolves upon you to uproot by law what the sword has felled, and to preside over the more difficult work of political reconstruction and social regeneration. The profound consciousness of your great mission will preserve you from all weakness in the execution of your stern duties. You will never forget that the American people at the inauguration of the new era of the emancipation of labor placed the burden of leadership on the shoulders of two men of labor—Abraham Lincoln, the one, and the other, Andrew Johnson." [16]

In 1865, September, another address over the signature of Marx declared boldly: "Injustice against a fraction of your people having been followed by such dire consequences, put an end to it. Declare your fellow citizens from this day forth free and equal, without any reserve. If you refuse them citizens' rights while you exact from them citizens' duties, you will sooner or later face a new struggle which will once more drench your country in blood."

The National Labor Union of workers was organized at Baltimore, Maryland, August 20, 1866. There were sixty delegates and on their banner was inscribed "Welcome to the sons of toil from the North, East, South and West." An address was issued on coöperation, trade unions, apprenticeship, strikes, labor of women, public land and political action. As to the Negroes, the union admitted that it was unable to express an opinion which would satisfy all, but the question must not be allowed to pass unnoticed. The Negro worker had been neglected. Coöperation of the African race in systematic organization must be secured. Otherwise, Negroes must act as scabs, as in the case of the colored caulkers, imported from Virginia to Boston, during the strike on the 8-hour question. There should be no distinction of race or nationality, but only separation into two great classes: laborers and those who live by others' labor. Negroes were soon to be admitted to citizenship and the ballot. Their ballot strength would be of great value to union labor. If labor did not accept them, capital would use the Negro to split white and black labor, just as the Austrian government had used race dissension. Such a lamentable situation should not be allowed to develop in America. Trade unions, eight-hour leagues, and other groups should be organized among Negroes.

Here was a first halting note. Negroes were welcomed to the labor movement, not because they were laborers but because they might be competitors in the market, and the logical conclusion was either to organize them or guard against their actual competition by other methods. It was to this latter alternative that white American labor almost unanimously turned.

This was manifest at the second annual meeting in Chicago in 1867, where the Negro problem was debated more frankly and less successfully. The President called attention to Negroes whose emancipation had given them a new position in the labor world. They would now come in competition with white labor. He suggested that the best way to meet this situation was to form trade unions among Negroes. A committee of three on Negro labor was selected. The Committee on Negro Labor reported that having had the subject under consideration, and after having heard the suggestions and opinions of several members of this convention—pro and con—they had arrived at the following conclusions:

"That, while we feel the importance of the subject, and realize the danger in the future of competition in mechanical Negro labor, yet we find the subject involved in so much mystery, and upon it so wide diversity of opinion amongst our members, we believe that it is inexpedient to take action on the subject in this National Labor Congress.

"Resolved, that the subject of Negro labor be laid over till the next session of the National Labor Congress. . . ."

The report of this committee brought a whirlwind of discussion which lasted throughout the whole day:

"The Negro will bear to be taught his duty, and has already stood his ground nobly when a member of a trades' union. . . .

"Did not like to confess to the world that there was a subject with which they were afraid to cope. . . .

"This very question was at the root of the rebellion, which was the war of the poor white men of the South, who were forced by the slaveholders into the war. . . .

"In New Haven, there were a number of respectable colored mechanics, but they had not been able to induce the trades' unions to admit them. . . . Was there any union in the states which would admit colored men?

"The colored man was industrious, and susceptible of improvement and advancement. . . .

"There was no need of entering on any discussion of the matter.

"There was no necessity for the foisting of the subject of colored labor, or the appointment of a committee to report thereon. . . . The blacks would combine together of themselves and by themselves, without the assistance of whites. God speed them; but let not the whites try to carry them on their shoulders. . . .

"Time enough to talk about admitting colored men to trades' unions and to the Congress when they applied for admission. . . .

"Whites striking against the blacks, and creating an antagonism which will kill off the trades' unions, unless the two be consolidated. There is no concealing the fact that the time will come when the Negro 'will take possession of the shops if we have not taken possession of the Negro. If the workingmen of the white race do not conciliate the blacks, the black vote will be cast against them.'

"The capitalists of New England now employ foreign boys and girls n their mills, to the almost entire exclusion of the native-born population. They would seek to supplant these by colored workers. . . .

"Little danger of black men wanting to enter trades' unions any more than Germans would try to join the English societies in America. . . ." [17]

The whole question was finally dodged by taking refuge in the fact that the constitution invited "all labor."

Sylvis, President of the International Labor Movement, spoke out in 1868 on slavery:

"Whatever our opinions may be as to immediate causes of the war, we can all agree that human slavery (property in man) was the first great cause; and from the day that the first gun was fired, it was my earnest hope that the war might not end until slavery ended it. No man in America rejoiced more than I at the downfall of Negro slavery. But when the shackles fell from the limbs of those four millions of blacks, it did not make them *free* men; it simply transferred them from one condition of slavery to another; it placed them upon the platform of the white working men, and made all slaves together. I do not mean that freeing the Negro enslaved the white; I mean that we were slaves before; always have been, and that the abolition of the right of property in man added four millions of black slaves to the white slaves of the country. We are now all one family of slaves together, and the labor reform movement is a second emancipation proclamation." [18]

In the meeting of the National Labor Union in New York in 1868, there was no mention of Negroes, but in 1869 at Philadelphia among 142 representatives, there appeared nine Negroes representing various separate Negro unions and organizations. This pointed a way out which labor eagerly seized. Contrary to all labor philosophy, they would divide labor by racial and social lines and yet continue to talk of one labor movement. Through this separate union, Negro labor would be restrained from competition and yet kept out of the white race unions where power and discussion lay. A resolution was adopted saying that the National Labor Union would recognize neither color nor sex in the question of the rise of all labor, and the colored laborers were urged to form their own organizations and send delegates to the next conference. The Negroes responded and declared that all Negroes wanted was a fair chance and no one would be the worse off for giving it. Isaac Myers, their leader, said: "The white laboring men of the country have nothing to fear from the colored laboring men. We desire to see labor elevated and made respectable; we desire to have the highest rate of wages that our labor is worth; we desire to have the hours of labor regulated as well to the interest of the laborer as to the capitalist. Mr. President, American citizenship for the black man is a complete failure if he is proscribed from the workshops of the country." [19]

In 1869, the General Council of the National Working-Men's Association sent a letter signed by Karl Marx to the President of the National Labor Union.

"The immediate tangible result of the Civil War was of course a deterioration of the condition of American Workingmen. Both in the United States and in Europe the colossal burden of a public debt was shifted from hand to hand in order to settle it upon the shoulders of the working class. The prices of necessaries, remarks one of your statesmen, have risen 78 per cent since 1860, while the wages of simple manual labor have risen 50 and those of skilled labor 60 per cent. 'Pauperism,' he complains, 'is increasing in America more rapidly than population.' Moreover the sufferings of the working class are in glaring contrast to the new-fangled luxury of financial aristocrats, shoddy aristocrats and other vermin bred by the war. Still the Civil War offered a compensation in the liberation of the slaves and the impulse which it thereby gave your own class movement. Another war, not sanctified by a sublime aim or a social necessity, but like the wars of the Old World, would forge chains for the free workingmen instead of sundering those of the slaves." [20]

Sylvis, President of the International Labor Movement, acknowledged this letter but said nothing about slavery, confining himself to attacking the monied aristocracy.

Thus American labor leaders tried to emphasize the fact that here was a new element; new not in he sense that it had not been there,—it had been there all the time—but new in the sense that the Negro worker must now be taken account of, both in his own interest and particularly in their interest. He was a competitor and a prospective under-bidder. Then difficulties appeared; the white worker did not want the Negro in his unions, did not believe in him as a man, dodged the question, and when he appeared at conventions, asked him to organize separately; that is, outside the real labor movement, in spite of the fact that this was a contradiction of all sound labor policy.

As the Negro laborers organized separately, there came slowly to realization the fact that here was not only separate organization but a separation in leading ideas; because among Negroes, and particularly in the South, there was being put into force one of the most extraordinary experiments of Marxism that the world, before the Russian revolution, had seen. That is, backed by the military power of the United States, a dictatorship of labor was to be attempted and those who were leading the Negro race in this vast experiment were emphasizing the necessity of the political power and organization backed by protective military power.

On the other hand, the trade union movement of the white labor in the North was moving away from that idea and moving away from politics. They seemed to see a more purely economic solution in their demand for higher wages and shorter hours. Ira Stewart spoke for "men who labor excessively . . . robbed of all ambition to ask for anything more than will satisfy their bodily necessities, while those who labor moderately have time to cultivate tastes and create wants in addition to mere physical comforts." [21] But Stewart was not thinking of Negroes and only once barely mentioned them:

"That we rejoice that the rebel aristocracy of the South has been crushed, that we rejoice that beneath the glorious shadow of our victorious flag men of every clime, lineage and color are recognized as free. But while we will bear with patient endurance the burden of the public debt, we yet want it to be known that the workingmen of America will in future claim a more equal share in the wealth their industry creates in peace and a more equal participation in the privileges and blessings of those free institutions, defended by their manhood on many a bloody field of battle. . . ."

Not a word was said of Negro suffrage and the need of the labor vote, black and white, if the demands of labor were to be realized. Indeed, at the very time that Southern labor was about to be enfranchised, Northern labor realized that the right to vote meant little under the growing dictatorship of wealth and corporate control. It made little difference what laws were made as long as their interpretation by the courts and administration was dictated by capital. Some proposed, therefore, to fight their battle out directly with the employer, on the one battle ground of economic bargaining, with strikes, violence and secret organization as the methods.

The National Labor Union veered from consumers' and producers' coöperation into a fight to control credits and capital and afterward through the Greenback party into an attempt to gain these ends by manipulating money. With falling prices and unemployment directly after the war, and rising prices and normal employment in 1868-1873, labor leaders became increasingly petty bourgeois and turned their backs on black labor. Farmers organized the Grange but not for black farm tenants and laborers, not for the struggling peasant proprietors among the freedmen. The Knights of Labor did not turn their attention to Negroes until after 1876.

There was, too, no rapprochement between the liberal revolt against big industry and Northern labor. Horace Greeley, a pioneer of the labor leaders, drew little labor support. The labor leaders went into the labor war of 1877 having literally disarmed themselves of the power of universal suffrage. And thus in 1876, when Northern industry withdrew military support in the South and refused to support longer the dictatorship of labor, they did this without any opposition or any intelligent comprehension of what was happening on the part of the Northern white worker.

Labor and Negro history illustrate these paradoxes. For instance in 1869, there came up the celebrated case of Lewis H. Douglass, the son of Frederick Douglass, who worked in the government printing office and was not allowed to join the Printers' Union. Rather than face the question, the matter was postponed for three years and all sorts of excuses given. This and other cases led and practically compelled the Negroes to form not only separate local trade unions but to work toward a separate national organization. White labor was organizing to fight against the new industrial oligarchy, which was growing in the North; but it was this same oligarchy which in its own self-defense had forced the South to accept Negro suffrage, allying itself temporarily with the abolition-democratic movement in the North.

This placed the white and black labor movement in a singularly contradictory position. The alliance of the black labor movement with the Republican Party was simply the political side of an economic fact. The Republican Party had given the black man the right to vote. This right to vote he was going to use to better his economic and social position. To oppose the Republican Party, then, was to oppose his own economic enfranchisement.

On the other hand, the white Labor Party had allied themselves with the Democrats, chiefly because the Democratic Party had opposed the "Know-nothing Party." The anti-foreign immigration movement was now the only organized political opposition to the great industrial forces represented by the Republicans in the North. It represented in some degree and voiced the radical demands of the West for low tariff and cheap money; but it was at the same time violently opposed to the new enfranchisement of black labor in the South. These two sets of facts alone put white and black labor in direct opposition, and because their leaders did not altogether understand the basis of this opposition, it made the attempt to achieve a common platform for white and black workers exceedingly difficult, especially when the anomalous position of the Northern Negro worker was taken into account.

Negro leaders, naturally, resented the attack made by white labor organizations on the Republican Party. Nor did they understand how far this new Southern labor government was dependent on Northern industrial reaction and capitalistic oligarchy. Northern labor was equally ignorant and did not dream that in the South the Republican Party was par excellence the party of labor.

This matter came to a crisis at the meeting of the National Labor Union in Cincinnati in 1870. A number of Negroes were present, including Isaac Myers, Josiah Weirs and Peter H. Clark. John M. Langston wanted to speak, but the labor leaders opposed him because he was a Republican politician. The motion to grant him the privilege to speak was lost by a vote of 29 to 23. There was excitement. Weirs remarked that a Democrat had been allowed to speak and that he regarded the Republican Party as a friend of the workingman. Myers lauded the Republicans amid cries of approval and disapproval. Senator Pinchback, colored leader of Louisiana, was also denied the privilege of the floor. Nevertheless, in the resolutions adopted after much debate, it was said, "The highest interest of our colored fellow-citizens is with the workingmen, who, like themselves, are the slaves of capital and politicians."

The Negroes, especially the Northern artisans, tried to keep in touch with the white labor movement. In September, 1870, Sella Martin, a colored man, went as delegate of the colored workers to the World Labor Congress in Paris. In 1871, the International Workingmen's Association, with its headquarters in London, and under the influence of Karl Marx, began to organize labor in the United States on a large scale, and in a parade held in New York in 1871, Negro organizations appeared.

The international movement, however, took no real root in America. Even the white National Labor Union began losing ground and ceased to be active after 1872. The main activity of the International was in the North; they seemed to have no dream that the place for its most successful rooting was in the new political power of the Southern worker.

Negroes, however, increased their attempts to organize and to think in groups. In 1865, an Equal Rights League met in Pennsylvania and tried to influence Negroes to secure real estate and give their sons business education.

In the District of Columbia, in 1867, a meeting of colored workers took place. They asked Congress to secure equal apportionment of employment to white and colored labor. Their petition was printed and a committee of fifteen was appointed to circulate it. In 1868 a similar petition was sent to Congress asking for equal share in work on public improvements authorized by law. There was a state colored convention in Indiana in 1865, another one in Pennsylvania in 1866, and in July, 1869, a Negro convention was held in Louisville, Kentucky, as a result of the agitation for immigrant workers. At this last convention there were 250 delegates who discussed political, economic and educational matters. They asked for the final abolition of slavery, equal education, rights in the courts, equality of taxation, the ratification of the Fifteenth Amendment. They recommended the purchase of land and the learning of trades.

A national convention of Negroes met in Washington in January, 1869. This convention was more really national than most Negro conventions hitherto. It was not simply a convention of Southern Negroes as that at Louisville, nor of Northern Negroes like the various conventions at Philadelphia and New York. In 1869, Negroes, representing a number of trades, met in Baltimore in July to form a state organization. Later, colored representatives in the same city urged Negroes to enter the movement for the formation of labor unions. In the Washington convention, there were a number of colored delegates from the South, including Henry M. Turner, a black political leader of Georgia, and in all, 130 delegates, including many men of intelligence and ability, came together. Frederick Douglass was elected permanent President and resolutions were passed in favor of the Freedmen's Bureau, a national tax for Negro schools, universal suffrage, and the opening of public land especially in the South for Negroes. The reconstruction policy of Congress was commended and there was opposition to colonization.

This was not primarily a labor convention, but it illustrated the connection in the Negroes' minds between politics and labor. They were beginning, more and more clearly, to see that their vote must be used for their economic betterment, and that their right to work and their income depended upon their use of the ballot. They were consequently groping for leadership in industry and voting, both within and without the race. In their conception of the ballot as the means to industrial emancipation, they were ahead of the Northern labor movement. But in their knowledge of the lurking dangers of the power of capital, they were far behind. This January convention was followed the same year by a national Negro labor convention sponsored by the Baltimore meeting which assembled in Washington in

December. This had been called by Negro artisans of the North, and was again national in its membership. This national labor convention assembled in Union League Hall, Washington, December, 1869. There were 159 delegates present, and Isaac Myers called the meeting to order.

While the committees were at work, James H. Harris addressed the convention. He was an astute and courageous Reconstruction leader of North Carolina and saw politics and labor in clear alliance. He stated that several millions of colored men were looking to the convention with much interest, and that the South, having passed through a political reconstruction, needed another reconstruction in the affairs of the laboring classes. John M. Langston spoke of the treatment of Negroes in public places and at their work. He especially scored the Printers' Union for its action toward Lewis H. Douglass. Remarks were made also by Richard Trevellick, the President of the white National Labor Convention, and A. M. Powell, the editor of the *Anti-Slavery Standard*.

The convention was permanently organized with James M. Harris of North Carolina as President. Committees were appointed on education, finance, business, platform and address, female labor, homesteads, travel, temperance, coöperative labor, bank savings, and agriculture. The platform of the convention covered the following subjects:

1. The dignity of labor. 2. A plea that harmony should prevail between labor and capital. 3. The desirability of an interchange of views between employers and employees. 4. Temperance in liquor consumption. 5. Education, "for educated labor is more productive and commands higher wages." 6. Political liberty for all Americans. 7. The encouragement of industry. 8. The exclusion from the trades and workshops regarded as "an insult to God, injury to us." 9. Immigrant labor should be welcomed, but coolie labor was an injury to all working classes. 10. The establishment of coöperative workshops, building and loan associations. 11. Gratitude to the agencies interested in Negro education. 12. Protection of the law for all. 13. The organization of workingmen's associations which should coöperate with the National Labor Union. 14. Capital must not be regarded as the natural enemy of labor.

At the third day's session, a special committee of five was appointed to draft a plan for the organization of mechanics and artisans, in order to secure recognition for them in the workshops of the country. Langston addressed the meeting concerning his observations in the South. There he had found skilled workers among the Negroes in gold, silver, brass, iron, wood, brick, mortar and the arts. He stated that all these workmen were asking for themselves and their children was that the trades should be open to them and that no avenue of industry should be closed, whether in workshops, printing offices, factories, foundries, railroads, steamboats, warehouses or stores.

On the fifth day, a resolution was passed which urged the delegates to call and organize state labor associations so that they might work in full coöperation with a committee which was to conduct its work as a labor bureau. This bureau was planned to serve as a clearing house for all questions of Negro labor and it was to aid in opening new labor opportunities. Isaac Myers was selected permanent President of the organization, and in his acceptance he stated that he expected to rely upon the Labor Bureau in reaching the Negro workingmen of the United States.

It is interesting to note that this convention was more representative of the large groups than the first general convention, and it deserves for this reason, as well as for its work, to be called the first organized national group of Negro laborers. Many political and religious leaders were not present at its sessions. These absentees included Douglass, Garnett, William Wells Brown, Purvis and Whipper. The definite results of this meeting included the organization of a permanent national Labor Union and a Bureau of Labor. Before the sessions were ended it was stated that there were 23 states represented and 203 accredited delegates in attendance during the period of five days.

The *American Workingman* of Boston called attention to the fact that this separate Negro organization had been formed and the writer said: "The convention of colored men at Washington last week was in some respects the most remarkable one we ever attended. We had always had full faith in the capacity of the Negro for self-improvement, but were not prepared to see, fresh from slavery, a body of two hundred men, so thoroughly conversant with public affairs, so independent in spirit, and so anxious apparently to improve their social condition, as the men who represented the South, in that convention."

There were some white fraternal delegates present and Langston attacked them as emissaries of the Democratic Party, but Sella Martin replied and told the convention plainly that they could not afford to repel the sympathy of white friends of the labor cause, and that the interests of the laboring classes, white and black, on this continent, were identical. Of the presiding officer, the writer in the *American Workingman* says:

"And here we feel impelled to say that in all our experience in tumultuous public assemblies, we have never seen a presiding officer show more executive ability than Mr. Harris, and certainly he does not owe it to white blood, as he is evidently a full-blooded Negro, so far as color and features are any evidence of being so. His success was largely owing, we think, to the fact that he possessed the entire confidence of the convention, as well as superior ability for the position."

He is sorry that a separate union has been formed. "But we are convinced that for the present at least, they could not do better. It is useless to attempt to cover up the fact that there is still a wide gulf between the two races in this country, and for a time at least they must each in their own way work out a solution of this labor problem. At no very distant day they will become united, and work in harmony together; and we who have never felt the iron as they have must be slow to condemn them because they do not see as we do on this labor movement. For ourselves, we should have felt better satisfied had they decided to join the great national movement now in progress, but fresh as they are from slavery, looking as they naturally do on the Republican Party as their deliverers from bondage, it is not strange that they should hesitate joining any other movement. Although they did not distinctly recognize any party in their platform, yet the sentiment was clearly Republican, if their speeches were any indication. Still, strange as it may seem, parties were ignored in their platform, and this course was taken mainly through the influence and votes of the Southern delegates."

The resolutions of this body stressed education as one of the strongest safeguards of the republic; advocated industrious habits, and the learning of trades and professions, and declared:

"That the exclusion of colored men and apprentices from the right to labor in any department of industry or workshops, in any of the states and territories of the United States, by what is known as 'trades unions,' is an insult to God, injury to us, and disgrace to humanity; while we extend a free and welcome hand to the free immigration of labor of all nationalities, we emphatically deem imported, contract, coolie labor to be a positive injury to the working people of the United States—is but the system of slavery in a new form, and we appeal to the Congress of the United States to rigidly enforce the Act of 1862, prohibiting coolie importations, and to enact such laws as will best protect free American labor against this or any similar form of slavery."

They recommended the establishment of coöperative workshops, building and loan associations, the purchase of land "as a remedy against their exclusion from other workshops on account of color, as a means of furnishing employment, as well as a protection against the aggression of capital, and as the easiest and shortest method of enabling every man to procure a homestead for his family; and to accomplish this end we would particularly impress the greatest importance of the observance of diligence in business, and the practice of rigid economy in our social and domestic arrangements.

"RESOLVED, that we regard education as one of the greatest blessings that the human family enjoys, and that we earnestly appeal to our fellow citizens to allow no opportunity, no matter how limited and remote, to pass unimproved; that the thanks of the colored people of this country is due to the Congress of the United States for the establishment and maintenance of the Freedman's Bureau, and to Major General Howard, commissioner; Reverend J. W. Alvord, and John M. Langston, Esq., general inspectors, for their coöperative labors in the establishment and good government of hundreds of schools in the Southern States, whereby thousands of men, women and children, have been, and are now being taught the rudiments of an English education . . . and we appeal to the friends of progress and to our citizens of the several states to continue their efforts to the various legislatures until every state can boast of having a free school system, with no distinction in dissemination of knowledge to its inhabitants on account of race, color, sex, creed or previous condition."

The low wages of labor in the South were cited, and according to the New York *Tribune,* December 11, 1869, it was said:

"To remedy this, labor must be made more scarce, and the best way to do that was to make laborers landowners. Congress is to be asked, therefore, to subdivide the public lands in the South into twenty-acre farms, to make one year's residence entitle a settler to a patent, and also to place in the hands of a Commission a sum of money, not exceeding two million dollars, to aid their settlement, and also to purchase lands in states where no public lands are found, the money to be loaned for five years, without interest. Congress will also be asked not to restore to Southern railroads the lapsed land grants of 1856, and to require that Texas, prior to readmission to representation, shall put her public lands under the operations of provisions similar to the United States Homestead Law of 1866. . . ."

". . . Mr. Downing from the Committee on Capital and Labor, submitted the following. . . . Your committee would simply refer to the unkind, estranging policy of the labor organizations of white men, who, while they make loud proclaims as to the injustice (as they allege) to which they are subjected, justify injustice, so far as giving an example to do so may, by excluding from their benches and their workshops worthy craftsmen and apprentices only because of their color, for no just cause. We say to such, so long as you persist therein, we cannot fellowship with you in your struggle, and look for failure and mortification on your part; not even the sacred name of Wendell Phillips can save you, however much we revere him and cherish toward him not only profound respect, but confidence and gratitude. . . ."

In February, 1870, the Bureau of Labor issued an address to the colored people which stressed the need of organizing Negro labor, and said that the lack of organization was the cause of low wages. It stated the following purposes of the Colored National Labor Union and the Bureau of Labor:

"1. To encourage and superintend the organization of labor.

"2. To bring about legislation which would secure equality before the law for all and enforce the contracts for labor.

"3. To secure funds from bankers and capitalists for aid in establishing coöperative associations.

"4. To overcome the opposition of white mechanics who excluded workers from their unions and shops.

"5. To organize state labor conventions.

"6. To organize, where there were seven or more mechanics, artisans and laborers of any particular branch of industry, separate labor associations and to advertise their labor in the daily papers.

"7. To encourage independent effort in creating capital, buying tools, building houses, forging iron, making brick.

"8. To own a homestead.

"The address was signed by Isaac Myers, President, and G. T. Downing, Vice-President. . . ." [22]

Local organizations were formed, meetings held, and a weekly paper, *The New Era,* was made the national organ. On February 21, a plan was adopted to send an agent South to organize Negro labor. Isaac Myers, President of the Union, was selected. He held a meeting in Norfolk, Virginia, urging the union of white and colored workmen in the same trade. Other labor meetings took place in 1870 in New York and the District of Columbia.

The second annual meeting of the National Labor Union took place January 9, 1871, with delegates from North and South, including Alabama, Virginia, Texas and North Carolina. Congress was petitioned for a national system of education with technical training. The convention desired to see industries and factories because the South was confined to a few staples, which created ignorance and poverty among both white and colored laborers and among the owning classes fear that industry would help elevate the status of the laborer.

The next annual meeting of the National Labor Union was called at Columbia, South Carolina, coincidental with the Southern convention which was a political gathering. Here there began to appear rivalry between the economic and political objects of the Negro. *The New Era,* national organ of the National Labor Union, inquired into the real objects of this meeting. It wanted to know if this union was another name for communism, or if it was a colored offshoot of the International, which intended eventually to impose a mobocracy on America?

The convention at Columbia was presided over by H. M. Turner of Georgia. Committees were appointed on education and labor, on printing, finance, civil rights, organization, immigration, and on Southern outrages. The committee on the address made a report which called for political rights, justice, protection of the courts, and advancement in the industrial arts.

In 1872, in April, a Southern states' convention assembled at New Orleans with Frederick Douglass presiding. Evidently, the National Labor Union was steadily becoming political in its influences and leadership. Efforts were made to show that Negro labor could only achieve its end by political organization. Frederick Douglass wrote an editorial to this effect, and concluded with the words: "The Republican Party is the true workingmen's party of the country." This sounded strange for the North but it was at the time true of the South. The National Labor Union issued an address to its state unions, saying that while it was not a political organization, it regarded it as the duty of every colored man to be interested in the Republican Party and stand by it. " 'By its success, we stand; by its defeat, we fall. To that party we are indebted for the Thirteenth, Fourteenth and Fifteenth Amendments, the homestead law, the eight-hour law and an improved educational system.' The presidents of the state labor unions were directed to read this address before their organizations."

As the Negroes moved from unionism toward political action, white labor in the North not only moved in the opposite direction from political action to union organization, but also evolved the American Blindspot for the Negro and his problems. It lost interest and vital touch with Southern labor and acted as though the millions of laborers in the South did not exist.

Thus labor went into the great war of 1877 against Northern capitalists unsupported by the black man, and the black man went his way in the South to strengthen and consolidate his power, unsupported by Northern labor. Suppose for a moment that Northern labor had stopped the bargain of 1876 and maintained the power of the labor vote in the South; and suppose that the Negro with new and dawning consciousness of the demands of labor as differentiated from the demands of capitalists, had used his vote more specifically for the benefit of white labor, South and North?

If the basic problem of Reconstruction in the South was economic, then the kernel of the economic situation was the land. This was clear to the sophisticated leadership of Stevens and to the philanthropy of Sumner and Oliver Howard; but it was equally clear to the ignorant and inexperienced of the freed slaves.

The Northern labor leaders and the mass of the North were slow in realizing that the center of the South's labor problem was the land, and not as yet industry. Here in the South, after the war, was a chance to keep the economic balance between farm and factory. And if it had been done, the result would have been fateful for the nation and for the world.

The Negro unerringly and insistently led the way. The main question to which the Negroes returned again and again was the problem of owning land. It was ridiculed as unreasonable and unjust to the impoverished landholders of the South, and as a part of the desire for revenge which the North had. But in essence it was nothing of the sort.

Again and again, crudely but logically, the Negroes expressed their right to the land and the deep importance of this right. And as usual here the government played fast and loose because it had two irreconcilable ideas in mind. Thaddeus Stevens and Charles Sumner were perfectly clear; the Negroes must have land furnished them either for a nominal sum or as a gift, and this land should be furnished by the government and paid for either out of taxation, or as Stevens repeatedly insisted, as an indemnity placed on the South for civil war. Moreover, for 250 years the Negroes had worked on this land, and by every analogy in history, when they were emancipated the land ought to have belonged in large part to the workers.

On the other hand, to the organized industry of the North, capital in machines or land was sacred; they did not wish to appear to punish the South by taking any more of its already partly confiscated capital. They did not want to set an example of confiscation before a nation victimized by monopoly; and they were bitterly opposed to giving capital to workers or redistributing wealth by public taxation. The result was that the nation moved backward and forward according as to one or the other idea gained the upper hand. Sir George Campbell said:

"All that is now wanted to make the Negro a fixed and conservative element in American society is to give him encouragement to, and facilities for, making himself, by his own exertions, a small landowner; to do, in fact, for him what we have sought to do for the Irish farmer. Land in America is so much cheaper and more abundant, that it would be infinitely easier to effect the same object there. I would by no means seek to withdraw the whole population from hired labor; on the contrary, the Negro in many respects is so much at his best in that function, that I should look to a large class of laborers remaining; but I am at the same time confident that it would be a very great benefit and stability to the country if a large number should acquire thrift and independent position as landowning American citizens." [23]

Most writers and speakers thought of the land problem so far as the Negro was concerned as an incidental thing; it was something that "would come." On the other hand, the former slave holders knew that land was the key to the situation and they tried desperately to center thought on labor rather than on land ownership. "One universal opinion is that they shall not be allowed to acquire or hold land. I have heard that expressed from the first. They say that unless Negroes work for them they shall not work at all." [24]

The freed slaves were desperately poor; the poor whites had always been poor except insofar as they were pensioners of the planters. How could industry be set going again and what was the relation of free Negro labor to this industry? Of course, the full realization of freedom could not be accomplished in a minute. Unless crops were raised and the wheels of industry started, emancipation would have been an experiment so costly that no nation could have supported it. And we must remember that in the end and as a logical matter of dollars and cents, emancipation paid. This is so much a matter of common knowledge today that we forget how bitterly and with what absolute certainty the South and even many in the North declared that free Negro labor was economically impossible.

What they insisted on during Reconstruction was labor, continuous, steady labor to continue production of high-priced crops. What they slurred over or refused to discuss was the object of this labor and the distribution of its product. Of labor for the economic benefit of the laborer except to the extent of the lowest possible wage that would sustain him they had no conception; and to any transfer of capital in land to the laborer as a basis of his right to demand a fairer share of the products, they were bitterly opposed.

The white South believed that it was being deliberately insulted in a petty spirit of vengeance by the North. But this was a childish way of attributing human emotions to an economic situation. The North as a whole harbored no thoughts of vengeance. Sumner wrecked his career on a deed of forgiveness; and Stevens punished the slave system and its promoters only insofar as they still interfered with freedom, or kept the ill-gotten capital accumulated by exploiting slaves.

The party of Northern industry watched the beginnings of democratic government in the South with distrust. They did not expect Negro suffrage to succeed, but they did expect that it would soon compel the Southern oligarchy to capitulate to the dictatorship of industry. Their hopes were fulfilled in 1876.

The abolition-democracy faced the Southern conventions of 1867 with fear. It was the greatest test of democracy that the nation had known. Even after the great Reform Bill of 1832, England had less than one million voters. It was not until 1867 that a million or more skilled laborers in England got the vote.

Here, at the stroke of the pen, more than one million Negroes were given the right to vote, of whom probably three-fourths could not read or write; and at the same time more than one million whites were given the same right, and at least one-third of them were equally illiterate. This was a desperate venture forced by a slave-minded régime; it had refused to grant complete physical freedom to black workers; it refused them education and access to the land and insisted on dominant political power based on the number of these same serfs. Under these circumstances the experiment had to be made. For to surrender now was to have sacrificed blood and billions of dollars in vain.

But, it was the American Blindspot that made the experiment all the more difficult, and to the South incomprehensible. For several generations the South had been taught to look upon the Negro as a thing apart. He was different from other human beings. The system of slave labor, under which he was employed, was radically different from all other systems of labor. There could be no comparison between labor problems in the South and in the North; between the Negro and white laborer.

"It must be confessed that the representatives of the white oligarchy are having a hard time, being forced to consider their own former slaves no longer as Negroes, 'niggers,' that is to say, members of a category unrecognized in any natural history, somewhere between men and monkeys in the animal scale, but as men, who have, as Jefferson phrased it, equal rights with them in the free development of their talents and in the pursuit of happiness; or, in other words, as citizens on an equal footing with themselves." [25]

"The Northern Democrats encouraged resistance on the part of the South, and yet some of them saw the situation clearly. The intrinsic difficulties of the situation are not to be denied. The ruling classes of the Southern people had attempted to disrupt the Union in order to establish their own independence. The overthrow of their armies had not changed their opinions nor their feelings. Necessity compelled their submission, but necessity could not make them love a union with the victorious North, nor make them cordially recognize and support the rights of the freedmen." [26]

During the winter and spring of 1867-1868 in accordance with the legislation of Congress, Southern conventions met and adopted new constitutions. These constitutions provided for equal civil rights, established universal suffrage and disfranchised disloyal whites. After the framing of these constitutions, they were voted on by the people. Also, state officers and members of the legislature were chosen at the same election and by the same voters. The army commanders did their best to bring out the vote and to counteract various devices for keeping Negroes away from the polls. The polls were kept open two and three days and in Georgia even five days.

Officials of the Freedmen's Bureau helped in the enforcement of the Reconstruction Acts. The act of March 23 provided that registration and elections should be conducted by boards of three loyal officers or persons appointed by the district commander. They were required to take the "Iron Clad Oath." Bureau officials were often appointed as members of these boards and Negroes were often used. The bureau officials advised Negroes about registration and voting and disabused their mind of fears of taxation or military service or reënslavement. They promised to protect them in case of a boycott of employers against those that voted.

Thus in 1867 there took place in the South a series of elections in which a new electorate registered and expressed its desire as to constitutional conventions to reconstruct the states. One million, three hundred and sixty-three thousand, six hundred and forty persons voted, of whom 660,181 were whites, and 703,459 were Negroes, as compared with a total vote of 721,191 whites voting in 1860.[27]

| | Registered | | | Vote on Holding Convention | | Total Vote 1860 |
	White	Colored	Total Vote	For	Against	
Virginia	120,101	105,832	225,933	107,342	61,887	167,223
North Carolina	106,721	72,932	179,653	93,006	32,961	96,230
South Carolina	46,882	80,550	127,432	68,768	2,278	
Georgia	96,333	95,168	191,501	102,283	4,127	106,365
Alabama	61,295	104,518	165,813	90,283	5,583	90,357
Florida	11,914	16,089	28,003	14,300	203	14,347
*Mississippi	62,362	77,328	139,690	69,739	6,277	69,120
*Arkansas	49,722	17,109	66,831	27,576	13,558	64,053
Louisiana	45,218	84,436	129,654	75,083	4,006	50,510
Texas	59,633	49,497	109,130	44,689	11,440	62,986
Total	660,181	703,459	1,363,640			721,191

* Division by race estimated; total official.

At first, the planters thought to defeat Reconstruction by refusing to vote and thus making the whole experiment a failure at the very start. Many leading whites, small in total number but large in influence and in former wealth and power, were disfranchised, perhaps 200,000 in all.

On the other hand, the poor whites must have voted widely, especially when we note the large white vote in most of the states despite war, mortality, abstentions and disabilities. It is probable that in 1868 not only did Negroes vote freely, but more poor whites than ever before exercised the franchise. Democracy for the first time in at least a century succeeded oligarchy in the South. The voting of nearly three-fourths of a million Negroes was especially significant and represented a very large proportion of, perhaps, a million eligible black voters.

The elections which reconstructed the South under the Congressional plan were fair and honest elections, and probably never before were such democratic elections held in the South and never since such fair elections. Indeed, as a special champion of the South says: "It would be hard to deny that, so far as the ordinary civil administration was concerned, the rule of the generals was as just and efficient as it was far-reaching. Criticism and denunciation of their acts were bitter and continuous; but no very profound research is necessary in order to discover that the animus of these attacks was chiefly political." [28]

As a result of the elections, constitutional conventions were decided on in all the Southern states and the following number of members of the Conventions elected:

	Delegates—1868			*Per Cent*
State	*Black*	*White*	*Total*	*Negro*
South Carolina	76	48	124	61
Louisiana	49	49	98	50
Florida	18	27	45	40
Virginia	25	80	105	24
Georgia	33	137	170	19
Mississippi	17	83	100	17
Alabama	18	90	108	17
Arkansas	8	58	66	12
North Carolina	15	118	133	11
Texas	9	81	90	10

As these conventions were being voted on, the presidential election approached. The campaign began in May, 1868. The Republican national platform did not dare to stand squarely for Negro suffrage but evolved this illogical compromise: "The guaranty by Congress of equal suffrage to all loyal men at the South was demanded by every consideration of public safety, of gratitude, and of justice, and must be maintained; while the question of suffrage in all the loyal states properly belongs to the people of these States." [29]

Grant and Colfax were nominated. Colfax declared that peace had been prevented by "executive opposition, and by refusals to accept any plan of reconstruction proffered by Congress. Justice and public safety at last combined to teach us that only by an enlargement of suffrage in those States could the desired end be attained, and that it was even more safe to give the ballot to those who loved the Union than to those who had sought ineffectually to destroy it."

In 1865-1868, the Democratic Party controlled from 44 per cent to 50 per cent of the voters in the North, so that if the white people of the South had been included, undoubtedly the Democratic Party would have been in the majority. By the exclusion of the South, the Democratic Party had been beaten in 1866, and in 1867 had carried only Maryland and Kentucky, Connecticut, New York, Pennsylvania, New Jersey and California; nevertheless, on the whole, the Democratic vote increased, as compared with the Republican.

The elections of 1867 made it clear that if the Democrats won in 1868, the entire system of Reconstruction would be changed. The business elements of the North, therefore, while not willing to follow abolition-democracy to the extreme, were even less willing to put Reconstruction entirely in the hands of Southerners. Congress, therefore, prepared to clinch its political hold on the South, and reconstruct Southern states on a basis of Negro suffrage.

While, then, the conservative and commercial elements in the North went into the Republican Party, on the other hand, former Democrats began to return to the Democratic Party, where they were received with more or less suspicion. Meetings began to be held by Democratic leaders to determine candidates and procedure. On Jackson Day, January 8, 1868, a meeting was held in Washington, at which President Johnson spoke and many Democratic leaders. This meeting was dominated by the War Democrats, rather than by Copperheads, and emphasis was laid upon coöperation between the War Democrats and the Johnson administration, on the one hand, and the Democratic organization on the other. New measures and new men were sought. August Belmont, the banker, was chairman of the National Committee. New York was chosen as the seat of the convention, and a general invitation was issued to former Democrats.

The New York *Herald* enumerated the elements of the new democracy: merchants who opposed the protective tariff, the unemployed, the foreign born, the Catholics, the women opposed to Negro suffrage, the opponents of military control in the South. Many papers warned the pro-Southern elements in the Democratic Party not to oppose the loyal sentiment in the nation. The Springfield *Republican*, July 1, mentioned "the mere stupid, causeless, aimless hatred of the Negro" in the Democratic Party.

The opposition of the Democrats to Negro suffrage was not clearly expressed. Evidently, the tide in favor of democracy had risen so high in the country that as a party the Democrats did not dare oppose it. The party, therefore, would not come out flatly in opposition to Negro suffrage but simply declared that suffrage was a question to be settled by the states. Twenty-two state Democratic conventions were held in 1868. Eleven of these opposed Negro suffrage anywhere. Only the convention of South Carolina in April approved it. Ten other conventions either were silent on the subject or announced their belief that this was a matter of state control.

The various state platforms illustrated local Northern thought. California Democrats declared that they "now and always confide in the intelligence, patriotism, and discriminating justice of the white people of the country to administer and control their Government, without the aid of either Negroes or Chinese." [30]

The Democrats of Washington territory agreed with California in opposing the extension of the elective franchise to Negroes, Indians and Chinese.

The Ohio Democrats declared that the attempt to regulate suffrage in Ohio was "subversive of the federal Constitution." The Democrats of Pennsylvania were opposed to conferring upon the Negro the right to vote. Most of the Republican conventions approved the Fifteenth Amendment. A minority report of the Virginia Conservatives called for white control and said: "We call upon white men, whether native or adopted citizens, to vote down the Constitution, and thereby save themselves and their posterity from Negro suffrage, Negro office-holding, and its legitimate consequence—Negro social equality."

This was a time of changing of political allegiance. The Johnson movement collapsed. Conservative Republicans, like Fessenden and Trumbull, united with the Republicans. Seward, McCulloch, and Welles, former supporters of Lincoln, stood staunchly by President Johnson. Other Republicans, like the Blairs, Doolittle, and Chase, drifted toward the Democrats. But the Democratic Party, by its action during the campaign, repelled many of the Conservatives on account of its attitude on money, and its radical attitude on Reconstruction. State and local elections in the spring of 1868 encouraged the Democrats. The Republican vote was reduced in New Hampshire; in Michigan Negro suffrage was defeated by a vote of 110,000 to 71,000, and the Democrats triumphed in Connecticut.

Before the war, Salmon P. Chase was a prominent Abolitionist, and after the war, a Radical Republican. He advocated Negro suffrage, and in May, 1865, made a trip to the South to investigate the position of the Negro. In Charleston, he spoke to the Negroes, and urged them to deserve the suffrage, even if they did not get it.

On the other hand, Chase did not like the military governments of the South, and favored state rights as against the increased power of the Federal Government. He said once: "While we freed the Negro, we enslaved ourselves." Becoming Chief Justice, he presided at Johnson's impeachment and favored Johnson possibly on account of his dislike of Benjamin F. Wade of Ohio. Wade would have become President if Johnson had been impeached. Chase's daughter Kate was said to have made some fiery declarations at "the idea of that horrid Ben Wade being put over my father." For his stand in this trial, he was practically read out of the Republican Party, and became a formidable candidate for the Democratic nomination.

The Chase supporters had headquarters in New York, and his daughter was there in person. It was suggested that Chase should declare Reconstruction acts unconstitutional "as the Supreme Court would probably decide." This statement, of course, Chase could not make, and he had to warn his daughter against too great activity. A small group of some twenty Negroes assisted the Chase movement, and argued that Chase would carry many Southern Negro votes. After a long deadlock, Seymour of New York, the former Copperhead Governor of Draft Riot fame, was nominated chiefly because he failed to swing his followers to Chase, as he had promised.

The platform of the convention recognized slavery and secession as closed questions. It demanded the immediate restoration of all states, amnesty for all political offenses, and the regulation of suffrage in the states by their citizens. It asked for the abolition of the Freedmen's Bureau and all agencies for Negro supremacy. It said that the Republicans, instead of restoring the Union, had dissolved it, subjecting ten states to military despotism and Negro supremacy; and that the corruption of the Radical Party had been unprecedented.

The New York *Herald* called Seymour "the embodiment of copperheadism." Greeley declared that Seymour had proposed resisting secession by force; had declared that if the Union could only be maintained by abolishing slavery, then the Union should be given up; had given grudging support to the government while war governor, and had opposed the draft. The New York *Sun* said that he represented fairly the average sentiment of his party. Seymour accepted the platform but did not discuss it in detail. He attacked Congressional Reconstruction, but pointed out that no violent change could take place since the

Republicans would continue to control the Senate. Frederick Douglass, writing in the *Independent*, August 20, 1868, said that Seymour's letter of acceptance "was smooth as oil and as fair-seeming as hypocrisy itself, containing every disposition to deceive but without the ability. It was cunning and cowardly." Seymour made no reference to finance or suffrage.

Blair, the Democratic candidate for Vice President, was a wild Missourian given to drink, who openly advocated that the new President "disperse the carpetbag governments" by force as soon as his party triumphed.

President Johnson was disgusted and chagrined at not receiving the nomination and said that Seymour had not lifted a finger to sustain his administration. In the campaign, he was finally induced to give some support to the Democratic ticket. Seymour, on the other hand, practically offered Johnson an appointment if he should be elected. Seward took little part in the campaign, although he spoke once for the Republican ticket, and included praise for President Johnson.

Thus the campaign started with contradictions inside the Democratic Party. Seymour opposed the greenback idea before the national convention, and then ran on a platform that advocated it. Blair advocated revolution; Hampton opposed Negro suffrage, and appealed to Negro voters. Chase asked universal suffrage, and remanded the question to the states. There were charges that the Democrats proposed to repudiate the national debt and pay for emancipated slaves and property lost during the war. Southern Democrats were prominent. Toombs, Cobb, and Forrest took part. The New York *Nation* said that "these Southerners were of more service to the Republicans than all of their orators and literature." Many of them were accused of incendiary speeches. Vance of North Carolina was accused of saying that Seymour and Blair would win what the Confederates fought for. Hill of Georgia declared that the South was going to regulate its own internal democratic affairs in its own way. Toombs declared that if the Democrats were victorious, the Reconstruction governor and legislators would be made to vacate at once. Howell Cobb said that those in control of the Southern states would be ousted, while Albert Pike of Arkansas wrote in the Memphis *Appeal:* "The day will come when the South will be independent." [31]

Violence and intimidation were widespread in the South during this election, and bribery and fraud were prevalent in the North. In Philadelphia, a Supreme Court justice issued over five thousand naturalization papers within two weeks.

The *Nation,* November 12, charged that Georgia and Louisiana were carried by "organized assassination, and New Jersey and New York by fraud." The Democratic majority of 165 in Oregon was due, it was said, to voters brought in from neighboring states. Late in October, there was a movement to get Seymour to withdraw and substitute Chase or Johnson. The New York *World* led the movement, but nothing came of it. Grant was elected by 214 electoral votes to 80 for Seymour, and 3,012,833 to 2,703,249 popular votes. Thus Grant received 52.71%. Seymour carried Delaware, Georgia, Kentucky, Louisiana, Maryland, New Jersey, New York and Oregon. Virginia, Mississippi and Texas did not vote. During this campaign, Negro suffrage was defeated in Missouri by 74.053 to 55,236. In Minnesota, it was carried. In Nevada, it was carried by the Republican legislature.

At Christmas, 1868, President Johnson proclaimed general amnesty, pardoning every person engaged directly or indirectly in the rebellion. His last presidential message was an interesting and rather curious argument. He declared, in effect, that the dictatorship of labor, attempted in the South under the Reconstruction acts, had led to corruption and bloodshed and, therefore, prevented the rise of industry in the South, which was the real solution of the race problem. He believed that the bondholders had already received an amount larger than the principal which they owed and that, hereafter, the interest paid should be applied to the reduction of that principal.

Johnson thus illustrated again the way in which the color problem became the Blindspot of American political and social development and made logical argument almost impossible. The only power to curtail the rising empire of finance in the United States was industrial democracy—votes and intelligence in the hands of the laboring class, black and white, North and South.

The chief act of the third session of the 40th Congress was the Fifteenth Amendment. Early in 1867, two amendments on the suffrage were introduced: one which prohibited any color distinction, and the other requiring $250 property qualification or an additional tax. The victory of the Republican Party in 1868 made the passage of the Fifteenth Amendment paramount.

In 1868, eleven amendments were introduced to extend the right of suffrage to the freedmen. Of these amendments, seven were presented in the House and four in the Senate. All except one were referred to the Committee on Judiciary in each House. The House Committee on the Judiciary reported June 11, 1869, a proposed Fifteenth Amendment. This caused long debate in the House and many proposed modifications. Among the propositions was that no educational attainment or possession of property should be made the test of any citizen's right to vote. The resolution proposed by the committee with a minor change was passed by the House by a vote of 150-42, January 30, 1869.

Meantime, the Senate had been discussing a similar proposition and many modifications had been proposed. January 30, on reception of the House Amendment, the Senate discussed it. Eight other amendments were offered, and some fifteen substitute propositions. Finally, a substitute suggested by Wilson was adopted by a vote of 31-27. It read:

"No discrimination shall be made in any State among the citizens of the United States in the exercise of the elective franchise or in the right to hold office in any State, on account of race, color, nativity, property, education or religious creed." [32]

This was amended so as to insure Congress power to direct the manner in which the election should be conducted, and thus the Senate agreed to the House proposition with amendments. The House refused to concur. The Senate declined to recede and the measure failed.

Thereupon, February 17, 1869, the Senate resumed consideration of its own resolution and eleven amendments were proposed and rejected. Finally, the Fifteenth Amendment was passed 35-11, in its present form, except that the words "to hold office" were added after "the right to vote."

February 20, the House considered this proposal and there were five attempts to amend it, of which one was successful and added "nativity, property and creed," to the other qualifications. It then passed the House 140-37. The Senate rejected the House amendment and asked for conference. Finally, the present Fifteenth Amendment was agreed upon, and it passed the House 145-44, and the Senate 39-13. It was thus recommended to the states February 26, 1869.

Some Americans think and say that the nation freed the black slave and gave him a vote and that, unable to use it intelligently, he lost it. That is not so. To win the war America freed the slave and armed him; and the threat to arm the mass of the black workers of the Confederacy stopped the war. Nor does this fact for a moment deny that some prophets and martyrs demanded first and last the abolition of slavery as the sole object of the war and at any cost of life and wealth. So, too, some Americans demanded not simply physical freedom but votes, land, and education for blacks, not only in order to compass the economic emancipation of labor, but also as the only fulfillment of American democratic ideals; but most Americans used the Negro to defend their own economic interests and, refusing him adequate land and real education and even common justice, deserted him shamelessly as soon as their selfish interests were safe. Nor does this for a moment deny that unselfish and far-seeing Americans, poor as well as rich, by supplying public schools when the Negroes demanded them and establishing higher schools to train teachers, saved the Negro from being entirely reënslaved or exterminated in an unequal and cowardly renewal of war.

We are the hewers and delvers who toil for another's gain,—
The common clods and the rabble, stunted of brow and brain.
What do we want, the gleaners, of the harvest we have reaped?
What do we want, the neuters, of the honey we have heaped?

What matter if king or consul or president holds the rein,
If crime and poverty ever be links in the bondman's chain?
What careth the burden-bearer that Liberty packed his load,
If Hunger presseth behind him with a sharp and ready goad?

JAMES JEFFREY ROCHE

---

1. McPherson, *History of United States During Reconstruction*, pp. 141, 142.
2. Herberg, *The Heritage of the Civil War*, p. 8.
3. *Congressional Globe*, 40th Congress, 1st Session, p. 55.
4. Pierce, *Memoirs and Letters of Charles Sumner*, Vol. IV, pp. 311, 312.
5. Pierce, *Memoirs and Letters of Charles Sumner*, Vol. IV, pp. 285-290.
6. Pierce, *Memoirs and Letters of Charles Sumner*, Vol. IV, pp. 313, 314.
7. Pierce, *Memoirs and Letters of Charles Sumner*, Vol. IV, p. 307.
8. Clemenceau, *American Reconstruction, 1865-1870*, p. 65.
9. Pierce, *Memoirs and Letters of Charles Sumner*, Vol. IV, p. 317.
10. Clemenceau, *American Reconstruction, 1865-1870*, pp. 104, 131.
11. Porter, *Ohio Politics*, p. 244.
12. McCall, *Thaddeus Stevens, American Statesmen*, p. 336.
13. Burgess, *Reconstruction*, p. 191.
14. McCall, *Thaddeus Stevens, American Statesmen*, pp. 352-353.
15. McCall, *Thaddeus Stevens, American Statesmen* (footnote), p. 336.
16. Schlüter, *Lincoln, Labor and Slavery*, pp. 196, 197, 200.
17. Commons and Andrews, *Documentary History of American Industrial Society*, IX, pp. 185, 186, 187, 188.
18. Schlüter, *Lincoln, Labor and Slavery*, p. 235.
19. Wesley, *Negro Labor in the United States*, pp. 162, 163.
20. Schlüter, *Lincoln, Labor and Slavery*, pp. 231, 232.
21. Commons and Andrews, *Documentary History of American Industrial Society*, Vol. IX, pp. 243, 256, 268, 285.
22. Wesley, *Negro Labor in the United States*, pp. 180, 187.
23. Campbell, *Black and White in the Southern States*, p. 160.
24. Haynes, in the *Report of the Joint Committee on Reconstruction*, 1866, Part IV, p. 62.
25. Clemenceau, *American Reconstruction, 1865-1870*, pp. 291-292.
26. Cox, *Three Decades of Federal Legislation*, pp. 378, 379.
27. Dunning, *Essays on the Civil War and Reconstruction*, p. 188. The registration figures by states are after the McPherson *History of United States During Reconstruction*, p. 374. Other sources give slightly different totals in some cases.

28. Dunning, *Essays on the Civil War and Reconstruction*, p. 174.
29. McPherson, *History of United States During Reconstruction*, pp. 364, 366.
30. McPherson, *History of United States During Reconstruction*, pp. 479, 483, 486.
31. Coleman, *Election of 1868*, pp. 311-312.
32. Ames, *Amendments to the Constitution*, Vol. II, pp. 233, 235.

X. THE BLACK PROLETARIAT*
IN SOUTH CAROLINA

How in the years from 1868-1876, in a state where blacks outnumbered whites, the will of the mass of black labor, modified by
their own and other leaders and dimmed by ignorance, inexperience and uncertainty, dictated the form and methods of government

A great political scientist in one of the oldest and largest of American universities wrote and taught thousands of youths and readers
that "There is no question, now, that Congress did a monstrous thing,
and committed a great political error, if not a sin, in the creation of
this new electorate. It was a great wrong to civilization to put the
white race of the South under the domination of the Negro race. The
claim that there is nothing in the color of the skin from the point
of view of political ethics is a great sophism. A black skin means
membership in a race of men which has never of itself succeeded in
subjecting passion to reason; has never, therefore, created any civilization of any kind." [1]
Here is the crux of all national discussion and study of Reconstruction. The problem is incontinently put beyond investigation and historic proof by the dictum of Judge Taney, Andrew Johnson, John
Burgess and their confreres, that Negroes are not men and cannot
be regarded and treated as such.
The student who would test this dictum by facts is faced by this
set barrier. The whole history of Reconstruction has with few exceptions been written by passionate believers in the inferiority of the
Negro. The whole body of facts concerning what the Negro actually
said and did, how he worked, what he wanted, for whom he voted,
is masked in such a cloud of charges, exaggeration and biased testimony, that most students have given up all attempt at new material
or new evaluation of the old, and simply repeated perfunctorily all
the current legends of black buffoons in legislature, golden spittoons

* The record of the Negro worker during Reconstruction presents an opportunity to
study inductively the Marxian theory of the state. I first called this chapter "The Dictatorship of the Black Proletariat in South Carolina," but it has been brought to my attention that this would not be correct since universal suffrage does not lead to a real dictatorship until workers use their votes consciously to rid themselves of the dominion of
private capital. There were signs of such an object among South Carolina Negroes, but
it was always coupled with the idea of that day, that the only real escape for a laborer
was himself to own capital.

for fieldhands, bribery and extravagance on an unheard-of scale, and the collapse of civilization until an outraged nation rose in wrath and ended the ridiculous travesty.

And yet there are certain quite well-known facts that are irreconcilable with this theory of history. Civilization did not collapse in the South in 1868-1876. The charge of industrial anarchy is faced by the fact that the cotton crop had recovered by 1870, five years after the war, and by 1876 the agricultural and even commercial and industrial rebirth of the South was in sight. The public debt was large; but measured in depreciated currency and estimated with regard to war losses, and the enlarged functions of a new society, it was not excessive. The legislation of this period was not bad, as is proven by the fact that it was retained for long periods after 1876, and much of it still stands.

One must admit that generalizations of this sort are liable to wide error, but surely they can justifiably be balanced against the extreme charges of a history written for purposes of propaganda. And above all, no history is accurate and no "political science" scientific that starts with the gratuitous assumption that the Negro race has been proven incapable of modern civilization. Such a dogma is simply the modern and American residue of a universal belief that most men are sub-normal and that civilization is the gift of the Chosen Few.

Since the beginning of time, most thinkers have believed that the vast majority of human beings are incorrigibly stupid and evil. The proportion of thinkers who believed this has naturally changed with historical evolution. In earliest times all men but the Chosen Few were impossible. Before the middle class of France revolted, only the Aristocracy of birth and knowledge could know and do. After the American experiment a considerable number of thinkers conceived that possibly most men had capabilities, except, of course, Negroes. Possibly never in human history before or since have so many men believed in the manhood of so many men as after the Battle of Port Hudson, when Negroes fought for Freedom.

All men know that by sheer weight of physical force, the mass of men must in the last resort become the arbiters of human action. But reason, skill, wealth, machines and power may for long periods enable the few to control the many. But to what end? The current theory of democracy is that dictatorship is a stopgap pending the work of universal education, equitable income, and strong character. But always the temptation is to use the stopgap for narrower ends, because intelligence, thrift and goodness seem so impossibly distant for most men. We rule by junta; we turn Fascist, because we do not believe in men; yet the basis of fact in this disbelief is incredibly narrow. We know perfectly well that most human beings have never had a decent human chance to be full men. Most of us may be convinced that even with opportunity the number of utter human failures would be vast; and yet remember that this assumption kept the ancestors of present white America long in slavery and degradation.

It is then one's moral duty to see that every human being, to the extent of his capacity, escapes ignorance, poverty and crime. With this high ideal held unswervingly in view, monarchy, oligarchy, dictatorships may rule; but the end will be the rule of All, if mayhap All or Most qualify. The only unforgivable sin is dictatorship for the benefit of Fools, Voluptuaries, gilded Satraps, Prostitutes and Idiots. The rule of the famished, unlettered, stinking mob is better than this and the only inevitable, logical and justifiable return. To escape from ultimate democracy is as impossible as it is for ignorant poverty and crime to rule forever.

The opportunity to study a great human experiment was present in Reconstruction, and its careful scientific investigation would have thrown a world of light on human development and democratic government. The material today, however, is unfortunately difficult to find. Little effort has been made to preserve the records of Negro effort and speeches, actions, work and wages, homes and families. Nearly all this has gone down beneath a mass of ridicule and caricature, deliberate omission and misstatement. No institution of learning has made any effort to explore or probe Reconstruction from the point of view of the laborer and most men have written to explain and excuse the former slaveholder, the planter, the landholder, and the capitalist. The loss today is irreparable, and this present study limps and gropes in darkness, lacking most essentials to a complete picture; and yet the writer is convinced that this is the story of a normal working class movement, successful to an unusual degree, despite all disappointment and failure.

South Carolina has always been pointed to as the typical Reconstruction state. It had, in 1860, 412,320 Negroes and 291,300 whites. Even at the beginning of the nineteenth century, the 200,000 whites were matched by 150,000 Negroes, and the influx from the Border and the direct African slave trade brought a mass of black slaves to support the new Cotton Kingdom. There had always been small numbers of free Negroes, a little over 3,000 at the beginning of the century, and nearly 10,000 in 1860.

"Slavery was the driving force of the state's industrial and social life; it was the institution which made South Carolina different from the states of the North; it was the principal reason why the white manhood of the state had fought so desperately." [2]

The economic loss which came through war was great, but not nearly as influential as the psychological change, the change in habit and thought. Imagine the 54th Massachusetts Colored Regiment, heading the Union troops which entered Charleston, and singing "John Brown's Body." A nun writes from that city concerning the changes which have come, and which seem to her unspeakable:

"Could you but see these delicate ladies in houses void of furniture, reduced to the wash-tub and the cook-pot, your heart would bleed." There were other Carolina women—not, to be sure, "ladies"—to whom the chance to wash and cook for themselves spelled heaven in these days.

The hatred of the Yankee was increased. The defeated Southern leaders were popular heroes. Numbers of Southerners planned to leave the country, and go to South America or Mexico. And yet, the slaveholders had not lost all by any means. There were 638 persons in South Carolina who were later pardoned by President Johnson because they had taxable property worth more than $20,000. They had their land, their tools, and while certain cities had been wrecked and pillaged, the great mass of the plantations had not been touched. The railroads had been injured but not destroyed. Most of the eighteen cotton factories were not touched.

The labor situation, the prospect of free Negroes, caused great apprehension. It was accepted as absolutely true by most planters that the Negro could not and would not work without a white master.

"The nigger, sir, is a savage whom the Almighty Maker appointed to be a slave. A savage! With him free, the South is ruined, sir, ruined. . . ."

On the other hand, these apprehensions were not fulfilled. William Henry Trescot said: "When Negroes heard that freedom was coming, there was no impatience, no insubordination, no violence. They have received their freedom quietly and soberly. They remained pretty steadily on the farms of their masters, a very general disposition being manifest to adjust the terms of compensation on a reasonable basis."

One great and real loss which the state suffered was the 12,922 men killed in battle, and dead of wounds. "Perhaps it can be concluded that the lack of distinctive achievements by South Carolinians since the war is in no small measure due to this loss."

It was estimated by the census that land values declined 60% between 1860-1867, and that all farm property, between 1860-1870, decreased from $169,738,630 to $47,628,175. In May, 1865, a meeting was held in Charleston, and a committee was sent to talk with President Johnson. He asked them to submit a list of names from which he might select a Provisional Governor, and he finally selected Benjamin F. Perry. This was, on the whole, an unfortunate selection. Perry was a devoted follower of Johnson, and believed that Johnson had the power and backing to put his policies through. He immediately succeeded in having all Negro troops withdrawn, and he was certain that the North was with him and Johnson in standing for a purely white man's government.

The Johnson convention met and took some advance steps. By a small majority, they did away with property qualifications for members of the legislature, but refused to count Negroes as basis of apportionment. This was a blow at the former slaveholders, and a step toward democracy so far as the whites were concerned, but it was coupled with absolute refusal to recognize the Negroes. Perry insisted on letting property retain its right of representation in the legislature, despite the opposition of President Johnson.

The convention wanted to abolish slavery only on condition that Negroes be confined to manual labor, and that slave owners be compensated. They were given to understand, however, that Johnson would not accept this, and they finally declared that since the slaves had been emancipated by the United States, slavery should not be reëstablished. In the elections for this convention, there was little interest. Only about one-third of the normal vote was cast on the coast, and inland, there were, in many cases, no elections at all.

In the election which followed again only 19,000 votes were cast. Ex-Governor Orr received a small majority, and would have been beaten by Wade Hampton, if Hampton had not refused the use of his name. Orr was a man of striking personality, and had once been Speaker of the United States House of Representatives.

The legislature which met after this election passed one of the most vicious of the Black Codes. It provided for corporal punishment, vagrancy and apprenticeship laws, openly made the Negro an inferior caste, and provided special laws for his governing.

"Neither humanity nor expediency demanded such sharp distinctions between the races in imposing punishments. The restriction of Negro testimony to cases in which the race was involved was not common sense. The free admission of such testimony in all cases would not have involved the surrender of power by the whites since they were to be the judges and jury. The occupational restrictions, instead of tending to restore order, created the impression that the dominant race desired to exclude the blacks from useful employment. It was impractical for a poverty-stricken commonwealth to have projected such elaborate schemes of judicial and military reorganization." [3]

There was increased difficulty in the economic situation. The war had ended late in the spring of 1865, so that the crops of that year were short, and there were crop failures for the next two years. All this complicated matters. In addition to this, the splendid start which the Negroes had on the lands of Port Royal, and on the Sea Islands, was interrupted. Johnson's proclamation and orders of 1865 provided for the early restoration of all property except property in slaves and such of the Port Royal lands as had been sold for taxes. The landlords hurried to get their pardons and to take back their lands. The Negroes resisted sometimes with physical force. When some of the landlords visited Edisto Island, the Negroes told them:

"You had better go back to Charleston, and go to work there, and if you can do nothing else, you can pick oysters and earn your living."

But these white men were not used to earning their own living. They were used to having Negroes do that for them, and now they had the Federal Government back of their claims. General Howard came down to facilitate the transfer and explain the condition to the Negroes. Still the black folk were dissatisfied. They drew up a petition to President Johnson, asking for at least an acre and a half of land. The planters became overbearing and the Negroes angry. Saxton, who had placed them on the land, was dismissed, and Howard deprived of his power. So that finally, by Federal force, Negroes were compelled to leave most of the lands and to make contracts as common laborers. The third Freedmen's Bureau Bill gave this the force of law. Thousands of Negroes migrated to Florida during 1866-1867, because of the land difficulties, the labor contracts, and the crop failures. Two thousand five hundred migrated to Liberia.

Landholders used force, fraud and boycott against farm labor. It was declared in 1868 that in South Carolina:

"The whites do not think it wrong to shoot, stab or knock down Negroes on slight provocation. It is actually thought a great point among certain classes to be able to boast that one has killed or beaten a Negro." [4]

The following resolutions were passed at public meetings of planters in South Carolina:

"Resolved, That if inconsistent with views of the authorities to remove the military, we express the opinion that the plan of the military to *compel the freedman* to contract with his former owner, when desired by the latter, is wise, prudent, and absolutely necessary.

"Resolved, That we, the planters of the district, pledge ourselves not to contract with any freedmen unless he can produce a certificate of regular discharge from his former owner.

"Resolved, That under no circumstances whatsoever will we rent land to any freedmen, nor will we permit them to live on our premises as employees." [5]

In the Abbeville district of South Carolina it was said:

"Here a planter worked nearly one hundred (100) hands near Cokesburg, ten (10) of them on the South Carolina railroad for six (6) months (the planter receiving their wages), and the remainder on his plantation, raising a crop of corn, wheat, rice, cotton, etc. After the crop was harvested the laborers were brought to Charleston, where, being destitute, they had to be rationed by the government. After their arrival in this city the planter distributed fifty dollars ($50) among them. The largest amount any one received was one dollar and twenty-five cents ($1.25) and from that down to fifty cents (50¢), some receiving nothing. One peck of dry corn a week was the only ration furnished the farm hands." [6]

Meantime, the growth of sentiment in favor of Negro suffrage was quickened because of the action of South Carolina and other states. Chief Justice Chase visited the state and spoke to the Negroes. He said, "I believe there is not a member of the Government who would not be pleased to see universal suffrage."

The Negroes were already bestirring themselves. In May, 1864, at Port Royal, they held a meeting which elected delegates to the National Union Convention, which was to be held in Baltimore in June. In November, 1865, the colored people met at Zion Church, Charleston, and protested against the work of the convention and of the legislature. The legislature refused to receive this petition, and determined to ignore the matter of Negro suffrage entirely. Orr attended the National Union Convention in Philadelphia in 1866, and advised the legislature to reject the Fourteenth Amendment. This the legislature did with only one negative vote in both Houses.

The military commanders, under the Reconstruction legislation, did much to abolish discrimination. One captain of a vessel was fined who refused to allow a colored woman to ride as a first-class passenger, and General Canby, a Kentuckian, whom Johnson appointed in March, 1867, ordered that Negroes serve on juries. This led to excitement and protests.

Northern capitalists began to appear in the state. They were, at first, welcomed:

"Men of capital are coming from the North by every steamer in view of investing in cotton and rice. We are glad to see such a lively trade in South Carolina; it benefits everyone."

Later, and especially when they began to take part in politics, they were loaded with every accusation. Some of them were army officers; others, employees of the Freedmen's Bureau; some were farmers, and some religious and educational leaders. The Negroes, naturally, turned to them for leadership and received it. They helped organize the

Negroes in Union Leagues in order to teach them citizenship and united action. Northern visitors continued to come. Senator Henry Wilson of Massachusetts spoke at Charleston:

"After four bloody years, Liberty tiiumphed and slavery has died to rise no more. . . . The creed of equal rights, equal privileges and equal immunities for all men in America is hereafter to be the practical policy of the Republic. . . . Never vote unless you vote for the country which made you free. Register your names. Vote for a united country. Vote for the old flag. Vote for a change in the constitution of the state that your liberties may be consummated."

Under the Reconstruction law of 1867, 46,882 whites and 80,550 blacks voted; the planter class refrained from participation in hope that the scheme would fail.

	Whites	Blacks	Total
Total Registration	46,882	80,550	127,432
"For the Convention"	2,350	66,418	68,768
"Against a Convention"	2,278		2,278
Not Voting	42,354	14,132	56,486
Majority "For a Convention"			66,490

In ten of the thirty-one counties there were white majorities, and in the remaining twenty-one counties, black majorities.

Party conventions began to meet. The first one was that of the Union Republican Party, which met in Charleston with nine county representatives. It adjourned to Columbia, where nineteen counties were represented. It was attended by colored and white men, including some Southern men like Thomas J. Robertson, a wealthy native.

The reaction among the whites led to three parties. Governor Orr and his party accepted the Reconstruction acts, and planned to work with the Negroes. Wade Hampton proposed to accept the acts, but only with the idea of finally dominating the Negro vote and having Negroes follow the lead of their former masters. Hampton owned large plantations in South Carolina and Mississippi.

The New York *Herald* summarized his views as follows: "He appeals to the blacks, lately his slaves, as his political superiors, to try the political experiment of harmonizing with their late white masters before going into the political service of strangers. . . . The broad fact that the two races in the South must henceforth harmonize on a political basis to avoid a bloody conflict is the ground covered by Wade Hampton."

A third party was led by former Governor Perry and Thomas W. Woodward.

" 'Strange to say,' wrote Perry, 'there are many persons in the Southern States whose high sense of honor would not let them adopt the Fourteenth Amendment, who are now urging the people to swallow voluntarily the Military Bill, regardless of honor, principle, or consistency.' If the state were forced to acquiesce in the tyranny of Congress, he added, 'she need not embrace the hideous thing. . . . If we are to wear manacles, let them be put on by our tyrants, not ourselves.' He argued the folly of attempting to control the Negro vote. 'General Hampton and his friends,' he asserted, 'had just as well try to control a herd of wild buffaloes as the Negro vote.' Woodward was violent in denouncing the compromisers. 'Why, oh, why, my Southern nigger worshippers,' he cried, 'will you grope your way through this worse than Egyptian darkness? Why not cease this crawling on your bellies and assume the upright form of men? . . . Stop, I pray you, your efforts at harmony, your advice about conventions, your pusillanimous insinuations about confiscations, etc., or you will goad these people by flattery to destruction, before they have a chance to pick out the cotton crop.' " [7]

Perry proposed to appeal to the courts, and advised the whites to register and vote against the constitutional convention. The convention of whites was held a week before the constitutional convention, with twenty-one of the thirty-one districts represented. This convention made coöperation on the part of Negroes of any intelligence utterly impossible. It declared:

"The fact is patent to all . . . that the Negro is utterly unfitted to exercise the highest function of a citizen. . . . We protest against this subversion of the social order, whereby an ignorant and depraved race is placed in power and influence above the virtuous, the educated, and the refined." The nation was informed that the white people of South Carolina "would never acquiesce in Negro Equality or supremacy." The president of the convention complained that the declarations were filled with adjectives and epithets, which put a weapon in the hands of the enemies of the movement.

The state convention, when it met, had Negro members for the first time in the history of the state. Seventy-six of the one hundred and twenty-four delegates were colored. As in Mississippi and elsewhere, a number of the planter class had early contemplated an effort to control the Negro vote, and thus quickly to get rid of military rule. On the other hand, the Negroes, because of the educated free Negro element, some considerable talent among the slaves, and the influx of Negroes from the North, showed unusual foresight and modesty. The convention was earnest, and on the whole, well-conducted. Of the seventy-six colored men, it is said, fifty-seven had been slaves.

"The native whites felt," said the correspondent of the New York

Times, "that the destinies of the state were safer in the hands of the unlettered Ethiopians than in those of the whites of the body." "Beyond all question," was the effusive comment of the Charleston *Daily News,* "the best men in the convention are the colored members. Considering the influences under which they were called together, and their imperfect acquaintance with parliamentary law, they have displayed, for the most part, remarkable moderation and dignity. . . . They have assembled neither to pull wires like some, nor to make money like others; but to legislate for the welfare of the race to which they belong."

There were twenty-seven Southern white members of the convention, some of them honest and earnest, and some of them with questionable antecedents. One of them had made up a purse to buy a cane for Brooks, after he had assaulted Sumner; another had assisted in hauling down the Union flag from Fort Sumter; a third had been a slave trader. Among the Northerners were colored and white men of education and character, as well as some adventurers.

To the chagrin of many white onlookers, the convention was not a disorderly group; "the delegates did not create 'the Negro bedlam' which tradition has associated with them. President Mackey said that he had 'no unpleasant reminiscences of those acrimonious bickerings which, in all deliberative assemblies, are often incidental to the excitement of debate and the attrition of antagonistic minds.' " [8] There was no tendency to insult the white South, and even deference was paid to the defeated Confederate soldiers.

This was in striking contrast to the wild and unscrupulous attacks made by the press upon this convention. Some called the experiment "the maddest, most unscrupulous, and infamous revolution in history," and said that it was snatching power from the hands of the race that settled the country and transferring it to its former slaves, an "ignorant and feeble race."

The representative of one paper was expelled from the floor for sneering at the "ringed, striped, and streaked convention." Other papers received all possible courtesies.

The real basis of opposition to the new régime was economic. Nothing showed this clearer than one fact, and that is that the chief and repeated accusations against the convention and succeeding legislatures was that they were composed of poor men, white and black. The white 47 delegates were said to have paid altogether $761 in annual taxes, of which one conservative paid $508. The total taxes paid by the 74 Negroes were $117, of which a Charleston Negro paid $85. Twenty-three of the whites and fifty-nine of the colored paid no taxes whatever.[9]

In a day when property was sacred no matter how secured, and in a state where it had been politically supreme, this attitude was understandable. Yet one wonders just what was expected. Since the great majority of the white people of the state had been kept in ignorance and poverty, and practically all of the Negroes were slaves, whose education was a penal offense, one would hardly expect universal suffrage to put rich men in the legislature. It was singularly to the credit of these voters that poverty was so well represented; it showed certain tendencies toward a dictatorship of the proletariat. The taxpayers' convention of 1871 frankly proposed to restore the power of property by giving 60,000 taxpayers voting power equal to 90,000 non-taxpayers!

What was the black man thinking and saying in these days? There was abundant evidence of clear and logical thought among his leaders. The South Carolina Negroes approached their new responsibilities with a due sense of difficulty and responsibility.

Beverly Nash, a black ex-slave and member of the constitutional convention, born in slavery, said: "I believe, my friends and fellow-citizens, we are not prepared for this suffrage. But we can learn. Give a man tools and let him commence to use them, and in time he will learn a trade. So it is with voting. We may not understand it at the start, but in time we shall learn to do our duty. . . . We recognize the Southern white man as the true friend of the black man. You see upon that banner the words, 'United we stand, divided we fall,' and if you could see the scroll of the society that banner represents, you would see the white man and the black man standing with their arms locked together, as the type of friendship and the union which we desire.

"It is not our desire to be a discordant element in the community, or to unite the poor against the rich. . . . The white man has the land, the black man has the labor, and labor is worth nothing without capital. We must help to create that capital by restoring confidence, and we can only secure confidence by electing proper men to fill our public offices.

"In these public affairs we must unite with our white fellow-citizens. They tell us that they have been disfranchised, yet we tell the North that we shall never let the halls of Congress be silent until we remove that disability. Can we afford to lose from the councils of state, our first men? Can we spare judges from the bench? Can we put fools or strangers in their positions? No, fellow-citizens, no! gloomy, indeed, would be that day. We want in charge of our interest only our best and ablest men. And then with a strong pull, and a long pull and a pull together, up goes South Carolina." [10]

Both Sumner and Stevens had encouraged the Negroes of South

Carolina to seek sympathetic Southern whites as their leaders, but neither they nor others suggested any plans of union with white labor White Carolina labor was dumb with absolutely no intelligent leadership except the planters and carpetbaggers.[11]

When the convention opened, ex-Governor Orr was invited to address them. In his speech he stressed the fact that the freedmen needed education, and that they did not represent the intelligence nor wealth of the state, and he recommended limited suffrage, a homestead law and education.

The plight of debtors after the losses and changes of war brought much debate in the constitutional convention. A white delegate advocated a three months' moratorium on debt collections, and a colored member supported the proposal. But Cardozo, a colored man, and later the Treasurer of the State, said:

"I am opposed to the passage of this resolution. The convention should be certain of the constitutionality of their acts. The law of the United States does not allow a state to pass a law impairing the obligations of contracts. This, I think, is therefore a proper subject for the judiciary. I am heartily in favor of relief, but I wish the convention to have nothing to do with the matter."

R. G. DeLarge, a colored delegate, afterward Land Commissioner, said. "It has been said in opposition to this measure, that the proposed legislation was for a certain class; however, no gentlemen can rise and argue that the proposed measure is for the benefit of any specific class. I hold in my hands letters from almost every section of the state addressed to members of the convention, crying out for relief. These letters depict in strong language the impoverished condition of the people, and demand that something should be done to relieve them. I deny in toto that this is a piece of class legislation, and I believe nothing but the zeal of the members who spoke yesterday induced them to speak of it as such. It is simply a request to General Canby to relieve the necessities of a large part of the people of the state. Some members have gone farther, and said it was a shame to keep the freedmen from becoming purchasers and owners of land. . . .

"It has been argued that the execution of the laws compelling the sale of the lands will benefit the poor man by affording him an opportunity to get possession of the lands. That argument, I am confident, cannot be sustained. If they are sold, they will be sold at public sale, and sold in immense tracts, just as they are at present. They will pass into the hands of the merciless speculators, who will never allow the poor man to get an inch without first drawing his life's blood in payment. The poor freedmen are the poorest of poor and unprepared to purchase lands. The poor whites are not in condition to purchase lands. The facts are, the poor class are clamoring, and their voices have been voiced far beyond the limits of South Carolina, away to the seat of the government, appealing for assistance and relief from actual starvation."

The problem of the land came in for early consideration. The landless, it was felt, should be aided in the acquirement of property and the landed aristocracy discriminated against. It was proposed that Congress be petitioned to lend the state one million dollars to be used in the purchase of land for the colored people; that the legislature be required to appoint a land commission; and that homesteads up to a certain value be exempt from the levy of processes.

One must view this action in light of what had taken place with regard to land in South Carolina. When Northern forces captured Port Royal in November, 1861, the Federal authorities took over 195 plantations and employed over 10,000 former slaves in raising cotton. Early in 1862, they imported labor superintendents from the North, and organized the enterprise. In July, 1862, Congress laid a direct tax on the land of the states in rebellion. When the absentee landholders of Port Royal failed to pay, their plantations were sold at public auction to satisfy a part of the debt of $363,570 which had been imposed upon South Carolina. Considerable other property, which was regarded as abandoned, was seized in Charleston. The lands that were auctioned off were bought largely by Northerners, although a few Negroes who had got hold of a little money from their labor bought certain plantations.

On January 16, 1868, General Sherman issued his celebrated Field Order, Number 15. All the Sea Islands, from Charleston to Port Royal, and adjoining lands to the distance of thirty miles inland, were set aside for the use of the Negroes who had followed his army. General Saxton executed this order, and divided 485,000 acres of land among 40,000 Negroes. They were given, however, only possessory titles, and in the end, the government broke its implied promise and drove them off the land.

In the convention, the whole matter of land for the landless came up for considerable debate. Cardozo said that he did not believe in the confiscation of property, but since slavery was gone, the plantation system must go with it. Whipper, another colored man, was more inclined to protect the interests of the planters, and reminded the members that they were representatives of all classes in the community and not simply of a particular class.

This debate on the economic situation was prolonged. All contracts and liabilities for the purchase of slaves, where the money had not yet been paid, were annulled. J. J. Wright, colored, and later a state

Supreme Court judge, said of this measure: "I know it is said by our opponents that we are an unlawful assembly, and that we are an unconstitutional body. I know we are here under the laws of Congress, lawfully called together for the discharge of certain duties, and the repudiation of debts contracted for slaves. . . .

"It is the duty of the convention to do what? It is our duty to destroy all elements of the institution of slavery. If we do not, we recognize the right of property in man."

A homestead law to the value of $1,000 in real estate and $500 in personal property was passed. Rainey declared that Congress would probably never pass an act confiscating the land, but the other colored members, including Ransier, wanted to petition Congress for a loan of a million dollars to purchase land.

A colored delegate said on this matter: "My colleague presented a petition asking the Congress of the United States to appropriate one million dollars for a specific purpose—to purchase homesteads for the people of South Carolina; not the colored people, as the gentleman from Barnwell has attempted to prove, but to all, irrespective of color. He has also attempted to prove that the money cannot be obtained, but has failed to carry conviction to the minds of any of the members. There is plenty of land in the state that can be purchased for two dollars an acre, and one million will buy us five hundred thousand acres; cut this into small farms of twenty acres and we have twenty-five thousand farms. Averaging seven persons to a family that twenty acres can sustain, and we have one hundred and seventy-five thousand persons, men, women and children, who for a million dollars will be furnished means of support; that is, one-fourth of the entire people of the state."

Mr. R. C. DeLarge, colored, continued on the same subject:

"There are over one thousand freedmen in this state who, within the last year, purchased lands from the native whites on the same terms. We propose that the government should aid us in the purchase of more lands, to be divided into small tracts and given on the above-mentioned credit to homeless families to cultivate for their support. It is well-known that in every district the freedmen are roaming from one side to the other, not because they expect to get land, but because the large landholders are not able to employ them, and will not sell their lands unless the freedmen have the cash to pay for them. These are facts that cannot be contradicted by the gentleman from Barnwell. I know one large landholder in Colleton District who had twenty-one freedmen working for him upon his plantation the entire year. He raised a good crop but the laborers have not succeeded in getting any reimbursement for their labor. They are now roaming to Charleston and back, trying to get remuneration for their services. We propose to give them lands, and to place them in a position by which they will be enabled to sustain themselves.

"In doing this, we will add to the depleted treasury of the state, and the large plantation system of the country will be broken up. The large plantation will be divided into small farms, giving support to more people and yielding more taxes to the state. It will bring out the whole resources of the state. I desire it to be distinctly understood that I do not advocate this measure simply for the benefit of my own race."

After much discussion by various white members on the same subject, Mr. F. L. Cardozo, colored, voiced the thought of colored men who demanded that the government furnish land for the freedmen:

"The poor freedmen were induced, by many Congressmen even, to expect confiscation. They held out the hope of confiscation. General Sherman did confiscate; gave the lands to the freedmen; and if it were not for President Johnson, they would have them now. The hopes of the freedmen have not been realized, and I do not think that asking for a loan of one million, to be paid by a mortgage upon the land, will be half as bad as has been supposed. I have been told by the Assistant Commissioner that he has been doing on a private scale what this petition proposes. I say every opportunity of helping the colored people should be seized upon. I think the adoption of this measure should be seized upon. We should certainly vote for some measure of relief for the colored men, as we have to the white men who mortgaged their property to perpetuate slavery, and whom they have liberated from their bonds."

Mr. W. J. Whipper, colored, was more conservative, and only wanted protection from immediate monopoly:

"The present owners will be compelled before long to sell portions of their land, and sell them to freedmen or whoever can pay for them. But if sold now, they will be sold in large bodies, or large tracts, so that nobody but a capitalist will be able to buy."

This demand for land was characterized as demagoguery by the property holders, but land was, as many speakers suggested, the economic means of raising the level of the electorate. A petition was passed by a great majority, asking Congress to appropriate funds for buying land. But Senator Wilson replied that this was impractical, and the convention, thereupon, created a state commission for buying lands and selling them to the freedmen.

The convention attacked race discrimination squarely. A colored man, Dr. B. F. Randolph, offered the following amendment: "Distinction on account of race or color in any case whatever shall be prohibited, and all classes of citizens, irrespective of race and color, shall enjoy all common, equal, and political privileges." He said:

"It is, doubtless, the impression of the members of the convention that the Bill of Rights as it stands secures perfect political and legal equality to all the people of South Carolina. It is a fact, however, that nowhere is it laid down in the instrument, emphatically and definitely, that all the people of the state, irrespective of race and color, shall enjoy equal privileges. Our forefathers were no doubt anti-slavery men, and they intended that slavery should die out. Consequently, the word color is not to be found in the Constitution or Declaration of Independence. On the contrary, it stated 'all men are created free and equal.' In our Bill of Rights, I want to settle the question forever by making the meaning so plain that a wayfaring man, though a fool, cannot misunderstand it. The majority of the people of South Carolina, who are rapidly becoming property-holders, are colored citizens—the descendants of the African race—who have been ground down by three hundred years of degradation, and now that the opportunity is afforded, let them be protected by their political rights. The words proposed as an amendment were not calculated to create distinction, but to destroy distinction, and since the Bill of Rights did not declare equality, irrespective of race or color, it was important that they should be inserted."

Thus, discriminations of race and color were abolished by the constitution, and practical application was attempted in the case of the public schools, and the militia.

The convention framed the most liberal provisions for the right of suffrage that any of the Southern constitutions provided. They did not attempt, as in Virginia, Alabama, and Mississippi, to restrict the voting of whites further than was provided by the Reconstruction acts. Indeed, Whipper, a colored delegate, wished to petition Congress to remove all political disabilities from the white citizens. In this Cardozo and Nash agreed, and the motion was passed.

Of course, they made no distinction in race and color. The rights of women were enlarged. The property of married women could not be sold for their husbands' debts, and for the first time in its history, the state was given a divorce law.

Education was discussed at length, and a free common school system voted for.

"It is sufficient to say here that for the first time the fundamental law of the state carried the obligation of universal education and demanded the creation of a school system like that of Northern states." [12] Nothing that the convention did aroused more opposition among property-holding whites. In the first place, as a white woman told a Northern teacher:

"I do assure you that you might as well try to teach your horse or mule to read as to teach these niggers." [13]

In the second place, the whites calculated that the school system would cost $900,000 a year, and that the new taxation would fall upon them.

In the debate on the school system, there was not a moment's hesitation, but there was considerable difference of opinion as to whether education should be made compulsory or not.

R. C. DeLarge, colored, said in the debate, "The schools may be open to all, but to declare that parents shall send their children to them whether they are willing or not is, in my judgment, going a step beyond the bounds of prudence. Is there any logic or reason in inserting in the constitution a provision which cannot be enforced?"

Mr. A. J. Ransier, colored, said, "I am sorry to differ with my colleague from Charleston on this question. I contend that in proportion to the education of the people so is their progress in civilization. Believing this, I believe that the committee has properly provided for the compulsory education of all children in this state between the ages named in the section."

Mr. J. A. Chesnut, colored, spoke on separation in schools: "Has not this convention the right to establish a free school system for the poorer classes? Then if there be a hostile disposition among the whites, an unwillingness to send their children to school, the fault is their own, not ours. Look at the idle youth around us. Is the sight not enough to invigorate every man with a desire to do something to remove this vast weight of ignorance that presses the masses down? I have no desire to curtail the privileges of freedmen, but when we look at the opportunities neglected, even by the whites of South Carolina, I must confess that I am more than ever disposed to compel parents, especially of my own race, to send their children to school. If the whites object to it, let it be so."

Mr. F. L. Cardozo said, "It was argued by some yesterday with some considerable weight that we should do everything in our power to incorporate in the constitution all possible measures that will conciliate those opposed to us. No one would go further in conciliating others than I would. But we should be careful of what we do to conciliate.

"In the first place, there is an element that is opposed to us no matter what we do, which will never be conciliated. It is not that they are opposed so much to the constitution we may frame, but they are opposed to us sitting in the convention. Their objection is of such

a radical and fundamental nature, that any attempt to frame a constitution to please them would be abortive.

"In the next place, there are those who are doubtful; and gentlemen
here say if we frame a constitution to suit these parties, they will
come over to our side. They are only waiting to see whether or not
it will be successful.

"Then there is the third class who honestly question our capacity to
frame a constitution. I respect that class, and believe if we do justice
to them, laying our corner-stone on a sure foundation of republican
government and liberal principles, the intelligence of that class will
be conciliated, and they are worthy of conciliation.

"Before I proceed to discuss the question, I want to divest it of
all false issue of the imaginary consequences that some gentlemen have
illogically thought will result from the adoption of this section with
the word 'compulsory.' They affirm that it compels the attendance of
both white and colored children in the same schools. There is nothing
of the kind in the section. It simply says that all the children shall
be educated; but how, it is left with the parents to decide. It is left
to the parent to say whether the child should be sent to a public or
private school. There can be separate schools for white and colored.
It is left so that if any colored child wishes to go to a white school,
it shall have the privilege of doing so. I have no doubt, in most localities colored people will prefer separate schools, particularly until some
of the present prejudice against their race is removed."

The committee proposed that persons coming of age after 1875
must be able to read and write before voting, but Cardozo opposed
it because he said it would take more than ten years and a great deal
of money to complete the system, and he wanted to extend the time
to 1890. Three other colored members spoke against any qualification,
and it was, therefore, stricken out.

To bridge over the interval before the state school system could
be installed, Mr. B. F. Randolph, colored, presented the following petition, which was referred to the Committee on Miscellaneous Provisions
of the Constitution: "We, the undersigned, people of South Carolina,
in convention assembled, do hereby recommend that the Bureau of
Refugees, Freedmen and Abandoned Lands be continued until the
restoration of civil authority; that then a Bureau of Education be
established, in order that an efficient system of schools be established."

"Perhaps the convention's achievement of greatest permanent importance was the reform of local and judicial administration." [14]

Judicial circuits were to be called counties, and some new counties
were arranged. A Court of Probate was established in each county,
and justices of the peace were given wider jurisdiction. Judges were

to be elected, instead of appointed, and in spite of much criticism, the new system worked well. From 1870 to 1877 the Supreme Court was composed of a Negro, a native Southerner, and a Northerner. Its administration was fair and its decisions just. Most of the circuit judges were native whites and honest men. Mixed juries were the rule, and no fault was found with them. They did not hesitate to convict colored prisoners. The trial judges came in for the greatest criticism. Among them were numbers of ignorant and unqualified persons, and there were a good deal of misappropriation of fees and costs. On the other hand, it was difficult to get proper trial judges, because so many qualified whites refused to serve.

Wright, the Negro who was on the Supreme Court, was the first colored man admitted to the bar in Pennsylvania. He had been connected with the Freedmen's Bureau; then became a member of the constitutional convention, and a state senator. He was elected to the bench in February, 1870, to fill out an unexpired term, and was reelected in December, 1870, for the full term. He resigned under Hampton in August, 1877.

"Although he lisped, Wright was a good speaker, decidedly intelligent, and generally said to be the best fitted colored man in the state for the position."

Some reforms were made in the county government. Most of the officers were to be elected by popular vote, and boards of commissioners were appointed for the highways, and for collection and disbursement of taxes.

Some of the delegates wanted to legislate concerning wages, which caused great indignation among the planters. It was suggested, for instance, that planters be required to pay back wages from the time of the issue of the Emancipation Proclamation, and that the division of one-half of the crop for tenant farmers be made compulsory. Such legislation was inherently just and reasonable but fifty years too early for public opinion in any modern country.

Among other things, the constitution abolished imprisonment for debt, and dueling, and did away with property qualifications, for voting or holding office. The colored members, despite their inexperience, gave evidence, here and there, of care and thrift. For instance, when the question of the pay of members of the convention came up, a discussion arose. Mr. L. S. Langley moved that the pay per diem of $12 in bills receivable be laid on the table. J. J. Wright moved that $10 be inserted. N. G. Parker, white, moved to fix the pay at $11. C. P. Leslie, colored, demurred: "I desire to say a word before that resolution be passed, and be put right on record. I am perfectly willing to receive $3 per day in greenbacks for my services. I think that sum all they are worth, and further, if I got any more, it would be so much more than I have been in the habit of receiving, I might possibly go on a spree and lose the whole of it. Now I ask any of the delegates in this body if they were called upon to pay a similar body of men out of their pockets, how much they would be willing to pay each member. I will stake my existence on it they would not pay more than $1.50 per day to each member. I want to be recorded as always being opposed to a high tariff, but not against any reasonable compensation. But this eight or nine dollars a day, when we consider all the surroundings and conditions of the people, looks too much like a fraud."

The new constitution for South Carolina was adopted by the Convention in April, 1868. It was eventually adopted by the people— 70,000 voting for it, 27,000 against it, and 35,000 abstaining.

The constitution was written in good English and was an excellent document, "embodying some of the best legal principles of the age. In letter it was as good as any other constitution the state has ever had, or as most American states had at that time. This assertion is supported by the practical endorsement which a subsequent generation of South Carolinians gave it; the conservative whites were content to live under it for eighteen years after they recovered control of the state government, and when in 1895 they met to make a new constitution, the document they produced had many of the features of the constitution of 1868." [15]

It was not, of course, an original document, either in form or wording, but copied largely from Northern state models. But colored men discussed it, amended it, and voted for its adoption. They shared in the capacity and thought that made it.

A convention of whites held in Columbia April 2, condemned the constitution, as " 'the work of sixty-odd Negroes, many of them ignorant and depraved, together with fifty white men, outcasts of Northern society, and Southern renegades, betrayers of their race and country.' Its franchise provisions were declared to be designed to further the ambitions of 'mean whites'; its judicial system 'repugnant to our customs and habits of thought'; the homestead provision 'a snare and deceit'; and 'the stupendous school arrangement' 'a fruitful source of peculant corruption.' " Here spoke Capital, Land and Privilege against white and black labor.

In the spring of 1868, the Fairfield *Herald* declared the Revolution "the maddest, most unscrupulous and infamous revolution in history," which "has snatched the power from the hands of the race which settled the country . . . and transferred it to its former slaves, an ignorant and feeble race." [16]

Indeed, the criticism here was just as boundless and intemperate as that directed later toward the expenditures of the legislature, only in this case, we have the evidence of the constitution itself to show how excellent a document it was.

The economic revolution which Reconstruction involved overshadowed and guided all thought and action. Usury laws had been repealed by the planters in 1866, and rates of interest rose to 25 and 30 per cent. Banks commonly charged from 18 to 24 per cent. The owners of land and property, the persons of intelligence and social prestige, despite their partial impoverishment of the war, were strong and well-organized. They put the whole blame on abolition of slavery, enfranchisement of labor, and refusal of black men to work under essentially the same conditions as formerly. But colored Congressman Rainey of South Carolina well said in the 42nd Congress:

"If the country there is impoverished, it has certainly not been caused by the fault of those who love the Union, but it is simply the result of a disastrous war madly waged against the best Government known to the world. The murder of unarmed men and the maltreating of helpless women can never make restitution for the losses which are the simple inevitable consequence of the rebellion. The faithfulness of my race during the entire war, in supporting and protecting the families of their masters, speaks volumes in their behalf as to the real kindliness of their feelings toward the white people of the South." [17]

South Carolina property had been valued in 1860 at $489,319,128. All the capital in slaves was lost, but the remainder was $278,116,128. This shrank to $90,888,436 in 1866. In 1870, the property of South Carolina was assessed at $183,913,337. Besides this, millions were lost in bank stocks, endowments, and investments. One newspaper estimated that the gross property values shrank from $400,000,000 in 1860 to $50,000,000 in 1865. Of course, much of this was guesswork. The values of 1860 were inflated; the values of 1865-1870, perhaps unduly depressed. The builders of the new state wanted to make taxes uniform and, therefore, provided for a revaluation of lands and improvements. A committee was appointed to investigate the financial status, and the new school system, which was expected to be the largest item of expense (a splendid commentary upon the new spirit which had arisen in the state), was guaranteed an annual levy on all property and a poll tax. The property holders wanted to limit state indebtedness and prevent the legislature from extending credit to private corporations, but these suggestions were not approved of. The convention had a vision of prosperity, and they wanted railroads, schools, and poorhouses, and a distribution of land.

"In a progressive age," said Judge Wright, "the legislature must do its part, and the responsibility of that body to the people was sufficient check against extravagance." [18]

A committee of property holders was alarmed, and estimated that it would cost $2,230,950 annually to run the state, instead of $350,000, which had sufficed before the war. This was true, but when later the expenditure of the state reached this sum, these same people complained that the expenditure must on its face be fraudulent.

Singularly enough, it is conveniently forgotten that a good proportion of the white officials of South Carolina during Reconstruction were not Northerners, but Southerners, and several of them had served in the Confederate army. Moses, who became Governor; Robertson, United States Senator; and Neagle, Comptroller and former Confederate officer, were Southern white men. Bowen, a Congressman, while born in the North, had lived in Georgia before the war, and served as captain in the Confederate army. Of the white Northerners, Chamberlain, shrewd and able, but not over-scrupulous, was the leader. Among the others were Scott, well-meaning but not a strong governor; the pliable Parker, inefficient State Treasurer; and Patterson, who bribed his way to defeat a Negro for the United States Senate.

The first governor, under the new régime, was Robert K. Scott, born in Pennsylvania, a colonel of Union troops during the war, and assistant commissioner of the Freedmen's Bureau. Scott faced great difficulties, and is generally conceded to have been a well-meaning man. A well-born native Southern white was Franklin J. Moses, Jr. His father had been a prominent South Carolinian, Senator before the war, and was respected by all people. Moses married the daughter of a distinguished Southerner; was private secretary to one of the former Governors, and became a lawyer and an editor in favor of Johnson's Reconstruction. When the Reconstruction acts were passed he went over to the side of the carpetbaggers and Negroes; he took a prominent part in the constitutional convention, and afterward became Speaker of the House, and in 1872, Governor. He was denounced as unscrupulous and dishonest, and extravagant in his manner of living.

The colored leaders formed a very interesting group. Francis L. Cardozo was free-born of Negro, Jewish and Indian descent. He was educated at the University of Glasgow, and in London, and went to New Haven, where he served as a Presbyterian minister. After the war, he came to Charleston and was Principal of Avery Institute. He was secretary of state during 1868-1872, and treasurer of the state during 1872-1876. He was a handsome, well-groomed man, with cultivated manners, and honest in official life. He was accused in several instances, but no dishonest act was ever proven against him.

Joseph H. Rainey was the first Negro to represent South Carolina in the House of Representatives. Robert Brown Elliott, born in Massachusetts, was educated at Eton College, in England. He was a first-rate lawyer; served in the legislature, and was twice elected to Congress. He had a commanding presence, and a fine gift of oratory. Richard A. Cain was a leader, and afterward bishop in the A. M. E. Church. His paper, *The Missionary Record*, was the most influential Negro paper in South Carolina. He served in the Senate and two terms in Congress. Robert C. DeLarge was a tailor from Charleston, and had been an agent in the Freedmen's Bureau. He served in the legislature, and while his education was limited, he had large influence. Beverly Nash had been a slave before the war, and afterward a waiter. When grown he learned to read and write, and became an earnest and hard-working leader.

Alonzo J. Ransier was elected lieutenant-governor in 1870. He was a free Negro, and became a member of the constitutional convention of the legislature, and auditor of Charleston County. In 1872, he went to Congress. He made a good presiding officer of the state senate, being dignified and alert. Richard H. Gleaves was lieutenant-governor in 1872-1876. He was from Pennsylvania, and had acted as probate judge. He was intelligent and knew parliamentary law. Samuel J. Lee was a Negro Speaker of the House, in 1872-1874. He was born in the state, worked as a farmer and laborer in lumber mills, and was self-educated. He was polished and a good lawyer. Stephen A. Swailes, a colored man of Pennsylvania, was a Union soldier, and school-teacher. He became a senator, and was known for his integrity and ability as a speaker. Robert Smalls was the one who stole the Confederate ship *Planter* and delivered it to the Union authorities. He was self-educated and popular. He was a member of Congress until after Reconstruction. These men were all poor and doubtless some of them accepted bribes and shared in graft. But very few of them were thoroughly venal or purchasable against their convictions. When it came to personal favors or sharing in gifts and gains which followed legislation of which they honestly approved, some of them were certainly approachable.

Negroes were conspicuous members of the legislatures. "There was a large proportion of former slaves, and at first perhaps two-thirds of them could not write, but by 1871, most of them had learned at least to read and write. Many of them were speakers of force and eloquence, while others were silent or crude. In the Senate, it was said that some of the colored members spoke exceedingly well, with great ease and grace of manners. Others, were awkward and coarse." [19]

One observer recorded that "The President of the Senate and the Speaker of the House, both colored, were elegant and accomplished men, highly educated, who would have creditably presided over any commonwealth's legislative assembly."

"The majority of the voters of the state were Negroes, and in every session but one that race had a majority in the legislature. They outnumbered, and in many cases outshone, their carpetbag and scalawag contemporaries." [20]

In the first legislature there were 127 members, of whom 87 were colored, and 40 white. According to the available figures, the composition of Reconstruction legislatures in South Carolina seems to have been as follows: [21]

| | Senate | | House | | Total | | |
	Negroes	Whites	Negroes	Whites	Negroes	Whites	Total
1868-1869	10	21	78	46	88	67	155
1870-1871	10	20	75	49	85	69	154
1872-1873	16	17	80	42	96	59	155
1874-1875	16	17	61	63	77	80	157
1876-1878	4	14	58	64	62	78	130

It will be seen from these figures that the white members of the legislature, from their control of the Senate, were always able to block Negro legislators; and that Negro control of the legislature was only possible because most of the white Senators voted with the Negroes. In the legislature of 1874, the whites had a majority in both Houses. It can hardly be said, therefore, that the Negroes of South Carolina had absolute control of the state at any time.

The economic status of the legislature of 1870-1871 is shown by their given occupations: 10 lawyers, 31 farmers, 9 physicians, 17 clergymen, 12 teachers, 16 planters, 13 merchants, 3 merchant tailors, 3 clerks, 2 masons, 8 builders, 1 engineer, 1 marble dealer, 8 carpenters, 2 hotel keepers, 1 druggist, 1 bookkeeper, 1 wheelwright, 4 coachmakers, 1 tanner, 2 mechanics, 1 chemist, 1 auditor, 1 hatter, 1 blacksmith, 1 tailor.

The state sent seven Negroes to Congress; made two of them lieutenant-governors; and for four years, two of them were speakers of the House. One was secretary of state and treasurer of the state. Another was adjutant and inspector general. These men were of various colors and mixtures of blood, and there was a good deal of difference of opinion, as to whether the mulattoes or the full-blooded blacks were superior. But one observer asserted that "the colored men generally were superior in decency and ability to the majority of the native white Radical legislators." [22] And another said that "the quadroons and octoroons of the Senate are infinitely superior in personal appearance to their white Yankee and native compeers." [23]

Most of these men had been slaves, although a few of them were well-educated. They had ability, and in some cases, more than ordinary ability. But above all, they were in the midst of a mighty social and economic change, and were swayed by the social and political revolution around them. "The bottom rail was on the top," and the former ruling oligarchy was now displaced by those who represented neither the wealth nor the traditions of the state.

The bitterness of this campaign against the Reconstruction governments was almost inconceivable.

"One unfamiliar with the situation would think the editors and their correspondents had gone crazy with anger or were obsessed with some fearful mania, so great was the ridicule, contempt, and obloquy showered upon the representatives of the state. With the deepest scorn for a scalawag, with all the Southern hatred for an adventuring Yankee, and with either sympathy or shame for the ignorant, misled Negro, the press, the aristocracy, the poor whites, the up-country, the low-country—all with one voice protested against the 'unlawful assembly' in Columbia maintained in power, they said, by the Federal bayonet. The Fairfield *Herald* battled 'against the hell-born policy which has trampled the fairest and noblest States of our great sisterhood beneath the unholy hoofs of African savages and shoulderstrapped brigands—the policy which has given up millions of our free-born, high-souled brethren and sisters, countrymen and countrywomen of Washington, Rutledge, Marion, and Lee, to the rule of gibbering, louse-eaten, devil-worshiping barbarians, from the jungles of Dahomey, and peripatetic buccaneers from Cape Cod, Memphremagog, Hell, and Boston." [24]

A new system of taxation came in with the Reconstruction government. It provided for a uniform rate of assessment on all property at its full value. This was a departure from the system previous to the war, which put a low valuation on land and slaves and heavy taxation on merchants, professions and banking. The merchant before the war paid five or six times as great a rate of taxation as the planter. In 1859, the total tax value of lands in the state was $10,257,000, while lots and buildings in Charleston were valued at $22,274,000. The tax on all the land of the state averaged less than five cents an acre in 1860. When the new system came in, it was difficult to find persons to administer it and every landholder objected to it.

The new system met all sorts of opposition from unsympathetic administrators and the newspapers of the state. Governor Scott expected $300,000,000 worth of property as a basis of taxation, but less than $115,000,000 were returned. This the Board of Equalization raised to $180,000,000. As the assessments decreased, the rate of taxation increased. The total assessment in 1869 was $181,000,000, and in 1877, under Hampton, $101,000,000. As the average rate of taxes rose, the property holders said that the Negro government wanted to raise taxes so as to confiscate the land.

The new government could not collect the tax levied. It met an organized and bitter boycott of property. In 1868, $175,688 of assessed tax was uncollected; in 1869, $248,165, and in 1870, $524,026—a total of nearly a million dollars in three years. Part of this delinquency was due to real poverty; but part was due to deliberate obstruction on the part of property holders. Taxation had to be increased to cover delinquency and to meet new expenses. In 1860, taxation on a half billion of property was $1,280,383; in 1870, $2,767,675 was assessed on $183,000,000. The increase of taxation was partly accounted for by gradually increased expenditures for education, construction, and charitable institutions.

At the same time, the inflation of the currency makes comparison with conditions previous to the war difficult. More money was certainly raised by the state during Reconstruction. But, on the other hand, a much larger proportion of the expenditures was designed to aid the laboring poor, and did aid them largely. Indeed, it might have changed the whole economic position of the proletariat if it had been efficiently and honestly expended.

In the legislature in 1868, the free common school system was organized temporarily, and permanently in 1870. Relief was extended to various classes of citizens, especially poor laborers. In 1868 and 1869, an act was passed providing for a land commissioner, who was to act under a board. Land was to be purchased in various parts of the state, and was to be sold in plots of not less than twenty-five and not more than one hundred acres to actual settlers. Two hundred thousand dollars' worth of bonds were provided to finance this proposal, and later this was increased to $500,000. The land commissioner was to hold office at the pleasure of an Advisory Board, consisting of chief state officers.

One of the chief sources of corruption in nearly all the reconstructed states was railroad building. And the reasons for this are easily misconceived because of the changed economic status of railroads today. It must be remembered that at the beginning throughout the country and the world, the railroad was a public highway, and for this reason a public enterprise toward whose building and maintenance the public rightly contributed. It was only after the railroad was built and established by public funds, that private interests monopolized it and sequestered its income to make individual millionaires.

In the South, the railroads had lagged. The planters would not submit to public taxation, and they would not divert funds from their private luxury consumption, in order to furnish capital. South Carolina was particularly a case in point. Charleston, by all rules of commerce, should have been one of the great ports of the United States. It was a gateway to the West; it should have at least connected its own uplands with the coast, and it might have tapped the West through Cincinnati, and the great cotton belt through the Southern South. But efforts toward this end before the war had but small success.

It was perfectly natural that the first thought of those who were reconstructing the state should turn toward railroad building as a means of economic rehabilitation. The usual method was the old one of loaning credit of the state. It meant, not that the state invested money, but simply that the state permitted the issue of bonds and guaranteed the payment of interest and principal. On a sound economic proposition, conducted by honest men, this was simply a way of securing private capital for a semi-public enterprise, which would greatly increase the prosperity of the state.

Railway mileage in South Carolina had increased from 289 to 973, between 1850-1860. By 1865, there were 1,007 miles. Then construction practically stopped, and effort was turned toward rebuilding the railroads and giving them new equipment.

The difficulty was that a flock of cormorants whose business was cheating and manipulation in the issue and sale of bonds and other certificates of enterprise, moved first West and then South, and took charge of railroad promotion. They were largely Northern financiers, in some cases already discredited in the centers of finance and driven out of the overworked investment fields North and West. They came South with an address and a technique which only trained, experienced, and honest administrators could have withstood. They flaunted the chances of quick and easy money before the faces of ruined planters, small Northern investors, and the few Negroes who had some little capital. The result was widespread graft, debt and corruption in South Carolina and North Carolina, in Florida and Georgia, in Louisiana, and in other states.

There was, however, in the reorganization, for instance, of the Greenville and Columbia Railroad, nothing worse than the ordinary stock-jobbing enterprise common all over the nation; and prominent Southerners, like ex-Governor Orr and J. P. Reed, were concerned in it. Instead of concentrating efforts on the rebuilding of the railroad and its equipment, most of the time and energy was spent in seeking to market stock in New York. This failed and the road was bankrupt by the end of the Reconstruction era, just as it was at the beginning.

In the same way, the Blue Ridge road, backed not only by carpetbaggers but by leading white Southerners, was prostrate after the war and sued for state aid. The legislature authorized aid in 1868, but the contract for rebuilding demanded much more money than the bonds provided for. Eventually the road was sold to a private company composed as usual not only of carpetbaggers but of planters. Matters were so manipulated that a state contingent liability of $4,000,000 of bonds was transmuted into an actual state indebtedness of $1,800,000. Again little was done actually to restore the road, and the company went into bankruptcy.

Thus in most cases, bankrupt corporations bequeathed to the Reconstruction régime by ante-bellum organizers, came before the Legislature to secure capital for rebuilding, and then fell into the hands of speculators who tried to make money out of the stock, rather than out of the rebuilding of the road; and these speculators were largely men trained in shady finance in Wall Street, and helped by much of the best element of the Southerners in South Carolina, as well as by the new carpetbag capitalists.

This was a difficult situation, calling for blame and criticism, but to place the blame of it mainly upon the Negro voter and the Negro laborer is a fantastic distortion of the truth. The money misused went primarily to Northern promoters and Southern white administrators. And while, of course, a poverty-stricken electorate was gripped and bribed by such organized thieves, the remedy for this was not the disfranchisement of labor but its education, and such an increased share of the product of industry as to make life livable, without theft or sale of soul.

The appropriations to meet the new expenses had to grow. The fact is that South Carolina had been a state absolutely dominated by landed property. It is said that the ante-bellum state was ruled by 180 great landlords. They had made the functions of the state just as few as possible, and did by private law and on private plantations most of the things which in other states were carried on by the local and state governments. The economic revolution, therefore, which universal suffrage envisaged for this state, was perhaps greater than in any other Southern state. It was for this reason that the right of the masses to vote was so bitterly assailed, and expenditures for the new functions of the state denounced as waste and extravagance.

The result of all this had to be increased taxation. The rate of taxation in 1868-1872 was 9 mills; in 1872-1876 over 11 mills. Yet this was excessive only by comparison with the past and because of recent severe losses. In Northern states, like Illinois, Massachusetts, New York and Pennsylvania, the average was 21½ mills on the dollar.

The grip of poverty was on the South and poverty always is felt most poignantly by those to whom poverty has been unknown. The planters, used to ease and a certain degree of luxury, were the ones that felt the new poverty as a terrible, heaven-shattering thing. They looked upon any action as justifiable if it restored to them the income which they had lost.

On the other hand, both the poor whites and the Negroes were not only poverty-stricken, but, for that reason, peculiarly susceptible to petty graft and bribery. Economically, they had always been stripped bare; a little cash was a curiosity, and a few dollars a fortune. The sale of their votes and political influence was therefore, from the first, simply a matter of their knowledge and conception of what the vote was for and what it could procure. With experience, their conception of its value rose until some of them conceived the idea of making the ballot a power by which they could change their social and economic status, and live like human beings. But before most of them rose to this conception, there were thousands to whom their vote and petty office-holding were simply a means of adding to their small incomes. And when one considers that this was a day when the line between using political power for personal advantage and using it for social uplift was dim and difficult to follow throughout the whole nation, the wonder is that the labor vote of South Carolina so easily ranged itself behind the new school system, the orphanages, the land distribution, and the movements toward reform in public efficiency.

The ascendancy of property over labor and the suffrage was in this day openly maintained by bribery, and if this had been uncommon in the pre-war South, it was simply because universal suffrage had not been established and capital ruled by social sanction rather than by money. In the new situation, property began systematically to attack labor in two ways: First, it deliberately encouraged extravagance, graft and bribery, so as to hasten the downfall of the labor régime. And secondly, it utterly upset the credit of the state, so as to prevent the new state from importing capital.

The failure of taxation to raise the required revenue compelled the state to borrow, and here it fell into the hands of Northern money sharks and Southern repudiators. The state debt October 1, 1867, was $8,378,255. The Constitutional Convention of 1868 repudiated $3,000,-000 of this as a Confederate debt, and made the total debt $5,407,306. From this beginning, the state debt increased to $10,665,908 in 1871, while committees claimed that there was evidence of total liabilities outstanding to the amount of 15 or even 30 millions.

"The exact amount of the debt was not known; the figures from the reports of the treasurer, comptroller-general, and financial agent did not agree; and it was claimed by the opposition press and even by some of the state officials that there were large issues of fraudulent bonds on the market, and that certain of the state officials had profited thereby."

"While the Conservative press continually reviled the Radical government, on no topic was it so prolific or bitter as that of finances and taxation." [25]

The total debt, bonded and contingent, seems to have been:

1860	$12,027,090
1865	15,892,946
1868	14,896,040
1871	22,480,914

In this case, the total indebtedness in 1871 is not clear. The Governor's report makes it a little less than twelve million, but the investigation committee insists that because the state government had printed and issued certain bonds, the amount of which was not definitely known, it was possible that the state might eventually be liable for thirty million dollars.

This did not mean, as many assume, that the state officials received or squandered any such sums. The methods by which small amounts of actual cash received became a paper debt of huge amounts is explained in the Governor's special message of January 9, 1865.

"In the fall of 1868, I visited New York City for the purpose of borrowing money on the credit of the state on coupon bonds, under the provisions of the acts of August 26, 1868. I had the assistance of Mr. H. H. Kimpton, United States Senator F. A. Sawyer, and Mr. George S. Cameron. I called at several of the most prominent banking houses to effect the negotiation of the required loan, and they refused to advance any money upon our state securities, for those securities had been already branded with the threat of a speedy repudiation by the political opponents of the administration, who have ever since howled the same cry against the state credit. As the persons who made this threat controlled the press of the state, they were enabled to impress capitalists abroad with the false idea of a speedy reaction that would soon place them again in authority.

"As the capitalists well knew that these persons when in power in 1862 did repudiate their debts due Northern creditors, their distrust of our bonds was very natural and apparently well-founded. It soon became evident to every man familiar with our financial standing in New York that to negotiate the loan authorized, the question was not what we would take for the bonds, but what we could get for them. After much effort, and the most judicious management, I succeeded in borrowing money, through Mr. Cameron, at the rate of four dollars in bonds for one dollar in currency, the bonds being rated at 75 per cent below their par value, or at 25 cents on the dollar. This loan, however, was only effected at the extravagant rate of 1½ per cent per month, or 18 per cent a year—a rate only demanded on the most doubtful paper, to cover what is deemed a great risk—for the money loaned.

"Subsequent loans were effected at a higher valuation of the bonds, but at the rates of interest varying from 15 to 20 per cent, in addition to commissions necessarily to be paid the financial agent. If, then, $3,200,000 in money has cost the state $9,514,000 in bonds, it does not, therefore, follow that the financial board has criminally conspired against the credit of the state, and still less, that any one member of the board can justly be held up to public execration or stigmatized by an accusation of 'high crimes and misdemeanors' for the assumed results of its action. It is proper that I should add that the armed violence which has prevailed in this state for the past three years has had upon our bonds the same effect as actual war in lessening their purchasing-value, as money is dearer in war than in peace. Ku-Kluxism made capitalists shrink from touching the bonds of this state, as a man would shrink from touching a pestilential body." [26]

If there were outstanding in 1874 twenty or even thirty millions of evidences of debt, it is unlikely that this represented more than ten millions in actual cash delivered, and all monies collected and paid beyond that were not the stealing necessarily of South Carolinians, white or black, but the financial graft of Wall Street and its agents, made possible by the slander and reaction of the planters.

The rise of a group of a people is not a simultaneous shift of the whole mass; it is a continuous differentiation of individuals with inner strife and differences of opinion, so that individuals, groups and classes begin to appear seeking higher levels, groping for better ways, uniting with other like-minded bodies and movements. Every indication of this was present among Negroes during Reconstruction times. There was not a single reform movement, a single step toward protest, a single experiment for betterment in which Negroes were not found in varying numbers. The protest against corruption and inefficiency in South Carolina had in every case Negro adherents and in many cases Negro leaders.

The responsibility of Negroes for the government of South Carolina in Reconstruction was necessarily limited. They helped choose the elected officials and furnished a large number of the members of the legislature. But most of the administrative power was in the hands of the whites, and these were either Northerners, who had come South as officers or officials or to invest money, or native Southerners, both aristocrats and poor whites, who had undertaken to guide the Negro vote.

As a majority of the electorate, Negroes were responsible for the officials elected, but their choice was limited. They had among themselves a few notable leaders, some educated in the North, a few educated Southern Negroes, and other Southern Negroes with little formal education, but much hard sense.

Three groups gradually formed themselves among the whites, those like General Orr, who represented the planters and who were willing to accept Negro suffrage as a fact; others, like Wade Hampton, proposed to control the Negro vote, but to control it in the interest of the planters, and eventually to limit it in various ways. Then, there was a third party led by men like B. F. Perry, who wanted to exclude the Negro entirely from the ballot and do this as soon as possible, frankly on lines of race and color.

Perry feared a union of poor whites and Negroes, and saw in this a menace of proletarian revolution and an attack on property. "I greatly fear there are many white persons in South Carolina who will vote for a convention under the hope of its repudiating the indebtedness of the state. This class may influence the Negro vote to unite with them, and then, in return, they can unite with the Negro in parceling out the lands of the state. One step leads to another: stay-law first—repudiation next; and then follows a division of lands and an equal appropriation of property amongst all persons. And last of all, the honest, hardworking, industrious, and prudent class must support the idle, dissipated, extravagant and roguish class." [27]

It was this last group that eventually dominated and transported to South Carolina the "Mississippi plan" of overthrowing the Negro vote by brute force.

The path of black leaders under these circumstances was exceedingly difficult. Many Negroes of importance, such as Rainey, Lomax and King, openly attacked the course of Republican administration. R. H. King formed a Negro reform movement and said: "We would favor to send to the legislature honest mechanics and farmers whose minds are not biased by chicanery, at any rate, have honest men who are identified with prosperity and the people's interest." But on the other hand, most Negroes were afraid of combination with the white planters, who clearly would disfranchise them if they had the chance.

As the state debt increased, a taxpayers' convention met in Columbia in May, 1871, with thirty counties represented and a few Negro delegates. It protested against the increase in the public debt and the high taxation, and attacked the financial legislation. It warned persons not to buy bonds or obligations issued by the present state government because the property holders were not adequately represented in the legislature. Several Negroes were members of this convention, and the same year leading Negroes, including DeLarge, Nash and Robert Smalls, tried to form a new political party. It was admitted that there were abuses which needed reformation, but, on the whole, the Republican party was gratified at the result of the taxpayers' convention. A Joint Committee of the legislature made an examination of the financial condition of the state in 1871. This extended over several months. It declared that the total bonded debt of the state was $15,767,908.

This Joint Committee denounced the state officials, the Land Commission and the Financial Agent. An attempt was made to impeach Scott and Parker, the treasurer, and it was charged that they bribed members of the legislature to stop the proceedings. In this way, doubt was spread upon the validity of much of the bonded debt, and the credit of the state was almost entirely destroyed. There was no money in the Treasury and no way of meeting expenses. Northern capitalists were warned repeatedly about taking the bonds.

With all this went undoubted efforts to improve the state; an orphan asylum was authorized in 1869, the poor of the state were provided for in 1870; and this system was kept after the whites came into power. An institution for the deaf, dumb and blind was started in 1871. It lasted until 1873, and then the faculty resigned because they were ordered to accept colored students. A lunatic asylum was provided and colored patients admitted. "Casting aside all questions of race and forgetting temporarily its setting among a severely defeated and hostile people, but bearing in mind the uniqueness of this new experiment, an experiment of universal education among persons unaccustomed to such, this free public school system, and this relief for unfortunates, transformed the rôle of the poor whites in the educational and political history of South Carolina, and inculcated in the hearts of the blacks a vision which the citizenry of the world must admire." [28]

In 1872, the Republican party split; Moses ran for Governor, while the reform Republicans nominated Chamberlain. Negroes were on both tickets. Moses, a white Southerner with aristocratic connections, won and his administration was the most corrupt of the Reconstruction period. Negroes were alarmed and despite the risk to their status, turned toward reform. They saw that it was not enough to vote, they must exercise greater control over administration of affairs.

Moses was eventually criminally indicted while in office, but he escaped conviction on a technical point. "Since his retirement from executive cares, ex-Governor Moses' adventures and financial exploits in Northern cities have furnished the local reporters of police courts with not a few disgraceful items. Had it not been for the Southern men of this and the Swepson type—men of high social standing (and they were in every reconstructed state), the Northern adventurers would have been far less successful in their spoliations." [29]

A second taxpayers' convention met in February, 1874. The legislature replied to its charges, that the cost of government had increased only 38 cents per capita. It said that appropriations for schools, lunatic asylums, penitentiaries and orphan asylums had been increased, while the public debt had been increased only about $5,000,000; and that the taxpayers' convention was composed of the former ruling class which wanted to regain power.

The effort of Negroes at reform was severely and definitely handicapped by the attitude of the whites. If they joined with the whites in reform, they joined a party which was more and more determined to disfranchise them and eliminate them from public life, and impoverish them in economic life. It was this consideration that kept leaders like Elliott and Cardozo fighting within their own party, because they saw only in the Republican party any protection for their rights, and they believed that the matter of Negro suffrage and economic progress was more important than even the driving out of the grafters and inefficient politicians.

It was a difficult and desperate alternative, but they saw no way out. Even when reform movements under Chamberlain began, Negroes were apprehensive. Reform was in sight. In 1874, progressive and intelligent leaders of the party, including many of the colored leaders, elected D. H. Chamberlain as Governor, and the reforms which he inaugurated and carried through were attested by the white people of the state. The Charleston *News and Courier* said: "He stands like a wall of granite between an obstinate people and those who seek by a foul move to rob them." The Charlotte *Observer* called him "a model Governor." The *Grange,* 1875, declares: "He was fulfilling the pledges made alike to Conservative and Republican." The Barnwell *Sentinel* said that "the Governor will support no measure or policy that does not tend to advance the interest of South Carolina." A public meeting in Charleston gave him thanks "for the bold and statesmanlike struggle he has made in the cause of reform and the economic administration of the government." The *News and Courier* in June says: "By supporting Mr. Chamberlain, the whole country will secure without revolution a government in every way satisfactory." [30]

The Chamberlain reforms consisted in retrenchment of the annual expenses of the state by nearly $2,000,000, and in an attempt to drive out the grafters who had been robbing the state. Many leading Negroes supported him, but others did not. Those who would not, like Elliott, had no confidence in the white Southerners behind him.

Here was a chance for white Carolina to unite with the progressive Northerners and Negroes, and usher in honest and efficient government, without disturbing the right of black men to vote, and the right of labor to strive through universal suffrage for its interests. When some Negro leaders refused to follow Chamberlain, this was from no opposition to reform. It was because they saw Chamberlain surrendering in many respects to those white elements in the state who were pledged to degrade Negroes, and who were using reform as a stepping stone and an excuse for disfranchisement. It was a cruel dilemma, but their fears and suspicions proved true.

The colored Speaker of the House in 1874 said of the colored voters: "We, as a people, are blameless of misgovernment. It is owing to bad men, adventurers, persons who, after having reaped millions almost from our party, turn traitors and stab us in the dark. Ingratitude is the worst of crimes, and yet the men we have fostered, the men we have elevated and made rich, now speak of our corruption and venality, and charge us with every conceivable crime." [31]

Independent Radicals met October 2, 1874, and nominated John T. Green and Martin R. Delany as Governor and Lieutenant-Governor. They said:

"We cordially invite the whole people of the State to support the nominees of the Convention as the only means of preserving their common interests—especially requesting the Conservatives that have persistently declared that their desire was only for good government without regard to partisan politics, to support the independents." [32]

Colored Congressman Ransier of South Carolina said in his speech at Charleston, March 9, 1871: "I am no apologist for thieves; for if I were, I do not think I would have occupied for so long a time a place in your confidence. On the contrary, I am in favor of a most thorough investigation of the official conduct of any and every public officer in connection with the discharge of whose duties there is anything like well-grounded suspicion; and to this effect have I spoken time and again. Nor am I lukewarm on the subject of better government in South Carolina than that which seems to be bearing heavily on all classes and conditions of society today. Still, recognizing that which I believe to be true, that such is the determined opposition to the Republican Party and its doctrines by our opponents that no administration of our affairs, however honest, just and economical, would satisfy any considerable portion of the Democratic masses in the State of South Carolina, and satisfied that the principles and policy of the great Republican Party to which I belong are best adapted for the promotion of good government to all classes of men, our party leaders should be judicious in dealing with the situation. . . .

"And, again, when you are called upon in your primary meetings in your county and State nominating conventions, let each man act as if, by his individual vote, he could wipe out the odium resting upon our party, and help to remove the evils that afflict us at present. Let him feel, black or white, that the country holds him responsible for the shortcomings of his party, and that it demands of him the elevation to public positions of men who are above suspicion. Let each man feel that upon him individually rests the work of reform; let each man feel that he is responsible for every dollar of the public money fraudulently used; for every schoolhouse closed against his children; for every dollar of taxation in excess of the reasonable and legitimate expenses of the State; in short, let every man feel that society at large will hold him and the party accountable for every misdeed in the administration of government, and will credit him with every honest effort in the interest of the people, and in the interest of good government, whereby the community as a whole is best protected and the equal rights of all guaranteed and made safe. . . ." [33]

The curious charge is often made that Negroes devoted all their energies to politics. Had this been true their labor could never have restored the cotton crop, the naval stores industry and the whole economic fabric in the state. In their fight they sought to use not only political but other economic weapons. The pressure for land and the taxation of landholders gradually yielded results.

"By 1880 the 33,000 plantations of 1860 were divided among 93,000 small farmers." [34]

In 1866, the Charleston branch of the Freedmen's Bank had deposits of $18,000; in 1870, $165,000, and in 1873, $350,000 belonged to 5,500 depositors, showing that this was the savings of the poor and not the capital of the petty bourgeois. Only about 200 of the depositors were white. The colored people had accounts ranging from 5 cents to $1,000. When the bank failed in 1874, the Charleston branch owed 5,296 depositors a total of $253,168. The Beaufort branch owed 1,200 depositors $77,216.

A Negro labor movement began. In November, 1869, a state labor convention met in Columbia, with Robert B. Elliott as President. They asked for one-half share of the crop for farm laborers, or a stated wage of seventy cents to one dollar a day. They demanded a commissioner to supervise labor contracts, reduce rates, and stop the postponement of suits to recover portions of crops due for services. They tried to secure laws to prevent the discharge of laborers before they were paid, or the removal of crops before satisfactory settlement. They objected to the working of plantations by gangs, and wished to lease farms.

There were serious labor difficulties in 1876, through a strike of farm laborers in Colleton County; they threatened to destroy the crops of the planters. Another strike occurred in the rice fields of Buford County, where 200 Negroes at harvest time demanded an advance of 50 per cent in wages. They imprisoned scabs in the out-houses, and overpowered a sheriff and his posse; but the Governor sent the colored leader, Robert Smalls, with a company of militia, and the mob was dispersed.

"I inquired whether the black laborers have shown any disposition to violent outbreaks such as have occurred in several West Indies islands, but I could only hear of one such case, when the hired laborers in some of the rice-plantations of South Carolina struck for wages, and used much violence toward non-strikers, hunting them about with whips. The whites attempting to apprehend the rioters were mobbed, and the affair at one time looked very serious; but, by the aid of influential black politicians, the matter was accommodated, and the laborers have since worked well and quietly. I am told that though in their immediate demands the blacks were in the wrong, they had much ground of complaint, owing to the practice of some of the employers, who not being able to pay the wages earned and due, put the laborers off with checks upon stores kept on the truck principle." [35]

One of the best Negro unions was the Longshoremen's Protective Association of Charleston. In 1875 it was described as "the most powerful organization of the colored laboring class in South Carolina." Five hundred of its eight hundred members held an "exceedingly creditable" parade, with members well-dressed and good-looking. It had successfully conducted a number of strikes, and it was the most successful labor union among Negroes.

Under exceedingly difficult circumstances, and handicapped by their necessary ignorance and lack of experience, often deliberately misled, both by Northerners and Southerners, planters and poor whites, the Negroes, in legislation and in self-control, had made an excellent record. The group control exercised by the South Carolina Negroes was remarkable. Their leadership distinctly showed more ability and character than that of either the carpetbaggers or the scalawags.

It is interesting to remember that the Negro officials repeatedly were commended by various papers and persons in South Carolina. Charles M. Wilder, postmaster of Columbia, was commended in the *Daily News*, April 13, 1869, as a man "well-known" and "universally respected." The *Courier* said January 25, 1869, that R. C. DeLarge spoke "ably and logically," and that Elliott spoke "ably." December 2, 1869, the *Courier* gave prominence to the opinion of Judge Woodland of Pennsylvania, a member of Congress, who received a very favorable impression of Robert Brown Elliott, and regarded him "as the ablest man in the legislature." The *Daily News,* November 30, 1869, called Whipper "an intelligent man and very popular in the party." The *Chesterfield Democrat,* 1870, called Henry L. Shrewsbury "an opponent of corruption," and declared that "he sustained a good reputation which he has kept intact under great temptations" and that "he has exerted himself zealously and courageously to guard his people from compulsion and vengeance, and establish their claim to decency and respectability." The *Courier,* in 1870, spoke of W. H. Jones, and said that "he speaks well and to the point." It said also that Jamison had sound, practical sense. Later, it called Dr. Boseman an "intelligent educated man." The *Abbeyville Press* commended Cardozo for trying to prevent waste of money and said, "The treasurer is an able officer of undoubted integrity." The *News and Courier,* September 4, 1874, called Samuel Lee "tolerably well educated," and said that he spoke "fearlessly and forcibly." Some visitors, like F. Barham Zinkle, found Negro members of the Assembly superior to white members. James S. Pike, a violent hater of Negroes, said that "all of the best speakers in the House are quite black" and added that Senator Beverly Nash "has more native ability than half the white men in the Senate." [36]

It is asserted beyond all question that the best men of the legislature were colored men. They knew more about parliamentary law and carried themselves with moderation. On the other hand, among the white members, were some strange bedfellows. Rutland was the one who gave a cane to Brooks after he had beaten Sumner. Moses helped pull down the flag at Fort Sumter. There were, of course, illiterate and ignorant men among the Negro speakers, but, on the other hand, there were some of poise and eloquence, who spoke with ease and grace.

These were the men and this the effort which have been endlessly blamed and reviled. There is that celebrated tirade by Pike:

"The members of the Assembly issued forth from the State House. About three-quarters of the crowd belonged to the African race. They were such a looking body of men as might pour out of a market-house or a courthouse at random in any Southern state. Every Negro type and physiognomy was here to be seen, from the genteel serving-man, to the rough-hewn customer from the rice or cotton field. Their dress was as varied as their countenances. There was the second-hand, black frockcoat of infirm gentility, glossy and threadbare. There was the stovepipe hat of many ironings and departed styles. There was also to be seen a total disregard of the proprieties of costume in the coarse and dirty garments of the field." This is, of course, the jibe of property and gentility at poverty and ignorance. Most men always have been poor and unkempt.

Then comes the real attack. "The Speaker is black, the Clerk is black, the doorkeepers are black, the little pages are black, the chairman of the Ways and Means is black, and the chaplain is coal black. At some of the desks sit colored men whose types it would be hard to find outside of the Congo."

Then comes this acknowledgment: "It is not all sham, nor all burlesque. They have a genuine interest and a genuine earnestness in the business of the assembly which we are bound to recognize and respect. . . . They have an earnest purpose, born of conviction that their conditions are not fully assured, which lends a sort of dignity to their proceedings." [37] It is surely not all "sham" and "burlesque"—indeed was any of it sham and burlesque, save in minds like Pike's?

Take out the accusation of being black, which is still a crime in the United States, and there remains in such tirades as this only a protest against ignorance and poverty presuming to rule intelligence and wealth; and yet, under the circumstances, how else was the necessary economic and social revolution to be effected?

The charge against the Negro legislators manifestly could not be simply the charge of being black. The question was, how did they govern? Sir George Campbell, a member of Parliament, says that whatever violence and disturbance there was, was not on the part of the black majority, but on the side of the white minority, who instead of trying constitutional methods to gain power, preferred Ku Klux organizations and such violent methods. He continues, "Before I went South, I certainly expected to find that the Southern states had been for a time a sort of Pandemonium in which a white man could hardly live, yet it was certainly not so. . . . 'Well, then,' I had gone on to ask, 'did the black Legislatures make bad laws?' My informants could not say that they did. . . . What, then, is the practical evil of which complaint is made? The answer is summed up in the one word, 'corruption.' . . . I believe that there can be no doubt at all that a great deal of corruption did prevail—much more than the ordinary measure of American corruption. It was inevitable that it should be so under the circumstances; but to what degree it was so, it was very difficult to tell." [38] His conclusion is that the carpetbag rule did no permanent injury to the state; that the black men used their victory with moderation.

This brings us to the center of the corruption charge, which was in fact that poor men were ruling and taxing rich men. And this was the chief reason that ridicule and scorn and crazy anger were poured upon the government. There was after the war a severe economic strain upon the former wealthy ruling class, and if South Carolina had been ruled by angels during 1868-1876, the protest of wealth and property would have been shrill and angry, and it would have had all the justification that the war-ridden always have.

On the other hand, great as was the stress upon the former owners of wealth, the condition of the Negroes was infinitely worse. The Negro was desperately poor. Outside of the three or four thousand free Negroes, he inherited no property, no tools, no land. His chance to make a decent labor contract was about as small as could be imagined. A number worked for the army and bought land; some earned a living on land furnished them. But the vast majority remained poor, landless laborers.

The people best qualified to help and advise in the reconstruction of the state refused even when there was no legal barrier. The attitude of most of the whites was childish. They complained then and afterward that they were not asked to lead the Negroes; that they were not chosen to be leaders, when it was their clear duty to place themselves at the head of Negro groups and white groups and lead them aright. In fact, they wanted labor government to fail. Nothing would have disgusted most of them more than to have a government, in which Negro slaves and Northern interlopers and poor whites participated, succeed. They had there, therefore, every motive for making progress difficult, and for using charges of failure for propaganda in the North.

The wilder charges have all the stigmata of propaganda and are in some respects intrinsically unbelievable. It is impossible to be convinced that the people who gave South Carolina so excellent a constitution, who founded good social legislation, a new system of public schools, and who were orderly and earnest in their general demeanor, could at the same time in all cases be stealing, carousing and breaking every law of decency. Yet the accusers in the case of South Carolina reconstruction attacked everybody, and when one Reynolds runs out of accusations in attacking the character of a leading Negro statesman, he turns around and without adducing a single line of proof, calls his wife a "strumpet." Scarcely a single person, white or black, Northern or Southern, connected with the government of South Carolina during 1868-1876 has escaped being called a "scoundrel," a "rascal," and a "thief." This does not sound reasonable. As two of the younger and later and more honest students of the situation frankly admit, the accusations do not sound true.

However, many believe that the main charges were substantiated. This report was made by the investigating committee appointed in 1877 by the Democratic legislature, and it was an attempt to justify everything that had been done in South Carolina to overthrow the rule of labor and its allies. If this report is to be believed in its entirety, then the people of South Carolina were the most extraordinary set of thieves in the United States; and this applied mainly to the native white South Carolinians, belonging both to the old aristocracy and the poor whites; next to the carpetbaggers, necessarily limited in numbers, but large in influence; and least to the Negroes—to the Negroes in small measure as actual recipients of money, but in larger responsibility as dupes and victims of their white leaders.

The interpretation that has grown out of this report has tended to identify the scalawags with the carpetbaggers; to say comparatively little concerning the part which white native Carolinians played, and to transfer the main guilt of dishonesty almost entirely to the Negroes. This is not only a falsification of history; it is not even a fair interpretation of the Fraud Report.

But the Fraud Report, moreover, in itself is not convincing.

Sir George Campbell said:

"In South Carolina I was given the report of the committee of Investigation disclosing terrible things, and said to be most impartial and conclusive. The general result was to leave on one's mind the belief that undoubtedly a very great deal of pilfering and corruption had gone on, but the tone of the report was far too much that of an indictment, rather than of a judgment, to satisfy me that it could be safely accepted in block." [39]

The report was made by a committee of the Democratic legislature of South Carolina, just after their party, by force and fraud, had driven the Negroes and the Republicans out of power. It was the bounden duty of this legislature to prove that their action was justified. No considerations of human life, character or desert, had deterred them from this bloody revolution, and it is not conceivable that any considerations of exact truth or fidelity to fact would deter them from defending it to such an extent that the Federal government should not interfere.

The men who made the report had in their hands all of the governmental records and documents to use or suppress as they wished. They gave accused persons no real or safe opportunity to reply. They could call as witnesses persons upon whom they were able to put the severest pressure. The unsupported testimony of these witnesses, so long as it was against the overturned government, was received as final authority. Some of these witnesses were acknowledged thieves. Yet their testimony was given full credence, with the curious assumption that such thieves would not lie, when it was to their distinct advantage to deceive. Why, for instance, should A. O. Jones, the colored clerk of the House, acknowledge systematic bribery, unless it was made distinctly to his interest to do so? And if it was to his interest to give this testimony, how can we know that the testimony was absolutely true?

The report piled charge upon charge; it grouped together sworn testimony, gossip and suspicion. It put down as facts the statements of men who were incriminated by the facts. It accepted as proof of articles and supplies furnished, the lists and statements of those who sold them, and who profited by the sale and bribed the purchasers. This committee, as a matter of fact, constituted itself judge and jury in an indictment which nobody since has had opportunity to scrutinize and criticize carefully. No court in Christendom would, without further data, receive the fraud report of South Carolina as the exact truth.

There was nothing in their general conduct during this time to leave any doubt that men would go to any limit of deception in order to prove that Negroes were not fit to vote and that all Northern men in the state were thieves. The whole story of this era has not been revealed nor studied with impartial and scientific accuracy. Perhaps at this late day it never can be.

In South Carolina, the charges of stealing were primarily sixty thousand dollars in bribery to pass the phosphate bill; forty thousand dollars to elect John J. Patterson to the United States Senate; $200,000 in four years for furnishing the capital; $200,000 as appropriations for state printing; large sums for supplies; the issue of fraudulent and excessive pay certificates to members of the legislature; the increase of needless clerks; a saloon in the State House and fraud in the sale of land to the state.

In none of these charges do colored men appear as principals accused except, possibly, in the case of Jones, a member of the printing ring, upon whose own testimony some of the charges are based. In the case of the phosphate bill, there was, doubtless, general bribery of both colored and white members of the legislature, but it was to establish an industry which the state sorely needed, and which it seemed able to get only by granting a monopoly to Southern white men. In the case of the Patterson election, the graft was dispensed by a white man in order to defeat his colored opponent, Eliott, who refused a $10,000 bribe to withdraw.

White Northerners who owned the two leading dailies got contracts for the public printing, but, later, clerks of the two Houses, one of whom was colored, got in on this graft and shared at least a part of it. In the case of the land commission, an excellent and needed movement to furnish small farmers land at reasonable prices was turned into a theft by which white land-holders were the chief gainers. Whatever stealing of land funds was done cannot be charged to

Robert D. DeLarge, the colored Land Commissioner. He says in his first report:

"It will be seen that I have never been in possession of the bonds as contemplated in the Act, and that I am consequently in no wise responsible for any disposition that may have been made of them. The lands I have purchased have been paid for, through orders of the State treasurer, approved by the chairman of the advisory board." [40]

He reported February 23, 1871, that nearly two thousand small farms were occupied or ready to be settled, and that settlers would have eight years to make payments. The greater portion of the farms bought were already occupied, and numbers of thrifty and industrious farmers, white and black, were eagerly securing homes. Over three hundred certificates of purchase had been issued.

It was said that the legislative sessions were unduly prolonged; that unnecessary clerks were employed; that a liquor saloon was maintained, and that under the head of supplies, all sorts of personal things were furnished individual members of the legislature, and charged to the state. But it is not usually added that merchants got the contracts for these furnishings, some Northern, some Southern. They furnished the money to bribe committees and members of the legislature in order to secure for themselves the right to charge taxpayers outrageous prices for shoddy materials. They were doing no more in this case than business men of New York and Philadelphia; but, also, it is perfectly clear, they were doing no less. The state got a capitol decked out in the flamboyant taste of the day, but we must not forget that for the first time in their drab life, representatives of black and white labor, toiling in the fields and swamps and living in the unpaved slums of the towns, saw something that meant to them beauty and luxury—saw it and touched it, and owned it. And somehow, I have more respect for the golden spittoons of freed Negro lawmakers in 1872, than for the chaste elegance of the colonial mansions of slave-drivers in 1860.

Graft and bribery spread in the state, but the "worst feature of corruption in South Carolina is that members of both parties and men of all classes are involved in it, and that public abhorrence of corruption, which is the safeguard of popular government, seems wanting or dormant. Even the old aristocratic class, to whom we had been taught to attribute sentiments of chivalric honor, have not scrupled to bribe officials."

Dr. R. M. Smith of Spartanburg County, an old citizen and Democratic member of the legislature, testified that he could see no wrong in bribing a public officer, and compared the transaction to the purchase of a mule. In the taxpayers' convention, held at Columbia, South

Carolina, Mr. F. F. Warley of Darlington County, an old citizen of high standing, spoke as follows:

"As I said on yesterday, public frauds would not exist were it not for private individuals who act the part of corruptors. Were none of these engaged in bribing members of the legislature, we would hear nothing of such frauds, as the one I have endeavored to expose.

"Mr. President, one prominent feature in this transaction is the part which native Carolinians have played in it; and it is to this feature that I ask to be allowed to address myself in closing. I say, sir, and I say it in sorrow, that some of our own household, men whom the state in the past has delighted to honor, but whose honors have been withered by the atmosphere of corruption that they breathe, are involved in this swindle.

"A legislature, composed chiefly of our former slaves, has been bribed by these men—to do what? To give them the privilege, by law, of plundering the property holders of the state, now almost bankrupt by reason of the burden of taxation under which they labor.

"It is difficult for citizens of other States to realize such prevalent corruption, affecting all classes of society, bringing to the same level, patriot and rebel, white and black, the old citizens and the new. Probably one cause contributing to produce this result is the condition of civil war which has prevailed in the state, in which the power has been almost exclusively in the hands of one class, and the property in the hands of the other. While open hostilities have not generally and continually existed, there has been mutual enmity more bitter than usually accompanies flagrant warfare. Hence, some of the men in office may have regarded what was taken from the treasury as taken from the property holders, enemies of the Government, and therefore spoils of war; and, on the other hand, some property holders have come to consider what they procure by bribery and corruption as a right of which they are wrongfully deprived, and which they are justified in recovering by any means. Another cause seems to be the contempt which the old property-holding class manifest and feel for freedmen and all who coöperate with them politically. This gives to bribery of such persons, in the eyes of the old native class, the semblance of the purchase of a slave." [41]

Many other Southern white speakers of the day were clear and frank in assessing blame. C. W. Dudley said in 1871: "The colored population must give us their assistance in any reforms which are contemplated. This they will do just as soon as they discover that their former owners are completely reconciled to their new condition. If they have turned from us heretofore, from a suspicion that their newly-acquired rights had been grudgingly granted, and were not safe in the hands of those who had never recognized them as equals, this was but natural; and we are compelled to admit that under similar circumstances we would have done so ourselves. They have looked for protection to others, because they were afraid to trust their all to those who might have a motive to betray that trust." [42]

Major F. F. Warley said the same year:

"I scorn the idea that the rich man in his glory, and the mighty man in his power, may indulge in crime with impunity and be passed by the world with a smile of recognition; while the poor tool he uses is consigned to prison and made the associate of felons. If I have displayed zeal and ardor in this exposure of fraud and vice, it is because I would save the State, not from ignorant and corrupt legislators so much as from rich, aspiring, and unprincipled men, some of them imported, it is true, but many of them degenerate and unworthy sons of that noble, though now impoverished, mother whom they rob." [43]

There was, then, without doubt, theft and incompetence in the government of South Carolina during Reconstruction times. But there is good ground for saying that this was no more due to Northern white men than to native Southerners; and least of all was it the guilt of Negroes. Moreover, in method and amount, it was no worse than the same kind of stealing in Northern states, and even in the United States government itself.

If we allow for depreciated currency, and for the monies which the state did not actually receive and did not spend, but for which it may have been legally responsible, South Carolina doubled its debt between 1865 and 1871. But it more than doubled its social responsibilities. That the proceeds of debt thus accumulated were not spent wholly to meet these social demands, is undoubtedly true; but it is also true that every cent which South Carolina raised in Reconstruction times, and much more, was needed for the uplift of its laboring classes.

It is interesting to note that $17,500,000 of the South Carolina debt, or almost the exact amount of its probable increase over 1865, was eventually repudiated by the state, and the property of the state thus put itself on record as refusing to recognize its obligation to pay the expense even of necessary Reconstruction, and at the same time, it had the satisfaction of spoiling the Egyptians in the Northern money market.

Two sorts of reform faced the state: first the elimination of theft and waste in the handling of the public funds; and secondly the continuation of the efforts for social uplift in land distribution, institutions for social reform, educational equipment and modern labor legislation. With the last category the reformers would have nothing to do. What they meant by reform was lower taxes, and this, Chamberlain gave them.

It is easy to prove that this part of the effort to reform the situation in South Carolina had the earnest effort of both white men and black men, and resulted in distinct advance. It was overthrown at just the time when there was every reason to think that reform would be triumphant, not simply in honest government but in more efficient social uplift.

No one has expressed this more convincingly than a Negro who was himself a member of the Reconstruction legislature of South Carolina and who spoke at the convention which disfranchised him in 1895, against one of the onslaughts of Tillman:

"The gentleman from Edgefield [Mr. Tillman] speaks of the piling up of the state debt; of jobbery and peculation during the period between 1869 and 1873 in South Carolina, but he has not found voice eloquent enough, nor pen exact enough to mention those imperishable gifts bestowed upon South Carolina between 1873 and 1876 by Negro legislators—the laws relative to finance, the building of penal and charitable institutions, and, greatest of all, the establishment of the public school system. Starting as infants in legislation in 1869, many wise measures were not thought of, many injudicious acts were passed. But in the administration of affairs for the next four years, having learned by experience the result of bad acts, we immediately passed reformatory laws touching every department of state, county, municipal and town governments. These enactments are today upon the statute books of South Carolina. They stand as living witnesses of the Negro's fitness to vote and legislate upon the rights of mankind.

"When we came into power, town governments could lend the credit of their respective towns to secure funds at any rate of interest that the council saw fit to pay. Some of the towns paid as high as twenty per cent. We passed an act prohibiting town governments from pledging the credit of their hamlets for money bearing a greater rate of interest than five per cent.

"Up to 1874, inclusive, the State Treasurer had the power to pay out State funds as he pleased. He could elect whether he would pay out the funds on appropriations that would place the money in the hands of the speculators, or would apply them to appropriations that were honest and necessary. We saw the evil of this, and passed an act making specific levies and collections of taxes for specific appropriations.

"Another source of profligacy in the expenditure of funds was the law that provided for and empowered the levying and collecting of special taxes by school districts, in the name of the schools. We saw its evil and by a constitutional amendment provided that there should only be levied and collected annually a tax of two mills for school purposes, and took away from the school districts the power to levy and to collect taxes of any kind. By this act we cured the evils that had been inflicted upon us in the name of the schools, settled the public school question for all time to come, and established the system upon an honest, financial basis.

"Next, we learned during the period from 1869 to 1874, inclusive, that what was denominated the floating indebtedness, covering the printing schemes and other indefinite expenditures, amounted to nearly $2,000,000. A conference was called of the leading Negro representatives in the two Houses together with the State Treasurer, also a Negro. After this conference, we passed an act for the purpose of ascertaining the bona fide floating debt and found that it did not amount to more than $250,000 for the four years; we created a commission to sift that indebtedness and to scale it. Hence when the Democratic Party came into power they found the floating debt covering the legislative and all other expenditures fixed at the certain sum of $250,-000. This same class of Negro legislators, led by the State Treasurer, Mr. F. L. Cardozo, knowing that there were millions of fraudulent bonds charged against the credit of the State, passed another act to ascertain the true bonded indebtedness, and to provide for its settlement. Under this law, at one sweep, those entrusted with the power to do so, through Negro legislators, stamped six millions of bonds, denominated as conversion bonds, 'fraudulent.' The commission did not finish its work. There were still to be examined into and settled under the terms of the act passed by us providing for the legitimate bonded indebtedness of the state, a little over two and a half million dollars' worth of bonds and coupons which had not been passed upon.

"Governor Hampton, General Hagood, Judge Simonton, Judge Wallace, and in fact, all of the conservative thinking Democrats, all aligned themselves under the provision enacted by us for the certain and final settlement of the bonded indebtedness and appealed to their Democratic legislators to stand by the Republican legislation on the subject and to conform to it. A faction in the Democratic Party obtained a majority of the Democrats in the legislature against settling the question, and they endeavored to open up anew the whole subject of the state debt. We had a little over thirty members in the House, and enough Republican Senators to sustain the Hampton conservative faction, and to stand up for honest finance; or by our votes, place the debt question of the old state into the hands of the plunderers and speculators. We were appealed to by General Hagood, through me, and my answer to him was in these words: 'General, our people have learned the difference between profligate and honest legislation. We have passed acts of financial reform, and with the assistance of God when the vote shall have been taken, you will be able to record for the thirty odd Negroes, slandered though they have been through the press, that they voted solidly with you all for the honest legislation and the preservation of the credit of the state.' The thirty odd Negroes in the legislature and their senators by their votes did settle the debt question and saved the state $13,000,000.

"We were eight years in power. We had built schoolhouses, established charitable institutions, built and maintained the penitentiary system, provided for the education of the deaf and dumb, rebuilt the jails and courthouses, rebuilt the bridges and reëstablished the ferries. In short, we had reconstructed the State and placed it upon the road to prosperity and, at the same time, by our acts of financial reform, transmitted to the Hampton Government an indebtedness not greater by more than $2,500,000 than was the bonded debt of the state in 1868, before the Republican Negroes and their white allies came into power." [44]

It seemed fairly clear that what South Carolina wanted was not reform even in its narrower sense; that what it was attacking was not even stealing and corruption. If there was one thing that South Carolina feared more than bad Negro government, it was good Negro government.

In fine, dishonesty in South Carolina was not racial. It was not even a matter of the lower economic classes, white or black. It was the child of an age of extravagance and characteristic of a state where the mass of the voters were poverty-stricken, and the property holders angry and ruthless in their methods.

"The fact that the best men of the South (unlike the Abolitionists of John Brown's time) were unwilling to strike openly and trust that the end and the future would justify the means, is very good evidence that the methods by which Negro rule was overthrown had not as yet been proved to be necessary, and, therefore, were unjustifiable. Goldwin Smith has said that statesmanship is the art of avoiding revolution. Of the Democrats of Mississippi and South Carolina in 1875 and 1876 one might well say, "Their revolution was the art of avoiding statesmanship." [45]

Beneath the race issue, and unconsciously of more fundamental weight, was the economic issue. Men were seeking again to reëstablish the domination of property in Southern politics. By getting rid of the black labor vote, they would take their first and substantial step. By raising the race issue, they would secure domination over the white labor vote, and thus the oligarchy that ruled the South before the war would be in part restored to power. It would, of course, lack capital. But the North stood ready to furnish capital if profit could be obtained, and it was being made more and more clear that this furnishing of capital, far from being contingent upon universal suffrage in the South, could be made more available even if the black labor vote was disfranchised completely, and white labor directed in the South by the same methods that were dominating it in the North.

<hr/>

> 'Tis not in the high stars alone,
> Nor in the cups of budding flowers;
> Nor in the redbreast's mellow tone,
> Nor in the bow that smiles in showers,
> But in the mud and scum of things
> There alway, alway something sings.
>   RALPH WALDO EMERSON

<hr/>

1. John W. Burgess, *Reconstruction and the Constitution*, p. 133.
2. For the main facts in this chapter, consult Simkins and Woody, *South Carolina During Reconstruction;* the *Proceedings of the Constitutional Convention of 1868,* and Williams' *History of Public Education,* etc., in South Carolina.
3. Simkins and Woody, *South Carolina During Reconstruction*, pp. 51-52.
4. Simkins and Woody, *South Carolina During Reconstruction*, p. 326.
5. *Congressional Globe,* 39th Congress, 1st Session, Part I, p. 93.
6. *Report of the Joint Committee on Reconstruction, 1866,* Part II (Abbeyville District), p. 225.
7. Simkins and Woody, *South Carolina During Reconstruction*, pp. 85-87.
8. Simkins and Woody, *South Carolina During Reconstruction*, p. 105.
9. *Ku Klux Conspiracy, South Carolina,* Part 2, pp. 1238-1250.
10. *Proceedings of the Constitutional Convention of 1868,* Charleston, S. C. The following speeches are quoted from this source.
11. "That a number of colored men met and appointed a committee which was sent to Washington to get the advice of Charles Sumner and Thaddeus Stevens concerning the formation of the political organization for the newly enfranchised Negro citizen, shortly after the adoption of the 14th Amendment.
    "Pains were taken to keep the plans from both the native whites and the so-called carpetbaggers from the North. That both Mr. Sumner and Mr. Stevens advised the committee to tender the leadership to native whites of the former master class of conservative views; but this plan was frustrated because they were not able to secure the consent of desired representatives of the former master class to assume the proffered leadership." (*Journal of Negro History,* V, p. 111.)
12. Simkins and Woody, *South Carolina During Reconstruction*, p. 100.
13. Simkins and Woody, *South Carolina During Reconstruction*, p. 424.
14. Simkins and Woody, *South Carolina During Reconstruction*, p. 101.
15. Simkins and Woody, *South Carolina During Reconstruction*, pp. 93-94.
16. *Fairfield Herald,* April 29, 1868.
17. C. G. Woodson, *Negro Orators and Their Orations*, p. 307.
18. Simkins and Woody, *South Carolina During Reconstruction*, p. 103.
19. Simkins and Woody, *South Carolina During Reconstruction*, pp. 128-129.
20. Simkins and Woody, *South Carolina During Reconstruction*, p. 128.
21. These figures are from Taylor, Simkins and Woody, and Work's compilation in

the *Journal of Negro History*, V, p. 63. Simkins and Woody's figures have many inaccuracies, and the figures of Taylor and Work are incomplete. Compare also Reynolds, *Reconstruction in South Carolina*.

22. *News*, March 17, 1870, in Simkins and Woody, *South Carolina During Reconstruction*, p. 130.
23. *News*, March 10, 1871, in Simkins and Woody, *South Carolina During Reconstruction*, p. 130.
24. Simkins and Woody, *South Carolina During Reconstruction*, pp. 121-122.
25. Simkins and Woody, *South Carolina During Reconstruction*, pp. 154-155.
26. 42nd Congress, 2nd Session, House Reports, II, No. 22, Part I, p. 120.
27. Lewinson, *Race, Class and Party*, p. 39. Letter to the Columbia *Phoenix*, reprinted in the Charleston *Courier*, May 4, 1867.
28. Williams, *A History of Public Education and Penal Institutions in South Carolina During Reconstruction*, p. 66.
29. S. S. Cox, *Three Decades of Federal Legislation*, p. 506.
30. Cited in Allen, *Governor Chamberlain's Administration in South Carolina*, pp. 63, 159, 201, 278.
31. Simkins and Woody, *South Carolina During Reconstruction*, p. 471. S. J. Lee in *House Journal*, 1873, pp. 551, 552.
32. Simkins and Woody, *South Carolina During Reconstruction*, p. 472.
33. C. G. Woodson, *Negro Orators and Their Orations*, pp. 412-416.
34. *Handbook of South Carolina*, 1883, p. 660.
35. Sir George Campbell, *White and Black in the United States*, p. 145.
36. Cf. Taylor, *Reconstruction in South Carolina*, pp. 153-157.
37. Fleming, *Documentary History of Reconstruction*, II, pp. 53-54.
38. Sir George Campbell, *White and Black in the United States*, pp. 176-178.
39. Sir George Campbell, *White and Black in the United States*, pp. 179-180.
40. *Ku Klux Report, South Carolina*, Part II, pp. 833-839.
41. 42nd Congress, 2nd Session, House Reports, II, No. 22, Part I, p. 123.
42. *Ku Klux Report, South Carolina*, Part I, p. 484.
43. *Ku Klux Report, South Carolina*, Part II, p. 502.
44. Thomas E. Miller, *Speech*. This speech may be found in the Occasional Papers of the American Negro Academy, No. 6, pp. 11-13.
45. F. A. Bancroft, *A Sketch of the Negro in Politics, Especially in South Carolina and Mississippi*, p. 71.

XI. THE BLACK PROLETARIAT IN MISSISSIPPI AND LOUISIANA

How in two other states with black majorities enfranchised labor led by educated men and groups of their own blood sought so to guide the state as to raise the worker to comfort and safety, and failed before land monopoly, the new power of imported capital and organized force and fraud

Mississippi has been called a peculiarly typical state in which to study Reconstruction. But this should be modified. In direct contrast to South Carolina, Mississippi was the place where first and last Negroes were largely deprived of any opportunity for land ownership. The great black belt plantations on the Mississippi had hardly been disturbed by war. The barons ruling there, who had dictated the policy of the state, were to the last degree reactionary because they entirely misconceived the results of the war. They were determined not to recognize even the abolition of slavery, and as for establishing peasant-proprietors on their land or granting even civil rights, they were adamant. To the proposition of political rights for Negroes, they simply would not listen for a moment.

Mississippi was in all respects a curious state. It was the center of a commercialized cotton kingdom. The graciousness and ease of the plantation system had scarcely taken root there. Mississippi plantations were designed to raise a profitable cotton crop and not to entertain visitors. Here and there the more pretentious slave manor flourished, but, on the whole, the level of the state in civilization and culture was distinctly below that of Virginia and South Carolina, and smacked more of the undisciplined frontier.

In this state there were, in 1860, 353,899 white people and 437,404 Negroes, of whom less than 1,000 were free. The population had only been a few thousand at the beginning of the century and small in 1820. Then from 1840 on, the Cotton Kingdom spread over Mississippi, greatly increasing its population. The result was that after the war, there was in this state a group of planters whose great plantations dominated the rich Black Belt. From Memphis to the Gulf were a succession of counties with 60% or more of black population, while on the poor lands of the northeast and southeast were the poor whites.

The planters had always dominated the state in its political and

431

economic aspects, and it was suddenly required after the war that this state should not only assimilate a voting population of nearly 450,000 former slaves, but also that the mass of poor whites should have a political significance which they had never had before. It was a project at which Mississippi quailed. Sterling Price prayed "to God that my fears for the future of the South may never be realized; but when the right is given to the Negro to bring suit, testify before the courts and vote in elections, you all had better be in Mexico."

Mississippi had a bad financial reputation long before the Civil War; Reconstruction actually improved this. In 1839, less than one-tenth of the money collected from fines and forfeitures by the sheriffs and clerks throughout the state ever reached the treasury. In 1840, the Senate Journal had the names of 26 tax collectors who were defaulters to an average amount of $1,000 each. In 1858, the auditor of the state was a defaulter for $54,000. The endowment of Jefferson College, valued at $248,748, disappeared without record, and the college had to be closed. The money realized from the 16th Section Fund donated to schools by the Congress of the United States was lost or embezzled to the amount of $1,500,000. The Mississippi Union Bank sold bonds to the amount of $5,000,000, and later repudiated the debt.

The effect of war on property in the state was marked. The assessed valuation of Mississippi property in 1860 was over $500,000,000. Subtracting $218,000,000 as the value of the slaves, we have $291,472,912. This was reduced in 1870 to $177,278,890. The whole industrial system was upset, and the cotton crop, which was 1,200,000 bales in 1860, was in 1870 only 565,000 bales.

Naturally, these planter-capitalists proposed to protect themselves from further loss by dominating the labor of their former slaves and getting their work as cheaply as possible, with the least outlay of capital, and selling their crops at prevailing high prices.

William L. Sharkey, former Chief Justice of the State, was appointed Provisional Governor, June 15, 1865, and the state held a constitutional convention the same year, the first to be held in the South under the Johnson plan. The Governor complained that there was "an unprecedented amount of lawlessness in the state." The convention consisted of 100 delegates, most of them representing former Whigs, largely opposed to the secession of 1861. This convention recognized slavery as abolished, but did not wish to assume responsibility "for whatever honor there may be in abolishing it." An ordinance, therefore, was passed declaring that slavery had been abolished by the United States, and that hereafter it should not exist in the state. Further concessions to the Negro were fought. The Negroes of the state met October 7 and protested to Congress, expressing fear lest they be reënslaved. President Johnson wrote to Governor Sharkey suggesting that Negroes of education and property be given the right to vote so as to forestall the Radicals in the North.

Johnson pointed out that such a grant "would completely disarm the adversary," the Radical Republicans in Congress. The suggestion did not "receive any attention whatever" from the convention. "It is highly probable that the unanimous sentiment of the convention was against the idea of political rights for the Negro in any form." But a whole arsenal of reasons against enfranchisement was already prepared. Most of them started from the assumption of a general Negro franchise, and consequent "Negro domination"; the intelligent freedman was considered but "a drop in the bucket."

"It was argued that 'this is a white man's government,' and that in the sight of God and the light of reason a Negro suffrage was impossible." [1]

The real fight in the convention was on the subsidiary question as to whether Negro testimony would be allowed in court, and it was on this question that the campaign for electing a Governor and legislature turned. It was remarkable that throughout the South, far from envisaging Negro suffrage for a moment, the states fought first to see how few civil rights must be granted Negroes; and this gradually boiled down to the momentous question as to whether a Negro could be allowed to testify against a white man in court.

The election took place October 2, 1865, and Humphreys, a general in the Confederate Army, was elected Governor by the party opposed to letting Negroes testify in court, which also secured a majority of the members of the legislature. This defeated Sharkey's candidacy for the United States Senate. Humphreys had received no pardon from the President when elected but received one afterward.

Sharkey notified the President that a Governor and legislature had been elected, but the President made him retain his powers, and warned him that the legislature must accept the Thirteenth Amendment and a code for the protection of Negroes. There was continued friction between the military and civil authorities, and the President allowed the writ of habeas corpus to remain suspended. "Anarchy must in any case be prevented." The presence of Negro troops in the state caused bitter complaint. On January 5, 1866, there were 8,784 Negro troops and 338 Negro officers. The President promised to remove them as soon as possible. Sharkey declared that they encouraged the belief among Negroes that lands were going to be distributed among them. By the 20th of May, 1866, all black troops had been mustered out and removed from Mississippi.

The legislature then proceeded to adopt the celebrated Black Code of 1865, and completed the set of laws by reënacting all the penal and criminal laws applying to slaves, "except so far as the mode and manner and trial of punishment has been ordained by law." The North was incensed, and the Chicago *Tribune* said that the North would convert Mississippi "into a frog pond before they will allow any such laws to touch one foot of soil in which the bones of our soldiers sleep." Back of this sentiment was the conviction that Mississippi, whose political population for Congressional apportionment was 616,040 in 1860, would now be increased to 900,000, and this new power was going to be arrayed against Northern industry, thrift and power.

The whole reactionary course of Mississippi helped the abolition democracy in the North. General Ord assumed command in Mississippi in March, 1867, and on April 15, he began to register the new electorate, colored and white. Among Ord's appointees was Isaiah T. Montgomery, formerly a slave of Jefferson Davis. He was made a Justice of the Peace and was perhaps the first Negro in the state to hold public office. Ord appointed a number of civil officials, and was compelled practically to nullify the Black Code by military order. The result of the registration showed the white people that contrary to their firm and happy belief, the Negro was not becoming extinct; 46,636 white voters registered, and 60,137 Negroes. This showed the political situation plainly.

In 1867, the cotton crop was almost a total failure on account of weather conditions and other reasons. Ord issued an order requiring investigation of charges against landholders of driving off freedmen in order to prevent paying back wages. There was a great deal of theft of cotton and horses. Later, the abundant crop of 1868 induced Mississippi to begin to believe in free labor.

At Christmas, 1867, there had been widespread rumor of a Negro insurrection due to the idea that land was going to be distributed among them. Humphreys, then Governor, issued a proclamation reciting the apprehensions of combinations or conspiracies formed among the blacks to seize the lands, unless Congress should arrange to plan a distribution by January 1. Ord told General Gillem, commander in the sub-district of Mississippi, that Congress was not going to seize the lands of planters, but that the Governor had already plenty of land in Mississippi for freedmen and that they could settle on it when they chose to do so.

The election was set for the first Tuesday in November, 1867. Negroes were given representation among the election officials; this brought bitter protest.

"We hoped this shameful humiliation would be spared our people, at least until the freedmen of Mississippi decide whether they will submit to Negro equality at the ballot box or elsewhere. General Ord has heretofore exhibited a wisdom in his administration which has been highly approved by the people, but we doubt not the lovers of peace throughout the country will condemn the order as injudicious, if not insulting, to that race whom God has created superior to the black man, and whom no monarch can make his equal. The general commanding cannot surely have forgotten that the Negro has no political rights conferred on him by the state of Mississippi, although he is given the privilege by a corrupt and fragmentary Congress to cast a ballot in the coming farce dignified by the name of election." [2]

White Mississippi fought Reconstruction tenaciously at every step. The legislature stubbornly refused to adopt the Thirteenth Amendment, declaring that they had already abolished slavery and that they would not consent to the second section, which gave Congress the right to enforce freedom.

"Shall Mississippi ratify the Thirteenth Amendment?" asked the Vicksburg *Herald* on November 9. "We answer, no, ten thousand times, no." [3]

Then came the question as to who might register and who was to decide on the eligibility of a former Confederate. The Commanding General, in accordance with Johnson's instructions, declared that the Board of Registrars had no power; he was overruled by General Grant and by the Act of Congress of July 19.

Immediately, Mississippi tried to bring the matter before the Supreme Court by seeking to enjoin President Johnson from enforcing the Reconstruction Acts. The Supreme Court refused to entertain the case on the ground that it would interfere with a coordinate branch of the government in the performance of its duties. Thereupon, another action was brought by the State of Georgia, which tried to enjoin the Secretary of War, but the court held that it was without jurisdiction. Finally, the celebrated case *Ex parte McCardle* was started on appeal from a military decision at Vicksburg, but Congress forestalled the case by depriving the court of jurisdiction in this particular case and others of similar character.

There had been a plan for the white people to refrain from voting in 1867, a plan widespread through the other Southern states. The idea was that by refraining from taking any part in this convention, the whole thing might go by default and Reconstruction fail. But that seemed to many too much of a risk, and in its place there came a movement on the part of some of the planters to acquiesce in the situation, and to organize and plan the control of the Negro vote. In other words, certain leaders, like the editor of the Jackson *Clarion*,

General Alcorn and Judge Campbell, were in favor of recognizing the right of the Negroes to vote in 1868, and said that the policy of the Democrats would drive the Negroes into the Republican Party. Ex-Senator Brown agreed, and many other white leaders. The most advanced Reconstructionist was General Alcorn, who asked if it would not be wise to yield something to black suffrage, and then to control the votes in the interests of such an organization of industry and society as they thought best.

This was no wild scheme. The Negroes were used to subordination to the great planters. If the planters did not form an alliance with the Negroes, the planters would be threatened by the pretensions of the poor whites and possible leadership from Northern white men, ex-soldiers and investors, who were largely represented in the state. It was a matter to consider carefully; in the end Mississippi went further along this line than any other Southern state, and found it easier to do this because of the compulsion and intimidation that could be exercised over the Negro vote on the great plantations of the Black Belt.

The so-called "Black and Tan" convention met at Jackson, January 9, 1868. It was the first political organization in Mississippi with colored representatives. There were in all one hundred delegates, of whom 17 were colored, although 32 counties had Negro majorities. There were 29 native white Republicans, and 20 or more Northern Republicans. This was interesting and characteristic. It showed in the first place that the Negroes were not even trying, much less succeeding in any effort to use their numerical preponderance in order to put themselves in political power. Under strong economic pressure, the Negro voter designated white men to represent him. The large majority of the members of this convention were elected by black voters.

Seven or eight of the colored delegates were ministers. Four of the Northern Republicans had lived in the South before the war, and two had served in the Confederate Army. It characterizes the times to know that five of the members afterward met violent deaths. Members were paid $10 a day in depreciated scrip worth 65¢-70¢ on a dollar, making their pay about equal to the convention of 1865.

During the organization of the convention, it was moved that the word "colored" be added to the name of each Negro delegate. Thereupon, the Reverend James Lynch, a colored man, afterward Secretary of State, moved to amend it so that the color of each delegate's hair should be added also.

There was here as in South Carolina the same charge against this convention and against succeeding legislatures, that they did not sufficiently represent wealth; they represented poverty; and the majority of the members, white and black, were not taxpayers. They represented labor, and were voting and working as far as they intelligently could to improve their condition and not to increase the profits of the hirers of labor.

In the convention, the colored people clung to the idea that the government intended to divide the land among them. One of the first acts of the convention was to appoint a committee of five to report what legislation was needed to afford relief and protection to the state and its citizens. This committee reported early in February, and found an alarming amount of destitution among the laboring class. They thought that the number of the destitute was at least 30,000, and perhaps was 40,000. There was distress and suffering, which in some cases bordered on actual starvation.

The Commanding General, who was at the time Gillam of Tennessee, sided with the planting interests, refused to coöperate with the convention in this matter, and declared that the demand for labor exceeded the supply. In other words, labor must work for food or starve. It was reported that the Negroes were still expecting the distribution of land. Suspension of taxes imposed upon freedmen prior to January 1, 1868, was demanded, and the repudiation of all debts, contracts and judgments incurred or made prior to April 28, 1865. The Commanding General was requested to issue an order "directing the restoration of property alleged to have been unlawfully taken from colored persons on the grounds that property accumulated by them in a state of slavery belonged to their masters." This the General declined to do.

The Commanding General was again requested, in a report signed by three colored members, to furnish from the public funds means to return slaves sold into Mississippi to their former homes, and Congress was asked to set aside, through the Freedmen's Bureau, one-half of the cotton tax collected in the state. They asked the Governor of the state to let Negroes share in the donations sent him for the relief of the destitute; but the Governor refused, saying that it was a private gift.

After this preliminary discussion, which was afterward criticized as beside the point, when in fact it was the main point, the convention turned toward making a new Constitution, as they had refused to adopt the old. They framed a Constitution under which Mississippi lived for twenty-two years. It did away with property qualifications for office or for suffrage; it forbade slavery; it provided for a mixed public school system; it forbade race distinctions in the possession and inheritance of property; it prohibited the abridgment of civil rights in travel;

and in general, it was a modern instrument based on universal suffrage.

A minority tried to disfranchise the mass of ignorant Negroes, and there was considerable quarreling and some fighting. Universal suffrage was adopted by a large majority, and on account of that, 12 of the white delegates resigned. Other ordinances forbade property qualification for office, or educational qualification for suffrage.

The civil government under Reconstruction increased the powers of the Governor and made a more elaborate governmental organization and function for the state. It provided for a Lieutenant-Governor, a State Superintendent of Education, and numerous other officials. Some of the counties were consolidated to form larger legislative districts. Evidently, the success of the planters in controlling the Negro vote alarmed the carpet-baggers and the poor whites, and they determined to suppress the ring-leaders of the rebellion far more drastically than was required by the Reconstruction Acts.

The convention consequently determined to deny the right to vote and hold office to practically all whites who had anything to do with the Rebellion, and thus the proposed Constitution disfranchised perhaps 20,000 or more of the leading white citizens of the state. This has been represented as petty jealousy and desire for vengeance on the part of the carpet-baggers. It was more than this. It was an attempt to end the oligarchy of landlords who still advocated slavery and the rule of wealth.

After sitting 115 days, the Convention adjourned and submitted the Constitution to the people. The proceedings in this convention had undoubtedly been dominated by the wishes of the Northern men and the poor whites, with the support of the Negroes. But instead of cementing the alliance, the Negroes were ignored, and when preparations were made for the campaign, were given little recognition. The chief evidence of this was failure to nominate Negroes for office; the real policy beneath this was ignoring the plight of Negro labor, and making the Republican Party chiefly the mouthpiece of the new Northern capital. The opposition organized as the Democratic White Men's Party of Mississippi and declared that the Republicans were trying to degrade the Caucasian race. The provision for a mixed school system particularly came in for widespread criticism.

Meantime, Humphreys was removed as Governor on account of opposition to the Reconstruction Acts, and General Adelbert Ames appointed Acting Governor. Humphreys refused to give up, and was removed by the soldiers. But reaction was not beaten. The vote of the Black Belt was cast largely under the dictation of the land-holders and hirers of black labor. The result of the election was a surprise. Fifty-six thousand, two hundred and thirty-one votes were cast for the Constitution, 63,860 were cast against it, and Humphreys had been re-elected Governor.

A committee of five from the Convention announced that the election had been carried by fraud and intimidation, accompanied by social proscription and threats to discharge laborers from employment. The Republicans held meetings in various counties, declaring that the late election had been the work of terrorism and fraud.

On the other hand, the result of the election was to show all parties that a more sincere attempt to recognize the Negro and enable him to vote had to be made. Negroes could not be ignored. Their right to vote meant something. If they were intimidated and coerced by force and economic means, the planters would soon be back in power. Moreover, even in this election, certain leading Negroes, like John R. Lynch, had deliberately voted with the planters, and an alliance of planters and Negroes was not impossible. It would have been an alliance based partly on labor control and partly on understandings consummated between black labor leaders and white land-holders. Working out from the old slavery, it might have gradually negotiated an industrial emancipation for the intelligent blacks, while using the solid black vote to keep white labor and Northern capital subordinate. One group of Negroes recommended, therefore, another constitutional convention. They said they wished to cultivate kindly relations with their white friends, and declared that they would support capable and honorable men, even if they were former Confederates.

The 40th Congress adjourned with the question of Mississippi unsettled. Finally, in April, 1869, a bill was agreed upon which directed that Mississippi was to be admitted when she adopted the Fifteenth Amendment, and that the President was authorized to submit the Constitution as a whole and also the same Constitution with its provisions disfranchising the bulk of Confederates left out. Gillam was removed, and General Ames, who had been acting Civil Governor, was made Provisional Governor of the state. He reported that certain men, backed by public opinion, were committing murders and outrages. Under direction of Congress, Ames removed a large number of officers, and made appointments of state and local officers, including several Negroes. Among other things, he declared freedmen to be competent jurors. He said of his work at this time:

"I found when I was Military Governor of Mississippi, that a black code existed there; that Negroes had no rights, and that they were not permitted to exercise the rights of citizenship. I had given them the protection they were entitled to under the laws, and I believed I could render them great service. I felt that I had a mission to perform in the r interest, and I hesitatingly consented to represent them and unite ny fortune with theirs." [4]

Ames thus made a counter bid for Negro support, reversing the indifferent stand of the Mississippi Republicans. In July, President Grant issued a proclamation ordering the Constitution to be submitted for ratification November 30. The Radical Republicans held their convention July 2 and attempted a platform of several resolutions. These resolutions declared: "In favor of an impartial and economic administration of the government; the unrestricted right of speech to all men at all times and places; unrestrained freedom of the ballot; a system of free schools; a reform of the 'iniquitous and unequal' system of taxation and assessments which discriminated against labor; declared that all men without regard to race, color or previous condition of servitude were equal before the law; recommended removal of political disabilities as soon as the 'spirit of toleration now dawning upon the state' should be so firmly established as to justify Congress in taking such action; declared in favor of universal amnesty, universal suffrage, and encouragement of immigration." [5]

Ex-Governor Brown and the Conservatives were in favor of ratifying the Constitution without the proscriptive provisions and of accepting the Fifteenth Amendment. They secured Judge Dent, a brother-in-law of Grant, as their candidate, thinking in that way to secure the good will of Grant: but Grant repudiated the party that nominated Dent The Dent party nominated Thomas Sinclair, a colored man, for Secretary of State. The Republicans nominated General J. L. Alcorn for Governor, and the Reverend James Lynch, a mulatto preacher, for Secretary of State.

The whole election showed the increasing political importance of the Negroes, and this undoubtedly explains the increased activity of the Ku Klux Klan in 1869. There were some riots in three or four counties. The Constitution was ratified almost unanimously, but the proscriptive sections disfranchising members of the Secession Convention and other active Confederates were defeated. The provision forbidding the loan of state funds was ratified.

The first Reconstruction legislature met at Jackson, January 11, 1870. The legislature elected in 1868 had never been convened because of the defeat of the Constitution. Negro membership in the new legislature was larger than in the convention. There were forty colored members, some of whom had been slaves before the war; but among them were some "very intelligent" men. Particularly, there was considerable representation of ministers. In the Senate, there were five colored members.

Many of the wealthiest counties were represented by ex-slaves. Yet as Lynch shows, Negroes never controlled Mississippi. "No colored man in that state ever occupied a judicial position above that of Justice of the Peace, and very few aspired to that position. Of seven state officers, only one, that of Secretary of State, was filled by a colored man, until 1873, when colored men were elected to three of the seven offices, Lieutenant-Governor, Secretary of State, and State Superintendent of Education. Of the two United States Senators, and the seven members of the Lower House of Congress, not more than one colored man occupied a seat in each House at the same time. Of the thirty-five members of the State Senate, and of the one hundred and fifteen members of the House,—which composed the total membership of the State Legislature prior to 1874,—there were never more than about seven colored men in the Senate and forty in the Lower House. Of the ninety-seven members that composed the constitutional convention of 1868, but seventeen were colored men. The composition of the Lower House of the State Legislature that was elected in 1871 was as follows:

"Total membership, one hundred and fifteen; Republicans, sixty-six; Democrats, forty-nine; colored members, thirty-eight; white members, seventy-seven; white majority, thirty-nine.

"Of the sixty-six Republicans, thirty-eight were colored men and twenty-eight, white. There was a slight increase in the colored membership as a result of the election of 1873, but the colored men never at any time had control of the State Government, nor of any branch or department thereof, nor even that of any county or municipality. Out of seventy-two counties in the State at that time, electing on an average twenty-eight officers to a county, it is safe to assert that not over five out of one hundred of such officers were colored men. The State, district, county and municipal governments were not only in control of white men, but white men who were to the manor born, or who were known as old citizens of the state, those who had lived in the state many years before the War of the Rebellion. There was, therefore, never a time when that class of white men, known as Carpetbaggers, had absolute control of state government, or that of any district, county or municipality, or any branch or department thereof. There was never, therefore, any ground for the alleged apprehension of Negro domination as a result of a free, fair, and honest election in any one of the Southern or Reconstructed States."[6]

At the same time, the Negroes were laborers, and if at any time the white and black labor vote united, property and privilege in Mississippi were bound to suffer. And on the other hand, if property controlled black labor, white labor would be as helpless as before the war. These two fears explain Reconstruction in Mississippi.

The legislature ratified the Fourteenth and Fifteenth Amendments and elected three United States Senators, one for the full term, and two for unexpired terms. For the full term, Alcorn was chosen, and for one unexpired term, General Ames; while Hiram R. Revels, a colored minister, was chosen to fill the unexpired term of Jefferson Davis.

Revels came from North Carolina and was educated in Indiana; he was a minister in Baltimore at the opening of the war, and there helped to organize two colored regiments. He came South with the Freedmen's Bureau, and was surprised when selected to represent the state in the Senate. He was a man of intelligence, but the Republican United States debated three days on his credentials. Finally, after one of Sumner's ablest speeches, he was admitted. Even after that, Philadelphia refused the use of her Academy of Music for a meeting at which he was to speak.

Ames now turned over the government to Alcorn and went to the Senate. Alcorn took a firm and advanced stand. In his inaugural speech, he spoke of his attachment for Mississippi. He declared that it was the duty of the government to protect all its citizens, white and black, before the ballot box, the jury box and public office, and to give industrial opportunity to the honest and competent without discrimination of color. He said:

"In the face of memories that might have separated them from me, as the wronged from the wronger, they offered me their confidence, offered me the guardianship of their new and precious hopes, with a trustfulness whose very mention stirs my nerves with emotion. In response to that touching radiance, the most profound anxiety with which I enter my office as Governor of this state is that of making the colored man the equal before the law of every other man—the equal, not in dead letter, but in living fact." He had a word to say for the poor whites. "Thousands of our worthy white friends have ever remained to a great extent strangers to the helping hand of the state." [7]

Unfortunately, Alcorn instead of staying and finishing this job thus well outlined, had the universal Southern ambition of the day to go to the United States Senate. He was, therefore, in office only a little over a year, when he went to Washington to succeed Revels. The legislature, meantime, went to work to set up the government.

The part which the Negro played in this Reconstruction was as extraordinary as it was unexpected. There were far fewer Negroes of education and ability in Mississippi than in South Carolina or Louisiana. But there were a few, perhaps a bare half-dozen, who gave universal and epoch-making service.

One of these leaders, and perhaps the best, tells of the task before them:

"The new administration had an important and difficult task before it. A State Government had to be organized from top to bottom; a new judiciary had to be inaugurated,—consisting of three Justices of the State Supreme Court, fifteen Judges of the Circuit Court, and twenty Chancery Court judges,—who had all to be appointed by the Governor, with the consent of the Senate; and, in addition, a new public school system had to be established. There was not a public school building anywhere in the state, except in a few of the larger towns, and they, with possibly a few exceptions, were greatly in need of repairs. To erect the necessary school-houses and to reconstruct and repair those already in existence so as to afford educational facilities for both races was by no means an easy task. It necessitated a very large outlay of cash in the beginning, which resulted in a material increase in the rate of taxation for the time being, but the Constitution called for the establishment of the system, and of course the work had to be done. It was not only done, but it was done creditably and as economically as possible, considering the conditions at that time. That system, though slightly changed, still stands,—a creditable monument to the first Republican state administration that was organized in the State of Mississippi under the Reconstruction Acts of Congress.

"It was also necessary to reorganize, reconstruct and, in many instances, rebuild some of the penal and charitable institutions of the State. A new code of laws also had to be adopted to take the place of the old code and thus wipe out the black laws that had been passed by what was known as the Johnson Legislature, and in addition, bring about other changes so as to make the laws and statutes of the state conform with the new order of things. This was no easy task, in view of the fact that a heavy increase in the rate of taxation was thus made necessary for the time being at least. That this important task was splendidly, creditably, and economically done no fair-minded person who is familiar with the facts will question or dispute.

"That the state never had before, and has never since had, a finer judiciary than that which was organized under the administration of Governor Alcorn and which continued under the administration of Governor Ames is an indisputable and incontrovertible fact." [8]

"When the Alcorn administration took charge of the state government, the war had just come to a close. Everything was in a prostrate condition. There had been great depreciation in the value of real and personal property. The credit of the state was not very good. The rate of interest for borrowed money was high. To materially increase the bonded debt of the State was not deemed wise, yet some had to be raised in that way. To raise the balance a higher rate of taxation had to be imposed, since the assessed valuation of the taxable property was so low." [9]

The legislature of 1871 was in session about six months, and passed 325 acts and resolutions. The increase of citizenship, and the revolution through which the state had passed, called without doubt for more laws. The expenses of the legislative department were large and the session long. Yet it can hardly be said, considering the work done and the depreciated value of currency, that it was an extravagant assembly. [10]

The legislature of 1872 had John R. Lynch, a Negro, as Speaker of the House. There were 28 white and 38 colored Republicans and 49 Democrats, and it took a trip of Senator Alcorn from Washington to induce enough white Republicans to support Lynch in order to elect him. At the close of the session, however, Lynch was presented with a gold watch and chain. On motion of a prominent white Democrat, a resolution was adopted thanking him "for his dignity, impartiality and courtesy as a presiding officer." The *Clarion* declared: "His bearing in office had been so proper, and his rulings in such marked contrast to the former conduct of the ignoble whites of his party, who had been aspiring to be leaders of the blacks, that the Conservatives cheerfully joined in the testimonial." [11]

Civil rights measures constituted a considerable part of the legislation between 1868 and 1876. In his inaugural address, Governor Alcorn "asserted positively that so long as he was governor, all citizens, without respect to color or nativity, should be shielded by the law as with a panoply." [12]

In 1870, "all laws relative to free Negroes, slaves and mulattoes, as found in the Code of 1857 and the laws constituting the so-called Black Codes," were declared to be forever repealed. It was declared to be the true intent and meaning of the legislature to remove from the records of the state all laws "which in any manner recognized any natural difference or distinction between citizens and inhabitants of the state." [13]

The legislature elected in 1873 had 37 members of the Senate, of whom nine were colored, and nine white carpetbaggers. In the House over 115 members, of whom 55 were colored and 60 white, including 15 carpetbaggers. This election went further than any toward a fusion of planters and Negroes, and this was only prevented by the rivalry of Alcorn and Ames.

When Alcorn went to the Senate, he was succeeded by a carpetbagger, R. C. Powers. Finally in 1873, Ames, who had been in the United States Senate, was elected Governor over Alcorn, who was again candidate. With Ames, three colored men went to office: A. K. Davis, Lieutenant-Governor; James Hill, Secretary of State; and T. W. Cardozo, Superintendent of Education. B. K. Bruce had been selected for Lieutenant-Governor, but refused, and afterward went to the Senate.

This greatly disappointed Alcorn, who wished to remain in the Senate, and who, therefore, refused to escort Bruce to take the oath. Bruce had been County Assessor, Parish and Tax Collector in Bolivar County, one of the wealthiest counties in the state.[14]

"Davis, the new Lieutenant-Governor, had made a creditable record as member of the legislature, but he was not a strong man. Hill was young, active and aggressive, and above the average colored man in intelligence. Cardozo was capable but not well-known."[15]

As to the colored men in the Legislature of 1873, Garner says:

"Relative to the course of the colored members in this legislature, a prominent Democrat writes me as follows: 'In my opinion, if they had all been native Southern Negroes, there would have been little cause of complaint. They often wanted to vote with Democrats on non-political questions, but could not resist the party lash. The majority of whites in both parties exhibit the same weakness."[16]

The real meaning of this criticism was that the Negroes wanted to coöperate with the planters, but knew that the planters would disfranchise them at the first opportunity, and only welcomed their alliance now for economic reasons. On the other hand, the Republicans were torn with factions, jealousies and suspicions, and the Negroes did not know how far they could be trusted.

With a few exceptions, the colored members took little part in the work of legislation, although some of the principal chairmanships were held by them. There were few educated men among them, and they watched only for efforts to abridge their privileges as voters and citizens. On the other hand, there were no charges of venality or bribery, and their efforts to learn were intense. They were too willing to take advice and follow leadership, once their confidence had been obtained. The number of prominent planters in Mississippi who entered the Republican party to lead the Negroes was unusually large as compared with other states.

Ames immediately began a program of retrenchment in expenditures, and recommended many reforms. Taxes had been increased from one mill on the dollar in 1869 to fourteen in 1874. The credit of the state was still impaired. He recommended a cut of 25% in appropriations, and especially curtailing the bill for public printing. "The recommendations," says Garner, "do credit to the Governor who made them. They do not sound like the utterance of a carpetbagger bent on peculation and plunder."

There were the usual charges of extravagance against the Reconstruction government.

"It should, however, be said that if the testimony of Governor Ames may be followed relative to the expenses of the state government during the two years in which he was at its head, his was the most economical administration since 1856, with the exception of two years, 1861 and 1869." [17]

It was charged that the public debt of Mississippi increased from almost nothing to $20,000,000 during the Reconstruction régime, but this was easily disproved by ex-Governor Ames, who had the figures; and the committee of Democratic legislators that sought to impeach him had to acknowledge the truth of what he said.

"Thus it will be seen that the actual indebtedness of the state is but little over a half million dollars, and that during the two years of Governor Ames' administration, the state debt had been reduced from $821,292.82 on January first, 1874, to $520,138.33, on January first, 1876; or a reduction of more than three hundred thousand dollars in two years—upwards of one-third of the state debt wiped out in that time. Not only has the debt been reduced as above, but the rate of taxation for general purposes has been reduced from seven mills in 1873 to four mills in 1875." [18]

"It should also be said by way of explanation, that the work of restoration which the government was obliged to undertake, made increased expenses necessary. During the period of the war, and for several years thereafter, public buildings and state institutions were permitted to fall into decay. The state house and grounds, the executive mansion, the penitentiary, the insane asylum, and the buildings for the blind, deaf and dumb, were in a dilapidated condition, and had to be extended and repaired. A new building for the blind was purchased and fitted up. The Reconstructionists established a public school system and spent money to maintain and support it, perhaps too freely, in view of the impoverishment of the people. When they took hold, warrants were worth but sixty or seventy cents on the dollar, a fact which made the price of building materials used in the work of construction correspondingly higher." [19]

Garner admits there were no great railroad swindles and no charge of excessive debt. The only charge which is perhaps true was that the number of offices and agencies was needlessly increased.

The one center of undoubted graft under Ames was the public printing contracts, which increased from $8,675 a year, 1867-1868, to sums varying from $50,000 to $127,000 in 1870-1875. This seems, however, to have been largely due to one white man and it is not clear whether he was Northern- or Southern-born.

Rhodes declares that few Negroes were competent to perform their duties and that one who was sheriff of DeSoto County for four years could neither read nor write and farmed out his office to a white deputy for a share of the revenue. John R. Lynch proves that this statement is absolutely false. The Reverend J. J. Evans, a colored Baptist minister and a Union soldier, who held that position, gave entire satisfaction; he left office with a spotless record, accounted for every cent of the funds, and he had, as he wrote, a letter from Evans before him, which showed that Evans could read and write.

Mr. Lynch goes on to say that of the seventy-two counties of the state, not more than twelve ever had colored sheriffs, and that he knew ten of these; and that "in point of intelligence, capacity and honesty, the colored sheriffs would have favorably compared with the whites." When one considers that over one-half of the electors had been slaves, now for the first time given a voice in government, Reconstruction in Mississippi certainly seems like a success.

The Negro leaders who came to the front were in most cases admirable and honest men; and only a few were corrupt. The advance of the masses of the people was shown in the increase of marriage licenses. In 1865, licenses were issued to whites, 2,708, and to blacks, 564, while in 1870, 2,204 were issued to whites, and 3,427 to blacks. In those two years, churches built increased from 105 to 283.

A curious feud between the Governor and his colored Lieutenant-Governor began in the summer of 1874, when Governor Ames went North on his vacation. The Lieutenant-Governor discharged certain appointees, and appointed several judges. Governor Ames, upon returning, revoked these appointees. Lieutenant-Governor Davis also issued a large number of pardons to persons in jail.

Singularly enough, while one of the accusations in the attempted impeachment of Ames was his dismissal of Davis' judicial appointees, Davis was also removed from office in 1876. It was alleged that he had accepted a bribe for granting a pardon. On the other hand, the Governor's action in revoking Davis' appointments was called by this legislature of 1876 "willful, corrupt and unlawful."

It was the especial grievance of the whites that officials and voters were not taxpayers, and that a comparatively small number of the colored voters owned real estate. The most that was charged was that the number of offices and agencies with high salaries was needlessly multiplied. The break came, however, between labor and capital inside the Democratic party.

"Of course a stubborn and bitter fight for control of the Democratic organization was now on between the antagonistic and conflicting elements among the whites. It was to be a desperate struggle between former aristocrats, on one side, and what was known as 'poor whites' on the other. While the aristocrats had always been the weaker in point of numbers, they had been the stronger in point of wealth, intelligence, ability, skill and experience. As a result of their wide experience, and able and skillful management, the aristocrats were successful in the preliminary struggles, as illustrated in the persons of Stephens, Gordon, Brown and Hill, of Georgia; Daniels and Lee, of Virginia; Hampton and Butler of South Carolina; Lamar and Walthall of Mississippi, and Garland, of Arkansas. But in the course of time and in the natural order of things the poor whites were bound to win. All that was needed was a few years' tutelage, and a few daring and unscrupulous leaders to prey upon their ignorance and magnify their vanity, in order to bring them to a realization of the fact that their former political masters were now completely at their mercy, and subject to their will." [20]

"After the Presidential election of 1872, Southern white men were not only coming into the Republican party in large numbers, but the liberal and progressive element of the democracy was in the ascendency in that organization. That element, therefore, shaped the policy and declared the principles for which that organization stood. This meant the acceptance by all political parties of what was regarded as the settled policy of the National Government. In proof of this assertion, a quotation from a political editorial which appeared about that time in the Jackson, Mississippi, Clarion,—the organ of the Democratic Party,—will not be out of place. In speaking of the colored people and their attitude towards the white, that able and influential paper said:

" 'While they [the colored people] have been naturally tenacious of their newly acquired privileges, their general conduct will bear them witness that they have shown consideration for the feelings of the whites. The race line in politics would not have been drawn if opposition had not been made to their enjoyment of equal privileges in the government, and under the laws after they were emancipated.'

"In other words, the colored people had manifested no disposition to rule or dominate the whites, and the only Color Line which had existed, grew out of the unwise policy which had previously been pursued by the Democratic Party in its efforts to prevent the enjoyment by the newly-emancipated race of the rights and privileges to which they were entitled, under the Constitution and laws of the country. But after the state and congressional elections of 1874, the situation was materially changed. The liberal and conservative element of the democracy was relegated to the rear and the radical element came to the front and assumed charge." [21]

Here is a record which is not bad. There was no violent revolution in Mississippi. There was no attack upon civilization and culture. There was increased expense, partly for legitimate objects, partly, without doubt, by injudicious and careless expenditure; possibly in some cases by corrupt expenditure.

"In the fall of 1875 just at the time when the whole state rang with assertions of Radical misrule, taxation and robbery, the Author traveled through Mississippi, east and west, north and south, traveled quietly and was personally unknown. At every town and village, at every station on the railroads and every rural neighborhood in the country, he heard Governor Ames and the Republican Party denounced for oppressions, robberies and dishonesty as proved by the fearful rate of taxation. He asked what was the per cent of taxes on the dollar, but never got an answer. One citizen replied: 'Our taxes are enormous.' Another said: 'They are ruinous.' Another: 'They amount to confiscation.' Such were the only replies given. Every form of words that could be used to express excessive taxation was employed. 'Awful,' 'Fearful,' 'Intolerable,' 'Monstrous,' 'Unheard of,' 'Incredible,' but no man answered the question. For the true answer would have been: 'The average taxation since Reconstruction has been a little less than nine mills on the dollar, for all purposes. Of this average of less than nine mills on the dollar almost one-fifth was for public schools so that the total annual taxation for all other purposes has been a little over seven mills on the dollar.' This was the true answer, but every White Leaguer knew better than to answer the question, for one of the originators of that order wrote confidentially to an associate that they must appeal to the world 'as a wretched, downtrodden and impoverished people.' " [22]

On the whole, one cannot escape the impression that what the whites in Mississippi feared was that the experiment of Negro suffrage might succeed. At any rate, they began a revolution known as the "Mississippi plan." Here was no labor dictatorship or dream of one. White labor took up arms to subdue black labor and to make it helpless economically and politically through the power of property.

Senator Revels, of Mississippi, said in the 41st Congress:

"Mr. President, I maintain that the past record of my race is a true index of the feelings which today animate them. They bear toward their former masters no revengeful thoughts, no hatred, no animosities. They aim not to elevate themselves by sacrificing one single interest of their white fellow citizens. They ask but the rights which are theirs by God's universal law, and which are the natural outgrowth, the logical sequence of the condition in which the legislative enactments of this nation have placed them. They appeal to you and to me to see that they receive that protection which alone will enable them to pursue their daily avocations with success and enjoy the liberties of citizenship on the same footing with their white neighbors and friends." [23]

John R. Lynch said, when he was counted out of his election:

"You certainly cannot expect them [the Negroes] to resort to mob law and brute force, or to use what may be milder language, inaugurate a revolution. My opinion is that revolution is not the remedy to be applied in such cases. Our system of government is supposed to be one of law and order, resting upon the consent of the governed, as expressed through the peaceful medium of the ballot. In all localities where the local public sentiment is so dishonest, so corrupt, and so demoralized, as to tolerate the commission of election frauds, and shield the perpetrators from justice, such people must be made to understand that there is patriotism enough in this country and sufficient love of justice and fair play in the hearts of the American people to prevent any party from gaining the ascendency in the government that relies upon a fraudulent ballot and a false return as the chief source of its support.

"The impartial historian will record the fact that the colored people of the South have contended for their rights with a bravery and a gallantry that is worthy of the highest commendation. Being, unfortunately, in dependent circumstances with the preponderance of the wealth and intelligence against them in some localities, yet they have bravely refused to surrender their honest convictions, even upon the altar of their personal necessities." [24]

With riot, fraud, boycott and intimidation, Negro rule was overthrown. William L. Hemingway was nominated against Captain George M. Buchanan, an able and well-qualified man. In an honest election, Buchanan would have been given the office, but Hemingway was declared elected. However, he had been in office only a brief time, when the discovery was made that he was a defaulter to the amount of $315,612.19. Thus "Reform" began. [25]

In the back districts of Mississippi, the world moved on. In May, 1874, at Burleigh a Southern lady writes:

". . . Last Wednesday, the Bishop, assisted by Mr. Douglass and Heber Crabe, ordained a Mr. Jackson, a Negro as black as any on this land, a deacon in the church. The ceremony was very interesting, and Mr. Jackson preached in the afternoon to as enlightened an audience as ever goes to our church. His sermon was admirable and admirably delivered. I have heard but few who read so well, and fewer who have so good a manner. He is a well-educated man, having a considerable knowledge of Latin, Greek and Hebrew. He has been living in one of the rectory houses for two years, and is a hard student under Mr. Douglass, and is without reproach." [26]

Louisiana came into the possession of the United States because Toussaint L'Ouverture and the blacks of Haiti so broke the French colonial power and Napoleon's plans for American empire that he practically gave away French America to the United States and turned his whole attention to Europe.

At the first census after the admission of the state, 1810, there were 34,000 whites and the same number of black slaves, and in addition to this, 7,585 free Negroes. In 1820, when Louisiana entered the Union, the white and black population were about equal, both being under 80,000. In 1860, there were 350,373 Negroes and 357,456 whites. By 1870, the colored population exceeded the whites by nearly 2,000. The great influx came between 1840 and 1860.

Among the Negro population, 18,647 in 1860 were free, and represented mainly descendants of the free Negroes in the territory at the time of the annexation. They were many of them rich and educated, and they formed a most interesting element in the population.

The migration to Louisiana after 1840 was of a distinctly lower grade than before—exploiters of commercial slavery, slave traders and smugglers, gamblers and desperadoes. They made the situation for free Negroes much more difficult. Rich colored folk, even those who were well known, were often arrested and mistreated.

In 1857, Wickliffe "informed the Legislature that the immigration of free Negroes from other states of the Union into Louisiana had been steadily increasing for years; that it was a source of great evil, and demanded legislative action. Public policy dictates, the interest of the people requires, that immediate steps should be taken at this time to remove all free Negroes who are now in the State, when such removal can be effected without violation of law. Their example and associations have a most pernicious effect upon our slave population."

As a result, in 1858, Emile Desdunes acted as agent for emigration to Haiti, then under the rule of Soulouque. Desdunes worked energetically to arrange for the deportation of a large number of colored Louisianians. Unfortunately, a revolution in Haiti stopped the project.

The ante-bellum society of Louisiana, and particularly of New Orleans, was brilliant and lawless; dueling, gambling and murder were widespread, and there were notorious outbreaks in political life, like the Plaquemine Riot of 1844 and the scenes of violence and intimidation at an election for sheriff in 1853. As late as 1855, the city was in the hands of rival political factions which fought behind barricades in the streets.

Governor Hebart said in 1856 that the riot of 1855, if repeated, would "sink us to the level of the anarchical governments of Spanish America; that before the occurrence of those great public crimes, the hideous enormity of which he could not describe, and which were committed with impunity in mid-daylight and in the presence of hundreds of persons, no one could have admitted even the possibility that a bloodthirsty mob could have contemplated to overawe any portion of the people of this state in the exercise of their most valuable rights; but that which would then have been denied, even as a possibility, is now an historical fact." [27]

The following year, Governor Wickliffe added:

"I is well-known that at the last two general elections many of the streets and approaches to the polls were completely in the hands of organized ruffians, who committed acts of violence on multitudes of our naturalized fellow-citizens, who dared venture to exercise the rights of suffrage. Thus nearly one-third of the registered voters of New Orleans have been deterred from exercising their highest and most sacred prerogative. The suppression of such elections is an open and palpable fraud on the people, and I recommend you to adopt such measures as shall effectually prevent the true will of the majority from being totally silenced."

The New Orleans *Delta* said, May 6, 1860:

"For seven years the world knows that this city, in all its departments, Judicial, Legislative, and Executive, has been at the absolute disposal of the most godless, brutal, ignorant and ruthless ruffianism the world has ever heard of since the days of the great Roman conspirator. By means of a secret organization, emanating from that fecund source of political infamy, New England, and named Know-Nothingism or Sammyism from boasted exclusive devotion of the fraternity to the United States, our city, far from being the abode of decency, of liberality, generosity, and justice, is a sanctum for crime. The ministers of the law, nominees of blood-stained, vulgar, ribald caballeros and licensed murderers, shed innocent blood on the most public thoroughfares with impunity; witnesses of the most atrocious crimes are either spirited away, bought off, or intimidated from testifying; perjured associates are retained to prove alibis, and ready bail is always procurable for the immediate use of those whom it is not immediately prudent to enlarge otherwise. The electoral system is a farce and fraud; the knife, the sling-shot, the brass knuckles determining, while the shame is being enacted, who shall occupy and administer the offices of the municipality and the Commonwealth."

Governor Wells said in 1866:

"It is within the knowledge of all citizens resident here before the War, that for years preceding the Rebellion, elections in the Parish of Orleans were a cruel mockery of free government. Bands of organized desperadoes, immediately preceding and during an election, committed every species of outrage upon peaceful and unoffending citizens, to intimidate them from the exercise of the inestimable privilege of free men, the elective franchise. A registry of 14,000 names, in the days alluded to, could scarcely furnish one-fourth of that number of legal votes at the polls, although six or seven thousand votes were usually returned as cast." [28]

Even the system of slavery in Louisiana differed from the southern South, and many slaveholders frankly made it their policy to work the slaves to death and buy new ones instead of taking care of the old and sick.

Intermixture of races was reduced to a recognized system by the regular importation of handsome colored slave girls for sale from the Border States, and by a carefully regulated system of colored common-law wives. One must add to this, the mulatto free Negro group in most cases descended from white fathers who had taken colored wives and whose children were often educated abroad. The grandchildren became now white, now colored, according to the choice or tint of skin. As a result, to this day it is difficult in Louisiana to draw the line between the races. Not long ago, when a prominent white man of a certain parish was "accused" of Negro blood, the court house, with all its vital records, was burned down that night.

Recently, a small group of colored people in New Orleans, all born since 1880, sat down and compared notes as to people whom they knew personally. They made a list of sixty families of Negro descent, who, in their knowledge and in their time, had gone over to the white race, and whose children had no knowledge of their Negro descent.

The condition of Louisiana after the war was desperate. The Federal Commander said:

"The resources of this state are infinitely reduced by the casualties of the war. The commerce, whose innumerable wheels used to vex the turbid current of the Mississippi, has passed away—the result of war. Plantations which used to bloom through your entire land, until the coast of Louisiana was a sort of repetition of the Garden of Eden, are now dismantled and broken down. Trade, commerce, everything, crippled. . . . You have to make revenues where the taxable property of the state is reduced almost two-thirds. You have to hold the appliances and surroundings of government, and maintaining and keeping up to a great extent nearly every charity which belongs to the city or state. The levees, on which the life of your country depends, which from local causes cannot be repaired by civil authorities, must be attended to by the United States, and a sum of $160,000 is being laid out now by the United States for the purpose of preventing this delta of the Mississippi from being subject to overflow." [29]

We have seen in Chapter VII how Banks and Shepley, under Lincoln, had attempted to reconstruct Louisiana in 1864. At the same time, a rival Confederate government at Shreveport recognized the right of all whites to vote; voted $500,000 to pay for slaves lost by death or otherwise, or while impressed for public works of the state; and decreed the death penalty for any slave bearing arms against the Confederate states.

When Hahn was elected to the Senate, Wells became Governor, March 14, 1865. Wells was a native Louisianian, a large planter, and had been an opponent of secession. His ambition was to restore the planters to power and have them recognize the new dispensation. As a result, he was caught between two fires; Sheridan told Stanton that Wells was a political trickster and a dishonest man; while the planters, once they got hands on power, overrode his advice, until he had to take refuge with the radicals.

On April 14, Lincoln was assassinated. President Johnson recognized Wells as Provisional Governor of Louisiana. The Governor at once ordered an election for state and national officers, on the ground that the previous registration of 1864 was fraudulent and that many Negroes were on the list, although Wells refrained from mentioning this fact explicitly. There appeared three political parties: the National Republicans, headed by Durant; the Conservative Union, headed by Wells; and the Democratic Party.

The Democratic Party held a state convention and adopted a platform which declared that Louisiana is "a government of white people, made and to be perpetuated for the exclusive political benefit of the white race, and in accordance with the constant adjudication of the United States Supreme Court, that the people of African descent cannot be considered as citizens of the United States, and that there can in no event nor under any circumstances by any equality between the whites and other races."

The Democratic or Conservative candidates were overwhelmingly elected and the new legislature was composed almost entirely of ex-Confederates. The Republican Party put no candidate in the field. At the first session of the legislature, a resolution was adopted declaring that the Constitution of 1864 was a creation of fraud, violence and corruption, and protested against seating Hahn and Cutler in the United States Senate. The legislature tried to reorganize the city government; the bill was vetoed by Wells, but was promptly passed over the Governor's veto and John T. Monroe was elected Mayor. He had led the mobs of ruffians in 1854-1856. Two governors had complained about him, and Butler had been obliged to put him in jail. He later engineered the riot of 1866.

The government now proceeded to oppress Negroes and Union men. Thousands were insulted and assaulted. Organized violence was common throughout the state. Negroes were whipped and killed, and no one was punished. Rebel sympathizers were rapidly replacing loyal officials, and the public schools were reconstructed. One hundred and ten of the Northern or loyal teachers were dismissed and their places filled by intolerant Southerners. Union men of business began to give up and move out of the state.

The principal departure of General Hancock, who succeeded Sheridan, from the policy pursued by his predecessors, related to the organization of juries. General Sheridan had issued an order requiring the state authorities to make no distinction as to race or color in the organization of juries. General Hancock superseded this order by one remanding the subject to the state authorities and the civil courts; and in order to avoid the annoyance of frequent applications to him for his intervention in private suits and controversies, he issued an order declaring that "the administration of civil justice appertains to the regular courts."

By decision of the State Supreme Court, there could never be any equality between white and other races. Above all, this legislature passed the Black Codes. Ficklen questions whether all this proposed legislation was actually enacted into law. Certainly, it represented the clear wish of the legislature, and was regarded as law. Afterward, the Reconstruction legislature took especial pains to repeal these enactments.

They were among the worst of the Black Codes, and virtually reenacted slavery. They were supplemented by extraordinary local ordinances like that of the town of Franklin.[30]

"All of these acts of the Legislature and municipal regulations meant the practical reëstablishment of slavery in the State of Louisiana. The acts were passed within the first fifteen days of its first session. This legislation and the various instances of widespread wanton violence and ostracism aroused the Union men of the state and the nation, and they determined to organize for their own protection, and for the protection of the freedmen and the old free Negroes before the War."[31]

The free Negro group early organized to guide the Negroes. Three colored refugees from San Domingo published and edited an unusually effective organ for the Negroes, called the New Orleans *Tribune*. One was Dr. J. T. Roudanez, who spent $35,500 to keep this paper going. He was an eminent physician, and his companions were men of intelligence. The paper was published in French and English, from 1864 until sometime in 1869. Most of the time it was published weekly, but it ran as a daily during 1865, and was thus the first Negro daily in America. It attacked the serfdom under Banks; planned for Negro economic coöperation, and opposed the Freedmen's Bureau when it was turned over to Southerners under General Fullerton. It carried on a war against the Johnson legislature, sending copies to every member of Congress, and printing all of the iniquitous labor laws. For a long time its editor was Paul Trevigne, a colored man born in 1825; his father had fought in the War of 1812, and he was well-trained, speaking several languages. At great personal peril and with dauntless courage, he battered his way to Negro freedom.

On January 8, 1865, the *Tribune* called attention to a convention of colored men of Louisiana, "which will meet tomorrow in this city." It pointed out that "Three principal points, for some time past, have been kept in view, by our leading men, and will unquestionably be brought before the convention. The first is the permanent organization and centralization of our leagues and societies; the second is the foundation upon a solid basis of a Permanent Board, intrusted with the interests of our population; and the third is the particular welfare of the freedmen."

This convention attacked the economic situation directly and with far-sighted prudence. It organized a Bureau of Industry in New Orleans under a superintendent and assistants. It was for the relief of distress, for establishing a Bureau of Information especially for colored soldiers and their relatives, and for buying and selling produce and other necessaries on a coöperative basis. Direct trade with France was planned.

The *Tribune,* from the first, strongly defended Negro suffrage. January 17, the *Tribune* said: "At the present time, when our state is entering into a new period of her social career, we must spare no means at our command to bring her under a truly democratic system of labor, glancing at the attempt recently made in Europe to organize a plan of credit for the people, which is worthy of our studies and investigations. We, too, need credit for the laborers; we cannot expect complete and perfect freedom for the working men, as long as they remain the tools of capital, and are deprived of the legitimate product of the sweat of their brow.

"We have denied time and again that the right of suffrage was confined—among the whites—to those distinguished by a high degree of civilization. But we assert that the sons and grandsons of the colored men who were recognized French citizens, under the French rule, and whose rights were reserved in the treaty of cession—taken away from them since 1803—are not savages and uncivilized inhabitants of the wild swamps of Louisiana. We contend that the freedmen, who proved intelligent enough to shed their blood in defense of freedom and the National Flag, are competent to cast their votes into the ballot-box."

April 2, the *Tribune* said: "The colored man will have to be called to the ballot-box, as he has been called in the ranks. The black man had to fight the battles of Union and Freedom with his musket; he will have to fight them too with the ballot. Loyalty does not dwell in the white population of the South—taken as a mass. But loyalty lives in the hearts of the colored men. Can the United States find friends where they have none or very few? They cannot. But the cause of universal freedom will find friends and defenders in the class of men who are longing for their liberties. . . .

"Louisiana and all the Southern states want an entire renovation of the political element, a renovation of the masses of voters.

"This superior understanding places the future into the hands of the Radical party. The game that the 'Free State' party has lost by its incompetency, the Radicals will win by their understanding of the times. They are still in the background; but one day, and one single act of Congress, or a single change of policy in the military ruling of the conquered territory, will bring them into power."

February 22, 1865, the efforts of this group culminated in the formation of a "Freedmen's Aid Association." It was an ambitious coöperative effort, thus described by the *Tribune*, February 24:

"Several plantations were leased to 'gangs' of laborers working for their own account. Seeds, mules, and agricultural implements were distributed among these freedmen—not as a gratuitous gift, but in the character of a loan, leaving to the laborer all his dignity and independence. . . .

"These associations of capital, furnished by small shares to freedmen who possess nothing more than their industry, good faith and courage, are destined not only to become powerful, but they will also enrich the state. They will inaugurate a new régime, and for the first time give a chance to field-laborers to obtain their rightful share in the proceeds of the sweat of their brows. Time will bring up a legislation appropriate to the necessities of the case. But now, at the start, we have to prepare the ground, under all disadvantages, for this important economical and social reform."

The free Negro group, and the intelligent freedmen, were thus bidding for the economic leadership of the mass of freed slaves, and offering them democratic sharing in the profits. For this rôle, they had many rivals—the planters, the military commanders and their agents, and the immigrant Northern capitalists.

Of the planters, the *Tribune* said, March 1:

"The planters are no longer needed in the character of masters. But they intend still to be needed as capitalists, and through the necessity of moneyed help, to retain their hold on the unfortunate people they have so long oppressed. It is that hold that every friend of justice and liberty is bound to break. As capital is needed to work the plantations, let the people themselves make up this capital. Our basis for labor must now be put on a democratic footing. There is no more room, in the organization of our society, for an oligarchy of slaveholders, or property holders."

These efforts of the free colored people to lead the freedmen toward economic emancipation soon ran afoul of the military authorities and their plans for using Negro labor. Banks had inaugurated a system of serfdom with schools and many excellent features, but with other provisions which insulted the free Negroes and hindered real emancipation.

Negroes, free and freed, especially objected to the pass system established ostensibly to stop the spread of smallpox, but kept at the demand of the planters in order to hold Negroes on the plantations. The *Tribune* said, April 30:

"The 'smallpox passes' will remain as an instructive feature in the history of abolition in Louisiana. It is one of those marks of servitude which are enforced upon us in view of controlling a population that has been declared free—that has to be let free. It is a deception practiced upon the emancipated slaves, who receive from one hand their liberty, and are deprived by the other hand of one of their most precious privileges—the right of moving at will. It is an outrage upon the old free colored men, who used that right during the darkest and most gloomy years of the slavery régime, and now are deprived of the exercise of their traditional liberties. It is well for the world at large to know how practical liberty is understood in Louisiana."

When in 1865, appeal was made to General Hurlburt for closer cooperation between the Negro leaders and the army, he replied: "If instead of assembling in mass meetings and wasting your time in high sounding resolutions, you would devote yourselves to assisting in the physical and moral improvement of the freedmen, you would do some practical good." He added:

"There has always been a bitterness of feeling among the slaves and the free colored people."

Junius ("not a rich Creole") answered him, March 31: "I am sure it is a well-known fact, and that too, beyond successful controversy, that the old free colored people of this city and state have done and are doing all that is in their power to morally and physically improve the condition of the new freedmen.

"Ever since the occupation of this city by the military forces of the United States in April, 1862, the free colored people of this city and state, have night and day been working for and in the interest of the new freedmen. Even under the administration of Major General B. F. Butler, when slavery was recognized by the authorities of the United States government, free public schools were opened under the auspices of the free colored people, and no distinction was made in regard to the former status of the pupils—and numerous other evidences can be produced showing that no sooner was slavery killed and the Black Code destroyed in this state, all who were formerly afraid to do anything in the direction of moral or physical assistance of the former bondsmen, entered into the work vigorously, and have accomplished great good. The work is still going on—increasing from day to day; and more would have been accomplished, but for the poverty of our people, who have been in the midst of war and all its dissolution for over four years—more would have been accomplished but for the 'Policy' of certain intriguers who have ingratiated themselves into our confidence, and have in the end deceived us. . . .

"All that is required by the free colored people of Louisiana is Justice, and without it, they are not free. . . .

"The free people of color own over twenty millions of taxable property acquired honestly under a system of oppression worse than ever existed since the foundation of the world, and but for the 'free labor system' [established by Banks] would now be paying taxes on over double the amount. The Freedmen's Aid Association has now in hand four plantations. They will soon have twenty; every one of these plantations is a death blow to this 'free labor system,' and the cultivation of the plantations by freedmen will show their capacity in their new career."

When Johnson became President, the colored leaders had firm faith in his economic program. "There is, in fact, no true republican government, unless the land, and wealth in general, are distributed among the great mass of the inhabitants. The policy of the new President will be, therefore, of enforcing the laws of confiscation, granting homesteads to Northern immigrants, soldiers, and Southern Loyalists, and dividing the property among a great number of freeholders, who will feel interested to support the new order of things, and to defend the Federal Government."

To enforce this faith, the Negroes knew it was necessary to be represented in Washington, and in May they communicated with several Southern states on the matter of sending such delegations. The *Tribune,* May 31, said: "Such a delegation at Washington this winter, from each of the Southern states, would have a great tendency toward answering any objections that might be adduced against a Reconstruction policy that would admit the justness of the black man's right to equality before the law; and most of all, the moral of such delegations will show that the colored people of the South are really awake to their interests. For Messrs. Editors, if civil authority again assumes sway legitimately here, and is acknowledged by the executive and legislative authorities, we may expect and prepare also for mobs of white against colored laborers, and white mechanics against colored mechanics, like the 'Iron Mongers of Cincinnati,' the 'Plug Uglies of Baltimore,' the 'Flat Heads of New York,' the 'Moyamensing Boys of Philadelphia,' and the 'Irish mobs' of Detroit, Chicago, and New York City. But more of mobs hereafter. If we desire to prevent these outrages from being our future inheritance, on account of our active and exerted influence and friendship and love of the Union, send a delegation to Washington, and say to Congress: 'There never will be domestic tranquillity in Louisiana so long as the most truly loyal portion of the people of this state are left at the mercy of the men who have for four years been attempting to destroy the Union!' "

When the campaign was on for the election of 1865, the colored leaders criticized the Conservative address in the *Tribune,* August 11:

"It is signed by ex-Judge Louis Davigneaud and Spencer G. Hamilton. It gives us the astounding news that at the breaking out of the rebellion, Louisiana was governed by 'wholesome and just laws.' Give us your authority for this, gentlemen; point us to the book and page. The fact that you immediately afterward refer us to the 'abundant harvest' with which we used to be blessed, leads us to suppose that in your opinion these 'wholesome and just laws' were found in the infamous Black Code, by virtue of which the life of the poor man was worn out in laboring for the princely planters. The address assures us that before the war, we enjoyed 'Life, Liberty (!) and the pursuit of happiness!' We were plunged into war by 'ambitious men' upon 'supposed and contemplated wrongs.' Why not name the men? It could do no harm to know their names. It labors under great fears from the party, which it admits exists in this state, 'advocating the pernicious doctrine of universal suffrage, with a view of conferring upon the emancipated Negro the right of suffrage.' The address does not, however, say a word in favor of the Negro not 'emancipated,' and who was always free. Why use the word 'emancipated'? Are the men of color who were born free entitled to suffrage in your opinion? If so, why not make the admission."

At the same time, the *Tribune,* September 14, attested the growing unity of the Negro group.

"We no longer hear of classes of colored men—some to claim the electoral franchise because they are rich, some because they are lettered, some because they bore an Uncle Sam's musket. All this was sheer aristocracy, and among those neglected there were men as good, as true, as patriotic and as intelligent, as among the privileged classes. When citizens undertake to claim a right for themselves, they must claim it as a principle, and therefore speak in the name of all who are deprived of the same immunities. As long as they do not consider the question from a high standpoint, as long as they overlook the principle for a mere expediency, they will have no force whatever."

It was this year that the new element of carpetbaggers began to be felt in Louisiana. Hitherto, there had been the planter class, the military authorities, and the free colored people, all striving for leadership of the freedmen. Now came the disbanded Union officers, the new small capitalists of the North, or those who represented them, although themselves without capital. Foremost among these was Henry Clay Warmoth.

Warmoth took up his residence in Louisiana in 1865. He was a young Union officer, then only 23 years of age, and had an astonishing career. He was an unmoral buccaneer, shrewd, likable, and efficient, who for ten years was practical master of the state of Louisiana. He represented those white men, Northern and Southern, currently called carpetbaggers and scalawags, who were either small capitalists or aspired to become rich, and whose business it was to manipulate the labor vote, white and black.

Some of them in many states, we have shown, were men of ability and vision, but most of those in Louisiana who were honest and forthright were early driven out by the turmoil and lawlessness. Types like Warmoth and Carter, who stayed, represented the carpetbagger and scalawag at their worst. A Negro preacher described the types: He said that the carpetbagger came South and stole enough to fill his carpetbag; but that the scalawag, knowing the woods and swamps better, succeeded in stealing the full carpetbag.[32]

Warmoth was a poor white of Southern extraction, whose great-grandfather was born in Virginia, and whose grandfather moved to Illinois.

His father was in the Mexican War, and Warmoth was born in Illinois in 1842. He declares in his biography, that he had "not a drop of any other than Southern blood in my veins. I think I may say at eighty-seven years of age, that I was never a 'Louisiana Carpetbagger,' though I might, in common parlance, be termed a 'scalawag.' " [33]

The Republican Party of Louisiana had been organized in 1863. It was composed of twenty-six members, of whom 21 were Union white men, and five free Negroes who had never been slaves and who were all nearly white, men of wealth and education. This committee issued a call for a convention which assembled in New Orleans, September 27, 1865. A state committee was formed which proceeded to organize the Union Republican Party of Louisiana. There were 111 delegates, of whom 19 were free Negroes, and one a freedman. Warmoth was Corresponding Secretary of the State Committee, and some of the free colored men were on the committee. Two of the resolutions said:

"Resolved—That the system of slavery heretofore existing in Louisiana, and the laws and ordinances passed from time to time to support it, have ceased to exist; and we protest against any and all attempts to substitute in their place a system of serfdom, or forced labor in any shape.

"Resolved—That the necessities of the nation called the colored men into public service in the most honorable of all duties—that of the soldier fighting for the integrity of his country and the security of the constitutional government; this, with his loyalty, patience and prudence, is sufficient to assure Congress of the justice and safety of giving him a vote to protect his liberty." [34]

This convention conceived the idea of adopting the Congressional theory that Louisiana was a territory, and holding a voluntary election for a delegate to Congress. The colored people, especially, fell in with the idea, and carried it through. The *Tribune,* September 2, bore testimony to the unity of effort and feeling and the work of two colored men who originated the idea—Crane and Dunn:

"Too much praise cannot be given to the Central Executive Committee for their strenuous efforts toward the organization of such a move, without the force of law, and on the basis of voluntary coöperation. It has taken several weeks to complete the preliminary arrangements. All members of the committee have heartily contributed their shares. We must, however, mention in a more particular manner the services of two of these members. When the importance of the move will be fully understood and its consequences developed, their names will remain more particularly connected with that work. It is with Mr. W. R. Crane that the first idea originated. It is the same member who prepared the various resolutions bearing on the subject. He advocated his plan with the conviction of its usefulness, and through industry and perseverance, has succeeded in removing all objections, and in carrying it through.

"Next to him, Mr. O. J. Dunn has a fair right to our gratitude. With private means only, he organized a machinery covering the whole city of New Orleans, and secured the voluntary and gratuitous concourse of the numerous commissioners and clerks. These two names will ever remain connected with the history of Reconstruction in 1865."

It was the first successful effort of the whole Negro group in political coöperation, and the "disfranchised citizens" expressed their debt of gratitude in the *Tribune,* November 4, to the "Commissioners and Clerks of Registration, who, during two months, attended with a zeal equal only to their disinterestedness, to the tedious business of registering the names of the political 'pariahs.' This debt will be paid by the just esteem and well-earned respect of their fellow-citizens."

On the crest of this wave of unprecedented effort, rose the figure of Warmoth. Thomas J. Durant, a Southern Unionist who had coöperated with Lincoln in restoring Louisiana, was the nominee by acclamation. He declined the doubtful honor, and Warmoth, handsome, charming and of fine military bearing, was finally substituted, since it was political wisdom to send a white man to Washington, and few others were willing to take the risk. Warmoth was more than willing. He was a born gambler, of unflinching courage in causes good and bad. The election was held just before the Johnson Reconstruction state legislature met, and Warmoth received 19,396 votes in thirteen parishes, or nearly twice as many as the number which Lincoln had recognized as sufficient to admit the state.

Naturally, most of these votes were cast by Negroes. Warmoth was careful, however, to have the Secretary of State affix his seal to a certificate attesting that the election had been held. He then went to Washington and spent several months getting acquainted with the Reconstruction leaders. He was accorded a seat on the floor of the House, while the Senators and Representatives elected by Johnson's legislature had to cool their heels in the galleries.

This election was a shrewd move on the part of the Negroes, and brought the rivalry of Johnson and Congress conspicuously to the fore in Louisiana. Governor Wells found himself soon in an untenable position. He had opposed secession before the war; but as a planter and Southerner, when he came into power, he tried to unite the leading white persons of the state back of his administration, on a platform acceptable to President Johnson. Once in power, his followers broke away and were determined to reëstablish the ante-bellum status in all essential particulars. It was this movement that was back of the Black Codes and the oppression of Union whites and Negroes.

Said the *Tribune,* May 10, 1865:

"Were the planters willing to bestow the same amount of money upon the laborers as additional wages, as they pay to runners and waste in dishonest means of compulsion, they would have drawn as many voluntary and faithful laborers as they now obtain reluctant ones. But there are harpies, who, most of them, were in the slave trade, and who persuade planters to use them as brokers to supply the plantations with hands, at the same time using all means to deceive the simple and unsophisticated laborer."

The planters in the legislature elected in 1865, proposed April 7, 1866, a convention for a new Constitution. Wells vetoed the bill. Then a bill passed the House by a two-thirds majority to restore the ante-bellum constitution by legislative enactment. Two members of the House were sent to Washington to confer with Johnson. Johnson was in the midst of his fight with Congress, and he strongly advised against the move.

Governor Wells was desperate. If the planters engineered a new constitutional convention, such a convention would be dominated by reaction and invite the vengeance of Congress. Wells, therefore, determined to reconvene the Constitutional Convention of 1864. He had a more or less shadowy legal right to do this, but the meeting of this convention meant that Negro suffrage would be recognized, at least to some extent. Probably, according to the Lincoln formula, Negroes of intelligence, those who owned a certain amount of property, and former soldiers, would get the right to vote.

If such a convention could have met in Louisiana in 1866, it would have been epoch-making; it would have turned the flank of the Johnson phalanx and anticipated and softened the rigor of the Reconstruction acts. The prospect of such a consummation was too much for the Louisiana Bourbons and they determined to meet it by reopening civil war. Wells was a man of no courage, and instead of placing himself resolutely at the head of this movement, he kept out of the way and induced a member of the convention of 1864 to issue a call summoning a meeting July 30 in the Mechanics' Institute, New Orleans. He followed this by a proclamation ordering special elections in the large number of parishes not represented in 1864.

The excitement was intense. A prominent judge harangued the Grand Jury against the meeting. The Mayor told the general in command of the United States Army that he proposed to prevent the assembly. General Baird doubted the mayor's authority, but did nothing.

Most of the leaders in this movement stayed away from the opening, and in fact, only a small number of members accepted the call; but Monroe, also chief of a secret society known as "The Southern Cross," armed his police and the mob, who wore white handkerchiefs on their necks.

A signal shot was fired, and the mob deployed across the head of Dryades Street, moved upon the State House, and shot down the people who were in the hall.

"The Reverend Dr. Horton waving a white handkerchief, cried to the police: 'Gentlemen, I beseech you to stop firing; we are non-combatants. If you want to arrest us, make any arrest you please, we are not prepared to defend ourselves.' Some of the police, it is claimed, replied, 'We don't want any prisoners; you have all got to die.' Dr. Horton was shot and fell, mortally wounded. Dr. Dostie who was an object of special animosity on account of his inflammatory addresses was a marked victim. Shot through the spine, and with a sword thrust through his stomach, he died a few days later. There were about one hundred and fifty persons in the hall, mostly Negroes. Seizing chairs, they beat back the police three times, and barred the doors. But the police returned to the attack, firing their revolvers as they came. Some of the Negroes returned the fire, but most of them leaped from the windows in wild panic. In some cases they were shot as they came down or as they scrambled over the fence at the bottom. The only member of the convention, however, that was killed was a certain John Henderson. Some six or seven hundred shots were fired. Negroes were pursued, and in some cases were killed on the streets. One of them, two miles from the scene, was taken from his shop and wounded in the side, hip, and back. The dead and wounded were piled upon drays and carried off." [35]

Some say that forty-eight were killed outright, sixty-eight were severely wounded, and ninety-eight slightly wounded in the hall and on the streets. Other reports say that thirty-eight people were killed and 148 wounded; and of the thirty-eight, all but four were colored.

As Sheridan said: "It was no riot. It was an absolute massacre." Too late, General Baird and the Federal soldiers arrived and proclaimed martial law. Mayor Monroe's threat to break up the convention succeeded completely and, but for the appearance of United States troops, "the killing would undoubtedly have been much greater than it was." [36]

After this, many Union men left the state permanently, and the new rule of organized anarchy ensued. The New Orleans riot was a characteristic gesture of the time and place. Most of the elected white members of the convention kept in the background to see what trouble was brewing. Negroes assembled, most of them as spectators, to find out what was going to be done for their enfranchisement. It was these black spectators upon whom the brunt of murder and assassination fell. There was an unusual moral aftermath to this inexcusable slaughter, in that it helped turn the national election of 1866 overwhelmingly against Andrew Johnson.

It was against this background of lawlessness and murder, this practical reopening of the Civil War, that Congressional Reconstruction began. Under the National Reconstruction Act in Louisiana, 127,639 registered, of whom 82,907 were blacks.

When Negro suffrage seemed inevitable, some effort was made on the part of the planters to gain the Negroes' support. They began by cajoling the field hands. In a meeting in Rapides Parish, held by the planters, they said they would "hold in high esteem the freedmen among us who range themselves on our side." Duncan F. Kenner, a prominent politician, urged the people to accept Negroes and to try and gain their vote for the South. General P. G. T. Beauregard, who began the fighting at Fort Sumter and wanted to raise the black flag after Emancipation, said: "If the suffrage of the Negro is properly handled and directed, we shall defeat our adversaries with their own weapons. The Negro is Southern born. With a little education, and a property qualification, he can be made to take an interest in the affairs of the South and in its prosperity. He will fight with the whites." [37]

On March 18, General Longstreet, a Confederate General, published two open letters advising submission to Congress. "It becomes us to insist that suffrage be extended in all the states and fully tested." [38] Other prominent Confederates agreed. Longstreet's wife afterward declared that this was the noblest act of her husband's life.

But these overtures of a few planters were more than neutralized by the bulk of white Southern opinion, which was bitter beyond description. All Republicans were bitterly assailed: "The shameless, heartless, vile, grasping, deceitful, creeping, crawling, wallowing, slimy, slippery, hideous, loathsome, political pirates who, in the name of God and Liberty, rob the South and put the Southern states under a black government." [39] "Everything was said that would disparage or discredit the officials. Nothing was said to explain, or justify their acts or their conduct." [40]

On the 25th of April, seven days after the election of officers under the new Constitution, the *Courier* of the Teche said: "Fourteen men, having a covering of white skin over their flesh, have voted for the mongrel constitution in the parish of St. Martin. May they be pointed out with the finger of scorn by all honorable men. May they be despised and hated by every living creature. May their wives, if such creatures can have wives, remain barren, that their descendants may not rot in jail or die of exhaustion in houses of ill-fame."

The *Banner,* the leading paper in its congressional district, said on the 20th of June, as the Republican members of the legislature and state government were assembling in New Orleans: "These miserable devils are worse than the itch, small-pox, measles, overflow, draughts and pestilence."

On the other hand, Negroes kept hammering at their economic condition. A meeting was held in the First African Church in May, 1867, to colonize colored laborers on colored homesteads. From this time until the new Constitutional Convention met, the *Tribune* pled for a high class of delegates to the Convention. "From the President down to the doorkeeper, and from the clerk and the chief reporter down to the printer, the choices should be made so as to convince the people of the State that the supremacy of a privileged class will be no longer fostered, and the time has come when the representatives of the colored race can find favor as well as white men. It is to be demonstrated that long services and unfaltering devotion to the cause of radicalism shall obtain the reward, irrespective of color or race, and to that effect it is important to choose officers from among both populations.

"But there is something more. It is important to show that the oppressed race will not be overlooked; that from this time forward the rights of the neglected race will be recognized to share in all departments of our state government. The Convention will have many things to do to break the spell under which we were laboring. The choice of officers will, therefore, have a political bearing, and cannot be dictated by fitness only.

"The Convention will meet under very peculiar circumstances—circumstances of originality and grandeur. It will be the first constitutional assembly, the first official body ever convened in the United States without distinction of race or color. It will be the first mixed assemblage, clothed with a public character. As such this Convention has to take a position in immediate contradiction with the old assemblies of the *white man's government.* They will have to show that a new order will succeed the former order of things, and that the long-neglected race will, at last, effectually share in the government of the state. . . ."[41]

By agreement, the 98 delegates to the Louisiana convention consisted of 49 Negroes and 49 whites. Among the Negroes were many free colored men of intelligence, property, and character. But when it was suggested that subordinate officers be equally divided between the races, P. B. S. Pinchback, one of the colored leaders, objected, and declared that was placing race above merit.

The Negro members of the constitutional convention took a prominent and effective part. They were largely represented on committees, such as the Committee of 13 on rules and regulations, where they had four members. In several cases, they acted as chairmen of committees, as in the case of the committee on the militia, and the committee on the Bill of Rights.

Their attitude, however, is best seen in the report of the committee to draft a constitution. The five white members of the committee, and the four colored members, differed in certain essential particulars, and sent in respectively a majority and minority report.

The chief points of difference were these: the white men wished to deprive all of the leaders of the Confederacy of the right to vote or hold office, while the colored men would allow them to vote, but restricted their right to hold office. The white men wished to prevent any law being passed regulating labor, or fixing wages. The colored men wished no such restrictions and also demanded that children bound out under the former black laws should be returned to their parents and relatives. The white men made provisions for the education of youth, but the colored men were more specific and demanded at least one free public school in every parish, to be provided for by public taxation, and with no distinction as to race and sex. They also asked for a university with six faculties, and a state lottery for the support of education and charity. While the white men wanted ninety-eight state representatives, the colored men wanted one hundred and two, which probably gave certain colored sections a larger representation.

In the final constitution, a compromise provided that no law should be passed fixing the price of manual labor; that there should be one hundred and one representatives; that Confederate leaders could neither vote nor hold office, and that the colored men's proposal for education, including no separation in schools and a university, should prevail.

The colored men assented to this constitution, but two of them, Pinchback and Blandin, together with two white men, protested against the disfranchisement of former Confederates, "as we are now and ever have been advocates of universal suffrage." [42] It is interesting to note that the colored men who published the *Daily Tribune* were the official printers of the Convention Journal.

The Convention adopted the Constitution, March 19, 1868. This Constitution made the Negroes equal to the whites and provided equal rights and privileges; public schools were thrown open to both races.

All adult male citizens resident in Louisiana for one year could vote, except certain classes of Confederates. The labor laws passed by the Democratic legislature of 1865 were declared null and void.

The planters reviled the Constitution, and called it "the work of the lowest and most corrupt body of men ever assembled in the South. It was the work of ignorant Negroes, coöperating with a gang of white adventurers, strangers to our interests and our sentiments. It was originated by carpetbaggers, and was carried through by such arguments as are printed on greenbacked paper. It was one of the long catalogues of schemes of corruption which make up the whole history of that iniquitous Radical Conclave." [43]

In the face of this, the laws of Louisiana, as codified on the basis of this Constitution and subsequent legislation, were finally adopted in three main codes, signed by the black Lieutenant Governor of the state, Oscar J. Dunn, and remain to this day as the basic law of the state!

The free Negroes had since the war increased in numbers, wealth and intelligence. On the other hand, the mass of the freedmen were ignorant and inexperienced and much lower in status, because of their harsh slavery, than even the Negroes of South Carolina. They had, however, two ever-insistent demands: land to cultivate and public schools. They had almost impoverished themselves under Banks to keep their schools going; and while their demand for land never reached the definite expression that it did elsewhere, it was always the great motivating ideal.

The colored people produced some notable leaders during Reconstruction. Oscar J. Dunn ran away from slavery and finally bought his freedom; he had laid the foundation for a good education before he became free. Dunn "was the only one of the seven colored men who sat in the State Senate in 1868 who had been a slave." [44] He was Lieutenant-Governor, 1868-1870, and was a man of courage and firmness. He was admitted by the Democrats to be incorruptible: "In the view of the Caucasian chiefs, the taint of honesty, and of a scrupulous regard for the official proprieties, is a serious drawback and enervating reproach upon the Lieutenant-Governor." [45] His sudden death in November, 1871, was a severe loss.

Pinchback, son of a white man, and himself indistinguishable from white in personal appearance, was born in Georgia, educated in Cincinnati, and had been a captain in the army. He was intelligent and capable, but a leader of different caliber from Dunn. He was a practical politician, and played the politician's game. Yet there were limits beyond which he would not go. To all intents and purposes, he was an educated, well-to-do, congenial white man, with but a few drops of Negro blood, which he did not stoop to deny, as so many of his fellow whites did. Pinchback succeeded Dunn as Lieutenant-Governor, and when Warmoth was impeached in December, 1872, Pinchback became for a few days Governor of the state.

C. C. Antoine later was also Lieutenant-Governor. The legislature sent J. H. Menard, a colored man, as one of the representatives of the Lower House and Congress, but he was refused his seat.

Antoine Dubuclet was State Treasurer during 1868-1879. He conducted his office for eighteen years without mistake or criticism. Politicians tried to find something wrong with his records; and the Aldiger committee was appointed to examine the archives of the Treasury. They secured three expert accountants to investigate the Treasury for six months. The honesty and efficiency of the Treasurer was confirmed.

There were the following colored officials in Louisiana: [46]

Charles E. Nash, Congressman, 1874-76 (44th Congress).

P. B. S. Pinchback, Governor, 1872, 43 days; Lieutenant-Governor, 1871-72.

Oscar J. Dunn, Lieutenant-Governor, 1868-71.

C. C. Antoine, Lieutenant-Governor, 1872-76.

P. G. Deslonde, Secretary of State, 1872-76.

Antoine Dubuclet, State Treasurer, 1868-69.

W. G. Brown, Superintendent of Public Education, 1872-76.

Augustin G. Jones, once chancery clerk of Assumption Parish, was a direct descendant of the hero John Paul Jones of Revolutionary War fame who was captain of the *Bonhomme Richard*. Several of his daughters are now teachers in the New Orleans public schools.[47]

In addition there were, between 1863 and 1896, 32 colored state senators and 95 representatives.

These colored leaders had a task of enormous difficulty, much more so than those of South Carolina or Mississippi. They differed in origin and education. Some looked white, some black, some born free and rich, the recipients of good education; some were ex-slaves, with no formal training. They were faced with an intricate social tangle among the whites. Economic and social differences were, in Louisiana, more complicated than in any other American state, and this makes the history of Reconstruction more difficult to follow.

First of all, there were the planters, rich before the war, largely officers and leaders in the Confederate Army, and now returned, embittered and widely impoverished. Then there were "the host of traders, capitalists and adventurers, who had come down during and just after the war to seek a new field for investment in the conquered country, who were, naturally, regarded more or less as harpies. The number was formidable, for already by the fall of 1866, Ficklen says between five and ten thousand Union soldiers had settled in the State." [48] Among these were Warmoth and Kellogg. Add to these, the scalawags—the large number of whites, both planters and others, who became Union men during and after the war.

"Another factor was the numerous poor whites in the northern part of the State. Living close to the subsistence line on the thin soil of the pine hills back of the bottom lands, without schools, with but few churches, given to rude sports and crude methods of farming, their ignorance and prejudice bred in them after the emancipation of the Negro, a dread of sinking to the social level of the blacks. The dread, in turn, bred hatred, and it was from this class, instigated very probably by the class above them, that the Colfax and Conshatta murders took their unfortunate rise.

"And still one other element, mischievous in the extreme, must be added to the social complex—men who pursued no occupations, but preyed on black and white alike, as gamblers and tenth-rate politicians, drinking and swaggering at the bar, always armed with knife and revolver, shooting Negroes now and then for excitement. This class, recruited largely from the descendants of the old overseer and Negro-trader of ante-bellum days, had just enough education to enable them to dazzle the Negro by a political harangue. They became demagogic leaders of the Negroes, on the one hand, and murderers and fighters for the planters. It was this element that more than anything else kept up the turmoil in the state."

According to Nordhoff, "the first duty of the Republican leaders in Louisiana was 'to hang them by the dozen.' And it was because they were not crushed out, except so far as the respectable Conservative could combat them, that Louisiana had to endure such a drawn-out purgatory before she was reconstructed." [49]

The number of Negroes in the legislature of Louisiana is not exactly known, chiefly on account of the great mixture of blood. In the first legislature, there were said to be 42 Negroes, about half of the House, and seven Negro Senators. The election showed the predominant influence of the carpetbaggers over the Negroes, who had good reason to be convinced of the bad faith of the planters.

"There was never a majority of Negroes in either House of the Legislature during my four years of service as Governor. The Legislature elected in 1868, at the same time I was elected Governor, had but six colored men in the Senate out of its thirty-six members; and though the House of Representatives had more colored men in it than did the Senate, they never constituted more than one-third of the membership.

"So it was in the general election of 1870. Only six out of the thirty-

six members of the Senate were colored men, and there were fewer
Negroes in the House of Representatives than in the House elected in
1868. Whatever legislation may have been worthy of criticism during
[this] administration was the work of white men in which the Negro
members played but a modest part." [50]

The real fight that developed in Louisiana was between the planters,
on the one hand, and the newcomers, Northern and Southern, on the
other. And these two factions fought to dominate both the poor whites
and the Negroes, usually by characteristically different methods. The
planters resorted to the old method of cajoling the poor whites, giving
them some political and social recognition, and using them as thugs
and murderers to carry out their ends. The carpetbaggers flattered
Negroes, bribed those whom they could and gave them some recognition, but always at some crucial point broke their promises because
they knew the Negro had no choice. Especially in Louisiana the question of social equality between whites and mulattoes was an insistent
source of bitter feelings.

Two factions soon developed among the Republicans; Warmoth
tried to appease the planters and avoid too great dependence on the
Negro. But the *Tribune,* leading the "Pure Radicals," said in 1868:
"The Republican Party in Louisiana is headed by men, who for the
most part are devoid of honesty and decency, and we think it right
that the country should know it. The active portion of the party in
Louisiana is composed largely of white adventurers, who strive to
be elected to office by black votes. . . . Some of these intend, if elected,
to give a share of office to colored men. We admit that, but they will
choose only docile tools, not citizens who have manhood." [51]

When the Republicans came to select their candidate for Governor,
the Pure Radicals proposed a wealthy colored man, Major F. E.
Dumas. Dumas received 43 votes and Warmoth 45. Dumas refused
the position of Lieutenant-Governor and Dunn was nominated. Five
white men and two colored men constituted the ticket, the other colored man being Antoine Dubuclet for treasurer. This ticket was
elected. The new legislature met June 29, 1868, and the temporary
Speaker was a Negro, R. H. Isbell. He and Dunn tried to enforce the
test oath, as they were legally bound to do, to the great anger of the
rebels, who asked if they were to be excluded "by a nigger" from the
seats to which they were elected.

The legislature spent some time discussing a civil rights bill. This
bill went over until the next session, and caused high feeling and long
discussion. The Conservatives protested against the colored people
forcing themselves in where they were not wanted. Pinchback insisted
only on equal accommodation.

"I consider myself just as far above coming into company that does not want me, as they are above my coming into an elevation with them. . . . I do not believe that any sensible colored man upon this floor would wish to be in a private part of a public place without the consent of the owners of it. It is false; it is wholesale falsehood to say that we wish to force ourselves upon white people." [52]

The bill passed both houses, but the Governor was almost afraid to sign it, and the newspapers tried to frighten Negroes. " 'Will any Negro, or gang of Negroes, attempt to exercise the privilege it confers?' belligerently asked the *Commercial Bulletin*. 'If they do, it will be at their peril. . . . He may be able to obtain a ticket of admission, but no New Orleans audience will ever permit him to take his seat except in the places allotted for colored persons.' "

It continued: "Apparently this state of calm does not suit the Radical leaders. Their continual control over the State must depend on the jealousy of the black toward the white people. They feel that the colored race have more confidence in the old citizens of Louisiana than in any newcomers. Hence the effort to revive a strife which would readily quiet itself without much stimulus." [53]

Warmoth in his inaugural address ventured "to urge immediate measures for the repression of lawlessness and disorder now rife in many parts of the State. From many parishes we have almost daily accounts of violence and outrage—in many cases most brutal and revolting murders—without any effort on the part of the people to prevent or punish them." [54]

In a special address to the colored people, Warmoth said:

"My friends, this is a great day for the colored men of Louisiana. It is full of good for you if my hopes and expectations in your favor are well founded. If you are honest, industrious and peaceable, you will have millions of friends who will stand by you, and see that you are protected in all the political rights which they themselves enjoy. You do not wish to intrude yourselves socially upon those who do not want your society, any more than you want other people to obtrude themselves upon you without your consent. The contest from which we are emerging has not been for social equality, but for civil and political equality. This last you now have, and it will be my duty to see that you are protected in it, and if I am not mistaken in my opinion of your race, it will be cheerfully accorded to you very soon by everybody; and remember that the roads that lead to prosperity for every man, whether white or black, are those of virtue and education, of honesty and sobriety, of industry and obedience to law." [55]

Unfortunately, the state government, inaugurated in July, was almost immediately confronted by a Presidential election in November,

1868. Skilfully, and with calculation, the economic problems of Reconstruction were being changed by planters and capitalists to look like problems of politics and social recognition. Beneath this deliberate camouflage, the industrial plans of the *Tribune* were being slowly submerged, until finally murder and mob-law seized the state.

The whole South was in a blaze of excitement in the 1868 election. Tremendous and frequent meetings were held in every city and parish in Louisiana. Every Confederate sympathizer was encouraged, and had hopes of what would happen to the South as a result of the election. The Republican Party in Louisiana was paralyzed. Secret semi-military organizations were set up, and riots broke up Republican meetings. Clubrooms were raided and destroyed. It was believed that if Seymour and Blair were elected, Reconstruction would be overthrown.

A civil war of secret assassination and open intimidation and murder began and did not end until 1876, and not entirely then. Strong as the hatred of the reactionaries was toward Negroes, it was stronger toward carpetbaggers. The Democratic State Central Committee sent out a letter: "And we would earnestly declare to our fellow-citizens our opinion that even the most implacable and ill-disposed of the Negro population, those who show the worst spirit toward the white people, are not half as much deserving our aversion and non-intercourse with them as the debased Whites who encourage and aid them, and who become through their votes the officeholding oppressors of the people. Whatever resentment you have should be felt toward the latter, and not against the colored men; but in no case should you permit this resentment to go further than to withdraw from them all *countenance, association,* and *patronage,* and thwart every effort they may make to maintain a business and social foothold among you." [56]

Secret Democratic organizations were formed, and all well armed: the Knights of the White Camellia, the Ku Klux Klan, and an Italian organization called "The Innocents." They all paraded nightly. In the election, Seymour and Blair received 88,225 votes, while Grant and Colfax received 34,859. Out of 21,000 Republican voters in New Orleans, only 276 Republican votes were cast. There were in 1870, 726,915 persons in the state. A map of the state showing where violence and intimidation occurred leaves less than a third of the state in peace. [57]

Because of the experiences in the Presidential election of 1868, the legislature was asked to change the election and registration laws, and approved the law of March 16, 1870, conferring great power upon the Governor. The Governor was authorized to appoint a chief election officer, who should make a registration of voters in each parish, and a board before which the Governor should lay all the election returns.

This Returning Board was composed of three state officers and two state Senators, and it could throw out fraudulent votes or returns secured by violence. This device made government by the mob impossible, but it substituted a possible dictatorship in the hands of an unscrupulous Governor.

Governor Warmoth's attitude toward the finances of the state was characteristic and original. There was need of money, and he raised it. His statement of the needs was unexceptional: "I found the State and the city of New Orleans bankrupt. Interest on the State and City bonds had been in default for years; the assessed property taxable in the State had fallen in value from $470,164,963.00 in 1860, to $250,063,-359.63 in 1870; taxes for the years 1860, 1861, 1862, 1863, 1864, 1865, 1866 and 1867 were in arrears. The City and State were flooded with State and City shinplasters, which had been issued to meet current expenses. Among the first acts of the new legislature was one to postpone the collection of all back taxes, and later they were postponed indefinitely." [58]

"The public roads were mud trails. There was not a hard surfaced road in the whole state. There was the one canal, and very limited telegraphic facilities. The mails were usually carried on horseback. New Orleans had but four paved streets. The amount of the state and city debt was unknown, and state securities were selling from 22¢ to 25¢ on a dollar. There was no money in either state or city treasury.

"New Orleans was a dirty, impoverished, and hopeless city, with a mixed, ignorant, corrupt, and bloodthirsty gang in control. It was flooded with lotteries, gambling dens and licensed brothels. Many of the city officials, as well as the police force, were thugs and murderers. Violence was rampant, and hardly a day passed that someone was not shot, out under the Oaks, in defense of his honor." [59]

There was a demand by business men for more railroads. The legislature granted charters and voted aid for construction. In the past, every railroad in the state had been built in this way. Ten years later, the Democratic legislature of 1878 granted $2,000,000 in bonds to aid in the building of a road to Shreveport, and the bill was signed by Governor Nichols.

A great deal of state indebtedness was represented by this attempt to promote railroad building, and in this attempt both parties were responsible for making the appropriations. The bill aiding the New Orleans, Mobile and Texas Railroad passed unanimously in a Senate composed of 21 Republicans and 9 Democrats, and in the House were 50 Republicans and 9 Democrats who voted for it, and only three members voted against it.[60]

In the bill incorporating the New Orleans, Baton Rouge and Vicksburg line, where the state assumed a liability of six million dollars, the introducer was a Democrat, and it passed unanimously in both Houses; the same thing was approximately true in five other cases, where the state assumed large financial responsibility.

The money which Warmoth raised did not go wholly or even perhaps mostly for public objects. He allowed all elements to feed at the public trough. Public debt and taxes mounted. Warmoth, his friends, and many of his enemies, began to get rich in the midst of the surrounding poverty. When he was approached about this, and bitter complaint made at the mounting costs of government, he had a suave and effective series of answers. First, he said that a great many of the members of the legislature were ignorant Negroes, and easily influenced by lobbyists, and that the men of the community ought to assist him in restraining them.

Then he turned around and reminded property holders and capitalists that many of the bills which the legislature was charged with passing corruptly were for the aggrandizement of individuals and corporations representing their "very best people." Their bank presidents and the best people of New Orleans were, he said, "crowding the lobbies of the legislature, continually whispering into these men's ears, bribes." [61] How was the state to be defended, he asked, against the interposition of these people who were potent in their influence in the community? It is apparent that Governor Warmoth understood the term "best people" to be synonymous with the term "richest people." He instanced the case of the five-million bond bill (to take up the city notes) which he had vetoed, which had been passed in the House over his veto.

"The bill went to the Senate. I walked into the Senate chamber and saw nearly every prominent broker of the city engaged in lobbying that bill through the Senate, and it was only by exposing the fact that one of their emissaries had come into this very chamber and laid upon the desk of my secretary an order for $50,000, that I was able to defeat it. Mr. Conway, the Mayor of your city, came here and offered me any consideration to induce me to sign this bill." [62] He also said that another Senator of New Orleans had offered him a bribe of $50,000, and a share of profits for his signature to the Nicolson Pavement Bill. [63]

It was not only the fact that unsuccessful jobbers had tried to bribe him, but that successful jobbers and prominent Southern men without reasonable doubt had bribed him and knew it. And their mouths were closely shut when it came to details and special instances of stealing.

Without a doubt many of the colored leaders shared in this graft, but from the very nature of the case it was not a large share. Many members of the legislature, white and black, were regularly paid small sums, but on the other hand, leaders like Dunn and Roundanez were incorruptible and lashed the thieves on all sides. Thomas G. Davidson of Livingston Parish, who had been a Democrat in the state since 1826, said: "That there was corruption in the legislature, no one doubts; but it was not confined to the Republicans alone." [64]

It was a colored man, W. F. Brown, who as State Superintendent of Education called attention in his report of 1873 to the way in which school funds were being stolen. New Orleans, as a legacy from Banks and the Freedmen's Bureau, was one of the few Southern states that had a system of public schools. In 1865, there were 141 schools for the freedmen, and 19,000 pupils. A school law had been passed in 1869, providing a system of public education without distinction of race or color. This system was not being carried out. W. F. Brown reported:

"Stolen in Carroll Parish in 1871, $30,000; in East Baton Rouge, $5,032; in St. Landry, $5,700; in St. Martin, $3,786.80; in Plaquemines, $5,855; besides large amounts in St. Tammany, Concordia, Morehouse and other parishes." [65] The entire permanent school funds of many parishes disappeared during this period.

Many colored voters tried to swing their vote so as to stop corruption, save the schools, and improve their economic condition; but if this was difficult in South Carolina and Mississippi, it was almost impossible in Louisiana, because there was so little choice between the parties aspiring to power.

Under these circumstances, it was exceedingly difficult for colored voters to know what to do. There is no question but that if the Negroes had been offered a chance to make their leadership effective in alliance with some party of social uplift, they would have followed it in large and increasing numbers. They would have become an honest and teachable electorate, and rapidly expelled most of their venal, careless, and dishonest fellows. But what could one choose between men like Warmoth, McEnery and Carter—a carpetbagger, a planter and a scalawag; a buccaneer, a slavedriver, and a plain thief?

The expenses of the Warmoth government increased to a total of $26,394,578 in four years and five months. The state debt was $10,099,074 in 1860, and $26,920,499 in 1865. Subtracting the Confederate debt, there was a total debt of $17,347,051 in 1868. This, in 1872, had increased to $29,619,473. Besides this, bonds voted but not yet issued would increase the real and contingent debt to $41,194,473.

The tax rate in 1864 was 3.75 mills; in 1869, 5.25 mills; in 1871, 14.5 mills, and in 1872, 21.5 mills. This expense was based on property valuation of $435,487,265 in 1860, which, with emancipated slaves, sank to $200,000,000 in 1865, and rose to $251,696,017 in 1870.

George W. Carter, the typical Louisiana scalawag, was a discovery of Warmoth, who maneuvered him into the legislature. He came to New Orleans soon after Warmoth was inaugurated. He was a Virginian, but had lived in Texas. He "was an apostatized preacher and ex-Confederate colonel, who [later] turned loyal patriot and anti-Warmoth leader." Carter was a man of education and polish, a good speaker, but an absolutely unscrupulous grafter. He was made Speaker of the House of Representatives in 1871, and became head of a ring proposing to control legislation that offered a chance for blackmail.

The history of Louisiana, from 1870 to 1876, reads like a Chinese puzzle to those who forget the great forces below. Beneath the witch's cauldron of political chicanery, it is difficult to remember the great dumb mass of white and black labor, the overwhelming majority of the citizens of Louisiana, groping for light, and seldom finding expression. Historians quite unanimously forget and ignore them, and chronicle only the amazing game of politicians.

Under the election laws of 1869, Warmoth secured control of Louisiana elections. The Governor, through the Returning Board which he appointed, could at his discretion throw out any votes anywhere in the state on any pretext. It was to no purpose, so far as results were concerned, that voters were intimidated, mobbed and killed. Consequently, the election of 1870 was unusually quiet.

Then, trouble began to brew. The colored men who formed the bulk of Warmoth's following were not willing to be simply his dumb followers. Led by Lieutenant-Governor Dunn, they began a revolt in the Republican convention of August, 1870.

The convention elected Dunn chairman; passed over Warmoth; and especially opposed a Constitutional amendment which would make the Governor eligible for reëlection. Warmoth took the stump, adroitly flattered the white planters, and eventually carried his amendment.

When the new legislature met in January, 1871, he faced a new dilemma. Several hundred colored men joined in a large meeting at the Louisiana Hotel to protest against his despotism. All the best elements of the state were arrayed against him, one wing of his own party and at least a part of the Negro population. In addition, economic conditions were crying for reform. The colored men nominated Pinchback for the term in the United States Senate, after the term of Harris expired March 4, 1871. At the same time, a brother-in-law of President Grant, Controller of Customs at New Orleans, also wanted to be Senator, and the President wanted him. Warmoth allowed a white planter to be elected. The result was that the Republican convention split in August, 1871, with Dunn at the head of one faction, and Warmoth at the head of the other.

While Warmoth was temporarily out of the state, Lieutenant-Governor Dunn discharged the duties of Governor, although Warmoth resented it. Some of the Democratic papers said that they preferred a "nigger" Governor to a carpetbagger. A state convention was called, and Dunn wrote to the leading colored Republicans:

"I write to you to ask of you your support and influence in behalf of the colored people. We have a great work before us, and in order to be successful we need the aid and coöperation of every colored man in the State. An effort is being made to sell us out to the Democrats by the Governor, and we must nip it in the bud. . . .

"I ask you to use your influence to elect good, honest men that will look out for the interests of the colored man, and not be duped by the money or the promises of Governor Warmoth, and above all do not elect as a delegate any of his officeholders, who being under obligations to him for position, will be compelled to support his policy." [66]

Warmoth retaliated by joining with the Democrats in depriving Lieutenant-Governor Dunn of his right to appoint committees in the Senate.

Dunn wrote Horace Greeley in 1871, after Greeley's visit South, and his strictures on carpetbaggers: "There are 90,000 voters in this state, 84,000 of whom are colored. In my judgment, a fair and untrammeled vote being cast, nineteen-twentieths of the Republican Party in the state, including a majority of the elective state officers and all of the Federal officers, with a few exceptions, are opposed to the administration of the present state executive. . . .

"We want for ourselves, and for the people of all parties, better laws on the statute-books, and better men to administer the same, and we are persuaded that neither of these wants will ever be met so long as the present executive exercises any material control over the politics of Louisiana. We are engaged in no strife of factions, but the people gravely and earnestly are fighting for their personal and political rights against the encroachments of impudent and unfaithful public servants. . . .

"Would you be greatly surprised, Mr. Greeley, to be informed that in the judgment of the good people of this state, irrespective of party, the young man who now occupies the executive chair of Louisiana, whose crimes against his party and his people you charitably ignore, and whose championship you so boldly assume, is preëminently the prototype and prince of the tribe of carpetbaggers, who seem to be your pet aversion." [67]

Just at this point, November 21, 1871, Oscar Dunn died, and the Louisiana Negroes lost an unselfish, incorruptible leader. This was Warmoth's chance, and he secured Pinchback's support, and at the same time avoided the contingency of having Carter, the scalawag, become Governor, by securing Pinchback's election as Lieutenant-Governor. This aroused another factional fight in the Republican Party for office and patronage, with the planters ready to take advantage of every opportunity, and the Negroes deprived of their leaders. Warmoth rode this storm until his following failed, when he adroitly leaped to the Liberal Republican revolt of the North, headed by Horace Greeley. When Chamberlain of South Carolina joined the Northern reform wave, he backed his move by excellent reform efforts, despite his dangerous and ultimately fatal alliance with disloyal planters. Warmoth had no program of reform.

On the other hand, scalawags like Carter joined the anti-Warmoth Republican faction and urged them to armed revolt. In came the United States troops, and down came a Congressional investigating committee and scored Warmoth.

The result was that in the campaign of 1872, Warmoth took 125 delegates, one-fifth of whom were colored, to the Cincinnati convention; this was the largest delegation that any state sent. This again was a shrewd move, because the Liberal Republicans were attacking graft and theft, both North and South, when this arch-grafter ranged himself on their side. Pinchback, under the advice of Sumner, was disposed to follow Warmoth into the Liberal Republican Party; but he was alienated when he saw that Warmoth, instead of leading a real third party movement, was about to surrender to the planters.

A curious campaign ensued. The reactionary Democrats nominated John McEnery, from one of the worst anti-Negro parishes of the state, where Negroes and white Republicans had been murdered by the dozens. No self-respecting colored man or liberal of any stamp could vote for him. On the other hand, there was a Reform Party, led by Beauregard, which displayed at its convention a placard: "Justice to all races, creeds and political opinions." [68] J. Sella Martin, the colored labor leader from the North, addressed this convention, and also Warmoth, who was working to have this movement and the Democrats unite with the Liberal Republicans. The Liberal Republicans nominated Penn for Governor, and a colored man, Dumas, for Secretary of State, while the regular Republicans nominated Kellogg and a colored man, Antoine.

Warmoth tried to get the reactionary Democrats and the Liberal Republicans to unite with McEnery and Penn as nominees, a colored man, Armistead, as Secretary of State, and Pinchback as Congressman-at-Large. Such a ticket Warmoth was sure would, with his power over the Returning Board, win, as he said, by thirty thousand majority. But the reactionary planters refused the coalition, and Warmoth capped the climax by surrendering to them completely, and backing McEnery. There was nothing for Pinchback to do but join the Grant Republicans. He said:

"It is well-known, as far as I am concerned, that I have no partiality for the Governor of the State; I have not stood at his back as one of the supporters or admirers of that distinguished gentleman. I am not a lover or worshiper of his." [69]

"If I thought we could secure a Republican government in Louisiana by supporting Mr. Greeley, I would support him; but after a careful observation, I tell you, fellow-citizens, if you wish a Republican government and the success of the Republican Party, you can only secure that under the Grant and Wilson ticket. Everybody knows how bitter I am against the custom-house and its party; but I tell you, my friends, if it is necessary to secure the success of the Republican Party, I will swallow it." [70]

All parties took great pains to assure the colored people that they would sustain and protect them in all their civil and political rights. The Reform Party, headed by General P. G. T. Beauregard, and other distinguished white men, with the written approval of several thousands of the best white citizens, declared:

"1. That henceforth we dedicate ourselves to the unification of our people.

"2. That by 'our people' we mean all men, of whatever race, color or religion, who are citizens of Louisiana, who are willing to work for her prosperity.

"3. That we shall advocate by speech, pen and deed, the equal and impartial exercise by every citizen of Louisiana of every civil and political right guaranteed by the Constitution and laws of the United States, and by the laws of honor, brotherhood and fair dealing.

"4. That we shall maintain and advocate the right of every citizen of Louisiana and of every citizen of the United States to frequent at will all places of public resort, and to travel at will on all vehicles or public conveyances, upon terms of perfect equality with any and every other citizen; and we pledge ourselves, so far as our influence, counsel and example may go, to make this right a live and practical right, and that there may be no misunderstanding of our views on this point:

"We shall further recommend that hereafter no distinction shall exist among citizens of Louisiana in any of our public schools, or state institutions of education, or in any other public institution supported by the State, City or Parish.

"We shall also recommend that the proprietors of all foundries, factories, and other industrial establishments, in employing mechanics or workmen, make no distinction between the two races." [71]

When the returns came in, Warmoth sought to count in McEnery, and immediately the opposition set up a rival Returning Board, and counted in Kellogg. They also got a United States judge to back them. Again, there was practically civil war, with two returning boards and two governments, until President Grant sent down United States soldiers and backed the Kellogg government.

The Louisiana elections of 1868, 1872, 1874 and 1876, were of one cloth: intimidation, fraud, open violence and murder, so that there was no real expression of public opinion. Three remedies were evident: first, a dictator working through a returning board; secondly, supervision of elections and repression of mob violence by the Federal government; thirdly, arming of the black militia.

Carpetbaggers were too corrupt and planters too selfish to be successful dictators. The nation recoiled at Federal supervision, not only in the drastic form proposed by Sheridan, but even in the milder form of supervised elections; finally, arms in the hands of the Negro aroused fear both North and South. Not that the Negroes could not and would not fight, for these same blacks, largely under their own officers, had beaten back Louisiana whites at Port Hudson and Milliken's Bend. But it was the silent verdict of all America that Negroes must not be allowed to fight for themselves. They were, therefore, dissuaded from every attempt at self-protection or aggression by their friends as well as their enemies.

Congress hesitated and refused to take action despite the pleas of President Grant. Under the law, he had no alternative but to use Federal troops to enforce the Reconstruction laws. The result was open war. Three times the soldiers restored to power Republican candidates who had been ousted from office by force and fraudulent elections. In retaliation, the planters murdered Negroes and Republicans in cold blood at Colfax, Coushatta and other places, and fought pitched battles in the streets of New Orleans. It was a humiliating and disgraceful situation. Kellogg attempted reforms, and succeeded in reducing the tax rate from 21 to 14 mills. But many parishes refused to pay taxes, and while the New Orleans Board of Trade and leading business men approved Kellogg's policy, his reforms could not go far. In fact, just as in South Carolina, there was nothing that Louisiana wanted less at that time than reform through Negro voters and Republican officeholders.

Evidently, the Negro voter, and even the office-holder, could not be held to blame for the anarchy and turmoil which are the history of Reconstruction in Louisiana. Practically, so-called Reconstruction in Louisiana was a continuation of the Civil War, with the Negro as pawn between the two forces of Northern and Southern capitalists. The

Northerners were determined to use the state for their own interest, but willing to admit universal suffrage under property control; while planters, united in secret organizations with poor whites, were determined to reduce the labor vote by disfranchising the Negro. Between these two forces, the Negro was victim and peon. His intelligent and sacrificing leadership was beaten back, deceived and ham-strung, and finally discredited by charging it with plans to "Africanize" Louisiana. The shrewd and venal and dishonest Negro elements were characterized as typical and used as an excuse for cheating and lawlessness by elements in the white population just as dishonest and much more influential. Back of this smoke screen lay the real charge, which was the attempt to subject this state so rich in raw materials, and so strategic for trade, to a dictatorship of labor, rather than an oligarchy of capitalists.

The panic of 1873 and the Democratic House elected to Congress in 1874 settled the matter. The Louisiana Democratic State Convention frankly called itself "we, the white people of Louisiana"; and a committee of Congress sent down to investigate revealed the new temper of the nation. One part of the committee was completely in favor of the planters, while the other part declared the White League an unscrupulous engine of fraud and murder.

The crucial election of 1876 came and with it came anarchy. As John Sherman and his fellows reported: "Organized clubs of masked, armed men, formed as recommended by the central Democratic committee, rode through the country at night, marking their course by the whipping, shooting, wounding, maiming, mutilation, and murder of women, children, and defenceless men, whose houses were forcibly entered while they slept, and, as their inmates fled, the pistol, the rifle, the knife and the rope were employed to do their horrid work. Crimes like these, testified to by scores of witnesses, were the means employed in Louisiana to elect a President of the United States."

The result was two sets of returns for presidential electors and for state offices, two governors and two legislatures. The whole nation waited on the outcome in Louisiana which would settle the presidential contest.

There followed an extraordinary period of negotiation, probably unparalleled in modern government. The white folk of Louisiana with threat of civil war entered into negotiations with the President and President-elect and arranged a filibuster of 116 Congressmen to prevent counting the electoral vote.

The Hayes party promised to work for the "material prosperity" of the South and allay sectional feeling. Nicholls and the legislature gave every assurance. They solemnly agreed not to deprive the Negro of any political or civil rights enjoyed by any other class and to educate white and black children with equal advantages. Finally the filibuster was dropped and the electoral count was finished March 2.

Hayes became President. An extra-legal commission went to Louisiana in April. By means of money furnished by the Louisiana Lottery Company and large business establishments, the Kellogg government was bribed to disband and the Nicholls legislature obtained a nominal quorum. On April 24, the Federal troops withdrew to their barracks and Louisiana was free for a new period of unhampered exploitation of the working classes.

In South Carolina, Mississippi and Louisiana, the proportion of Negroes was so large, their leaders of sufficient power, and the Federal control so effective, that for the years 1868-1874 the will of black labor was powerful; and so far as it was intelligently led, and had definite goals, it took perceptible steps toward public education, confiscation of large incomes, betterment of labor conditions, universal suffrage, and in some cases, distribution of land to the peasant.

Ignorant and vicious leadership, white and black, hindered and even stopped this progress, and gradually tended toward a duel between Northern and Southern capitalists to effect control of labor. This succeeded first in Louisiana, then in Mississippi, and finally in South Carolina. In each case, labor control passed into the hands of white Southerners, who combined with white labor to oust Northern capitalists.

> O twin of monarchy that lives to rob and kill,
> What deviltry here that prostitutes at will,
> That keeps a robber gang in kingly rights enthroned,
> Then turns their robberies to legal acts condoned?
> Is not the blood as pure of him who lives by toil
> As he who waxes fat—on idleness and spoil?
>
> L. S. OLLIVER

---

1. Garner, *Reconstruction in Mississippi*, p. 109, 111.
2. Garner, *Reconstruction in Mississippi*, p. 177.
3. Vicksburg *Herald*, Nov. 9, 1867; Garner, *Reconstruction in Mississippi*, p. 120.
4. Garner, *Reconstruction in Mississippi*, p. 277.
5. Garner, *Reconstruction in Mississippi*, p. 238.
6. Lynch, *The Facts of Reconstruction*, pp. 92-94.

7. Garner, *Reconstruction in Mississippi*, p. 280 (also footnote).
8. Lynch, *The Facts of Reconstruction*, pp. 33-35.
9. Lynch, *The Facts of Reconstruction*, p. 86.
10. Garner, *Reconstruction in Mississippi*, p. 286.
11. Garner, *Reconstruction in Mississippi*, p. 296 (footnote).
12. Garner, *Reconstruction in Mississippi*, p. 279.
13. Garner, *Reconstruction in Mississippi*, p. 285.
14. Lynch, *The Facts of Reconstruction*, p. 78.
15. Lynch, *The Facts of Reconstruction*, p. 75.
16. Garner, *Reconstruction in Mississippi*, p. 295.
17. Garner, *Reconstruction in Mississippi*, p. 320.
18. Lynch, *The Facts of Reconstruction*, pp. 88-89; Harris, Garner, *Reconstruction in Mississippi*, p. 322.
19. Garner, *Reconstruction in Mississippi*, p. 322.
20. Lynch, *The Facts of Reconstruction*, pp. 123, 124.
21. Lynch, *The Facts of Reconstruction*, pp. 114-115.
22. Brewster, *Sketches of Southern Mystery, Treason and Murder*, pp. 188-189.
23. Woodson, *Negro Orators and Their Orations*, p. 288.
24. Woodson, *Negro Orators and Their Orations*, p. 282.
25. Lynch, *The Facts of Reconstruction*, pp. 165-166.
26. Smedes, *Memorials of a Southern Planter*, p. 257.
27. Warmoth, *War, Politics and Reconstruction*, Appendix C, p. 272.
28. Warmoth, *War, Politics and Reconstruction*, Appendix B, p. 271.
29. Ficklen, *History of Reconstruction in Louisiana*, pp. 102-103.
30. Warmoth, *War, Politics and Reconstruction*, p. 275.
31. Warmoth, *War, Politics and Reconstruction*, p. 43.
32. Lonn, *Reconstruction in Louisiana*, p. 10 (cf. footnote).
33. Warmoth, *War, Politics and Reconstruction*, p. 270.
34. Warmoth, *War, Politics and Reconstruction*, p. 44.
35. Ficklen, *History of Reconstruction in Louisiana*, p. 168.
36. Warmoth, *War, Politics and Reconstruction*, p. 49.
37. Ficklen, *History of Reconstruction in Louisiana*, p. 185.
38. The New Orleans *Republican*, June 6, 1867.
39. Brewster, *Sketches of Southern Mystery, Treason and Murder*, p. 163.
40. Warmoth, *War, Politics and Reconstruction*, p. vii.
41. Warmoth, *War, Politics and Reconstruction*, pp. 53-54.
42. Official Journal of the Proceedings of the Convention for Framing a Constitution for the State of Louisiana, New Orleans, 1867-1868.
43. Lonn, *Reconstruction in Louisiana*, p. 9.
44. Perkins, *Who's Who in Colored Louisiana*, p. 63.
45. Lonn, *Reconstruction in Louisiana*, p. 93.
46. Perkins, *Who's Who in Colored Louisiana*, p. 49.
47. Perkins, *Who's Who in Colored Louisiana*, p. 58.
48. Lonn, *Reconstruction in Louisiana*, pp. 11-12.
49. Lonn, *Reconstruction in Louisiana*, p. 16.
50. Warmoth, *War, Politics and Reconstruction*, p. xii.
51. Ficklen, *History of Reconstruction in Louisiana*, p. 196.
52. Lonn, *Reconstruction in Louisiana*, p. 40.
53. Bulletin, February 17, 1869 (in Lonn, *Reconstruction in Louisiana*, pp. 40-41).
54. Warmoth, *War, Politics and Reconstruction*, p. 61.
55. Warmoth, *War, Politics and Reconstruction*, p. 64.
56. Warmoth, *War, Politics and Reconstruction*, p. 66.
57. Lonn, Map No. I.
58. Warmoth, *War, Politics and Reconstruction*, p. 79.
59. Warmoth, *War, Politics and Reconstruction*, p. 80.
60. Bragdon, *Facts and Figures, New Orleans*, 1871.
61. 42nd Congress, 2nd Session, House Reports II, No. 22, Part I, p. 202.
62. Lonn, *Reconstruction in Louisiana*, p. 68.

63. Cox, *Three Decades of Federal Legislation*, pp. 553-554.
64. Warmoth, *War, Politics and Reconstruction*, p. 168.
65. Herbert, *Why the Solid South*, p. 406.
66. Warmoth, *War, Politics and Reconstruction*, pp. 113-114.
67. Warmoth, *War, Politics and Reconstruction*, pp. 144-145.
68. Warmoth, *War, Politics and Reconstruction*, p. 180.
69. Senate Debates, 1879; Lonn, *Reconstruction in Louisiana*, p. 147.
70. Lonn, *Reconstruction in Louisiana*, p. 163.
71. Warmoth, *War, Politics and Reconstruction*, pp. 240-241.

XII. THE WHITE PROLETARIAT IN ALABAMA, GEORGIA, AND FLORIDA

How in those Southern States where Negroes formed a minority
there ensued strife between planters, poor whites, Negroes and
carpetbaggers which after varying forms of alliance finally ended
in the subjection of black labor

We have studied Reconstruction in three states where the preponderance of Negro population, and the political part which it played during Reconstruction, makes it fair to say that the Negro during part of the time exercised a considerable dictatorship over the state governments of South Carolina, Mississippi, and Louisiana. In these states, the material for studying the participation of the Negro in Reconstruction is large, although by no means complete.

We now come to states where the Negro population is large, but where from the beginning the political influence of the Negro was comparatively small.

In Virginia, North Carolina, Alabama, Georgia, Arkansas, Texas and the Border States, the interests of black labor were never in the ascendent; but from the first there was a battle between carpetbaggers and planters to control white and black labor. For a time, the ancient breach between planters and poor whites gave control to carpetbaggers and scalawags supported by Negroes. But war and poverty had depleted the old planter families; and some poor whites, eager for land and profits, and jealous of Negroes, came to join the planters. They gradually drove the carpetbaggers to the wall, and took forcible control of colored labor, with the help of the whole labor vote which they controlled. The carpetbaggers made the hardest fight in North Carolina, Alabama and Georgia.

Alabama had 85,451 whites when it entered the Union in 1820, and 42,450 Negroes. By 1860, there were 526,271 whites and 437,770 Negroes.

There was competition for appointment to the provisional governorship of Alabama, but Louis E. Parsons was appointed June 1, 1865. He called an election for a convention based on white suffrage. The convention in September admitted that "the institution of slavery has been destroyed in the State of Alabama." It adjourned September 30, and the legislature met November 20. This legislature adopted the

Thirteenth Amendment, "with the understanding that it does not confer upon Congress the power to legislate upon the political status of freedmen in this State." [1]

The Black Code adopted by the legislature was one of the most severe in the South. Most of these laws, however, were vetoed by Governor R. M. Patton, who saw the reaction in the North, and was trying to keep in careful touch with Washington. He warned the lawmakers that the Negro was at work, and that such severe legislation was not needed. Patton said with regard to these bills:

"I have carefully examined the laws which under this bill would be applied to the freedmen; and I think that a mere recital of some of these provisions will show the impolicy and injustice of enforcing it upon the Negroes in their new condition." [2]

The final code contained the usual provisions for vagrancy, apprenticeship, enticing labor, etc., but was drawn without obvious color discrimination, although there naturally was that in fact.

The chief characteristic of Reconstruction in Alabama was the direct fight for mastery between the poor whites and the planters. The poor whites of Alabama were largely segregated in the Northern part of the state. A correspondent of *The Nation,* who traveled among them in August, 1865, said: "They are ignorant and vindictive, live in poor huts, drink much, and all use tobacco and snuff; they want to organize and receive recognition by the United States government in order to get revenge—really want to be bushwhackers supported by the Federal government; they 'wish to have the power to hang, shoot, and destroy in retaliation for the wrongs they have endured'; they hate the 'big nigger holders,' whom they accuse of bringing on the war and who, they are afraid, would get into power again; they are the 'refugee,' poor white element of low character, shiftless, with no ambition." [3]

The poor whites won their first victory after the Constitution of 1865, when a law was passed providing for a census in 1866, and for apportionment of Senators and Representatives according to the white population. The delegates from the white counties of north and southeast Alabama voted in favor of this, and thirty white delegates from the Black Belt voted against it. This measure destroyed the political power of the Black Belt, and if the Johnson government had survived, the state would have been ruled by the white counties, instead of by the black counties.

The planters were thus thrown into involuntary alliance with Negro labor, and the matter of Negro suffrage was discussed. The planters were sure they could control the Negro vote, while the poor white merchants and farmers opposed Negro voters.

Brooks, once President of the Secession Convention of 1861, and a brother of Bully Brooks of South Carolina, who nearly killed Sumner, introduced a bill in the lower house providing for a qualified Negro suffrage, based on education and property. He represented Lowndes County in the Black Belt. This bill was indorsed by Governor Patton and Judge Goldthwaite, but there were two difficulties: first, the unbending opposition of the triumphant poor whites, and secondly, the suspicion of the planters themselves that their ability to dictate to the blacks was not so certain. The movement did not get far.

"From 1865 to 1868, and even later, there was for all practicable purposes over the greater part of the people of Alabama, no government at all. . . . From 1865 to 1874, government and respect for government were weakened to a degree from which it has not yet recovered. The people governed themselves extra-legally, and have not recovered from the practice." [4] In 1866 the Negroes held a convention in Mobile and complained of lawless aggression and the refusal of the legislature to receive their petitions.

There was continual fear of insurrection in the Black Belt. This vague fear increased toward Christmas, 1866. The Negroes were disappointed because of the delayed division of lands. There was a natural desire to get possession of firearms, and all through the summer and fall, they were acquiring shotguns, muskets, and pistols, in great quantities. In several instances, the civil authorities, backed by the militia, searched Negro houses for weapons, and sometimes found supplies which were confiscated.

The financial condition of Alabama was difficult. There was not only loss of slaves, destruction, and deterioration of property, but the cotton tax and war confiscation fell heavily on this cotton section. "The cotton spirited away by thieves and confiscated by the government would have paid several times over all the expenses of the army and the Freedmen's Bureau during the entire time of the occupation. Many times as much money was taken from the Negro tenant, in the form of this cotton tax, as was spent in aiding him." [5]

At the end of the war, at least five thousand Northern men were in Alabama engaged in trade and farming. They brought with them a good deal of capital, and since cotton was selling for 40¢ to 50¢ a pound, they naturally expected to make large profits. After the Reconstruction laws, these capitalists sought to control the labor vote. Encouraged by them, the Negroes called a convention in Mobile, which met in May, 1867. The convention declared itself in favor of the party of the new capitalists, and asked protection in their civil rights

and schools supported by a property tax. They declared that it was
the undeniable right of the Negro to hold office, sit on juries, ride
in public conveyances, and visit places of public amusement.

That same month, Senator Henry Wilson of Massachusetts made
a political speech in Montgomery to a great crowd of black and white
people. He made a plea for coöperation between whites and Negroes.
The Confederates objected that this would lead to a union of alien
capitalists and colored people, and the state thus would be taken out
of the control of natives. Later, May 14, when Judge Kelley of Pennsylvania tried to speak in Mobile, there was a race riot.

General Pope wrote in 1867 from Alabama:

"It may be safely said that the marvelous progress made in the education of these people, aided by the noble charitable contributions of
Northern societies and individuals, *finds no parallel in the history of
mankind*. If continued, it must be by the same means, and if the
masses of the white people exhibit the same indisposition to be educated that they do now, *five years will have transferred* intelligence
and education, so far as the masses are concerned, to the colored people of this District." [6] His district included Georgia, Florida, Alabama
and Mississippi.

In July, General Clanton formed the Conservative party of Alabama,
and knowing what this represented in reaction, there was a widespread desire among colored people around Montgomery to prevent
the meeting of this convention. A few leading colored people formed
themselves into a special committee, and resolved that they would "use
all the influence they may choose to counteract any acts of violence
to the convention." The result was that the meeting was held without
the fact being known that there was any movement against it.

In the election under the Reconstruction laws, 61,295 Negroes and
104,518 whites registered. But of the whites, only 18,533 voted in favor
of a convention. In the convention were 31 Northerners, of whom 18
were officials of the Freedmen's Bureau and 18 Negroes; the rest
were Southern whites. The Alabama Negroes had few educated leaders in their ranks and were, in the main, poor, ignorant field hands.

The Negro members of the convention are noted as follows: Ben
Alexander of Greene, field hand; John Carraway of Mobile, assistant
editor of the Mobile *Nationalist;* Thomas Diggs of Barbour, field
hand; Peyton Finley, formerly doorkeeper of the House; James K.
Green of Hale, a carriage driver; Ovid Gregory of Mobile, a barber;
Jordan Hatcher of Dallas, Washington Johnson of Russell, field
hand; L. S. Lathan of Bullock; Tom Lee of Perry, field hand, who
had a reputation for moderation; Alfred Strother of Dallas; and J. T.
Rapier of Lauderdale. Rapier was educated in Canada and was a man

of power. Several of his proposals are embodied in the present Constitution of Alabama.

Of these members, two were well educated, and one, Rapier, a national leader; about half could not write. Nevertheless their actions, their votes and their speeches, were encouraging. They were, as in practically all cases, conservative, and willing to follow leadership.

The debates touched the disfranchisement of Confederate leaders, mixed schools, and inter-marriage. Many white people at this time proposed to leave the state, but the elections of 1867 in the North encouraged them, especially the defeat of Negro suffrage in several states.

"The majority of the Scalawags were ready to revolt after finding that the carpetbag element had control of the Negro vote; the Negroes with a few exceptions made no unreasonable and violent demands unless urged by the carpetbaggers; the carpetbaggers, with a few extreme Scalawags, were disposed to resort to extreme measures of proscription in order to get rid of white leaders and white majorities, and to agitate the question of social equality in order to secure the Negroes, and to drive off the Scalawags." [7]

The debates on suffrage were long, and many took part. Duston White, formerly of Iowa, proposed that the new Constitution should admit former rebels to the ballot, but his resolution was voted down by a vote of 30 to 51. Some of the Negroes voted for it. Rapier proposed that the convention memorialize Congress to remove the political disabilities of those who might aid in Reconstruction, according to the plan of Congress. This was adopted, and Griffin, a radical member, was made chairman of the committee to make these recommendations.

The Majority Report of the committee did not wish to go beyond the acts of Congress in disfranchising former Confederates, but attempts were made to disfranchise all Confederates above the rank of captain, and all who held any civil office anywhere. Sisby wanted to exclude from suffrage those who had killed Negroes during the last two years, or opposed Reconstruction, or persuaded voters not to take part in the election.

It was finally settled that in addition to those disfranchised by the Reconstruction Acts, others should be excluded for violation of the rules of war. Such persons could neither register, vote, nor hold office, until relieved by the vote of the General Assembly, and until they had "accepted the civil and political equality of men."

"Lee, Negro, said that such a course would endanger the ratification of the Constitution and if the Negroes did not get their rights now, they would never get them. He wanted his rights at the court-house and at the polls and nothing more." [8]

The colored representative of Dallas County demanded that the Negroes be empowered to collect pay from those who held them in slavery at the rate of ten dollars per month for service rendered, from January 1, 1863, the date of the Emancipation Proclamation, to May 20, 1865. An ordinance to this effect was adopted by a vote of 53 to 31.

The scalawags, as a rule, wished to prohibit inter-marriage of the races, and Simple of Montgomery reported an ordinance to that effect. Carraway, a Negro, wanted life imprisonment for any white man marrying or living with a black woman, but he said it was against the civil rights bill to prohibit inter-marriage. Gregory, a Negro of Mobile, wanted all regulations, laws and customs wherein distinctions were made on account of color or race to be abolished.

Carraway succeeded in having an ordinance passed, directing that church property used during slavery for colored congregations be turned over to the latter. Some of the property was paid for by Negro slaves and held in trust for them by white trustees. Some of it had belonged to the planters, who had erected churches for the use of their slaves.

The Negro members demanded free schools and special advantages for the Negro, and a few carpetbaggers spoke of the malign influence of the old régime in keeping so many thousands in ignorance. The scalawags demanded separate schools for the races, but pressure was brought to bear, and most of them gave way. Sixteen of the native whites finally refused to sign the Constitution, and united in a protest against the action of the convention in refusing to provide separate schools.

The protest said that the Constitution agreed upon "tended to the abasement and degradation of the white population of the state," because it authorized mixed schools, and because the convention had refused to prohibit the inter-marriage of the races. The protest pointed out, as evidencing the degree in which leading white Republicans deferred to their colored colleagues, that "though the Judiciary Committee had *unanimously* reported a measure providing against amalgamation, yet the Convention tabled it; and *many members of the Committee, who had concurred in the report of the Committee,* receding from their position, voted to lay it on the table." [9]

The Constitution was adopted by the convention by a vote of 66-6, twenty-six not voting. Just before the convention adjourned, Carraway, a Negro, offered a resolution, which was adopted, stating that the Constitution was founded on justice, honesty, and civilization, and the enemies of law and order, freedom and justice, were pledged to prevent its adoption.

This Constitution was afterward repudiated by the convention of 1875, when the Negroes had been driven from political power. Nevertheless it was a more modern and democratic instrument than any of the preceding Constitutions of the state, and the new Constitution of 1875 retained many of its provisions.

On the first, second and third of February, 1868, the new Constitution was to be voted on. According to the Reconstruction Act, the adoption of the Constitution required a majority of the registered vote. A conference of Conservatives was held in Montgomery, January 1; it was decided that as many as possible should register, and then stay away from the polls. The time of voting was extended to five days; the Constitution received 70,812 affirmative votes and only 1,005 negative; yet this was not a majority of the registered vote, so that the plan of the Conservatives was successful. However, Congress changed the law so as to make a majority of the vote cast valid for adopting the Constitution, and thus declared it adopted. Alabama was admitted to the Union, June 25.

On July 13, the General Assembly convened. The Fourteenth Amendment was ratified, and William H. Smith elected Governor. The legislature held three sessions during 1868, on July 13, September 16, and November 2. There were twenty-six Negroes in the House and one in the Senate. One of the first things that the legislature did by means of the Negro votes was to relieve the disabilities of those disfranchised by the state Constitution. In 1869, a general state system of schools was put into operation, and the private schools of Mobile merged into the system. November 25, the Fifteenth Amendment was ratified.

At the beginning of the Reconstruction government, the debt of the state was $8,355,683. At the first session of the legislature there was no important legislation, but at the second session of the legislature, the previous custom of Alabama, of aiding railroads, was taken up, and the aid increased from $12,000 to $16,000 a mile. The argument was that under the old law capitalists had not been attracted, but that now they would come in. Under this law, there was a good deal of waste of money through railroads failing to complete building for which they had been paid.

These railroad acts were adopted by votes of men of both parties; the first by the Democratic provisional legislature of 1867, and those of 1868-1879 by the Republicans; additional aid to one railroad was opposed and many charges of corruption made.

Railroad building increased in Alabama. In 1860, there were 743 miles; in 1867, 851 miles. In 1871-1872, 1,697 miles were completed, with other lines in construction. The cost of the miles completed, with equipment, was over $60,000,000.

One peculiarity of the dispute about railroad legislation during Reconstruction is that money secured on the credit of the state was controlled and spent very largely by Southern men. The question, therefore, of the liability of the states in the future to pay such of these debts as the railway corporations did not pay, was really, in most cases, a question as to how far Southern people were going to conduct railroads so as to pay debts owed their own state. Thus the large contingent railway debts of North Carolina, South Carolina, Alabama and Georgia, would not have been debts at all if Southern people had handled investments efficiently and wisely. Yet their failure to do this enabled them to make the charge of extravagance against the carpetbaggers all the greater.

Election for Governor and for the Lower House in the legislature was held in November, 1870. Lindsay, a Democrat, was elected in November, and after some contest with the Republican incumbent, was seated. His administration was admittedly not a success, and there was as much railroad graft as ever. In 1872, Lewis, a Republican, was elected, but two bodies, one Democratic and the other Republican, both claimed to be the legislature of the state. The Democrats met at the State House, and the Republicans at the United States Court House. Both appealed to the President, and December 11, 1872, the President submitted an unofficial plan for compromise. The Republicans finally secured a majority in both Houses.

In 1874, the debt, including railroad bonds, amounted to $25,503,593. There were conflicts between whites and blacks during the election, but the Democrats carried all the state officers, and had majorities in both Houses of the legislature. A new Constitution was adopted; the number of officers was cut down and the salaries; and the school funds were seriously curtailed, and the system weakened.

The Ku Klux Klan was rampant in Alabama. In one district, six churches were burned by incendiaries before the election of 1870. Many schoolhouses were burned. Between 1868 and 1871, there were 371 cases of violence, including 35 murders.

The planters and poor whites after their first enmity early made alliance in Alabama, and their concentrated social weight descended on whites who dared to vote with the blacks. Such persons were warned and attacked until they fled the state or made peace with the new masters. Later, Northern capital poured into the poor white belt to develop coal and iron. Convict labor was widely used and exploitation developed, with labor divided by race, and helpless.

" 'It is absolutely essential,' declared a great Negro convention in Montgomery, December, 1874, 'to our protection in our civil and political rights that the laws of the United States shall be enforced so as to compel respect and obedience for them. Before the state laws and state courts, we are utterly helpless.' The force acts were failing, and to the Negro, the question presented by the failure of their execution was whether his constitutional rights as a citizen were to be 'a reality or a mockery; a protection and a boon, or a danger and a curse'; whether they were to be 'freemen in fact or only in name'; whether the last two amendments to the Constitution were to be 'practically enforced,' or to become nullities, and stand only as dead letters on the statute books." [10]

The state of Georgia had, in 1790, 52,886 whites and 29,662 Negroes. The increase was rapid, but fairly uniform up until 1850, when there were 384,613 Negroes and 521,572 whites. In 1860, this had increased to 465,698 Negroes and 591,550 whites. There were, in 1860, 3,500 free Negroes in the state.

The assets of the state of Georgia in 1860 included $600,000,000 of taxable property, besides stock in banks and railroads amounting to about $800,000. The state debt in 1861, including nearly $15,000,000 worth of currency, came to a total of $18,035,775. Georgia lost forty thousand of its white population during the war.

Georgia clung to slavery. Howell Cobb wrote in June, 1865: "The institution of slavery, in my judgment, provided the best labor system that could be devised for the Negro race." [11] He had his capital invested in thousands of Negroes and hundreds of acres of land in middle and southwestern Georgia.

In 1866, there was a sufficient migration of Negroes from Georgia to the West to cause some alarm. The Georgia Land and Immigration Company was formed in 1865 to encourage white immigrants. It was not successful. Some who came demanded better wages and were dissatisfied with the food. The project was given up.

By May, 1866, 1,200 citizens of Georgia had received special pardons from the President under the $20,000 exemption clause, and as early as 1865 and 1866, there was evident in Georgia a transition of leadership from the old landed aristocracy to the new commercial class.

In June, James Johnson, a lawyer of Columbus, was appointed Provisional Governor of Georgia, instead of Joshua Hill, who had been strongly urged, and had urged himself. Former Governor Brown had summoned the State Legislature, acting on the assumption that the state was already restored. The State Legislature was prevented from assembling by military order, and Brown resigned the Governorship. He had, however, great influence with Andrew Johnson, and "may have been one of the influences that changed Johnson from severe to moderate measures toward the rebels."[12]

Elections for the Convention were held in October, 1865. Nearly three hundred delegates assembled at Milledgeville, of whom the great majority were insignificant men. They were "a conservative body, unprogressive, mostly old men and rising politicians."[13]

This convention repealed but refused to nullify the ordinance of secession, and abolished slavery with the proviso that "this acquiescence in the action of the Government of the United States, is not intended to operate as a relinquishment, waiver or estoppel of such claim for compensation or loss sustained by reason of the emancipation of his slaves, as any citizen of Georgia may hereafter make upon the justice and magnanimity of that government."[14] The Convention adjourned and in the November election C. J. Jenkins was elected Governor, after Alexander Stephens and former Governor Brown had refused to be candidates. The legislature convened in Milledgeville in December, 1865, and elected two leading former Confederates, Alexander Stephens and H. V. Johnson, as Senators. President Johnson wanted Governor Johnson, and Joshua Hill greatly desired the place. The New York *Times* regretted that two men had been selected apparently because of their prominence in the rebellion.[15]

The first work of the legislature was a series of eleven laws which formed the Black Code. Georgia, however, under ex-Governor Brown's advice, was more careful than the other states, and listened to the storm of criticism against the other black codes.

The Black Code contained an apprentice law in the usual form; a vagrancy law with heavy penalties; various alterations in the penal laws, and laws about the "enticing" of labor. Civil rights were established for Negroes, giving them the right to testify in courts, but only where colored people were concerned. Every colored child hereafter born was declared the legitimate child of his mother and also of his *colored* father, if acknowledged by that father.[16]

Alexander Stephens suggested extending the franchise to the Negro, after he had reached a certain cultural standard and acquired an amount of wealth, but no one paid the slightest attention to this proposal. The Fourteenth Amendment was rejected in 1866 unanimously in both Houses.

In the summer of 1867, Toombs suddenly returned from Europe, where he had been hiding. He declared: "I regret nothing in the past, but the dead and the failure; and I am ready today to use the best means I can command to establish the principles for which I fought."[17]

The Negro early began to organize. Meetings were held in Macon and in Savannah, and a particularly large convention was assembled in Augusta, in 1866, before the Reconstruction legislation. There were over 100 delegates from 18 counties. James Porter was elected President, and the convention went on record as not asking universal suffrage, but advocating property and educational tests as qualifications for the right to vote. It appointed a board to look after the education of the Negroes within the state, and finally formed itself into a body to be called the Equal Rights Association of Georgia. The platform of the Association sought to inculcate principles of honesty, industry and sobriety among Negroes, and a kindly feeling toward former masters. Negroes were advised to work hard, to learn to read and write, and to buy homes.

There were two other important resolutions passed: one, that the coast lands held by Negroes were not to be regarded as territories, and that land was not to be confiscated from its owners; the other, that the Georgia legislature should give equal rights to Negroes before the Courts.[18]

Another meeting was held in Macon, March 26, 1867, two months after the Reconstruction Acts. The Macon *Telegraph* carried a long account of this gathering. The meeting was to be held at the Second Colored Baptist Church, but this was not large enough, and it convened in a grove near Rose Hill cemetery. Here a huge platform was erected for the speakers, Federal officials and school teachers. There were speeches by white and colored men, and the procession carried banners. On one banner was the inscription: "As we have got to live and vote together in one state, let us be friends."[19]

This was followed by another meeting in Savannah. On the platform were ex-Governor Johnson, several army officers, and three colored men. Ex-Governor Johnson was made President. Five resolutions were passed recognizing the power of Congress, the enfranchisement of colored people, the education of the whole people as of the highest importance, and early registration and election for the convention.[20]

The last of this series of meetings was held in Augusta with an attendance of one thousand people. Again ex-Governor Johnson was the principal speaker; but the meeting was not quite as harmonious as the former meetings. In the other meetings, there had been evidently a careful attempt to reconcile the desires of the white and colored people. But in this meeting, the wishes of the colored people were more frankly expressed. The resolutions asked for equal political rights and the abolition of corporal punishment. White papers reported that "many intelligent colored men disapproved of the spirit of the resolutions," but this was evidently white propaganda.[21]

When the military reconstruction of Georgia was ordered by General Pope, Governor Jenkins went to Washington to seek an injunction before the Supreme Court on the part of the state of Georgia against the Secretary of War, General Grant, and General Pope. His petition was dismissed May 13 for want of jurisdiction.

Later, the Governor returned to Washington, carrying the Great Seal of the state and about $400,000 in cash which disappeared. He filed a Bill of Complaint in the Supreme Court, against General Grant, General Meade, and others, for illegal seizure of the property of the state, and again asked for an injunction but was unsuccessful. General Pope gave Negroes the right to serve on juries in August, and in January, he was removed by President Johnson, and General Meade substituted.

In the registration under the Reconstruction laws, 93,457 Negroes registered and 95,214 whites. This meant that the whites were registering in spite of the advice of leading men like Ben Hill. Joseph Brown, on the other hand, counseled the whites not to let the new-comers and Negroes sweep on to victory unopposed, and Brown's advice was evidently followed. Notwithstanding this, 24,000 Negroes were persuaded or intimidated into not voting, and 60,000 whites did not take part.

While it is often stated that the great mass of white people were debarred by the Reconstruction Acts, it is notable in Georgia that the average vote, before the war, was 102,585, while the registration of whites was 95,214. Thus those debarred from registering were estimated at between 7,000 and 10,000.

The convention met in Atlanta on December 9, 1867, and sat until the middle of March, 1868. Of the 169 delegates to the convention, 37 were Negroes, 9 were white carpetbaggers, and 12 Conservative whites. The great majority, then, were native whites. This convention therefore was not controlled by carpetbaggers and Negroes, but by native whites. A reporter of the Savannah *News,* December 14, 1867, declared that "the Negroes in the convention appeared well-dressed and well-behaved, with few exceptions." [22]

The convention was interested in suffrage, qualifications for office-holding, relief, and a liberal Constitution. In these matters, Negroes took active part in the discussions, and used their political privilege intelligently, and with caution.

Among the most capable colored members of this meeting were Aaron A. Bradley, Tunis George Campbell, J. B. Costin and Henry McNeal Turner. Bradley was a fighter, and attacked both Democrats and Republicans when they tried to coerce the Negroes. He was, therefore, given much publicity as a dangerous and undesirable Negro, who would cause trouble.

Bradley had a colorful and eventful career and was a man of great eloquence, and the Negroes could not be made to lose confidence in him. He attacked racial discrimination on public carriers, and requested the General in command to have the jails and prisons examined so as to release persons unlawfully deprived of their liberties. Bradley left the convention because of charges that he had deceived Negroes on an island off the coast of Savannah. As a matter of fact, he was trying to protect their land, and they had so much confidence in him that they sent him back as Senator in 1888.[23]

Turner was the most prominent of the Negroes. He was born in South Carolina in 1833 and was appointed Chaplain in the army by President Lincoln. He was a preacher in the African M. E. Church, of which he eventually became Bishop. In 1865, he was appointed to the Freedmen's Bureau in Georgia. He traveled over the whole state, and when he became a part of the Republican organization in 1867, was well-known for his speeches in all parts of Georgia.

Turner was not liked by the whites. The Atlanta *Intelligencer* called him an "unscrupulous fellow, shrewd enough to deceive the poor, deluded Negro." He had to withstand all sorts of attempts to involve him in difficulties. He said that the whites accused him "of every crime in the catalogue of villany; I have even been arrested and tried on the wildest and most groundless accusations ever distilled from the laboratory of hell." He was acquitted, however, in every case.[24]

Turner, nevertheless, sought to win the confidence of the Conservatives. He tried to prevent the sale of property on which owners were unable to pay taxes; and he introduced a resolution for the relief of banks. Both these passed the convention. He desired civil rights, but did not wish the downfall of the aristocracy. There was enthusiasm in his efforts to secure pardon for Jefferson Davis. He tried to secure internal improvements by state action rather than by private companies. As a member of the education committee, he sought to insert provisions that five years after the common school system had come into full operation, no person on becoming 21 years of age should vote, unless he possessed an educational qualification.

Another Negro leader was Tunis Campbell. He was born in Massachusetts, and came South as an agent of the Freedmen's Bureau. He first established himself on an island off the coast of Savannah, where he established his own government, and armed force was necessary to remove him. He then went to Darien, where he acquired wide control over the Negroes, and virtually ruled them. In the Constitutional Convention, he was particularly interested in relief, seeking unsuccessfully to abolish imprisonment for debt.[25]

The convention prohibited slavery, established a single citizenship without discrimination, and gave the right to vote to all males born or naturalized in the United States and resident in Georgia six months. In laying down qualifications for voters, it was said especially that all voters should be eligible to office. This stipulation was afterward stricken out by an almost unanimous vote on the ground that it was unnecessary. This was probably a trick engineered by ex-Governor Brown for election purposes, and was the basis of the subsequent expulsion of colored men from the legislature.

In the Constitution, a general system of education free to all children of the state was provided. There was no attempt to disqualify Confederates for office, beyond the demands of the Reconstruction Acts.

The convention devoted much of its efforts at first toward relief from taxes, foreclosures, executions for debt, etc.

On April 20, 1868, the Constitution was adopted by a majority of 17,699 votes, and Rufus B. Bullock was elected Governor. Bullock is usually classed as a carpetbagger; but he had lived in Georgia before the war, and served as an officer in the Confederate army.

In the election of 1868, the Democratic Conservatives attacked the Constitution because they claimed that it established social, political and educational equality of whites and blacks, and that it would result in depreciation of property and a fearful increase of taxation. They declared it was framed by adventurers, convicts, and ignorant Negroes.

Both parties appealed to the poor whites, the Conservatives through race prejudice and the Republicans by class prejudice. One of the latter appeals was:

"Be a man! Let the slave-holding aristocracy no longer rule you. Vote for a constitution which educates your children free of charge; relieves the poor debtor from his rich creditor; allows a liberal homestead for your families; and more and more than all, places you on a level with those who used to boast that for every slave they were entitled to three-fifths of a vote in congressional representation. Ponder this well before you vote." [26]

The result of the election was mixed, but the Conservative Democrats had seventeen of the forty-four members of the Senate, and eighty-eight of the 170 members of the House. There was evidence of fraud and intimidation of the Negroes in many counties where the Negroes were in the majority, and the electoral vote of the state was given to Seymour. In this legislature, three Negroes were elected to the Senate, and twenty-nine to the House.

Bullock was installed as Governor, June 28, but he complained to the Military Commander that many men ineligible to office under the Fourteenth Amendment were seated in the legislature. The legislature investigated, but finally found none ineligible.

The Fourteenth Amendment was ratified July 21. Georgia was duly restored to the Union by the Omnibus Bill, passed by Congress, June 25, 1868. Military authority was withdrawn. Seven Congressmen from Georgia were seated in the House, but the Senators were elected too late to take their seats before Congress adjourned.

Just as soon as Congressional power was withdrawn, the Georgia legislature turned upon its Negro members, of whom there were three in the Senate, and twenty-nine in the House. "Their presence was an offense." [27]

Former Governor Brown had maintained during the campaign that Negroes were not eligible to office, and the Conservatives immediately took up the question, citing ex-Governor Brown's opinion, and asking investigation. Led by Milton Candler, a white Democratic Senator, a movement was started to declare that since Negroes were not citizens, they could not hold office. There was long and heated discussion. Bradley, one of the black Senators, argued forcibly and ably in the Senate on the Negro's eligibility, and after his speech, it was moved that Candler's resolutions be expunged from the minutes.

Later Bradley's own eligibility to his seat was attacked because of an alleged previous criminal conviction in New York. A majority of a special committee (all white men) sustained the accusation, but a minority declared that the evidence was incomplete. Nevertheless, Bradley was not allowed to defend himself, and resigned. Thereupon in September, the effort was continued to declare Campbell and Wallace, the other two colored Senators, ineligible. The Negroes were given one hour for defense. After vigorous debate, the three colored Senators were expelled by a vote of 24-11.

The following protest was sent in by Wallace and Campbell: "We claim to be the legally elected representatives of a very large portion of—nearly one-half of—the legal electors of the State of Georgia. Sirs, the Constitution and the laws of Georgia strictly provide that no laws shall be made or enforced which shall abridge the privileges or immunities of citizens of the United States, or of this state, or deny to any person within its jurisdiction the equal protection of its laws.

"Therefore, in behalf of ourselves, our constituents, and also in behalf of nearly five hundred thousand loyal citizens of this State, we do enter our solemn protest against the illegal, unconstitutional, unjust and oppressive action of this body, based upon the resolutions of the Senator from the 35th Senatorial District, declaring us ineligible on account of color." [28]

In the House, the resolution was introduced in August, and passed in September by a vote of 83-23. The Negroes refused to vote. Four of the colored members, who were so white that their Negro blood could not be proven, were permitted to remain. They were Beard, Belcher, Davis and Fyall.

Turner made an elaborate defense of the right of the Negro to hold office:

"Cases may be found where men have been deprived of their rights for crimes and misdemeanors; but it has remained for the State of Georgia in the very heart of the Nineteenth Century, to call a man before the bar and there charge him with an act for which he is no more responsible than for the head which he carries upon his shoulders. The Anglo-Saxon race, sir, is a most surprising one. No man has ever been more deceived in that race than I have been for the last three weeks. I was not aware that there was in the character of that race so much cowardice, or so much pusillanimity. . . .

"The Negro is here charged with holding office. Why, sir, the Negro never wanted office. I recollect that when we wanted candidates for the Constitutional Convention, we went from door to door in the 'Negro belt,' and begged white men to run. Some promised to do so; and yet, on the very day of election, many of them first made known their determination not to comply with their promises. They told the black men, everywhere, that they would rather see *them* run; and it was this encouragement of the white men that induced the colored man to place his name upon the ticket as a candidate for the Convention. In many instances, these white men voted for us. . . .

"It is very strange, if a white man can occupy on this floor *a seat created by colored votes,* and a black man cannot do it. Why, Gentlemen, it is the most short-sighted reasoning in the world. . . .

"If Congress has simply given me merely sufficient civil and political rights and made me a mere political slave for Democrats, or anybody else—giving them the opportunity of jumping on my back in order to leap into political power—I do not thank Congress for it. Never, so help me God, shall I be a political slave. . . . You have all the elements of superiority upon your side; you have our money and your own; you have our education and your own; and you have our land and your own, too. We, who number hundreds of thousands in Georgia, including our wives and families, with not a foot of land to call our own—strangers in the land of our birth; without money, without education, without aid, without a roof to cover us while we live, nor sufficient clay to cover us when we die! It is extraordinary that a race such as yours, professing gallantry, chivalry, education, and superiority, living in a land where ringing chimes call child and sire to the Church of God—a land where Bibles are read and Gospel truths are spoken, and where courts of justice are presumed to exist; it is extraordinary, I say, that with all these advantages on your side, you can make war upon the poor defenseless black man." [29]

This speech was not printed in the minutes of the legislature, but issued as a pamphlet in Augusta the same year.

In September, 1868, the legislature declared all colored members ineligible, and it then proceeded to put in their seats the persons who had received the next largest number of votes. The outrages of the Ku Klux Klan on Negroes and whites became widespread. Bullock protested and appealed to Congress, citing that members of the legislature had not all taken the test oath. Bullock's letter was accompanied by the memorial of the convention of colored people held in Macon in October.

The Republicans brought the case to the state Supreme Court in June, 1869. Two of the three judges decided that the Negroes were eligible. Immediately there came the question as to whether this decision affected the legislature. Alexander Stephens and many others thought it did not.

Negroes immediately began a movement to reseat their members. A closed convention was held at Macon with 136 delegates, many of whom walked from ten to forty miles to attend the meeting. The *Constitution* said that there were "venomous" and "incendiary" speeches, but these largely unlettered men went about to do their work of recovery of their privileges in extraordinarily practical ways. Eighty-two counties were represented, and Turner presided. Reports of outrages and conditions were brought together and sent to Congress. Turner and Sims went to carry the report and relate their hardships before the Committee on Reconstruction. [30]

There was a disposition in Georgia to stand firm and not to reseat the Negroes. Several papers advised the Assembly to persist in the attitude which it had adopted, and to reseat the Negroes only under compulsion. In spite of such advice, Nelson Tift, Democratic Representative-elect to Congress, from the Second District, had pledged certain parties in Washington that Georgia would reseat the colored members and ratify the Fifteenth Amendment, if Congress would not interfere. This rumor ruined Tift's chance for a seat in Congress, for the Democrats said that they had not granted him such power and never would do so, for they did not intend to reseat the Negroes, unless Congress should use force. [31]

Joshua Hill, one of the Senators elected by the Georgia legislature in July, presented his credentials to the United States Senate, December 7, 1868. It was recommended that Hill be not admitted on the ground that Georgia had failed to comply with the Omnibus Act.

In the House of Representatives, the Committee on Reconstruction was instructed to examine public affairs in Georgia; they took testimony during January, 1869, hearing Governor Bullock, James Sims, a colored preacher, H. M. Turner, and others. The lawlessness in the treatment of blacks was emphasized, there being 260 cases of outrages between January and November. Meantime, there was a grave question as to whether Georgia's vote could be cast in the Presidential election of 1868. It was finally decided that if Georgia's vote did not effect the result, the final vote should be announced in two ways, with and without the vote of Georgia.

On a technicality, the members of the lower house who had already been representing Georgia were excluded, as not entitled to sit in the 41st Congress. Several bills concerning Georgia were introduced into Congress. Finally, in March, 1869, when Georgia refused to ratify the Fifteenth Amendment, a bill was passed making the ratification of the Fifteenth Amendment necessary before Georgia was admitted. The testimony as to the lawlessness in Georgia helped the passage of this bill, which became a law December 27, 1869. Georgia thus came again under military authority, and all persons elected to the legislature were called to meet in special session by General Meade. A legislature convened January 10, and the test oath was administered under military supervision.

This legislature ratified the Fourteenth and Fifteenth Amendments, and not only recognized the twenty-four colored members, but paid them for lost time. There was thus a double expense for the salary of members that year, since both sets of members were paid, the white members on the motion of a colored Senator.

There was a question as to how long members of this legislature, originally elected in 1869, but stopped by the expulsion of colored members, should hold office; and many attempts were made to bribe members of the legislature to secure their votes for and against prolonging their terms.

Georgia members were admitted to the 3rd session of the 41st Congress, and Georgia entered her third and final stage of Reconstruction, January 10, 1870. The one colored Congressman from Georgia, Jefferson Long (1869-1871), opposed removing Confederate disabilities. Speaking in the House, he said, February 1, 1871:

"What do those men say? Before their disabilities are removed, they say: 'We will remain quiet until all of our disabilities are removed, and then we shall again take the lead.' Why, Mr. Speaker, in my state since emancipation there have been over five hundred loyal men shot down by the disloyal men there, and not one of those who took part in committing those outrages has ever been brought to justice. Do we, then, really propose here today, when the country is not ready for it, when those disloyal people still hate this government, when loyal men dare not carry the 'Stars and Stripes' through our streets, for if they do they will be turned out of employment, to relieve from political disability the very men who have committed these Ku Klux outrages? I think that I am doing my duty to my constituents and my country, when I vote against any such proposition. . . ." [62]

The parties in Georgia were now three: the Conservatives, who represented the former planters; the scalawags and carpetbaggers, or Radicals, who stood together as a commercial, capitalistic group; and a moderate group who held the balance of power.

The legislature of 1868 was evenly divided between Conservatives and Radicals in the Senate, but the House had a majority of the Conservatives, and after the exclusion of colored members, the Conservatives had a majority in both, 25-19 in the Senate, 127-48 in the House. When the legislature was reorganized in 1870, the Radicals had a majority in both Houses, 27-17 in the Senate, 87-83 in the House. In the election of 1871, the Moderates threw their power to the Conservatives; and the combination gained two-thirds of the seats.

Negroes in the Georgia legislature introduced numbers of bills. Senator Campbell not only introduced bills for education, but on the jury system, in regard to churches, concerning the city government of Savannah and of Reidville, on pleading and practice in the courts, and on better government of cities and towns. Most of these were reported back by the various committees with recommendations that they pass.

The number of Negro members was reduced to 26 by the death of Representative Lumpkin, of Macon County. He had spoken little but his vote could be counted on always for worthy bills. Although several of the members of the General Assembly, 1868-1870, had died, in no case was the resolution of eulogy so pronounced as that concerning Lumpkin: "We cheerfully record our appreciation of his modest worth, his integrity as a man, a citizen and a Representative." [33]

Turner introduced the following bills:

"To establish a state police; to secure chaplains for convicts; to enforce an act donating lands to the Georgia State Orphan's Home; to amend the Constitution of Georgia so as to enable females to vote; to appropriate the State Capitol and the Governor's mansion, at Milledgeville, to educational purposes; to repeal an act to amend the several acts now in force, regulating the fees of magistrates and constables in the State of Georgia, so far as relates to the counties of Bibb, Richmond, Monroe and Lee, and to provide for the mode of collecting the same, approved January 22, 1852; and the several acts amendatory thereof, and to prescribe the costs in insolvent cases due magistrates and constables in this state; to add an additional section to the 9th division of the Penal Code; also, a bill declaring certain persons husband and wife." [34]

Turner's resolution extending sympathy to the inhabitants of Richmond, Virginia, who had just suffered a terrible disaster, was adopted by the House.

The Negroes in the General Assembly seem to have had a special interest in correcting the methods of maintaining and managing the penitentiary of this state. Representative Turner offered several resolutions for reform in the system.

This penitentiary system began to characterize the whole South. In Georgia, at the outbreak of the Civil War, there were about 200 white felons confined at Milledgeville. There were no Negro convicts, since under the discipline of slavery, Negroes were punished on the plantation. The white convicts were released to fight in the Confederate armies. The whole criminal system came to be used as a method of keeping Negroes at work and intimidating them. Consequently there began to be a demand for jails and penitentiaries beyond the natural demand due to the rise of crime.

Federal officials began the custom of leasing the convicts to private persons for work. This system was extended by Bullock, who leased 500 victims to a firm of contractors. The legislature of 1871 confirmed this lease, and in 1876, the Democrats hastened to order a twenty-year lease of convicts, which began the horrible system of convict leasing, and gave to the state a profit in crime, not to mention the vast profits which came to the private contractors.

Naturally, then, the colored members of the legislature, even before this system was settled, were interested in securing better conditions for convicts. Senator George Wallace and Representative James Sims served on a joint committee from the Senate and the House respectively, to ascertain the number of inmates, and how they were treated. Peter O'Neal offered a bill for the abolishment of the penitentiary system.

As a result of this movement, changes were made in the drastic methods used to punish convicts. This amelioration led to the issuing of many pardons, for which the Bullock administration was severely criticized.

The most energetic Negro on the standing committee on penitentiary investigation was Representative J. M. Sims of Chatham

County. He had spoken only twice in 1868. On his return to the General Assembly in 1870, Sims offered many bills:

"To amend an act for the more efficient preservation of peace and good order on election days in this State; to repeal an act prohibiting the sale and purchase of agricultural products in the counties of Lowndes and Macon; to incorporate the Chatham Mercantile, Loan and Trust Company; to repeal the act passed in 1869 to encourage immigration into this state; to repeal the local laws of Savannah and Chatham County, so far as relates to the fees and costs of Justices of the Peace, Notaries, ex-officio Justices and Constables in criminal cases and warrants; to provide for the re-opening of the books of registration by the Clerk of the Common Council of the city of Savannah." [35] Two of these bills passed; the last two were indefinitely postponed.

Representative Porter was prominent. He "was born in Charleston, South Carolina, of free parents. Before the war he was a member of the Underground Railroad, and he opened a secret school in his home. He was a music teacher and tailor by trade. In 1856 he had won some distinction in music, which led the Bishop of the Episcopal Church in Savannah to have him to come there to train a choir for the Saint Stephens Episcopal Church. . . . After the war between the States, Porter opened an eight-grade private school, and later on, he was called to be the principal of the first Negro public school in Savannah. He left this position to become the first principal in the public school of Thomasville, Georgia. While there, he published his first book, 'English Grammar for Beginners.' Finally, he became principal of a school in Yazoo, Mississippi." [36] Porter was especially prominent in the Negro conventions which preceded the state conventions of 1867.

Jefferson Long was sent to Congress from Georgia. He was born in Crawford County in 1836; educated himself, and went into business as a merchant tailor in Macon, Georgia. He was elected a Representative from Georgia to the Forty-first Congress, by a majority of nine hundred over Lawton, a Democrat. He was admitted to his seat January 16, 1871.

The record of the Negro in the Georgia legislature is creditable, and yet Clark Howell afterwards declared Negro members of this legislature were "unlettered," ignorant politicians, who seemed a "stack of puppets and harlequins of a menagerie."

Outrages and guerrilla warfare against Negroes were widespread in Georgia. General Lewis of the Freedmen's Bureau reported 260 attacks, whippings and murders of freedmen between January and November, 1868. In September, there was a race riot at Camilla.

Nordhoff found about 1875 that the Negroes in and near the cities and towns were usually prosperous. "There are many colored mechanics, and they receive full wages where they are skillful. Near Atlanta and other places, they own small truck-farms, and supply the market with vegetables. There are fewer black than white beggars in the cities; and a missionary clergyman surprised me by the remark that the blackberry crop, which was ripening, was 'a blessing to dozens of poor white families whom he knew,' who lived half the year, he said, in a condition of semi-starvation."

"There are many colored mechanics, and they are all thrifty people, and very commonly own the houses they live in, and often a town lot besides. In the cotton country, an increasing number of colored men own farms of from forty to a hundred acres, but many of these were free before the war. In the towns and villages, the colored people have a prosperous look; they dress neatly, and very commonly live in frame houses. On the whole, their condition appears to me very comfortable and satisfactory." [37]

He gives these facts: "In an official report of the Comptroller-General of the state for 1874, giving the character and value of property and amount of taxes returned by colored taxpayers for that year, the number of colored polls listed was 83,318. These returned an aggregate value of taxable property amounting to $6,157,798, on which they actually paid $30,788 in taxes. They owned 338,769 acres of agricultural land, and city and town property to the amount of $1,200,115. Now, remembering that these people were slaves only nine years before . . . I think it clearly establishes that, first, they have labored with creditable industry and perseverance, and, second, that they have been fairly protected in the rights of life and property by the Democratic rulers of the State. I do not think the colored people in any other State I have visited own half as much real estate, or indeed, a quarter as much, as those of Georgia." [38]

The difficulty of securing adequate wages led to a Negro labor movement. This step was undertaken by two Negro leaders: Congressman Jeff Long and State Representative H. M. Turner. Their purpose was to organize a union among Negroes, demanding a minimum wage of $30 a month for fieldhands, and $15 for women. The convention received considerable notice, and the employers condemned it. There were strikes in Macon and Dougherty County. In Houston County, there was agitation, and county associations of fieldhands were attempted. But this movement for rural unions was not very successful.

Georgia was thus a state where a coalition of planters and Negroes began before Reconstruction. But while the planters advised the Negroes and made fair promises, they took no active part with them.

When the new political life began, the planters and the poor whites combined to put the Negroes out of the legislature.

The carpetbaggers and scalawags formed a "Moderate" bloc and fought with the planters to gain control of the poor whites. In this way they succeeded and were able to ignore the Negroes, bribe white labor with silence and make commerce and business triumphant in the state.

The carpetbaggers and scalawags spent money extravagantly, but they spent it, in their printing and contingent funds, with Southern merchants and supply houses, thus combining capitalistic interests. Georgia does not present the stock picture of a state looted by outsiders. It looted itself.

"Reviewing the events recorded from the beginning of this chapter, we observe that the period of reconstruction in Georgia was not a period when a swarm of harpies took possession of the state government and preyed at will upon a helpless people. The constitutional convention of 1867-1868 forebodes such a period, but when the Conservatives rouse themselves, from that time on the stage presents an internecine war between two very well matched enemies. This struggle is usually represented as between a wicked assailant and a righteous assailed. That it was a struggle between Republicans and Democrats is much more characteristic. In such a contest mutual vilifying of course abounded, and it is not to be supposed *a priori* that the vilifying of one party was more truthful than that of the other." [39]

None were more proud of the extravagance that accompanied this building of the commercial state than white Georgians. They welcomed the bearers of Northern capital then as now. The most extraordinary man in the Reconstruction history of Georgia was Hannibal I. Kimball, who was a capitalist interested in railroads, and often associated for business purposes with ex-Governor Brown. He was especially close to Governor Bullock, and was a focus of bribery and corruption. He was a type "of a class of aspiring Northern men who have rushed to the South since the war, some to run plantations, some to open mines of coal and iron, some to build railroads, others to establish great hotels, and all to give a grand impulse to Southern progress, and show the 'old fogies' in the South how to do it. Many of these enterprising men have already come to grief and left the country, while others are in full career to Fortune, or—her eldest daughter —Miss Fortune." [40]

Kimball has been of course represented as bribing Negroes; but what Kimball and his kind bribed was the city of Atlanta, the state of Georgia, and the whole South. And while he doubtless gave his tens and hundreds to Negro legislators, his thousands and tens of thousands went to that vast majority of white men who saw in him and his methods the salvation of the new capitalistic South, and who made the wealth and advertising of Atlanta overshadow the old-fashioned conservatism of Savannah and Macon.

Moreover, Georgia was not ruled by carpetbaggers. "Facts do not warrant the description of the Reconstruction government of Georgia as a Negro-carpet-bagger combination. There were some of both classes in the constitutional convention and in the legislature of 1868, already mentioned, and many in the Federal service, particularly as internal revenue officers, but they generally held minor positions." [41] The planter candidate for Governor, who opposed Bullock, testified that in 1870 no more than a dozen former non-residents were holding office in Georgia, and that the judges appointed by Bullock were entirely satisfactory. The economic boom of Georgia was evident. The value of total property rose steadily from 191 million in 1868 to 234 million in 1871. By 1870, the cotton crop of Georgia had surpassed the largest crop raised under slavery; a proof that Negro labor had not been demoralized by emancipation. Manufactures increased during 1860-1870, and the lumber business greatly increased. There had been 643 miles of railroad in 1850, and 1,420 in 1860. By 1870, this had increased to 1,845 miles, and 2,160 in 1872.

This business and industrial prosperity of Georgia was largely at the expense of the laboring classes. The educational system was started, but it received little support. Instead of preventing crime, crime was deliberately increased by the convict lease system. The poor, the blind, and the insane were neglected, and although peasant-farmers, because of the high price of produce, were able to buy some land, there was no effort to place large numbers of small owners on their own farms. There was no real labor legislation.

On the other hand, capital began to receive large returns, and speculation was rife. It is of especial interest to note that in Georgia, where the native white man never lost control, there was practically the same increase in debt, and the same railway scandals. There was graft in printing, advertising and attorney's fees, and the state debt was greatly increased, so that including endorsed railway bonds, it reached a total liability of over twenty million dollars in 1872.

It may be gathered from this that extravagance and theft in the Reconstruction South was a matter neither of race nor of geography; rather it was a question of poverty, opportunity, and current American morals. Nevertheless there were in Georgia the same charges of theft and waste as elsewhere and the same final desire to shoulder the blame on the Negroes.

In the election of December, 1870, there was a large Democratic majority in both Houses of the legislature, and the Democrats continued in power. Bullock, foreseeing impeachment, resigned in October, 1871. The legislature met in November. In December, there were several investigating committees. Robert Toombs became prosecuting attorney, and the investigations were thoroughly partisan.

Railroad manipulation in Georgia as elsewhere led to Wall Street and many financiers of New York, like Henry Clews and Company, and Russell Sage. The acts granting aid to railroads "were passed by votes of members of both political parties, and the State is considered secure against loss if the law be properly enforced." [41a] The lease of the state-owned railroad, undoubtedly involved corruption, but among the lessees were former Governor Brown, Alexander Stephens, and Ben Hill, in addition to H. I. Kimball and others. Naturally, no Negroes were involved, except as possible recipients of bribes. Representative Turner seems to have worked hard to secure more reasonable terms—payment only after the work was actually finished. Bullock himself was charged with many financial frauds but none of them were ever proven; his worst deed, the establishment of the convict lease system, was not held against him but adopted by the state with avidity.

Florida had long been a refuge for runaway slaves, and the desire to reclaim these slaves had led to the so-called Seminole Wars and the final annexation. There were 27,943 whites and 26,534 Negroes in 1840, the first census after the state entered the Union. In 1860 there were 77,746 whites and 62,677 Negroes. There never were as many as 1,000 free Negroes in the state before emancipation.

Florida was a poor state with a small population. It had been dominated by rich planters and the poor whites had had little opportunity. The state therefore in many respects resembles South Carolina rather than Alabama in that the black man was the dominant labor and no white proletariat ever ruled. On the other hand black labor never came to self-assertion, while planters and carpetbaggers manipulated it from the first and gerrymandered its representation. White rule was ever in control, but it was only partially proletarian in character.

Although there were hundreds of Negro soldiers in the state at the time of Johnson's proclamation, he ordered a convention based on white suffrage, and the convention met October 2, 1865. It was composed almost entirely of Confederates, and the message of the provisional governor, Marvin, gave them encouragement.

It is doubtful if there was any noticeable opinion among the whites in favor of Negro suffrage. Certainly Marvin spoke decidedly against it.

"'It does not appear to me that the public good of the State or of the nation at large, would be promoted by conferring at the present time upon the freedmen the elective franchise.' 'Neither the white people nor the colored people are prepared for so radical a change in their social relations.' 'Nor have I any reason to believe that any considerable number of the freedmen desire to possess this privilege.' " [42]

The convention finally said: "The people of the State of Florida, in general convention assembled, do ordain and declare, that while we recognize the freedom of the colored race, and are desirous of extending to them full protection . . . we declare it the unalterable sentiment of this convention, that the laws of the State shall be made and executed by the white race." [43]

The convention sat twelve days and adjourned for the ensuing election. E. S. Walker was elected governor. He recommended the removal of black soldiers from the state and advocated various black laws. He said with regard to Negro suffrage:

"Each one of us knows that we could not give either an honest or conscientious assent to Negro suffrage. There is not one of us that would not feel that he was doing wrong, and bartering his self-respect, his conscience and his duty to his country and to the Union itself, for the benefits he might hope to obtain by getting back into the Union." [44]

A commission of three was appointed to report laws concerning the Negro. They recommended a County Criminal Court mainly for Negro offenders and the same discrimination against emancipated slaves which had been used formerly against free Negroes. They were not sure how they could keep the Negro at work, and they were tearful concerning his future:

"If, after all, their honest efforts shall prove unavailing, and this four millions of the human family but recently dragged up from barbarism, and through the influence of Southern masters elevated to the status of Christian men and women, shall be doomed by the inscrutable behest of a mysterious Providence to follow in the footsteps of the fast fading aborigines of this continent; and when the last man of the race shall be standing upon the crumbling brink of a people's grave, it will be some compensation to the descendants of the Southern master to catch the grateful and benignant recognition of this representative man, as he points his withered finger to the author of his ruin and exclaims, 'Thou didst it.' " [45]

The black laws of Florida followed: "To save them from the ruin which inevitably awaits them if left to the 'tender mercy' of the canting hypocrisy and mawkish sentimentality which has precipitated them to the realization of their present condition." [46]

There were the usual vagrancy and apprenticeship laws, and laws against firearms. On the other hand, there were laws regarding marriage and the right to testify in court, but only in matters in which Negroes were concerned.

After the Federal law of June 21, 1866, a large number of Negroes flocked to Florida. From 1865 to 1867, the chief thought of the freedmen of Florida, as in other states, concerned itself with what the government was going to do for them with regard to farms, and they were victims of many speculators.

The duel in Florida for the control of labor was between two sets of Northern men, mostly Federal officeholders of various sorts and the planters. The policy of the planters was so to shift their influence between the Northerners so as to gain their ends by political strategy, which they finally did. At the same time, they made some effective efforts to keep in touch with the Negroes so that they retained a good deal of influence over their vote.

When the elections of 1867 under the Reconstruction laws were about to take place, the Negroes sought to get in touch with leading white Southerners. One meeting was held in Leon County and several white planters invited to address it and give the Negroes information as to their newly acquired duties as citizens. This increased the rivalry between the planters and the carpetbaggers, with the result that the planters made few further open efforts to coöperate with the Negro voters. The Southern whites tried to kill the convention by refraining from voting, so that the total vote cast was 14,503, of which all but 1,220 was cast by Negroes.

In the convention of 1868, forty-six delegates were returned. Eighteen of these were Negroes. Of the twenty-seven whites two were Conservatives, fifteen carpetbaggers, and the rest Southern whites. "The most cultured member of the convention, probably, was Jonathan Gibbs, a Negro. Gibbs was a tall and slightly-built black with a high forehead and a color indicating mulatto origin. His voice was clear and ringing. He possessed some of the qualities of a born orator and a genuine sentimentalist." [47]

E. Fortune, another colored member, was a native of Florida with a fair education, courageous in his opinions. Among other colored leaders were Armstrong, Oats, and Wallace, who wrote the history of Reconstruction in Florida.

The convention which met January 20, 1868, had a colored man of Tallahassee, C. H. Pearce, as temporary president. He was not a strong man and was later convicted of technical bribery. But, on the whole, his advice and effort seem to have been sincere and he had the confidence of large numbers of colored people. Of the 46 delegates there were only 20 present. Richards, a white man of Illinois, who,

as Wallace says, had been only two days in the county from which he
had been returned, was elected permanent chairman.

Richards, however, struck the right note in his speech. He said:
We should provide for a system by which all may obtain homes of
their own and a comfortable living, and also provide for schools in
which all may be educated free of expense; clothe honest industry
with respectability; inaugurate a public sentiment that shall crown
the man with honors as the benefactor of his race who makes two
blades of grass grow where one grew before, and prohibit all laws
that are not equal and just to all within our State." [48]

The first difficulty was a matter of money. There was only $500
in the treasury, and the convention had to issue scrip to pay its expenses. This scrip circulated at less than par value and made the expenses appear much larger than they actually were. Two factions early
developed among the carpetbaggers, and the policy of the planters was
to wait and take advantage from time to time of the outcome of
this internal fight. This left the Negroes in a peculiarly helpless condition, and it was only the ability and sanity of men like Gibbs that
enabled them to make any headway at all.

On the second day of the convention, an ordinance was passed
forbidding the sale of property for debt, suspending the collection of
taxes, releasing all persons held to labor for non-payment of taxes,
but not forbidding the laborer the right to collect wages from his
employer. It was distinctly legislation in the interest of labor.

The convention had been in session about two weeks when the
planters took a hand. The two factions among the Northern white
leaders were the conservative Osborne faction, which leaned toward the
planters, and the more radical Billings faction which sought complete
control of the Negroes. The Osborne faction and the planters, under
the leadership of ex-Governor Walker, succeeded in breaking up the
convention so that nearly half of it seceded and went off secretly to
a neighboring town to work on a constitution. This rump convention
adopted a constitution and sent it to the Federal General of the District
for his approval. They then took a recess. Afterwards they returned
to Tallahassee, broke into the legislative hall at midnight, and declared
themselves the rightful convention.

General Meade intervened and made the two factions come together
and adopt a constitution which proved to be mainly the constitution
drawn by the seceders. This constitution was a peculiar document. It
put vast appointing power in the hands of the Governor, making him
a practical dictator of the state, and it was also charged that the basis
of representation was so unfair that less than one-fourth of the registered voters would elect a majority in the state Senate and less than

one-third a majority of the Assembly. "6,700 voters in the rebel counties elect as many Senators . . . as 20,282 voters elect in Union counties. Seven Senators are elected by 3,027 voters in rebel counties, and only one Senator is elected by 3,181 in Union County [Leon], and twenty-three voters elect one Senator in a rebel district.

"In the assembly, 8,330 voters in rebel counties choose *twenty-seven* members. . . . Madison County [Union], with 1,802 voters sends *two* representatives, while the rebel sent from Dade County has a constituency of *eight* registered voters." [49]

This was accomplished by discriminating against the localities where the Negro vote was large so that the Negroes never had in the legislatures a representation anywhere near as large as their population called for. The constitution relieved the former Confederates from taking the registration oath. Charles Sumner and others opposed the admission of the state under this constitution but, nevertheless, after a delay from February to June, the state was admitted.

In the election on the constitution and for state officers, Billings was the candidate of the radical branch of the Northern white leaders, and the planters nominated a Confederate cavalry colonel, but in reality threw their support to Harrison Reed, the candidate of the Osborne faction which had made the constitution. The Republican ticket, headed by Reed, received 14,421 votes; the Democratic ticket, headed by Scott, 7,731; and the Independent Radical ticket, 2,251.

In the first legislature there were 17 Republicans and 8 Democrats in the Senate, and 36 Republicans and 15 Democrats in the House. Of these 76, 19 were Negroes, 13 carpetbaggers, 21 Southern loyalists, and 23 Conservatives.

Harrison Reed was a Johnson Democrat and formerly chief postal agent in Florida. He was present at Johnson's inauguration, as an unofficial representative of the state, and was a strong opponent of Chase. He was a curious character. Like Warmoth of Louisiana, he was an adroit politician and was repeatedly threatened with impeachment. But he was not as unscrupulous a grafter as Warmoth and exercised his great power with considerable care. His policy always was to favor the planters as much as possible, and then, when the Negroes or Northern whites revolted, to yield to them sufficiently so as to retain their support. In his cabinet, the more important places went to exslaveholders.

The number of Negro members in subsequent Florida legislatures is not clear. Wallace mentions twenty-five colored members of the House in the legislature of 1873. The number of representatives in the legislature who could neither read nor write, during the seven years of carpetbag rule in Florida, was six, of whom four were white.

Under the constitution, the Governor appointed all of the chief state officers except the lieutenant-governor and judges; and also he named most of the county officers. Nevertheless, the constitution of 1869 gave the Negroes the right to vote and gave Florida its first approach to a real government of the people.

Reed's administration started out with strength and respectability, but it was weak because of lack of recognition of the colored people. His opponents, therefore, tried one method of attacking him by introducing a civil rights bill, compelling hotel keepers and railroad companies to receive Negroes on the same terms as whites. The bill was passed in the assembly, but the Governor called in members of the Senate and explained why he thought it was not wise to push such legislation. Colored people became alarmed, but through Pearce and other leaders their apprehensions were allayed.

The ill-will against Reed began when electors were chosen in November, 1868. Impeachment proceedings against him were begun, but the Supreme Court ruled that there was no quorum in the Senate at the time. The Secretary of State, Alden, had joined in the opposition to Reed and was removed; Gibbs, the colored leader, was selected as his successor, which greatly increased the strength of Reed among the freedmen.

The ensuing turmoil in Florida cannot be understood unless one keeps carefully in mind just what was taking place. The planters were encouraging lawlessness and inciting the Negroes to make extravagant demands for equality in order to embarrass the carpetbaggers and excite the poor whites. The carpetbaggers and Northern capitalists were seeking to get rid of Reed, and bribing white and black members of the legislature in order to get through special legislation for capital. The Negroes were trying to find a program of labor legislation, which would help and uplift the masses; Reed was playing capital, labor and planters against each other, and in the midst of these contradictory and opposing forces, the state staggered on. The Governor informed the legislature that the past seven years of anarchy and insurrection had left nothing in the treasury, with $600,000 of debts and a large amount repudiated. The former inadequate school fund had been robbed of its last dollar to aid the Confederate forces. The railroad system, half completed, was bankrupt, the revenue laws inadequate, no schools or school systems, no benevolent institutions, no almshouses, penitentiaries, and scarcely a jail.

In the first Reconstruction legislature, Negro leaders, Harmon and Black, tried to pass a school law for the education of the masses. At the second session of the legislature a homestead law was passed and the school laws amended. Acts of violence throughout the state continued and there was considerable bribery in the legislature.

The second session of the legislature met January 5, 1869. There was a second attempt to impeach Reed, foiled by the action of two colored members, H. S. Harmon and E. Fortune, and finally defeated by a vote of 43 to 5. An extraordinary session of the legislature was called May 17, 1869, on account of financial difficulties and matters connected with the sale of the Pensacola and Georgia Railroad and the Tallahassee Railroad.[50]

Railroad legislation was introduced, Littlefield and Swepson, already operating in North Carolina, being connected with the matter. State aid was asked at the rate of $12,000 a mile for these railroads, which would amount to $4,000,000. Wallace says that members of the legislature were openly bought, white men receiving from $2,000 to $6,000 and colored men $500 or less.

There were disturbances in various counties and open violence and bloodshed in 1868-1869. Reed was asked to declare martial law, but instead he sent Secretary Gibbs to the centers of disturbance. Gibbs received close attention from the colored people and openly attacked the carpetbagger leaders.

The legislature met in January, 1870, in its third regular session. The Governor repeated a statement which he had made before. "In several counties organized bands of lawless men have combined to over-ride the civil authorities, and many acts of violence have occurred; but these have been incidental to the State in all its past history, and arise less, perhaps, from special enmity to the present form of government than from opposition to the restraints of law in general." [51]

"It is true that these same localities, being, to all intents, border sections, have from time immemorial been the resorts of lawless and reckless men, and in some of them, as in earlier periods of the existence of the Western and South-western States, the law of Judge Lynch and the 'Regulators' for years before the war, had been the only code of much efficacy.

"I had hoped better results from the reorganization of government under Republican auspices; but the bitterness resulting from the war, the noxious teachings of disappointed and defeated political opponents, assisted by the occasional lack of discretion on the part of injudicious political friends, succeeded for a long time in setting at naught the advice and the efforts of the better men of all classes, until improvement at times seemed to be hopeless; and I have been strongly and forcibly urged to the declaration of martial law." [52]

Again an attempt was made to impeach Reed but the colored members stood by him. The impeachment committee sent in two reports;

a majority report signed by four, and a minority report signed by one. The minority report, which was adopted, said: "Looking back over the history of the State for the last ten years, so full of excitement, agitation, and turmoil, we are profoundly impressed with a sense of the value of the results of the reconstructive legislation of the National Government, and its subsequent result in the organization of our own State government. . . .

"We feel bound in duty to call attention to the many difficulties and embarrassments, particularly of a financial description, with which in the administration of a newly organized government, Governor Reed has found himself continually surrounded. Without sympathy, with scanty resources, without the support from a portion of his Cabinet, as it appears from the testimony and from official documents, called to fill a multitude of offices by the appointment of comparative strangers, he must have been seriously embarrassed and hampered on every hand.

"After deliberate consideration of the charges, the evidence, the surrounding and difficult circumstances, and in view of the results that may be expected to follow the action taken, we do not find the charges preferred to be so far sustained by the evidence given as to warrant us in recommending an impeachment." The report was adopted by a vote of 27 to 22; all the colored members of the legislature except one voted against impeachment.[53]

In 1870 the Democratic party put in nomination Bloxham for Lieutenant-Governor. The Republican politicians declared that if Bloxham was elected they would unite with the Democrats so as to impeach Governor Reed and make Bloxham Governor. Wallace thinks that Bloxham was in fact elected but counted out by the Returning Board, of which Gibbs, the colored Secretary of State, was a member. He says that Gibbs consented with great reluctance and under threat of impeachment if he did not yield. It must be remembered, however, that Bloxham was the friend and mentor of Wallace and edited his book.

The legislature met in January, 1872, and again sought to impeach the Governor. The more ignorant of the members of the assembly were secured to vote for the impeachment. A Southern county judge was promised appointment as a circuit judge, and a Democratic member of the assembly was promised a share of the new bonds. Ex-Governor Walker promised the support of the Democrats.

The Governor in his message complained that more than two-thirds of the bonds issued in aid of Littlefield roads had been wasted without any real progress. The bonds were intrusted to firms of swindlers in New York. Impeachment proceedings were based on this, and the

Governor was suspended from office; but the trial was never held and at an extra session of the legislature he was restored to office.

There had been much corruption in every legislature under Reed, but Wallace says: "The colored members at this session began to show more manhood by openly denouncing the tricks of the carpetbaggers and refusing to be enslaved by caucus rule." They showed their independence by this resolution introduced by Daniel McInnis, colored, of Duval County: "Whereas it appears that after several attempts to have a Civil Rights bill, which gives to every citizen the same protection in the enjoyment of his liberties; and, whereas it has become a painful fact from the action of Liberty Billings, acting president *pro tem.* of the Senate of the State of Florida, and others who are opposed to seeing the colored citizens of this State enjoy the same rights that he and his associates do, we again witness on today another defeat of the Civil Rights bill, caused by only those who profess to be our friends in connection with this great cause of civil rights; therefore:

"Resolved that we, the colored members, and those who honestly sympathize with us, do unhesitatingly repudiate such friendship, and do now and henceforth withdraw from and decline from ever affiliating with, politically, or to aid in electing any such man or men who have so basely misrepresented our people." [54]

These resolutions were ruled out of order; McInnis was fought and denounced in his county, and lost the next election to the legislature, although "one of the most faithful and honest representatives of the colored people."

The delegation elected from Leon County, all colored, "stood opposed to the system of plunder which had been inaugurated in almost every county of the state." This was shown when Gleason introduced a bill to authorize corporations to change their names and consolidate their capital stock, etc. The measure was adopted by the Republican caucus, but when the matter came up for final consideration, the Leon County delegates opposed the bill and John W. Wyatt, a Negro, made a speech which was the first ordered spread on the minutes of the legislature of Florida.

"We want no *Tom Scotts*, *Jim Fisks* or *Vanderbilts* in this State to govern us, by means of which they would influence legislation tending to advance personal interests.

"The great curse of Florida has been dishonest corporations, rings and cliques, with an eye single to their central interest, and if this bill is suffered to pass this Assembly, in my opinion we may look for a continuation of abuses and a usurpation of the rights of citizens who may be opposed to the evil machinations such as are generally exerted by consolidated bodies. . . .

"The recent exposé of the Tammany Ring in New York has satisfied all right thinking men that the power exercised by strong bodies, composed of many corporations, is the most dangerous to the public good and safety. Therefore, it ill becomes us to pass a bill enveloped in darkness as the title to this bill indicates it to be. . . ."

A last attempt was made in this session to impeach Reed. Wallace says: "As one of the members of the committee, I never saw the report of the investigating committee nor any other evidences upon which the subsequent articles of impeachment presented by the committee were based." [55]

After a long and intricate fight, Reed, supported loyally by his Secretary of State, Gibbs, out-generaled his opponents. However, Reed was not renominated, although the colored people wanted him. The planters now felt strong enough to assert themselves, and secured the selection, as Republican candidate for Governor, of Justice O. B. Hart. The carpetbaggers filled the rest of the ticket, except that the freedmen received recognition by the nomination of J. T. Walls, as one of the candidates for United States Representative. The campaign was bitter and the results of the election close. The Republicans carried it by a small margin. Hart was the first native governor of Florida in Reconstruction times, but was a vacillating and uncertain man.

The legislature met in January, 1873, and nominated a colored man, Scott, for speaker. He was defeated by the revolt of the colored delegation from Leon County on account of his connection with politicians. In return, the white leaders insisted that no colored man was fit for a cabinet position except Jonathan C. Gibbs, and he, they charged, had attempted to count in Bloxham in the previous election. The Negroes insisted on Gibbs. Hart refused until the colored members in caucus demanded Gibbs' appointment, with a threat that they would otherwise combine with the Democrats and clog the wheels of the administration. Colored members of both branches of the legislature went to Hart in a body and finally he had to accede to their demand. Gibbs was appointed Superintendent of Public Instruction.

Gibbs held this office during 1872-1874, when the school system was tottering and the collection of funds difficult. He virtually established the public schools of the state as an orderly system; but when a student of Florida history recently tried to examine the records of his administration, he discovered that they had all disappeared from the state archives.

The extraordinary political complications of the day are illustrated by Hart and his cabinet. Hart was a Southern planter backed by carpetbaggers and his Secretary of State was McLin. Wallace says:

"The Cabinet was a very fair one, with the exception of McLin, who was a deserter from the rebel army, and being self-condemned for his own treachery for having volunteered in the Confederate service and then deserted before he smelled gunpowder, he was satisfied that neither the Democrats nor the carpetbaggers cared to trust him, and he was therefore the tool of the most rabid and unprincipled members of the carpetbag dynasty of the State." [56]

In 1873, Gibbs and the trustees of the Agricultural College frustrated an attempt to invest the $100,000 received from the general government in bonds which would have put the cash in possession of the politicians.

When Hart died in 1874, Stearns became Governor. He wanted to ask the resignation of Gibbs, but Gibbs was too popular. Stearns had promised to nominate Gibbs for Congress but was afraid that he could not control him. Gibbs was in perfect health before the meeting of the convention and during its sitting. He delivered a powerful speech in the Stearns convention, attacking one of his supporters. He went home and ate a hearty dinner, after which he suddenly died. "It was whispered and generally believed that he was poisoned by some of the carpetbaggers, because they dreaded his growing popularity."

His brother, Judge Mifflin Gibbs of Arkansas, gives a different cause for his death but notes his fear of assassination.

"My brother, Jonathan C. Gibbs, was then Secretary of State of Florida, with Governor Hart as executive. He had had the benefit of a collegiate education, having graduated at Dartmouth, New Hampshire, and had for some years filled the pulpit as a Presbyterian minister. The stress of Reconstruction and obvious necessity for ability in secular matters induced him to enter official life. Naturally indomitable, he more than fulfilled the expectations of his friends and supporters by rare ability as a thinker and a speaker, with unflinching fidelity to his party principles. I found him at Tallahassee, the capital, in a well-appointed residence, but his sleeping place in the attic resembled, as I perceived, considerably an arsenal. He said that for better advantage it had been his resting place for several months, as his life had been threatened by the 'Ku Klux.' . . . It was my last interview or sight of my brother. Subsequently after a three hours' speech, he went to his office and suddenly died of apoplexy." [57]

In the legislature of 1873 there were twenty-five colored members of whom 19 were in revolt against the political leaders. The methods of the white politicians were illustrated in the case of two colored members who wished to inspect the state prison. Everything was done to impede them. A special train was prepared for the comfort of the visiting guests, but it left just two hours before the time designated and the colored men were left behind. But the Negroes were energetic and determined and reached the grounds by other means. The warden at once set out liquors and cigars, but the colored men refused to partake and went about their investigation.

The Civil Rights Bill finally passed at this session without great opposition. The matter of land distribution continued to come up, and the Northern politicians assured the freedmen that they favored high taxes upon the lands of the ex-slaveholders so as to compel them to sell these lands cheaply. On the other hand, they accused the planters of being in favor of low taxes so that the whites could hold the land and rent it to the colored people. This propaganda influenced Negro votes but resulted in no real action.

In the legislature of 1875, most of the minor offices were filled with colored men. The Republican state convention renominated Stearns for Governor and adopted a platform arraigning both state and national governments for corruption, extravagance and oppression. The state debt was only $1,329,757.68; the state taxation, which had been less than 2 mills on a dollar in 1861, had increased to 5 mills in 1867 and 13$\frac{7}{10}$ mills in 1872. It was then reduced to seven mills in 1875. The expenditures were but $190,000 against receipts of about $220,000. Thus the Democratic cry of extravagance was not particularly effective.

In the campaign of 1876, the Democrats won. McLin, the ex-Confederate in the Cabinet, celebrated in the Tallahassee *Sentinel* the victory of Hayes.

In general, Florida presents no abnormal picture. There was some waste and high taxation but it did not reach extremes; it had, as in other states, to contend with deliberate efforts to sabotage its advance. The *Floridan* said in 1871:

"No greater calamity could befall the State of Florida, while under the rule of its present carpetbag, scalawag officials, than to be placed in good financial credit. . . . Our only hope is in the state's utter financial bankruptcy; and Heaven grant that that may speedily come! On the other hand, establish for the State financial credit on Wall Street, so that Florida bonds can be sold by Reed & Company, as fast as issued, and you give these foul harpies a life-tenure of these offices. . . . The temporal salvation of the taxpayers is having scrip low, so that they can buy it to pay taxes with, and in having the State's financial credit low so that Reed & Co. can't sell State bonds so as to raise money with which to perpetuate their hold on office."

There was bribery of Negro legislators, as Wallace frankly shows, but he also says of his history: "The design of this work is to correct the settled and erroneous impression that has gone out to the world that the former slaves, when enfranchised, had no conception of good government, and therefore their chief ambition was corruption and plunder. . . .

"That it was white men, and not colored men, who originated corruption and enriched themselves from the earnings of the people of the State from the year 1868 to 1877; that the loss of the State to the National Republican Party was not due to any unfaithfulness of the colored people to that party, but to the corruption of these strange white leaders termed 'carpetbaggers'; that the colored people have done as well as any other people could have done under the same circumstances, if not better." [58]

Wallace particularly laments the effect of corrupt leaders on the Negro:

"The Northern machine politicians assert that it was the incompetence and unfaithfulness. of the Negro voter to the Republican Party that brought about the unhealthy condition of things which made the Solid South—it was these and kindred acts of the carpetbaggers which furnish the key to unlock the door that reveals the secrets of the Solid South, while these very carpetbaggers were sustained by the Northern machine politicians. From the beginning to the end of Stearns' so-called administration it was contaminated with packed juries for political purposes, and during the last two years of his term it became a patent fact that scarcely a person brought before the courts in the Black Belt counties could be convicted from the fact that the petit juries were mostly composed of the very worst element among the freedmen." [59]

This is not the whole truth. The reactionary planters, in whom Wallace and other colored men pathetically believed, were not honest or sincere in their advice to and support of Negroes. They encouraged lawlessness among poor whites, extravagance among carpetbaggers and bribery among Negroes. They deliberately befouled the whole political nest in order to discredit its rulers and voters.

Shall I sing of Liberty when there is no liberty?
Shall I sing of Freedom when there is none?
Shall I sing love-songs to young lovers who are slaves?
My soul thrills even as I think the laburnum

In Spring-time thrills to link her chains of gold,
I am lost in the great miracle which Nature
Has endlessly wrought out of freedom.
But Man sits amid his own ruins, eating husks.

CHARLES ERSKINE SCOTT WOOD

1. McPherson, *History of United States During Reconstruction*, p. 21.
2. McPherson, *History of United States During Reconstruction*, pp. 21-22.
3. Fleming, *Civil War and Reconstruction in Alabama*, p. 352.
4. Fleming, *Civil War and Reconstruction in Alabama*, p. 406.
5. Fleming, *Civil War and Reconstruction in Alabama*, p. 304.
6. Herbert, *Why the Solid South?*, p. 43.
7. Fleming, *Civil War and Reconstruction in Alabama*, p. 530.
8. Fleming, *Civil War and Reconstruction in Alabama*, p. 525.
9. Herbert, *Why the Solid South?*, p. 46.
10. Davis, *The Federal Enforcement Acts* (in *Studies in Southern History and Politics*), pp. 227-228.
11. Thompson, *Reconstruction in Georgia*, p. 52.
12. Thompson, *Reconstruction in Georgia*, p. 145 (footnote).
13. Thompson, *Reconstruction in Georgia*, p. 149.
14. Thompson, *Reconstruction in Georgia*, p. 151.
15. Cf. Thompson, *Reconstruction in Georgia*, pp. 153-154.
16. McPherson, *History of United States During Reconstruction*, p. 33; cf. Thompson, *Reconstruction in Georgia*, p. 158.
17. Thompson, *Reconstruction in Georgia*, p. 174.
18. Cf. Christler, *Participation of Negroes in the Government of Georgia*, p. 5.
19. Christler, *Participation of Negroes in the Government of Georgia*, p. 7.
20. Cf. Christler, *Participation of Negroes in Government of Georgia*, p. 7 (footnote).
21. Christler, *Participation of Negroes in the Government of Georgia*, p. 8.
22. Thompson, *Reconstruction in Georgia*, p. 191.
23. Cf. Christler, *Participation of Negroes in the Government of Georgia*, p. 19.
24. Christler, *Participation of Negroes in the Government of Georgia*, p. 21.
25. Cf. Christler, *Participation of Negroes in the Government of Georgia*, pp. 24-25.
26. Thompson, *Reconstruction in Georgia*, p. 204.
27. Woolley, *The Reconstruction of Georgia*, p. 56.
28. Christler, *Participation of Negroes in the Government of Georgia*, pp. 34-35.
29. Turner, *Speech on the Eligibility of the Colored Members*.
30. Cf. Christler, *Participation of Negroes in the Government of Georgia*, pp. 43, 44.
31. Cf. Christler, *Participation of Negroes in the Government of Georgia*, p. 48.
32. Woodson, *Negro Orators and Their Orations*, p. 294.
33. Christler, *Participation of Negroes in the Government of Georgia*, p. 64.
34. Christler, *Participation of Negroes in the Government of Georgia*, pp. 64-65.
35. Christler, *Participation of Negroes in the Government of Georgia*, p. 66.
36. Christler, *Participation of Negroes in the Government of Georgia*, p. 67.
37. Nordhoff, *The Cotton States in the Spring and Summer of 1875*, p. 106.
38. Nordhoff, *The Cotton States in the Spring and Summer of 1875*, p. 104.
39. Woolley, *The Reconstruction of Georgia*, p. 99.
40. Somers, *The Southern States Since the War*, p. 97.
41. Thompson, *Reconstruction in Georgia*, p. 216.
41a. House of Representatives Report, 42nd Congress, 2nd Session, No. 22, p. 130.
42. Wallace, *Carpetbag Rule in Florida*, p. 13.
43. Cf. *New York Times*, November 17, 1865. (Laws of Florida Convention, 1865.)
44. Wallace, *Carpetbag Rule in Florida*, p. 24.
45. Wallace, *Carpetbag Rule in Florida*, p. 35.
46. Wallace, *Carpetbag Rule in Florida*, p. 34.
47. Davis, *Reconstruction in Florida*, p. 494.

48. Wallace, *Carpetbag Rule in Florida*, p. 52.
49. Wallace, *Carpetbag Rule in Florida*, p. 73.
50. Wallace, *Carpetbag Rule in Florida*, p. 102.
51. Wallace, *Carpetbag Rule in Florida*, p. 113.
52. Wallace, *Carpetbag Rule in Florida*, pp. 144-145.
53. Wallace, *Carpetbag Rule in Florida*, p. 123.
54. Wallace, *Carpetbag Rule in Florida*, pp. 151-152.
55. Wallace, *Carpetbag Rule in Florida*, pp. 156-158, 160.
56. Wallace, *Carpetbag Rule in Florida*, p. 268.
57. Gibbs, *Shadow and Light*, pp. 111-112.
58. Wallace, *Carpetbag Rule in Florida*, pp. 3-4 (preface).
59. Wallace, *Carpetbag Rule in Florida*, p. 297.

XIII. THE DUEL FOR LABOR CONTROL
ON BORDER AND FRONTIER

How in North Carolina and Virginia, in the Border States and
on the southwestern frontier, the dominant white worker after the
war sealed the fate of his black fellow laborer

North Carolina presents quite a different situation and method of
Reconstruction from the states studied. The war left the state in economic bankruptcy. The repudiation of the Confederate debt closed
every bank, and farm property was reduced in value one-third. The
male population was greatly reduced and the masses were in distress.

In 1800, North Carolina had 337,764 whites and 140,339 Negroes;
in 1840, 484,870 whites and 268,549 Negroes. In 1860 there were 629,-
942 whites and 361,544 Negroes. There were 30,000 free Negroes in
1860, a class who had in the past received some consideration. Up until
1835 they had had the right to vote and had voted intelligently. In the
nineteenth century one of the best schools in the state for children of
the white aristocracy was conducted by John Chavis, a Negro, educated at Princeton. Many Negroes had come into the state during the
war so that their proportion of the population increased in 1870 and
1880. In general, however, Emancipation was not attended by any great
disorders, and the general tide of domestic life flowed on.

The Freedmen's Bureau issued rations to white people as well as
colored, and many were kept from starvation. Large sums of money
were received from the North in 1866-1867 and grain and provisions
as well.

When President Johnson called North Carolina whites into consultation concerning his proposed plan of Reconstruction, many of
them were highly indignant, some even leaving the room. They did
not propose to share power even with the President but wanted to
put their own legislature back in power.

They finally acquiesced and William W. Holden was appointed
Provisional Governor, May 29. He ordered an election for a convention with a white electorate September 21. By June 27, 1,912 pardons
had been granted in North Carolina, 510 of which came under the
$20,000 exemption. Here, as in other states, there came the preliminary
movement of planters to secure control of the Negro vote. Alfred M.
Waddel, in July, 1865, editor of the *Herald* before the war and a colo-

nel in the Confederate army, spoke to the colored people of Wilmington and denounced taxation without representation. He advocated the extension of the suffrage to qualified Negroes. The *Sentinel* said it was opposed to Negroes' voting, but would open its pages for discussion. Favorable articles appeared by Victor C. Barringer and David L. Swaint.

The idea was to forestall any attempt of Northern white leaders and capitalists to control the Negro vote. The Negroes, however, had thought and leadership, both from the free Negro class, who had some education, and from colored immigrants from the North, many of whom had been born in North Carolina but had escaped from slavery.

During the year 1865, Negroes circulated petitions asking the President for equal rights. The convention of 1865 met October 2. The Ordinance of Secession was repudiated and slavery abolished but no action at first was taken on the Confederate debt. Johnson interfered and at last the debt was formally repudiated, although the leading papers of the state called the action "humiliating." The General Assembly met in November, when the Thirteenth Amendment was ratified, but the vote explained that this amendment did not give Congress power to legislate on the civil and political status of the freedmen.

A commission was appointed to report on new legislation for the freedmen. This commission reported in 1866, and the General Assembly passed a bill which defined Negroes and gave them the civil rights that free Negroes had had before the war. An apprenticeship law disposing of young Negroes "preferably to their former masters and mistresses" was passed and Negroes could be witnesses only in cases in which Negroes were involved. In 1867 there were acts to prevent enticing servants, harboring them, breach of contract, and later seditious language and insurrection.

The adjourned session of the convention in May made a significant change in the basis of representation. Formerly, three-fifths of the Negroes had been counted in the representation, but the new constitution changed the basis to the white population alone, and allowed only white persons to vote or hold office.

During the state convention, the Negroes had met in Raleigh and adopted a set of resolutions which "asked in moderate and well-chosen language that the race might have protection and an opportunity for education." [1] They also asked that discrimination before the law be abolished. They said nothing about the suffrage.

In the fall election of 1866, Worth was chosen Governor. He advocated the rejection of the Fourteenth Amendment. The legislature agreed. Holden, the former Provisional Governor and now leader of the Republicans, changed his attitude toward Negro suffrage, and in December, 1866, openly advocated votes for Negroes.

Holden says: "The people of North Carolina had rejected President Johnson's plan of Reconstruction on the white basis. They had also rejected the Howard Amendment under which they could have returned to the Union as Tennessee did. Nearly three years from the close of hostilities had elapsed and we were still under provisional forms with the national military paramount. What was to be done? In a conversation which I had with Thaddeus Stevens in December, 1866, he told me he thought it would be best for the South to remain ten years longer under military rule and that during this time we would have territorial Governors and territorial legislatures and the government at Washington would pay our general expenses as territories and educate our children, white and colored. I did not want that state of things in North Carolina. I did not want to run the risk of a practical confiscation of our property to pay the expenses which would have been entailed upon us by these military governments. I did not want North Carolina to cease to exist as a state. I confess I feared confiscation of property to a greater or less extent, especially as President Johnson had said to me in May, 1865: 'I intend to confiscate the lands of these rich men whom I have excluded from pardon by my proclamation, and divide the proceeds thereof among the families of the wool hat boys, the Confederate soldiers, whom these men forced into battle to protect their property in slaves.' " [2]

When the Reconstruction Act was under consideration in Congress, the North Carolina Negroes sent a delegation to Washington asking for the removal of Worth, and that Holden be relieved of his disabilities so that he could again be put in office. In September, 1867, after the Reconstruction Act had passed, the Negro leaders called another convention in Raleigh. Among these leaders was James H. Harris, born in North Carolina but educated in Ohio. Even the whites acknowledged that "he had great ability." Another leader was James Walker Hood, born in Pennsylvania and sent South as a missionary by the African Zion Church. He became eventually a leading official in the organization of the public schools of North Carolina, and finally was elected bishop of his church. Other Negro leaders were A. H. Galloway, Isham Sweat and J. W. Ward. This Raleigh convention asked for full rights and full protection and the abolition of all discrimination before the law. They especially demanded ample means and opportunity for education. The convention resolved itself into an Equal Rights League and established a newspaper.

The order for general registration was published in May, 1867, and the registration was to begin in July in 170 registration districts. In the appointment of the boards, Governor Worth wanted to avoid the appointment of Negroes but recommended a few. For the general board, G. W. Broody, a colored minister from the North, was selected by General Sickles.

There were 106,721 whites who registered and 72,932 Negroes. Ninety-three thousand and six voted for the constitutional convention, and 32,961, all of them white, voted against the constitution. The constitution was ratified April 21, 1868, by a vote of 93,084 against 74,015.

In the registration, nineteen counties had Negro majorities and in several other counties the white majority was less than 100. Immediately there was an attempt to organize political parties. A people's convention met March 27 with white and black delegates. It was denounced by the planters as a meeting of "Holden's Miscegenationists." The colored delegates took a prominent part and made many speeches, and a Republican Party was organized. On the other hand, an attempt was made in Raleigh to call a colored mass meeting at which Governor Worth and other Conservatives were to speak, the idea evidently being to divide the Negro vote between the parties, but the Conservatives did not respond.

Among the colored people there was growing a strong feeling about the land. Some wanted the land confiscated and given to small farmers. But many of the Northern capitalists opposed this. Harris advocated taxation of large estates so that the land could be sold and opportunity given Negroes to buy. On the other hand, he wanted the disabilities of the planters removed, while most of his followers were opposed to this. The election was held in November, 1867, and resulted in a large majority for the convention, although over fifty thousand people, mostly whites, did not vote.

On January 14, 1868, the constitutional convention on the Congressional plan convened at Raleigh. Of the one hundred and thirty-three members of the body, eighteen were Northern carpetbaggers and fifteen were Negroes. The leading carpetbaggers were: H. L. Grant of Rhode Island and the Rev. S. S. Ashley of Massachusetts, afterwards the Superintendent of Public Instruction. The Rev. James Walker Hood of Pennsylvania was the outstanding Negro delegate. The Rev. Ashley was made Chairman of the Committee of Education and from this position he greatly influenced the educational provisions of the constitution of 1868. The leading Negro members were: James H. Harris, J. W. Ward, J. W. Hood and A. H. Galloway. The next year Hood was made an agent of the Bureau of Education, and there did his life work.

In the convention, the chief matters of discussion were segregation in schools, inter-marriage, and propositions concerning holding of state offices by Negroes.

The records of the proceedings of the convention adhere strictly to parliamentary form. There were no speeches by any of the members of the convention recorded.

The constitution which was adopted had a Bill of Rights in which men were declared equal, slavery prohibited, and the people's right to education asserted. Property qualifications for office were abolished, and universal suffrage and a system of public schools ordered to be established. There were also provisions for vagrants, a penitentiary, public charities and orphanages.[3]

The convention wrangled over the question of separate schools for Negroes, and finally refused to make separation of races in schools compulsory. They discussed inter-marriage and universal suffrage. There was a proposition to get loans from Congress for agricultural purposes and buying land and homes. This was declared to be pay for Negroes for their long labor without reward and for their services during the war. Loans from $3,000,000 to $10,000,000 were proposed. The convention passed 75 ordinances and 56 resolutions and sat for 55 days.

The reception of this constitution and the work of the convention was characteristic. The planter press in the state was strong and it insulted the convention in every way possible. The real brunt of the attack, however, fell not on the Negroes but on the Northern capitalists and leaders. The Republican *Standard* called the convention one of "the ablest, most dignified and most patriotic bodies" that ever assembled in the state. The reactionary *Sentinel* called it "the socalled" convention of "Ethiopian minstrelsy, Ham radicalism in its glory." Some said that "the pillars of the capitol should be hung in mourning for the murdered sovereignty of North Carolina." And Josiah Turner, who has the chief credit for finally overthrowing Reconstruction in North Carolina, said: "In the legislative halls, where once giants sat, are adventurers, manikins, and gibbering Africans." The *North Carolinian,* February 11, 1868, said: "The Cowles Museum contains baboons, monkeys, mules, Tourgée, and other jackasses."[4]

Evidently the state, by a combination of Northern capitalists and Negroes, and by a corresponding refusal of the whites to coöperate, was passing under a new régime. In the convention the carpetbaggers had large influence in the committees, and when the state was organized they undertook to run it upon a larger scale, spending more money, certainly, in part for the reason that the state had more things to do, as, for instance, public education, internal improvements, the extension of the credit of the state and public improvements.

By 1868, the ex-planters in North Carolina had begun to organize themselves as Democrats, although some of them for financial reasons became scalawags and allied themselves with the carpetbaggers.

The Conservatives fought the constitution on the ground that it made the Negro a social equal and while it gave representation to the Negro, it did not give representation to property. In Wilmington, for instance, it was said that Negroes cast the majority of votes; that thirty-nine-fortieths of the real estate belonged to the white people. Property was thus arrayed against labor, while labor was allied with the new carpetbag capital. This new capital was in the hands of persons who had but lately come to the state. In no state was the fight of the planters against carpetbaggers more bitter. Due to the long presence of the army in the state during the war, with the easy communication by water, a large number of Northerners after the war chose North Carolina as a likely home and place for work and investment.

Holden summoned the legislature to meet July 1, 1868. In his inaugural address, he defended the carpetbaggers and stated that in the history of the state most of the leaders had come from the outside. This legislature ratified the Fourteenth Amendment and voted down a provision for separate Negro schools. There were 3 Negro members of the Senate out of a total of 15, and 16 members of the House, out of a total of 120. Two of the Negroes acted as Speakers at various times. Among both Negro and white members there was considerable illiteracy, and among the local officials throughout the state it was said that few of the Negro appointees were competent and many of the white ones were not.

Thus the Reconstruction problem in North Carolina, while it had to deal with ignorance and inefficiency, was only to a very small extent a Negro problem.

The real fight in North Carolina was between the old régime and the white carpetbaggers, with the poor whites as ultimate arbitrators, and Negro labor between, struggling for existence. The brunt of attack was the Northern newcomers. The combination by which the white immigrants gained control of the state with the support of the Negroes had to meet, as in all Southern states, a charge of extravagance if not corruption. During the two years of the government of Holden the debt of North Carolina was increased from $16,000,000 to $32,000,000. It is doubtful, however, if Holden could be held responsible for this, and certainly the Negroes could not.

Most of this debt was to aid railroads. The aid granted to railroads by the convention of 1868, and the legislatures of 1868-1869, "was generally approved and passed by votes of members of both parties. The object was to extend and complete the general railroad system,

and the popular belief was that immigration and consequent development would justify the improvement and secure the State against loss.
"These expectations have been disappointed. Immigration was checked
and prevented. Part of the bonds were sold as a sacrifice, and the proceeds misapplied by the officers of the companies. Among the men
managing the railroads and converting the proceeds were members of
both political parties." [5] The planters who bore the taxation raged with
cries of fraud and theft. The *Sentinel* said: "Rave on, ye Radical plunderers; but your days of iniquity and fraud and corruption are fast
coming to an end. The people, insulted and robbed, will not much
longer suffer you to pursue your foul practices and elude public justice." [6]

"The North Carolina served, loved and honored by Gaston, Hash,
Badger, Swain and Ruffin is the same North Carolina no more. She
is now the 'hog trough' of the Union where Littlefield, Deweese,
Laflin, Tourgée, Heaton, Ashley, Brewer and Abbott, and such swine,
come to wallow with native hogs like Holden, Victor, and Greasy
Sam." [7]

Many things show that in North Carolina land and capital were
bidding for the black and white labor vote. Capital with universal suffrage outbid the landed interests. The landholders had one recourse,
and that was to draw the color line and convince the native-born white
voter that his interests lay with the planter-class and were opposed to
those of the Northern interloper and the Negro. The boycott on the
part of the planters against Negro labor, unless it voted right, was
severe. When the legislature of 1868 adjourned, 88 of the Republican
members signed a bitter address to the people, which was militant
labor striking back:

"Did it ever occur to you, ye gentlemen of property, education, and
character—to you, ye men, and especially ye women, who never received anything from these colored people but services, kindness, and
protection—did it never occur to you that these same people who are
so very bad, will not be willing to sleep in the cold when your houses
are denied them, merely because they will not vote as you do; that
they may not be willing to starve, while they are willing to work for
bread? Did it never occur to you that revenge which is sweet to you,
may be sweet to them? Hear us, if nothing else you will hear, did it
never occur to you that if you kill their children with hunger they
will kill your children with fear? Did it never occur to you that if
you good people maliciously determine that they shall have no shelter,
they may determine that you shall have no shelter?

"And now, be it remembered that in the late election there were
more than twenty thousand majority of the freemen of North Caro-

lina who voted in opposition to the Democratic party. Will it be safe
for the landholders, householders, and meatholders to attempt to kick
into disgrace and starve to death twenty thousand majority of the
freemen of this state?" [8]

Again, later, as the power of the planters became stronger, the
Standard, representing the c~~petbaggers, said:

"Can there be any remedy under the forms of law? We think so,
unquestionably. Of course it is not to be supposed that men and
women and children will starve to death while corn is still standing
in the fields and while hogs and cattle are not kept under lock and
key! But these are matters of minor importance and are to be expected, however much the necessity may be deplored. What we mean
is, that there is one efficient remedy for this wholesale crusade of oppression carried on against the colored race to starve him into voting
against his choice. The remedy is this:

"Whenever the Republicans have control of a county, let a meeting
of the commissioners be called at once. Let them make out a list of
all the colored stonemasons, bricklayers, plasterers, painters and carpenters. Then let them select a site of sufficient dimensions for a village of from five to fifteen hundred colored paupers, as the case may
be. The work itself will give employment to a considerable number
of persons, and some time will be required to complete it. Then let the
county paupers be moved in and be provided with houses and food
at the expense of those who have made them paupers. Let the tax be
so laid as to affect only the large landholders. Not one in twenty owns
any land at all, and the large landholders are much rarer. This tax
will fall lightly upon the great mass of people, while the oppressive
landholder will be compelled to throw his broad acres upon the market to raise money to pay the taxes. And in addition to this, let the
legislature deprive these exacting tyrants of the benefit of the stay law
and compel them to pay their debts, to pass their lands under the
sheriff's hammer and give the poor a chance to buy land." [9]

Governor Holden was accused of being the head of the Union
League, which was the organization of white and colored voters, of
believing in social equality and of being corrupt. The Ku Klux Klan
increased their activities and the Congressional Investigating Committee reported 260 outrages, including 7 murders and the whipping of 72
whites and 141 Negroes.

Holden says:

"These combinations were at first purely political in their character,
and many good citizens were induced to join them. But gradually
under the leadership of ambitious and discontented politicians and
under the pretext that society needed to be regulated by some authority

outside or above the law, their character was changed, and those secret Klans began to commit murder, to rob, whip, scourge, and mutilate unoffending citizens. . . . They met in secret, in disguise, and arms, in a dress of a certain kind intended to conceal their persons and their horses, and to terrify those whom they menaced or assaulted. They held their camps, and under leaders they decreed judgment against their peaceable fellow-citizens from mere intimidations to scourgings, mutilations, the burning of churches, schoolhouses, mills, and in many cases to murder. This organization, under different names but cemented by a common purpose, is believed to have embraced not less than 40,000 voters in North Carolina." [10]

Governor Holden said in his proclamation of July 19, 1870: "For months past there has been maturing in these localities, under the guidance of bad and disloyal men, a dangerous secret insurrection. I have invoked public opinion to aid me in suppressing this treason! I have issued proclamation after proclamation to the people of the State to break up these unlawful combinations! I have brought to bear every civil power to restore peace and order, but all in vain! The Constitution and the laws of the United States and of this State are set at naught; the civil courts are no longer a protection to life, liberty and property; assassination and outrage go unpunished, and the civil magistrates are intimidated and are afraid to perform their functions.

"To the majority of the people of these sections the approach of night is like the entrance into the valley of the shadow of death; the men dare not sleep beneath their roofs at night, but abandoning their wives and little ones, wander in the woods until day." [11]

The legislature met in 1870 with three Negro Senators and nineteen Negro members of the House. This small proportion of Negroes was continued up until 1876, the number of Senators remaining about the same, but the number of Representatives being reduced to seven. The appropriations for schools and relief were not sufficient and there was continued complaint. A system of public schools had been inaugurated in April, 1869.

The impeachment of Holden was repeatedly demanded. Seventeen colored members of the legislature issued an address in 1870 in which they defended Holden. "The only offense of Governor Holden and that which has brought down the wrath of the dominant party upon him, is that he thwarted the designs of a band of assassins who had prepared to sacrifice this State in the blood of the poor people on the night before the last election on account of their political sentiments and to prevent them from voting. Because he dispersed this murderous host organized by the so-called Conservative party, they proposed to destroy him. First proposed to suspend him, then to go through with a mock trial before the Senate as they have already done before the House, where a true bill has been found without taking testimony.

"After impeachment his enemies will not be satisfied until he is hanged, unless happily their own gallows should overtake them. When Governor Holden is disposed of, those whom he protected will be the next victims. For the blood of one man will not satisfy their thirst. They are mad because Reconstruction measures have triumphed and we are permitted to represent you in this body. They are mad because we refuse to bow the knee to them." [12]

The legislature which convened in the capital in the fall of 1870 was made up of a Senate of thirty-six Conservatives, three Negroes, and two carpetbaggers, and a House of seventy-five Conservatives, nineteen Negroes, and two carpetbaggers.

One of the first things which this new legislature did was to take steps leading to the impeachment of the Governor. He was accused of being the head of the Union League in North Carolina, of believing in the social and the political equality of the two races, and of conducting the affairs of the state of North Carolina in a wasteful way. As members of the Union League, it was to be expected that Negroes would give their full support to the only political organization which made any pretense at wanting them among its membership and which they believed to be the one thing standing between them and reënslavement. In a letter to Captain Pride Jones of Hillsboro, Holden said: "Every citizen, no matter of what color, or how poor or humble, has a right to labor for a living without being molested; to express his political opinions without let or hindrance; and to be absolutely at peace in his own house." [13]

But the strategy of North Carolina became increasingly clear: to drive out Northerners who dared to take political leadership of Negroes and to unite all whites against Negroes on a basis of race prejudice and mob law. Thus under "race" they camouflaged a dictatorship of land and capital over black labor and indirectly over white labor.

The Albemarle Register said: "This paper in the future is in favor of drawing the line between whites and blacks regardless of consequences."

Despite all the charges of fraud, corruption and stealing, Holden when finally impeached was charged not with dishonesty, but with using and paying troops to put down insurrection in the state. He said in defense: "That as regarded the white militia, we all agreed, at least those of us who took part in this discussion, that the Governor would be employing a militia composed of Ku Klux to put down Ku Klux; that as regards the colored militia it was inexpedient and impolitic to use them, owing to the prejudice in regard to race and color.

It was then suggested, by whom I do not recollect, that it would be best to organize a regular force." [14] White Northerners added that far from the Ku Klux trying to stamp out corruption, "that to punish or prevent corruption is no part of the object of the Ku Klux, but that they tolerate those who rob the State. This may be because among the robbers are members of both political parties, including some who direct and others who control and might easily suppress the Klan, and if the Ku Klux were to punish corruption impartially they would strike men in sympathy with themselves, even their own members. Another reason for the indulgence of public robbers by Ku Klux is, that the doings of both tend to the same result—the overthrow of the State government. The one assaults while the other undermines." [15]

In the ensuing constitutional convention, Tourgée, one of the ablest and most honest of the carpetbaggers, defended the carpetbaggers and said that Columbus, the Pilgrims and even Jesus Christ were carpetbaggers. O'Hara, a Negro delegate, moved to make the cohabitation of a white person and a Negro a felony. This was rejected 59 to 46. Tourgée proposed to make it a misdemeanor. This was rejected 61 to 43.

From 1870 on, North Carolina was in the power of the Democratic Party, so that radical Reconstruction controlled the state for only two years. Wages were low during Reconstruction and probably would have been under any government. In 1860, $110 a year was the wages of a man hired out; in 1867, $104; in 1868 and 1870, $89. The value of the chief crops was $38,000,000 in 1867, $31,000,000 in 1870. In 1860, the value of manufactured products was $9,011,050; in 1870, $19,021,327.

Concerning this whole North Carolina struggle, Tourgée expressed the truth when he said that democratic methods of government were "never indigenous to Southern soil. In truth, it has never become acclimated there, but has remained from the first an exotic. A few thousand of the white people of North Carolina accepted it in 1868, simply as the equivalent of the Unionism which has always held so dear a place in their hearts. A few hundred Adullamites accepted it as the alternative of political bankruptcy and the shibboleth of profitable power; and a few score of earnest natives accepted it with a clear perception of its basic principles, and a *bona fide* belief in their beneficence and righteousness. A few hundred carpetbaggers received it as the spontaneous product of their native States, the sentiments for which they fought and bled. The African race in bulk received it as the incarnation and sheet anchor of that liberty which they had just tested. . . . Ignorance, poverty and inexperience were its chief characteristics." [16]

At the beginning of the nineteenth century, Virginia had something over 300,000 Negroes, of whom 285,369 were slaves and 20,124 free Negroes. By 1860, the slaves had increased to 490,865 and the free Negroes to 58,042.

The western counties of Virginia, beyond the mountains, opposed secession, and at a meeting held in August, 1861, they called themselves the restored government of Virginia, and made F. H. Pierpont Governor. This body gave the consent of Virginia to the forming of a new state of West Virginia.

Governor Pierpont then moved his capital to Alexandria, under the protection of the Federal armies, but actually had only a small part of Virginia under his control. In May, 1864, this restored government adopted a constitution with white suffrage. President Lincoln recognized the government, and President Johnson, May 9, 1865, restored Federal functions in Virginia. A session of the legislature met in June, 1865, passed some black laws, and congratulated itself on escaping Negro suffrage.

The government was moved from Alexandria to Richmond, and immediately there appeared a split between the former Confederates and the Unionists. The freedmen were especially disappointed and held a convention in Alexandria in August, 1865.

"The body reviewed 'the indignities, brutalities and inhumanities,' to which the Negroes were subjected as slaves. It asserted that a large number of Virginians bore the Negroes an undeserved malice because they were black, and had been freed by the United States Government. As a protection against such people, the freedmen demanded the rights, privileges and immunities common to citizens, including the right to vote. The freedmen declared that they were prepared to exercise the suffrage intelligently; and they pledged their loyalty to the interests of the State and to the United States. They presented a claim to citizenship on the ground that they should not be regarded as a separate class, but granted the considerations prayed as an evidence of the natural equality of all men." [17]

In the congressional election of October 12, the reactionaries were completely successful and in January, 1866, passed a stern black code with the usual vagrancy law and contract labor law. Ordinary civil rights were granted the Negro, but he could testify in court only when he was himself involved. Even some of the Confederates thought these laws too drastic and General Terry prohibited their application. The Congressional Committee of Fifteen began an inquiry into affairs in Virginia in January, 1866, and had 49 witnesses of all shades of opinion.

The reactionaries were bitter toward the Negroes and there were several riotous outbreaks. The Unionists called a convention at Alexandria May 17 and took a stand in favor of public schools and Negro suffrage. Late in 1866, Pierpont, recognizing the trend of affairs, recommended modification of the vagrancy law and ratification of the Fourteenth Amendment; but the Legislature at first refused, and then in extra session debated the matter. Before they had come to any final decision, the Reconstruction laws became operative.

The Reconstruction Act of March 2 had been passed when the legislature met again. On March 5, the Negroes had attempted to vote in a municipal election at Alexandria. The mayor and judge asked advice of President Johnson and of the Attorney-General, but received no answer. The Negroes cast 1,400 votes; the white Conservatives, 1,000 votes; and the white Radicals, 72 votes. The Negro votes were not counted; and the military commander forbade further local elections until after registration.

Meantime the considerable immigration of white politicians and officeholders began to organize the Negro vote. Among those who early took leadership was James W. Hunnicutt, a native of South Carolina, who became the Radical leader of the Negroes. John C. Underwood became a more moderate leader, and John Minor Botts, a Conservative leader. At first, Botts was not in favor of Negro suffrage.

Various Republican papers were established which told the Negroes that they were in danger of being reënslaved, and they were given to understand that the plantations would be broken up and every freedman given a forty-acre farm. The reactionaries were strongly against Negro suffrage. They wanted the Negro neither to vote nor hold office, but would grant him some civil and economic rights. They nevertheless insisted that Negroes coöperate with their former masters.

There was a great deal of sickness, poverty and death among Negroes at this time and some crime. There was also much philanthropic effort, fraternal and insurance societies, attempts at theatrical exhibitions, and some inter-marriage between the races. Negro churches and schools were built and burned. A riot took place in Alexandria on Christmas Day, 1865, in which two whites were injured and fourteen Negroes killed.

Yet Whitelaw Reid said: "The Negroes 'were everywhere found quiet, respectful and peaceable; they were the only class at work; and in, perhaps, most respects their outward conduct was that of excellent citizens.'"[18] "With regard to their deportment, the Alexandria *Gazette* expressed the consensus of press opinion that 'the Negroes generally behave themselves respectfully toward the whites.'"[19]

The economic oppression of the Negro led during 1865-1867 to considerable migration. Perhaps as many as 200,000 left the state, and there were attempts to organize unions and strikes for higher wages,

particularly in the tobacco factories. In Richmond there was a stevedores' strike and another strike on the Richmond and Danville Railroad. In 1875, a state convention of Negroes assembled which organized the Laboring Men's Mechanic Union Association to protect
Negro labor.

The Superintendent of Public Instruction in his report for 1871
said: "The more striking evidences of thrift are, of course, given by
comparatively a small proportion of the race, and the general willingness to labor which exists among them is to be partly accounted for
by the habit having been formed in slavery. But in the past history of
the race in America, there have always been examples of Negro
shrewdness and enterprise in every neighborhood. . . . With the very
limited opportunities which a slave had for getting money, it is astonishing how many of them bought themselves and their families, in
order to enjoy freedom. And how common it was for them to gain
money for themselves by extra work, by little manufactures and other
honest means. And it is not to be forgotten that during the late war,
the Negroes of Richmond contributed thousands of dollars to sustain
the Confederacy, and many stood the test of the battlefield on both
sides." [20]

In 1868, the Negroes of Richmond organized the Virginia Home-
Building Fund and Loan Association, and in 1875 there was a Land
and Financial Association chartered by the legislature to purchase
land in small parcels for Negroes. It is estimated that during the late
'60's and the early '70's, Virginia Negroes bought between 80,000 and
100,000 acres of land, and there were many individuals who owned
considerable quantities. Schools were started, at Hampton and Norfolk,
and were greatly extended by the Freedmen's Bureau.

Two political factions now appeared: one consisting of the planters
and a few Negroes, and the other of the Liberals, Negroes, and Northern and native whites. Hunnicutt became a Radical champion.

At an Emancipation Day celebration held in Richmond, 1867, Hunnicutt spoke: "He urged Negroes to register in order to vote in the
fall elections. Where they were organized, he said, they should elect 'a
loyal Governor and loyal Congressmen.' Negroes were advised not to
support white men who had opposed their liberty. Union men also
should be tested. Those refusing to sit in a constitutional convention
with Negroes should not be supported for office. Negroes who voted
for rebels invited the perpetuity of the whipping post, the chain gang,
and the vagrant law. Hunnicutt regarded with suspicion the praise of
Negroes emanating from journals which formerly abused and ridiculed them. He counseled unity of action among the blacks and ex-

pressed the hope that whites and Negroes might live together in harmony." [21]

A Republican state convention was held April 10, 1867. "Some of the Negroes were intelligent looking men and neatly attired." [22] There were 210 delegates, including 160 Negroes. The Negroes took an active part in the convention. Many wanted land confiscation and distribution but some opposed it. Fields Cook, a Negro of Richmond, especially warned the Negroes against any ill-advised measures approving confiscation. The resolutions thanked Congress, advocated public schools and universal suffrage, and made special effort to attract the white laboring class.

"Hunnicutt denied that he had given the Negroes advice detrimental to the whites. He asserted that the Negroes were the bone and sinew of the land, but the pay they received was inadequate. This was an imposition that should not be permitted to continue. He opposed a white landed aristocracy. He opposed injustice to the Negroes in the courts. Whites, he said, were not executed for murdering, but Negroes were hanged for killing whites. Hunnicutt opposed the restitution of the State to native white control. He asserted that Pierpont was a political disloyalist and should not be trusted. He flayed the legislature, stating that its sentiment was attested in the passage of the vagrant law, galling alike to poor whites and Negroes. Summing up his contentions, Hunnicutt stated that he did not desire to place Negroes above whites, but he believed that whites and Negroes should be accorded exactly equal rights." [23]

The ascendancy of Hunnicutt was feared in the North. The New York *Tribune* spoke against it, and Senator Wilson of Massachusetts was sent to Virginia to counteract him. On the other hand, the planters began to threaten economic proscription against Negroes, if they did not work and vote with the native whites. But coöperation was made difficult by Negro agitation for civil rights on street cars, and on juries, which incensed the reactionaries. The freedmen arranged a political meeting at Amelia Courthouse where prominent whites and Negroes spoke. Consequently the Republicans became more and more divided. Moderate Republicans tried to organize and leave out the Hunnicutt faction. They held a meeting at Charlottesville in July and elected delegates to a convention in Richmond. Meetings for coöperation among blacks and whites were held throughout the state. The Richmond meeting was held in the African Baptist Church and was completely captured by Hunnicutt. This defeated coöperation.

In the registration 225,933 persons registered, of whom 120,101 were white and 105,832 were Negroes. The whites had majorities in fifty-two counties and the Negroes in fifty counties. The election took place

October 18, 19 and 20, 1867. The whites cast 76,084 votes and the Negroes 93,145. The call for a convention was authorized. The planters had thirty-three delegates, the Liberals seventy-two delegates, and among the latter were twenty-five Negroes. Hunnicutt was arrested for inciting the Negroes to insurrection but released on bail.

The reactionary press boldly advocated proscription of Negro labor, and the discharge of workmen who supported the Liberal cause. One hundred and fifty Negroes employed in iron mines were discharged because they voted for the Radical ticket. Lewis Lindsay said to this that "before any of his children should suffer for food, the streets of Richmond should run knee-deep in blood; and he thanked God that the Negroes had learned to use guns, pistols, and ramrods." "Commenting on this, the editor of the *Enquirer* deplored that 'the capitalist was threatened with murder if he dared to discharge men who had declared themselves his implacable enemies. He is to house, feed and cherish the black vipers who meet in midnight conclave, and not content with heaping foul epithets upon him, conspire to defraud him of his property. Undaunted by the presence of the military, the Negroes openly avow sentiments, which deserve death upon the gallows.'" [24]

"The Petersburg *Index* asserted: 'The Negroes are the last men who should complain if their white employers were to discharge them and supply their places with white men.' The Lynchburg *Virginian* said: 'They [the native whites] should concert measures without delay to fill the State with white laborers from the North and from Europe. *They must crowd the Negro out.* They must rid the State of an element that will hinder its prosperity, an element that, under the influence of base white demagogues—themselves without property—would tax the property of others to relieve themselves of obligation to educate their children and care for their paupers.'" [25]

A white man's convention was held in Richmond, November 11. It appealed to the North not to permit the "disgrace" of Negro suffrage to be inflicted upon the state, and urged the organization of a party to bring the state under a white man's government.

The constitutional convention with 105 members met in Richmond, December 3, 1867. There were thirty-five Reactionaries and sixty-five Liberals and five doubtful. Among the Liberals were twenty-five Negroes. The native press ridiculed the convention, calling it the convention of "Kangaroos" and the "Black Crook Convention." The convention began work in January and first took up a Bill of Rights with a statement of the natural equality of men.

When the first section of the preamble was brought up for discussion on January 6, 1868, James W. D. Bland (colored) moved that in place of the word "men" in the clause "that all men are by nature equally free and independent," as reported from the committee, be substituted the words "mankind, irrespective of race or color."

Mr. Bland said: "When I recollect that the word 'men,' as written in this first section, has been construed to mean white men only in Virginia, and as the word mankind takes in all the men, women and children on earth, I propose that as an amendment, as men upon this earth are of different races and colors and as we are here to propose a Bill of Rights for the people of Virginia which will make no distinction. I think it right and proper that we should state distinctly what we mean by mankind, or what we mean by men."

Mr. Bayne, another Negro, replied: "I rise to state emphatically that when I was elected to the convention, I pledged the good people of my section that I should endeavor to aid in making a constitution that should not have the word black or white anywhere in it. I told them that I wanted a constitution which our children fifteen years hence might read and not see slavery, even as a shadow, remaining in it. I am here to carry out that agreement. . . .

"All that was necessary, in my judgment, for this nation to do to abolish slavery was simply to place men in power that would interpret that constitution as an anti-slavery instrument which I always believed it was. The word 'slave' was not found in it, but bad men in the nation and bad men in power placed such wicked constructions upon it that it worked death to the nation, and that is the cause of our being here today."

The convention discussed free public education and held a long debate on the matter of race separation in schools. The Negroes especially insisted upon mixed schools and the final report made no specific reference to whether the schools were to be mixed or segregated.

When the debates over mixed schools were in progress, Bayne proposed an amendment to the committee's plan so as to place blacks and whites in the same schools. The amendment failed to get the support of enough Radicals to be adopted, in spite of the efforts on the part of the Negro delegates, and the threats of Bayne, Lindsay, Hodges and others, that if it were not supported by the white Radicals, the Negroes would withdraw from the Republican Party.

The suffrage was the paramount question. The liberals stood for universal suffrage, while the reactionaries declared that government was the prerogative of white men. Finally, the enfranchisement of all males twenty-one years of age was adopted.

Mr. Bayne said: "Does the gentleman mean that the black men are not to have any rights in this country? Does he mean to set us free today and in fifty or sixty years to come, then to give us the right of suffrage? I want it distinctly understood that the old slaveholders' coach moves too slow for us. They design to enslave the blacks again if they can. They design to make him a slave by cutting him off from all opportunities for labor, by starving and oppressing him. Set the Negro free now and let him remain here. No, that is too much for him. He will enjoy it too much. A hundred years to come will be time enough for him to have these rights. In order to carry out their ideas and designs they have commenced just like they did with secession. They are preaching the danger of a war of races in this hall. They are preaching it in Congress, in the cities and over the country, in the streets, and on the seas, on the steamboats, in the cars, in the taverns, and everywhere. This war of races is being preached up constantly, but nobody preaches it up but that side of the House which hates the Republican Party and hates the Federal government. . . ."

Lewis Lindsay, a Negro, said: "We want to give to the poor classes in this state, blacks and whites, every right to which they are entitled, and we will go home satisfied. I want this black race to have every right that is conferred upon every other man."

Mr. Bayne said: "In one breath he tells the convention that this boon is given to us by the blessed Providence of God, and in the next, he says that the Northern fanatics have clothed us with these rights. If the Northern fanatics are the means with which God wishes to confer upon us these rights, I will take the rights whether they or the devil brought them to us. I know that we have them. There is no power on earth or in hell that can deprive the black man of his right to vote. . . ."

The economic problems appear in many guises. One resolution was introduced:

"Resolved: That the Committee on Limitations and Guarantees, when appointed, be entrusted to consider and report the propriety or impropriety of incorporating in the proposed constitution a provision clothing the General Assembly with power to declare and punish as a misdemeanor, the discharge of any person employed as a laborer on account of his political opinions."

Mr. Bayne said: "I claim to be an ignorant man, one not wholly acquainted with this kind of work. . . .

"I give this convention notice that unless they settle the question mentioned at this time and in the commencement of the sessions, we ignorant men will settle it ourselves and to satisfy ourselves. If we are to be bound and obligated at this time, let us know it."

Mr. Marye (white) asked: "Why is it that the cry is coming up from the colored men, actually now taking the form of a petition to Congress, that they cannot get employment because the white people hustle them out of it?"

Mr. Bayne answered: "Will the gentleman allow me to answer his question? The colored people will not work because the employers do not pay them. Six dollars a month will not pay a man and feed and clothe his wife and children."

Former Confederates were disfranchised by a test oath and for participation in the rebellion as officers. The constitution was adopted by a vote of 51-36, only one Negro voting against it.[26]

The reactionary members of the convention joined in a statement: "For nearly five months we have patiently sat in this convention listening to the encomiums upon the Negro race, to wholesale denunciations against the whites of the South, to propositions and speeches leveled against property, and addressed to the cupidity of enfranchised slaves suddenly invested with the controlling power in the state." "It was the subject of remark among us during the progress of the convention," said they, "that the Negroes grew more and more impracticable. The reported debates of the convention will show how active they gradually became in the proceedings of the body."[27]

This constitution was especially opposed because the test oath went further than congressional legislation. It also provided for the reorganization of counties which interfered with the rule of certain families who had dominated various county governments. Income taxes were imposed on incomes over $600, a poll tax on all males, and a homestead exemption. Civil and political rights were guaranteed, and a system of free public schools.

Voting on this constitution was postponed by the military commander, Gen. J. M. Schofield, who was hostile to it, and refused to let money for the election be taken from the state treasury. The election, therefore, could not be held unless Congress made a special appropriation. Political parties, nevertheless, began to prepare for the election and the Republicans nominated H. H. Wells over Hunnicutt. The Conservative Party condemned the "abominable" constitution and nominated Withers, a Confederate colonel. Withers pledged himself to fight against Negro suffrage and said: "I appear before you as the standard-bearer of the white man's party. . . . I do not ask the support of the Negroes, nor do I expect it, for I consider them unfit to exercise the right of suffrage."[28]

In the meantime, the Republicans appealed to Congress and the House of Representatives passed a bill to hold the election in August, 1868, and then afterward another bill to hold it in May, 1869; but the Senate would not assent. Meantime, more moderate men in Virginia proposed that Negro suffrage be accepted, but that the new constitution be rejected. This led to a convention in December in Richmond which stated that while it did not believe in Negro suffrage it would accept it. A committee went to Washington and also a Republican party committee was sent. They appeared before the Committee of Fifteen.

Finally, the Republicans held a new convention, again nominating Wells, but with him as lieutenant-governor, a Negro, Dr. J. D. Harris. This convention split, and the seceders nominated a white man, Walker, for Governor. President Grant ordered an election to be held July 6, 1869, with a separate vote as to the test oath and disfranchisement of Confederates. The reactionaries supported Walker and the ensuing campaign turned entirely on the Negro. Walker was elected, the whites casting 125,114 votes and the Negroes 97,201 votes. Harris was defeated by a vote of 99,600 to 120,068 for his white opponent. The disfranchisement and test oath clauses were rejected, but the constitution was ratified.

"Among the white people there was great rejoicing over the result. The Petersburg *Index* said: 'Virginia has accepted restoration, has rebuked proscription, has vindicated her right to a voice in the control of her affairs, and by a vote unprecedentedly large, places at the head of the government the ticket of peace and equality.' The Danville *Register* said: 'Let us all now go to work, white and colored, looking forward hopefully to a just and liberal system of legislation and an impartial administration for the protection of all alike.' The Lynchburg *Virginian* said: 'The deluded Negroes have been taught a lesson which will bring them to their senses, and we shall have no more trouble with them.' The Norfolk *Journal* rejoiced that Virginia was 'redeemed, regenerated and disenthralled.' " [29]

The colored Conservative Republican group sought to encourage the depressed Negroes and appealed to the whites not to take economic revenge upon the Negroes and drive them away from their jobs because they had voted in accordance with their convictions.

October 5, the General Assembly came together and ratified the Fourteenth Amendment. But the Liberal Republicans continued dissatisfied and declared that the election held in July resulted in a Confederate triumph and was achieved by "artifice, intimidation and fraud." They tried to keep the Federal government from admitting the state, but Grant recommended its admission and Virginia was restored February 8, 1870.

The new constitution was on the whole an excellent instrument. Taylor says that it "gave Virginia the only democratic instrument of government it has ever had. In spite of some of its cumbrous provisions and its imperfect machinery, the Underwood Constitution was as far ahead of that of the old régime or that of the present Virginia caste system as a modern steamship is of an Indian canoe. Such an innovation, of course, struck the reactionaries as a disaster, destructive of all that the gods had ordained as equitable and just." [30]

An Englishman in 1870 said of the legislature:

"I counted among the delegates," he said, "three or four colored men, one of whom was a pure Negro, very well attired, and displaying not more jewelry than a gentleman might wear; while another, who seemed to have some white blood in his veins, was a quite masculine-looking person, both physically and mentally. The Senate was presided over by the Lieutenant-Governor of the State, who was altogether like a young member of the British House of Lords, as the Senate itself had a country-gentleman sort of air not perceptible in the Lower House, which more resembled a Town Council or Parochial Board than the House of Commons. There were two colored Senators among the number, quite black, but senatorial enough, and like men who in Africa would probably have been chiefs. In the Lower House the colored delegates mingled freely with the other members, but in the Senate these two sat in a corner by themselves." [31]

Here, then, was a state in which the Negroes never had control, and nevertheless its chief difficulty under white control was the progressive piling up of an enormous debt which in January, 1872, amounted to $43,690,542. Nothing illustrates better than this the fact that there was no necessary connection between debt and Negro control. The subsequent history of Virginia for many years was the question of paying or repudiating this debt. Meantime, gradually, the Negroes were disfranchised by continued economic pressure, by appeals from their white friends and connections, and by force and fraud.

Arkansas had 12,597 whites and only 1,676 Negroes in 1820. In 1860 it had 324,143 whites and 111,259 Negroes. There was a brief military rule in Arkansas under John S. Phelps in 1862, followed by a year of civil war in 1863; then came four years of civil state government under Governor Murphy, 1864-1867. In 1867, the civil government was subordinated to a military régime under brigadier-generals of the United States Army. Then came the Republican government under Powell Clayton, 1868-1871, and four additional years of Republican rule, after which came the revolution in which the Republicans were driven from power by the local Democrats, assisted by Republican influences at Washington.

At the outbreak of the Civil War, the Negroes resided mainly in the lowlands where most of the plantations were located. During the war, the slaves remained with their masters until the Federal military operations of 1863 took place in sections containing the largest numbers of Negroes. All territory along the White River from Pea Ridge to Helena and westward to Little Rock came under Federal control; and the southeastern counties and lower Arkansas also were captured. The Negroes in these sections then began to enter the Federal lines in large numbers.

A group of Union sympathizers determined to reorganize the State and sought Lincoln's coöperation. He cautiously gave it under his military power, but the group went ahead boldly, held a convention in January, 1864, adopted a constitution and elected Isaac Murphy governor. Two Senators were sent to Washington but Congress called a halt on this summary action and would not admit them. In 1866, the returned Confederates practically took charge of the Murphy government and sent a commission to Washington to confer concerning the condition of the state. The most important change in the constitution during this time was the abolition of slavery and the prohibition of indenture of any Negro except as an apprentice. Some of the leaders preferred permanent despotism to restoration under Negro suffrage. General Albert Pike said Negro suffrage would make "a hell on earth, a hideous, horrid pandemonium filled with all the devils of vice, crime, pauperism, corruption, violence, political debauchery, social anarchy." [32]

Meantime, congressional Reconstruction was begun. Registration began in May, 1867, but progressed slowly. A few whites told the Negroes registration was for the purpose of enrolling them for taxes, but the Freedmen's Bureau sent out agents to instruct them in the purpose of voting.

The total number of registered voters in Arkansas was 66,805; 41,134 voted at the election, and of these 27,756 voted for and 13,558 against holding a constitutional convention. Upon these figures, General Ord announced the names of delegates elected to the convention.

The Arkansas constitutional convention convened January 7, 1868, in the city of Little Rock, and adjourned February 14, 1868. There were eight Negro delegates to the convention: J. W. Mason, Richard Samuels, William Murphy, Monroe Hawkins, William Grey, James T. White, Henry Rector, and Thomas P. Johnson.

Hempstead County had one Negro out of four delegates; Jefferson, one out of four; Lafayette, one out of two; Phillips and Pulaski each had two out of four. Of the Negro delegates, one was a postmaster, two were farmers, four ministers, and one a planter.

Cypert, leader of the white Conservatives, proposed in the convention of 1868 the adoption of the Constitution of 1864. Cypert claimed to be a friend of the Negro. He had been a Freedmen's Bureau agent for a while, and "had always been desirous of advancing the interests of this unfortunate race. He knew the Negro in all his attributes; that their people were now being misled. He appealed to the Negro members present."

Mr. Brooks (white) interrupted, to rise to a point of order. It was disrespectful to style the gentlemen of the convention Negroes.

Mr. Grey (colored), of Phillips County, said "he took no objection to the appellation; his race was closely allied to the race which built the great pyramids of Egypt, where slept the remains of those whose learning had taught Solon and Lycurgus to frame the systems of their laws, and to whom the present ages are indebted for the hints of art and knowledge."

"Mr. Cypert (white) said he was glad that the rebellion had been crushed. He was glad the Negro was free, but while he would have the Negroes protected, as they now are by law, in all their just rights, he could never consent to see them entrusted with the elective franchise, and made the rulers of white men."

Mr. Grey of Phillips replied: "I must confess my surprise at the action of the gentleman from White County (Mr. Cypert). I am here as the representative of a portion of the citizens of Arkansas whose rights are not secured by the ordinance offered by the gentleman from White,—men, sir, who have stood by the government and the old flag in times of trouble, when the republic trembled with the thought of civil war, from center to circumference, from base to cope. From this and other considerations, we are here not to ask charity at the hands of this honorable body, but to receive at the hands of the people of Arkansas in convention assembled, the apportionment of our rights, as assigned by the Reconstruction Acts of Congress.

"I am here, sir, to see those rights of citizenship engrafted upon the organic law of this state; the gentleman from White does not seem to recognize the fact that the present Constitution is not in accordance with the Constitution of the United States, guaranteeing to each state a Republican form of government; the gentleman from White says the Negro cannot become a citizen. The fact is patent that we have exercised the rights of citizenship under the Constitution, in all the states except South Carolina; and that we voted for that time-honored instrument—the Federal Constitution—by voting for the men that ratified it. . . .

"Before the revolution, all native-born free persons were British subjects and hence citizens, as the British government did not base allegiance or citizenship on color or complexion. Hence, we passed from British subjects to American subjects, without changing our relative status as to citizenship. This, I think, disposes of the assertion that we cannot be citizens under the Constitution. But, sir, I claim that it is ours, not only on constitutional grounds, according to the rulings of distinguished American jurists, but ours by right of purchase on the numerous battlefields of our country. It is ours, because from the Revolution down to and through the rebellion, we have stood unswervingly by our country and the flag. We fought for liberty. That liberty cannot be secured to us without the right of suffrage. The government owes the debt, acknowledges it, and apportions it out among the several states. We are here, sir, to receive the amount due us from the State of Arkansas.

"The troubles now on the country are the result of the bad exercise of the elective franchise by unintelligent whites, the 'poor whites' of the South. I could duplicate every Negro who cannot read and write, whose name is on the list of registered voters, with a white man equally as ignorant." [33]

James T. White, a colored man, spoke on social equality:

"I cannot think that the extension of the right of suffrage to colored men could be construed as opening the parlors of white people to a forcible entrance of colored men; but, on the contrary, their virtue and pride of race will be a sufficient safeguard to prevent them from anything like social intercourse. Who is to blame for the present state of affairs? When I look around I see an innumerable company of mulattoes, not one of them the heir of a white woman. This is satisfactory evidence of the virtue of white women. In the late bloody war, these gentlemen left their wives and daughters in the care of colored men for four years, and I defy the gentleman to cite me a single instance where they have failed to live up to their integrity. Gentlemen, the shoe pinches on the other foot—the white men of the South have been for years indulging in illicit intercourse with colored women, and in the dark days of slavery this intercourse was largely forced upon the innocent victims, and I think the time has come when such a course should end." [34]

Mr. William Murphy, a colored man, said February 10:

"When the late war resulted in the issuing of the Emancipation Proclamation by Abraham Lincoln, four millions of our enslaved brethren were called to aid in the establishment of this union of loyalty. For the colored troops have proved their loyalty; they protected the Union flag. So they stood; and white gentlemen have been compelled to surrender the sword, at the same time they will rise here, under the same flag, after they have dropped their swords and their bayonets, and seek to limit our privileges. I would never have spoken, but to say this to the men that have been our masters, men whom we have brought to the very condition they are now in, and have not only fed them, but have clothed them, have tied their shoes, and finally have fought until they are obliged to surrender. Yet now that they have surrendered, they say we have no rights. Has not the man who has conquered upon the battlefield gained any rights? Have we gained none by the sacrifice of our brethren?"

Concerning the adoption of the constitution, James P. Johnson, a colored man, said:

"I believe this constitution to be the best one that Arkansas ever had. The gentleman from Ashley [Mr. Moore] has undertaken to show us that the class of men of whom he is a representative are our best friends. My God! I hope he will put his hand over his mouth and never speak that word again. We are very much inclined to believe the men who are trying to secure equal rights of voting according to the true Republican doctrine of the equal rights of all men; you do not want us to have any rights, but just let us stay in slavery as we were before the war."

James Mason, another colored delegate, read the following explanation of his vote, which he asked to have spread upon the journal:

"I object to the continued disfranchisement of all persons who are now disfranchised by the present Reconstruction Acts of Congress and I believe many are now disfranchised who ought not be; but in the face of the reiterated assertions of gentlemen of the Conservative Party, that they are not to give us the right of suffrage under any circumstances, I am forced to accept this constitution as being good as a whole and as being the best that I can get under the circumstances; and give up my ideas of limited disfranchisement and qualified suffrage."

James White, the colored delegate, added:

"Another reason why I shall vote, and why if I had 10,000 votes I would give them all for the constitution, is that I see in it a principle that is intended to elevate our families—the principle of schools—of education. That is the only way that these Southern people can be elevated. Were they properly educated they would not be led from any prejudice to oppress other men. Were they educated they would not hate us because we have been slaves; but like these gentlemen, if they should puzzle their brains and risk their lives upon the battlefield for the Union, they would stand up for our rights. Away with Union men who will not give all men their rights! Talk about friendship! The devil has such friends locked up, and hell is full of them!" [35]

In the course of convention sessions, a Conservative taunted a carpetbagger with the assertion that the Negro vote was his only way to ride into Congress. Thereupon, Negro members said their race was ready both to vote and fight for the whites who would grant them political rights. Brooks, leader of the Radicals, declared: "We, the great Republican Party, hold that they [the Negro] should have the ballot;

and we intend that they should have it, and we will sustain the government based upon the principles of universal franchise and universal equality." On the other hand, Hinkle, a scalawag, exclaimed: "Great God! Is there no help for the widow's son?" and asserted that "all the devils in hell could not keep him from making himself a record by voting against adoption of the constitution." [36] Despite this, the final vote was 45 to 21 in favor of adoption.

On April 1, it was announced that the constitution had been ratified by a vote of 30,380 to 41. On May 7, a bill for the readmission of Arkansas was presented in Congress by Thaddeus Stevens. It was finally passed in both Houses and over the President's veto on June 22, 1868. Before the bill was presented to Congress, however, the state legislature had met April 2, 1868, and adopted the Fourteenth Amendment which was one of the prerequisites to her admission.

The constitution of Arkansas, like that of Florida, was a document which centralized power in the state government. The governor appointed nearly all the local officers in counties and townships, and he had the power to fill vacancies even in the few offices he did not originally fill. He appointed judges, collectors, and assessors of taxes, justices of the peace, prosecuting attorneys, registrars of elections who in turn appointed the judges of elections.

In April, 1867, a Union convention at Little Rock nominated a state ticket and succeeded in electing Powell Clayton as Governor. One Negro, John Payton of Pulaski County, was on the Committee of Resolutions; otherwise the Negro was not represented among the officials in this party convention.

During 1868-1873, Clayton ruled Arkansas with an iron hand, while the Ku Klux Klan practically carried on civil war. In 1869 an anti-Ku Klux Klan law of great severity was passed which prevented all secret political organizations, and declared their members public enemies. Even the possession of a Ku Klux Klan costume was a criminal offense. The law was sternly enforced, and the Klan disbanded after a season of martial law. In February, 1873, a severe civil rights law was passed which compelled hotels and places of public amusement to admit colored people and insured them equal school facilities in separate schools. Fines of $200-$1,000, or imprisonment of 3 to 12 months, were provided:

"Officers of the law may be prosecuted for failure to enforce it, and prosecuting attorneys, sheriffs, coroners, justices of the peace and even constables, are to institute proceedings, and are obliged to do so. Many of these officers throughout the State are colored men. I was told there had been but a single case under this act, in which a saloon-keeper was fined twenty-five dollars. I noticed that some drinking—

saloons had two bars, one for each color; but I also saw in several cases black and white men drinking together. The Negroes have shown no disposition to make the law offensive." [37]

The rulers of the state constituted a closed ring which had no Negro members, but its power depended on controlling the Negro vote, and on the disfranchisement of about 20,000 of the former Confederates. Those disfranchised were given the right to vote by a constitutional amendment in 1872.

In April, 1874, a civil war broke out in Arkansas between Baxter, the regular Republican, and Brooks, a reform Republican. Each claimed to be Governor. Baxter was recognized by the legislature but Brooks took possession of the state buildings by force. They appealed to President Grant. Grant refused to take part but the Federal forces prevented the two parties from fighting. Grant finally recognized Baxter as Governor because the legislature had, and ordered the Brooks forces to disperse. A constitutional convention was held which cut down the length of the Governor's term and his power.

Brooks now allied himself with the Democrats and declared that the constitutional convention had not been called according to law and was the result of conspiracy. The Democratic convention nominated Garland; the Republican convention, not recognizing the election as lawful, made no nominations. Garland was therefore elected. Grant came to the conclusion that the constitutional convention was illegal and that Brooks was still Governor. But Congress declared against Federal interference. Finally in 1874, the Democrats secured complete control of the state.

Arkansas thus was a contrast to Louisiana. Law and order conquered, but it conquered not for the purpose of giving the Negro any economic power, or, in fact, anything at all except schools and the civil rights bill. The government dictatorship was frankly capitalistic and for the benefit of capital and the protagonists who represented it.

Texas had, in 1860, 182,921 Negroes and 420,891 whites, thus putting this state among those where the Negro population was a decided minority, and white immigration destined greatly to increase the preponderance of the whites. The division of the planters and poor whites was less distinct in this state than in many others. There was plenty of rich land and the poorest white men could get a start; this increased the demand for labor.

Texas was one of the Southern States that had considerable prosperity during the war. She was outside the area of conflict; excellent crops were raised and slave labor was plentiful. Many slaves were deported to Texas for protection, especially from Louisiana and

Arkansas, so that Texas could furnish food and raw material for the Confederate States; and on the other hand, when the blockade was strengthened, Texas became the highway for sending cotton and other goods to Europe by way of Mexico. There were many losses because of the distance, the dishonesty of traders, and lawlessness. Nevertheless, these were offset by the high prices.

When the war neared its end, the Confederate troops in Texas got out of hand and began rebelling and looting. Towns like Houston were burned, and clothes and food and all sorts of goods stolen. The Texas *Republican* stressed "the ruinous effect of freeing four million of ignorant and helpless blacks," and said that the people of the North would be glad to witness a return of slavery, because it would raise "larger crops and a richer market for Yankee manufacturers."

This paper did not think that slavery would be abolished for at least ten years, and that in the meantime compulsory labor would continue. Under the army officials, the compulsory labor did continue, but when the officials of the Freedmen's Bureau arrived, they began to supervise contracts. There was the usual complaint that Negroes were not keeping their contracts, together with reports that they were working well.

President Johnson appointed A. J. Hamilton as Provisional Governor. He was a native of Alabama but had come to Texas before the war. He had refused to join the seceding states and fled to Louisiana, where he became a brigadier-general in the Federal army. When he arrived in Texas, he found everything in confusion. Money had been stolen from the treasury, the capitol building was without a roof, and there was general anarchy. Hamilton protested to Johnson against the tendency of the farmers to keep the Negroes as slaves. The question of the legal status of the Negroes the Governor left to the courts, and the courts contradicted themselves in their decisions, some of them admitting Negro testimony and others refusing it altogether. There continued the strong feeling that either the Negroes were going to remain in bondage, or compensation was going to be paid for their emancipation. The lawlessness continued, robbery and murder of Unionists and freedmen were common, and outlaws defied arrest. One county reports that "the civil authorities are helpless because the country is full of ruffians and lawless men," another that the "laws cannot be enforced without the aid of the military."

The Inspector-General on the staff of General Howard declared, early in 1866, "that Texas was in the worst condition of any state that he had visited; that almost the whole population was hostile in feeling and action to the United States; that there was a mere semblance of government, and that the whites and the Negroes were everywhere ignorant, lawless and starving."

The Assistant Commissioner for Texas under the Freedmen's Bureau arrived in Texas in September, 1865, and began to appoint local agents in December. He found the freedmen "not only willing but anxious to improve every opportunity offered for their moral and intellectual advancement." [38]

In January, 1866, one Black Belt county reports "that two-thirds of the freed population were then at work at good wages and that seven thousand contracts had been filed already and that unemployed freedmen were becoming scarce."

By the end of January there were twenty-six day and night schools and 1,600 Negro pupils enrolled. There was the usual bitter attack upon the presence of Negro troops, late in 1865 and early in 1866.

After much delay, an election was held January 8, 1866, and a convention was scheduled to meet in Austin in February. There were strong differences of opinion among the delegates. Dalrymple said:

"My opponents . . . each and all, concede something to the Negroes; some more, some less, approximating to equality with the white race. I concede them nothing but the station of 'hewers of wood and drawers of water.' . . . If a republican form of government is to be sustained, the white race must do it without any Negro alloy. A mongrel Mexico affords no fit example for imitation. I desire the perpetuation of a white man's government . . . !"

Colonel M. T. Johnson of Tarrant County "declared his opposition to granting the Negro any political rights whatever, and insisted that he should be made to work by uniform laws regulating pauperism, labor and apprenticeship; but at the same time asserted the necessity of treating him with justice and kindness in his helpless condition." There seems to have been only one candidate, E. Degener, a prominent German of San Antonio, who openly advocated Negro suffrage.

One prominent Texan, John H. Reagan, a prisoner of war at Fort Warren, Massachusetts, wrote a thoughtful letter in August which was published in Texas in October. He pointed out that the South was in the position of a conquered nation, that Texas would not be restored until it did what the North demanded, and that the North demanded protection against secession, the abolition of slavery, and civil rights for the freedmen. Moreover, it was probable that this alone would not satisfy the North and that it would demand Negro suffrage. Reagan, therefore, advised that Negro testimony be admitted in courts, and that an intelligence and, possibly, a property test be set for admission to the right to vote regardless of race or color, provided that no persons previously entitled to vote should be deprived of the right by the new requirements. President Johnson secured a parole for Reagan and it was hoped that he would have influence on the state, but his wise advice raised such opposition that he long refrained from further discussion. "A refusal to accede to these conditions would only result in a prolongation of the time during which you will be deprived of the civil government of your own choice, and will continue subject to military rule." [39]

When the convention assembled, the former secessionists were in control. The Governor in his message stressed the necessity of giving full civil rights to the Negro and the possibility of political suffrage. He said:

"I do not believe that the great mass of the freedmen in our midst are qualified by their intelligence to exercise the right of suffrage, and I do not desire to see this privilege conferred upon them; [but] if we fail to make political privileges depend upon rules of universal application, we will inevitably be betrayed into legislation under the influence of ancient prejudices and with a view only to the present. I think that human wisdom cannot discern what is to be the future of the African race in this country. . . . I would not be willing to deprive any man, who is qualified under existing laws to vote, of the exercise of that privilege in the future; but I believe it would be wise to regulate the qualifications of those who are to become voters hereafter by rules of universal application." [40]

The convention dawdled and spent most of its time electioneering for the Senatorships, and entered into a metaphysical discussion as to whether secession was illegal from the beginning or should simply be disavowed at present. Finally, the usual Southern circumlocutions were adopted: African slavery had been terminated by the United States government, and therefore it should be discontinued in Texas. Negroes were to have property rights but could testify only in cases involving Negroes, although the legislature could, when it wished, give them full rights of testimony. The German Degener was alone in his advocacy of Negro suffrage. There was some debate on repudiating the civil debt which had been recklessly increased to nearly $8,500,000.

After a session of eight weeks, the convention adjourned, having failed to take any really advanced step, except the grudging recognition of Emancipation. Immediately preparations were made for the coming elections, and a considerable party wanted to drive out all Union men and nullify the emancipation of Negroes. The planters supported the president of the Convention as Governor and opposed Negro suffrage. Their ticket was elected by a large majority and eventually recognized by the President. Former Confederates, elected as Senators, were unable to take the test oath. They and the Representatives were refused seats in Congress. The Thirteenth and Fourteenth Amendments were presented to the legislature, the first without comment and the second with unqualified disapproval. The Fourteenth Amendment was rejected by a vote of 70-5 in the House, and a large majority in the Senate.

Reagan again called attention to the trend of events, and advocated qualified Negro suffrage and the right of Negroes to testify in the courts. His letter produced only irritation.

The new head of the Freedmen's Bureau, General Kiddoo, favored the employers as against the Negro laborers and established heavy fines for "enticing" laborers away from employers. A black code gave certain rights to freedmen not prohibited by the Constitution, but forbade inter-marriage, voting, holding public office, serving on juries, or testifying in cases where Negroes were not concerned. Johnson urged that civil rights be extended to the colored people if it had not already been done.

Violence continued in the spring and summer of 1866. The town of Brenham was burned, soldiers broke up a Negro ball, and there was general lawlessness. Gangs of horse thieves and desperadoes were roaming about. Federal officials reported that Union men and Negroes were fleeing for their lives and that murders and outrages on Negroes were on the increase, while criminals were always acquitted.

Kiddoo substituted yearly contracts instead of monthly contracts in the cotton districts, and tried to assure the freedmen of their wages. He repudiated the labor law passed by the legislature, but his successor adopted some of its provisions. March 19, 1867, Sheridan was made commander of the 5th Military District, consisting of Louisiana and Texas. Unable to secure the release of large numbers of Negroes imprisoned on trivial charges, Sheridan issued his jury order excluding from juries persons who were unable to take the test oath. Sheridan declared that one trial of a white man for killing a Negro was a farce.

Meantime, the registration of voters under the new Congressional legislation began. The Negroes were eager to vote. A new state Republican Party was organized, and there was advocacy of free common schools and free homesteads from the public lands to all without discrimination of color. E. M. Pease was appointed Governor by Sheridan July 30, 1867, and Throckmorton removed. Pease was a native of Connecticut but had been in Texas since 1835, and during 1853-1857 had been Governor of the state. He opposed secession. There arose among the Republicans a severe difference of opinion as to how far the former Confederates should be disfranchised.

The President in August removed Sheridan from command and substituted Thomas; ten days later he substituted Hancock for Thomas. Hancock assumed command in November. He was a Democrat, and a follower of Johnson. He reversed Sheridan's order concerning juries, and declared that the country was "in a state of profound peace." Pease flatly contradicted this and said there had been one hundred murders during the past year, with only ten arrests and five trials. He declared that, because of Hancock's order concerning juries, there had been an increase in crime and hostility to the government.

Agitation arose because it was said that Negroes were carrying arms, although it was well known that every white Texan was habitually armed. A Negro meeting which was addressed by a Supreme Court judge was broken up, and the judge complained: " 'None but a Johnson man could be tolerated here. He must cuss Congress and damn the nigger. . . . General Hancock is with the President politically and will only execute the letter of the law to escape accountability. . . . There is not an intelligent rebel in all the land who does not understand him. . . .' " [41] During 1867 there was bad feeling between the races. The whites especially resented arms in the hands of the Negro soldiers. And the impossibility of convicting white aggressors upon black men was continually manifest.

A judge declared that it was impossible to convict a white man of any crime on Negro testimony; where the crime was against a Negro, to convict a white man of murder in the first degree was out of question.

Registration of voters had begun early in the summer of 1867 but went on slowly. The Conservatives first proposed not to register, and then afterward changed their minds and registered with the plan of staying away from the election. The election was held in February, 1868, and showed that comparatively few whites had been disfranchised.

Fifty-nine thousand, six hundred and thirty-three, or 14% of the white population, registered in 1867, and 49,497 Negroes, or 27% of the colored population. A majority of the whites voted against the convention but the blacks carried it. The total registration was 109,130, and the white registration was about equal to the total vote in the campaign of 1866.

The election was quiet, and the convention won by an overwhelming vote of 44,689 to 11,440. In the Constitutional Convention, it was characteristic that among the 90 members there were twelve reactionary white members from the Black Belt, elected undoubtedly by all too common methods. There were nine Negroes, and delegates from the black districts bordering on the Brazos and Trinity Rivers.

J. T. Ruby came from Galveston. He was an educated Negro and was elected from the white district of Galveston. Ruby was a mulatto from Philadelphia and for fifteen years was the leader of the Negroes. He was rated as an astute politician and a man of unusual ability. He was very popular in Galveston, where his brother held a position in the custom house.

E. J. Davis was a new white leader of the Unionists. He had been an opponent of secession and an officer in the Union army during the war. He was one of the first to defend Negro suffrage. Governor Pease sent in a message in which he declared that from December 1, 1867, to June 1, 1868, in sixty-seven counties out of 127, two hundred and six murders had taken place with few attempts to punish the offenders. He recommended schools and homesteads and the encouragement of immigration. Ralph Long of Limestone, a Negro, was an outstanding leader. It was he who offered the resolution annulling certain court decisions which declared that the Emancipation Proclamation should not take universal effect. His resolution was rejected by a two-thirds vote.

On July 2, the committee on lawlessness and violence reported 509 whites and 486 Negroes killed, 1865-1868. More than 90% of these murders were committed by white men. The report continues:

"In other words, according to the lowest calculation, the peace administration of Generals Hancock and Buchanan has to account for twice the number of murders committed under the Sheridan-Throckmorton administration, and three times the number committed under the Sheridan-Pease administration. Moreover, fuller reports show that since the policy of General Hancock was inaugurated, sustained as it is by President Johnson, the homicides in Texas have averaged fifty-five per month; and for the last five months they have averaged sixty per month. It is for the Commander of the Fifth Military District to answer to the public for at least two-thirds of the 330, or more, homicides committed in Texas since the first of December, 1867. Charged by law to keep the peace and afford protection to life and property, and having the army of the United States to assist him in so doing, *he has failed*. He has persistently refused to try criminals, rejected the prayers of the Executive of the State and of the Commanding General of the District of Texas for adequate tribunals, and turned a deaf ear to the cry of tried and persecuted loyalists. And knowing whereof we affirm, and in the face of the civilized world, we do solemnly lay to his charge the death of hundreds of the loyal citizens of Texas—a responsibility that should load his name with infamy, and hand his very memory to coming years as a curse and an execration." [42] Delegates were sent to Congress with this report, while the Houston *Telegraph* advocated their assassination.

The convention in making the constitution came to the question of the suffrage in August, and then postponed it until after the recess, which took place after ninety-two days of work. The reason for the recess was differences among the Republicans and fear of mob law among the Democrats before the presidential election. Mobs appeared. G. W. Smith, a white New Yorker and leader of the Negroes, was jailed and lynched, together with several of his black followers. Feuds were rife in many of the counties. Bands of Ku Klux roamed about. Negroes were boycotted or given employment as they joined Democratic groups.

In January, when the convention came together again, the question of suffrage was discussed. The Democrats proposed to exclude Negroes, while unrestricted suffrage was defeated by a vote of 34-31. The final proposition allowed Negroes to vote and disqualified only those classes mentioned in the Fourteenth Amendment. This finally passed by a vote of 30-26.

The whole fight on suffrage was not a fight against Negro suffrage, but a question as to how far former Confederates were to be allowed to vote. The measure finally passed admitted the great mass of these. Hamilton, the former Provisional Governor, secured the final triumph of a policy of leniency toward the ex-Confederates. This divided the Republicans into two factions: one which wished to disqualify the Confederates more completely, and the other which was willing to share the practical control with the Confederates. Three Negro members, Ruby, Williams and Newcomb, revolted against the prolonging of the session of the convention and resigned, declaring that the convention was prolonged for the purpose of subsidizing a venal press. Ruby declared "that the present Reconstruction convention has lost, through many of its members, all regard for dignity and honor as a legislative assembly, and that its continued assemblage will only terminate in disgust to the entire country."

The convention never actually adjourned nor was the constitution ever adopted by actual vote. The most meritorious features of the constitution were the abolition of slavery and the liberal provisions for the schools. The constitution established free public schools and decreed that the receipts from public lands should go to the school fund, besides other revenues. A State Superintendent of Public Instruction was appointed. As a final result, Davis became the leader of the radical Republican Party, while Hamilton was the leader of the Conservatives and was backed by Johnson. The result was a contest in which Hamilton could only hope to win by getting a large number of white Democratic votes, while Davis sought the bulk of the Negro votes, because of their fear of disfranchisement at the hands of the ex-Confederates. The election took place in 1869. It was quiet, although there were accusations of fraud in various parts of the state. E. J. Davis, by the efforts of Ruby, who marshaled the Negro votes, was elected Governor by a small plurality.

In the ensuing legislature, the Fourteenth and Fifteenth Amendment were adopted almost without opposition, and March 30, 1870, the representatives of Texas were admitted to Congress. Thereupon, E. J. Davis became Governor instead of Provisional Governor. In April Governor Davis complained of the continuance of lawlessness in many parts of the state. Ruby, the colored leader, was still active in Galveston, working for a new charter for the city. Every effort was made to aid the railroads by renewing land grants and making appropriations of $16,000 in state bonds for every mile built. Davis favored railroads but opposed subsidies and vetoed some of the bills. He kept on declaring that a slow civil war was going on in Texas, and pressed for a state police force. Later, a railroad grab involving $6,000,000 subsidy was passed through the legislature and indignantly vetoed by the Governor.

"In counting up the charges against Davis's administration, not a suspicion can rest against his financial honesty, of which this veto message is an enduring monument." [43]

There was a small increase of debt. When Davis came into office in 1870, the state was out of debt, and when he left office in 1874, the debt was $4,414,095. The rate for state taxes had risen from 15¢ in 1860 to $2.17½ on $100 valuation in 1866, exclusive of about 60¢ in addition, which was interest on bonds donated to railroads.

There had been an ineffectual effort to establish a free public school system in Texas in 1845. In 1869, provision was made to give to the public school fund the proceeds of the sale of all the public lands, which resulted in a magnificent endowment. The constitution of 1869 authorized the legislature to divide the state into school districts and appoint school directors. Every effort was made to wreck the school system in order to exclude Negroes, but gradually it became solidly established.

As the election of 1873 approached, there was great excitement. Davis's chief reliance was on the Negro vote, and he strove especially to get out the Negro vote in the Black Belt counties, where it was largely suppressed. The whites were determined to drive him out. "It was in a sense a revolution. There is no shadow of a doubt of fraud and intimidation at this election. 'Davis Negroes' were in many communities ordered to keep away from the polling places, while white men under age were voted." [44]

The total vote was surprisingly large, probably because it was fraudulent. Davis was defeated by a vote of 85,549 to 42,663, and the majority of the legislature were Democrats. The State Supreme Court held the election irregular because of the case of a single individual, and Governor Davis attempted to prolong his term; but this meant civil war. Negro militia was on hand to prevent Democrats from taking possession of the capitol, and open hostilities were imminent. Davis telegraphed Grant, but military aid was refused, and finally Davis retired.

The problem in this frontier state never reached its vital economic phases until long after Reconstruction.

During this Reconstruction period many Negroes held office. There was a lack of whites who could take the test or oaths or who were willing to act as supervisors, registrars and clerks. The Negroes were usually on these boards and sometimes were appointed even when whites were available. They became indeed so outstanding as officeholders for a while that the Houston *Telegraph* sounded a warning that unless the full strength of the whites should be enlisted, there would be large numbers of Negro officeholders, and that they would try to take the land out of the hands of the present owners. There were Negroes in the state militia and on the various police forces, and they formed a military guard when Davis was trying to keep the Democrats from taking forcible possession of the capitol.

In 1872, for the first time, Negroes voted for President. Norris Wright Cuney, a young colored man, born in 1846, became sergeant-at-arms in the Texas legislature, and warmly attached to Governor Davis. In 1871, Cuney became one of the school directors of Galveston County; in 1872 he was Inspector of Customs for the state. Cuney ran for Mayor of Galveston in 1875, and his successful Democratic opponent testified to Cuney's interest in sound policy and honest government. He continued for many years to be the incorruptible and intelligent leader of the Negroes of Texas.

The border land between slavery and free labor, including the District of Columbia, Delaware and Maryland, West Virginia, Kentucky and Tennessee, Missouri and the Indian Territory, was vitally affected by the abolition of slavery. Its history during and after the Civil War is not usually included in Reconstruction, and yet it had analogous problems arising from abolition and enfranchisement.

Unfortunately, however, monographic material upon which a study of the Negro in these states might be based is lacking in many particulars. There is practically nothing about Negroes in Delaware and the Indian Territory; and in the case of the other states, the problems are insistently conceived as being exclusively problems of the white population, so that the development of the Negro is followed with great difficulty. Here remains, therefore, a most interesting and neglected field of historical and economic exploration.

The District of Columbia is of especial interest because it is the seat of the United States government. The status of slavery there not only was of intrinsic importance, but the nation and the world actually saw slavery in Washington and judged the whole system largely from what they saw.

At the beginning of the nineteenth century, there were 4,027 Negroes in the District. They increased to 10,425 in 1820, and 13,746 in 1850. At the beginning of the war, the Negro population stood at 14,316. Of this population, there were 783 free Negroes in 1800; 6,152, or a majority of the black population, in 1830; and 11,131 in 1860, when they largely outnumbered the 3,000 slaves.

Immediately after the war, the Negro population greatly increased, reaching 43,404 in 1870 and 59,596 in 1880. During these years, however, the proportion of Negroes in the total Washington population did not vary greatly. It formed one-third in 1810 and one-third in 1880. It fell to its lowest point, 19%, in 1860.

Because of the prominence of the city, the abolition campaign was early concentrated upon slavery in the District, and gained partial triumph when the slave trade was abolished in 1850. In 1861, a bill to abolish slavery in the District of Columbia was introduced by Senator Wilson, and after much opposition from the Border States, it passed the Senate and the House in April, 1862, and was signed by President Lincoln, April 16. The result of this law made Washington a mecca for free Negroes, and in a single decade, the Negro population increased 200%. These Negroes had begun their own self-supported schools in 1807.

The civil rights of Negroes in the District were fought for continuously by Charles Sumner. He secured the law of April 3, 1865, to make valid Negro testimony in the District courts. He fought segregation on railroad and streetcar lines and the law which prevented Negroes from carrying mail. On his motion, a Negro was admitted to practice before the Supreme Court in 1865, and another in 1867. The right to serve as jurors was not conferred on Negroes until March, 1869.

After the abolition of slavery in the District of Columbia, there came an agitation to give the Negroes the right to vote. A large mass meeting was held at the Asbury M. E. Church in 1865. A petition signed by Negroes who could read and write was sent to Congress, and after long debate and postponement for a year, the Negro was finally enfranchised in December, 1866; the bill passed over a veto by President Johnson.

In November, 1867, there were 13,294 white voters, and 6,648 Negroes. In 1871, at the election of a delegate to Congress, 17,757 whites and 10,772 Negroes voted.

The economic status of the Negro in the District was made very difficult during and after the war because of the large increase in the Negro population. Nevertheless, Negroes accumulated a good deal of property. When, for instance, it was charged in 1865 that they did not own $40,000 worth of property in the whole city, it was proven that in one square their holdings aggregated $45,592. Yet there were poverty and suffering among the Negroes. In 1867, it was estimated that of 32,000 Negroes in the district, one-half were destitute. Congress appropriated $15,000 on March 16, 1867, to relieve the freedmen.

In February, 1871, an act was passed changing the government of the District of Columbia. The old charters and courts which had been inherited from the Maryland government were discarded and a territorial form of government established with a Governor and legislative assembly composed of a Council and House of Delegates. The Governor and Council were appointed by the President, and the House elected by the people. The powers were similar to those granted to new territories, including the right to borrow money, assess taxes, and carry on the government: Alexander R. Shepherd, a personal friend of President Grant. He ran a plumbing business, and was a native of the District; Grant appointed him Governor. He changed Washington from a poorly paved, badly lighted, unattractive city into a model and beautiful capital. The work was done rapidly and was accompanied by all the current political jobbery. Under any circumstances, the transformation would have cost large sums of money, but with graft and misappropriation of funds, the District was plunged into a debt of many millions of dollars. After sharp agitation, the government was changed again, all the people disfranchised, and the District put under the rule of three commissioners. Naturally, in this case, as in the Southern states, the harm and dishonesty of the Shepherd régime was charged to the colored voter, while the beauty and accomplishment of the re-born city was put to the credit of white civilization. There was about as much sense in one charge as in the other. Disfranchisement in the District came at the demand of over-taxed real estate and of reactionary property interests hiding behind the color bar.

Maryland had at the beginning of the nineteenth century 125,222 Negroes. This number increased gradually to 155,932 in 1830; decreased in 1840; rose in 1850 to 165,091, and in 1860, was estimated at 171,131.

The free Negroes in this population numbered 19,587 at the beg...
ning of the century, and increased rapidly and steadily to 83,942 in
1860. Thus, the black population of Maryland was almost evenly
divided at the opening of the war between free Negroes and slaves.

Maryland, along with Virginia and the other Border States, had
some part in the business of raising slaves for sale further South, but
not as large a part as these other states. On the whole, her Negro population were artisans, laborers and servants, and the institution of slavery
was insecure because of the ease of escape to Northern states.

The Black Code of Maryland forbade the immigration of free
Negroes, although in 1862, the penalty for sale into slavery was abolished. In 1865, immigration was permitted. The Assembly of 1867
repealed many parts of the Black Code, but among other things, did
not allow a colored woman to be a competent witness against the
white father of her child.

During the war, nothing was done to interfere with the institution
of slavery. But the convention of 1864, charged with forming a new
Constitution, had a considerable number of delegates in favor of
abolition. Finally, a clause for immediate abolition of slavery was
passed by a vote of 2-1. When the Constitution went before the people,
it was accepted by a narrow margin.

A constitutional convention was held in Annapolis in 1867, and
another Constitution adopted by an overwhelming popular vote. It
did not declare that men were "created equally free," and compensation for freed slaves was demanded. This represented a reactionary
movement, as compared with the Constitution of 1864.

During the campaign, the Unconditional Union Party, in 1866,
pledged itself against Negro suffrage, while the Republican Party
Convention, in 1867, had colored men among the 200 delegates from
Baltimore and a large number from the counties. A colored clergyman
opened this convention.

"A colored veteran said there was no need to tell his people how
to vote. 'We have not,' he said, 'the ability among us to occupy high
positions of honor; we are like a new-born babe, taking our first steps
to political life and strength, supported by the Radical party.' Another
prominent leader said, 'It is because we are a minority of the voting
population of Maryland that the necessity has been forced upon us
of casting around to see by what means we can extricate ourselves
from our present position'; and another still, 'Whenever we can get
the suffrage for the colored man, I am satisfied there is no man that
can ever betray us again.' " [45]

"The resolutions of the convention called for the equality of all
American citizens in all civil and political rights, and urged the Re-

publican party, as a last resort, should the coming conservative constitution not give impartial suffrage, to appeal to Congress for support.

"One colored delegate, a member of the Committee on Resolutions, rejoiced to see a day of real political equality between whites and blacks; another said he was ready, like Simeon of old, to depart in peace, now that he had seen salvation."[46]

In 1866, Governor Swann, the man who wanted to arm his militia with Federal artillery, addressed an open letter to the editors of the Baltimore *American* in which he said:

"I am utterly opposed to universal Negro suffrage and the extreme radicalism of certain men in Congress and in our own State, who have been striving to shape the platform of the Union Party in the interests of Negro suffrage. . . . I look upon Negro suffrage and the recognition of the power in Congress to control suffrage within the States as the virtual subordination of the Negro in the State of Maryland. . . . I consider the issue upon this subject . . . as well made in the fall elections, and the most important that has ever been brought to the attention of the people of the State of Maryland."[47]

Governor Swann was answered in an editorial in the *American,* a few days later, which read:

". . . At least nine-tenths of the Union men of Maryland have taken position with the Congress of the United States. . . . The Governor will find, when too late, that he will not be followed by a corporal's guard of those who placed him in his present position in the course he has taken, and that his future affiliation must be with the disloyal, whilst his antagonists will be the true and loyal men of Maryland. . . ."[48]

Notwithstanding the effort of the Republicans, the Conservative Constitution, without Negro suffrage, was adopted a few months later. Negroes did not get the right to vote until after the Fourteenth and Fifteenth Amendments. Few colored men have been nominated to elective offices in Maryland. In 1872, a Negro ran for Congress in the 5th District, but withdrew in favor of a white candidate.

Negro labor had a larger chance in Baltimore because of skilled work by the blacks in brickmaking, oyster shucking, work as stevedores; and they practically had a monopoly on ship-caulking. After the Civil War, there came a good deal of competition with foreign labor.

"From the testimony of many persons, the colored people of Baltimore appear to have been actively engaged in all manner of business ventures even before the Civil War. These ante-bellum enterprises were carried on generally by individual ownership. But immediately after the Civil War, numerous coöperative movements sprang up among the people all over the city. Coöperative grocery stores, coal yards, beneficial societies and other kinds of business met with marked success for short periods, but each one in its turn finally failed, owing either to lack of capital, or trained business management, or both." [49]

Prior to the war, the colored people of Baltimore had no place, aside from the churches, in which to hold public entertainments. To meet this need, several colored men, John H. Butler, Simon Smith and Walter Sorrell, formed a partnership, and purchased in 1863 a large three-story brick building on Lexington Street, near North, and had it converted into a hall. They named it Douglass Institute, after the grand old man from Maryland. Besides public entertainments of all sorts, the hall was used as a meeting place for fraternal orders.

The Chesapeake Marine Railway and Dry Dock Company, a company owned and controlled by colored men, was organized in the year 1865. The company was capitalized at $40,000. The stock was divided into 8,000 shares at $5 a share. The corporation lived for a period of eighteen years, or from 1865 to 1883, and was for many years very successful.

It finally gave up business in 1883. The organization of the ship company saved the colored caulkers, for they became members of the white caulkers' union. The failure of the whites to drive out the colored caulkers lessened their efforts to drive colored labor out of other fields. Changing economic conditions ended this company but it was an object lesson to the whites, as well as to the blacks, of the power and capability of the colored people in their industrial development. [50]

Before 1865, the public schools depended on local authorities. Then an educational revolution took place, and the state began to control the schools. The law of 1865 provided that the part of the school taxes paid by colored men should be used for Negro schools. The law of 1868 ordered a 10¢ tax on $100 for state schools, and this was all the colored schools could expect down to 1872, except by donations from philanthropists.

In 1872, the state appropriated $50,000 for the colored schools, in addition to the colored tax; but the white schools received all the regular school tax. In 1878, the sum of $100,000 was appropriated, to be taken from the state school fund at the expense of the white schools. This remained the law until 1888. Baltimore had before the war at least six private schools taught by colored people, and later, Northern philanthropists founded schools for the freedmen.

Kentucky was a state with 41,082 Negroes at the beginning of the century, 170,130 in 1830, and 226,167 in 1860. The Negroes formed a little over one-third of the population. There were comparatively few free Negroes, the number being only 10,684 in 1860. Kentucky was so situated between the two sections that it was in the main current of trade movements. Not only was it vitally interested in the slave trade to the South, but also in the trade in food stuff and manufactured materials from the North. The economic problem, therefore, for Kentucky during the Civil War, was difficult. Her chief interest was to keep the sections from falling apart and thus spoiling her favored economic position. Then, too, she had several important crops, chief of which was tobacco, and next, corn; besides these there were hemp, flax, and live stock. In all these economic, industrial activities, the Negro figured largely. On the other hand, Kentucky was near the border, and the loss of capital through runaway slaves was a constant menace to the system.

No sooner did the war open than this menace was increased by the action of the slave owners themselves.

"This practice of putting slaves to work on military projects was first begun with the slaves of Southern sympathizers. . . . A network of wagon roads had to be constructed over which military supplies should go; fortifications had to be built. Large numbers of slaves were early set to work on a road from central Kentucky to Cumberland Gap; and by the middle of 1863, Boyle was calling for 6,000 slaves to extend the railway from Lebanon to Danville." [51]

In 1863, there was a rumor that the slaves would rise in insurrection at Christmas time, and that Northern troops would aid them. This was followed by the policy of enlisting colored troops into Northern armies.

The enlistment of slaves ended the slave system. The cash bounty and offer of freedom brought droves of black volunteers. "The Negroes deserted the fields in the midst of growing crops in many parts of the state, and in western Kentucky where they were under better control, steamboats threatened the rivers and with squads of troops raided the plantations, and forcibly took 'hundreds of Negroes from the fields.' In Madison County Negro regiments were used to scour the fields and force the slaves into the army. Ten thousand slaves left the state during the year 1863; slaves enlisted at the rate of a hundred a day, and after the war, were freed at the rate of 500 a day." [52]

Still the legislature refused to ratify the Thirteenth Amendment. Kentucky regarded the Emancipation Proclamation, issued January 1, 1863, as unwise, unconstitutional and void. Legislation was passed to nullify its execution, and in 1864, slaves were still being sold for $350 to $500 apiece.

The Freedmen's Bureau set up the first state organization for Negroes at a convention held in Lexington, March 22-23, 1866. It was bitterly opposed because of its attempt to secure colored men justice in the courts. General Fisk announced that Freedmen's Courts would be established for the protection of the Negroes, and in the following months, these courts found much to do. This activity scared the legislature into granting the Negro partial civil rights, and abolishing the slave code.

During 1867, the Bureau arrested 89 persons charged with crimes against Negroes, and handed them over to the Federal courts for trial.[53]

The legislature stubbornly refused to ratify the Thirteenth Amendment; after it had been ratified, Kentucky passed a Civil Rights Act, February, 1866, which repealed the old slave code. The bill was passed as the result of a refusal on the part of Congress to remove the Freedmen's Bureau from that state until Negroes had been granted civil rights. The freedmen were given all the civil rights enjoyed by white persons with the exception of sitting on juries and testifying against whites.[54]

White labor rivalry was widespread. Guerrilla bands spread all over the state following the war. In March, 1865, a band of men stopped a train on the Ohio and Mississippi Railroad by tearing up the track north of the Ohio River; secured $30,000 in United States bonds; robbed the passengers, and fled across into Boone County. A similar crime was committed in 1867, in Simpson County. Some of the members of this gang were arrested. Some of the names these gangs assumed were "Regulators," "Rownee Band," and "Skagg's Men." In Madison County, which the "Regulators" terrorized for three or four years, a wealthy farmer was hanged; in Mercer County, one was shot and then hanged; another 70 years old was killed; and later, two cousins were also hanged. In western Kentucky, the Negroes were warned to leave the country and landowners threatened with having their homes burned if they rented to them.

In the election of 1864, the two parties were the Conservatives and the Radicals. The Radical Party was the champion of the rights of the Negroes. A great storm of complaint came from the Conservatives: "The military authorities had acted outrageously; they had assumed control of the election, as if it were wholly an affair of the army, and had assumed to decide who should vote, and who should not. Soldiers were stationed around the polls, and at many places, they were Negroes, holding lists of names of people who some Radicals thought should not vote. . . . None of these were permitted to approach the ballot box. . . . All were simply people who were opposed to the Thirteenth Amendment."[55]

In the meantime, Negroes began their political organization and on Emancipation Day and the Fourth of July held celebrations with parades. The celebration of July 4, 1868, was attended by 15,000 Negroes, from Fayette and surrounding counties. Radicals estimated that there would be over 50,000 Negro votes, and that only through these votes could they overcome the Conservatives.

The proposed Fourteenth and Fifteenth Amendments encouraged the Radicals to anticipate victory by organizing Negro voters. "It was predicted that there would be 100,000 Negro votes. The Louisville *Commercial* declared that elections thereafter would not be the 'one-sided affairs of 1867, 1868 and 1869.' Picnics and celebrations were held on the passage of the Fifteenth Amendment, where the Negroes gathered in great numbers, and where the Radicals used their full opportunities to make speeches and to organize and control the new voters. One of the celebrations was held in Paris, Kentucky, and was attended by more than 6,000 Negroes.

"The most ambitious move to organize the Negroes was made in a convention in Frankfort in February, 1870, where Negroes from almost every county in the state gathered together. This 'First Republican Convention of the Colored Citizens of the State of Kentucky' was refused the legislative halls, but it seems to have lost no prestige by meeting elsewhere, for one of its members boldly declared, 'The eye of the world is upon Major Hall,'" where they finally met.

The planters and capitalists made a counter stroke by starting a noisy agitation for Chinese and other foreign labor. Many Negroes were alarmed. Partly as an answer to this, and for other purposes, a Negro convention was held in "Louisville, Kentucky, on July 18, 1869. There were 250 delegates in attendance. The subjects discussed were political and economic as well as educational. They included the abolition of the relics of slavery, equal education, the rights in the courts, equal taxation, the ratification of the Fifteenth Amendment, and the purchase of real estate." [56]

The Negroes advised the young men and youth of Kentucky to "learn trades and engage in agricultural pursuits as a proper mode of supporting themselves and giving encouragement to mechanics and agriculture, and by all means to procure homes for themselves and families."

In Fayette County, a meeting of Negroes was held in which they expressed their willingness to work and enter into labor contracts with whites. An Intelligence Office of the ex-soldiers maintained a labor agency. During the first half of 1869, 3,000 Negroes were supplied with jobs through them. On August 20, 1869, the Negroes observed a day of thanksgiving for their success. Evidently, the whites were praised for their cooperation; they contributed ham, beef, flour, and other provisions for the celebration.

The first test of Negro suffrage came in 1870, when county offices were to be filled. The Democrats attempted to arouse the Negroes to demand offices so that the Radicals would be estranged.

The Democrats did not intend to invite Negro support, and they "early saw that it would be dangerous to interpose violent opposition to Negro voting. What then should be their position toward inviting his support? Henry Watterson believed that the Negro suffrage should be accepted as an established fact and that Negro voters should be welcomed as much as others. . . .

"But the whole idea of Negro suffrage was so fearful and repulsive to the Democrats that they plead with the reasonable Radicals, 'as sensible men . . . to halt and think seriously for at least one minute.' . . . They sought to drive out of the party many Radicals by holding up to them the specter of Negro officials. In fact they pushed the logic with great emphasis on every occasion that if the Radicals embraced the Negroes they must give them offices. They hoped to arouse the Negro on this point to demanding offices, and thereby imperil his relations with his allies." [57]

Cheating and fraud were eventually resorted to. Many Negroes were prevented from voting by requiring receipts for taxes which had been assessed on them. There were insufficient facilities for voting, purposely leaving the Negroes waiting until the sun went down. An endless number of irrelevant questions were asked, requiring in one place from twenty to twenty-five minutes for four Negroes to vote, while ten to fifteen whites could vote during that time.

The question of offices became increasingly important for the Negroes. It was not merely a matter of personal ambition, but here, as in the deep South, a question of the administration of the law which they with perfect right feared to trust entirely to the hand of whites. In 1873 a Negro convention declared that since they had voted for the Radicals, they should now have "a reasonable portion of the offices," and if claims were to be ignored, they would "cease to be indebted to this party any more than to any other."

In 1867, the Negroes owned $1,000,000 of taxable property on which they paid a tax of $3,661. Most of this wealth consisted in land, which they greatly coveted. By 1871, Negro agricultural fairs were held in many of the counties. The freedmen were encouraged by Bureau agents and by other people to be frugal and begin to save money. The branches of the Freedmen's Saving and Trust Company, located in Louisville and Lexington, contained $171,000 in savings belonging to Negroes when the crash came. [58]

The economic rebirth of the state went on with Negro help. The number of farms increased in this decade (1860-1870) from 90,000 to

118,000. The last year of the war (1864-1865) tobacco dropped from 127 million pounds to 54 million; wheat from 8 million bushels to 3 million; hemp from 10 million pounds to 2 million; hay from 135,-000 tons to 127,000; barley from 161,000 bushels to 137,000. Corn increased from 39 million bushels to 58 million. An increase in crops began in 1867 and attained the pre-war mark by 1871. A comparison of the produce of these two years shows an increase: in tobacco from 54 million to 103 million pounds; hay from 127,000 to 320,000 tons; barley from 161,000 to 243,000 bushels. Corn fell from 58 million to 54 million bushels.

Tennessee was a Border State which formed in many respects an economic complement to Kentucky. The state had at the beginning of the century 3,778 Negroes. They increased rapidly to 146,158 in 1830, chiefly through the development of the Cotton Belt in the western part of the state near the Mississippi. At the opening of the war, Tennessee had 283,019 Negroes. The number of free Negroes was small, being only 7,300 in 1860. During the decade 1850-1860, Shelby County, of which Memphis was the center, gained its great mass of Negro population. From this point the Cotton Kingdom spread West and South. In strong contrast to this, in Nashville and in the middle and eastern part of the state, and in similar parts of Kentucky, there was strong emancipation sentiment in early times, chiefly with the motive of getting rid of the competition of Negro labor. This was manifested by opposition to the custom of slaves' hiring out at times, which was prevalent in this part of the state.

In the constitutional convention of 1796, there was an attempt to prohibit slavery after 1864, which did not pass, but free Negroes who met the requirements of residence and land holding were allowed to vote. They enjoyed this right until 1834. At the convention of 1834 another attempt to abolish slavery was defeated and the vote was denied free Negroes, with some exceptions.

The slave trade in Tennessee was even more lucrative than in Kentucky, and there was strong trade in both slaves and materials down the Mississippi to New Orleans.

The Confederates seized most of Tennessee at the beginning of the war, but with the retreat of the Confederate army after the surrender of Fort Donelson, in 1862, a territory of 30,000 square miles was opened to Federal occupation, and a population of 1,000,000 souls was left without government and in possible danger of a slave insurrection. To meet the emergency, President Lincoln, March 3, appointed Senator Andrew Johnson, a former Governor of Tennessee, Military Governor, with the rank of brigadier-general.

In 1863, Rosecrans needed every available man for the winter campaign. Lincoln telegraphed September 8, and urged all Union officers to get every man he could, black and white, to guard the roads and bridges and send all the better-trained soldiers forward to Rosecrans. On October 21, Johnson and Stearns of Massachusetts were authorized to raise troops in Tennessee. Six regular Negro regiments, and two garrison and hospital regiments, were thus raised.

Governor Johnson made attempts immediately and at several times thereafter to reorganize the civil government of the state, but all these attempts failed, until the people of East Tennessee undertook the task in the summer of 1864. In November, 1864, the East Tennessee Union Executive Committee called a convention to meet in Nashville in December. Meantime, the Confederates captured Knoxville, and when it was time for the convention to meet, Hood was threatening Nashville. The convention was, therefore, postponed until January 8, 1865. By that time, the Confederates had been driven out, Johnson had been elected Vice President, and Congress had refused to count Tennessee's scattering presidential vote. The convention met and voted for amendments to the Constitution: 1. Abolishing slavery. 2. Providing that all citizens who had borne arms for the United States should be allowed to vote; color should not disfranchise any person who was a competent witness in the courts.

Johnson favored the amendments and they were put through "with slight modification." This is the story of Winston, but by consulting Hall, one learns that that slight modification was the dropping of the amendment which allowed Negroes to vote.[59]

The report finally adopted by the convention proposed two amendments to the State Constitution, one to abolish slavery, and another forbidding the Legislature to make any law recognizing it. The report directed that all who voted should take the iron-clad oath and that the convention should nominate a candidate for Governor and a complete legislative ticket.

In the ensuing election, 20% of the vote in 1860 was cast: William G. Brownlow was chosen Governor by 23,352 votes, against 35 scattering ones. Four days after his inauguration, Lee surrendered and the new government was safe.

The constitutional convention had declared in favor of disfranchising all who had fought against the United States. Governor Brownlow was determined to make this declaration into a law. After recommending the ratification of the Thirteenth Amendment to the Federal Constitution, he reminded the Legislature that the loyal people who had entrusted the qualifications of voters to them wanted them to act decisively in the matter. He asked the Legislature for military force to enforce the law when enacted.[60]

The law provided that white persons of lawful age and residence, who had entertained unconditional Union sentiments from the outbreak of the war, or who had arrived at the age of 21 years since November 4, 1865, or who could prove their loyalty, or had been honorably discharged from the Union Army, or were Union men conscripted into the Confederate Army, or had voted at the elections of 1864-1865, should be entitled to the privileges of the elective franchise.

At the next session of the Legislature, the Governor recommended the amendment of the franchise bill and the colonization of the Negroes in Texas or Mexico, or their admission to full citizenship and suffrage, in case the franchise law restricting the vote of former Confederates should be repealed. The result was that a bill which the first legislature had refused to consider became law on January 21, 1866. This said:

"That persons of African and Indian descent are hereby declared to be competent witnesses in all the courts of this state, in as full a manner as such persons are by an act of Congress competent witnesses in all the courts of the United States, and all laws and parts of laws of the State, excluding such persons from competency are hereby repealed: *Provided, however,* That this act shall not be so construed as to give colored persons the right to vote, hold office, or sit on juries in this State; and that this provision is inserted by virtue of the provision of the 9th Section of the amended Constitution, ratified February 22, 1865."

Race prejudice was strong in East Tennessee, based on the economic rivalry of Negroes and poor whites.

"East Tennesseeans, though opposed to slavery and secession, do not like 'niggers.' There is at this day more prejudice against color among the middle and poor classes, the 'Union' men of the South who owned few or no slaves, than among the planters who owned them by scores and hundreds." [61]

On the other hand, the planters had not surrendered their ideas on slavery.

"The *designs* of the great secession majority of Tennessee may have been changed by the events of the war, and so may have been their opinions of their own strength and of the strength of the government, but, unless your memorialists greatly misunderstand them, their sentiments, sympathies, and passions remain unchanged. They welcome peace because they are disabled from making war; they submit because they can no longer resist; they accept results they cannot reject, and profess loyalty because they have a halter around their necks. They *recognize* the abolition of slavery because they see it before them as a fact; but they say it was accomplished by gross violations of the

Constitution, that the Negro is free only in fact, but not in law or of right." [62]

The attitude of the state toward Negroes was bad. "The predominant feeling of those lately in rebellion is that of deep-seated hatred, amounting in many cases to a spirit of revenge towards the white Unionists of the State, and a haughty contempt for the Negro, whom they cannot treat as a freeman. The hatred for the white loyalist is intensified by the accusation that he deserted the South in her extremity, and is, therefore, a traitor, and by the setting up of a government of the minority. The spirit of revenge is called forth by the attempt to disfranchise them, and by the retaliatory acts of the returned Union soldiers for wrongs done them during the war. The Negro is the Mordecai who constantly reminds them of their defeat, and of what they call a 'just, but lost cause.' And the sight of him in the enjoyment of freedom is a constant source of irritation." [63]

On the first of May, 1866, a riot broke out in Memphis between the whites and blacks, which continued two days and resulted in the death of 24 Negroes and the wounding of 1 white man. As a result of this the Legislature passed the Metropolitan Police Bill, May 14, which provided that the police regulations of the city of Memphis should be in the hands of three commissioners appointed by the Governor, and made it a crime for anyone else to attempt to exercise any control in the city not subordinate to this board. The provisions of this act were also extended to Nashville and Chattanooga.[64]

The Negroes of Tennessee were not content. On Friday, June 23, 1865, they sent out notice of a state convention in August:

"Great efforts are being made to oppress (and in our judgment in relation to House Bill, No. 47) and reënslave us. Let us lay our grievances before the General Government. Under the government of the noblest patriot of the country—Andrew Johnson—the friend of humanity and liberty, we feel assured that our cause will succeed. We enter anew upon our duties as men, trusting in God. Come one, come all. Rally to the cause of liberty, and to the rescue." [65]

The convention was in session four days, and

"RESOLVED, That we protest against the Congressional delegation from Tennessee being received into the Congress of the United States, if the Legislature of Tennessee does not grant the petition before it prior to December 1, 1865." [66]

A month before the opening of Congress in December, 1865, the Clerk of the House announced his decision not to put on the official roll the names of any men claiming to be elected from any Southern state. This decision of the Clerk was endorsed by the Republican caucus held at the opening of the session.

Congress assembled at noon, December 4, and when the Clerk, in calling the roll, reached Indiana, Mr. Maynard, from the First District of Tennessee, rose and attempted to speak, but the Clerk would allow no interruption of the roll.

A report of the Joint Committee on Reconstruction, March 5, 1866, proposed to allow the admission of Tennessee with white suffrage; but it was recommitted. July 20 it reappeared and was amended by the Senate so as to require acceptance of the Fourteenth Amendment. In this form, the resolution was passed July 23, and was approved July 24, although the President denied that Congress had any right to pass laws preliminary to the admission of qualified representatives from any of the states and objected to certain words in the preamble. Tennessee complied by promptly accepting the Fourteenth Amendment, July 11-12, 1866, the vote being 15-6 in the Senate and 43-11 in the House.

Subsequently, February 6, 1867, the House of Representatives of Tennessee passed a bill striking the word "white" from the franchise law of the state by a vote of 38-25. The Senate concurred February 18, by a vote of 14-7. And in March, the Supreme Court of the state upheld the constitutionality of Negro suffrage. The Republican platform in February, 1867, severely attacked Andrew Johnson, as an unprincipled adopted son, but said nothing directly about the Negro. The Conservative platform of April 17 said:

"That our colored fellow-citizens, being now citizens of the United States and citizens of the State of Tennessee, and voters of this State, are entitled to all the rights and privileges of citizens under the laws and Constitution of the United States, and of the State of Tennessee."

In a race for Congress in 1872, Johnson made a bid for the Negro vote.

"In the western counties crowds of Negroes attended the speaking, some evidently anxious to make good citizens. Addressing these colored people, Andrew Johnson explained his position. 'If fit and qualified by character and education, no one should deny you the ballot,' he said. 'I have been ridiculed for saying I would be your Moses,' he continued. 'Yet I say again, I will be your Moses; and if you have a certificate to vote you should be allowed to vote.' " [67]

There were two or three Negroes in the Tennessee legislature during Reconstruction, while others served as state and city officers. Nashville at one time had a third of its city council composed of Negroes.

Missouri was a Western state which became "Southern" because it was on the great national highway to the South and its political weight was needed by the Southern oligarchy. It was thought that if Missouri remained a slave state, Kansas, Colorado and California would follow, and the Southern empire would be safe; but if Missouri was lost, slavery would be restricted, with its whole Western dependence on Texas.

Missouri had few Negroes—3,618 at her first census; 59,814 in 1840; and 118,503, about a tenth of her population, in 1860. Only 3,572 of them were free. Most slaveholding families had only 3 or 4 Negroes. Slavery was not a system—it was a survival, a sentiment, and a matter of common labor and service.

This made a sharp economic division, at the outbreak of the war, between those who said slavery was industrially useless in Missouri, but that the South had a right to it, and those who cared neither for slavery nor for the South. There arose a bitter internecine strife, family against family, and neighbor against neighbor. To the Union went 109,000 troops; to the Confederates, 30,000. There were 244 battles and 2,261 engagements in the state, which devastated the land and killed over 30,000 people. War routed thousands of settlers, and spread robbery and crime, lying and murder, mistreatment of women and children, disease and death.

The legislature of 1860 favored the South, but not secession. The new Governor, Jackson, who sought to force the state into secession, was opposed by F. P. Blair, a leader of the new industrial development. The Civil War came, and Blair was victorious. A constitutional convention in 1865 abolished slavery, without compensation.

The convention which emancipated the Negro drew up a new constitution which provided for the establishment and the maintenance of free public schools for the instruction of all persons in the state who were between the ages of five and twenty-one. Later, the legislature passed a law requiring one or more segregated schools to be set up in cities and villages. This law, like many other laws relating to the Negro, was overlooked. During the period, however, there was a growing sentiment in favor of public schools. The school system grew. Negro troops founded the first school of Negro higher training at Jefferson City—Lincoln Institute.

The Radicals carried the elections of 1866 and 1868, but nevertheless, the state constitutional amendment enfranchising the Negro in Missouri was defeated. The amendment was submitted by the legislature, but was lost by more than 19,000 votes. The opposition came from the Democrats, who voted solidly against it, and from a goodly number of Radicals, also. The question of enfranchising the Negroes had been an important issue in the state ever since they had been freed in 1865, but it was submitted to the people in the form of a constitutional amendment but once.

The Fifteenth Amendment of the United States, conferring suffrage upon the Negro, was ratified and put in force before the amendment to the Constitution of Missouri could be brought up again. This settled the issue without any further contest in the state.

Here, then, is a sketch of the part which Negroes took in the reconstruction of various Southern states, together with some indication of their action along the border. It is incomplete, and for that reason, inconclusive. And yet, no one can read these records, and the documents upon which they are based, without concluding that this was a perfectly normal development, that these black men were ordinary men who, according to their training and experience and particularly according to their economic condition, did extraordinarily well and do not in the slightest degree deserve the contempt and unbridled abuse that has been put upon them. They were not primarily responsible for the exceeding waste and corruption in the South any more than the laboring class was to blame for the greater waste and dishonesty in the North. They were not proven incapable of self-government. On the contrary, they took decisive and encouraging steps toward the widening and strengthening of human democracy. It is only the Blindspot in the eyes of America, and its historians, that can overlook and misread so clear and encouraging a chapter of human struggle and human uplift.

Then speed the day and haste the hour,
Break down the barriers, gain the power
To use the land and sail the sea,
To hold the tools, unchecked and free;
No tribute pay, but service give,
Let each man work that all may live.
Banish all bonds and usury,
Be free! Set free!
Democracy! Democracy!

A. W. THOMAS

---

1. Hamilton, *Reconstruction in North Carolina*, p. 150.
2. Holden, *Memoirs* (John Lawson Monographs of the Trinity College Historical Society, Durham, N. C., 1911), pp. 83-84.
3. Hamilton, *Reconstruction in North Carolina*, p. 274.
4. Cited in Hamilton, *Reconstruction in North Carolina*, pp. 256, 257, 378.
5. Report Number 22, 42nd Congress, 2nd Session, House of Representatives, II, Part I, p. 107.
6. The *Sentinel*, Feb. 9, 1870 (cited in Hamilton, p. 405).
7. The *Sentinel*, Feb. 19, 1870 (cited in Hamilton, p. 405).
8. Hamilton, *Reconstruction in North Carolina*, p. 365.
9. Hamilton, *Reconstruction in North Carolina*, pp. 368-369.

10. Holden, *Memoirs* (John Lawson Monographs), pp. 138-139.
11. Holden, *Memoirs* (John Lawson Monographs), p. 544.
12. Holden, *Memoirs* (John Lawson Monographs), p. 544.
13. Clement, *A History of Negro Education in North Carolina*, p. 57.
14. Holden, *Memoirs* (John Lawson Monographs), pp. 191-192.
15. Report Number 22, 42nd Congress, 2nd Session, House of Representatives, II, Part I, p. 124.
16. Hamilton, *Reconstruction in North Carolina*, p. 664.
17. Taylor, *The Negro in the Reconstruction of Virginia*, p. 14.
18. Reid, *After the War: A Southern Tour*, pp. 302-303 (quoted in Taylor, p. 84).
19. Taylor, *The Negro in the Reconstruction of Virginia*, p. 84.
20. Cited in Taylor, *The Negro in the Reconstruction of Virginia*, p. 129.
21. Taylor, *The Negro in the Reconstruction of Virginia*, p. 210.
22. *Enquirer*, April 18, 1867 (cited in Taylor, p. 210).
23. Taylor, *The Negro in the Reconstruction of Virginia*, pp. 211-212 (reported in Richmond *Times*, April 18, 1867).
24. Taylor, *The Negro in the Reconstruction of Virginia*, p. 223 (reported in Richmond *Times*, April 18, 1867).
25. Taylor, *The Negro in the Reconstruction of Virginia*, p. 224 (reported in Richmond *Times*, April 18, 1867).
26. Documents of the Constitutional Convention of Virginia, 1867, No. XV.
27. Quoted in Taylor, *The Negro in the Reconstruction of Virginia*, p. 237.
28. Taylor, *The Negro in the Reconstruction of Virginia*, p. 246.
29. Taylor, *The Negro in the Reconstruction of Virginia*, p. 257.
30. Taylor, *The Negro in the Reconstruction of Virginia*, p. 262.
31. Quoted in Taylor, *The Negro in the Reconstruction of Virginia*, pp. 263-264.
32. Staples, *Reconstruction in Arkansas*, p. 129.
33. Arkansas Constitutional Convention, 1868.
34. Arkansas Constitutional Convention, 1868.
35. Arkansas Constitutional Convention, 1868.
36. Arkansas Constitutional Convention, 1868.
37. Nordhoff, pp. 35-36.
38. Ramsdell, *Reconstruction in Texas*, pp. 69, 73, 75.
39. Ramsdell, *Reconstruction in Texas*, pp. 86, 87.
40. Ramsdell, *Reconstruction in Texas*, pp. 92-93.
41. Ramsdell, *Reconstruction in Texas*, p. 189.
42. Ramsdell, *Reconstruction in Texas*, pp. 220-223.
43. Ramsdell, *Reconstruction in Texas*, p. 308.
44. Ramsdell, *Reconstruction in Texas*, p. 315.
45. Brackett, *Colored People of Maryland Since the War*, p. 13; Johns Hopkins Studies in Historical and Political Science, VIII, p. 359.
46. Brackett, *Colored People of Maryland Since the War*, pp. 13-14; Johns Hopkins Studies in Historical and Political Science, VIII, pp. 359-360.
47. Myers, *The Self-Reconstruction of Maryland*, p. 55 (Johns Hopkins Studies, XXVII).
48. Myers, *The Self-Reconstruction of Maryland*, pp. 55-56 (Johns Hopkins Studies, XXVII).
49. Du Bois, *Atlanta University Studies*, II, p. 150.
50. Du Bois, *Atlanta University Studies*, II, pp. 152-153.
51. Coulter, *The Civil War and Reconstruction in Kentucky*, pp. 157-158.
52. Coulter, *The Civil War and Reconstruction in Kentucky*, p. 247.
53. Coulter, *The Civil War and Reconstruction in Kentucky*, p. 348.
54. Coulter, *The Civil War and Reconstruction in Kentucky*, p. 340.
55. Coulter, *The Civil War and Reconstruction in Kentucky*, p. 283.
56. Wesley, *Negro Labor in the United States*, p. 173.
57. Coulter, *The Civil War and Reconstruction in Kentucky*, pp. 425, 426.
58. Coulter, *The Civil War and Reconstruction in Kentucky*, p. 358.
59. Hall, *Andrew Johnson*, pp. 167-170.
60. Fertig, *Reconstruction in Tennessee*, p. 65.
61. Trowbridge, *The South*, p. 239.

62. Report of Joint Committee on Reconstruction, 1866, p. 91.
63. Report of Joint Committee on Reconstruction, 1866, pp. 92-93.
64. Fertig, *Reconstruction in Tennessee*, p. 75.
65. New Orleans *Tribune*.
66. New Orleans *Tribune*.
67. Winston, *Andrew Johnson*, pp. 497-498.

XIV. COUNTER-REVOLUTION
OF PROPERTY

How, after the war, triumphant industry in the North coupled with privilege and monopoly led an orgy of theft that engulfed the nation and was the natural child of war; and how revolt against this anarchy became reaction against democracy, North and South, and delivered the land into the hands of an organized monarchy of finance while it overthrew the attempt at a dictatorship of labor in the South

The abolition-democracy of the North had been willing to try real democracy in the South because they believed in the capabilities of the Negro race and also because they had passed through war, oligarchy, and the almost unbridled power of Andrew Johnson. Relatively few of them believed in the mass of Negroes any more than they believed in the mass of whites; but they expected that with education, economic opportunity and the protection of the ballot, there would arise the intelligent and thrifty Negro to take his part in the community, while the mass would make average labor. Perhaps they did not expect the proportion of thrift and intelligence to equal that of the whites, but they knew certain possibilities from experience and acquaintance.

The machinery they were compelled to set up, with the cooperation of Northern industry, was a dictatorship of far broader possibilities than the North had at first contemplated. It put such power in the hands of Southern labor that, with intelligent and unselfish leadership and a clarifying ideal, it could have rebuilt the economic foundations of Southern society, confiscated and redistributed wealth, and built a real democracy of industry for the masses of men. When the South realized this they emitted an exceeding great cry which was the reaction of property being despoiled of its legal basis of being. This bitter complaint was all the more plausible because Southern labor lacked sufficient intelligent and unselfish leadership. Some in truth it got—from black men who gave their heart's blood to make Reconstruction go; from white men who sacrificed everything to teach and guide Negroes. But for the most part their leaders were colored men of limited education, with the current honesty of the times and little experience, and Northern and Southern whites who varied from conventional and indifferent officeholders to demagogues, thieves, and scoundrels.

The next step would have been, under law and order, gradually to have replaced the wrong leaders by a better and better sort. This the Negroes and many whites sought to do from 1870 to 1876. But they failed because the military dictatorship behind labor did not function successfully in the face of the Ku Klux Klan and especially because the appeal of property in the South got the ear of property in the North.

After the war, industry in the North found itself with a vast organization for production, new supplies of raw material, a growing transportation system on land and water, and a new technical knowledge of processes. All this, with the exclusion of foreign competition through a system of import taxes, and a vast immigration of laborers, tremendously stimulated the production of goods and available services. But to whom were the new goods and the increased services to belong, and in whose hands would lie the power which that ownership gave?

An almost unprecedented scramble for this new power, new wealth and new income ensued. It broke down old standards of wealth distribution, old standards of thrift and honesty. It led to the anarchy of thieves, grafters, and highwaymen. It threatened the orderly processes of production as well as government and morals. The governments, federal, state and local, had paid three-fifths of the cost of the railroads and handed them over to individuals and corporations to use for their profit. An empire of rich land, larger than France, Belgium and Holland together, had been snatched from the hands of prospective peasant farmers and given to investors and land speculators. All of the national treasure of coal, oil, copper, gold and iron had been given away for a song to be made the monopolized basis of private fortunes with perpetual power to tax labor for the right to live and work. Speculation rose and flourished on the hard foundation of this largess.

Senator George Hoar said: "When the greatest railroad of the world, binding together the continent and uniting the two great seas which wash our shores, was finished, I have seen our national triumph and exaltation turned to bitterness and shame by the unanimous reports of three committees of Congress that every step of that mighty enterprise had been taken in fraud."

William N. Tweed became New York State Senator in 1868 and his candidates for Governor and Mayor were swept into office that year. Tweed became director in numbers of great corporations and regularly bribed the legislature; graft crept into all city business. He and his partners stole something like $75,000,000. Public opinion was silenced; real estate owners, merchants and the propertied class were afraid to complain lest they be highly assessed and taxed. Offices were sold and men nominated for what they could pay. Directors of corporations plotted and nominated judges; men were sent to the United States Senate because they were lawyers for railroads, mining companies and banks; Congressional leaders were on the pay rolls of corporations. Great lawyers hired their services to rascals who were stealing, and such persons included distinguished names like David Dudley Field, who was nearly expelled from the Bar Association because of his identification with Fisk and Gould at a salary of $125,000. Editors of publications received stocks and bonds and railroad passes for publicity. Appointment to cadetships at West Point was on sale and federal offices given in return for contributions to campaign funds. The whole civil service became filled with men who were incompetent and used to paying political debts. It was common for members of Congress to take stocks and bonds in railroad and other companies when they were in position to favor these companies by voting for certain laws. A Western governor was impeached for embezzlement. The President of the United States and his family received gifts and loans from financiers.

Consolidation of railway systems began with fighting, stealing and cheating. The New York Central was financed; the Erie went through an extraordinary series of manipulations in which millions were spent; judges were bought and members of the legislature were bribed. The new method of stock-watering came into use by which actual invested capital was doubled and trebled in face value by issuing stock, and the public was compelled to pay fabulous interest on fictitious investments.

"When the annals of this Republic show the disgrace and censure of a Vice-President; a late speaker of the House of Representatives marketing his rulings as a presiding officer; three Senators profiting secretly by their votes as lawmakers; five chairmen of the leading committees of the late House of Representatives exposed in jobbery; a late Secretary of the Treasury forcing balances in the public accounts; a late Attorney-General misappropriating public funds; a Secretary of the Navy enriched or enriching friends by percentages levied off the profits of contracts with his departments; an Ambassador to England censured in a dishonorable speculation; the President's private secretary barely escaping conviction upon trial for guilty complicity in frauds upon the revenue; a Secretary of War impeached for high crimes and misdemeanors—the demonstration is complete."[1] All this was not simply the corruption of the Republican Party, as some writers insist; it ran across all lines of party and geography; it embraced all sections, classes and races. It was the disgrace of a whole nation.

The slime of this era of theft and corruption, which engulfed the nation, did not pass by the South. Legislators and public officials were bribed. Black men and white men were eager to get rich. In every Southern state white members of the old planting aristocracy were part and parcel of the new thieving and grafting. But the South did not lay the blame of all this on war and poverty, and weak human nature, or on the wretched example of the whole nation. No. After first blaming greedy and vengeful Northerners and then holding up to public execration those Southerners who accepted Negro suffrage, THE SOUTH, FINALLY, WITH ALMOST COMPLETE UNITY, NAMED THE NEGRO AS THE MAIN CAUSE OF SOUTHERN CORRUPTION. THEY SAID, AND REITERATED THIS CHARGE, UNTIL IT BECAME HISTORY: THAT THE CAUSE OF DISHONESTY DURING RECONSTRUCTION WAS THE FACT THAT 4,000,000 DISFRANCHISED BLACK LABORERS, AFTER 250 YEARS OF EXPLOITATION, HAD BEEN GIVEN A LEGAL RIGHT TO HAVE SOME VOICE IN THEIR OWN GOVERNMENT, IN THE KINDS OF GOODS THEY WOULD MAKE AND THE SORT OF WORK THEY WOULD DO, AND IN THE DISTRIBUTION OF THE WEALTH WHICH THEY CREATED.

Throughout the North, reaction followed, directed mainly at two impossible goals; first, to reëstablish old standards of honesty in a new field: property was taking new forms and called for a new morality, not a reëstablishment of the old. Secondly, an attempt was made to curb production by breaking down tariff walls, the monopoly of raw materials and the privileges of special laws and exclusive techniques. But this was also difficult if not impossible so long as the rewards of monopoly and privilege were so spectacular and the powers bestowed so tremendous.

Thus the old dictatorship carried on by property interests failed, while at the same time a new super-dictatorship arose. The dictatorship of property, as represented by the wild freebooting from the close of the war to the panic, had proven to many minds that free competition in industry was not going to bring proper control and development.

Far from turning toward any conception of dictatorship of the proletariat, of surrendering power either into the hands of labor or of the trustees of labor, the new plan was to concentrate into a trusteeship of capital a new and far-reaching power which would dominate the government of the United States. This was not a petty bourgeois development, following the overthrow of agrarian feudalism in the South. It was, on the contrary, a new feudalism based on monopoly—but not monopoly of the agricultural possibilities of the land so much as of its wealth in raw material, in copper, iron, oil and coal, particularly monopoly of the transportation of these commodities on new public iron roads privately sequestered, and finally, of the manufacture of goods by new machines and privileged technique. This new feudalism was destined to crush the small capitalist as ruthlessly as it controlled labor, and even before the panic of 1873, it was beginning to consolidate its power.

The copper of Michigan, the coal, steel and oil of Pennsylvania, came under control, and at the same time the bankers and financiers began to bend the manufacturers and the railroads to their will by their monopoly of investment capital and direction of its distribution which they secured by guaranteeing income to small investors.

Great corporations, through their control of new capital, began to establish a super-government. On the one hand, they crushed the robber-barons, the thieves and the grafters, and thus appeased those of the old school who demanded the old standards of personal honesty. Secondly, they made treaty with the petty bourgeoisie by guarantying them reasonable and certain income from their investments, while they gradually deprived them of real control in industry. And finally, they made treaty with labor by dealing with it as a powerful, determined unit and dividing it up into skilled union labor, with which the new industry shared profit in the shape of a higher wage and other privileges, and a great reservoir of common and foreign labor which it kept at work at low wages with the threat of starvation and with police control.

This control of super-capital and big business was being developed during the ten years of Southern Reconstruction and was dependent and consequent upon the failure of democracy in the South, just as it fattened upon the perversion of democracy in the North. And when once the control of industry by big business was certain through consolidation and manipulation that included both North and South, big business shamelessly deserted, not only the Negro, but the cause of democracy; not only in the South, but in the North.

To the leaders of the Republican revolt of 1872, big business offered law and order, greater efficiency of the "business man in politics" and security of salaries and investment. To the insurgent West, it offered combinations which would give lower railway rates, wider and better markets and rising land values. To the South, it offered the withdrawal of the national army and the restoration of political control to property. Before this dominant power the meaning of party designations faded. When the old Democratic party secured a majority in Congress in 1874, the majority sat under the dictatorship of big business. When the Republicans were seated in 1876, the Empire of Industry was completed.

To the student of government who fastens his attention chiefly on politics, the years 1866 to 1876 were years when the power of the national government remained exclusively democratic, with ultimate control in the hands of the mass of citizens who had the right to vote. But the student who realizes that human activity is chiefly exercised in earning a living and, thus, particularly in the present industrial age, the actions of groups and governments have to do mainly with income—this student will see that the Civil War brought anarchy in the basic economic activities which were gradually hammered and forced into a new and vast monarchy of tremendous power and almost miraculous accomplishment.

Forms of democratic government went on but they were almost fantastic in their travesty on real popular control. Industrial freebooters and bandits, now as lone and picturesque masked highwayman, now hunting in packs and mercenary armies, gripped and guided the efforts of a vast nation to get rich after the indiscriminate murder and destruction of four years' war. All this led to disaster which threatened the industrial machine. Those who still believed in democracy came to the rescue and saw salvation, in the North as in the South, in universal suffrage.

In the South universal suffrage could not function without personal freedom, land and education, and until these institutions were real and effective, only a benevolent dictatorship in the ultimate interests of labor, black and white, could establish democracy. In the North, democracy ceased to function because of corruption and bribery, the open buying of elections, low and selfish ideals, and officials chosen to misgovern in the interest of industrial freebooters. The party of democracy saw salvation in increased freedom of industrial competition through the uprooting of tariff-nurtured monopoly and civil service reform which would replace knavery and selfishness by character and ideal in public office; then, with an electorate of growing intelligence, democracy would truly function.

But the electorate, despite schools and churches, was not intelligent; it was provincial and bigoted, thinned by poverty-stricken and ignorant peasant laborers from abroad, and impregnated with the idea that individual wealth spelled national prosperity and particularly with the American assumption of equal economic opportunity for all, which persisted in the face of facts. Only a vast and single-eyed dictatorship of the nation could guide us up from murder in the South and robbery and cheating in the North into a nation whose infinite resources would be developed in the interest of the mass of the nation—that is, of the laboring poor.

Dictatorship came, and it came to guide the industrial development of the nation by an assumption of irresponsible monarchial power such as enthroned the Caesars, by methods of efficiency of accomplishment and control never surpassed among so many millions of men.

But the object of this new American industrial empire, so far as that object was conscious and normative, was not national well-being, but the individual gain of the associated and corporate monarchs through the power of vast profit on enormous capital investment; through the efficiency of an industrial machine that bought the highest managerial and engineering talent and used the latest and most effective methods and machines in a field of unequaled raw material and endless market demand. That this machine might use the profit for the general weal was possible and in cases true. But the uplift and well-being of the mass of men, of the cohorts of common labor, was not its ideal or excuse. Profit, income, uncontrolled power in My Business for My Property and for Me—this was the aim and method of the new monarchial dictatorship that displaced democracy in the United States in 1876.

Part and parcel of this system was the emancipated South. Property control especially of land and labor had always dominated politics in the South, and after the war, it set itself to put labor to work at a wage approximating as nearly as possible slavery conditions, in order to restore capital lost in the war. On the other hand, labor was in open revolt by army desertions, by the general strike and arming of black labor, by government employment through the army and the Freedmen's Bureau; but its revolt could only be shown by refusal to work under the old conditions, and it had neither permanent organization nor savings to sustain it in such a fight.

Into this situation, Northern capital projected itself through the agency of the so-called carpetbagger. The carpetbagger tried to stimulate production on the Northern model. He offered the laborer higher wages and yielded him political power. He tried to establish wide systems of transportation and to exploit new raw materials. His efforts involved the same overthrow of old standards of honesty and integrity prevalent in the North, and this was emphasized in the South by the post-war bitterness and war losses of capital. The orgy of graft, dishonesty and theft, North and South, was of the same pattern and involved the same sorts of people: those scrambling to share in the distribution of new goods and services which the new industry in the North and the restoration of the old agriculture in the South poured out, and those trying to get legal titles to the new forms of property and income which were arising.

The South, however, had two peculiar elements: a capitalist class deprived of most of its capital except land; and a new class of free black labor with the right to vote. Into the hands of this body of labor, the North had been compelled by the intransigeance of the planters themselves to place a tremendous dictatorship, and this dictatorship of labor was gradually being set to change the whole pattern of distribution of wealth. But Southern labor was thinking in terms of land and crops and the old forms of wealth, and was but dimly conscious of the new industry and the new wealth.

The landholder, therefore, in the South, was caught in a curious vise: impoverished by the war, he found labor in control of the remaining parts of his wealth and determined to distribute it for the uplift of the mass of men. He found carpetbaggers encouraging this by yielding to the political power of laborers, and manipulating that power so as to put into the hands of carpetbaggers the new wealth arising from corporations, railroads, and industries. He found the carpetbagger trying to raise the capital necessary for new investment through spending money borrowed by the state, and thus increasing the taxation on him which already new social legislation on behalf of the laborers had increased. The result was that a scramble ensued in the South as mad as that in the North, but different, more fundamental, more primitive.

It had been insistently and firmly believed by the best thought of the South: (1) that the Negro could not work as a free laborer; (2) that the Negro could not really be educated, being congenitally inferior; (3) that if political power were given to Negroes it would result virtually in the overthrow of civilization.

Now, it is quite clear that during the period we are studying, the results failed to prove these assumptions. First of all, the Negro did work as a free laborer. Slowly but certainly the tremendous losses brought on by the Civil War were restored, and restoration, as compared with other great wars, was comparatively rapid. By 1870, the Cotton Kingdom was reëstablished, and by 1875, the South knew that with cheap labor and freedom from government control, it was possible for individuals to reap large profit in the old agriculture and in new industry.

The restoration of Southern industry varied according to crops and conditions. The cotton crop, for instance, which was 2,469,093 in 1850 and leaped to the high mark of 5,387,052 in 1860, dropped to 3,011,996 in 1870, but had surpassed by 1880 the high mark of 1860 by reaching 5,755,359 bales and then went on to ten, twelve and fourteen million bales. The sugar production did not recover as quickly, but its decline began before the war. There were 247 million pounds raised in 1850, 230 million in 1860, and only 87 million in 1870; but by 1880, it had reached 178 million and from then kept on its path of recovery. Tobacco was at 434 million pounds in 1860 and 472 million pounds in 1880. The production of corn had recovered by 1880 and the average value of live stock on farms had very nearly recovered by 1870.

The production of wool in the South did not greatly decline and had rapidly recoverd by 1880. Rice continued a decline begun before the war from 215 million pounds in 1850 to 178 million in 1860, 73 million in 1870, and up to 110 million in 1880.

It is true that after the war a larger and larger proportion of white laborers was in part responsible for the increased crops. But this simply proved that emancipating one class of laborers emancipated all and was to the credit of abolition. Nevertheless, the free black laborer was the main constituent labor force in the South and as such, largely responsible for results.

The land holdings in the South decreased, showing a tendency toward peasant proprietorship. The average acreage of 335 acres in 1860 fell to 214 acres in 1870 and 153 acres in 1880. The increase in the value of machinery and implements per acre, while not as great, showed gradual progress.

The average value of farm land did not recover from its high speculative value of 1860 until thirty years later; but on the other hand, its decrease in value, 1860-1870, was not large. The land, for instance, in 1870 in the South, was worth more in average value per acre, including improvements and live stock, than in 1850.

The testimony of unprejudiced visitors as to the work of the Negro as a free laborer during these days is practically unanimous. Nordhoff said in 1875: "The Negro in the main is industrious; free labor is an undoubted success in the South. . . . The Negro works; he raises cotton and corn, sugar and rice, and it is infinitely to his credit that he continues to do so, and according to universal testimony, works more steadfastly and effectively this year than ever before since 1865, in spite of the political hurly-burly in which he has lived for the last te 1 years." [2]

Somers said: "The testimony generally borne of the Negro is that they work readily when regularly paid. Wherever I have consulted an effective employer, whether in the manufacturing works of Richmond or on the farms and plantations, such is the opinion, with little variation, that has been given.

"The testimony borne of the Negroes by candid and substantial people is that, while they do not afford the supply of steady labor necessary, and there is room for more of them, or of more efficient laborers, they are doing much better than was expected before emancipation.

"That the Negroes are improving, and many of them rising under freedom into a very comfortable and civilized condition, is not only admitted in all the upper circles of society, but would strike even a transient wayfarer like myself in the great number of decent colored men of the laboring class and of happy colored families that one meets." [3]

Manufactures began to develop in the South. The manufacture of pig iron assumed importance in Alabama in 1874 and the output arose from $64,000 to $1,405,000 in 1875. The manufacture of cotton goods increased in North and South Carolina. The number of mills in South Carolina was 270 in 1860 and 720 in 1880.

The railroad mileage southeast of the Mississippi was 8,838 miles in 1860 and 11,501 in 1870. West of the Mississippi the growth was even larger. In every Southern state, 1860-1866, the railroad mileage increased, sometimes only slightly, as from 973 to 1,007 in South Carolina and from 1,420 to 1,502 in Georgia; but all these figures include the rebuilding of railroads destroyed during the war. White labor was of increased importance in these lines, but colored labor was never negligible.

With regard to education, the testimony is equally clear. Grant that the Negro began as almost totally illiterate, the increase in schools and education, largely by his own initiative, is one of the most extraordinary developments of modern days and will be treated more in detail in the next chapter. It is enough to say here that the question as to whether American Negroes were capable of education was no longer a debatable one in 1876. The whole problem was simply one of opportunity.

The third problem, of the Negro's use of his political power, was not so clear because it involved matters of norm and ideal. Whose civilization, whose culture, whose comfort, was involved? The Negro certainly did not attempt to "overthrow civilization" in the sense of attacking the fundamental morals and habits of modern life. Sir George Campbell said in 1879: "During the last dozen years the Negroes have had a very large share of political education. Considering the troubles and the ups and downs that they have gone through, it is, I think, wonderful how beneficial this education has been to them, and how much these people, so lately in the most debased condition of slavery, have acquired independent ideas; and, far from lapsing into anarchy, have become citizens with ideas of law and property and order. The white serfs of European countries took hundreds of years to rise to the level which these Negroes adopted in America." [4]

"Before I went South I certainly expected to find that the Southern States had been for a time a sort of Pandemonium in which a white man could hardly live. Yet it certainly was not so. . . . When I went to South Carolina I thought there at least I must find great social disturbances; and in South Carolina I went to the county of Beaufort, the blackest part of the State in point of population, and that in which black rule has been most complete and has lasted longest. It has the reputation of being a sort of black paradise, and *per contra,* I rather expected a sort of white hell. There I thought I should see a rough Liberia, where blacks ruled roughshod over the whites. To my great surprise I found exactly the contrary. At no place that I have seen are the relations of the two races better and more peaceable. . . . All the best houses are in the occupation of the whites—almost all the trades, professions, and leading occupations. White girls go about freely and pleasantly as if no black had ever been in power. Here the blacks still control the elections and send their representatives to the State Assembly. . . .

"In Mississippi alone did I find politicians silly enough to talk about the superiority of the Caucasian race, and the natural incapacity of the Negro for self-government; but even there the best Republicans told that these noisy Democratic demagogues were but a small, though aggressive and not unpowerful, minority." [5]

Sir George Campbell, however, makes one interesting observation: "Not only is the Negro labor excellent, but also there is among the Southern proprietors and leading men accustomed to black labor, and not so used to whites, a disposition greatly to rely on black labor as a conservative element, securing them against the dangers and difficulties which they see arising from the combinations and violence of the white laborers in some of the Northern States; and on this ground the blacks are cherished and protected by Democratic statesmen, who now hold power in the South." [6]

If we include in "morals" and "culture" the prevailing manner of holding and distributing wealth, then the sudden enfranchisement of a mass of laborers threatens fundamental and far-reaching change, no matter what their race or color. It was this that the South feared and had reason to fear. Economic revolution did not come immediately. Negro labor was ignorant, docile and conservative. But it was beginning to learn; it was beginning to assert itself. It was beginning to have radical thoughts as to the distribution of land and wealth.

If now it is true that the enfranchisement of black labor in the South did not crush industry but gave the South a working class capable of being trained in intelligence and did not disturb the essential bases of civilization, what is the indictment—the bitter and deepseated indictment brought against the Negro voter?

The indictment rests upon this unquestioned fact: Property in the South had its value cut in half during the Civil War. This meant that property was compelled, after the war, not simply to attempt to restore its losses, but to bear a burden of social expense largely because of the widened duties of the state and the greatly increased citizenship due to emancipation and enfranchisement. The bitter conflict, therefore, which followed the enfranchisement of Negro labor and of white labor, came because impoverished property holders were compelled by the votes of poor men to bear a burden which meant practically confiscation of much of that property which remained to them and were denied opportunity to exploit labor in the future as they had in the past. It was not, then, that the post-bellum South could not produce wealth with free labor; it was the far more fundamental question as to whom this wealth was to belong to and for whose interests laborers were to work. There is no doubt that the object of the black and white labor vote was gradually conceived as one which involved confiscating the property of the rich. This was a program that could not be openly avowed by intelligent men in 1870, but it has become one of the acknowledged functions of the state in 1933; and it is quite possible that long before the end of the twentieth century, the deliberate distribution of property and income by the state on an equitable and logical basis will be looked upon as the state's prime function.

Put all these facts together and one gets a clear idea, not of the failure of Negro suffrage in the South, but of the basic difficulty which it encountered; and the results are quite consistent with a clear judgment that Negro and white labor ought to have had the right to vote; that they ought to have tried to change the basis of property and redistribute income; and that their failure to do this was a disaster to democratic government in the United States.

To men like Charles Sumner, the future of democracy in America depended on bringing the Southern revolution to a successful close by accomplishing two things: the making of the black freedmen really free, and the sweeping away of the animosities due to the war.

What liberalism did not understand was that such a revolution was economic and involved force. Those who against the public weal have power cannot be expected to yield save to superior power. The North used its power in the Civil War to break the political power of the slave barons. During and after the war, it united its force with that of the workers to uproot the still vast economic power of the planters. It hoped with the high humanitarianism of Charles Sumner eventually to induce the planter to surrender his economic power peacefully, in return for complete political amnesty, and hoped that the North would use its federal police power to maintain the black man's civil rights in return for peaceful industry and increasing intelligence. But Charles Sumner did not realize, and that other Charles—Karl Marx—had not yet published *Das Kapital* to prove to men that economic power underlies politics. Abolitionists failed to see that after the momentary exaltation of war, the nation did not want Negroes to have civil rights and that national industry could get its way easier by alliance with Southern landholders than by sustaining Southern workers. They did not know that when they let the dictatorship of labor be overthrown in the South they surrendered the hope of democracy in America for all men.

Doggedly to the end of his days and with his dying breath Charles Sumner strove for his peaceful revolutionary ideal. As early as 1870, he had tried to have the names of Civil War battles taken from the army register and the regimental colors. He introduced the matter in Congress again in 1872. He was unsuccessful, and not only that, he was publicly censured by his own Massachusetts legislature.

When Congress met in the fall of 1871, Sumner made his last effort to carry his civil rights bill. The first civil rights bill of April 9, 1866, after varied experience in the courts, was superseded by the first section of the Fourteenth Amendment. The present bill was aimed at the North as well as the South, and Sumner proposed to secure equality of civil rights to colored people and prohibit discrimination against them in railroads, theaters, hotels, schools, cemeteries and churches and in serving as jurors. He presented a series of petitions favoring the bill and tried to make action on the bill a condition of adjournment. Finally, he sought to make the pressure for reconciliation with the South a part of his movement for civil rights. He therefore moved his civil rights bill as an amendment to the amnesty bill which had been passed in the House.

"He thought the two measures should be associated in history—the one an act of justice, and the other an act of generosity; and it was his opinion, not however, justified by the result, that the desire for amnesty was so strong that when once his civil rights measure had been incorporated in it, the bill thus amended would pass by a two-thirds vote. His amendment was lost in committee of the whole by a single vote; and moving it again after the bill was reported, he said: 'I entreat Senators over the way [the Democrats] who really seek reconciliation now to unite in this honest effort. Give me an opportunity to vote for this bill. I long to do it. Gladly would I reach out the olive branch; but I know no way in which that can be done unless you begin by justice to the colored race.' " [7]

Colored people held meetings to popularize the measure but there was no wide interest in it. After the Christmas recess, Sumner made his final appeal: "I make this appeal also for the sake of peace, so that at last there shall be an end of slavery, and the rights of the citizen shall be everywhere under the equal safeguard of national law. There is beauty in art, in literature, in science, and in every triumph of intelligence, all of which I covet for my country; but there is a higher beauty still—in relieving the poor, in elevating the downtrodden, and being a succor to the oppressed. There is true grandeur in an example of justice, making the rights of all the same as our own, and beating down prejudice, like Satan, under our feet. Humbly do I pray that the republic may not lose this great prize, or postpone its enjoyment." [8]

He read documents, letters and newspaper extracts to show the necessity for the bill; the galleries were filled with colored people. But industry and the new finance looked askance. Their attitude toward the abolition-democracy was plainly expressed in 1876 by Henry Cooke, brother of Jay Cooke, the great banker:

"You know how I have felt for a long time in regard to the course of the ultra-infidelic radicals like Wade, Sumner, Stevens et id omne genus. They were dragging the Republican Party into all sorts of isms and extremes. Their policy was one of bitterness, hate and wild agrarianism. These reckless demagogues have had their day and the time has come for wiser counsel. With Wade uttering agrarian doctrines in Kansas and fanning the flames of vulgar prejudices, trying to array labor against capital and pandering to the basest passions; with Butler urging wholesale conscription throughout the South and wholesale repudiation throughout the North . . . ; with Stevens . . . advocating the idea of a flood of irredeemable paper money . . . ; with Pomeroy and Wade and Sprague and a host of others clamoring for the unsexing of woman, [the load] was too heavy for any party to carry." [9]

Even Schurz did not sympathize with Sumner and said little during the debate. Sumner pushed the bill throughout the session, but despite his efforts the bill failed. Another bill came from the House three months later but was lost by a Senate vote. Just after that, Sumner again sought to attach his civil rights proviso to the amnesty bill. He lost in the committee of the whole by a single vote.

He placed the civil rights bill on the calendar with the amnesty bill but his strategy was finally defeated by a ruse, and the amnesty bill passed without the civil rights bill.

On the first day of the new Congress, December, 1873, Sumner pressed two measures: a national civil rights bill and a bill for equal rights in the schools of the District of Columbia. He traced, in debate, the history of the civil rights bill from 1870 to 1874, when he made his last appeal. The bill was not reported until after his death and then Senator Frelinghuysen said:

"Would that the author of the measure were here to present and defend it! To our view it would have been becoming that he, who was in the forum the leader of the grandest victory of the nineteenth century in the western hemisphere—the victory of freedom over slavery—should have completed the work he so efficiently aided. But it was otherwise decreed." [10]

It passed the Senate but was not voted on in the House. In February, 1875, a new House bill omitting schools and cemeteries became a law. In 1883, the Supreme Court pronounced this law unconstitutional.

Sumner passed before the effect of the new alignment of big business on the Southern situation was clear. He was taken ill in March, 1874; at his death-bed stood three Negroes: Frederick Douglass, George T. Downing and Sumner Wormley, together with distinguished senators and officials. Three times he said hoarsely and in a tone of earnest entreaty: "You must take care of the civil rights bill—my bill, the civil rights bill—don't let it fail!" This was his last public message. [11]

Frederick Douglass led his funeral procession and colored soldiers guarded his body at the State House in Boston. So died, as Sherman said, "the foremost man in the civil service of the United States." William Lloyd Garrison had written: "Your blood staining the floor of the Senate Chamber, was the blood of a martyr; now it is given to you to wear a martyr's crown! This is no human, but divine triumph; this is not in the wisdom of man, but in the power of God." [12]

The dream of democracy died hard. The final ratification of the Fifteenth Amendment brought a special message from President Grant, March 30, 1870, which has a curious historical significance:

"Such notification is unusual, but I deem a departure from the usual custom justifiable. A measure which makes at once four millions of people voters, who were heretofore declared by the highest tribunal in the land not citizens of the United States, nor eligible to become so (with the assertion that, 'at the time of the Declaration of Independence, the opinion was fixed and universal in the civilized portion of the white race, regarded as an axiom in morals as well as in politics, that black men had no rights which the white man was bound to respect'), is indeed a measure of grander importance than any other one act of the kind from the foundation of our free government to the present day."

Blaine, who preëminently represented that Northern plutocracy which was throttling democracy, still spoke with the voice of wisdom: "The Fifteenth Article of Amendment to the Constitution, now pending and about to be adopted, would confirm the colored man's elective franchise and add the right of holding office. One of the Senators just admitted from Mississippi in advance of the ratification on the amendment [Hiram R. Revels] was a colored man of respectable character and intelligence. He sat in the seat which Jefferson Davis had wrathfully deserted to take up arms against the Republic and become the ruler of a hostile government. Poetic justice, historic revenge, personal retribution were all complete when Mr. Revels' name was called on the roll of the Senate. But his presence, while demonstrating the extent to which the assertion of equal rights had been carried, served to increase and stimulate the Southern resistance to the whole system of Republican reconstruction. Those who anxiously had studied the political situation in the South could see how unequal the contest would be and how soon the men who organized the rebellion would again wield the political power of their states—wield it lawfully if they could, but unlawfully if they must; peaceably if that would suffice, but violently if violence in their judgment became necessary." [13]

The Reform movement in the North which Sumner joined was abortive. First it split the combination of industry and abolition-democracy which had won the Civil War and reconstructed the South, and it threatened to put the Copperhead-Democratic party back in power. This latter party had not only supported the South against the East in the Civil War, but had fought the Thirteenth, Fourteenth and Fifteenth Amendments, and now was seeking to unite with the radical West.

The abolition-democracy itself was largely based on property, believed in capital and formed in effect a powerful petty bourgeoisie. It believed in democratic government but only under a general dictatorship of property. Most of the leaders of the revolt of 1872 in the North lived on investments or received salaries from investments. They did not believe in a democratic movement which would confiscate and redistribute property, except possibly in an extreme case like slavery. But even here, while they seized stolen property in human bodies, they never could bring themselves to countenance the redistribution of property in land and tools, which rested in fact on no less defensible basis. Not only, then, did the property complaint of the South fall on their sensitive and responsive ears, they were the more aroused at familiar complaints of theft and corruption in public office because this was precisely the thing they were fighting in the North. They found themselves in dilemma; they could not join the ex-slave Democratic party and repudiate their own investments in government bonds and industry. They could not maintain further political alliance with the industrial and political order eventually responsible for the Crédit Mobilier, the Whiskey Ring and the gold corner. Their logical path lay toward organized labor, leading to a combination of Eastern intellectuals, Western peasant farmers and the great army of labor. But the panic of 1873 altered the face of society; the era of business depression which followed helped this consolidation of industrial control in a few hands.

The panic of 1873 changed, too, the history of the South. Already, in 1870, the Republicans had lost their two-thirds majority in Congress, and in 1874, for the first time in twenty years, the Democrats had a majority in the House of Representatives. They looked forward confidently to controlling the nation in 1876.

Even in the face of catastrophe, the North had moral courage and the spirit of faith among large numbers of its best citizens. The history of abolition is full proof of this. But Sacrifice must build on Faith. A saving nucleus of the North believed in the Negro from experience and study—but this same class had lost faith in democratic methods in the North. The experience with the Irish in Massachusetts and New York, misgovernment, crime and dirt in the great industrial cities, were attributed to the laboring masses. How could they rightly exercise the power to rule? New England lost faith in democracy and cherished something like a race hatred for the Irish. Her Puritan past kept her just—she gave them schools, she refused discriminatory laws in religion; but she doubted; and even if she knew the end was mass rule, it was a long, long, bitter way, and a crisis was already here.

The system of capital and private profit smashed in 1873, and all property and investment were in dire danger; labor was at the edge of starvation, and democracy and universal suffrage could function only through revolution. But a new savior appeared. Already Industry had been undergoing a process of integration, alliance and imperial domination. Instead of lawless freebooters, there were appearing a few strong purposeful kings with vast power of finance and technique in their hands. They promised law and order; they promised safe income on a sure property base with neither speculative bubbles nor criminal aggression. In other words a new Empire of Industry was offering to displace capitalistic anarchy and form a dictatorship of capital to guide and repress universal suffrage.

The conquest of the new industry in the ranks of labor was quick and certain. The growth of the National Labor Union into a labor party along Marxist lines, which had been developing from the close of the war, began to become petty bourgeois. It began to fight for capital and interest and the right of the upper class of labor to share in the exploitation of common labor. The Negro as a common laborer belonged, therefore, not in but beneath the white American labor movement.

Craft and race unions spread. The better-paid skilled and intelligent American labor formed itself into closed guilds and, in combination with capitalist guild-masters, extorted fair wages which could be raised by negotiation. Foreign-born and Negro labor was left outside and tried several times, but in vain, to start a class-conscious labor movement. Skilled labor proceeded to share in the exploitation of the reservoir of low-paid common labor, and no strikes nor violence by over-crowded competing beggars for subsistence could move the industrial machine so long as engineers and skilled labor kept it going. To be sure the skilled labor guilds and capital had bitter disputes and even open fighting, but they fought to share profit from labor and not to eliminate profit.

Big business with high-salaried engineers, well-paid skilled labor and a mass of voiceless common labor then offered terms to the nation. Profiteering, graft and theft had run wild in the North under the extreme individualism of post-war industry. Northern business had protected its monopoly by high tariff, profit from investments in railroad and government bonds, and new ventures. It had held its political power by the Fourteenth Amendment and Reconstruction Acts. But its dominion and advance were threatened by loss of all moral standards, cut-throat competition; political revolt threatened, which might result in lowering the tariff, attacking the banking and money system, and strengthening government control of business freedom. One way to forestall this was to effect inner control and coördination of business by centralizing the control of the power of capital. regaining the confidence of investors by sure and steady income, and driving from power the irregular banditti and highwaymen of industry.

Fortunately for them, the panic of 1873 checked the reform movement of 1872, and delivered the country into the power of the great financiers without seriously breaking the power of capital. Reform became liberal, attacking theft and graft, and calling for freedom of the South from military control. Thus, the radical revolution of controlling capital and forcing recognition of the rights of labor by government control was lost sight of. Labor war ensued in the North, and serfdom was established in the South.

But what of the South in this development? The planters had expected Negro governments to fall in confusion at the very beginning of the attempted dictatorship of labor. This did not happen.

Writing in the *American Historical Review* I said, "In legislation covering property, the wider functions of the state, the punishment of crime and the like, it is sufficient to say that the laws on these points established by Reconstruction legislatures were not only different from and even revolutionary to the laws in the older South, but they were so wise and so well suited to the needs of the new South that in spite of a retrogressive movement following the overthrow of the Negro governments the mass of this legislation, with elaboration and development, still stands on the statute books of the South.

"Reconstruction constitutions, practically unaltered, were kept in

Florida	1868-1885	17 years
Virginia	1870-1902	32 years
South Carolina	1868-1895	27 years
Mississippi	1868-1890	22 years

"Even in the case of states like Alabama, Georgia, North Carolina, and Louisiana, which adopted new constitutions to signify the overthrow of Negro rule, the new constitutions are nearer the model of the Reconstruction document than they are to the previous constitutions. They differ from the Negro constitutions in minor details but very little in general conception.

"Besides this there stands on the statute books of the South today law after law passed between 1868 and 1876, and which has been found wise, effective, and worthy of preservation." [14]

This compels us to begin with the fact that the basic difficulty with the South after the war was poverty, a depth of grinding poverty not easily conceivable even in these days of depression. In the first place, it goes without saying that the emancipated slave was poor; he was desperately poor, and poor in a way that we do not easily grasp today. He was, and always had been, without money and, except for his work in the Union Army, had no way of getting hold of cash. He could ordinarily get no labor contract that involved regular or certain payments of cash. He was without clothes and without a home. He had no way to rent or build a home. Food had to be begged or stolen, unless in some way he could get hold of land or go to work; and hired labor would, if he did not exercise the greatest care and get honest advice, result in something that was practically slavery. These conditions, of course, while true for the mass of freedmen, did not apply to workers in the army, artisans or laborers in cities and others who had exceptional chances to obtain work for cash at something like decent rates.

The white worker, in the mass, was equally poverty-stricken, except that he did usually hold, as a squatter, some land, and Emancipation gave him better chance to hire his labor in cities. Finally, there were the impoverished planters, merchants and professional men who came out of the war with greatly reduced income and resources. In this setting of poverty, as nearly universal as one could have under modern conditions, must come the effort to set up a new state, and it is clear to the unprejudiced observer that no matter who had conducted that state, if there had been no Negro or other alien elements in the land, if there had been no universal suffrage, there would have been bitter dissatisfaction, widespread injustice, and vast transfer of wealth involving stealing and corruption.

The freedman sought eagerly, after the war, property and income. He believed that his condition was not his own fault but due to Theft on a mighty scale. He demanded reimbursement and redress sufficient for a decent livelihood. This came partially from the Federal government, from religious bodies; and in one lamentable case, the new industry reached forth a careless helping hand, expecting profit from the venture. No more extraordinary and disreputable venture ever disgraced American business disguised as philanthropy than the Freedmen's Bank—a chapter in American history which most Americans naturally prefer to forget.

The organization of the Freedmen's Savings and Trust Company has been called "one of the few sensible attempts made at the close of the Civil War to assist the ex-slave." [15] During the Civil War, and when colored soldiers became numerous, the matter of their savings became of importance and military savings banks were created at Norfolk, Virginia, and at Beaufort, South Carolina. At the same time there were various sums of money held by the Departments of Negro Affairs in the different army headquarters of the South.

General Banks established a bank for Negroes at New Orleans in 1864, and General Butler and General Saxton in South Carolina established banks. Several efforts in 1865 were made to organize permanent savings banks; an army paymaster, A. M. Sperry, hoped to absorb the banks at Norfolk, Virginia, and Beaufort, South Carolina; and in New Orleans, Negroes planned a labor bank. In January, 1865, Alvord arranged a meeting of a number of interested persons and business men in New York, and the result was a bill to incorporate the Freedmen's Savings and Trust Company introduced into the Senate, February 13, 1865. Another bill was introduced into the House and the name of Chief Justice Chase added as a trustee. These bills were combined and passed and Lincoln signed the law, March 3. He said, "This bank is just what the freedmen need," at the same time that he signed the bill creating the Freedmen's Bureau.

The incorporators and trustees of the bank included Peter Cooper, William Cullen Bryant, A. A. Lowe, Garrett Smith, John Jay, S. G. Howe, George L. Stearns, Edward Atkinson and Chief Justice Chase. The business was confined to the Negro race and at least two-thirds of the deposits must be invested in United States securities. For a while, the success of the Freedmen's Savings Bank was phenomenal and the deposits extraordinarily encouraging. They came from day laborers, house servants, farmers, mechanics and washerwomen, and the proverbial thriftlessness of the Negro seemed about to be disproven. North as well as South, the whites were agreeably surprised.

Gradually difficulties developed; on the one hand, in the North, the bank was regarded as a philanthropy and not worth the careful control and oversight of those who had loaned their names to it. The Southern state governments began to oppose the branch banks because they were a sort of national system not under local control and took money away from local communities. The white banks were not disposed to coöperate, and were often unfair, while the white planter regarded the Freedmen's Bank as part of the Freedm..n's Bureau and did everything possible to embarrass it and curtail its growth.

Before 1871, there had been errors in the conduct of the bank and disregard of law. Indeed, it is not quite clear whether in the original charter the bank had any right to establish branches outside the District of Columbia. Soon the speculators of Washington were attracted by the assets of the bank and discovered how they were growing. These assets were, however, amply protected by provisions requiring investment mainly in government bonds. An amendment to the charter was introduced into Congress in 1870 which provided that one-half of the deposits invested in United States bonds might be invested in other notes and bonds secured by real estate mortgages. Immediately the pennies of poor black laborers were replaced by worthless notes. Money was loaned recklessly to the speculators in the District of Columbia. Jay Cooke and Company, the great bankers, borrowed half a million dollars, and this company and the First National Bank of Washington controlled the Freedmen's Bank between 1870 and 1873. Runs were started on the bank and then an effort was made to unload the whole thing on Frederick Douglass as a representative Negro. This was useless and the bank finally closed in June, 1874. The Commission of Three which liquidated the Freedmen's Savings Bank paid depositors 30% and charged for their services $318,753.

At the date of closing, so far as is known, there was due to depositors $2,993,790.68 in 61,144 accounts; this was never paid. The assets amounted to $32,089.35. The rest was represented by personal loans and loans on real estate which were practically uncollectable.

The total business transacted by the Freedmen's Bank was extraordinary, considering that the bulk of its clientele had just emerged from slavery; its total deposits at one time reached $57,000,000.

Thus, the most promising effort to raise the financial status of the best and thriftiest of Negroes went down in the maelstrom of national corruption. It is difficult to over-estimate the psychological effect of this failure upon Negro thrift.

But after all, the amount of cash handled by the freedman was small and by far the most pressing of his problems as a worker was that of land. This land hunger—this absolutely fundamental and essential thing to any real emancipation of the slaves—was continually pushed by all emancipated Negroes and their representatives in every Southern state. It was met by ridicule, by anger, and by dishonest and insincere efforts to satisfy it apparently.

The Freedmen's Bureau had much Confederate property in its possession. But the seizure of abandoned estates in the South came as a measure to stop war and not as a plan for economic rebirth. Just as the slaves were enticed from the South in order to stop the aid which they could give to rebels, in the same way the land of masters who ran away or were absent aiding the rebellion was seized; and this large body of land was the nucleus of the proposal to furnish forty acres to each emancipated slave family. The scheme was further advanced when Sherman, embarrassed by the number of Negroes who followed him from Atlanta to the sea and gathered around him in Savannah and South Carolina, as a war measure settled them upon the abandoned Sea Islands and the adjacent coast.

Confiscated property was in some cases condemned or sold on order of the Federal courts for unpaid taxes, and the title vested in the United States. Thus the Freedmen's Bureau came into possession of nearly 800,000 acres of farm land with control over it, except the right of sale. This land was in Virginia, Georgia, South Carolina, Louisiana, North Carolina, Kentucky and Tennessee. There was very little in Alabama and Florida and none in Texas. The Bureau intended to divide up this land and allot it to the freedmen and the white refugees, but much of it was tied up with leases, and, after all, despite the large amount, there was never enough to give the freedmen alone an acre apiece.

A million acres among a million farmers meant nothing, and from the beginning there was need of from 25 to 50 million acres more if the Negroes were to be installed as peasant farmers. Against any plan of this sort was the settled determination of the planter South to keep the bulk of Negroes as landless laborers and the deep repugnance on the part of Northerners to confiscating individual property. Even Thaddeus Stevens was not able to budge the majority of Northerners from this attitude. Added to this was the disinclination of the United States to add to its huge debt by undertaking any large and costly social adjustments after the war. To give land to free citizens smacked of "paternalism"; it came directly in opposition to the American assumption that any American could be rich if he wanted to, or at least well-to-do; and it stubbornly ignored the exceptional position of a freed slave.

Indeed it is a singular commentary on the attitude of the government to remember that the Freedmen's Bureau itself during the first year was financed not by taxation but by the toil of ex-slaves: the total amount of rents collected from lands in the hands of the Bureau, paid mostly by Negroes, amounted to $400,000, and curiously enough it was this rent that supported the Freedmen's Bureau during the first year!

Surprise and ridicule has often been voiced concerning this demand of Negroes for land. It has been regarded primarily as a method of punishing rebellion. Motives of this sort may have been in the minds of some Northern whites, but so far as the Negroes were concerned, their demand for a reasonable part of the land on which they had worked for a quarter of a millennium was absolutely justified, and to give them anything less than this was an economic farce. On the other hand, to have given each one of the million Negro free families a forty-acre freehold would have made a basis of real democracy in the United States that might easily have transformed the modern world.

The law of June 21, 1860, opened public land in Alabama, Mississippi, Missouri, Arkansas and Florida; but comparatively few of the freedmen could take advantage of this offer. The Bureau gave some assistance in transporting families, but most of the Negroes had neither stock nor farm implements, and the whites in those localities bitterly opposed their settling. Only about 4,000 families out of nearly four million people acquired homes under this act.

The Sherman order gave rise to all sorts of difficulties. The Negroes were given only possessory titles. Then the owners came back and immediately there was trouble. The Negroes protested, "What is the use of giving us freedom if we can't stay where we were raised and own our own house where we were born and our own piece of ground?" It was on May 25, 1865, that Johnson in his Proclamation of Pardon had provided easy means whereby all property could be restored, except the land at Port Royal, which had been sold for taxes. General Howard came to Charleston to make arrangements, and the story is characteristic—"At first," said a witness, "the people hesitated, but soon as the meaning struck them that they must give up their little homes and gardens and work for others, there was a general murmuring of dissatisfaction." [16]

General Howard was called upon to address them, and to cover his own confusion and sympathy he asked them to sing. Immediately an old woman on the outskirts of the meeting began "Nobody Knows the Trouble I've Seen." Howard wept. [17]

The colored landholders drew up an illiterate petition to Andrew Johnson, the poor white, expressing "sad feelings" over his decree, and begging for an acre and a half of land each; but naturally nothing came of it; for President Johnson, forgetting his own pre-war declaration that the "great plantations must be seized, and divided into small farms," declared that this land must be restored to its original owners and this would be done if owners received a presidential pardon. The pardoning power was pushed and the land all over the South rapidly restored. Negroes were dispossessed, the revenue of the Bureau reduced; many schools had to be discontinued. The Bureau became no longer self-supporting and its whole policy was changed.

In December, 1865, the Bureau had 768,590 acres of land; in 1868, there were only 139,644 acres left, and much of this unimproved and unfertile. For a long time there still persisted the idea that the government was going to make a distribution of land. The rumor was that this was to be made January 1, 1865, and for months before that Negroes all over the South declined to make contracts for work and were accordingly accused of laziness and insubordination. The restoration of the lands not only deprived Negroes in various ways of a clear path toward livelihood, but greatly discouraged them and broke their faith in the United States Government.

These disappointments and discouragements did not for a moment stop the individual efforts of exceptional and lucky Negroes to get hold of land, and the cheapness of the land enabled them to make purchases on a considerable scale where they could get hold of a money wage. The land holdings of Negroes increased all over the South. In South Carolina, the gradual subdivision of the land showed that poor people, colored and white, were slowly getting hold of the divided plantations. Some 33,000 plantations were divided among 93,000 small farmers.

Virginia Negroes acquired between 80,000 and 100,000 acres of land during the late sixties and early seventies. There were soon a few prosperous Negro farmers with 400 to 1,000 acres of land and some owners of considerable city property. Georgia Negroes had bought, by 1875, 396,658 acres of land, assessed at $1,263,902, and added to this they had town and city property assessed at $1,203,202.

Of Arkansas in 1875, Nordhoff said: "Of the forty thousand Negro voters in the State, it is believed that at least one in twenty owns either a farm, or a house and lot in town. This would give but two thousand such independent landholders—a small number, but yet a beginning, showing that, even amidst the intense and incessant political turmoil of the last seven years, a part of the colored men have been persistently industrious and economical." [18]

All this was the record of the exceptional and lucky freedmen. After all they owned in 1870 less than one-tenth of the land which they ought to have possessed, and the wages of nine-tenths of the black laborers were low and seldom paid in cash or with regularity. Wesley gives figures showing annual wages in Southern states to have ranged from $89 to $150 in 1867 and 1868. [19]

On the other hand this demand for land by government action and the increased disposition to vote public funds for the benefit of the pauperized masses incensed the planters. In every Southern state, the South from 1868 to 1876 stressed more and more the anomaly of letting people who had no property vote away the wealth of the rich. The strongest statement of the case against the black legislature of South Carolina was that they paid almost no taxes upon property, they who for the most part had only had the right to hold property since 1866.

This charge against the poor, frequent as it always is in democratic movements, is not valid. The first attempt of a democracy which includes the previously disfranchised poor is to redistribute wealth and income, and this is exactly what the black South attempted. The theory is that the wealth and the current income of the wealthy ruling class does not belong to them entirely, but is the product of the work and striving of the great millions; and that, therefore, these millions ought to have a voice in its more equitable distribution; and if this is true in modern countries, like France and England and Germany, how much more true was it in the South after the war where the poorest class represented the most extreme case of theft of labor that the world can conceive; namely, chattel slavery?

On the other hand, there is not the slightest doubt but that the South had a right to demand of the nation that the whole of the burden of this readjustment of wealth should not fall upon the planters; guilty as they were of supreme exploitation of labor, their guilt was shared by the rest of the nation, just as the rest of the nation had for centuries shared the profits of the slave system. It would have been fair and just for the cost of emancipating the slaves and giving them land to be equitably shared by the whole of the United States.

Moreover the increased taxation of which the South so bitterly complained was not wholly for social uplift. It took mainly the form of (1) restoration of injured property, (2) restoration of capital investment, lost or injured, as in the case of the railroads, (3) the expense of a new system of public education, (4) the expense of carrying on a government with enlarged functions. Only the last two directly benefited the black worker.

There had been a destruction and disappearance of invested capital, through war and emancipation, which represented the greater part of the whole invested capital of the South except land. The value of the land decreased enormously because of the disappearance of slave labor and the destruction of a whole industrial system.

Accurate figures are out of the question. A report to the House of Representatives, 42nd Congress, gives these estimates: the total assessed property of the South in 1860, including slaves, was $4,363,030,347.05; in 1870 it was $2,141,834,188.02, a loss of $1,634,105,341 in slaves and $586,990,218 in other property.[20] The total loss in the South by the war, in property, assets and debts, state and Confederate, has been estimated at $5,262,303,554.26.

These were the losses of capital; but what of the losses of nine million laborers, represented not so much by positive loss as by negative deprivation and exploitation for centuries?

The nineteenth century assumed that universal suffrage would prevent the state from falling into the power of forces inimical to the masses. It might and did leave power in the hands of property and invested capital, but it left them less chance to oppress unduly the laboring class, in so far as that class was thrifty and intelligent. But suppose labor was not intelligent and had been so long enslaved that shiftlessness became a virtue? It seemed clear that in America and in all leading countries in the latter half of the nineteenth century the dictatorship of wealth and capital would be modified in some degree by reference to the will of the mass of laborers. In this way industrial peace and progress toward high standards of living for the masses would be secured without disturbing the basis of capitalistic production. Thus the guidance and dictatorship of capital for the object of private profit were not to be questioned or overthrown; but it must maintain that ascendancy by controlling the public opinion of the laboring class. This was accomplished and, on the whole, easily accomplished by the power to give and withhold employment from people who were without capital, the power to fix wages within certain wide limits, the power to influence public opinion through the prestige of wealth, news and literature, and the power to dominate legislatures, courts, and offices of administration.

The building and buttressing of the new and more powerful capitalistic imperialism was slow and difficult, and with purposeful leadership, labor could enormously curtail the power of capital and bring nearer a critical time when the dictatorship of capital must yield to a dictatorship of labor—when general well-being would replace individual profit as the object of industry.

This was not so clear in detail in the middle of the nineteenth century as it is now. There were democrats, like Sumner and Stevens, who sensed the new power which super-capital was beginning to assert over labor and particularly over universal suffrage. Still it seemed to them that the right to vote in the hands of the intelligent mass could dictate the form of any state that it wished; the difficulty was that the mass of labor and particularly black labor was not intelligent. They freely admitted, therefore, that while it would be better to give the right of suffrage only to those Negroes who were intelligent and particularly those who by economic opportunity would amass some little capital, nevertheless they felt that since the South compelled them to choose between universal suffrage and disfranchised landless labor in the control of landholders and capitalists, with increased political power based on the disfranchisement of labor, the right of suffrage even in the hands of the poor and ignorant gave better chance for ultimate economic justice than their disfranchisement.

It was for this reason that they advocated universal suffrage for the emancipated slaves. They were offered no middle ground. There were in the South only spasmodic signs that any powerful body of public opinion was willing to admit the Negro to the right of suffrage, no matter how intelligent he became, or to admit white labor without nullifying its vote by giving to capital the power based on disfranchised blacks; yet without some acceptance of a labor vote the modern state could not endure; and while the cost of introducing this sudden change in the South was great, yet the action of the dominant South left no alternative. It was either universal suffrage or modified slavery, and in either case, increased political power in the nation for the former slave oligarchy.

Moreover, it is certain that unless the right to vote had been given the Negro by Federal law in 1867, he would never have got it in America. There never has been a time since when race propaganda in America offered the slightest chance for colored people to receive American citizenship. There would have been, therefore, perpetuated in the South and in America, a permanently disfranchised mass of laborers; and the dictatorship of capital would, under those circumstances, have been even more firmly implanted than it is today.

Certainly and naturally the slaves were far more ignorant and poverty-stricken than the mass of Northern white laborers. A dictatorship of Federal power was therefore set up in the first Freedmen's Bureau bill, which would have furnished them land and schools and protected their civil and economic rights until they were ready for universal suffrage or had learned by using it. The bill, as finally passed, left out the provision for land and most of the provisions for education. The Negroes themselves continued to demand land when they were enfranchised by the Reconstruction Bill of 1867; but this evoked shrieks of anger from property in the South and apprehension from property in the North.

There arose in the South an extraordinary situation which few scholars have studied in its economic aspects. First, there was black labor, in the main ignorant and poor, but with some leaders of intelligence, backed in part by the military power of the North; secondly there was white exploitation, which in the South had been based on the ownership of land and labor and which was now widely impoverished, but still left with most of the land, some capital and large social influence. There was in addition to these the mass of impoverished and ignorant white peasants and laborers. To this there were added a number of Northern immigrants with smaller or larger amounts of capital.

It is idle to speculate as to just how this situation could have been avoided. Of course, it would not have arisen if slavery had continued. Moreover, there would have been less evident catastrophe and turmoil immediately if slavery had been continued under another name, in accordance with the efforts of the Southern states under the Johnson Reconstruction plan.

But this simply meant a postponement of the trouble. Eventually the complete agrarian capitalistic system, based on the ownership of both land and labor, had to disappear from America and the world and its disappearance had to spell revolution involving a vast transfer of capital and of political power.

This revolution might have taken the form of annulling property in slaves with indemnity to the slave owners, and seeking to put into the South a laboring class without political power. This would have been an impossible solution, because this laboring class would have been thrown into even more direct competition with white laborers the land over, a fact which had already been a cause of civil war; and it would have involved an attempt at capitalist autocracy without the corrective of universal suffrage among a third of the American laboring class. Moreover, the capital to indemnify the slave owners must have come out of the wealth of that part of the country whose capital was being taxed to pay the staggering cost of a war to overthrow political power based on enslaved labor. Northern capital would not consent to restore Southern loss from investment in slaves, much less if this restored capital were to be used to compete with capital in the North.

There ensued in the South a contest for the ultimate dictatorship of the state in conjunction with universal suffrage for black and white. The temporary dictatorship set up by the Federal government represented and had to represent, in essence, the attitude of northern capitalists. The parties that hoped to dominate this dictatorship, all of them, lacked capital; the planter had been impoverished by the war; the small capitalist from the North who had come South brought little to invest, but expected to accumulate capital on the spot; and the poor white represented the impoverished peasantry and labor class as well as a petty bourgeois of small merchants and professional men.

Here, then, was the situation. And what had to follow? The planters had to move toward the control of the political power of newly enfranchised labor, both black and white. One can see such movements in the consent of Beauregard and Longstreet in Louisiana, Alcorn in Mississippi and Hampton in South Carolina, to Negro suffrage, and their willingness to concede something of economic power to the black voters. But this movement, which would have been comparatively simple under the ordinary organization of capital and labor in modern countries, was complicated by three facts:

First, there came in a new, eager class of competing capitalists who proposed to share with the planters the dictatorship of labor.

Secondly, the movement of the planter class to attract black labor with economic concession met the immediate and bitter fear and opposition of the poor whites, not simply of the mass of half-starved white peasants and farmers, but of the merchants, the former slave overseers and managers, men who proposed to join the planters as exploiters of labor.

These desperately feared the rise of black labor to a position which might equal and even surpass the poor whites'. This was shown in the voting in Alabama, under Johnson's reconstruction, where the poor white counties went solidly against the Black Belt on several occasions; and it was also shown in the bitter opposition to the counting of black folk as a basis of representation. If the whole population was to be counted as a basis of representation, then after the war as before, the Black Belt and its capitalistic dictators were going to dominate white labor; and it was for this reason that the poor whites long fought to exclude the Negro in apportioning the political power of the state, and after Reconstruction united in disfranchising him.

When the Negro received the right to vote and had to be counted, there arose a desperate effort on the part of the poor whites to keep the planters from controlling the Negro vote by their economic power. Sometimes this effort took the crude method of driving black labor off the plantations and intimidating it in various ways. Sometimes it took the form of trying to lead black labor through demagogues, like Hunnicutt in Virginia; and all the time, in the background, was the feeling that unless the planters united with the poor whites in a solid racial phalanx against the black voters, anarchy and destruction were preferable to the economic rise of the Negro.

How this interaction of former land monopolists, white peasant and Negro peasant, would have worked itself out if uncomplicated by other interests, is a question. But it seems almost inevitable that division would have had to take place along economic rather than racial lines, and that the planter-capitalists, reënforcing themselves with recruits from a poor white petty bourgeois, would have organized to control white and black labor endowed with universal suffrage, along the same lines that allowed capital in the North to control native white labor and new immigrants.

There entered, however, the small northern investor, usually and inaccurately comprehended under the term "carpetbagger," a phrase too vague for our use, but too much used to discard. When the war ended there were large numbers of Northern soldiers and officers in the South. There were civilian agents of the government and there were other Northerners who looked toward the South as a place of economic re-birth and investment. There was nothing extraordinary in this. Thousands upon thousands of Southerners had come into the North and had been welcomed to its freedom and opportunities; while this migration to the South had come mainly in time of war, with the resultant war hatred and bitterness, still its main reason was economic. Men with smaller or larger amounts of capital and many with no capital proposed to invest in land and free labor in the South at a time when the great staples of Southern agriculture were abnormally high and in wide demand throughout the world. These men, so far as they were investing capitalists, and most of them were, proposed to build up in the South the same kind of capitalistic democracy based on universal suffrage to which they had been used in the North. They were going to trade with free black labor and white labor and yield to it that amount of consideration and that economic share of the product which they would naturally have to yield in order to keep their dictatorship and yet get profit for themselves.

If, now, the new Northern capitalists and the Southern planter class had been united into one new capitalistic class, their only problem would have been to deal with a new laboring class composed of blacks and whites and to admit to their ranks those of either class who had or could get any amount of new capital.

But both capitalists and laborers were split in two; there was hatred and jealousy in the ranks of this new prospective capitalistic class, and race prejudice and fear in the ranks of the laborers. In the new capitalistic class, the hatred of the planters for Northerners, who apparently were planning to add to the conquests of war new conquests of economic power, was naturally intense. It was this same power of Northern capital which in Southern minds caused civil war. The new Northern capitalists, on the other hand, could not understand why they should not be welcomed as investors without sentiment, in a region where investment of new capital was sadly needed, and why this should not be accompanied by the same attitude toward labor which capital must take throughout the world if it were going to maintain its mastery.

Thirdly, the poor whites began a desperate and almost panic-stricken attempt to force themselves into this situation, either as allies of the old planter class which had for them the greatest contempt, or as allies of the carpetbagger capitalist, against whom they had just been fighting in the ranks of the army, and whose attitude toward black labor they did not understand and feared, or even as allies of black labor, which they might use as a club against both planter and capitalist.

The ensuing turmoil in the South was a fight of these three pretenders to economic power over the capitalistic state, and also it was further complicated by the fact that the Federal military dictatorship was in the hands of Northern capitalists and Northern social workers.

There ensued a fierce fight for mastery characterized by widespread graft, corruption, and violence; for what responsibility did any of these parties have to a state they did not own? And the greater the failure of government through any of the contenders, the more it justified radical change. When the planter class moved toward black labor its leaders made demands which the planters would not meet; namely, demands for land, education and the expense of social uplift. These demands of the black laborer might have been modified, if he had not found that they were easily promised and partially fulfilled by the carpetbag capitalist. He, therefore, turned to the carpetbagger for leadership and through him was given education and at least a possibility of buying land. The poor white could try to compete with the carpetbag capitalist in leadership and demagoguery over the Negroes; or he could seek alliance with the planter because the planter's property was bearing the main cost of the new educational-social program; or by sabotage he could seek to sink the government in anarchy.

Small wonder that the ensuing graft, stealing and renewal of civil war was widely misunderstood. But the very last place where the blame for the situation could, by the wildest imagination, be placed was upon the newly enfranchised black labor. What the Negro needed, and what he desperately sought, was leadership in knowledge and industry. In knowledge he wanted through his own irrepressible demand for education to become an intelligent citizen; and a start toward this he received through the splendid and unselfish coöperation of the Northern social workers connected with the Federal dictatorship and through their allies, the teachers who came down to man the Freedmen's Bureau schools. By straining his political power to the utmost, the Negro voter got a public school system and got it because that was one clear object which he understood and which no bribery or chicanery could seduce him from advocating and insisting upon in season and out.

On the other hand, in economic leadership, in the whole question of work and wage, he was almost entirely at sea. His higher schools based on New England capitalism and individualism gave little training for an economic battle just dawning in the world and far from the conception of leaders in Southern industry. Even his later industrial schools were tied hand and foot to triumphant capitalism unhampered by a labor vote.

He had, then, but one clear economic ideal and that was his demand for land, his demand that the great plantations be subdivided and given to him as his right. This was a perfectly fair and natural demand and ought to have been an integral part of Emancipation. To emancipate four million laborers whose labor had been owned, and separate them from the land upon which they had worked for nearly two and a half centuries, was an operation such as no modern country had for a moment attempted or contemplated. The German and English and French serf, the Italian and Russian serf, were, on emancipation, given definite rights in the land. Only the American Negro slave was emancipated without such rights and in the end this spelled for him the continuation of slavery.

Beyond this demand for land, economic leadership for the Negro failed. He appealed to his former master. The best of the planters, those who in slavery days had occupied a patriarchal position toward their slaves, were besieged not only by their own former slaves but by others for advice and leadership. If they had wished, they could have held the Negro vote in the palm of their hands. The Negroes would have followed them implicitly, and it was this that poor whites from Andrew Johnson down feared. But they forgot that the planters were estopped from this program by their own lack of capital; by the new and confiscatory taxation which the Negroes' demands entailed even under the most frugal and honest administration; by their own singular lack of knowledge of the methods of capitalistic democracy throughout the world, which was based on those very concessions to labor of which they could not conceive. They kept insisting on hard, regular toil, vague and irregular wages, and no exercise of political power; all this in a day when labor the world over demanded shorter hours, a definite high wage contract, and the right to vote.

To this attitude of the planters must be added the bitter jealousy, not only of the worst and more vicious and selfish of the planters, but of the poor whites. And when there was added to this the fact that they themselves were being supplanted as advisers of Negroes by the new white Northern capitalist, willing to grant labor's demands at the expense of the state, they, in most cases, utterly refused to lead Negro labor, and thus threw the Negroes back on the carpetbag capitalists for advice and leadership. Thither, too, Negroes were attracted by a trust that naturally grew out of the fact that these people represented their emancipation. They represented Abraham Lincoln and his government, and Negroes were naturally strongly inclined to do anything that this leadership told them to, even when the advice was dishonest and unwise. Thus were the freedmen landed in piteous contradiction and difficulty.

The Negro's own black leadership was naturally of many sorts. Some, like the whites, were petty bourgeois, seeking to climb to wealth; others were educated men, helping to develop a new nation without regard to mere race lines, while a third group were idealists, trying to uplift the Negro race and put them on a par with the whites. But how was this to be accomplished? In the minds of very few of them was there any clear and distinct plan for the development of a laboring class into a position of power and mastery over the modern industrial state. And in this lack of vision, they were not singular in America. Where else in the land, even among labor leaders, was there any such fixed and definite program of action?

The fight for the domination of the new form of state which Reconstruction was building took the direction of using the income for new forms of state expenses; and for that, public investment for private profit was the widespread custom in the North. The South had entered only to a small extent into such schemes and tended to regard them as outside the function of the state. Even the forms of expenditure for education, and the help of indigents, were kinds of expenditure to which the Southern taxpayers had not been used and in which for the most part they did not believe. There were consequently fierce outcries against the "waste" of such expenditures.

When in addition to that, there came widespread and deliberate investment of public funds in railroads and corporations where the profits went to speculators and grafters, the protest of landed property was intensified.

The results of this form of stealing bore hard upon the impoverished landholder and were particularly detestable to him because, monopolizing the government before the war, he had largely escaped taxation and had tried to transfer it to the shoulders of the small business man. Now the small business man, reënforced by the carpetbagger and black voter, was returning it to the landholder. Assessments were increased and the gradual disestablishment of the landed aristocracy became imminent.

Here is the crux of the matter: It was this large and, for the day and circumstances, overwhelming loss that lay at the bottom of the extraordinary charges of extravagance and stealing that characterize the Reconstruction controversy. For had there been no further loss, and no necessity nor effort to increase the customary taxation of the past, the planter would have felt hurt to his heart by the disappearance of the bulk of his capital. But when to this was added a new taxation for uplifting Negroes and enriching Northerners, he raised his protest to a shriek of bitterness.

When we try to get to the details of the Southern States' debts after the war and during Reconstruction, we are faced by the fact that there is no agreement among authorities. The reasons for this are several: First, What is a debt? Is it the amount which a state actually owes, or is it the amount for which a state may become liable in the future, by reason of present commitments and promises? In this latter case, for how much does it actually become liable?

A careful examination of such facts as seem established shows that the increase of debts under the Reconstruction régime was not large. In eleven Southern States there was little over $100,000,000 of debt in 1860, which rose to $222,000,000 on account of war. When the Confederate debt was repudiated, the recognized debts in 1865 stood at $156,000,000. To this should be added certain railroad liabilities of Alabama, which brings the total debt at the beginning of Reconstruction to $175,000,000. In 1871, this debt had increased nearly 100% to $305,-000,000; but $100,000,000 of this debt consisted in contingent and prospective liabilities due to the issue of railway bonds, which confuses the whole issue with regard to Reconstruction debts. The whole increase of debt, during 1860-1871, amounted apparently to less than 100%. [21] What now did this increase of debt due to the railway bonds mean? It meant that Southern and Northern men, Republicans and Democrats, had united to put the credit of the state back of their railway investments. The only way in which nine-tenths of Negro voters came into this matter was as their representatives were bribed by both parties to support this legislation for private profit. Such bribery undoubtedly was widespread. But it was widespread not only among Negro voters, but among white voters, and among all the voters of the United States, and among members of all legislatures and members of Congress. It could hardly be argued that in this respect, new and largely ignorant Negro voters should show a higher public morality than the rest of the country.

On the other hand, the wrath of the landholders against this increase in debt was the wrath of agrarian capitalists against the new industrialism; and yet they were unable to prosecute those who stole the state's money through the issue of railway bonds because there were too many Southern people, and Southern people of prominence, involved. This was shown in North Carolina, where despite the extravagant investment in railways, the hope of wide immigration and rapid development was disappointed, and the landholders put the commercialists out of power; but they did not dare prosecute them. In Mississippi, on the other hand, where the Negro was as powerful as in any state, there was no increase of debt, because from the first the landholders and Negroes refused to loan the credit of the state to railroads.

If the money raised by taxes had been spent carefully and honestly upon legitimate and necessary matters of restoration and government, the increase is not unreasonable. Or in other words, there is nothing on the face of the figures that proves unusual theft.

Over one hundred and fifty millions of this debt was repudiated by the reactionary governments which came into office after 1876. John F. Hume [22] claims that to this should be added $120,000,000 of debts repudiated before the Civil War, showing that the South was not unused to dealing in this way with borrowed funds.

This indebtedness must also be interpreted by considering the price of gold. South Carolina's debt of twenty-two million in 1871 was made when paper money was at 70 and was therefore equivalent to fifteen and a half million in 1860. Indeed the curve of the price of gold explains to some extent the curve of alleged extravagance.

The debt of these states between the time when it reached its highest point and 1880 was scaled down to $108,003,974. This meant that a sum of $155,525,856 was repudiated and it will be noted that this is almost exactly the increased indebtedness which the Reconstruction régime incurred in order to meet the increased burden of the state—public school education, charitable institutions, the restoration of public buildings, and increased social responsibilities.

There can be no possible proof that all of this increased indebtedness represented theft; nor is there any adequate reason for believing that most of it did. What happened in Southern repudiation after the war was that the Southern states proceeded to punish people who had dared to loan money to the Southern states under Negro suffrage, by confiscating the sums which they had loaned. This was what they had threatened to do, and they did it with vengeance.

There are certain other considerations. White Southerners were in practically complete control during the Reconstruction régime, in Virginia and Tennessee; yet in these two states, an indebtedness of $52,000,000 in 1860 increased to $88,000,000 before 1880, and $34,000,000 of this was repudiated. This could hardly be charged to Negro suffrage. Then, too, in North Carolina, Georgia and Alabama, the ex-Confederate South never lost all control, and was early restored to full control. Yet in these states, an indebtedness of $19,000,000 in 1860 reached $81,000,000 before 1880. And of this $56,000,000 was repudiated. A part of the blame of this may be shouldered on white Northerners, but very little of it could possibly be attributed to Negroes.

In the case of Florida and Mississippi, the debt was negligible, and on the face of it, absolutely defensible. Yet large amounts were repudiated by the reform party. In South Carolina, the debt stood at nearly $6,000,000 in 1865, before Reconstruction. It reached at its highest point, before 1880, nearly $25,000,000. And of this $17,000,000 was repudiated. If any large proportion of it represented theft, it represented as much the illegal graft of Northern moneylenders as the theft of money actually received by the state. Arkansas, under a government in which the Negro had almost no part, repudiated $12,000,000 out of $18,000,000 of indebtedness.

The whole debt transaction of the South after Reconstruction seemed to show that many of the accusations of unreasonable debt, and the haste at repudiation, were a blow aimed at Northern finance, rather than a proof of Negro extravagance. It was openly said in Louisiana that it was fitting that "the Northerners who tore down the basis of our former prosperity should share some of the ills." [23]

Sir George Campbell said: "All the Carpet-bag Governors are, as a matter of course, accused of the grossest personal corruption; and as soon as they fall from power it is almost a necessity that they should fly from criminal prosecutions instituted in the local courts under circumstances which give little security for fair trial. . . .

"On the whole, then, I am inclined to believe that the period of Carpet-bag rule was rather a scandal than a very permanent injury . . . ; and there was more pilfering than plunder on a scale permanently to cripple the State." [24]

Indeed, in most cases, the testimony concerning stealing and corruption in the South during this time was either given by bitter politi-

cal opponents who constituted themselves judge, witness, and jury
or by criminals who were clearing their own skirts by accusing others.

Note well the character of the stealing in the South. In the first
place, when money was appropriated even extravagantly, it was appropriated for railroads, which the South needed desperately, and it
was appropriated under the same terms that had enabled the North
and the West to get their railroads; it was appropriated for public
institutions; it was appropriated for the buying of land in order
to subdivide the great plantations; it was appropriated for certain
public services.

In all cases the graft and dishonesty came in the carrying out, the
fulfillment of these needs, and this was not only in the hands of white
men, but Southern white men as often as Northern; and Northern
white financial agents and manipulators in Wall Street helped to make
the bond sales of South Carolina, Alabama, Mississippi and Florida.
To charge this debt to the Negroes is idiotic. It was not so charged at
the time, but this came to be a popular version of Southern corruption
when it became unpopular to accuse the Northerners.

In the original charges of graft and corruption made by the Southerners, Negroes were mentioned only as tools. It was the carpetbagger and scalawags, Northern and Southern white men, who were
continually and insistently charged with theft and corruption.

Then as the carpet-baggers lost the power of military dictatorship,
and as the prospect of alliance with the poor whites showed the planters a way of re-securing the government, they turned and with the
poor whites concentrated all their accusations of misgovernment and
corruption upon the Negro, in order to deprive the Negro of his political power.

Southern corruption was not the exclusive guilt of scalawags and
carpet-baggers, nor were all carpet-baggers and scalawags thieves.
Some carpet-baggers were noble-hearted philanthropists. Some scalawags were self-sacrificing benefactors of both Negroes and whites.
Some of the scalawags and carpet-baggers lied and stole, and some
helped and coöperated with the freedmen and worked for real democracy in the South for all races. Indeed in graft and theft the skirts of
Southern whites of all classes were not clear before or after the war.

Before the war, the South was ruled by an oligarchy and the functions of the state carried on largely by individuals. This meant that
the state had little to do, and its expenses were small. The oligarchic
state does not need to resort to corruption of the government. Its leaders, having the right to exploit labor to the limit, receive an income
which makes them conspicuously independent of any income from

the government. The government revenues are kept purposely small and the salaries low so that poor men cannot afford to enter into government service.

On the other hand, when the oligarchy is broken down and when labor increases its power, revenue is raised by taxing the rich, and then the temptation to bribery and stealing increases according to the amount of poverty. The corruption in the South before the war did not usually touch the state governments. The income there was too small to be tempting; yet in Mississippi, after two receivers of public money had defaulted for $155,000, a United States treasury agent recommended that the last one be retained since another would probably be as bad. Other Southern states had defaulting officials, and shamelessly repudiated their public debts.

For thirty years, during 1830-1860, the South was ruled by its own best citizens and yet during that time there were defalcations in Tennessee, Mississippi, Georgia, Louisiana, Texas, Alabama and Arkansas among postmasters, United States marshals, collectors and surveyors, amounting to more than one million dollars.

How far, then, was post-bellum corruption due to Negroes? Only in so far as they represented ignorance and poverty and were thus peculiarly susceptible to petty bribery. No one contends that any considerable amount of money went to them. There were some reports of show and extravagance among them, but the great thieves were always white men; very few Negro leaders were specifically accused of theft, and again seldom in these cases were the accusations proven. Usually they were vague slurs resting on the assumption that all Negroes steal. Petty bribery of members of Reconstruction legislatures, white and black, was widespread; but Wallace in Florida shows the desperate inner turmoil of the Negroes to counteract this within their own ranks; and outstanding cases of notably incorruptible Negro leaders like Lieutenant-Governor Dunn of Louisiana, Treasurer Cardozo of South Carolina, Secretary of State Gibbs of Florida, and Speaker Lynch of Mississippi, are well known.

Certainly the mass of Negroes were unbribable when it came to demands for land and education and other things, the beneficent object of which they could thoroughly understand. But they were peculiarly susceptible to bribes when it was a matter of personal following of demagogues who catered to their likes and weaknesses.

The mass of Negroes were accused of selling votes and influence for small sums and of thus being easily bought up by big thieves; but even in this, they were usually bought up by pretended friends and not bribed against their beliefs or by enemies. To the principles that they understood and knew, they were true; but there were many things connected with government and its technical details which they did not know; in other words, they were ignorant and poor, and the ignorant and poor can always be misled and bribed. What made the Negro poor and ignorant? Surely, it was slavery, and he tried with his vote to escape slavery.

As Dunning says: "As to corruption under the Negro government of the South, this must be noted: first, the decade when the Negroes were ushered into political life, from 1867 to 1877, was probably the most corrupt decade in the history of the United States, and of all parts of the United States.

"The form and manner of this corruption, which has given so unsavory a connotation to the name 'reconstruction,' were no different from those which have appeared in many another time and place in democratic society. At the very time, indeed, when the administrations of Scott, in South Carolina, and Warmoth, in Louisiana, were establishing the Southern high-water mark of rascality in public finance, the Tweed ring in New York City was at the culmination of its closely parallel career." [25]

"When we come to examine them, the charges made by such men as Rhodes, Oberholtzer, Dunning, Bowers, etc., even if taken at their face value, which they assuredly should not be, are charges that might with equal force be leveled against every government, Federal, state and municipal, North and South, Republican and Democratic, of the time—and against the 'lily white' Restoration governments that followed in the South with reaction. Only compare the public moneys stolen by officers of the Reconstruction governments with the vast sums that found their way into the pockets of the Tweed Ring in the perfectly Conservative, Democratic, Copperhead City of New York!" [26]

It may be contended that the presence of a mass of unlettered and inexperienced voters in a state makes bribery and graft easier and more capable of misuse by malign elements. This is true. But the question is, is the situation any better if ignorance and poverty are permanently disfranchised? The whole answer of modern industrial conditions is—no, it is not. And the only alternative, therefore, is the one continually urged by Sumner, Phillips and Stevens: if ignorance is dangerous—instruct it. If poverty is the cause of stealing and crime, increase the income of the masses.

Property involves theft by the Rich from the Poor; but there comes a grave question; given a mass of ignorance and poverty, is that mass less dangerous without the ballot? The answer to this depends upon whose danger one envisages. They are not dangerous to the mass of laboring men. If they are kept in ignorance and poverty and dominated by capital, they are certainly dangerous to capital. To escape such revolution and prolong its sway property must yield political power to the mass of laborers, and let it wield that power more intelligently by giving it public schools and higher wages. It is naturally easier for capital to do this gradually, and if there could have been a choice in 1867 between an effective public school system for black labor in the South and its gradual enfranchisement, or even beyond that, a property qualification for such laborers as through free land and higher wage had some chance to accumulate some property—if this had been possible, it would have been, without doubt, the best transition program for capital and labor, provided of course that capitalists thus tamely yielded power. But there was no such alternative. Labor, black labor, must be either enfranchised or enslaved, unless, of course, the United States government was willing to come in with a permanent Freedmen's Bureau to train Negroes toward economic freedom and against the interest of Southern capital. This was revolution. This was force and no such permanent Freedmen's Bureau backed by a strongly capitalistic Northern government could have been expected in 1867.

The essential problem of Negro enfranchisement was this: How far is the poor and ignorant electorate a permanent injury to the state, and how far does the extent of the injury make for efforts to counteract it? More than a million Negroes were enfranchised in 1867. Of these, it is possible that between 100,000 and 200,000 could read and write, and certainly not more than 25,000, including black immigrants from the North, could be called educated. It was the theory that if these people were given the right to vote, the state, first of all, would be compelled to discontinue plans of political action or industrial organization which did not accord with the general plans of the North, and secondly, in self-defense, it would have to begin the education of the freedmen and establish a system of free labor with wages and conditions of work much fairer than those in vogue during slavery.

How far was this a feasible social program? It was not possible, of course, if the South had the right to continue its industrial organization based on land monopoly and ownership of labor. Conceding the emancipation of labor, that emancipation meant nothing if land monopoly continued and the wage contract was merely nominal. If a wage system was to be installed, it must receive protection either from an outside power, like that of the Federal government, or from the worker himself. So far as the worker was concerned, the only protection feasible was the ballot in the hands of a united and intelligently led working class. Could it be assumed now that the possession of the

ballot in the hands of ignorant working people, black and white, would lead to real economic emancipation, or on the other hand would it not become a menace to the state so great that its very existence would be threatened?

It had been the insistent contention of many that the basis of the state was threatened between 1867 and 1876 and, therefore, the revolution of 1876 had to take place. The known facts do not sustain this contention and it seems probable that if we had preserved a more complete story of the action of the Negro voter the facts in his favor would even be stronger. As it is, it must be remembered that the proponents of Negro suffrage did not for a moment contend that the experiment was not difficult and would not involve hardship and danger. The elections for the conventions went off, for the most part, without upheaval, with intelligence and certainly with unusual fairness. The conduct of the Negro voters, their selection of candidates, their action in conventions and early legislatures, was, on the whole, sane, thoughtful, and sincere. No one can, with any color of truth, say that civilization was threatened or the foundations of the state attacked in the South in the years from 1868 to 1876.

Then, however, came a time of decisions. Did the South want the Negro to become an intelligent voter and participant in the state under any circumstances, or on the other hand was it opposed to Negro voters no matter how intelligent and efficient?

It may be said, then, that the argument for giving the right to vote to the mass of the poor and ignorant still stands as defensible, without for a moment denying that there should not be such a class in any civilized community; but if the class is there, the fault is the fault of the community and the community must suffer and pay for it. The South had exploited Negro labor for nearly two and one-half centuries. If in ten years or twenty years things could be so changed that this class was receiving an education, getting hold of land, exercising some control over capital, and becoming co-partners in the state, the South would be a particularly fortunate community.

If, on the other hand, there had been the moral strength in the South so that without yielding immediate political power, they could have educated and uplifted the blacks and gradually inducted them into political power and real industrial emancipation, the results undoubtedly would have been better. There was no such disposition, and under the profit ideal of a capitalist organization, there could not have been. That would have required, after the losses of war, an industrial unselfishness of which capitalist organization does not for a moment admit. Force, therefore, and outside force, had to be applied or otherwise slavery would have persisted in a but slightly modified form, and the persistence of slavery in the United States longer than it had already persisted would have been a calamity worse than any of the calamities, real or imagined, of Reconstruction.

Consequently, with Northern white leadership, the Negro voters quite confounded the planter plan; they proved apt pupils in politics. They developed their own leadership. They gained clearer and clearer conceptions of how their political power could be used for their own good. They were unselfish, too, in wishing to include in their own good the white worker and even the ex-master. Of course, all that was done in Constitution-making and legislation at this time was not entirely the work of black men, and in the same way all that was done in maladministration and corruption was not entirely the fault of the black man. But if the black man is to be blamed for the ills of Reconstruction, he must also be credited for its good, and that good is indubitable. In less than ten years, the basic structure of capitalism in the South was changed by his vote. A new modern state was erected in the place of agrarian slavery. And its foundations were so sound and its general plan so good that despite bitter effort, the South had to accept universal suffrage in theory at least, and had to accept the public school system. It had to broaden social control by adding to the landholder the industrial capitalist.

Indeed the Negro voter in Reconstruction had disappointed all the prophets. The bravest of the carpetbaggers, Tourgée, declared concerning the Negro voters: "They instituted a public school system in a realm where public schools had been unknown. They opened the ballot-box and jury box to thousands of white men who had been debarred from them by a lack of earthly possessions. They introduced home rule in the South. They abolished the whipping post, and branding iron, the stocks and other barbarous forms of punishment which had up to that time prevailed. They reduced capital felonies from about twenty to two or three. In an age of extravagance they were extravagant in the sums appropriated for public works. In all that time no man's rights of person were invaded under the forms of laws." [27] The Negro buttressed Southern civilization in precisely the places it was weakest, against popular ignorance, oligarchy in government, and land monopoly. His schools were more and more successful. If now he became a recognized part of the state, a larger and larger degree of social equality must be granted him. This was apparent in his demand for a single system of public schools without discrimination of race—a demand that came for obvious reasons of economy as well as for advantages of social contact. It appeared also in the demand for equal accommodations on railroads and in public places.

Ultimately, of course, a single system of public schools, and state universities without distinction of race, and equality of civil rights was going to lead to some social intermingling and attacks upon the anti-intermarriage laws which encouraged miscegenation and deliberately degraded women. This was a possibility that the planter class could not contemplate without concern and it stirred among the poor whites a blind and unreasoning fury.

The dictatorship of labor in the South, then, with its establishment of democratic control over social development, education and public improvements, succeeded only at the expense of a taxation on land and property which amounted to confiscation. And it was accompanied by a waste of public funds partly due to inexperience, and partly due to the prevailing wave of political dishonesty that engulfed the whole country.

The singular thing about the wholesale charge of stealing and corruption during Reconstruction times is that when government was restored to the whites and to the Democratic Party, there were so few attempts at criminal indictment or to secure any return of the loot. In North Carolina, for instance, wholesale theft was charged against the carpetbaggers, and yet when the governor and leader of the Republican Party was impeached, no charge of stealing was in the indictment. He was impeached for using the militia to put down admitted and widespread disorder, and for the arrest of the men who openly and impudently encouraged the disorder.

In Mississippi, all that the restored government apparently wanted was to get rid of Governor Ames. They made no attempt to charge him with theft. In South Carolina, the restored government claimed to have documentary evidence of widespread stealing and graft, and they made a few indictments which were afterward quietly quashed. Why did not the fraud committee go into the courts which they now controlled, and find out where the money they alleged was stolen had gone, and who was now enjoying it? The conclusion is almost inescapable, that the fraud committee knew perfectly well that a large proportion of the thieves were now on the side of white rule, and that much of their theft had been designed and calculated to discredit Negroes and carpetbaggers.

These facts and similar ones show that the overthrow of Reconstruction was in essence a revolution inspired by property, and not a race war.

The echo of the Northern reform movement was felt in the South. It encouraged the Northern capitalists and the more intelligent Negroes to unite in a Southern reform movement. This was shown by the Chamberlain government in South Carolina, the Ames government in Mississippi, and less clearly by the Kellogg government in Louisiana.

The carpetbag reformers moved toward an alliance with the planters with an understanding that called for lower taxes and the elimination of graft and corruption. Negro voters began to support this program, but were restrained by distrust. They feared that the planters still planned their disfranchisement. If this fear could have been removed, and as far as it was removed, the power of the Negro vote in the South was certain to go gradually toward reform.

It was this contingency that the poor whites of all grades feared. It meant to them a reëstablishment of that subordination under Negro labor which they had suffered during slavery. They, therefore, interposed by violence to increase the natural antagonism between Southerners of the planter class and Northerners who represented the military dictatorship as well as capital, and also to increase the fear of the Negroes that the planters might try to reënslave them. The planters certainly were not disposed to make any permanent alliance with carpetbaggers like Chamberlain. After all they were Northerners, recent enemies, and were responsible for the taxation that had gone before reform.

The efforts at reform, therefore, at first widely applauded, one by one began to go down before a new philosophy which represented understanding between the planters and poor whites. This again was not an easy thing for the planters to swallow, but it was accompanied by deference to their social status, by eagerness on the part of the poor whites to check the demands of the Negroes by any means, and by willingness to do the dirty work of the revolution that was coming, with its blood and crass cruelties, its bitter words, upheaval and turmoil. This was the birth and being of the Ku Klux Klan.

Before the war, there had been violent Southern anti-Negro propaganda on racial lines; but that had been mainly for consumption in the North. Northerners, traveling in the South, were always astonished at finding it accompanied by peculiar evidences of social equality and closer intimacies; in other words, there was no deep racial antagonism except in the case of poor whites, where it had a tremendous economic foundation. After the war, the race division, so long as the economic foundation was equitable, would have become less and less pronounced had it not been emphasized with determination in the application of the "Mississippi Plan."

It is one of the anomalies of history that political and economic reform in the North and West after 1873 joined hands with monopoly and reaction in the South to oppress and reënslave labor.

Every effort was made by careful propaganda to induce the nation to believe that the Southern wing of the Democratic party was fighting the same kind of corruption as the North and that corruption was represented in the South solely by carpetbaggers and Negroes. This was only partly true in the South; for there labor too was fighting corruption and dishonesty, so far as land and capital, which were secretly abetting graft in order to escape taxation, would allow it to do so without disfranchisement. But the South now began to use the diplomacy so badly lacking in its previous leadership since the war. Adroitly it stopped attacking abolitionists and even carpetbaggers, and gradually transferred all the blame for post-war misgovernment to the Negroes. The Negro vote and graft were indissolubly linked in the public mind by incessant propaganda. Race repulsion, race hate, and race pride were increased by every subtle method, until the Negro and his friends were on the defensive and the Negro himself almost convinced of his own guilt. Negro haters and pseudo-scientists raised their heads and voices in triumph. Lamar of Mississippi, fraudulently elected to Congress, unctuously praised Sumner with his tongue in his cheek; and Louisiana solemnly promised to give Negroes full political and civil rights with equal education for Negro children—a deliberate lie which is absolutely proven by the revelations of the last fifty years.

The South was impelled to brute force and deliberate deception in dealing with the Negro because it had been astonished and disappointed not by the Negro's failure, but by his success and promise of greater success.

All this came at a time when the best conscience of the nation—the conscience which was heir to the enthusiasm of abolitionist-democracy —was turned against the only power which could support democracy in the South. The truth of the insistence of Stevens was manifest: without land and without vocation, the Negro voter could not gain that economic independence which would protect his vote. Unless, therefore, his political and civil rights were supported by the United States army, he was doomed to practical reënslavement. But the United States army became in the seventies the representative of the party of political corruption, while its political opponents represented land monopoly and capitalistic reaction in the South. When, therefore, the conscience of the United States attacked corruption, it at the same time attacked in the Republican Party the only power that could support democracy in the South. It was a paradox too tragic to explain and it deceived leading reformers, like Carl Schurz, into consenting to throw the poor, ignorant black workers, whom he had helped to enfranchise, to the lions of land monopoly and capitalistic control, which proposed to devour them, and did.

In the South, reform sought to follow the Northern model and the carpetbag capitalists turned toward the purging of the civil service and the throttling of monopoly. In this, they gained the backing of many intelligent Negroes. But for one thing they could have got the bulk of the Negro vote, and that one thing was the Negro's distrust of the honesty of the planters' objects. Did the planter want reform or did he want reënslavement of Negro labor? As a matter of fact, the planter got the beginnings of reform in the administration of government in South Carolina, in Mississippi, and even in Louisiana. But he was aware that if that movement went far, it would prove that the Negro vote could be appealed to and made effective in good government as well as bad. This he did not want. As the South Carolina Democratic convention said, April, 1868, in an address to the colored people: "It is impossible that your present power can endure, whether you use it for good or ill." [28]

Back of this was the knowledge that honest labor government would be more fatal to land monopoly and industrial privilege than government by bribery and graft.

The white South, therefore, quickly substituted violence and renewal of the war in order to get rid of the possibility of good government supported by black labor votes.

There was not a single honest Southerner who did not know that any reasonable political program which included a fair chance for the Negro to get an honest wage, personal protection, land to work, and schools for his children, would have received the staunch, loyal and unyielding support of the overwhelming mass of Negro voters; but this program, when ostensibly offered the Negro, concealed the determination to reduce him practicallly to slavery. He knew this and in his endeavor to escape floundered through bribery, corruption, and murder, seeking a path to peace, freedom, and the income of a civilized man.

The South has itself to blame. It showed no historic sign of favoring emancipation before the war, rather the contrary. It showed no disposition to yield to the offer of recompensed emancipation which Abraham Lincoln repeatedly made. It showed no desire to yield to emancipation with correspondingly curtailed political power as Congress suggested. It showed no disposition to reform democracy with the Negro vote. It relied on stubborn brute force.

Meantime, the leaders of Northern capital and finance were still afraid of the return of Southern political power after the lapse of the military dictatorship. This power was larger than before the war and it was bound to grow. If it were to be used in conjunction with Northern liberals, it might still mean the reduction of the tariff, the reduction of monopoly, and an attack upon new financial methods and upon concentrated control in industry. There was now no sentiment like "freedom" to which the Northern industrialists could appeal. It was, therefore, necessary for Northern capital to make terms with the dominant South.

Thus, both the liberal and the conservative North found themselves willing to sacrifice the interests of labor in the South to the interest of capital. The temporary dictatorship as represented by the Freedmen's Bureau was practically ended by 1870. This led to an increase of violence on the part of the Ku Klux Klan to subject black labor to strict domination by capital and to break Negro political power. The outbreak brought a temporary return of military dictatorship, but the return was unpopular in the North and aroused bitter protest in the South.

Yet the end that planters and poor whites envisaged and, as the fight went on, the end that large numbers of the Northern capitalists were fighting for, was a movement in the face of modern progress. It did not go to the length of disfranchising the whole laboring class, black and white, because it dared not do this, although this was its logical end. It did disfranchise black labor with the aid of white Southern labor and with the silent acquiescence of white Northern labor.

The white capitalist of the South saw a chance of getting rid of the necessity of treating with and yielding to the voting power of fully half the laboring class. It seized this opportunity, knowing that it thus was setting back the economic progress of the world; that the United States, instead of marching forward through the preliminary revolution by which the petty bourgeois and the laboring class armed with the vote were fighting the power of capital, was disfranchising a part of labor and on the other hand allowing great capital a chance for enormous expansion in the country. And this enormous expansion got its main chance through the thirty-three electoral votes which the counting of the full black population in the South gave to that section. It was only necessary now that this political power of the South should be used in behalf of capital and not for the strengthening of labor and universal suffrage. This was the bargain of 1876.

Reconstruction, therefore, in the South degenerated into a fight of rivals to control property and through that to control the labor vote. This rivalry between dictators led to graft and corruption as they bid against each other for the vote of the Negro, while meantime Negro labor in its ignorance and poverty was agonizing for ways of escape. Northern capital compromised, and Southern capital accepted race hate and black disfranchisement as a permanent program of exploitation.

In a certain way this great struggle of a laboring class of five black millions was epitomized by the appearance of sixteen of their representatives in the Federal Congress from 1869 to 1876. These are the men, their states and their service:

Hiram R. Revels, Senator, Mississippi, 1870-1871.

Blanche K. Bruce, Senator, Mississippi, 1875-1881.

Jefferson P. Long, Congressman, Georgia, 1869-1871.

Joseph H. Rainey, Congressman, South Carolina, 1871-1879.

Robert C. DeLarge, Congressman, South Carolina, 1871-1873.

Robert Brown Elliott, Congressman, South Carolina, 1871-1875.

Benjamin S. Turner, Congressman, Alabama, 1871-1873.

Josiah T. Walls, Congressman, Florida, 1873-1877.

Alonzo J. Ransier, Congressman, South Carolina, 1871-1873.

James T. Rapier, Congressman, Alabama, 1873-1875.

Richard H. Cain, Congressman, South Carolina, 1873-1875, 1877-1879.

John R. Lynch, Congressman, Mississippi, 1873-1877, 1881-1883.

Charles E. Nash, Congressman, Louisiana, 1875-1877.

John A. Hyman, Congressman, North Carolina, 1875-1877.

Jere Haralson, Congressman, Alabama, 1875-1877.

Robert Smalls, Congressman, South Carolina, 1875-1879, 1881-1887.

Several others, like Menard of Florida, Pinchback of Louisiana, Lee and others, had excellent titles to their seats, but did not gain them. Twelve of these men who were the earliest to enter Congress were ex-slaves or born of slave parents and brought up when Negroes were denied education. On the other hand the other four had received a more or less complete college education in the North and abroad. Five of the Congressmen were lawyers, and two, Elliott and Rapier, had unusual training and ability.

Rhodes sneers at these men: "They left no mark on the legislation of their time; none of them, in comparison with their white associates, attained the least distinction."

But Blaine, who knew them and served with most of them, said: "The colored men who took seats in both Senate and House did not appear ignorant or helpless. They were as a rule studious, earnest, ambitious men, whose public conduct . . . would be honorable to any race."

Most of the colored Congressmen had had experience in state legislatures and in public office. When these men entered Congress, questions of Reconstruction and of the economic and social condition in the North and West were before it. These included the exploitation of public lands, the development of railroads, the question of money, and the relation of the races in the South. The Negro Congressmen, especially, had three objects: to secure themselves civil rights, to aid education, and to settle the question of the political disabilities of their former masters.

This last question became of paramount importance. Long of Georgia was in favor of removing disabilities if the Southerners proved loyal to the new legislation. Revels supported amnesty, but Rainey felt that it had led to force and murder. Elliott protested against amnesty, saying that the men seeking relief were responsible for the crimes perpetrated against loyal men in the South, and that this proposal put a premium on disloyalty and treason.

All the Negro Congressmen plead for civil rights for their race. It was here that Robert Brown Elliott made one of his greatest speeches in a dramatic situation seldom equaled in Congress. Forney describes the incident: "Mr. Stephens, the Vice-President of the Confederacy, of which slavery was the corner-stone, spoke January 6, 1874, and Mr. Elliott, the colored champion of the liberated race, followed him the next day. I cannot describe the House when the two men addressed it, especially when the African answered the Caucasian. Here we have a new history—a history that may, indeed, be repeated, but which stands alone in the novelty of all its surroundings, and in the eloquence of all its lessons. . . .

"Mr. Elliott, the last speaker, is a full-blooded black, a native of Boston, Massachusetts, where he was born August 11, 1842. Educated in England, he was not of age when the Rebellion broke out; and in 1868, in his twenty-sixth year, was a member of the South Carolina Legislature, and elected to Congress from Columbia district in 1872. He received 21,627 votes, against 1,079 votes for the Democratic candidate, W. H. McCaw. Had any man predicted that this colored boy, while attending school in 1853, at High Holborn Academy, and Eton College, England, in 1855, would sit in Congress from the capital of the proud state of South Carolina in 1874, and would there confute the ablest apostle of the old slave power, he would have been pronounced a madman."

Elliott, defending against Stephens civil rights for Negroes, said:

"Sir, it is scarcely twelve years since that gentleman shocked the civilized world by announcing the birth of a government which rested on human slavery as its corner-stone. The progress of events has swept away that pseudo-government which rested on greed, pride, and tyranny; and the race whom he then ruthlessly spurned and trampled on are here to meet him in debate, and to demand that the rights which are enjoyed by their former oppressors—who vainly sought to overthrow a Government which they could not prostitute to the base uses of slavery—shall be accorded to those who even in the darkness of slavery kept their allegiance true to freedom and the Union. Sir, the gentleman from Georgia has learned much since 1861; but he is still a laggard. Let him put away entirely the false and fatal theories which have so greatly marred an otherwise enviable record. Let him accept, in its fullness and beneficence, the great doctrine that American citizenship carries with it every civil and political right which manhood can confer. Let him lend his influence, with all his masterly ability, to complete the proud structure of legislation which makes this nation worthy of the great declaration which heralded its birth, and he will have done that which will most nearly redeem his reputation in the eyes of the world, and best vindicate the wisdom of that policy which has permitted him to regain his seat upon this floor." [30]

In the matter of education, Rainey of South Carolina was one of the first Americans to demand national aid for education. Walls of Florida protested that national aid was not an invasion of state rights, and showed the discrimination in the distribution of state funds.

The colored Congressmen advocated local improvements, including distribution of public lands, public buildings, and appropriations for rivers and harbors, in Alabama, Florida, Mississippi and South Carolina.

Aside from these more personal questions, Negro Congressmen discussed national economic matters. Walls of Florida and Lynch of Mississippi asked protective tariffs for local products, including cotton, lumber and sugar. Walls voted for an appropriation for the centennial exposition of 1876, and urged the recognition of Cuba. Hyman championed relief of the Cherokee Indians. Bruce opposed the restriction of Chinese immigration, arraigned our selfish policy toward Indians, and especially advocated improving the navigation of the Mississippi and protecting life and property from its overflow.

The words of these black men were, perhaps, the last clear, earnest expression of the democratic theory of American government in Congress.

Congressman DeLarge of South Carolina said in 1871: "When I heard the gentleman from New York (Mr. Cox) on Tuesday last hurl his shafts against the members of my race, charging that through their ignorance they had brought about these excesses, I thought he should have remembered that for the ignorance of that portion of the people, he and his party associates are responsible, not those people themselves. While there may have been extravagance and corruption resulting from the placing of improper men in official positions—and this is part of the cause of the existing state of things—these evils have been brought about by men identified with the race to which the gentleman from New York belongs, and not by our race." [31]

Congressman Rainey of South Carolina said in the same debate: "Sir, I ask this House, I ask the country, I ask white men, I ask Democrats, I ask Republicans whether the Negroes have presumed to take improper advantage of the majority they hold in that State by disregarding the interest of the minority? They have not. Our convention which met in 1868, and in which the Negroes were in a large majority, did not pass any proscriptive or disfranchising acts, but adopted a liberal constitution, securing alike equal rights to all citizens, white and black, male and female, as far as possible. Mark you, we did not discriminate, although we had a majority. Our constitution towers up in its majesty with provisions for the equal protection of all classes of citizens." [32]

It was not, then, race and culture calling out of the South in 1876; it was property and privilege, shrieking to its kind, and privilege and property heard and recognized the voice of its own.

The bargain of 1876 was essentially an understanding by which the Federal Government ceased to sustain the right to vote of half of the laboring population of the South, and left capital as represented by the old planter class, the new Northern capitalist, and the capitalist that began to rise out of the poor whites, with a control of labor greater than in any modern industrial state in civilized lands. Out of that there has arisen in the South an exploitation of labor unparalleled in modern times, with a government in which all pretense at party alignment or regard for universal suffrage is given up. The methods of government have gone uncriticized, and elections are by secret understanding and manipulation; the dictatorship of capital in the South is complete.

The military dictatorship was withdrawn, and the representatives of Northern capital gave up all efforts to lead the Negro vote. The new dictatorship became a manipulation of the white labor vote which followed the lines of similar control in the North, while it proceeded to deprive the black voter by violence and force of any vote at all. The rivalry of these two classes of labor and their competition neutralized the labor vote in the South. The black voter struggled and appealed, but it was in vain. And the United States, reënforced by the increased political power of the South based on disfranchisement of black voters, took its place to reënforce the capitalistic dictatorship of the United States, which became the most powerful in the world, and which backed the new industrial imperialism and degraded colored labor the world over.

This meant a tremendous change in the whole intellectual and spiritual development of civilization in the South and in the United States because of the predominant political power of the South, built on disfranchised labor. The United States was turned into a reactionary force. It became the cornerstone of that new imperialism which is subjecting the labor of yellow, brown and black peoples to the dictation of capitalism organized on a world basis; and it has not only brought nearer the revolution by which the power of capitalism is to be challenged, but also it is transforming the fight to the sinister aspect of a fight on racial lines embittered by awful memories.

It is argued that Negro suffrage was bad because it failed, and at the same time that its failure was a proof of its badness. Negro suffrage failed because it was overthrown by brute force. Even if it had been the best government on earth, force, exercised by a majority of richer, more intelligent and more experienced men, could have overthrown it. It was not overthrown so long as the military dictatorship of the North sustained it. But the South proved by appropriate propaganda that Negro government was the worst ever seen and that it threatened civilization. They suited their propaganda to their audience. They had tried the accusation of laziness but that was refuted by a restoration of agriculture to the pre-war level and beyond it. They tried the accusation of ignorance but this was answered by the Negro schools.

It happened that the accusation of incompetence impressed the North not simply because of the moral revolt there against graft and dishonesty but because the North had never been thoroughly converted to the idea of Negro equality. When, therefore, the North, even granting that all the South said of the Negro was not true, contemplated possibilities, it paused. Did the nation want blacks with power sitting in the Senate and in the House of Representatives, accumulating wealth and entering the learned professions? Would this not eventually and inevitably lead to social equality and even to black sons and daughters-in-law and mulatto descendants? Was it possible to contemplate such eventualities?

Under such circumstances, it was much easier to believe the accusations of the South and to listen to the proof which biology and social science hastened to adduce of the inferiority of the Negro. The North seized upon the new Darwinism, the "Survival of the Fittest," to prove that what they had attempted in the South was an impossibility; and they did this in the face of the facts which were before them, the examples of Negro efficiency, of Negro brains, of phenomenal possibilities of advancement.

Moreover, Americans saw throughout the world the shadow of the coming change of the philanthropic attitude which had dominated the early nineteenth century, with regard to the backward races. International and commercial imperialism began to get a vision. Within the very echo of that philanthropy which had abolished the slave trade, was beginning a new industrial slavery of black and brown and yellow workers in Africa and Asia. Arising from this, as a result of this economic foundation, came the change in the attitude toward these darker people. They were no longer "Brothers in Black"; they were inferiors. These inferiors were to be governed for their own good. They were to be raised out of sloth and laziness by being compelled to work. The whole attitude of Europe was reflected in America and it found in America support for its own attitude.

The great republic of the West was trying an impossible experiment. They were trying to make white men out of black men. It could not be done. It was a mistake to conceive it. The North and Europe were still under the sway of individual laissez-faire in industry, and "hands off" in government. It was easy, therefore, for the North to persuade itself that whatever happened politically in the South was right. If the majority did not want Negro rule, or Negro participation in government, the majority was right, and they would not allow themselves to stop and ask how that majority was made. They knew that an organized inner group was compelling the mass of white people to act as a unit; was pounding them by false social sanctions into a false uniformity.

If that part of the white South which had a vision of democracy and was willing to grant equality to Negroes of equal standing had been sustained long enough by a standing Federal police, democracy could have been established in the South. But brute force was allowed to use its unchecked power in the actions of the whites to destroy the possibility of democracy in the South, and thereby make the transition from democracy to plutocracy all the easier and more inevitable.

Through the rift of the opposition, between votes for and against the Negro, between high and low tariff, between free land and land monopoly, plutocracy drove a silent coach and four.

What the South did in 1876 was to make good its refusal either to give up slavery or to yield the political power based on the counting of slaves.

· And so the South rode the wind into the whirlwind and accomplished what it sought. Did it pay? Did it settle either the Negro's problem or any problem of wealth, labor, or human uplift? On the contrary, it made the government of the South a system of secret manipulations with lying and cheating. It made its religion fundamental hypocrisy. And the South knows today that the essential Negro problem is just as it was—how far it dare let the Negro be a modern man.

It was all so clear and right and logical. A nation could not exist half-slave and half-free. If it tried, either its mass of laborers would by force of competition sink into the depths of exploited, ignorant poverty, or rising in bloody revolt break the monopoly of land and materials and endow the mass with more equal income and more political power to maintain their freedom.

So in America came Civil War over the slavery of labor and the end was not peace, but the endeavor really and honestly to remove the cause of strife—to give the black freedman and the white laborer land and education and power to conduct the state in the interests of labor and not of landed oligarchy. Labor lurched forward after it had paid in blood for the chance. And labor, especially black labor, cried for Light and Land and Leading. The world laughed. It laughed North. It laughed West. But in the South it roared with hysterical, angry, vengeful laughter. It said: "Look at these niggers; they are black and poor and ignorant. How can they rule those of us who are white and have been rich and have at our command all wisdom and skill? Back to slavery with the dumb brutes!"

Still the brutes strove on and up with silent, fearful persistency. They restored the lost crops; they established schools; they gave votes to the poor whites; they established democracy; and they even saved a pittance of land and capital out of their still slave-bound wage.

The masters feared their former slaves' success far more than their anticipated failure. They lied about the Negroes. They accused them of theft, crime, moral enormities and laughable grotesqueries. They forestalled the danger of a united Southern labor movement by appealing to the fear and hate of white labor and offering them alliance and leisure. They encouraged them to ridicule Negroes and beat them, kill and burn their bodies. The planters even gave the poor whites their daughters in marriage, and raised a new oligarchy on the tottering, depleted foundations of the old oligarchy, a mass of new rulers the more ignorant, intolerant and ruthless because of their inferiority complex. And thus was built a Solid South impervious to reason, justice or fact.

With this arose a Solid North—a North born of that North which never meant to abolish Negro slavery, because its profits were built on it; but who had been gradually made by idealists and laborers and freed slaves to refuse more land to slavery; to refuse to catch and return slaves; and finally to fight for freedom since this preserved cotton, tobacco, sugar and the Southern market.

Then this new North, fired by a vision of concentrated economic power and profit greater than the world had visioned, tried to stop war and hasten back to industry. But the blind, angry, bewildered South threatened to block the building of this new industrial oligarchy by a political power increased by the very abolition of slavery, until the North had to yield to democracy and give black labor the power with which white Southern landholders threatened Northern industry.

In return, Northern capital bribed black and white labor in the South and white and black labor in the North. It thrust debt, concessions and graft on the South, while in the North it divided labor into exploiting and exploited groups of skilled and highly paid craftsmen who might and did become capitalists, and a mass of ignorant, disfranchised imported foreign slaves. The West transformed its laboring peasant-farmers into land speculators and investors and united its interests through railways to the Solid South in return for non-interference with Big Business.

God wept; but that mattered little to an unbelieving age; what mattered most was that the world wept and still is weeping and blind with tears and blood. For there began to rise in America in 1876 a new capitalism and a new enslavement of labor. Home labor in cultured lands, appeased and misled by a ballot whose power the dictatorship of vast capital strictly curtailed, was bribed by high wage and political office to unite in an exploitation of white, yellow, brown and black labor, in lesser lands and "breeds without the law." Especially workers of the New World, folks who were American and for whom America was, became ashamed of their destiny. Sons of ditch-diggers aspired to be spawn of bastard kings and thieving aristocrats rather than of rough-handed children of dirt and toil. The immense profit from this new exploitation and world-wide commerce enabled a guild of millionaires to engage the greatest engineers, the wisest men of science, as well as pay high wage to the more intelligent labor and at the same time to have left enough surplus to make more thorough the dictatorship of capital over the state and over the popular vote, not only in Europe and America but in Asia and Africa.

The world wept because within the exploiting group of New World masters, greed and jealousy became so fierce that they fought for trade and markets and materials and slaves all over the world until at last in 1914 the world flamed in war. The fantastic structure fell, leaving grotesque Profits and Poverty, Plenty and Starvation, Empire and Democracy, staring at each other across World Depression. And the rebuilding, whether it comes now or a century later, will and must go back to the basic principles of Reconstruction in the United States during 1867-1876—Land, Light and Leading for slaves black, brown, yellow and white, under a dictatorship of the proletariat.

> Profit? What profit hath the sea
> Of her deep-throated threnody?
> What profit hath the sun, who stands
> Staring on space with idle hands?
> And what should God Himself acquire
> From all the æons' blood and fire?
>
> FANNIE STEARNS DAVIS
> From *Crack o' Dawn*, The Macmillan Company

---

1. Haworth, *The Hayes-Tilden Disputed Presidential Election of 1876*, p. 32.
2. Nordhoff, *The Cotton States in the Spring and Summer of 1875*, p. 20.
3. Somers, *The Southern States Since the Civil War*, pp. 30, 54.
4. Campbell, *White and Black*, p. 131.
5. Nordhoff, *The Cotton States in the Spring and Summer of 1875*, p. 10.
6. Campbell, *White and Black*, p. 143.
7. Pierce, *Sumner*, Vol. IV, p. 500.
8. Pierce, *Sumner*, Vol. IV, p. 500.
9. Oberholtzer, *Jay Cooke*, Vol. II, p. 28.
10. Pierce, *Sumner*, Vol. IV, p. 581.
11. Pierce, *Sumner*, Vol. IV, p. 598.
12. Pierce, *Sumner*, Vol. IV, p. 364.
13. Blaine, Vol. II, pp. 448-449.
14. *American Historical Review*, 1910. W. E. B. Du Bois, "Reconstruction and Its Benefits," pp. 798, 799.
15. Fleming, *The Freedmen's Savings Bank*, pp. 1, 26.
16. Simkins and Woody, *South Carolina During Reconstruction*, pp. 229-230.
17. *Slave Songs of the United States* (A. Simpson and Company, N. Y., 1867), p. 55.
18. Nordhoff, *The Cotton States in the Spring and Summer of 1875*, pp. 37-38.
19. Wesley, *Negro Labor in the United States*, p. 132.
20. 42nd Congress, 2nd Session, House Reports, II, No. 22, Part I, pp. 214-215.
21. *Ibid. Cf. Report on Valuation and Taxation and Public Indebtedness, 10th Census of U. S.*, pp. 281-294. "A very conservative figure in 1872 put the increase of indebtedness of the eleven states since their reconstruction at $131,717,777.81, of which more than two-thirds consisted of guarantees to various enterprises, chiefly railways." (*Reconstruction, Political and Economic*, W. A. Dunning, p. 208.)
22. *North American Review*, August-December, 1884.
23. Green, *Society for Political Education*, 1883, N. Y.
24. Campbell, *White and Black*, pp. 179-180.
25. Dunning, *Reconstruction, Political and Economic* (Vol. 22, American Nation Series, 1865-1877, Hart), p. 209.
26. Herberg, *The Heritage of the Civil War*, pp. 21-22.

27. *American Historical Review*, Vol. XV, No. 4, July, 1910, p. 796.
28. *Ku Klux Report*, S. C., Part II, p. 1253.
29. Taylor, "Negro Congressmen a Generation After" in *Journal of Negro History*, VII, p. 127.
30. Woodson, *Negro Orators and Their Orations*, pp. 323-324.
31. Woodson, *Negro Orators and Their Orations*, p. 298.
32. Woodson, *Negro Orators and Their Orations*, pp. 379-380.

XV. FOUNDING THE PUBLIC SCHOOL

How the freedman yearned to learn and know, and with the guiding hand of the Freedmen's Bureau and the Northern school-marm, helped establish the Public School in the South and taught his own teachers in the New England college transplanted to the black South

It was soon after the war that a white member of Johnson's restored Louisiana legislature passed one of the schools set up by the Freedmen's Bureau in New Orleans. The grounds were filled with children. He stopped and looked intently, and then asked, "Is this a school?" "Yes," was the reply. "What, for niggers?" "Evidently." He threw up his hands. "Well, well," he said, "I have seen many an absurdity in my lifetime, but *this is the climax!*"[1]

If a poor, degraded, disadvantaged horde achieves sudden freedom and power, what could we ask of them in ten years? To develop some, but surely not all, necessary social leadership; to seek the right sort of leadership from other groups; to strive for increase of knowledge, so as to teach themselves wisdom and the rhythm of united effort.

This latter accomplishment crowns the work of Reconstruction. The advance of the Negro in education, helped by the Abolitionists, was phenomenal; but the greatest step was preparing his own teachers —the gift of New England to the black South.

If the Negro public school system had been sustained, guided and supported, the American Negro today would equal Denmark in literacy. As it is, he surpasses Spain and Italy, the Balkans and South America; and this is due to the Negro college, which despite determined effort to curtail the efficiency of the Negro public school, and despite a sustained and violent attack upon higher education for black folk, nevertheless, through white Northern philanthropy and black Southern contributions, survived and furnished teachers and leaders for the Negro race at the time of its greatest crisis.

The eagerness to learn among American Negroes was exceptional in the case of a poor and recently emancipated folk. Usually, with a protective psychology, such degraded masses regard ignorance as natural and necessary, or even exalt their own traditional wisdom and discipline over "book learning"; or they assume that knowledge is for higher beings, and not for the "likes of us."

American Negroes never acted thus. The very feeling of inferiority which slavery forced upon them fathered an intense desire to rise out of their condition by means of education. Of the 488,070 free Negroes in the United States in 1860, 32,629 were attending school, and only 91,736 were unable to read and write. In the slave states, there were 3,651 colored children attending schools supported by the free Negroes.

The mass of the slaves could have no education. The laws on this point were explicit and severe. There was teaching, here and there, by indulgent masters, or by clandestine Negro schools, but in the main, the laws were followed. All the slave states had such laws, and after the Nat Turner insurrection in Virginia, these laws were strengthened and more carefully enforced.

As late as May, 1862, Edward Stanley, whom Lincoln appointed Provisional Governor of North Carolina, sought to conciliate the white people when he stopped a Negro school at New Bern. He said that he had been sent there to restore the old order of things, and that the laws of North Carolina forbade the teaching of slaves to read and write; and he could not expect success in his undertaking if he encouraged the violation of the law.

At the time of emancipation, not all the Southern Negroes were illiterate. In South Carolina, a majority of the nearly 10,000 free Negroes could read and write, and perhaps 5% of the slaves. But illiteracy among the colored population was well over 95% in 1863, which meant that less than 150,000 of the four million slaves emancipated could read and write.

The first great mass movement for public education at the expense of the state, in the South, came from Negroes. Many leaders before the war had advocated general education, but few had been listened to. Schools for indigents and paupers were supported, here and there, and more or less spasmodically. Some states had elaborate plans, but they were not carried out. Public education for all at public expense, was, in the South, a Negro idea.[2]

"Prior to the abolition of slavery, there was no general public educational system, properly speaking, in the Southern states, except perhaps, in North Carolina. In some populous centers, there were free schools; in some localities, academies and colleges, but for the most part, no adequate provision was made for the education even of the poorer whites. Emerging from their bondage, the Negroes in the very beginning manifested the utmost eagerness for instruction, and their hunger was met by a corresponding readiness on the part of the people of the North to make provisions for it."[3]

The original state constitution of North Carolina, in 1775, provided for public education, but there was no appropriation for the schools, and the only direct result was the establishment of the state university. In 1825, a literary fund was established toward defraying the cost of the public schools. A school system was sketched in 1839, but without an executive head, and with small funds. In 1852, a Superintendent of Public Instruction was appointed. His work for a long time was confined to propaganda, and he especially noted the lack of any demand for public schools, and the feeling that such schools were simply for paupers.

Nevertheless, the work of the first superintendent, C. H. Wiley, was important as propaganda, but only as propaganda, because at the time of the war, "only here and there in the state is there a schoolhouse for whites of very inferior description, and with long distance between." There was no state support of schools. The burden of public education, such as it was, rested on local authorities.

In South Carolina, there was even less effort. In 1811, there was "An Act to Establish Free Schools Throughout the State." It provided for as many free schools in each election district as the district was entitled to representatives in the Lower House. After forty-four years of operation (1811-1855), Governor J. A. Adams pronounced the system a failure, saying of the handling of funds: "Great inequalities prevailed, and during twenty-seven years, returns were made in only five years; the small districts and parishes did not receive regular sums, and the amounts received, did not have proportion to the number of schools, or to the population; after 1815, the annual appropriation was $37,000 annually, nearly $1,500,000 in all, of which only $109,-740 was accounted for." [4]

In December, 1855, Governor Adams plead for the appointment of a Superintendent of Education. "Let us make at least this effort, and if the poor of the land are hopelessly doomed to ignorance, poverty and crime, you will at least feel conscious of having done your duty." He was, of course, referring only to the whites, and did not himself seem to believe much in the educability of the poor.

In Virginia, Armstead reports that in 1851, less than one-half the poor white children were attending any schools, and those attended only eleven weeks in the year. "This pitiable result was obtained with a cost to the state of $69,000." Thomas Jefferson in the eighteenth century had evolved a school system for whites, with industrial schools for Negroes, "but there was bitter and successful opposition" and as Jefferson himself said, "Such a permissive scheme was doomed to failure from the very moment of its inception." [5]

In Georgia, the constitution of 1777 had spoken of schools, but nothing was done. Some private academies were incorporated in 1783, and permission given the Governor to grant a thousand acres of free land for erection of free schools, but few if any grants were made. In 1815, $250,000 was appropriated, known as the Poor School Fund. Nothing further was done until the legislature of 1851, when something was added to this fund to pay tuition for the children of parents too poor to pay anything.

The whole fund for education as late as 1865 was only $23,355. Governor Brown urged a system of public schools before the war, but the legislature did nothing but make a small increase of the poor school fund.

In 1858, a movement was started in Atlanta looking toward the establishment of a system of free schools in Georgia. A. N. Wilson went to Rhode Island to look into the public school system there, and on his return, held several meetings, culminating in a meeting October 6, 1858, called by the mayor. The chairman appointed a committee, but some of the members of the committee took charge of the entire movement and blocked it. The original movers, seeing that they had lost control, withdrew, and the proposal fell through. The constitution of 1865 under the provisional government gave the legislature permission to appropriate money for the "promotion of learning and science," and "for the education of the people," and provided "for the resumption of the regular exercises of the University of Georgia."

In the first session of the legislature after the war, a bill to establish public schools was introduced, but postponed until late in 1866. By a vote of 62-58, in the House, and an equally close vote in the Senate, a bill to establish a system of public schools was squeezed through but only on condition that nothing was to be done until 1868. This proposal lapsed because of the Reconstruction Acts of 1867.

Thus although there had been much talk and some legislation on the subject, there had been "no regularly organized system of common schools supported by public taxation in Georgia prior to the Civil War." [6]

Mississippi did lip service to the idea of public education in her earlier constitutions, but little tangible was accomplished. The Sixteenth Section fund given to the states by the Federal government for education, amounting to at least $15,000,000 in Mississippi, was totally mismanaged and lost, while tens of thousands of white children grew up in ignorance. Florida tried, about 1850, to obtain schools for whites, from taxes on certain sales of slaves, with small results.

Alabama and North Carolina had the best pre-war systems, due to the enthusiasm of certain teachers, but even here, there was no disposition among the planters to accept taxation for public education. Joel Riggs, comptroller of the state treasury in 1851, said: "Perhaps of all trust-funds, none has been so greatly mismanaged as the school-fund of Alabama." [6a]

The experience of the other Southern states shows similar neglect and indisposition to educate the poor whites.

The fact of the matter was that in the pre-war South, there were two insuperable obstacles to a free public school system. The first was the attitude of the owners of property. They did not propose under any circumstances to be taxed for the public education of the laboring class. They believed that laborers did not need education; that it made their exploitation more difficult; and that if any of them were really worth educating, they would somehow escape their condition by their own efforts.

The second obstacle was that the white laborers did not demand education, and saw no need of it, save in exceptional cases. They accepted without murmur their subordination to the slaveholders, and looked for escape from their condition only to the possibility of becoming slaveholders themselves. Education they regarded as a luxury connected with wealth.

It was only the other part of the laboring class, the black folk, who connected knowledge with power; who believed that education was the stepping-stone to wealth and respect, and that wealth, without education, was crippled. Perhaps the very fact that so many of them had seen the wealthy slaveholders at close range, and knew the extent of ignorance and inefficiency among them, led to that extraordinary mass demand on the part of the black laboring class for education. And it was this demand that was the effective force for the establishment of the public school in the South on a permanent basis, for all people and all classes.

If the planters opposed schools for poor whites, they all the more regarded Negro schools as absurd. The unalterable conviction of most white Southerners was that Negroes could not and would not learn, and thus their education involved an unjustifiable waste of private property for public disaster.

D. R. Grattan, a native Virginian, testified before the Reconstruction Committee in 1866: "They cannot educate themselves; they are not disposed to educate themselves." [7]

In the face of this, listen to the words of Booker T. Washington: "Few people who were not right in the midst of the scenes can form any exact idea of the intense desire which the people of my race showed for education. It was a whole race trying to go to school. Few were too young, and none too old, to make the attempt to learn. As fast as any kind of teachers could be secured, not only were day-schools filled, but night-schools as well. The great ambition of the older people was to try to learn to read the Bible before they died. With this end in view, men and women who were fifty and seventy-five years old, would be found in the night-schools. Sunday-schools were formed soon after freedom, but the principal book studied in the Sunday-school was the spelling-book. Day-school, night-school, and Sunday-school were always crowded, and often many had to be turned away for want of room." [8]

The first educational efforts came during the war, when the Negroes, refugees and soldiers were taught at various camps and places of refuge at their own pressing request. This was followed by the efforts of philanthropic societies. Schools were started among the Negroes of the peninsula of Virginia and of Port Royal, South Carolina, as soon as they were captured.

In Virginia, when Federal authority was established in the Southeast, the American Missionary Association asked to work among the freedmen and was welcomed by Governor Butler.

The first day-school was established on September 17, 1861, in the town of Hampton in a small brown house near the Seminary, a school formerly used by the whites. This school was taught by Mrs. Mary Peake under the auspices of the American Missionary Association. Mrs. Peake was a mulatto, whose father was an Englishman. She was born a free woman and received a fair education at her home in Alexandria. She wanted to help her race, and she had gone among the slaves during slavery to teach them to read and write. She held her school at Hampton, however, only until the next spring, when she died of consumption at the early age of 39. Her school was not only the first one at Hampton but the first of the kind in the South. Around the small school she began followed the other schools in the Hampton vicinity, all of which led to the Hampton Institute of today.[9]

In January, 1862, Solomon Peck had opened a school at Beaufort, South Carolina, and Barnard Lee, at Hilton Head. In February, 1862, "Edward L. Pierce and General Thomas W. Sherman, sent out a call to 'the highly favored and philanthropic people' of the North to send volunteers to teach 'both old and young the rudiments of civilization and Christianity.'" [10] Freedmen's Aid Societies were formed at Boston, New York and Philadelphia, and forty-one men and twelve women teachers went to Port Royal in March. Eight schools were in operation by May, and within a year, thirty, with three thousand students. Officers held schools for black soldiers; and many Negroes, who had bought abandoned lands, opened schools at their own expense. Port Royal schools in 1855 had sixty teachers.

Schools for their children had been supported by the free Negroes of Charleston since 1744, openly at first—clandestinely after the law

forbade them. When Johnson was inaugurated, the event was celebrated in Charleston, South Carolina, by opening the public schools
to all children without distinction of color. Twenty-five of the forty-
two teachers were colored. The *Tribune* said, March 10, 1865:

"So the thing is done. The loyal white people—the Irish and German population, have shown that they are quite willing to let their
children attend the same school with the loyal blacks; although it is
true, that no attempt to unite them in the same room or classes would
have been tolerated at the time. But in the play-grounds, white and
black boys joined in the same sports as they do in the public streets;
and there can be no doubt that now that this great step has been made,
all the prejudice against equal educational advantages will speedily
vanish, and indeed, it is the veriest hypocrisy in the city where very
old families have aided in obliterating all the complexional distinctions
by mingling their blood with that of their slaves.

"In the rooms where the colored children assembled, there were
many children with clear, blue eyes, pure, white skins, long, silky
hair without kinks, and yet, they were classed with the Negro population by the former rulers of the city." [11]

"A month later came a significant celebration. I walked to the
square with William Lloyd Garrison. Think of the great pioneer
Abolitionist of Boston in the streets of Charleston! As Mr. Garrison
entered the square, he was introduced to about two thousand children
by Mr. James Redpath, Superintendent of Public Instruction. When
the children were told who Mr. Garrison was, they surrounded him;
threw up their hats and caps; caught hold of him; fell down and
over each other, and sent up shout after shout of such welcome and
greeting as I may safely say was never before witnessed on the soil
of South Carolina." [12]

Many private schools were established; one by Jonathan C. Gibbs,
afterward Superintendent of Schools in Florida; another by F. L.
Cardozo, who became State Treasurer of South Carolina, and others
in various parts of the state. In the second year of freedom, 23 schools
in different localities were built by Negroes, aided by the Freedmen's
Bureau and philanthropy. The freedmen contributed to the support
of school teachers $12,252, and $500 to schoolhouses. In Beaufort, the
Negroes opened a building for a free high school bought and supported
entirely by them as early as 1867.

In the West, General Grant appointed Colonel John Eaton, afterwards United States Commissioner of Education, to be Superintendent
of Freedmen in 1862. He sought to establish and regulate schools and
succeeded in organizing a large system.

Louisiana had schools for free Negroes, supported by them before the war. Afterward, the army established a large system. On March 22, 1864, General Banks, on his own responsibility, had made provisions for the establishment of schools for freedmen by an order issued which did not meet the approval of many in Louisiana. He appointed a Board of Education of three persons, and granted it large powers. It was to establish one or more common schools in every school district defined by the provost-marshal; to acquire by purchase or otherwise, lands for school sites; to erect schoolhouses and to employ teachers as far as practicable among the loyal citizens of Louisiana; to furnish books; to provide every adult freedman with a library costing two dollars and fifty cents, this amount to be deducted from the wages of the said freedman; and, finally, to levy for these purposes a school tax on real and personal property in every school district.

When the collection of the general tax for Negro schools was suspended in Louisiana by military order, the colored people were greatly aroused and sent in petitions. One of these petitions, thirty feet in length, represented ten thousand Negroes, who signed mostly with marks. They offered to pay a special tax, if the schools could be kept going.

When the Confederates returned to domination, the public schools, which had attained a degree of efficiency never before reached in the South, were greatly curtailed. One hundred and ten of the teachers, many of them native-born, were dismissed at once, and their places filled with intolerant Confederates.

The most noted of the clandestine schools for free colored children was opened in Savannah in 1818 or 1819 by a colored Frenchman named Julien Froumontaine, from Santo Domingo. Up to 1829, this school was taught openly. After December 22, 1829, it was made a penal offense to teach a Negro or free person of color to read or write. Froumontaine's school, however, flourished clandestinely for many years, and in a sense, laid the foundation of the new state system of public instruction, which gave equal school privileges to all children regardless of race or color.

The public school system of Georgia started in the conference in Savannah, December, 1864, when Stanton, Secretary of War, and General Sherman met five or six leading Negroes, and decided upon schools. It was a notable gathering. The colored committee consisted of eight or ten leading colored ministers of Savannah. Secretary Stanton was astonished at the wisdom and tact of those untutored blacks and observed that the men's replies to his questions were "so shrewd, so wise, and so comprehensive. They were the picked men of the race in Georgia, of great native ability and would have attracted attention in any assembly." [13]

It was decided to have the schools opened at once for all the colored people who should apply. A time was set for examination of teachers, and a number of colored men and women applied. The colored citizens of Savannah were greatly encouraged and assisted in their efforts by the Rev. James Lynch, of the A.M.E. Church, an educated colored man, who afterwards became Secretary of the State for Mississippi. Early in January, 1865, the Rev. J. W. Alvord, Secretary of the American Tract Society, Boston, who had done business in Savannah for a number of years before, gave his assistance. He and Mr. Lynch examined the teachers. Ten colored persons were found competent. It was very difficult to find buildings in which to locate the schools. The most available place was the "Old Bryan Slave Mart," which had recently served as the pen from which relatives of many of these Negroes had been sold. The bars which marked the slave stalls were knocked down to make more space for seating. To this and other places flocked the freed people of every age and shade, eager for that book learning which really seemed to them the key to their advance.

By December, 1865, the colored people of Savannah had opened a number of schools with five hundred pupils, and they were contributing a fund of a thousand dollars for the support of the teachers.

In January, 1866, the Negroes of Georgia organized the Georgia Educational Association, whose object was to induce the freedmen to establish and support schools in their own counties and neighborhoods. In 1867, 191 day schools and 45 night schools were reported as existing. Of these, 96 were reported either wholly or in part supported by the freedmen, who also owned 57 of the school buildings.

Persistent propaganda represents the South after the war as being largely in favor of Negro education. This is a flat contradiction of plain historical evidence. Dunning says: "The Negroes were disliked and feared almost in exact proportion to their manifestation of intelligence and capacity"; and there were many reasons in the utterances of Southerners to support his generalization. "Education of the Negroes, they thought, would be labor lost, resulting in injury instead of benefit to the working class."

"The teachers of the Freedmen's Bureau or of private philanthropies 'interfered with labor—and encouraged directly or indirectly, insolence to employers.'"

"'Schooling,' felt the South, 'ruins a nigger.'" [14]

The American Freedmen's Commission reports that the Negroes' "attempts at education provoked the most intense and bitter hostilities, as evincing a desire to render themselves equal to the whites. Their churches and schoolhouses in many places were destroyed by mobs."

"'Nigger teachers' was one of the most opprobrious epithets that the Southern vocabulary furnished. Even in the North this prejudice existed among some of the avowed friends of the freed people, and it is a singular fact that one of the early Freedmen's Aid Societies was rent asunder by the unwillingness of a part of its members to co-operate in any movement looking toward the education of the Negro, though they were willing to provide him with food and clothing, in order to prevent suffering and death." [15]

"The teachers who went down from the North were soon disillusioned, if they were at all influenced by any other than the most serious missionary spirit. Ostracism is a mild term for the disesteem with which they were regarded as 'nigger teachers.' " [16]

"The white people of Virginia were shocked at the efforts of Northern philanthropists to educate Negroes, and the papers sneered at them." [17]

There was some gradual change of sentiment among the better class of whites in Virginia, but still the mass of whites remained bitterly opposed to the schools, and some had become brutal. Teachers were proscribed and ill-treated; schoolhouses burned, and threats so strong that many schools could not be opened. And others, after a brief struggle, had to be closed.

"In Virginia, I heard a man who did not know who I was, make a remark in reply to something that had been said about establishing a school at Wytheville for the teaching of colored children. He said that he hoped that the 'damned rascal who attempted to teach niggers would be shot.' " [18]

In North Carolina, instances are found where persons who taught in Negro schools were assaulted, schoolhouses burned, and threats made against the lives of those engaged in the work.

"Two women school-teachers who were recently sent from Wilmington to Fayetteville [North Carolina] to establish a school for colored children, were informed by the sheriff of the county that they would not be allowed to start their schools, nor would they be allowed to land; but they might remain on the steamer until her return to Wilmington, inasmuch as they were women; if they were men, they would receive such treatment as was awarded to such meddlesome characters before the war." [19]

In South Carolina, General Saxton said that teachers of colored schools throughout the state gave it as their opinion that they would be unable to remain there for a day, but for the protection of United States troops.

In Mississippi, bitter opposition was manifested against Negro schools. Colored men in some instances themselves gave the money to prepare and furnish a school, and then were forbidden to use it.

"Four young men in Adams County conspired to murder the teacher of a Negro school. . . . They maltreated him somewhat barbarously." [20] One wonders just what "somewhat barbarously" would be.

In Louisiana, it was said: "If military protection were withdrawn, our schools would cease." Conway said of Louisiana in 1866: "The feeling there is unanimous that they shall not own an acre of land or have any schools. They are more hostile to the establishment of schools than they are to owning lands. They had broken up some of our schools at the time of my departure, and since then I have official reports from those who have charge of the schools that upon the withdrawal of the military from the parishes of St. Mary and Lafourche the freedmen's school-houses in those parishes were, before night, burnt or pulled down, the schools disbanded, and the teachers frightened away." [21]

"In many regions, this opposition was very persistent. Along the coast it was usually tacit and suppressed. There teachers and schools for Negroes were ignored. But, in the interior of Texas, Alabama, Mississippi, Louisiana, Kentucky, Tennessee, and Maryland, it was given full and free expression. Negroes were dispossessed of their school buildings, teachers were not allowed to enter upon their duties, and churches and schoolhouses were sometimes burned." [22]

A few voices cried in the wilderness that "A due regard for the public weal imperatively requires that the Negroes be educated, taught at least to read and write—steeped in ignorance, they can never be made to understand the responsibilities that rest upon them as freedmen." [23]

But others only admitted that "The sole aim should be to educate every white child in the commonwealth." [24]

"I am in favor of providing ways and means for the education of freedmen—but not in favor of positively imposing upon any legislature the unqualified and imperative duty of educating any but the superior race of man—the white race . . . our pecuniary condition does not allow us to do it." Often this objection took an even more ungracious form: "I say that the levying of a tax upon us, to pay for the education of a race we expect to be torn from us, is an indignity. Why are we called upon to educate these Negroes? No, sir; I will never be so dishonest as to disgrace myself by such a vote." [25]

In the midst of these efforts of Negroes and the general opposition of whites came the Freedmen's Bureau. The Freedmen's Bureau found many schools for freedmen already in existence maintained by tax commissioners, by Negroes, and by the army. The original Freedmen's Bureau act made no provision for Negro education; but notwithstanding this, the funds derived from the rent of abandoned property was used for education, and government buildings were turned into schoolhouses. Transportation was given to teachers and subsistence granted. By act of 1866, the educational powers of the Bureau were greatly enlarged, coöperation with benevolent associations, teachers and agents was sanctioned, and buildings leased. The sum of $521,000 was appropriated for school purposes, and other sums provided by the sale and lease of property formerly belonging to the Confederate Government. Teachers were sent from the North, and the Quakers, Methodists, Baptists, Presbyterians, and especially Congregationalists, took part.

The efforts thus begun in the army and by philanthropists, and taken up later by the Freedmen's Bureau, expanded into a system which penetrated the whole South, although naturally it touched but a fraction of the Negro population.

Between 1865 (June 1st) and September 1, 1870, the Bureau spent on education a sum which represented about one-half of the expenses of the schools. The rest was met by benevolent associations and the freedmen themselves. For some years after 1865, the education of the Negro was well-nigh monopolized by the Freedmen's Bureau, and the missions sustained by the Northern churches and organizations allied with them. Schools of all grades, from the kindergarten to the college, were established in each state. The Freedmen's Bureau alone appropriated $3,521,934 to schools from 1868 to 1870, while the churches and societies spent $1,572,287 during the same period.

"Among the Northern teachers were many men and women of unusual sincerity of purpose, zealous as only religious enthusiasts can be. 'The Negro was only responsive to efforts in his behalf as far as his economic conditions would permit.'" [26] It is nevertheless both interesting and astonishing to realize that during 1866-1870 the freedmen contributed in cash $785,700 to their schools.[27]

In 1866, Alvord, the Superintendent of Education under the Freedmen's Bureau, reported that in eleven former slave states and the District of Columbia, there were 90,589 Negro pupils and 1,314 teachers in 740 schools. From 1865 to 1866, teachers in the Negro elementary schools were almost exclusively Northern whites. Gradually Negro teachers came to be used.

The annual amount which the Bureau voted to school purposes increased from $27,000 in 1865 to nearly $1,000,000 in 1870, and reached a total in 1865-1870 of $5,262,511.26. In July, 1870, there were 4,239 schools under their supervision, with 9,307 teachers and 247,333 pupils. Notwithstanding this, of the 1,700,000 Negro children of school age in 1870, only about one-tenth were actually in school.

The public school systems, in most Southern states, began with the enfranchisement of the Negro. For instance, in South Carolina, "the constitution of 1868 was a notable departure in the educational history of the state. Not only was education mentioned for the first time in the organic law, but the state for the first time was given the outline of an educational system in keeping with the advanced thought of the age. The General Assembly was obligated to establish a system of universal education as soon as practical." [28]

Perhaps no state illustrates the relation of the Negro and the public school system better than South Carolina, and the story of the debate in the convention of 1868 is worth following. "On Saturday, January 18, 1868, Beverly Nash, a colored member, offered a resolution on education; and A. J. Ransier on Tuesday, January 21, presented another resolution which read:

"*Resolved,* That the Committee on Education inquire into the expediency of establishing a Board of Education, consisting of three from each Congressional District. Such Board shall have power to divide the state into school districts, and provide for a thorough system of common schools, elect a Superintendent from among their number, and make all needful regulations for the education of youth, no distinction to be made in favor of any class of persons.' " [29]

The Committee on Education was named January 20, and F. L. Cardozo, the Negro leader, was chairman. Three white men and five colored men served on the committee.

Robert Smalls, of "Planter" fame, desired that a system of public schools be established, and that they be open to all classes of people, and he wanted compulsory education. B. F. Randolph wanted institutions for the insane, blind, deaf and dumb, and poor fostered and supported by the state.

The matter of compulsory attendance brought considerable discussion. Ransier, afterwards Congressman, supported compulsory attendance, contending that ignorance was a cause of vice and degradation, and that civilization and enlightenment were the consequence of the schoolmaster, and if force was necessary to secure the benefits of education, it ought to be resorted to. One or two able Negroes were against the compulsory feature, but two white delegates were in favor of it. One of them, Jillson, said: "In South Carolina, where there has never been any system of free public schools, there is one person in every eight who cannot read and write." [30]

Finally, it was decided that the compulsory feature should not be insisted upon until a thorough and complete system had been organized.

The Constitution as ratified provided for the establishment of universal education as soon as practical and for compulsory attendance for all children between the ages of six and sixteen, but this was not to become effective until the system had been completely organized. It provided for a normal school and a school for the deaf, dumb and blind.

After the termination of the convention, the General Assembly enacted a law to provide for the temporary organization of the education department. On November 20, 1869, one year after this, J. K. Jillson made a report on the school situation, incomplete because many counties had not reported. There were at that date 16,418 children in school, of whom 8,255 were white, and 8,165 colored. There were 381 schools with 528 teachers. Among the teachers, fifty were colored.

The temporary act proved inadequate, and Governor Scott urged in November, 1869, an efficient and comprehensive law. This led to the Act of February 16, 1870, " 'to establish and maintain a system of free schools for the state of South Carolina.' An examination of its provisions reveals that it is no gross exaggeration to state that it was the most comprehensive and most beneficial legislation the State of South Carolina has ever enacted.' " Textbooks were to be provided at cost or free to the poor.[31]

June 4, 1870, there were 30,448 children in 769 schools, and the average pay of the teachers was $35 a month. The superintendent complained of the inexperience of the school officers, want of suitable schoolhouses, scarcity of good teachers, and the apathy and opposition to the new system, and also of the inadequacy of the appropriation. Besides this, there was deep prejudice against mixed schools. The public press of the state had held the whole educational system up to ridicule, abused officials and belittled their efforts, or else had remained silent.

The number of colored pupils attending school in 1869 was 8,163; in 1870, there were 15,894. The number of white pupils in 1869 was 8,255; in 1870, 11,122.

"The repeated failure on the part of the State to meet in full its appropriations for school purposes had been a fruitful source of sore perplexity to these officers, and a very serious detriment to the cause." [32] Evidently, the "school system was operated in a most inefficient manner, and there was a gross misappropriation of the school funds." [33]

"From year to year, Jillson was able to report progress. . . . When he left office in 1876, there were 123,035 students attending 2,776 schools taught by 3,068 teachers, and the school revenue was $457,260. We may assume that had the reconstruction government not been overthrown in 1877, it would have given to the state an excellent school system." [34]

F. J. Moses, Jr., while governor, said: "No greater eulogy can be written upon the reconstructed administration of government in South

Carolina than that when it came into power it was a statutory offense against the law of the land to impart even the rudiments of a common school education to a South Carolinian, because, forsooth, he was black, while the reconstructed government has made it a statutory offense to hinder or prevent any child in the State, of whatever color, from obtaining a common school education. Nay, we have even gone further, and demanded, by our Constitution, that their attendance at school be compulsory." [35]

The Reconstruction Constitution of Georgia in 1868 provided for a "thorough system of general education to be forever free to all the children of the state," the details to be worked out by the Legislature.

In August, 1869, the Georgia Teachers' Association, composed of white and colored teachers, met for the first time at Atlanta; the subject of public education was thoroughly discussed and a plan proposed by which the educational provisions of the Constitution could be put into operation.

It was not until 1870 that the legislature took up the subject. Practically all of the Negro Senators and Representatives introduced bills on education. Senator Campbell, who was one of the group that met Stanton and Sherman at Savannah, presented a bill asking for a thorough system of a public education. He also presented a very lengthy resolution describing how the money for education was to be secured.

White Georgia, however, long resisted the establishment of the public school system. The first public school law was enacted in October, 1870, and amended in 1872. Its details were the result of recommendations made by a committee of the Georgia Teachers' Association. The plan was more elaborate than that of 1866 and had a state school commissioner and a State Board of Education, and a special school fund was provided. There would be separate schools for whites and blacks, but equal facilities. The first public schools were taught in the state during the summer of 1871. The schools were suspended in 1872 because of reaction and the alleged lack of funds. In 1871, there was $500,000 in the school fund, but the legislature had diverted it to other purposes. The schools were put in operation in 1873, and in 1874, there were 1,379 schools for whites, and 356 for Negroes.

It is a coincidence that the passage of the act of 1870 came on the hundredth anniversary of a previous act passed by the Georgia legislature, making it penal to teach a Negro to write or read. "This was a great day for Georgia."

There were over a half-million Negroes in the state, and less than 1% of them were able to read and write in 1870. Perhaps not over 500 colored people, when the public schools were opened, were more or less capable of taking charge of a primary school. In 1871, 6,664 colored children were enrolled in private schools while in 1880, after ten years of free schools, the enrollment of colored children was 86,399. By that time, too, most of them were taught by colored teachers. Along with the public school system, there were 3,719 pupils in private schools, and a few in college, making a total enrollment, in 1880, of 97,174.

The new state constitution of Mississippi of 1868 made it the duty of the legislature to establish "a uniform system of free public schools, by taxation or otherwise, for all children between the ages of 5 and 21 years." [36]

"Before this . . . the only free schools in the state were those maintained out of the proceeds arising from the sale or lease of the so-called sixteenth section lands, granted to the state by Congress in the early part of the century. But as most of these lands had been lost by mismanagement, the number of such schools was not very large."

The reconstruction convention was throughly imbued with the idea of education for all. The Constitution made it the duty of the legislature "to encourage by all suitable means the promotion of intellectual, scientific, moral, and agricultural improvement by establishing a uniform system of public schools for all children between the ages of five and twenty-one years. Constitutional provision was made for a permanent school fund, and the legislature was empowered to levy a poll tax not exceeding $2 per capita."

Many difficulties were encountered in the early life of Mississippi's new school system, and its progress was slow. Objections to Negro education were early apparent. The school report of 1873 says: "Again it is objected that a general tax compels white men of the state to educate the children of the Negro. But as the Negro forms a majority of the entire population of the state, and in an eminent degree a majority of the producing classes, as such classes of every population— the laborer, tenant and consumer—indirectly bear the burdens of taxation, it follows that an assessment upon the property of the state would be principally paid by the Negro and, therefore, the ground of complaint, if any, against a general tax is with the colored people and not with the white." [37]

During the first year of free education in Mississippi, State Superintendent Pease reported that more than 3,000 free schools had been opened with an attendance of 66,257 pupils. Of the 3,500 teachers employed, all except 399 were white. The total expenditure for public education for the year exceeded the government expenditures for all other purposes.

Alabama, in 1850, out of 176,657 persons 5-20 years of age, reported 62,728 pupils, mostly in private academies and pay schools; which meant that the bulk of the white poor had no schools. The established public schools were without a state board, and in 1854, spent only $2.50 a year on each enrolled pupil.

The public school system of Alabama was established by the State Constitution of 1867, and organized in the following year. It was in continual financial difficulty owing to the bitter opposition of the whites. Irregularities and defalcations in the educational department were charged, and finally, owing to the lack of funds and non-payment of taxes, as well as other conditions, the schools closed in 1873, as the result of the triumph of reaction. But the demand for education was now strong, and the effect of the Northern opinion too great, so that the new Constitution made by the Democrats in 1875 kept something of the system, but abolished the Board of Education, and sought, as far as possible, to return to the ante-bellum status. Separate schools for the races were ordered; the administrative expenses were reduced; no money was to be paid to any denominational school or private school. And the constitutional provision of one-fifth of the state revenue for school use was abolished. The United States Commissioner of Education gave a disapproving account of these changes, and said it was exchanging "a certainty for an uncertainty." [38]

This was in fact a restoration of education to local reactionary control, and cutting off all higher training of Negroes from public help. Alabama felt the result of this narrow policy for many years.

The Freedmen's Bureau schools in the state reached only a small portion of the Negroes, and there were a few missionary schools. "It is likely that for five years there were not more than two hundred Northern teachers in the state, and a majority of the white people were hostile toward the education of the Negro." [39]

In Florida, a school at Fernandina was established in 1862 by the Rev. Dr. Barrows, who was superintendent, with a half-dozen white Northern teachers. In Jacksonville, the Odd Fellows Hall was seized by the United States Provost General and turned over to Dr. Barrows for a school building. Here a school was opened both for Negroes and for whites. When the white children remonstrated against attending school with black children, Mrs. Hawks, the lady principal, said, "Very well, the colored children will be educated even if you will not." It is reported that this type of argument proved effective, and the two races got along harmoniously in school for a time.

Several disturbing factors prevented this experiment in democracy from continuing. First, the schools were built upon military force and outside workers, rather than the community itself, and secondly, public education was new to Florida, and came at a time when it could least afford to have it from the point of view of finances and personnel.

Schools were closed in 1864, but education continued in Federal military camps.[40]

Negro schools began again under the Freedmen's Bureau in 1865, helped by missionary societies, including two colored groups: the A.M.E. Church, and the African Colonization Society of New York. The Constitution of 1865 under Johnson's reconstruction established a uniform system of education without specific provisions. There were thirty schools at the close of 1865.

The committee on Negroes recommended immediate education for Negroes, but the legislature of 1866 compromised by establishing a state "system" of Negro schools under which Negroes were to pay for their own schools. E. B. Duncan eventually became Superintendent of both the state and the Freedmen's Bureau schools.

This system of schools was based on the plan of making the poor pay for their own education. The schools for freedmen were to be supported by a tax of one dollar upon all male persons of color, between one and fifty-five, and a tuition fee to be collected from each pupil, and the fee for a teacher's certificate, five dollars, was also to go to the school fund for freedmen. The superintendent was to establish schools for the freedmen when the number of children of persons of color in any county or counties should warrant it: "Provided, the funds provided for shall be sufficient to meet the expense thereof."[41] The freedmen themselves erected schoolhouses and provided further school funds.

Some good schools were established under the superintendency of the Rev. E. B. Duncan, an able and conscientious man, who worked hard to establish colored schools in every county. "At that time railroad facilities were very poor, and I have known him to walk from county to county in South Florida to establish colored schools."[42] Gradually, the Bureau schools were absorbed into the state system, although the Bureau was the paramount authority during the period of military rule, 1866-1868.

Under Negro suffrage came the law of 1869, and "all of Florida's educational historians grant that this was the real beginning of the public school system in this state."[43]

Near the end of the Radical Republican administration, conditions in education among Negroes of Florida were improved. The field of primary education was virgin; 71,000 inhabitants over ten years of age were illiterate; 18,000 of them were white. By the end of 1870, 331 schools were open with 14,000 pupils in attendance, one-third of whom were Negroes.

Probably the most outstanding character in the early life of the Florida public school system was a Negro, Jonathan C. Gibbs, whose colorful and efficient career has been noted in Chapter XII. After acting as Secretary of State for three years, he was appointed, late in 1872, Superintendent of Public Instruction, an office which he held until his death in 1874.

"It was then a post of considerable difficulty, as the first enthusiasm for a new school system had subsided and political complications and embarrassment about school funds had come in to hinder progress. But by his energy and enthusiasm in the cause he so far succeeded that, in the month of August, 1873, he had the pride and pleasure of saying before the National Educational Association: 'The census of 1860—ante-bellum—shows that Florida had in her schools, 4,486 pupils, at an expense of $75,412. Today, Florida has 18,000 pupils in school, at an expense of $101,820; fully four times as many pupils, at an increase of only 33 per cent expense.' " [44]

In 1876, when the Republicans were driven from power, 676 public schools had been established with 28,444 pupils, black and white, costing $158,846.36.

In North Carolina, Negroes early pushed toward public education. There had been private schools for free Negroes before the war and they had the example of John Chavis, who studied at Princeton and at what is now Washington and Lee University. Among his white pupils were a United States Senator, a governor of the state, and the sons of a Chief Justice. "All accounts agree that John Chavis was a gentleman." When the law stopped him from teaching white students, he taught a school for free Negroes in Raleigh. In 1867, it was reported that many instances had come to notice where the teachers of a self-supporting Negro school had been sustained until the last cent the freedmen could command was exhausted, and where these last had even drawn on their credit in the coming crop to pay the bills necessary to keep up the school.

The most severe critics of Reconstruction must admit that the convention of 1868 and the legislature of 1868-1869 set up a fine school system for North Carolina, so far as it could. The poverty of the state made the realization of this system immediately an impossibility, but no one can "place at their door the laxity and graft of the administrative officers which afterwards characterized the department of public instruction." Their work was to provide a system of public schools for the state of North Carolina, and this they did. "The only error with which one may charge them is that they did not set up a system calling for separate schools for Negro and white children, and many people there are, who would not class this as an error." [45]

Article IX of the new Constitution, the section dealing with education, made provision for a general system of public schools, with tuition free to all persons between the ages of six and twenty-one. The counties were to be divided into school districts in which at least one school must exist and run for a minimum term of four months. The entire state system was to be governed by a Board of Education, composed of the Governor of the State, the Lieutenant-Governor, the Secretary of State, the Treasurer, the Superintendent of Public Works, the Auditor, the Superintendent of Public Instruction, and the Attorney-General. The money to support this system was to come from appropriations from the State Treasury, from county taxation, certain fines from the courts, and certain other funds, such as the pre-war Literary Fund. "The school laws were more thoroughly set forth than at any other time in the history of the state." [46] S. S. Ashley, a Northern white man, who favored mixed schools, was selected superintendent.

The new Superintendent of Public Instruction made his first report ot the status of education in North Carolina in November of 1868. The new school laws had just been passed, and sufficient time had not elapsed for any considerable amount of constructive work to be accomplished. The act authorizing the organization of a system of schools was not passed until April, 1869. One hundred thousand dollars was appropriated, chiefly to come from the poll tax.

This report showed that there was a total of 330,581 children between the ages of six and twenty-one in the state; of this number 223,815 were white, and 106,766 were Negroes. There were 1,906 schoolhouses or buildings being used for school purposes, of which 178 could be definitely classed as "good," and 685 were just as definitely to be thought of as "bad"; the remainder of the buildings were probably neither very good nor particularly bad. On the assumption that the Legislature would appropriate the $100,000 called for in the school law, Superintendent Ashley apportioned this sum among the counties; the capitation tax was supposed to supplement this so that the total from the state to the counties was reckoned at $165,209.50, or fifty cents per census child. This was only an "apportionment," as the first money out of the State Treasury which actually went for the support of public education was not yet distributed.

Ashley's second report, issued in the autumn of 1869, gives one an idea of the general situation, and is especially helpful in the matter of Negro education, as it contains the report of the Rev. John Wesley Hood, the Negro who had been appointed as the Assistant Superintendent of Public Instruction in charge of the Negro schools.

J. W. Hood, afterward bishop in the A.M.E. Zion Church, had been given his position by the Board of Education, but it appears that no legal provision had been made for this office. In calling attention to this report, Ashley simply states that he had been secured as an agent of the Board of Education and as Assistant Superintendent of Public Instruction. Hood had visited every section of the state in compiling his report, and Ashley asked that attention be given to it, "as it represents a more intelligent and complete view of the work of education among the colored population of this state than has yet been given." [47]

Hood reported that there were 257 Negro schools, with an enrollment of 15,647, chiefly carried on by churches and missionary societies. Ashley estimated 25,000 colored pupils in all, but the financial support of the public schools was bad. It improved, however, by 1872. That year, $412,070 was appropriated, and a property tax helped to raise the funds. Just as success seemed in sight, the Democratic Party in North Carolina entered upon its historic policy of white control.

The results of the return of the whites to power were soon shown. In 1870, the salary of the Superintendent of Public Instruction was reduced from $2,400 to $1,500, and his appropriations for travel and clerks cut off. The state lost the services of both Ashley and Hood.

From yet another quarter was Negro education to receive a blow in the same year. The legal life of the Freedmen's Bureau had expired before this time, but the agents had remained in the field, winding up its affairs. The last of the reports dealing with the educational work of the Bureau is dated July, 1870.

"The very fact that it was generally disliked by the Southern whites is testimony in favor of its effectiveness. And though it did antagonize the whites on the question of educating the Negro, it stood behind the schools for these same Negroes until such time as they had become pretty well established. Without the support of the Bureau, it is doubtful if any of these schools for Negroes would have existed very long; reasons of local hostility and financial stringency make this seem probable." [48]

A professor of the faculty at the University of North Carolina, Alexander McIver, was appointed by the new governor to fill out the unexpired term of Ashley. McIver served in this position until January 1, 1875, when he was succeeded by Stephen D. Pool. Pool promptly stole the money of the Peabody Fund entrusted to his care, proving that theft in North Carolina was not confined to Negroes and carpetbaggers. He was removed from office the following year.

In 1872, there were 119,083 white pupils and 55,000 colored pupils in school. For a long time, there was continual fear of mixed schools, but an amendment to the Constitution finally eliminated this.

In Virginia, the Constitutional Convention of 1867-1868 had twenty-five Negroes, and they and some of the whites were eager to educate the children. The attempt to establish a public school system was vigorously opposed by the reactionaries, but with the backing of the Negroes, the Constitution provided for a uniform system of public schools to be established not later than 1876. This was adopted by the voters in 1869, and W. H. Ruffner became Superintendent of Public Instruction in 1871. The Constitution did not provide for separate schools, but the laws under it did, and the support of the schools was to be obtained from a corporation tax of $1 and a small property tax. The first schools were opened in 1870, and by the end of the year, there were 2,900 schools, with 130,000 pupils, and 3,000 teachers. Of these, 706 were Negro schools, with 38,554 pupils. The Negroes were eager for the schools, but the whites were largely indifferent. There was a scarcity of Negro teachers and many white teachers were used.

In Arkansas, there was a so-called school system before the war, but the Governor in 1860 called it "radically defective" and noted "only twenty-five common schools organized and kept up in the whole State, from the common school funds." The "beginnings of popular education in Arkansas" were under the Reconstruction government in 1868.[49]

Negroes themselves after 1865 established the first free schools in Arkansas. This they did at Little Rock, where after paying tuition for a short time, they formed themselves into an educational association, paid by subscription the salaries of teachers, and made the schools free.

In July, 1865, General Sprague appointed William M. Colby, General Superintendent of Refugees and Freedmen, to coöperate with the state authorities, and, if possible, work out a system of education for those classes. Little progress had been made in Negro education under the lessee system, and Colby had little to build on. Many Arkansas whites did not approve education under the Bureau because they feared it encouraged "social equality."

Under the Freedmen's Bureau, Negroes built schoolhouses and sometimes furnished as much as 33% of the cost of instruction. The civil government did little toward the encouragement of Negro education. As has been stated earlier, little free school education was furnished for anyone. The Legislature of Arkansas on July 2, 1867, provided for a rather pretentious public school system, but all benefits were limited to whites. This was in direct contradiction to the ordinance passed at the constitutional convention of 1864.

The Constitution of 1868 provided for the maintenance of a system of free public schools for the gratuitous instruction of all persons in the state between the ages of 5 and 20 years. On July 23, 1868, Governor Clayton approved the law under which education was to be carried on. A state board of education had been begun under the lessee system and continued under the Freedmen's Bureau, but this was the first time the civil government had made any provisions for it.

The expense of public school education was to be taken care of by taxation. The masses, black and white, were unprepared for this. Competent teachers were scarce, and school officials were often indifferent. This made the situation very trying. Nevertheless, the work of organization was begun August 1, 1868, with Thomas Smith as State Superintendent. The Freedmen's Bureau turned over to school authorities all schools under its control, and entered heartily into the development of Negro schools under the new order.

In March, 1869, a few schools were reported organized. On June 15, 1869, the *Daily Republican* claimed that there were "in successful operation nearly, if not quite, three hundred schools." [50]

The school funds were reduced somewhat in the fall of 1869 because of tax collectors' squandering the proceeds. As a result, many school terms were cut, and others were closed completely, but some continued. Teachers were, as a rule, inefficient. White teachers in Negro schools were held in contempt. The textbooks were usually fixed by the school board, and occasionally the Democratic press demanded that only books of Southern production be used.

J. C. Cordon, a Negro graduate of Oberlin, was State Superintendent of Education from January 16, 1873, to October 30, 1874.

Under the Democratic administration, the schools were closed during the years of 1874 and 1875, and the attendance in 1876 was only 8 per cent of the school population; but from that time onward, it gradually increased from year to year. "The year 1870 remained the high-water mark in school attendance for a period of at least twenty years."

In Texas, as a result of the work of the Freedmen's Bureau, the educational work, which was under the charge of Lieutenant E. M. Wheelock, advanced to such an extent that by the end of January, 1865, there were in operation twenty-six day and night schools with an enrollment of about sixteen hundred pupils. These schools were supported partly by voluntary contributions, partly by a small tuition fee. The number of pupils enrolled in the schools September 1, 1866, was over four thousand five hundred, with forty-three teachers.

When the State Republican party was organized, they advocated free common schools and free homesteads out of the public lands, open to all without distinction of color or race.

During the convention of 1868-1869, the Committee on Education reported that there were provisions for increasing the existing permanent school fund by adding to it all money to be received from the sale of the public domain, and for applying all the available fund to the education of all children within the scholastic age—from six to eighteen years—without distinction of race or color.

The public school system in Texas was at first in a large measure a failure because of popular hostility to the admission of Negroes to the public schools, coupled with inefficient management by counties.

In the convention which reconstructed Louisiana in 1864, the Banks system of schools was discussed, and there was a motion to declare it unconstitutional, but it was finally approved by a vote of 72 to 9. There was, however, a great diversity of opinion as to the ways and means of providing for the system. It was decided at first to establish schools for whites supported by the white taxation and schools for Negroes to be supported by black taxation. It was argued that unless this measure was adopted, whites and blacks might be compelled to attend the same schools.

The friends of the freedman feared that he would suffer by separate taxation. The mover of the previous resolution, Terry, moved some three weeks later that there should be no separate taxation of the races, and that the legislature should provide for the education of all children between the ages of six and eighteen by the maintenance, by taxation or otherwise, of free public schools. This provision, being adopted by a vote of 53 to 27, was incorporated into the Constitution.

By the Constitution of 1868, all children were admitted to the public schools regardless of color. The law thus provided for compulsory mixed schools, a condition which prevailed until 1877. As a matter of fact, there were not a great many cases where colored children were pupils in white schools, so that the mixed schools were not universally prevalent. The children of Governor Pinchback, for example, were escorted to a white school by a policeman, but often run off by white hoodlums after the policeman had disappeared.

The Freedmen's Bureau was the salvation of Negro education in Kentucky. By the middle of 1866, 35 Negro schools had been established with 58 teachers. The number increased to 139 in 1869. In 1866, there were 58 teachers with an enrollment of 4,122 pupils. An average attendance of 3,215 was maintained. In 1869, the number of teachers had reached 1,080, and the pupils 18,891.

Most of the teachers were Negroes with a few whites from the North. The revenue for these schools was obtained from state taxes levied on Negroes, private donations, and sometimes tuition fees. By a law passed in 1866, all Negro taxes, including a poll tax, were to be divided equally between Negro schools and Negro paupers. In 1867, an additional poll tax of $2 was levied on Negroes, but it was soon repealed in 1871, after considerable Negro opposition. In 1873, Negroes also threatened to appeal to the State and Federal courts to obtain, by legal process, equal school advantages.

Not until the advent of Sach F. Smith as State Superintendent of Education in 1867 did public school education in Kentucky take on new growth. In the 1869 elections, the people voted an increase in school taxes to 20 mills on the dollar. By 1871, the school receipts had increased from less than $400,000 in 1869 to almost one million dollars; the number of districts from 4,477 to 5,177; the number of pupils from 376,000 to 405,000.

In the District of Columbia, Negroes began their self-supported schools in 1807. Led by three former slaves, a great educational movement began. Other schools followed during the early nineteenth century, and finally, efforts to start a free school system for Negroes in the district were made in 1856. The project was overwhelmingly defeated by white voters at the polls. In 1862, May 21, Congress passed an act providing that 10% of the taxes collected from colored people be appropriated to establish public schools for Negroes.

Three trustees for the Negro schools in Washington and Georgetown were appointed by the Secretary of the Interior, but even the meager funds thus provided were only in part turned over to the Negroes. For two years, only $736 had been credited to the colored school fund, and the first public school for Negroes was not opened until March, 1864.

In 1864, another act became the fundamental school law for the whole district. This provided that the authorities should set apart every year from all its receipts for educational purposes "such proportionate part thereof, as the number of colored children between the ages of six to seventeen years in the respective cities bear to the whole number thereof, for the purpose of establishing and sustaining public schools in said cities for the education of colored children."

In 1866, Congress appropriated $10,000 to purchase school sites and erect buildings, and after these laws, the Negroes began to receive a just proportion of the school funds.

"It was not until the year 1867 that these trustees obtained sufficient funds to undertake the establishment of any considerable number of schools. Previous to that time, for about three years, from 60 to 80 colored schools had been maintained at a large expense by various benevolent associations in the Northern states." [51] There were 26 private schools in 1864, and between 1860-1864, $135,000 was contributed by philanthropists for the work.

After this, for several years, the white and colored school systems were practically separate, each with their own superintendent. Finally, about 1890, one general superintendent with white and colored assistants under him combined the two school systems.

In Delaware, early attempts at the education of the colored youth were made by the Negroes themselves, and it was not until 1875 that schools for Negroes had any recognition by the state. By personal taxes, tuition fees and voluntary contributions, these people were able to keep up the work of education until the general assembly of the state assumed the responsibility in 1881. Since that date, the work of educating Negroes has been a matter of public concern, with much discrimination against the colored schools.

In the other Border States, the development of the Negro schools was somewhat different. Missouri and West Virginia established free schools about the same time that the other states did, and made provisions for Negroes. Tennessee was slower, while Maryland, like Delaware, refused to provide for colored children at first, and for a long time granted them only the taxes raised among themselves. Not until 1880 were the colored children generally in Border States put on a legal footing with other children in education.

It will be noted that in nearly all the Southern states there were continual and well-proven charges of peculation and misuse of public school funds. This was not a part of the general charge of stealing and graft, but was the fault of local county officials. In most cases, the leading white landholders, who took no part in the administration of the state, nevertheless kept their hands upon local taxation and assessments, and were determined that the impoverished property-holder should not be taxed for Negro education. By various methods, direct and indirect, they thus continually diverted the school funds, and this class of white people were primarily the ones responsible for such dishonesty as there was in the administration of local school funds. On the other hand, there were Negro and poor white officials, here and there, who were guilty of waste and theft.

During and after Reconstruction, diversion of school funds was common. In North Carolina, $136,076 was collected for education in 1870, but the Department of Education received only $38,931. In Louisiana, $1,000,000 worth of bonds for the school fund were used to pay the expenses of the legislature in 1872. In Texas, a large part of the income and public lands which belonged to the education fund was lost. In 1870, the school funds in Georgia were partially used for other purposes, and in 1874, Alabama school funds were diverted. In Tennessee, from 1866-1869, only 47% of the school taxes were spent on schools.

In nearly every state, the question of mixed and separate schools was a matter of much debate and strong feeling. There was no doubt that the Negroes in general wanted mixed schools. They wanted the advantages of contact with white children, and they wanted to have this evidence and proof of their equality. In addition to this, they were strengthened in their stand by white Northern leaders, who pointed out the practical difficulty of two separate systems of schools, which must, to an extent, duplicate effort, and would certainly greatly increase cost. In many of the states, the matter was left in abeyance, and in some states, like Louisiana, mixed schools were established.

This raised a fury of opposition among the whites, but for reasons of economy and democracy it was obviously the best policy. The propaganda of race hatred made it eventually impossible, and the separate school systems so increased the cost of public education in the South that they resulted in the retardation of the whole system and eventually in making the Negro child bear the burden of the increased cost; so that even to this day throughout the South, the Negro child has from one-half to one-tenth as much spent on his education as the white child, and even then, the white child does not receive sufficient funds for a thorough elementary education.

Separation by race was prohibited in the Constitutions of South Carolina and Louisiana. In Atlanta, the Board of Education wanted mixed schools, but allowed separate schools when they were desired. The trustees of the Peabody Fund caused the dropping of a clause prohibiting separate schools in the original draft of the Federal Civil Rights Bill of 1875.

One Southern Congressman's speech represents the strength of this fear. "Woe be unto the political party which shall declare to the toiling yeoman, the honest laboring poor of this country, 'Your children are no better than a Negro's.' If you think so, you shall not practice on that opinion. We are the rulers; you are the servants! We know what is best for you and your children. We, the millionaires—we, who are paid out of your pockets, will take your money and will send our children to select high schools, to foreign lands, where no Negroes are, but you, you who are too poor to pay, shall send your ragged, hungry urchins to the common schools on such terms as we dictate, or keep them away to stray among the treacherous quick-sands and shoals of life; to wander on the streets and learn to syllable the alphabet of vice and crime, or stay at home, and like blind Samson, in mental darkness, tramp barefoot, the tread-mill of unceasing toil!" [52]

In the Reconstruction constitutions, state taxation for schools was a new feature, unknown in the previous school laws of Alabama, Florida, Arkansas, Georgia, Mississippi, North Carolina, and South Carolina. "The principle of direct taxation was undoubtedly the most important contribution of the Reconstruction régime to the public school movement in the South." It was perpetuated in all the revisions of these constitutions after 1876, except in Alabama. The victory of home rule in 1876 was followed by a period of hostility or at least indifference to public education. In 1879, in Virginia, $1,000,000 belonging to the school fund had been used for other purposes. In Georgia, the legislature of 1876 destroyed $350,000 worth of bonds belonging to the school fund. Tennessee, in 1869, abolished the general tax for school purposes, and the administrative system. The Alabama Constitution of 1875, instead of allocating one-fifth of the state revenue to education, which was the provision in the Constitution of 1868, substituted direct appropriation. In Arkansas, the income from land sales belonging to the school fund was used for other purposes. There were similar reductions of school revenue in Louisiana. In Texas, a voluntary county system was substituted for the state system in 1875 and 1876. The public school system of the South was helped by the gifts of the Peabody Fund in 1867 and 1869.

"On account of the influences mentioned, it became common throughout the South, for all parties to pledge themselves to the cause of public schools. Yet, by some of those strange fatalities of history, the strongest of all influences for educational progress was the very one which during and just after the Reconstruction period undoubtedly checked the cause. That was the race issue. The movement to eliminate the Negro as a factor in politics involved an appeal to passion, to prejudice, and sometimes a misrepresentation of the part of the colored man in Southern progress." [53]

It is fair to say that the Negro carpetbag governments established the public schools of the South. Although recent researches have shown many germs of a public school system in the South before the war, there can be no reasonable doubt that common school instruction in the South, in the modern sense of the term, was founded by the Freedmen's Bureau and missionary societies, and that the state public school system was formed mainly by Negro Reconstruction governments.

Dunning says: "Free public education existed in only a rudimentary and sporadic form in the South before the war, but the new constitutions provided generally for complete systems on advanced northern models." [54]

Colonel Richard P. Hallowell adds: "The whites had always regarded the public school system of the North with contempt. The freedman introduced and established it, and it stands today a living testimony." [55]

From the beginning of the public school system under Reconstruction, and after, the fight between local and state control and supervision has been bitter. Local control meant the control of property and racial particularism. It stood for reaction and prejudice; and wherever there was retrogression, particularly in Negro schools, it can be traced to the increased power of the county and district administrators. This accounts for the difficulties, corruption, and failures in Alabama and South Carolina, particularly, and in most of the other Southern states.

For the first success of the Negro schools, the South deserved little praise. From the beginning, most of the Southern states made the Negro schools just as bad as they dared to in the face of national public opinion, and every cent spent on them was taken from Negro rents and wages, and came back to the property-holders tenfold in increased opportunities for exploitation.

It is said, for instance, in one state: "There were to be free public schools. The blacks were to be the chief beneficiaries of the new system, but the whites would pay the taxes. Whites considered such education either useless or positively dangerous to society." Of free, self-sacrificing gifts for the sake of Negro uplift and intelligence, the vast majority of Southern white people contributed almost nothing.

In recent years under the influence of educational leaders like Atticus Haygood and James Dillard, the support of Negro education in some Southern states has become more enlightened and generous. This is particularly true in North Carolina, West Virginia, and Texas. Improvement over unusually bad conditions may be noted also in Louisiana, Virginia, and Delaware. The situation in South Carolina, Florida, Georgia, Alabama, and Mississippi is still reactionary and deplorable, while the improvement in Arkansas, Tennessee, and Kentucky is not great.

Finally, the movement that saved the Negro public school system was not enlightened Southern opinion, but rather that Northern philanthropy which at the very beginning of the Negro education movement contributed toward the establishment of Negro colleges. The reason for them at first was to supply the growing demand for teachers, and was also a concession to Southern prejudice, which so violently disliked the white teacher in the Negro school.

This led to the establishment by 1879 of eighty-four normal and high schools and sixteen colleges, with over twelve thousand students. But these institutions soon saw a higher mission. In the midst of reaction and disfranchisement, of poverty and growing caste, they became the centers of a training in leadership and ideals for the whole Negro race, and the only fine and natural field of contact between white and black culture.

"The fathers of forty years ago anticipated the criticisms of later years as to the wisdom of colleges for the development of a backward race. So, they said, let it be granted that other lines of education are imperative; colleges also certainly are needed, and we must set the standards for the education of the race now! Thorough training, large knowledge, and the best culture possible are needed to invigorate, direct, purify, and broaden life; needed for the wise administration of citizenship, the duties of which are as sure to come as the sun is to shine, though today or tomorrow may be cloudy; needed to overcome narrowness, one-sidedness, and incompleteness." [56]

Howard University and Freedman's Hospital are survivals of the Freedmen's Bureau. Howard University was chartered in 1867 and General O. O. Howard, head of the Freedmen's Bureau, was made its first president. Succeeding as presidents were W. W. Patton, J. E. Rankin, who wrote "God Be With You Until We Meet Again," and John Gordon, a lineal descendant of Jonathan Edwards. On its governing board have been Douglass, Langston and Bruce; it has the largest Negro medical center in the United States, and has furnished about half of the Negro lawyers.

Berea College was started by John G. Fee, a Kentuckian, who became an abolitionist. After the war, colored students were admitted, and a brother of the President of Oberlin was at the head of the school. For forty years, colored students attended Berea, but finally, in 1904, the institution was by law closed to Negroes.

Hampton Institute was founded by General S. C. Armstrong, near where the Negroes were first made "contraband of war," and where a colored woman founded the first colored school. Among its trustees were Mark Hopkins, Phillips Brooks, and John G. Whittier.

Atlanta University was founded by Edmund Ware in 1867. "To have gone on as President Ware did during those early years there must have been in his heart deathless love and pity for men who needed what he could give them—a faith in the gospel and eternal righteousness that never wavered, and a love for God that made work easy and suffering joy." [57]

Add to this the picture of DeForrest at Talledega, Cravath at Fisk, and others at Biddle, Knoxville, New Orleans, and Central Tennessee. There were those two influential schools at the edge of the South, Lincoln in Pennsylvania, and Wilberforce in Ohio.

Nearly all of these educational leaders were either nominated by Howard, head of the Freedmen's Bureau, as in the case of General S. C. Armstrong, or received from him the most thorough-going cooperation. There is no greater tribute to the Freedmen's Bureau than this.

Propaganda has centered the attention of the world upon these Northerners who took part in the political reconstruction of the South, and particularly upon those who were charged with dishonesty, while of the history of this astonishing movement to plant the New England college in the South, and to give the Southern black man a leadership based on scholarship and character, almost nothing has been said. And yet this was the salvation of the South and the Negro. These "carpetbaggers" deserve to be remembered and honored. Without them there can be no doubt that the Negro would have rushed into revolt and vengeance and played into the hands of those determined to crush him. As it was, when reaction triumphed in 1876, there was already present a little group of trained leadership which grew by leaps and bounds until it gripped and held the mass of Negroes at the beginning of the twentieth century.

Had it not been for the Negro school and college, the Negro would, to all intents and purposes, have been driven back to slavery. His economic foothold in land and capital was too slight in ten years of turmoil to effect any defense or stability. His reconstruction leadership had come from Negroes educated in the North, and white politicians, capitalists and philanthropic teachers. The counter-revolution of 1876 drove most of these, save the teachers, away. But already, through establishing public schools and private colleges, and by organizing the Negro church, the Negro had acquired enough leadership and knowledge to thwart the worst designs of the new slave drivers. They avoided the mistake of trying to meet force by force. They bent to the storm of beating, lynching and murder, and kept their souls in spite of public and private insult of every description; they built an inner culture which the world recognizes in spite of the fact that it is still half-strangled and inarticulate.

There is wide wide wonder in it all,
That from degraded rest and servile toil
The fiery spirit of the seer should call
These simple children of the sun and soil.
O black slave singers, gone, forgot, unfamed,
You, you alone, of all the long, long line
Of those who've sung untaught, unknown, unnamed,
Have stretched out upward, seeking the divine.

JAMES WELDON JOHNSON

---

1. J. J. Alvord in *Report of Joint Committee on Reconstruction*, Part II, p. 247.
2. Boyd, *Educational History in the South Since 1865*, Studies in Southern History and Politics, pp. 260-261. Boyd claims 595,306 pupils enrolled in Southern public schools in 1860. This is clearly an exaggeration and no detailed figures are adduced to prove the claim.
3. *Results of Emancipation in the United States*, p. 28.

4. Thomason, *The Foundation of the Public Schools of South Carolina*, p. 147. Cited in Williams, *A History of Education and Charitable Institutions in South Carolina During the Reconstruction Period*, p. 50.
5. Sadler, *The Education of the Coloured Race*, p. 13.
6. Wright, *Brief Sketches of Negro Education in Georgia*, p. 30.
6a. House Reports, No. 22, 42nd Congress, 2nd Session, p. 170.
7. *Report of the Joint Committee on Reconstruction, 1866*, Part II, pp. 162-163.
8. Sadler, *Education of the Coloured Race*, p. 21.
9. *Journal of Negro History*, X, p. 137.
0. Simkins and Woody, *South Carolina During Reconstruction*, p. 427.
11. New York *Tribune*, March 10, 1865.
12. New York *Tribune*, April 15, 1865.
13. Compare Wright, *Brief Sketches of Negro Education in Georgia*, pp. 16, 17.
14. Lewinson, *Race, Class and Party*, p. 36.
15. R*esults of Emancipation in the United States*, p. 29.
16. *Results of Emancipation in the United States*, p. 29.
17. B*ard, Reports of American Missionary Association.
18 Testimony of Wood, *Report of Joint Committee on Reconstruction, 1866*, Part II, p. 86.
19. *Congressional Globe*, 39th Congress, 1st Session, Part I, p. 93.
20. Garner, *Reconstruction in Mississippi*, p. 236.
21 Testimony of Conway, *Report of Joint Committee on Reconstruction, 1866*, Part IV, p. 82.
22. P*erce, *Freedmen's Bureau*, p. 80.
23. Fleming, *Documentary History of Reconstruction*, II, p. 177.
24. Charleston *Daily Courier*, July 4, 1865.
25. Lewinson, *Race, Class and Party*, pp. 35-36.
26 Boyd, *Educational History in the South Since 1865*, Studies in Southern History and Politics, p. 282.
27. Du Bois, *Atlanta University Studies*, No. 6, p. 32.
28. Simkins and Woody, *South Carolina During Reconstruction*, p. 434.
29. Williams, *A History of Education and Charitable Institutions in South Carolina During the Reconstruction Period. Proceedings of the Constitutional Convention of 1868*, Charleston, S. C.
30. *Proceedings of the Constitutional Convention of 1868*, Charleston, S. C.
31. Williams, *A History of Education and Charitable Institutions in South Carolina During the Reconstruction Period*, pp. 30, 32.
32. Williams, *A History of Education and Charitable Institutions in South Carolina During the Reconstruction Period*, pp. 48-49.
33. Williams, *A History of Education and Charitable Institutions in South Carolina During the Reconstruction Period*, p. 50.
34. Simkins and Woody, *South Carolina During Reconstruction*, p. 442.
35. Williams, *A History of Education and Charitable Institutions in South Carolina During the Reconstruction Period*, p. 51.
36. Garner, *Reconstruction in Mississippi*, pp. 354, 355.
37. Du Bois, *Atlanta University Studies*, No. 16, p. 72.
38. Fleming, *Civil War and Reconstruction in Alabama*, p. 634.
39. Fleming, *Civil War and Reconstruction in Alabama*, p. 468.
40. Davis, *Reconstruction in Florida*, p. 236.
41. McPherson, *History of the United States During Reconstruction*, p. 41.
42. Wallace, *Carpetbag Rule in Florida*, p. 35.
43. Lanier, *History of Negro Education in Florida*, p. 21.
44. Du Bois, *Atlanta University Studies*, No. 6, p. 39.
45. Clement, *A History of Negro Education in North Carolina*, p. 47.
46. Clement, *A History of Negro Education in North Carolina*, p. 45.
47. Clement, *A History of Negro Education in North Carolina*, p. 50.
48. Clement, *A History of Negro Education in North Carolina*, pp. 58, 59.
49. Powell, *The Aftermath of the Civil War in Arkansas*, pp. 221, 230.

50. *Daily Republican*, June 15, 1869.
51. Du Bois, *Atlanta University Studies*, No. 6, p. 37.
52. Norwood, Speeches delivered in the United States Senate on April 30 and May 4, 1874.
53. Boyd, *Educational History of the South Since 1865*, Studies in Southern History and Politics, p. 270.
54. Dunning, *Reconstruction, Political and Economic.*
55. Hallowell, *Why the Negro Was Enfranchised*, p. 33.
56. Beard, *A Crusade of Brotherhood*, p. 149.
57. *From Servitude to Service*, p. 166.

XVI. BACK TOWARD SLAVERY

How civil war in the South began again—indeed had never ceased; and how black Prometheus bound to the Rock of Ages by hate, hurt and humiliation, has his vitals eaten out as they grow, yet lives and fights

It must be remembered and never forgotten that the civil war in the South which overthrew Reconstruction was a determined effort to reduce black labor as nearly as possible to a condition of unlimited exploitation and build a new class of capitalists on this foundation. The wage of the Negro worker, despite the war amendments, was to be reduced to the level of bare subsistence by taxation, peonage, caste, and every method of discrimination. This program had to be carried out in open defiance of the clear letter of the law.

The lawlessness in the South since the Civil War has varied in its phases. First, it was that kind of disregard for law which follows all war. Then it became a labor war, an attempt on the part of impoverished capitalists and landholders to force laborers to work on the capitalist's own terms. From this, it changed to a war between laborers, white and black men fighting for the same jobs. Afterward, the white laborer joined the white landholder and capitalist and beat the black laborer into subjection through secret organizations and the rise of a new doctrine of race hatred.

It is always difficult to stop war, and doubly difficult to stop a civil war. Inevitably, when men have long been trained to violence and murder, the habit projects itself into civil life after peace, and there is crime and disorder and social upheaval, as we who live in the backwash of World War know too well. But in the case of civil war, where the contending parties must rest face to face after peace, there can be no quick and perfect peace. When to all this you add a servile and disadvantaged race, who represent the cause of war and who afterwards are left near naked to their enemies, war may go on more secretly, more spasmodically, and yet as truly as before the peace. This was the case in the South after Lee's surrender.

Emancipation loosed the finer feelings of some Southerners toward Negroes. They felt the fall of a burden—and expressed it. The nightmare was at last over. They need no longer apologize to the world for a system they were powerless to change or reconstruct. It had been changed and they were glad.

But Emancipation left the planters poor, and with no method of earning a living, except by exploiting black labor on their only remaining capital—their land. This underlying economic urge was naturally far stronger than the philanthropic, and motivated the mass of Southerners.

Carl Schurz said: "Some planters held back their former slaves on their plantations by brute force. Armed bands of white men patrolled the county roads to drive back the Negroes wandering about. Dead bodies of murdered Negroes were found on and near the highways and byways. Gruesome reports came from the hospitals—reports of colored men and women whose ears had been cut off, whose skulls had been broken by blows, whose bodies had been slashed by knives or lacerated with scourges. A number of such cases, I had occasion to examine myself. A veritable reign of terror prevailed in many parts of the South." [1]

Many testified that the Southern people seemed to have transferred their wrath at the Federal Government to the colored people. The disorder and utter lack of control was widespread. Governor Sharkey of Mississippi found an unprecedented amount of lawlessness in 1866. Mrs. Smedes, a Southern white woman, tells of incidents in Mississippi involving both whites and Negroes.

"At this time, incendiary fires were common. There was not much law in the land. We heard of the gin-houses and cotton houses that were burned in all directions. One day as Thomas came back from a business journey, the smoldering ruin of his gin-house met his eyes. The building was itself valuable and necessary. All the cotton that he owned was consumed in it. He had not a dollar. He had to borrow the money to buy a postage stamp, not only during this year, but during many years to come. It was a time of deepest gloom. Thomas had been wounded to the bottom of his affectionate heart by the perfidy of the [white] man who had brought this on his house. In the midst of the grinding poverty that now fell in full force on him, he heard of the reckless extravagance of this man on the money that should have been used to meet these debts." [2]

Bands of Confederate soldiers roamed in some states: "There have been a number of complaints made to Captain Glavis by citizens of Wayne, Green, and Sampson Counties of numerous robberies and acts of violence by a band of late rebel soldiers, who are inhabitants of Wynn County. They are said to be headed by one Frank Coley." [3]

"Some eight weeks ago, several returned rebel soldiers from Pitt County went into the village of Washington and commenced shooting and beating Union men. Several assaults were made, and at least one Union man was publicly whipped in the streets, and some Negroes were wounded. One of the party was badly wounded by a person whom they attacked. On their return, they met on the public highway a Negro. They first castrated him, and afterwards murdered him in cold blood." [4]

In Alabama, Mississippi and Louisiana, it was said in 1866: "The life of a Negro is not worth much there. I have seen one who was shot in the leg while he was riding a mule, because the ruffian thought it more trouble to ask him to get off the mule than to shoot him. There is a very large class of such people in Alabama, Mississippi and Louisiana. I had expected to find Texas in a much worse condition, but I found it much safer there than in Alabama and Mississippi. Particularly in Alabama, the people have been rendered desperate. The crops for the past year have been very poor. The rust and the army worm have destroyed their cotton crops, and there is much want and suffering among the people." [5]

"An argument frequently employed in justifying the outrages on the freedmen is that the whites were goaded into it by the evils of Negro domination. The argument holds good in part, but only in part, for unhappily, the outrages were committed before the suffrage was conferred upon the blacks; before such a step was even favored by any considerable number of Northern people." [6]

Clara Barton, who visited Andersonville, Georgia, in 1866, tells the story of a colored wife of 18, whom her husband, a blacksmith, brought to her, walking 30 or 40 miles. "I took his wife into my tent and examined her back: she was a young bright-colored woman, a little darker than he, with a fair, patient face, with nothing sulky in her look; I found across her back twelve lashes or gashes, partly healed and partly not, some of them cut into the bone. She must have been whipped with a lash half as large as my little finger—it may have been larger; and one of these lashes was from eight to ten inches in length; and the flesh had been cut completely out most of the way. It had been a curling whip; it had curled around her arms, cut inside the arm, over the back, and the same on the other side. There were twelve of those long lashes, partly healed and partly not; she could not bear her clothing on her at that time, except thrown loosely over her shoulders; she had got strong enough so as to be able to walk, but she was feeble and must have been unable to work before that occurred; she was in no condition to work." She had been "bucked and gagged" by her employer, thrown on her face, and lashed on her back; so that, when her husband found her, he said she was "a gore of blood." The offense was that, in the last months of pregnancy, she had proved unable to do the task of spinning which was given her.[7]

"There was in those Southern states which I have visited for some years after the war, and up to the year 1868, or in some cases 1870, much disorder, and a condition of lawlessness toward the blacks—a disposition, greatest in the more distant and obscure regions—to trample them underfoot, to deny them equal rights, and to injure or kill them on slight or no provocations. The tremendous change in the social arrangements of the Southern whites had suffered a defeat which was sore to bear, and on top of this, they saw their slaves—their most valuable and cherished property—taken away and made free, and not only free, but their political equals. One needs to go into the far South to know what this really meant, and what deep resentment and irritation it inevitably bred."[8]

The unrest and bitterness of post-war lawlessness were gradually transmuted into economic pressure. Systematic effort was made by the owners to put the Negro to work, and equally determined effort by the poor whites to keep him from work which competed with them or threatened their future work and income. Cotton and other crops were high in price, and hard work would soon restore something of the losses of war. The planters offered the ex-slave, therefore, a labor contract, and were surprised when he refused. He had to refuse. The plantation laborer, under the conditions offered, would still be a slave, with small chance to rise to the position of independent farmer, or even of free modern laborer.

On the other hand, the poor whites were determined to keep the blacks from access to the richer and better land from which slavery had driven the white peasants. A three-cornered battle ensued and increased lawless aggression. Recurrent crop failures due to the weather made more trouble, and at the same time, the wars of Europe, the Seven Weeks' War and the Franco-Prussian War, disturbed civilization.

In such an economic revolution, the cost of change and uplift ought to fall on the community, the nation, and the government. The plantation land should have gone to those who worked it, and the former owner should have been compensated in some part for a lost investment made with the social sanction of the nation. To this, should have been added economic opportunity and access to the land for the poor whites.

But such a possible outcome was frustrated by the economic selfishness of the North, and by the intransigent attitude of the vast majority of the planters. They did not believe in freedom for Negroes, and they sought to frustrate it by law, force, and deliberate cheating, and by arrogant demands for economic license and political power, such

as no sane nation could grant. This result was Federal Reconstruction.
A lawlessness which, in 1865-1868, was still spasmodic and episodic,
now became organized, and its real underlying industrial causes obscured by political excuses and race hatred. Using a technique of
mass and midnight murder, the South began widely organized aggression upon the Negroes.

"When Congress intervened by its reconstruction measures to defeat
the reactionary program of the South, there swept over that section a
crime-storm of devastating fury. Lawlessness and violence filled the
land, and terror stalked abroad by day, and it burned and murdered
by night. The Southern states had actually relapsed into barbarism.
During that period, a new generation was conceived and born to the
South of both races that was literally conceived in lawlessness, and
born into crime-producing conditions. Lawlessness was its inheritance,
and the red splotch of violence its birthmark." [9]

Armed guerrilla warfare killed thousands of Negroes; political riots
were staged; their causes or occasions were always obscure, their
results always certain: ten to one hundred times as many Negroes
were killed as whites.

Then differences began to arise. Instead of driving the Negroes to
work, bands of poor whites began to drive them from work. Private
vengeance was taken upon prosperous and hard-working Negroes. A
number of Negroes were employed in building the airline railroad
between Atlanta and Charlotte. Disguised men went there, took the
Negroes and whipped them, and forced them back to the farms to
work. They were receiving money wages for working on the railroad.

A man from Ohio, living in Clarendon County, South Carolina, had
his stock and business amounting to $40,000 a year entirely destroyed.
"There were a good many industrious men, who if they could get a
start, would make crops of their own and become independent farmers. In every such case, where colored men could bring proper recommendations there of evidences of industry, he would take advances to
them as well as to white men." The farmers about complained that in
this way he was taking away laborers and making Negroes independent farmers. They whipped him; ruined his business; and drove him
out of the state. [10]

In Choctaw County, Alabama, a colored man, Robert Fullerlove,
lived. Masked men shot into his house and burned it. He and his
neighbors were killed and driven away. "I have four hundred acres
of land. I have about twenty head of cattle, little and big. I have an
ox team, and in the lot of cattle there are seven milk cows. I have
corn and fodder and hogs. I had a very fine crop of cotton planted
and was going over it, when this last raid happened at my house.

I have lost my crop entirely, and it isn't worthwhile for me to stay. I am a hard-working man, and I love what I have worked for and earned." [11]

Augustus Blair of Huntsville, Alabama, was a hard-working old black man, who had stayed at home during the war and helped to take care of the little white children. The Ku Klux came to his house; seized his son, and beat and maltreated him.

"He got so he could get about a little. I hired a wagon and fetched him here, but directly he came here he was taken down with a hemorrhage that came from stamping him on the stomach and breast. They stamped him all over the stomach and breast. In two weeks after he was examined in the court-room there, he died. Everybody that saw him said he couldn't live, and they were surprised that he lived so long. I had the doctors to tend to him. I owe forty or fifty dollars to Doctor Henry Benford; he asked me for the money on Saturday. After all this was done, I knew every man of them, and I came here and made complaint. Mr. Wager assisted me, and Jim Common, of Athens, told me to have them arrested before the grand jury. . . . I had a good deal of property down there. I had thirty head of hogs and four bales of cotton; I had four bales ginned and fetched my cotton there and sold it. They looked for me to go back. I left my wife and young child there. I didn't want to go away. I hadn't done anything, but I believe they would have treated me just the same way, and I went away. I left thirty head of hogs and one good milk cow; four bales of cotton, and my corn in the field. Jim Common told me to sue for it. I went down there and all my things were gone." [12]

These happenings were not confined to particular regions. They spread all over the South. In 1866, the first church for colored people was opened by the American Missionary Association at Memphis, Tennessee. It was burned with all the colored churches in Memphis in the riot that year. [13]

In the eighteen months ending June 30, 1867, General Canby reported 197 murders, and 548 cases of aggravated assault in North and South Carolina.

"In reference to South Carolina, the report of the joint select committee of the two houses of Congress of 1872 contains such a mass of revolting details that one cannot decide where to begin their citation or where to stop. Murders, or attempts to murder, are numerous. Whippings are without number. Probably the most cruel and cowardly of these last was the whipping of Elias Hill. He was a colored man who had from infancy been dwarfed in legs and arms. He was unable to use either. But he possessed an intelligent mind; had learned to read; and had acquired an unusual amount of knowledge for one in his circumstances. He was a Baptist preacher. He was highly respected for his upright character. He was eminently religious, and was greatly revered by the people of his own race. It was on this ground that he was visited by the Ku Klux, brutally beaten and dragged from his house into the yard, where he was left in the cold at night, unable to walk or crawl." [14]

A report from South Carolina tells of 97 Negroes killed, and 146 shot and whipped. There are riots because of the arming of Negroes. White farmers who are displaced as tenants attack the Negro tenants. Negro churches are burned. In one community, four-fifths of the Negro men are sleeping out in the woods. Gins and ginhouses are burned in retaliation by Negroes. Colored women are whipped and raped by whites. In some cases, the white landholders try to protect Negroes, while the irresponsible poor whites lead the attack. In another community, eleven murders and more than 600 whippings have gone unnoticed, while there are seven cases of incendiary burnings. Negro artisans are stopped from following their trade, and the antagonism between poor whites and Negroes grows. Six Negro foundrymen are beaten and blacksmiths whipped.

In Edgefield and Laurens Counties, South Carolina, there were organized bands of "regulators"—armed men, who make it their business to traverse these counties and maltreat Negroes without any avowed definite purpose in view. They treat the Negroes, in many instances, in the most horrible and atrocious manner, even to maiming them, cutting their ears off, etc. In one case, two citizens of one of these counties testified against these parties, and were instantly compelled to leave the county, barely escaping with their lives. The citizens are bound in honor, by an understanding or compact among them, not to testify against these regulators; so that it is impossible to get evidence against them unless the Negro gives it. [15]

The report of the Ku Klux investigation published in 1871 said of South Carolina that "in the nine counties covered by the investigation for a period of approximately six months, the Ku Klux Klan lynched and murdered 35 men, whipped 262 men and women, otherwise outraged, shot, mutilated, burned out, etc., 101 persons. It committed two cases of sex offenses against Negro women. During this time, the Negroes killed four men, beat one man, committed sixteen other outrages, but no case of torture. No case is found of a white woman seduced or raped by a Negro."

The reasons given for the Ku Klux outrages were significantly varied: the victims should suffer in revenge for killing, and for some cases of arson; they were Republicans; they were radical; they had attempted to hold elections; they were carrying arms; they were "niggers"; they were "damn niggers"; they boasted that they would own land; they should be made to recant Republican principles; and they should give desired information.

In Georgia, in 1868, disturbances are reported in the Northwest section, where the poor whites are in the majority. Negroes were whipped for debt, for associating with white women, and for trying to vote. In the cotton belt, where the Negroes outnumber the whites, three white members of the legislature were killed, and there were insurrections and riots, culminating in the one at Camilla. In this case, 300 Republicans, mostly Negroes, with music and banner, were marching to hold a public meeting. They were met by the sheriff and told that they could not meet. A riot ensued, where eight or nine Negroes were killed, and twenty to forty wounded. No whites were killed.

The Negro Secretary of State, Jonathan Gibbs, in Florida, when called before a committee of Congress in 1871, reported 153 murders in Jackson County in that state.[16]

Conditions in Texas were particularly bad. In 1869, in thirty counties, there was no civil government, and in others, very imperfect organizations. During Sheridan's command of the state there were nine murders a month. If he owned both hell and Texas, Sheridan said upon one occasion, he would rent out Texas and live in hell—a statement which was repeated over the country for a generation. Benjamin F. Wade added to this that he was told by a native, "All that Texas needs to make it a paradise is water and good society." "Yes," answered Wade, "that's all they need in hell."[17]

A committee of the Constitutional Convention of 1868 on partial returns said that 1,035 men had been murdered in Texas since the close of the war, and a Federal attorney said that the number might have been two thousand. The Secretary of State reports to the Texas Senate that 905 homicides had taken place in the two years ending in 1870, and he believed that if all the facts were known, the total would be 1,500. In 1870, after the new state government was organized, it was officially reported that 2,970 persons charged with murder were evading arrest in the state, and two to seven murders were often attributed to the same individual.

From war, turmoil, poverty, forced labor and economic rivalry of labor groups, there came again in the South the domination of the secret order, which systematized the effort to subordinate the Negro.

The method of force which hides itself in secrecy is a method as old as humanity. The kind of thing that men are afraid or ashamed to do openly, and by day, they accomplish secretly, masked, and at night. The method has certain advantages. It uses Fear to cast out

Fear; it dares things at which open method hesitates; it may with a certain impunity attack the high and the low; it need hesitate at no outrage of maiming or murder; it shields itself in the mob mind and then throws over all a veil of darkness which becomes glamor. It attracts people who otherwise could not be reached. It harnesses the mob.

How is it that men who want certain things done by brute force can so often depend upon the mob? Total depravity, human hate and *Schadenfreude,* do not explain fully the mob spirit in America. Before the wide eyes of the mob is ever the Shape of Fear. Back of the writhing, yelling, cruel-eyed demons who break, destroy, maim and lynch and burn at the stake, is a knot, large or small, of normal human beings, and these human beings at heart are desperately afraid of something. Of what? Of many things, but usually of losing their jobs, being declassed, degraded, or actually disgraced; of losing their hopes, their savings, their plans for their children; of the actual pangs of hunger, of dirt, of crime. And of all this, most ubiquitous in modern industrial society is that fear of unemployment.

It is its nucleus of ordinary men that continually gives the mob its initial and awful impetus. Around this nucleus, to be sure, gather snowball-wise all manner of flotsam, filth and human garbage, and every lewdness of alcohol and current fashion. But all this is the horrible covering of this inner nucleus of Fear.

How then is the mob to be met and quelled? If it represents public opinion, even passing, passionate public opinion, it cannot permanently be put down by a police which public opinion appoints and pays. Three methods of quelling the mob are at hand: the first, by proving to its human, honest nucleus that the Fear is false, ill-grounded, unnecessary; or secondly, if its Fear is true or apparently or partially true, by attacking the fearful thing openly either by the organized police power or by frank civil war as did Mussolini and George Washington; or thirdly, by secret, hidden and underground ways, the method of the Ku Klux Klan.

Why do we not take the first way? Because this is a world that believes in War and Ignorance, and has no hope in our day of realizing an intelligent majority of men and Peace on Earth. There are many, many exceptions, but, in general, it is true that there is scarcely a bishop in Christendom, a priest in the church, a president, governor, mayor, or legislator in the United States, a college professor or public school teacher, who does not in the end stand by War and Ignorance as the main method for the settlement of our pressing human problems. And this despite the fact that they may deny it with their mouths every day.

But here again, open civil war is difficult, costly, and hard to guide. The Right toward which it aims must be made obvious, even if it is wrong. In 1918, in order to win the war, we had to make Germans into Huns. In order to win, the South had to make Negroes into thieves, monsters and idiots. Tomorrow, we must make Latins, Southeastern Europeans, Turks and other Asiatics into actual "lesser breeds without the law." Some seem to see today anti-Christ in Catholicism; and in Jews, international plotters of the Protocol; and in "the rising tide of color," a threat to all civilization and human culture. Even if these things were true, it would be difficult to bring the truth clearly before the ignorant mob and guide it toward the overthrow of evil. But if these be half true or wholly false, the mob can only be stirred to action by wholesale lying, and this is difficult and costly, and may be successfully answered; or by secret underground whispering, the methods of night and mask, the psychology of vague and unknown ill, the innuendo that cannot be answered, for it is not openly published.

Secret organization had long been a method of fastening dictatorship upon the South. It was seen in Louisiana early in the nineteenth century, and helped in the annexation of Texas; it was widespread in Kansas. Senator Douglass called the whole secession movement "the result of an enormous conspiracy." Charles Sumner said: "Not in all history, ancient and modern, is there any record of conspiracy so vast, so wicked, ranging over such spaces, both in time and history."

"The evidence taken by the Congressional committee which visited Kansas in 1856, furnished the most incontestable proof of the power and extent of those oathbound orders. . . . The different lodges were connected together by an effective organization, it embraced great numbers of the citizens of Missouri, and was extended into other slave states and into the territory. Its avowed purpose was not only to extend slavery into Kansas, but also into other territories of the United States. This dangerous society was controlled by men who avowed their purpose to extend slavery at all hazards." [18]

The renewed use of the secret orders to fasten the dictatorship of property over labor upon the South began in New Orleans in 1865, when the rebel armies were disbanded and began to return to the city. First, apparently, appeared the "Southern Cross," determined to drive out the new Northern capitalist, and reduce the Negroes to slavery. Governor Wells said in 1866: "Should the secret associations now organizing rapidly be able to regain the ascendancy which made it [New Orleans] a living hell for years before the rebellion, I shudder at the consequences."

Meantime, a larger and more inclusive secret order had been started in Tennessee known as the Ku Klux Klan. Tennessee, Alabama,

Texas, Arkansas and North Carolina, soon fell under its action by the same methods. The new technique of the plan solidified the various objects and efforts, and provided a new unity through emphasizing the importance of race.

The race element was emphasized in order that property-holders could get the support of the majority of white laborers and make it more possible to exploit Negro labor. But the race philosophy came as a new and terrible thing to make labor unity or labor class-consciousness impossible. So long as the Southern white laborers could be induced to prefer poverty to equality with the Negro, just so long was a labor movement in the South made impossible.

Some excuse the rise of the Ku Klux and the White League and the Knights of the White Camellia in the South with the plea that they were the answer to Negro suffrage, and that the Union Leagues started among Negroes were the cause of secret orders among whites. There is no historic foundation for this. The Union League in the North was the movement of Northern white aristocracy, including most of the rich and well-to-do, against defeatism and the menace of the copperhead. Its powerful and influential social clubs in New York, Philadelphia, and elsewhere, exist to this day. This Union League movement influenced the labor vote in the North. It came to the South with the carpetbaggers and used the Northern technique. It employed among Negroes some ceremonies and secrecy, but it never contemplated murder and force. By no stretch of imagination could it be called an organization similar to or provocative of the Ku Klux Klan.

The carpetbaggers organized the Negro voters and offered them more in wages and privileges than the whites. The logical answer of he planters, in a free industrial democracy, would have been to meet these offers by better ones. They chose instead force and secret revolution. It was not, then, the organization of Union Leagues that caused the Ku Klux Klan; it was the determination to deprive the Negroes, by force, of any real weapon for economic bargaining.

Their use of the ballot from 1868 to 1872 aroused the property-holders to a frenzy of protest, but it also attracted certain elements of white labor, and bade fair, with reform and efficiency, to build a Southern labor party.

There was but one way to break up this threatened coalition, and that was to unite poor and rich whites by the shibboleth of race, and despite divergent economic interests. The work of secret orders in 868 1872 frustrated any mass movement toward union of white and black labor.

Before 1874, the turmoil of Louisiana blazed the way. The New

Orleans riot in 1866, which stirred the nation and influenced a presidential election, was due primarily to the fact that the head of a secret order was also Chief of Police. The Knights of the White Camellia came into prominence after Negro enfranchisement and were especially aimed at excluding Negroes from voting by terrorism and killing the leaders.

The presidential election of 1868 spurred the planters and their allies to deliberate activity. They saw a chance to nullify the vote of black labor, unite with Northern copperhead Democracy and capture the government. Frank Blair egged them on to revolution.

"The testimony shows that over 2,000 persons were killed, wounded, and otherwise injured in Louisiana within a few weeks prior to the Presidential election in November, 1868; that half the state was overrun by violence; and that midnight raids, secret murders, and open riot kept the people in constant terror until the Republicans surrendered all claim. . . . But the most remarkable case is that of St. Landry, a planting parish on the river Teche. Here the Republicans had a registered majority of 1,071 votes. In the spring of 1868 they carried the parish by 678. In the fall they gave Grant no vote, not one—while the Democrats cast 4,787, the full vote of the parish, for Seymour and Blair. Here occurred one of the bloodiest riots on record, in which the Ku Klux killed and wounded over 200 Republicans, hunting and chasing them for two days and nights through fields and swamps. Thirteen captives were taken from the jail and shot. A pile of twenty-five dead bodies was found half-buried in the woods. Having conquered the Republicans and killed and driven off the white leaders, the Ku Klux captured the masses, marked them with badges of red flannel, enrolled them in clubs, made them vote the Democratic ticket, and then gave them a certificate of the fact." [19]

"In the parish of St. Bernard, a Negro was killed; a black mob killed a white man. Three steamboats filled with armed ruffians left New Orleans for the scene of the riot. Before the trouble could be composed, a dozen or fifteen men were slain." [20]

"Frightful conditions prevailed up the Red River around Shreveport, in Caddo and Bossier Parishes, a trading center for Texas, Arkansas, and the Indian Nations. A United States army officer on duty in this place saw two or three men shot down in the street in front of a store in which he sat. He picked up the bodies of eight men who had been killed in one night. Never had he heard of any one being punished for murder in that country." [21]

"One hundred and twenty corpses were found in the woods or were taken out of Red River after a 'Negro hunt' in Bossier parish." [22]

"For ten days prior to the election of November, the streets were filled with men carrying shot guns, rifles, pistols, and knives. A band of 'Sicilian cutthroats' called the 'Innocents' made up largely of fruit dealers, fishermen, oystermen and other elements drawn from the markets, roamed the city, hunting Negroes. Soon no one could be found in the streets. Then the ruffians entered the houses to drive out the blacks, shooting them like rabbits as they ran. A colored man feared to sleep two nights in the same place." [23]

"This bloody club had 2,000 members. There were more than 70 other clubs in New Orleans bearing such names as the 'Seymour Southrons,' the 'Seymour Infantas,' the 'Seymour Tigers,' the 'Blair Knights,' the 'Swamp Fox Rangers,' the 'Hancock Club,' and the 'Rousseau Guards.' Their appearance in parades led to riots in which many were killed and injured." [24]

"Disorder extended to other parts of Louisiana. In one month, said General Hatch, of the Freedman's Bureau, 297 persons were slain in the parishes adjacent to New Orleans." [25]

During election time, the gun stores of New Orleans were thronged with buyers, and the price of Colt's revolvers doubled.

A local paper said: "Thad Stevens is dead; the prayers of the righteous have at last removed the congressional curse. May old Brownlow, Butler and all such political monsters follow the example of their illustrious predecessor."

The coup d'état failed, and the Reconstruction government was established. But although conditions during the next two years showed improvement, General Mower, in command in New Orleans, said in 1869 that the country around Winnsboro in Franklin Parish was "infested by a gang of desperadoes and thieves" who totally defied the civil authorities.

All this was a challenge to the North and to democratic government. The response was only half-hearted. The North recoiled from force, and force alone could dislodge the planters and allied capitalists and firmly fasten labor government on the South. The North hesitated. Did it want labor government in the South? Should black rule white, even if it could?

To enforce the Fifteenth Amendment, a Federal law was passed May 31, 1870, after a long debate. There was an all-night session in the Senate, May 21; conferences between the two Houses, and finally, the bill became a law May 31. The law made minute provisions to protect by Federal action all citizens in the civil and political rights guaranteed by the Constitution. It enumerated 26 misdemeanors, 5 felonies, and 87 crimes. The punishments varied from $500 fine and one year's imprisonment, to $5,000 fine and ten years' punishment.

It was the intention of this law to protect the Negro in using his right to vote and this protection was to be carried out through Federal officials. It was known that the Southern whites were keeping the Negro from voting by methods which local officials and state courts could not touch. Witnesses were afraid to testify, and juries did not return verdicts, even on clear evidence. Registration was hindered, voters were bribed and intimidated, Negroes and white men were killed. The law brought the whole power of the government, militia, land and naval forces, and courts to bear upon persons who, by bribery or threat, sought to influence the Negro voter or to deprive him of his political rights. Meantime, the Ku Klux Klan, organized in Tennessee in 1865, became so widespread that in 1871 Congress appointed a Joint Committee to investigate it. This committee investigated conditions from April, 1871, to February 9, 1872, and issued a voluminous report in twelve volumes, covering most of the Southern states. This formed a tremendous and invaluable picture of the situation in the South at that time. A Federal election law was passed February 28, 1871, which provided for a national registration of voters—a necessary and inevitable step to rescue national democracy from local particularism and possible fraud. Such a law is still needed and still lacking.

President Grant was appealed to in March, 1871, for military aid to suppress violence in South Carolina. He recommended legislation, and as a result, the Ku Klux Klan enforcement law of April 20, 1871, was passed. It strengthened the act of 1870 and was designed to destroy conspiracies against the Fourteenth or Fifteenth Amendments. It empowered the President to suspend the writ of habeas corpus "when in his judgment the public safety shall require it." The President by proclamation of May 3, 1871, called the attention of the nation to this act, and said that it had been made necessary by persistent violations of the rights of citizens of the United States. He recognized the responsibility placed on him, and did not wish to use these extraordinary powers. But it was his duty to make it known that when it was necessary, he would use them. As a matter of fact, he only once suspended the writ of habeas corpus, in the case of certain lawless counties in South Carolina. The actual military forces at his disposal at this time were limited, amounting to only about nine thousand troops, or one-third of the army in the whole South.

To emphasize his wish to be fair to the South, Grant urged the removal of all political disabilities of former Confederates in December, 1871. A bill for this purpose had passed the House, but failed in the Senate, because Sumner tried to couple with it his Civil Rights bill, and the Northern Democrats voted against it. It finally passed Congress in May, 1872, with the Civil Rights feature omitted. Also, in

1872, the Ku Klux Klan law expired by limitation, and was not extended.

Meantime, in Tennessee, North Carolina and Texas, the writ of habeas corpus had been suspended in the summer of 1870 by the governors, and in 1871, United States courts were filled with Ku Klux cases. In Mississippi, 640 persons were indicted under these enforcement laws, and 200 arrested, but not a single one convicted. President Grant declared that in some of the counties of South Carolina two-thirds of the whites were organized and armed. In all, during 1870-1897, 5,172 cases were tried in the South, and 2,200 in the North. Of these, 5,046 were dismissed, 1,432 convicted, 903 acquitted. The testimony was overwhelming, but conviction was impossible in the South. With 1872, new forms of violence took the place of old—intimidation, threats and fraud. There were judicial discrimination, force and actual civil war. Federal officials were kept busy, and the President tried in vain to execute the Force Acts.

The election of 1872 and the panic of 1873 changed the face of affairs. The labor governments built on Negro votes had kept Grant in office, since the only alternative offered the Negroes was to vote for their own disfranchisement. The Northern reform movement had begun to unite itself with Big Business and Super-Finance, and to sympathize with the Southern planters. The planters had won this sympathy by denouncing the carpetbaggers as the cause of Southern corruption, and thus compelling these representatives of Northern capital either to unite with the planters or leave the South. The labor vote was divided along the color line, and the freedmen submerged beneath a wave of race prejudice and economic rivalry. The time was now ripe for open war on the labor of the Black Belt.

Seven states had been "redeemed" from labor domination under the leadership of carpetbaggers and scalawags; i.e., Virginia, North Carolina, Georgia, Alabama, Tennessee, Arkansas and Texas. This had been accomplished by unifying the white majority and suppressing the Negro vote by intimidation or economic pressure. It was now planned to move on the states where the Negro majority was such that only force could dislodge them.

Four states in 1874 remained under Reconstruction governments: Louisiana, Mississippi, South Carolina and Florida. It is said that consultations among white leaders took place throughout the South, and that in May, 1874, forty men assembled on Magazine Street, New Orleans, to arrange for the final drive. They represented all of the secret organizations. They consulted during May and June, and in July the "White League" was organized, under five comparatively unknown leaders, who were the chosen agents for the secret combinations. In less than sixty days after the formation of the New Orleans central of the White League, it spread to the furthest parts of the state, had before the end of the year 40,000 members, and was extending in all directions through the South.

In Mississippi, the White League began organized work in 1874. Seven organized armed groups were formed in Vicksburg to control the city election. The charge here was extravagance in building schoolhouses and "too many niggers in office." Armed companies patrolled the city, and yet there was perfect order at the polls. Voters were thus intimidated and kept at home while in the surrounding counties some 200 Negroes were killed. At Clinton, in 1875, another blow was struck when a mass meeting and barbecue was being held by the colored people. Five hundred armed white men assembled, food and wagons were destroyed, mules and horses stolen, hundreds of Negro homes searched, and fugitives driven away.

Grant wrote to the Senate, January 13, 1875, regarding the condition of Louisiana. He said:

"On the 13th of April [1873] . . . a butchery of citizens was committed at Colfax, which in blood-thirstiness and barbarity is hardly surpassed by any acts of savage warfare. . . . Insuperable obstructions were thrown in the way of punishing these murderers, and the so-called conservative papers of the state not only justified the massacre but denounced as Federal tyranny and despotism the attempt of the United States officers to bring them to justice." [26]

Concerning Mississippi, President Grant said: "As to the state election of 1875, Mississippi is governed today by officials chosen through fraud and violence, such as would scarcely be accredited to savages." [27]

In 1874, the President was asked for Federal troops in Mississippi and South Carolina. The President refused to send extra troops, and the result was the Vicksburg riot in Mississippi, where many were killed. Afterward, troops were sent there. In 1876, he promised South Carolina every aid on account of the Hamburg riot. He tried in February, 1875, to secure the passage of a bill to protect voters in United States elections, but it did not pass. Nevertheless, before the election of 1876, the House of Representatives asked him to enforce the remaining provisions of the Force Act with the utmost vigor. Grant kept appealing to the Southern people to stop this situation of their own initiative and make the exercise of his power unnecessary.

The South did not listen. Rather, it took note of the strong liberal opposition to Grant in the North, and counted on these liberals to favor withdrawal of that same protection of Southern labor which, in alliance with Northern business, they had helped institute in 1867. On the other hand, the South sensed the willingness of Big Business, threatened by liberal revolt, labor upheaval and state interference, to make new alliance with organized Southern capital if assured that the tariff, banks and national debt, and above all, the new freedom of corporations, would not be subjected to mass attack. Such a double bargain was more than agreeable to Southern leaders.

During the last session of the 43rd Congress in 1875, another Federal election bill, drawn so as to put Congress in control of the national elections, was introduced. The Speaker of the House, James G. Blaine, prevented its passage. He was candidate for the Republican nomination in 1876, and was afraid that the bill might defeat him. He told Lynch, the colored representative from Mississippi, that the passage of the bill would defeat the Republican Party throughout the country. But he was confident, on the other hand, that if a Solid South resulted from the failure to pass the bill, it would make a Solid North in opposition.

It did nothing of the sort. It did not prevent a South solidified by the determination to exploit disfranchised Negroes and it did leave a North hesitating between democracy with black voters and plutocracy with white supremacy.

In South Carolina, the situation was a little more difficult for the mob because of the efforts at reform that were being made by the Republicans. Despite Chamberlain's administration and the efforts at reform, the Democrats determined to carry the election of 1876 by force.

Hampton, shortly after the war, went to Mississippi to look after his large planting interests in the Yazoo Delta. He returned to South Carolina in 1876 at the earnest solicitation of Butler and Gary, former Confederate generals. Their plan of campaign was clear. "Every Democrat must feel honor bound to control the vote of at least one Negro, by intimidation, purchase, keeping him away or as each individual may determine, how he may best accomplish it.

"Never threaten a man individually. If he deserves to be threatened, the necessities of the times require that he should die. A dead Radical is very harmless—a threatened Radical or one driven off by threats from the scene of his operations is often very troublesome, sometimes dangerous, always vindictive.

"In the month of September, we ought to begin to organize Negro clubs, or pretend that we have organized them, and write letters from different parts of the county giving the facts of organization out from prudential reasons, the names of the Negroes are to be withheld. Those who join are to be taken on probation and are not to be taken into full fellowship until they have proven their sincerity by voting our ticket." [28]

Riots and labor troubles ensued. Addressing the Senate on August 1, 1876, on "the late disgraceful and brutal slaughter of unoffending men at the town of Hamburg, South Carolina," President Grant said: "Murders and massacres of innocent men for opinion's sake, or on account of color, have been of too recent date and of too frequent occurrence to require recapitulation or testimony here. All are familiar with their horrible details, the only wonder being that so many justify them or apologize for them." [29] "The scene at Hamburg," he wrote to the Governor of South Carolina, "as cruel, bloodthirsty, wanton, unprovoked, and as uncalled for as it was, is only a repetition of the course that has been pursued in other states within the last few years, notably in Mississippi and Louisiana." In September there was a race riot in Aiken County, where an unknown number of Negroes were killed; some said fifteen, some said 125. Federal troops intervened.

"No one ever knew how many were killed, but the best informed men estimate that between eighty and 125 lost their lives. In Charleston County, Negroes in October killed five white men and wounded sixteen others." [30]

Meantime, deliberate fraud carried the election of 1876. There was cheating, intimidation, bribery, and repeating in voting, especially in Edgefield and Laurens County. At Edgefield, several hundred armed men were ready to take possession of the Court House, and Negroes were kept from voting.

When a Negro leader, with several hundred followers, marched to the Court House to vote, the white leader "ordered his men to pack the steps and corridors so that entrance would be impossible." When the Negroes protested to General Ruger, he asked Gary to let the Negroes vote. Gary refused, and was reported to have replied:

"By God, sir, I'll not do it. I will keep the compact I made with you this morning that white men and Negroes should vote at separate boxes." [31]

Gary's doctrine of voting "early and often" changed the Republican majority of 2,300 in Edgefield to a Democratic majority of 3,900, thus giving Hampton a claim to the office of governor. It was Edgefield's majority alone which gave to Hampton a chance to claim to have been elected—the opportunity which he utilized so well.

"It will be recalled that the tissue ballots were used in the heavy Negro counties for the purpose of having the white men to vote several tickets at once by folding them all together in a way to have them drop apart in the boxes. The law provided on closing the polls that if there were more ballots found in the box than there were names on the poll lists the ballots should be returned to the box and one of the managers should draw out the excess to be destroyed. It is needless to say that the Democratic white manager did the drawing and the Negroes used to be very much surprised that he always drew a thick Republican ticket to be burned.

"We all went on each other's bonds, and it became a joke, causing great amusement, that Creighton Matheny, who did not own ten dollars' worth of property, had signed bonds to the extent of $20,000. In truth the whole performance was a perfunctory and in many respects a laughable travesty on law, for if they had attempted to put us in jail I am sure few or none of us would have acquiesced; and we would have probably killed every obnoxious radical in the court room and town and gone to Texas or some other hiding place. In an hour we had departed and gathering up our camp followers were on our way home." [32]

In Laurens County, the Democratic majority was 1,112 as against a Republican majority of 1,077 in 1874.

"To catch the unwary Negro, the Democrats counterfeited the Union Republican ticket in various ways. Some ballots were headed by the picture of Hayes and Wheeler but carried the name of no presidential candidate. Instead it carried the name of Hampton for Governor, along with Republican County candidates." [33]

In this way, Wade Hampton became Governor of South Carolina, but with the specific promise to protect the Negro in his political rights. After 1877, this Southern gentleman made no attempt to keep the promise. Seventeen Republican representatives in the legislature from Charleston were expelled, and Democrats replaced them in special elections. Thereafter, all sorts of fraud and intimidation kept the South Carolina Negro from voting.

A white South Carolinian, who went through the period and was violently partisan, says of the election of 1876: "It is not now denied, but admitted and claimed, by the successful party, that the canvass was systematically conducted with the view to find occasions to apply force and violence. The occasions came, and the methods adopted had their perfect work. The result is known, but must be stated here for historical purposes purely. By a system of violence and coercion, ranging through all possible grades, from urgent persuasion to mob violence, the election was won by Democrats."

It has been charged by Rhodes and others that there was deliberate exaggeration and misrepresentation concerning these outbreaks and atrocities. This might have been true in some cases, but no one can read the mass of testimony in the various Congressional reports and other sources without being convinced of the organized disorder and conspiracy that accompanied this revolution. The Majority Report of the Ku Klux Committee says:

"Obedient citizens they cannot be considered who, themselves, complaining of bad laws, excuse or encourage the masked and armed mobs that override all laws. Brave and magnanimous enemies, even they cannot be reckoned, who permit the remnants of rebellious feeling, the antagonisms of race, or the bitterness of political partisanships to degrade the soldiers of Lee and Johnston into the cowardly midnight prowlers and assassins who scourge and kill the poor and defenseless." [84]

And even the Minority Report admits that "we do not intend to deny that bodies of disguised men have in several states of the South been guilty of the most flagrant crimes." [85]

And this same Minority Report voices the object of the revolution:

"But whenever that party shall go down, as go down it will at some time not long in the future, that will be the end of the political power of the Negro among white men on this continent. Men in the phrensy of political passions may shut their eyes to this fact now, but it will come at any time when the Negro shall cease to be a party necessity in the politics of this country. Thousands of Republicans, even now, hate him for his insolence and for his arrogance in the ready self-assertion of his new-found rights and privileges. The truly sincere and rational humanitarian looks with sorrow upon the future status of the poor, deluded Negro; for in the near state of things which is to come, when the two great parties which now exist shall have passed away, he sees either the exodus or the extinction of this disturbing element in the social and political condition of the more powerful race." [86]

Systematic effort was made during the whole period of Reconstruction to prevent Negroes from bearing arms. First, there was the demand that Negro Federal troops be immediately disbanded or moved from the South. Then the white militia searched Negro dwellings for arms and took them away.

"The militia organizations in the opposite country of South Carolina [Edgefield] were engaged in disarming the Negroes. This created great discontent among the latter, and in some instances, they had offered resistance. In previous inspecting tours in South Carolina much complaint reached me of the misconduct of these militia companies towards the blacks. Some of the latter of the most intelligent and well-disposed came to me and said: 'What shall we do? These militia companies are heaping upon our people every sort of injury and insult unchecked. Our people are peaceably inclined and we are endeavoring to inculcate good feeling; but we cannot bear this treatment much longer.' Many are beginning to say:

" 'We have been patient long enough. We are free men now, and we have submitted to such usage as long as we can.' And again they ask: 'What shall we do?' I assured them that this conduct was not sanctioned by the United States military authorities, and that it would not be allowed." [37]

While the Negro was in power, most of the Southern states organized Negro militia. In South Carolina, 96,000 were thus nominally enrolled, and others in Louisiana and Texas in the militia and in the police. Nevertheless, the Reconstruction governors were afraid to use these militia lest they start race war, and the effort to arm and equip them efficiently was silently opposed. Usually it resulted that disarmed and unsuspecting black people were set upon by white forces superior in numbers, armed and disciplined, and with little chance of self-defense.

Meantime, a new power appeared upon the scene, or rather an old power of government paralyzed by the Civil War began to re-assert itself, and effectively stopped Northern Federal dictatorship to enforce democracy in the South. This was the Supreme Court. Johnson had had no chance to make appointments to the Supreme Court, although he had long relied upon that court to overthrow Reconstruction. The court, however, hesitated before overwhelming public opinion.

In 1870, Northern Big Business designated two railroad and corporation lawyers from Pennsylvania and New York for appointment. It was charged that they were purposely put on the bench in order to reverse the Legal Tender decision, and protect the bondholders in collecting at par debts contracted when paper money was at a discount of 30% to 60%. At any rate, they, together with one other appointment made in 1872-1874, changed the complexion of the Supreme Court, and when Waite was appointed Chief Justice, over the protest of Charles Sumner, the reconstructed court was ready for the appeals concerning the laws to enforce the Fourteenth and Fifteenth Amendments.

It is significant that the very center of Northern capitalistic power, which protected and buttressed the new monopoly of Big Business, turned, and with the same gesture freed land and capital in the South from any fear of control by black and white labor.

Cases on appeal reached that tribunal in 1876. Reverdy Johnson, Henry Stanbery, and others had striven to bring this to pass. They relied upon the court to do what Democratic members of Congress had failed to accomplish—and the court, through a process of reasoning very similar to that of Democratic legislators, deprived the enforcement legislation of nearly all its strength when it rendered its decisions in the cases of United States *vs.* Reese and United States *vs.* Cruikshank:

"The Fifteenth Amendment to the Constitution does not confer the right of suffrage," the court concluded in the first case. "The power of Congress to legislate at all upon the subject of voting at state elections rests upon this Amendment and can be exercised by providing a punishment only when the wrongful refusal to receive the vote of a qualified elector at such election is because of his race, color, or previous condition of servitude."

In the Cruikshank case, the court declared that "The right of suffrage is not a necessary attribute of national citizenship; but that exemption from discrimination in the exercise of that right on account of race, etc., is. The right to vote in the States comes from the States; but the right of exemption from the prohibited discrimination comes from the United States. The first has not been granted or secured by the Constitution of the United States; but the last has been. . . . The Fourteenth Amendment prohibits a state from denying to any person within its jurisdiction the equal protection of the laws, but this provision does not, any more than the one which preceded it, . . . add anything to the rights which one citizen has under the Constitution against another. The equality of the rights of citizens is a principle of republicanism. Every republican government is in duty bound to protect all its citizens in the enjoyment of this privilege if within its power. That duty was originally assumed by the state, and it still remains there. The only obligation resting upon the United States is to see that the states do not deny the right. This the amendment guarantees, but no more. The power of the national government is limited to the enforcement of the rights guaranteed." [37a]

Both the Fourteenth and Fifteenth Amendments were thus made innocuous so far as the Negro was concerned, and the Fourteenth Amendment in particular became the chief refuge and bulwark of corporations. It was thus that finance and the power of wealth accomplished through the Supreme Court what it had not been able to do successfully through Congress.

In 1876 came the bargain between Big Business and the South. At first, there was the attempt at direct bribery, in Louisiana, Florida and South Carolina. In one case in one state, a majority of the Board was said to have been secured if Tilden would pay $80,000. But this was rather too crude and direct. The work of 'Mr. Charles Foster, representative from the district of Rutherford Hayes in Ohio, was much more subtle and certain. Mr. Charles Foster, representative from Hayes' own district, stated in a speech in the Louisiana debate that it would be the policy of Mr. Hayes, if inaugurated, to wipe out "sectional lines; that under him the flag should wave over states, not provinces, over freemen, not subjects."

Negotiations were entered into and conferences held. On the 26th of February, 1876, there were three conferences. The outcome was an agreement. The Republicans guaranteed that Mr. Hayes, when he became President, would by non-interference and the withdrawal of troops allow the planter-capitalists, under the name of Democrats, to control South Carolina and Louisiana. They also agreed to induce President Grant to adopt the same policy before the end of his term. This meant that Southern landholders and capitalists would be put in complete control of disfranchised black labor. The Democrats promised to "guarantee peace, good order, protection of the law to whites and blacks"; or, in other words, exploitation should be so quiet, orderly and legal, as to assure regular profit to Southern owners and Northern investors. This bargain was so raw and obvious that it must not yet be submitted to public opinion. In order, therefore, to avoid bringing up the issue in the United States Senate, before the cabinet was confirmed, and perhaps preventing the confirmation of persons favorable to this Southern policy, the Democrats agreed not to elect the long-term Louisiana Senator until March 10th.

Other details were arranged next day. The Democratic assurances were ratified by Governor Nicholls of Louisiana, and a copy was sent North. Louisiana was told that Grant had promised that as soon as the count should be completed, to rescind or modify all orders to enforce the laws in the South. Foster sent an unsigned draft of a letter to Brown and to Senator Gordon:

"The Democrats thought the letter might be 'fuller and stronger,' but agreed to it. An hour later, the same letter signed was received from Foster."

The Democratic legislature, protected by armed members of the White League, declared Nicholls Governor. He was eventually recognized by the President, and Louisiana became Democratic. Federal troops were withdrawn under Hayes. The force behind the dictatorship of labor in the South disappeared. The last act was to appoint a Kentuckian and a Georgian to the Supreme Court. The deed was done.

Negroes did not surrender the ballot easily or immediately. They continued to hold remnants of political power in South Carolina and Florida, Louisiana, in parts of North Carolina, in Texas, Tennessee and Virginia. Black Congressmen came out of the South until 1895 and black legislators served as late as 1896. But it was a losing battle, with public opinion, industry, wealth, and religion against them. Their own leaders decried "politics" and preached submission. All their efforts toward manly self-assertion were distracted by defeatism and counsels of despair, backed by the powerful propaganda of a religion which taught meekness, sacrifice and humility.

But the decisive influence was the systematic and overwhelming economic pressure. Negroes who wanted work must not dabble in politics. Negroes who wanted to increase their income must not agitate the Negro problem. Positions of influence were only open to those Negroes who were certified as being "safe and sane," and their careers were closely scrutinized and passed upon. From 1880 onward, in order to earn a living, the American Negro was compelled to give up his political power.

There was an old remedy known since the eighteenth century, the colonization movement which had resulted in Liberia. In the first Negro convention held in Philadelphia in 1833, migration to Canada was discussed and recommended, and large numbers went there. In 1853, a convention at Rochester opposed emigration, but seceders called another convention, and this convention sent emissaries to Haiti, Africa and Central America. As a result, some two thousand Negroes went to Haiti.

The war stopped thoughts of emigration, except as Lincoln proposed it. After 1876, movements arose simultaneously in several states. The first conspicuous leader was Benjamin Singleton, a Negro undertaker in Tennessee, who took two colonies of 7,432 Negroes to Kansas. Henry Adams started an even greater movement in Louisiana, sending organizers into each state in the South. It claimed, by 1879, 92,800 members in Louisiana, Texas, Arkansas, Mississippi and Alabama. Altogether about 60,000 Negroes went to Kansas, two-thirds of whom were destitute when they arrived. Slow individual movements of Negroes from the South to the North kept up but there were no further mass movements until the World War.

Indeed, the whole matter of migration to escape the new régime in the South was complicated by the attitude of the North. Few Northern communities wanted Negro immigrants, and labor organizations opposed them, so that it was difficult to get work. Outside the United States, growing imperialism and the treatment of Liberia, Haiti and other small colored countries made emigration less attractive; and the United States government, by permitting the spreading of unfavorable reports and putting difficulties in the way of Negro travelers, has made colored migration to the West Indies and South America difficult even to this day.

The situation settled down to a new system and a new outlook in the South. The whole history of this post-Reconstruction development is yet to be written, but a few words concerning it may close this chapter.

First, there was systematic disfranchisement of the Negro. He was kept from voting by force, by economic intimidation, by propaganda designed to lead him to believe that there was no salvation for him in political lines but that he must depend entirely upon thrift and the good will of his white employers. Then came the series of disfranchisement laws discriminating against poverty and ignorance and aimed at the situation of the colored laborer, while the white laborer escaped by deliberate conniving and through the "understanding" and "Grandfather" clauses. To make assurance doubly sure, the "White Primary" system was built on top of this, by which the "Democratic" party confined its membership to white voters of all parties. The "White Primary" was made by law and public pressure the real voting arena in practically all Southern states.

This brings us to the situation when Booker T. Washington became the leader of the Negro race and advised them to depend upon industrial education and work rather than politics. The better class of Southern Negroes stopped voting for a generation. Then with the shift of population toward the North, there comes the present situation when out of 12,000,000 Negroes, 3,000,000 are in the North and 9,000,000 in the South. Those in the North and in Border States vote. Those in the South are seriously restricted in their voting, and this restriction means that their political power is exercised by the white South, which gives the white South an extraordinary political influence as compared with the voters of the North and East.

The disfranchisement of Negroes in the South became nearly complete. In no other civilized and modern land has so great a group of people, most of whom were able to read and write, been allowed so small a voice in their own government. Every promise of eventual recognition of the intelligent Negro voter has been broken. In the former slave states, from Virginia to Texas, excepting Missouri, there are no Negro state officials; no Negro members of legislatures; no judges on the bench; and usually no jurors. There are no colored county officials of any sort. In the towns and cities, there are no colored administrative officers, no members of the city councils, no magistrates, no constables and very seldom even a policeman. In this way, at least eight million Negroes are left without effective voice in government, naked to the worst elements of the community.

Beyond this, caste has been revived in a modern civilized land. It was supposed to be a relic of barbarism and existent only in Asia. But it has grown up and has been carefully nurtured and put on a legal basis with religious and moral sanctions in the South. First, it was presented and defended as "race" separation, but it was never mere race separation. It was always domination of blacks by white officials, white police and laws and ordinances made by white men. The schools were separate but the colored schools were controlled by white officials who decided how much or rather how little should be spent upon them; who decided what could be taught and what textbooks used and the sort of subservient teachers they wanted. In travel, separation compelled colored passengers to pay first-class fare for second- or third-class accommodations, and to endure on street cars and trains discrimination of all sorts. Ghettos were built up in nearly all Southern cities, not always sharply defined but pretty definite, and in these, Negroes must live, and in them white vice and crime might find shelter and Negro delinquency go unpoliced. Little attention was paid to lighting, sewerage and paving in these quarters.

Besides this, a determined psychology of caste was built up. In every possible way it was impressed and advertised that the white was superior and the Negro an inferior race. This inferiority must be publicly acknowledged and submitted to. Titles of courtesy were denied colored men and women. Certain signs of servility and usages amounting to public and personal insult were insisted upon. The most educated and deserving black man was compelled in many public places to occupy a place beneath the lowest and least deserving of the whites. Public institutions, like parks and libraries, either denied all accommodations to the blacks or gave them inferior facilities.

A distinguished white Southerner said in 1885:

"Is the freedman a free man? No. We have considered his position in a land whence nothing can, and no man has a shadow of a right to drive him, and where he is being multiplied as only oppression can multiply a people. We have carefully analyzed his relations to the finer and prouder race, with which he shares the ownership and citizenship of a region large enough for ten times the number of people. Without accepting one word of his testimony, we have shown that the laws made for his protection against the habits of suspicion and oppression in his late master are being constantly set aside, not for their defects, but for such merit as they possess. We have shown that the very natural source of these oppressions is the surviving sentiments of an extinct and now universally execrated institution; sentiments which no intelligent or moral people should harbor a moment after the admission that slavery was a moral mistake. We have shown the outrageousness of these tyrannies in some of their workings, and how distinctly they antagonize every State and national interest involved in the elevation of the colored race. Is it not well to have done so? For, I say again, the question has reached a moment of special importance. The South stands on her honor before the clean equities of the issue. It is no longer whether constitutional amendments, but whether the eternal principles of justice, are violated." [38]

With this went widespread and determined exploitation of black labor, and, of course, above all, taxation without representation. Taxation fell crushingly upon the poor, so that the proportion of taxes which the black laborer paid, according to income, was much larger than that borne by the rich whites or even the laboring whites. The Negro had no voice concerning this taxation, whether in the state, county, city, town, or district administration. He had little redress in the courts. The judges of the upper courts were usually selected from the better class of men whose fairness could be depended on so far as public opinion and their own sympathy with white exploiters would admit; but the police courts and magistrates' courts were in the hands of a wretched set of white Negro-hating politicians, and nine-tenths of the Negro court cases ended here and filled the chain-gangs with Negroes.

It was the policy of the state to keep the Negro laborer poor, to confine him as far as possible to menial occupations, to make him a surplus labor reservoir and to force him into peonage and unpaid toil.

In a report by the Hon. Charles W. Russell, Assistant Attorney General, to the Attorney General, in 1908, appears this language:

"I have no doubt from my investigations and experiences that the chief support of peonage is the peculiar system of State laws prevailing in the South, intended evidently to compel services on the part of the working man. From the usual condition of the great mass of laboring men where these laws are enforced, to peonage is but a step at most. In fact, it is difficult to draw a distinction between the condition of a man who remains in service against his will, because the State has passed a certain law under which he can be arrested and returned to work, and the condition of a man on a nearby farm who is actually made to stay at work by arrest and actual threats of force under the same law." [39]

The editor of the Macon, Georgia, *Telegraph* said recently:

"Since at least 1865, we have been holding back the Negro to keep him from getting beyond the white man. Our idea has been that the Negro should be kept poor. But by keeping him poor, we have thrown him into competition with ourselves and have kept ourselves poor.

"Of course, Governor Talmadge has the popular attitude. It is to hold the Negro down in order to make him work—to keep him poor. And Southerners are willing to keep themselves and their kind and section down and poor in order to keep the Negro that way." [40]

To make this policy effective it was necessary to keep the Negro ignorant and disorganized. Here, however, there were some difficulties. The Negroes had higher schools, supported largely by Northern philanthropy. They were turning out small but increasing numbers of educated men. There were, therefore, larger and larger numbers of trained teachers available for the public schools.

The North was not disposed at this time to defend universal suffrage or even democracy. But it did still believe in intelligence, so that the Negro public schools had to be kept open, and at the same time, the private schools which were furnishing teachers and leaders were depending not on state aid but on Northern philanthropy. This meant that a large and influential section of the North had direct contact and knowledge of the educated Negro. For a long time they defended the Negro college and normal school from all assaults. Indeed, it was not until the '90's that organized property in the North, uniting with Southern propaganda for Negro industrial education, made an assault upon the Negro college that almost overthrew it. But that is another story.

There were, nevertheless, numberless ways in which Negro schools could be and were decreased in efficiency; in the first place, the public school funds were distributed with open and unashamed discrimination. Anywhere from twice to ten times as much was spent on the white child as on the Negro child, and even then the poor white child did not receive an adequate education. In the Black Belt, particularly, large amounts of funds were drawn by the county officers because of black population and distributed among the whites to the extent of sending some to college. The Negro schools were given few buildings and little equipment. No effort was made to compel Negro children to go to school. On the contrary, in the country they were deliberately kept out of school by the requirements of contract labor which embraced the labor of wife and children as well as of the laborer himself. The course of study was limited. The school term was made and kept short and in many cases there was the deliberate effort, as expressed by one leading Southerner, Hoke Smith, when two Negro teachers applied for a school, to "take the less competent." The supervising officers paid little or no attention to Negro schools, and the education of the Negro for many years after the overthrow of Reconstruction proceeded in spite of their school system, not because of it.

An attempt was made through advocacy of so-called industrial education to divert the Negro schools from training in knowledge to training in crafts and industry. But here the white laborers, North and South, objected and practically no effective industrial training was ever given in the Southern public schools, except training for cooking and menial service.

Sickness, disease and death have been the widespread physical results of caste. The sick have had wretched care. Public hospitals supported by public funds turn Negroes away or segregate and neglect them in cellars and annexes. White physicians often despise their Negro clientele and colored physicians crowd into the larger towns and cities to escape the insult and insecurity to which the colored professional man is exposed in the country and smaller towns.

Above all, crime was used in the South as a source of income for the state. An English traveler wrote in 1871:

"I confess I am more and more suspicious about the criminal justice of these Southern states. In Georgia there is no regular penitentiary at all, but an organized system of letting out the prisoners for profit. Some people here have got up a company for the purpose of hiring convicts. They pay $25,000 a year besides all expenses of food and keep, so that their money is clear profit to the state. The lessees work the prisoners both on estates and in mines, and apparently maintain severe discipline in their own way, and make a good thing of it. Colonel P——, who is not very mealy-mouthed, admits that he left the concern because he could not stand the inhumanity of it. Another partner in the concern talked with great glee of the money he had made out of the convicts. This does seem simply a return to another form of slavery."

In no part of the modern world has there been so open and conscious a traffic in crime for deliberate social degradation and private profit as in the South since slavery. The Negro is not anti-social. He is no natural criminal. Crime of the vicious type, outside endeavor to achieve freedom or in revenge for cruelty, was rare in the slave South. Since 1876 Negroes have been arrested on the slightest provocation and given long sentences or fines which they were compelled to work out. The resulting peonage of criminals extended into every Southern state and led to the most revolting situations.

A Southern white woman writes:

"In some states where convict labor is sold to the highest bidder the cruel treatment of the helpless human chattel in the hands of guards is such as no tongue can tell nor pen picture. Prison inspectors find convicts herded together, irrespective of age; confined at night in shackles; housed sometimes, as has been found, in old box cars; packed almost as closely as sardines in a box. During the day all are worked under armed guards, who stand ready to shoot down any who may attempt to escape from this hell upon earth—the modern American bastile. Should one escape, the bloodhounds, trained for the purpose, are put upon his track, and the chances are that he will be brought back, severely flogged and put in double shackles, or worse."

"Of all the degrading positions, to our mind, that of the whipping boss in the Georgia penitentiary system is the worst. . . .

"He stands over his pinioned victim and applies the lash on the naked, quivering flesh of a fellowman. Plies it hard enough to lacerate the flesh and send the blood coursing down the bruised back and sides from the gaping and whip-cord cuts; and just think of the mercilessness, the inhumanity, the bestiality of the sentiment that can drive the lash deeper and deeper through the cuts and gashes on the body of a human being, white or black . . . just as a cool, calculating business for a very niggardly stipend." [41] Hundreds of Southern fortunes have been amassed by this enslavement of criminals.

George W. Cable protested in 1883 and wrote: "If anything may be inferred from the mortal results of the Lease System in other States, the year's death-rate of the convict camps of Louisiana must exceed that of any pestilence that ever fell upon Europe in the Middle Ages. And as far as popular rumor goes, it confirms this assumption on every hand. Every mention of these camps is followed by the execrations of a scandalized community whose ear is every now and then shocked afresh with some new whisper of their frightful barbarities. It is not for the present writer to assert that every other community where the leasing of convicts prevails is moved to indignation by the same sense of outrage and disgrace; yet it certainly would be but a charitable assumption to believe that the day is not remote when in every such region, the sentiment of the people will write, over the gates of the convict stockades and over the doors of the lessees' sumptuous homes, one word: Aceldama—the field of blood." [42]

The normal amount of crime which an ignorant working population would have evolved has been tremendously increased. Young criminals and vagrants were deliberately multiplied and this in turn made an excuse for mob law and lynching. Colored women were looked upon as the legitimate prey of white men and protection for them even against colored men was seldom furnished.

While all instruments of group control—police, courts, government appropriations and the like—were in the hands of whites, no power was left in Negro hands. If a white man is assaulted by a white man or a Negro the police are at hand. If a Negro is assaulted by a white man, the police are more apt to arrest the victim than the aggressor; if he is assaulted by a Negro, he is in most cases without redress or protection, and the group-will of the colored man has no power to express itself.

Inter-racial sex jealousy and accompanying sadism has been made the wide foundation of mobs and lynching. With thousands of white fathers of colored children, there is scarcely a case on record where such a father has been held legally responsible.

Such evils led to widespread violence in the South, to murder and mobs. Probably in no country in the civilized world did human life become so cheap. This condition prevails among both white and black and characterizes the South even to our day. A spirit of lawlessness became widespread. White people paid no attention to their own laws. White men became a law unto themselves, and black men, so far as their aggressions were confined to their own people, need not fear intervention of white police. Practically all men went armed and the South reached the extraordinary distinction of being the only modern civilized country where human beings were publicly burned alive. Southern papers specialized on Negro crime with ridicule and coarse caricature. The police court where hearts bled was a matter of hilarious newspaper laughter while a note of decency and success among Negroes was buried on a back page or ignored entirely.

The political success of the doctrine of racial separation, which overthrew Reconstruction by uniting the planter and the poor white, was far exceeded by its astonishing economic results. The theory of laboring class unity rests upon the assumption that laborers, despite internal jealousies, will unite because of their opposition to exploitation by the capitalists. According to this, even after a part of the poor white laboring class became identified with the planters, and eventually displaced them, their interests would be diametrically opposed to those of the mass of white labor, and of course to those of the black laborers. This would throw white and black labor into one class, and precipitate a united fight for higher wage and better working conditions.

Most persons do not realize how far this failed to work in the South, and it failed to work because the theory of race was supplemented by a carefully planned and slowly evolved method, which drove such a wedge between the white and black workers that there probably are not today in the world two groups of workers with practically identical interests who hate and fear each other so deeply and persistently and who are kept so far apart that neither sees anything of common interest.

It must be remembered that the white group of laborers, while they received a low wage, were compensated in part by a sort of public and psychological wage. They were given public deference and titles of courtesy because they were white. They were admitted freely with all classes of white people to public functions, public parks, and the best schools. The police were drawn from their ranks, and the courts, dependent upon their votes, treated them with such leniency as to encourage lawlessness. Their vote selected public officials, and while this had small effect upon the economic situation, it had great effect upon their personal treatment and the deference shown them. White schoolhouses were the best in the community, and conspicuously placed, and they cost anywhere from twice to ten times as much per capita as the colored schools. The newspapers specialized on news that flattered the poor whites and almost utterly ignored the Negro except in crime and ridicule.

On the other hand, in the same way, the Negro was subject to public insult; was afraid of mobs; was liable to the jibes of children and the unreasoning fears of white women; and was compelled almost continuously to submit to various badges of inferiority. The result of this was that the wages of both classes could be kept low, the whites fearing to be supplanted by Negro labor, the Negroes always being threatened by the substitution of white labor.

Mob violence and lynching were the inevitable result of the attitude of these two classes and for a time were a sort of permissible Roman holiday for the entertainment of vicious whites. One can see for these reasons why labor organizers and labor agitators made such small headway in the South. They were, for the most part, appealing to laborers who would rather have low wages upon which they could eke out an existence than see colored labor with a decent wage. White labor saw in every advance of Negroes a threat to their racial prerogatives, so that in many districts Negroes were afraid to build decent homes or dress well, or own carriages, bicycles or automobiles, because of possible retaliation on the part of the whites.

Thus every problem of labor advance in the South was skillfully turned by demagogues into a matter of inter-racial jealousy. Perhaps the most conspicuous proof of this was the Atlanta riot in 1906, which followed Hoke Smith's vicious attempt to become United States Senator on a platform which first attacked corporations and then was suddenly twisted into scandalous traducing of the Negro race.

To this day no casual and unsophisticated reader of the white Southern press could possibly gather that the American Negro masses were anything but degraded, ignorant, inefficient examples of an incurably inferior race.

The result of all this had to be unfortunate for the Negro. He was a caged human being, driven into a curious mental provincialism. An inferiority complex dominated him. He did not believe himself a man like other men. He could not teach his children self-respect. The Negro as a group gradually lost his manners, his courtesy, his light-hearted kindliness. Large numbers sank into apathy and fatalism! There was no chance for the black man; there was no use in striving; ambition was not for Negroes.

The effect of caste on the moral integrity of the Negro race in America has thus been widely disastrous; servility and fawning, gross flattery of white folk and lying to appease and cajole them; failure to achieve dignity and self-respect and moral self-assertion, personal cowardliness and submission to insult and aggression; exaggerated and despicable humility; lack of faith of Negroes in themselves and in other Negroes and in all colored folk; inordinate admiration for the stigmata of success among white folk: wealth and arrogance, cunning dishonesty and assumptions of superiority; the exaltation of laziness and indifference as just as successful as the industry and striving which invites taxation and oppression; dull apathy and cynicism; faith in no future and the habit of moving and wandering in search of justice; a religion of prayer and submission to replace determination and effort.

These are not universal results or else the Negro long since would have dwindled and died in crime and disease. But they are so widespread as to bring inner conflict as baffling as the problems of interracial relations, and they hold back the moral grit and organized effort which are the only hope of survival.

On this and in spite of this comes an extraordinary record of accomplishment, a record so contradictory of what one might easily expect that many people and even the Negroes themselves are deceived by it. The real question is not so much what the Negro has done in spite of caste, as what he might have accomplished with reasonable encouragement. He has cut down his illiteracy more than two-thirds in fifty years, but with decent schools it ought to have been cut down 99 per cent. He has accumulated land and property, but has not been able to hold one-tenth of that which he has rightly earned. He has achieved success in many lines, as an inventor, scientist, scholar and writer. But most of his ability has been choked in chain-gangs and by open deliberate discrimination and conspiracies of silence. He has made a place for himself in literature and art, but the great deeps of his artistic gifts have never yet been plumbed. And yet, for all that he has accomplished, not only the nation but the South itself claims credit and actually points to it as proof of the wisdom or at least the innocuousness of organized suppression!

It is but human experience to find that the complete suppression of a race is impossible. Despite inner discouragement and submission to the oppression of others there persisted the mighty spirit, the emotional rebound that kept a vast number struggling for its rights, for self-expression, and for social uplift. Such men, in many cases, became targets for the white race. They were denounced as trouble makers.

They were denied opportunity. They were driven from their homes. They were lynched.

It is doubtful if there is another group of twelve million people in the midst of a modern cultured land who are so widely inhibited and mentally confined as the American Negro. Within the colored race the philosophy of salvation has by the pressure of caste been curiously twisted and distorted. Shall they use the torch and dynamite? Shall they go North, or fight it out in the South? Shall they segregate themselves even more than they are now, in states, towns, cities or sections? Shall they leave the country? Are they Americans or foreigners? Shall they stand and sing "My Country 'Tis of Thee"? Shall they marry and rear children and save and buy homes, or deliberately commit race suicide?

Ordinarily such questions within a group settle themselves by laboratory experiment. It is shown that violence does not pay, that quiet persistent effort wins; bitterness and pessimism prove a handicap. And yet in the case of the Negro it is almost impossible to obtain such definite laboratory results. Failure cannot be attributed to individual neglect, and success does not necessarily follow individual effort. It is impossible to disentangle the results of caste and the results of work and striving. Ordinarily a group experiments—tries now this, now that, measures results and eliminates bad advice and unwise action by achieving success. But here success is so curtailed and frustrated that guiding wisdom fails. Why should we save? What good does it do to be upstanding, with self-respect? Who gains by thrift, or rises by education?

Such mental frustration cannot indefinitely continue. Some day it may burst in fire and blood. Who will be to blame? And where the greater cost? Black folk, after all, have little to lose, but Civilization has all.

This the American black man knows: his fight here is a fight to the finish. Either he dies or wins. If he wins it will be by no subterfuge or evasion of amalgamation. He will enter modern civilization here in America as a black man on terms of perfect and unlimited equality with any white man, or he will enter not at all. Either extermination root and branch, or absolute equality. There can be no compromise. This is the last great battle of the West.

Evil results of the revolution of 1876 have not been confined to Negroes. The reaction on the whites was just as significant. The white people of the South are essentially a fine kindly breed, the same sort of human beings that one finds the world over. Perhaps their early and fatal mistake was when they refused long before the Civil War to allow in the South differences of opinion. They would not let honest white Southerners continue to talk against slavery. They drove out the noncontormist; they would not listen to the radical. The result was that there has been built up in the South an intolerance fatal to human culture. Men act as they do in the South, they murder, they lynch, they insult, because they listen to but one side of a question. They seldom know by real human contact Negroes who are men. They read books that laud the South and the "Lost Cause," but they are childish and furious when criticized, and interpret all criticism as personal attack.

The result is that the South in the main is ranged against liberalism. No liberal movement in the United States or in the world has been able to make advance among Southerners. They are militaristic and will have nothing to do with a peace movement. Young Southerners eagerly crowd West Point and Annapolis. The South is not interested in freedom for dark India. It has no sympathy with the oppressed of Africa or of Asia. It is for the most part against unions and the labor movement, because there can be no real labor movement in the South; their laboring class is cut in two and the white laborers must be ranged upon the side of their own exploiters by persistent propaganda and police force. Labor can gain in the South no class-consciousness. Strikes cannot be effective because the white striker can be threatened with the colored "scab" and the colored striker can be clapped in jail.

The result of the disfranchisement of the Negro on the political life of the South has been pitiful. Southerners argued that if the Negro was disfranchised, normal political life would be possible for the South. They did not realize that a living working class can never lose its political power and that all they did in 1876 was to transfer that political power from the hands of labor to the hands of capital, where it has been concentrated ever since. Moreover, after that transfer the forms of republican government became a continuing farce.

As Chamberlain said: "Every present citizen of South Carolina knows, and those who are truthful and frank will confess that the ballot debauched in 1876 remains debauched; the violence taught them remains now, if not in the same, in other forms; the defiance of law learned then in what was called a good cause survives in the horrid orgies of degradation and of lynchings." [43]

There can be no doubt that the revolution of 1876 established fraud and oligarchy in the South and the remains of that régime are still with us. Local government in the South to this day is handicapped and frustrated by caste and by the use of the color line to divide the electorate and dominate the Negro. As late as 1931, the Atlanta *Constitution* said of the Georgia legislature: "Never in its history has Georgia been inflicted with so incompetent a legislature as the one just adjourned."

George W. Cable said in 1885: "The vote, after all, was a secondary point, and the robbery and bribery on one side, and whipping and killing on the other were but huge accidents of the situation. The two main questions were really these: on the freedman's side, how to establish republican state government under the same recognition of his rights that the rest of Christendom accorded him; and on the former master's side, how to get back to the old semblance of republican state government, and—allowing that the freedman was de facto a voter—still to maintain a purely arbitrary superiority of all whites over all blacks, and a purely arbitrary equality of all blacks among themselves as an alien, menial and dangerous class.

"Exceptionally here and there someone in the master caste did throw off the old and accept the new ideas, and, if he would allow it, was instantly claimed as a leader by the newly liberated thousands around him. But just as promptly the old master race branded him also an alien reprobate, and in ninety-nine cases out of a hundred, if he had not already done so, he soon began to confirm by his actions the brand of his cheek."

The paradox of this whole muddle is that what the South started to do in 1876 was never accomplished and never will be. The Negro cannot be disfranchised. He votes in every policy and the only result of disfranchisement is to bind the white South hand and foot and deliver it to its own worst self. Stevens and Sumner stand eternally vindicated.

Particularly has the South suffered spiritually by the effort to use propaganda and enforce belief. This always results in deliberate lying. Not that all white Southerners deliberately lie about the Negro, but to an astonishing degree the honest South allows known lies to stand uncontradicted.

The wide distortion of facts which became prevalent in the white South during and after Reconstruction as a measure of self-defense has never been wholly crushed since. For years Southerners denied that there was any fraud and cheating in elections. Henry Grady stood in Boston and told New England that the Negro was as free to vote in the South as the white laborer was in the North. Booker T. Washington repeatedly testified as to the good will and essential honesty of purpose of Southerners and put the whole burden of responsibility for advance upon the Negro himself. "The Southern white man is the Negro's best friend," scream all the Southern papers, even today. And this in the face of the open record of five thousand lynchings, jails bursting with black prisoners incarcerated on trivial and trumped-up charges, and caste staring from every train and street car.

This whole phantasmagoria has been built on the most miserable of human fictions: that in addition to the manifest differences between men there is a deep, awful and ineradicable cleft which condemns most men to eternal degradation. It is a cheap inheritance of the world's infancy, unworthy of grown folk. My rise does not involve your fall. No superior has interest in inferiority. Humanity is one and its vast variety is its glory and not its condemnation. If all men make the best of themselves, if all men have the chance to meet and know each other, the result is the love born of knowledge and not the hate based on ignorance.

The result of this upon the higher life in the South is extraordinary. Fundamentalism rules in religion because men hesitate openly to reason about the Golden Rule. Literature, art and music are curiously dominated by the Negro. The only literature the South has had for years is based largely upon the Negro. Southern music is Negro music. Yet Negroes themselves are seldom recognized as interpreters of art, and white artists must work under severe social limitations and at second hand; they thus lack necessary sincerity, depth and frankness.

Democracy in the South and in the United States is hampered by the Southern attitude. The Southerner, by winning the victory which the Fourteenth Amendment tried to deny, uses the Negro population as a basis of his political representation and allows few Negroes to vote; so that the white Southerner marches to the polls with many times as much voting power in his hand as the voter in the North.

The South does and must vote for reaction. There can be, therefore, neither in the South nor in the nation a successful third party movement. This was proven in the case of Theodore Roosevelt and LaFollette. A solid bloc of reaction in the South can always be depended upon to unite with Northern conservatism to elect a president.

One can only say to all this that whatever the South gained through its victory in the revolution of 1876 has been paid for at a price which literally staggers humanity. Imperialism, the exploitation of colored labor throughout the world, thrives upon the approval of the United States, and the United States gives that approval because of the South. World war waits on and supports imperial aggression and international jealousy. This was too great a price to pay for anything which the South gained.

The chief obstacle in this rich realm of the United States, endowed with every natural resource and with the abilities of a hundred different peoples—the chief and only obstacle to the coming of that kingdom of economic equality which is the only logical end of work is the determination of the white world to keep the black world poor and themselves rich. A clear vision of a world without inordinate individual wealth, of capital without profit and of income based on work alone, is the path out, not only for America but for all men. Across this path stands the South with flaming sword.

Of course, it would be humanly impossible for any such régime to be completely successful anywhere without protest and reaction from within. Alms-giving to Negroes in the South has always been almost universal. Even petty pilfering has been winked at. Beyond this, and of far greater social significance, have been the personal friendships between blacks and whites with aid and advice, even at great pecuniary and spiritual costs. Large-hearted Southern white men and women have in unnumbered cases quietly and without advertisement done enormous work to make life bearable and success possible for thousands of Negroes.

Most of the benevolence of this sort, however, has been of a personal and individual matter. In only a minority of cases have such Southern white people been willing to stand on principle and demand for all Negroes rights as men and treatment according to desert. When in some cases such opinion and clear advocacy has been made and has consequently evoked the usual social punishment, it is singular and almost peculiar to the South how seldom Southern whites have had the courage to stand up and suffer for righteousness' sake against the mass terror of public opinion.

In the South the iconoclast, the martyr, not only on the Negro question, but on other moral matters, have been conspicuously absent; and where they have arisen, they have soon either subsided into silence or retreated to the more tolerant atmosphere of the North, leaving the South all the poorer and all the more easily hammered into conformity with the mob.

If white and black in the South were free and intelligent there would be friendship and some intermarriage and there ought to be; but none would marry where he did not wish to, and there could be no greater intermingling in the future than in the shameful past, unless this union of races proved successful and attractive.

The revolution of 1876 was, in fine, a victory for which the South has every right to hang its head. After enslaving the Negro for two and one-half centuries, it turned on his emancipation to beat a beaten man, to trade in slaves, and to kill the defenseless; to break the spirit of the black man and humiliate him into hopelessness; to establish a new dictatorship of property in the South through the color line. It was a triumph of men who in their effort to replace equality with caste and to build inordinate wealth on a foundation of abject poverty have succeeded in killing democracy, art and religion.

And yet, despite this, and despite the long step backward toward slavery that black folk have been pushed, they have made withal a brave and fine fight; a fight against ridicule and monstrous caricature, against every refinement of cruelty and gross insult, against starvation, disease and murder in every form. It has left in their soul its scars, its deep scars; but when all is said, through it all has gone a thread of brave and splendid friendship from those few and rare men and women of white skins, North and South, who have dared to know and help and love black folk.

The unending tragedy of Reconstruction is the utter inability of the American mind to grasp its real significance, its national and world-wide implications. It was vain for Sumner and Stevens to hammer in the ears of the people that this problem involved the very foundations of American democracy, both political and economic. We are still too blind and infatuated to conceive of the emancipation of the laboring class in half the nation as a revolution comparable to the upheavals in France in the past, and in Russia, Spain, India and China today. We were worried when the beginnings of this experiment cost Eighteen Millions of Dollars, and quite aghast when a debt of Two Hundred and Twenty-Five Millions was involved, including waste and theft. We apparently expected that this social upheaval was going to be accomplished with peace, honesty and efficiency, and that the planters were going quietly to surrender the right to live on the labor of black folk, after two hundred and fifty years of habitual exploitation. And it seems to America a proof of inherent race inferiority that four million slaves did not completely emancipate themselves in eighty years, in the midst of nine million bitter enemies, and indifferent public opinion of the whole nation. If the Reconstruction of the Southern states, from slavery to free labor, and from aristocracy to industrial democracy, had been conceived as a major national program of America, whose accomplishment at any price was well worth the effort, we should be living today in a different world.

The attempt to make black men American citizens was in a certain sense all a failure, but a splendid failure. It did not fail where it was expected to fail. It was Athanasius contra mundum, with back to the wall, outnumbered ten to one, with all the wealth and all the opportunity, and all the world against him. And only in his hands and heart the consciousness of a great and just cause; fighting the battle of all the oppressed and despised humanity of every race and color, against the massed hirelings of Religion, Science, Education, Law, and brute force.

For he has a pall, this wretched man,
Such as few men can claim;
Deep down below a prison-yard,
Naked, for greater shame,
He lies, with fetters on each foot,
Wrapt in a sheet of flame! ...

OSCAR WILDE

1. 39th Congress, 1st Session, Senate Executive Documents No. 2, Report of Carl Schurz.
2. Smedes, *Memoirs of a Southern Planter*, p. 232.
3. *Reconstruction Report*, Part 2, p. 196.
4. *Reconstruction Report*, Part 2, p. 208.
5. *Reconstruction Report*, Part 3, p. 4.
6. Haworth, *The Hayes-Tilden Disputed Presidential Election of 1876*, p. 83.
7. *Reconstruction Report*, pp. 104-105.
8. Nordhoff, *The Cotton States*, p. 16.
9. Milner, *Ku Klux Klan*, p. 6.
10. *Ku Klux Klan Report, South Carolina*, Part 1, p. 285.
11. *Ku Klux Klan Report, Alabama*, Part 3, pp. 1649-1656.
12. *Ku Klux Klan Report, Alabama*, Part 2, p. 676.
13. Beard, *A Crusade of Brotherhood*, p. 139.
14. Haworth, *The Hayes-Tilden Disputed Presidential Election of 1876*, p. 125.
15. *Reconstruction Report*, Part 2, pp. 231-240.
16. *Ku Klux Klan Report*, XIII, pp. 221-224.
17. White, *Autobiography*, I, p. 489.
18. Brewster, *Sketches*, p. 41.
19. Cited in Cox, pp. 551-552.
20. Oberholtzer, *History of the United States Since the Civil War*, II, p. 366. Compare *Report of the Secretary of War*, 1868-1869, pp. 303-304.
21. Oberholtzer, *History of the United States Since the Civil War*, II, p. 366. Compare *House Miscellaneous Documents*, 41st Congress, 2nd Session, No. 154, Part I, p. 199.
22. Oberholtzer, *History of the United States Since the Civil War*, II, p. 366. Compare *House Miscellaneous Documents*, 41st Congress, 2nd Session, No. 154, Part I, p. 131.
23. Oberholtzer, *History of the United States Since the Civil War*, II, p. 365. Compare *House Miscellaneous Documents*, 41st Congress, 2nd Session, No. 154, Part I, p. 22.
24. Oberholtzer, *History of the United States During the Civil War*, II, pp. 365-366.
25. *House Mis. Documents*, 41st Congress, 2nd Session, No. 154, Part 1, pp. 32-33.
26. Woolley, "Grant's Southern Policy," in *Studies in Southern History and Politics*, p. 198.
27. Woolley, "Grant's Southern Policy," in *Studies in Southern History and Politics*, p. 199.
28. Simkins and Woody, *South Carolina During Reconstruction*, pp. 566-568.
29. Woolley, "Grant's Southern Policy," in *Studies in Southern History and Politics*, p. 198.
30. Tillman, *Struggles of 1876*, p. 66.
31. Simkins and Woody, *South Carolina During Reconstruction*, p. 515.
32. Tillman, *Struggles of 1876*, p. 38.
33. Simkins and Woody, *South Carolina During Reconstruction*, p. 515.
34. *House of Representatives Reports*, 42nd Congress, 2nd Session, Report No. 22, II, Part 1, p. 99.
35. *Ibid.*, p. 292.

36. *House of Representatives Reports*, 42nd Congress, 2nd Session, Report No. 22, II, Part 1, p. 517.
37. *Reconstruction Report*, Part 3, p. 46.
37a. U. S. *v.* Reese, 92, U. S. 214; U. S. *v.* Cruikshank, 92, U. S. 542.
38. Cable, *Silent South*, p. 36.
39. *Occasional Papers*, American Negro Academy, No. 15, p. 10.
40. Macon *Telegraph*, October 18, November 3, 1933.
41. Keeler, *American Bastilles*, pp. 7, 8.
42. Cable, *Silent South*, p. 171.
43. *Atlantic Monthly*, LXXXVII, p. 483.

XVII. THE PROPAGANDA OF HISTORY

How the facts of American history have in the last half century
been falsified because the nation was ashamed. The South was
ashamed because it fought to perpetuate human slavery. The North
was ashamed because it had to call in the black men to save the
Union, abolish slavery and establish democracy

What are American children taught today about Reconstruction?
Helen Boardman has made a study of current textbooks and notes
these three dominant theses:

1. *All Negroes were ignorant.*

"All were ignorant of public business." (Woodburn and Moran,
"Elementary American History and Government," p. 397.)

"Although the Negroes were now free, they were also ignorant and
unfit to govern themselves." (Everett Barnes, "American History for
Grammar Grades," p. 334.)

"The Negroes got control of these states. They had been slaves all
their lives, and were so ignorant they did not even know the letters
of the alphabet. Yet they now sat in the state legislatures and made
the laws." (D. H. Montgomery, "The Leading Facts of American History," p. 332.)

"In the South, the Negroes who had so suddenly gained their freedom did not know what to do with it." (Hubert Cornish and Thomas
Hughes, "History of the United States for Schools," p. 345.)

"In the legislatures, the Negroes were so ignorant that they could
only watch their white leaders—carpetbaggers, and vote aye or no
as they were told." (S. E. Forman, "Advanced American History,"
Revised Edition, p. 452.)

"Some legislatures were made up of a few dishonest white men
and several Negroes, many too ignorant to know anything about
law-making." (Hubert Cornish and Thomas Hughes, "History of the
United States for Schools," p. 349.)

2. *All Negroes were lazy, dishonest and extravagant.*

"These men knew not only nothing about the government, but also
cared for nothing except what they could gain for themselves." (Helen
F. Giles, "How the United States Became a World Power," p. 7.)

"Legislatures were often at the mercy of Negroes, childishly ignorant, who sold their votes openly, and whose 'loyalty' was gained by

allowing them to eat, drink and clothe themselves at the state's expense." (William J. Long, "America—A History of Our Country," p. 392.)

"Some Negroes spent their money foolishly, and were worse off than they had been before." (Carl Russell Fish, "History of America," p. 385.)

"This assistance led many freed men to believe that they need no longer work. They also ignorantly believed that the lands of their former masters were to be turned over by Congress to them, and that every Negro was to have as his allotment 'forty acres and a mule.'" (W. F. Gordy, "History of the United States," Part II, p. 336.)

"Thinking that slavery meant toil and that freedom meant only idleness, the slave after he was set free was disposed to try out his freedom by refusing to work." (S. E. Forman, "Advanced American History," Revised Edition.)

"They began to wander about, stealing and plundering. In one week, in a Georgia town, 150 Negroes were arrested for thieving." (Helen F. Giles, "How the United States Became a World Power," p. 6.)

3. *Negroes were responsible for bad government during Reconstruction:*

"Foolish laws were passed by the black law-makers, the public money was wasted terribly and thousands of dollars were stolen straight. Self-respecting Southerners chafed under the horrible régime." (Emerson David Fite, "These United States," p. 37.)

"In the exhausted states already amply 'punished' by the desolation of war, the rule of the Negro and his unscrupulous carpetbagger and scalawag patrons, was an orgy of extravagance, fraud and disgusting incompetency." (David Saville Muzzey, "History of the American People," p. 408.)

"The picture of Reconstruction which the average pupil in these sixteen States receives is limited to the South. The South found it necessary to pass Black Codes for the control of the shiftless and sometimes vicious freedmen. The Freedmen's Bureau caused the Negroes to look to the North rather than to the South for support and by giving them a false sense of equality did more harm than good. With the scalawags, the ignorant and non-propertyholding Negroes under the leadership of the carpetbaggers, engaged in a wild orgy of spending in the legislatures. The humiliation and distress of the Southern whites was in part relieved by the Ku Klux Klan, a secret organization which frightened the superstitious blacks." [1]

Grounded in such elementary and high school teaching, an American youth attending college today would learn from current textbooks of history that the Constitution recognized slavery; that the chance of getting rid of slavery by peaceful methods was ruined by the Abolitionists; that after the period of Andrew Jackson, the two sections of the United States "had become fully conscious of their conflicting interests. Two irreconcilable forms of civilization . . . in the North, the democratic . . . in the South, a more stationary and aristocratic civilization." He would read that Harriet Beecher Stowe brought on the Civil War; that the assault on Charles Sumner was due to his "coarse invective" against a South Carolina Senator; and that Negroes were the only people to achieve emancipation with no effort on their part. That Reconstruction was a disgraceful attempt to subject white people to ignorant Negro rule; and that, according to a Harvard professor of history (the italics are ours), "Legislative expenses were grotesquely extravagant; the *colored members in some states engaging in a saturnalia of corrupt expenditure*" (Encyclopaedia Britannica, 14th Edition, Volume 22, p. 815, by Frederick Jackson Turner).

In other words, he would in all probability complete his education without any idea of the part which the black race has played in America; of the tremendous moral problem of abolition; of the cause and meaning of the Civil War and the relation which Reconstruction had to democratic government and the labor movement today.

Herein lies more than mere omission and difference of emphasis. The treatment of the period of Reconstruction reflects small credit upon American historians as scientists. We have too often a deliberate attempt so to change the facts of history that the story will make pleasant reading for Americans. The editors of the fourteenth edition of the Encyclopaedia Britannica asked me for an article on the history of the American Negro. From my manuscript they cut out all my references to Reconstruction. I insisted on including the following statement:

"White historians have ascribed the faults and failures of Reconstruction to Negro ignorance and corruption. But the Negro insists that it was Negro loyalty and the Negro vote alone that restored the South to the Union; established the new democracy, both for white and black, and instituted the public schools."

This the editor refused to print, although he said that the article otherwise was "in my judgment, and in the judgment of others in the office, an excellent one, and one with which it seems to me we may all be well satisfied." I was not satisfied and refused to allow the article to appear.

War and especially civil strife leave terrible wounds. It is the duty of humanity to heal them. It was therefore soon conceived as neither wise nor patriotic to speak of all the causes of strife and the terrible results to which sectional differences in the United States had led. And so, first of all, we minimized the slavery controversy which convulsed the nation from the Missouri Compromise down to the Civil War. On top of that, we passed by Reconstruction with a phrase of regret or disgust.

But are these reasons of courtesy and philanthropy sufficient for denying Truth? If history is going to be scientific, if the record of human action is going to be set down with that accuracy and faithfulness of detail which will allow its use as a measuring rod and guidepost for the future of nations, there must be set some standards of ethics in research and interpretation.

If, on the other hand, we are going to use history for our pleasure and amusement, for inflating our national ego, and giving us a false but pleasurable sense of accomplishment, then we must give up the idea of history either as a science or as an art using the results of science, and admit frankly that we are using a version of historic fact in order to influence and educate the new generation along the way we wish.

It is propaganda like this that has led men in the past to insist that history is "lies agreed upon"; and to point out the danger in such misinformation. It is indeed extremely doubtful if any permanent benefit comes to the world through such action. Nations reel and stagger on their way; they make hideous mistakes; they commit frightful wrongs; they do great and beautiful things. And shall we not best guide humanity by telling the truth about all this, so far as the truth is ascertainable?

Here in the United States we have a clear example. It was morally wrong and economically retrogressive to build human slavery in the United States in the eighteenth century. We know that now, perfectly well; and there were many Americans North and South who knew this and said it in the eighteenth century. Today, in the face of new slavery established elsewhere in the world under other names and guises, we ought to emphasize this lesson of the past. Moreover, it is not well to be reticent in describing that past. Our histories tend to discuss American slavery so impartially, that in the end nobody seems to have done wrong and everybody was right. Slavery appears to have been thrust upon unwilling helpless America, while the South was blameless in becoming its center. The difference of development, North and South, is explained as a sort of working out of cosmic social and economic law.

One reads, for instance, Charles and Mary Beard's "Rise of American Civilization," with a comfortable feeling that nothing right or wrong is involved. Manufacturing and industry develop in the North; agrarian feudalism develops in the South. They clash, as winds and waters strive, and the stronger forces develop the tremendous industrial machine that governs us so magnificently and selfishly today.

Yet in this sweeping mechanistic interpretation, there is no room for the real plot of the story, for the clear mistake and guilt of rebuilding a new slavery of the working class in the midst of a fateful experiment in democracy; for the triumph of sheer moral courage and sacrifice in the abolition crusade; and for the hurt and struggle of degraded black millions in their fight for freedom and their attempt to enter democracy. Can all this be omitted or half suppressed in a treatise that calls itself scientific?

Or, to come nearer the center and climax of this fascinating history: What was slavery in the United States? Just what did it mean to the owner and the owned? Shall we accept the conventional story of the old slave plantation and its owner's fine, aristocratic life of cultured leisure? Or shall we note slave biographies, like those of Charles Ball, Sojourner Truth, Harriet Tubman and Frederick Douglass; the careful observations of Olmsted and the indictment of Hinton Helper?

No one can read that first thin autobiography of Frederick Douglass and have left many illusions about slavery. And if truth is our object, no amount of flowery romance and the personal reminiscences of its protected beneficiaries can keep the world from knowing that slavery was a cruel, dirty, costly and inexcusable anachronism, which nearly ruined the world's greatest experiment in democracy. No serious and unbiased student can be deceived by the fairy tale of a beautiful Southern slave civilization. If those who really had opportunity to know the South before the war wrote the truth, it was a center of widespread ignorance, undeveloped resources, suppressed humanity and unrestrained passions, with whatever veneer of manners and culture that could lie above these depths.

Coming now to the Civil War, how for a moment can anyone who reads the *Congressional Globe* from 1850 to 1860, the lives of contemporary statesmen and public characters, North and South, the discourses in the newspapers and accounts of meetings and speeches, doubt that Negro slavery was the cause of the Civil War? What do we gain by evading this clear fact, and talking in vague ways about "Union" and "State Rights" and differences in civilization as the cause of that catastrophe?

Of all historic facts there can be none clearer than that for four long and fearful years the South fought to perpetuate human slavery; and that the nation which "rose so bright and fair and died so pure of stain" was one that had a perfect right to be ashamed of its birth and glad of its death. Yet one monument in North Carolina achieves the impossible by recording of Confederate soldiers: "They died fighting for liberty!"

On the other hand, consider the North and the Civil War. Why should we be deliberately false, like Woodward, in "Meet General Grant," and represent the North as magnanimously freeing the slave without any effort on his part?

"The American Negroes are the only people in the history of the world, so far as I know, that ever became free without any effort of their own. . . .

"They had not started the war nor ended it. They twanged banjos around the railroad stations, sang melodious spirituals, and believed that some Yankee would soon come along and give each of them forty acres of land and a mule." [1a]

The North went to war without the slightest idea of freeing the slave. The great majority of Northerners from Lincoln down pledged themselves to protect slavery, and they hated and harried Abolitionists. But on the other hand, the thesis which Beale tends to support that the whole North during and after the war was chiefly interested in making money, is only half true; it was abolition and belief in democracy that gained for a time the upper hand after the war and led the North in Reconstruction; business followed abolition in order to maintain the tariff, pay the bonds and defend the banks. To call this business program "the program of the North" and ignore abolition is unhistorical. In growing ascendancy for a calculable time was a great moral movement which turned the North from its economic defense of slavery and led it to Emancipation. Abolitionists attacked slavery because it was wrong and their moral battle cannot be truthfully minimized or forgotten. Nor does this fact deny that the majority of Northerners before the war were not abolitionists, that they attacked slavery only in order to win the war and enfranchised the Negro to secure this result.

One has but to read the debates in Congress and state papers from Abraham Lincoln down to know that the decisive action which ended the Civil War was the emancipation and arming of the black slave; that, as Lincoln said: "Without the military help of black freedmen, the war against the South could not have been won." The freedmen, far from being the inert recipients of freedom at the hands of philanthropists, furnished 200,000 soldiers in the Civil War who took part in nearly 200 battles and skirmishes, and in addition perhaps 300,000 others as effective laborers and helpers. In proportion to population, more Negroes than whites fought in the Civil War. These people, withdrawn from the support of the Confederacy, with threat of the withdrawal of millions more, made the opposition of the slaveholder useless, unless they themselves freed and armed their own slaves. This was exactly what they started to do; they were only restrained by realizing that such action removed the very cause for which they began fighting. Yet one would search current American histories almost in vain to find a clear statement or even faint recognition of these perfectly well-authenticated facts.

All this is but preliminary to the kernel of the historic problem with which this book deals, and that is Reconstruction. The chorus of agreement concerning the attempt to reconstruct and organize the South after the Civil War and emancipation is overwhelming. There is scarce a child in the street that cannot tell you that the whole effort was a hideous mistake and an unfortunate incident, based on ignorance, revenge and the perverse determination to attempt the impossible; that the history of the United States from 1866 to 1876 is something of which the nation ought to be ashamed and which did more to retard and set back the American Negro than anything that has happened to him; while at the same time it grievously and wantonly wounded again a part of the nation already hurt to death.

True it is that the Northern historians writing just after the war had scant sympathy for the South, and wrote ruthlessly of "rebels" and "slave-drivers." They had at least the excuse of a war psychosis.

As a young labor leader, Will Herberg, writes: "The great traditions of this period and especially of Reconstruction are shamelessly repudiated by the official heirs of Stevens and Sumner. In the last quarter of a century hardly a single book has appeared consistently championing or sympathetically interpreting the great ideals of the crusade against slavery, whereas scores and hundreds have dropped from the presses in ignoble 'extenuation' of the North, in open apology for the Confederacy, in measureless abuse of the Radical figures of Reconstruction. The Reconstruction period as the logical culmination of decades of previous development, has borne the brunt of the reaction." [2]

First of all, we have James Ford Rhodes' history of the United States. Rhodes was trained not as an historian but as an Ohio business man. He had no broad formal education. When he had accumulated a fortune, he surrounded himself with a retinue of clerks and proceeded to manufacture a history of the United States by mass production. His method was simple. He gathered a vast number of authorities; he selected from these authorities those whose testimony supported his thesis, and he discarded the others. The majority report of the great Ku Klux investigation, for instance, he laid aside in favor of the minority report, simply because the latter supported his sincere belief. In the report and testimony of the Reconstruction Committee of Fifteen, he did practically the same thing.

Above all, he begins his inquiry convinced, without admitting any necessity of investigation, that Negroes are an inferior race:

"No large policy in our country has ever been so conspicuous a failure as that of forcing universal Negro suffrage upon the South. The Negroes who simply acted out their nature, were not to blame. How indeed could they acquire political honesty? What idea could barbarism thrust into slavery obtain of the rights of property? . . .

"From the Republican policy came no real good to the Negroes. Most of them developed no political capacity, and the few who raised themselves above the mass, did not reach a high order of intelligence." [3]

Rhodes was primarily the historian of property; of economic history and the labor movement, he knew nothing; of democratic government, he was contemptuous. He was trained to make profits. He used his profits to write history. He speaks again and again of the rulership of "intelligence and property" and he makes a plea that intelligent use of the ballot for the benefit of property is the only real foundation of democracy.

The real frontal attack on Reconstruction, as interpreted by the leaders of national thought in 1870 and for some time thereafter, came from the universities and particularly from Columbia and Johns Hopkins.

The movement began with Columbia University and with the advent of John W. Burgess of Tennessee and William A. Dunning of New Jersey as professors of political science and history.

Burgess was an ex-Confederate soldier who started to a little Southern college with a box of books, a box of tallow candles and a Negro boy; and his attitude toward the Negro race in after years was subtly colored by this early conception of Negroes as essentially property like books and candles. Dunning was a kindly and impressive professor who was deeply influenced by a growing group of young Southern students and began with them to re-write the history of the nation from 1860 to 1880, in more or less conscious opposition to the classic interpretations of New England.

Burgess was frank and determined in his anti-Negro thought. He expounded his theory of Nordic supremacy which colored all his political theories:

"The claim that there is nothing in the color of the skin from the point of view of political ethics is a great sophism. A black skin means membership in a race of men which has never of itself succeeded in subjecting passion to reason, has never, therefore, created any civilization of any kind. To put such a race of men in possession of a 'state' government in a system of federal government is to trust them with the development of political and legal civilization upon the most important subjects of human life, and to do this in communities with a large white population is simply to establish barbarism in power over civilization."

Burgess is a Tory and open apostle of reaction. He tells us that the nation now believes "that it is the white man's mission, his duty and his right, to hold the reins of political power in his own hands for the civilization of the world and the welfare of mankind." [4]

For this reason America is following "the European idea of the duty of civilized races to impose their political sovereignty upon civilized, or half civilized, or not fully civilized, races anywhere and everywhere in the world." [5]

He complacently believes that "There is something natural in the subordination of an inferior race to a superior race, even to the point of the enslavement of the inferior race, but there is nothing natural in the opposite." [6] He therefore denominates Reconstruction as the rule "of the uncivilized Negroes over the whites of the South." [7] This has been the teaching of one of our greatest universities for nearly fifty years.

Dunning was less dogmatic as a writer, and his own statements are often judicious. But even Dunning can declare that "all the forces [in the South] that made for civilization were dominated by a mass of barbarous freedmen"; and that "the antithesis and antipathy of race and color were crucial and ineradicable." [7a] The work of most of the students whom he taught and encouraged has been one-sided and partisan to the last degree. Johns Hopkins University has issued a series of studies similar to Columbia's; Southern teachers have been welcomed to many Northern universities, where often Negro students have been systematically discouraged, and thus a nation-wide university attitude has arisen by which propaganda against the Negro has been carried on unquestioned.

The Columbia school of historians and social investigators have issued between 1895 and the present time sixteen studies of Reconstruction in the Southern States, all based on the same thesis and all done according to the same method: first, endless sympathy with the white South; second, ridicule, contempt or silence for the Negro; third, a judicial attitude towards the North, which concludes that the North under great misapprehension did a grievous wrong, but eventually saw its mistake and retreated.

These studies vary, of course, in their methods. Dunning's own work is usually silent so far as the Negro is concerned. Burgess is more than fair in law but reactionary in matters of race and property, regarding the treatment of a Negro as a man as nothing less than a crime, and admitting that "the mainstay of property is the courts."

In the books on Reconstruction written by graduates of these universities and others, the studies of Texas, North Carolina, Florida, Virginia and Louisiana are thoroughly bad, giving no complete picture of what happened during Reconstruction, written for the most part by men and women without broad historical or social background, and all designed not to seek the truth but to prove a thesis. Hamilton reaches the climax of this school when he characterizes the black codes, which even Burgess condemned, as "not only . . . on the whole reasonable, temperate and kindly, but, in the main, necessary." [8]

Thompson's "Georgia" is another case in point. It seeks to be fair, but silly stories about Negroes indicating utter lack of even common sense are included, and every noble sentiment from white people. When two Negro workers, William and Jim, put a straightforward advertisement in a local paper, the author says that it was "evidently written by a white friend." There is not the slightest historical evidence to prove this, and there were plenty of educated Negroes in Augusta at the time who might have written this. Lonn's "Louisiana" puts Sheridan's words in Sherman's mouth to prove a petty point.

There are certain of these studies which, though influenced by the same general attitude, nevertheless have more of scientific poise and cultural background. Garner's "Reconstruction in Mississippi" conceives the Negro as an integral part of the scene and treats him as a human being. With this should be bracketed the recent study of "Reconstruction in South Carolina" by Simkins and Woody. This is not as fair as Garner's, but in the midst of conventional judgment and conclusion, and reproductions of all available caricatures of Negroes, it does not hesitate to give a fair account of the Negroes and of some of their work. It gives the impression of combining in one book two antagonistic points of view, but in the clash much truth emerges.

Ficklen's "Louisiana" and the works of Fleming are anti-Negro in spirit, but, nevertheless, they have a certain fairness and sense of historic honesty. Fleming's "Documentary History of Reconstruction" is done by a man who has a thesis to support, and his selection of documents supports the thesis. His study of Alabama is pure propaganda.

Next come a number of books which are openly and blatantly propaganda, like Herbert's "Solid South," and the books by Pike and Reynolds on South Carolina, the works by Pollard and Carpenter, and especially those by Ulrich Phillips. One of the latest and most popular of this series is "The Tragic Era" by Claude Bowers, which is an excellent and readable piece of current newspaper reporting, absolutely devoid of historical judgment or sociological knowledge. It is a classic example of historical propaganda of the cheaper sort.

We have books like Milton's "Age of Hate" and Winston's "Andrew Johnson" which attempt to re-write the character of Andrew Johnson. They certainly add to our knowledge of the man and our sympathy for his weakness. But they cannot, for students, change the calm testimony of unshaken historical facts. Fuess' "Carl Schurz" paints the picture of this fine liberal, and yet goes out of its way to show that he was quite wrong in what he said he saw in the South.

The chief witness in Reconstruction, the emancipated slave himself, has been almost barred from court. His written Reconstruction record has been largely destroyed and nearly always neglected. Only three or four states have preserved the debates in the Reconstruction conventions; there are few biographies of black leaders. The Negro is refused a hearing because he was poor and ignorant. It is therefore assumed that all Negroes in Reconstruction were ignorant and silly and that therefore a history of Reconstruction in any state can quite ignore him. The result is that most unfair caricatures of Negroes have been carefully preserved; but serious speeches, successful administration and upright character are almost universally ignored and forgotten. Wherever a black head rises to historic view, it is promptly slain by an adjective—"shrewd," "notorious," "cunning"—or pilloried by a sneer; or put out of view by some quite unproven charge of bad moral character. In other words, every effort has been made to treat the Negro's part in Reconstruction with silence and contempt.

When recently a student tried to write on education in Florida, he found that the official records of the excellent administration of the colored Superintendent of Education, Gibbs, who virtually established the Florida public school, had been destroyed. Alabama has tried to obliterate all printed records of Reconstruction.

Especially noticeable is the fact that little attempt has been made to trace carefully the rise and economic development of the poor whites and their relation to the planters and to Negro labor after the war. There were five million or more non-slaveholding whites in the South in 1860 and less than two million in the families of all slaveholders. Yet one might almost gather from contemporary history that the five million left no history and had no descendants. The extraordinary history of the rise and triumph of the poor whites has been largely neglected, even by Southern white students.[9]

The whole development of Reconstruction was primarily an economic development, but no economic history or proper material for it has been written. It has been regarded as a purely political matter, and of politics most naturally divorced from industry.[10]

All this is reflected in the textbooks of the day and in the encyclopedias, until we have got to the place where we cannot use our experiences during and after the Civil War for the uplift and enlightenment of mankind. We have spoiled and misconceived the position of the historian. If we are going, in the future, not simply with regard to this one question, but with regard to all social problems, to be able to use human experience for the guidance of mankind, we have got clearly to distinguish between fact and desire.

In the first place, somebody in each era must make clear the facts with utter disregard to his own wish and desire and belief. What we have got to know, so far as possible, are the things that actually happened in the world. Then with that much clear and open to every reader, the philosopher and prophet has a chance to interpret these facts; but the historian has no right, posing as scientist, to conceal or distort facts; and until we distinguish between these two functions of the chronicler of human action, we are going to render it easy for a muddled world out of sheer ignorance to make the same mistake ten times over.

One is astonished in the study of history at the recurrence of the idea that evil must be forgotten, distorted, skimmed over. We must not remember that Daniel Webster got drunk but only remember that he was a splendid constitutional lawyer. We must forget that George Washington was a slave owner, or that Thomas Jefferson had mulatto children, or that Alexander Hamilton had Negro blood, and simply remember the things we regard as creditable and inspiring. The difficulty, of course, with this philosophy is that history loses its value as an incentive and example; it paints perfect men and noble nations, but it does not tell the truth.

No one reading the history of the United States during 1850-1860 can have the slightest doubt left in his mind that Negro slavery was the cause of the Civil War, and yet during and since we learn that a great nation murdered thousands and destroyed millions on account of abstract doctrines concerning the nature of the Federal Union. Since the attitude of the nation concerning state rights has been revolutionized by the development of the central government since the war, the whole argument becomes an astonishing *reductio ad absurdum*, leaving us apparently with no cause for the Civil War except the recent reiteration of statements which make the great public men on one side narrow, hypocritical fanatics and liars, while the leaders on the other side were extraordinary and unexampled for their beauty, unselfishness and fairness.

Not a single great leader of the nation during the Civil War and Reconstruction has escaped attack and libel. The magnificent figures of Charles Sumner and Thaddeus Stevens have been besmirched almost beyond recognition. We have been cajoling and flattering the South and slurring the North, because the South is determined to re-write the history of slavery and the North is not interested in history but in wealth.

This, then, is the book basis upon which today we judge Reconstruction. In order to paint the South as a martyr to inescapable fate, to make the North the magnanimous emancipator, and to ridicule the Negro as the impossible joke in the whole development, we have in fifty years, by libel, innuendo and silence, so completely misstated and obliterated the history of the Negro in America and his relation to its work and government that today it is almost unknown. This may be fine romance, but it is not science. It may be inspiring, but it is certainly not the truth. And beyond this it is dangerous. It is not only part foundation of our present lawlessness and loss of democratic ideals; it has, more than that, led the world to embrace and worship the color bar as social salvation and it is helping to range mankind in ranks of mutual hatred and contempt, at the summons of a cheap and false myth.

Nearly all recent books on Reconstruction agree with each other in discarding the government reports and substituting selected diaries, letters, and gossip. Yet it happens that the government records are an historic source of wide and unrivaled authenticity. There is the report of the select Committee of Fifteen, which delved painstakingly into the situation all over the South and called all kinds and conditions of men to testify; there are the report of Carl Schurz and the twelve volumes of reports made on the Ku Klux conspiracy; and above all, the *Congressional Globe.* None who has not read page by page the *Congressional Globe,* especially the sessions of the 39th Congress, can possibly have any idea of what the problems of Reconstruction facing the United States were in 1865-1866. Then there were the reports of the Freedmen's Bureau and the executive and other documentary reports of government officials, especially in the war and treasury departments, which give the historian the only groundwork upon which he can build a real and truthful picture. There are certain historians who have not tried deliberately to falsify the picture: Southern whites like Frances Butler Leigh and Susan Smedes; Northern historians, like McPherson, Oberholtzer, and Nicolay and Hay. There are foreign travelers like Sir George Campbell, Georges Clemenceau and Robert Somers. There are the personal reminiscences of Augustus Beard, George Julian, George F. Hoar, Carl Schurz and John Sherman. There are the invaluable work of Edward McPherson and the more recent studies by Paul Haworth, A. A. Taylor, and Charles Wesley. Beale simply does not take Negroes into account in the critical year of 1866.

Certain monographs deserve all praise, like those of Hendricks and Pierce. The work of Flack is prejudiced but built on study. The defense of the carpetbag régime by Tourgée and Allen, Powell Clayton, Holden and Warmoth are worthy antidotes to the certain writers.

The lives of Stevens and Sumner are revealing even when slightly apologetic because of the Negro; while Andrew Johnson is beginning to suffer from writers who are trying to prove how seldom he got drunk, and think that important.

It will be noted that for my authority in this work I have depended very largely upon secondary material; upon state histories of Reconstruction, written in the main by those who were convinced before they began to write that the Negro was incapable of government, or of becoming a constituent part of a civilized state. The fairest of these histories have not tried to conceal facts; in other cases, the black man has been largely ignored; while in still others, he has been traduced and ridiculed. If I had had time and money and opportunity to go back to the original sources in all cases, there can be no doubt that the weight of this work would have been vastly strengthened, and as I firmly believe, the case of the Negro more convincingly set forth.

Various volumes of papers in the great libraries like the Johnson papers in the Library of Congress, the Sumner manuscripts at Harvard, the Schurz correspondence, the Wells papers, the Chase papers, the Fessenden and Greeley collections, the McCulloch, McPherson, Sherman, Stevens and Trumbull papers, all must have much of great interest to the historians of the American Negro. I have not had time nor opportunity to examine these, and most of those who have examined them had little interest in black folk.

Negroes have done some excellent work on their own history and defense. It suffers of course from natural partisanship and a desire to prove a case in the face of a chorus of unfair attacks. Its best work also suffers from the fact that Negroes with difficulty reach an audience. But this is also true of such white writers as Skaggs and Bancroft who could not get first-class publishers because they were saying something that the nation did not like.

The Negro historians began with autobiographies and reminiscences. The older historians were George W. Williams and Joseph T. Wilson; the new school of historians is led by Carter G. Woodson; and I have been greatly helped by the unpublished theses of four of the youngest Negro students. It is most unfortunate that while many young white Southerners can get funds to attack and ridicule the Negro and his friends, it is almost impossible for first-class Negro students to get a chance for research or to get finished work in print.

I write then in a field devastated by passion and belief. Naturally, as a Negro, I cannot do this writing without believing in the essential humanity of Negroes, in their ability to be educated, to do the work of the modern world, to take their place as equal citizens with others. I cannot for a moment subscribe to that bizarre doctrine of race that makes most men inferior to the few. But, too, as a student of science, I want to be fair, objective and judicial; to let no searing of the memory by intolerable insult and cruelty make me fail to sympathize with human frailties and contradiction, in the eternal paradox of good and evil. But armed and warned by all this, and fortified by long study of the facts, I stand at the end of this writing, literally aghast at what American historians have done to this field.

What is the object of writing the history of Reconstruction? Is it to wipe out the disgrace of a people which fought to make slaves of Negroes? Is it to show that the North had higher motives than freeing black men? Is it to prove that Negroes were black angels? No, it is simply to establish the Truth, on which Right in the future may be built. We shall never have a science of history until we have in our colleges men who regard the truth as more important than the defense of the white race, and who will not deliberately encourage students to gather thesis material in order to support a prejudice or buttress a lie.

Three-fourths of the testimony against the Negro in Reconstruction is on the unsupported evidence of men who hated and despised Negroes and regarded it as loyalty to blood, patriotism to country, and filial tribute to the fathers to lie, steal or kill in order to discredit these black folk. This may be a natural result when a people have been humbled and impoverished and degraded in their own life; but what is inconceivable is that another generation and another group should regard this testimony as scientific truth, when it is contradicted by logic and by fact. This chapter, therefore, which in logic should be a survey of books and sources, becomes of sheer necessity an arraignment of American historians and an indictment of their ideals. With a determination unparalleled in science, the mass of American writers have started out so to distort the facts of the greatest critical period of American history as to prove right wrong and wrong right. I am not familiar enough with the vast field of human history to pronounce on the relative guilt of these and historians of other times and fields; but I do say that if the history of the past has been written in the same fashion, it is useless as science and misleading as ethics. It simply shows that with sufficient general agreement and determination among the dominant classes, the truth of history may be utterly distorted and contradicted and changed to any convenient fairy tale that the masters of men wish.

I cannot believe that any unbiased mind, with an ideal of truth and of scientific judgment, can read the plain, authentic facts of our history, during 1860-1880, and come to conclusions essentially different from mine; and yet I stand virtually alone in this interpretation. So much so that the very cogency of my facts would make me hesitate, did I not seem to see plain reasons. Subtract from Burgess his belief that only white people can rule, and he is in essential agreement with me. Remember that Rhodes was an uneducated money-maker who hired clerks to find the facts which he needed to support his thesis, and one is convinced that the same labor and expense could easily produce quite opposite results.

One fact and one alone explains the attitude of most recent writers toward Reconstruction; they cannot conceive Negroes as men; in their minds the word "Negro" connotes "inferiority" and "stupidity" lightened only by unreasoning gayety and humor. Suppose the slaves of 1860 had been white folk. Stevens would have been a great statesman, Sumner a great democrat, and Schurz a keen prophet, in a mighty revolution of rising humanity. Ignorance and poverty would easily have been explained by history, and the demand for land and the franchise would have been justified as the birthright of natural freemen.

But Burgess was a slaveholder, Dunning a Copperhead and Rhodes an exploiter of wage labor. Not one of them apparently ever met an educated Negro of force and ability. Around such impressive thinkers gathered the young post-war students from the South. They had been born and reared in the bitterest period of Southern race hatred, fear and contempt. Their instinctive reactions were confirmed and encouraged in the best of American universities. Their scholarship, when it regarded black men, became deaf, dumb and blind. The clearest evidence of Negro ability, work, honesty, patience, learning and efficiency became distorted into cunning, brute toil, shrewd evasion, cowardice and imitation—a stupid effort to transcend nature's law.

For those seven mystic years between Johnson's "swing 'round the circle" and the panic of 1873, a majority of thinking Americans in the North believed in the equal manhood of black folk. They acted accordingly with a clear-cut decisiveness and thorough logic, utterly incomprehensible to a day like ours which does not share this human faith; and to Southern whites this period can only be explained by deliberate vengeance and hate.

The panic of 1873 brought sudden disillusion in business enterprise, economic organization, religious belief and political standards. A flood of appeal from the white South reënforced this reaction—appeal with no longer the arrogant bluster of slave oligarchy, but the simple moving annals of the plight of a conquered people. The resulting emotional and intellectual rebound of the nation made it nearly inconceivable in 1876 that ten years earlier most men had believed in human equality.

Assuming, therefore, as axiomatic the endless inferiority of the Negro race, these newer historians, mostly Southerners, some Northerners who deeply sympathized with the South, misinterpreted, distorted, even deliberately ignored any fact that challenged or contradicted this assumption. If the Negro was admittedly sub-human, what need to waste time delving into his Reconstruction history? Consequently historians of Reconstruction with a few exceptions ignore the Negro as completely as possible, leaving the reader wondering why an element apparently so insignificant filled the whole Southern picture at the time. The only real excuse for this attitude is loyalty to a lost cause, reverence for brave fathers and suffering mothers and sisters, and fidelity to the ideals of a clan and class. But in propaganda against the Negro since emancipation in this land, we face one of the most stupendous efforts the world ever saw to discredit human beings, an effort involving universities, history, science, social life and religion.

The most magnificent drama in the last thousand years of human history is the transportation of ten million human beings out of the dark beauty of their mother continent into the new-found Eldorado of the West. They descended into Hell; and in the third century they arose from the dead, in the finest effort to achieve democracy for the working millions which this world had ever seen. It was a tragedy that beggared the Greek; it was an upheaval of humanity like the Reformation and the French Revolution. Yet we are blind and led by the blind. We discern in it no part of our labor movement; no part of our industrial triumph; no part of our religious experience. Before the dumb eyes of ten generations of ten million children, it is made mockery of and spit upon; a degradation of the eternal mother; a sneer at human effort; with aspiration and art deliberately and elaborately distorted. And why? Because in a day when the human mind aspired to a science of human action, a history and psychology of the mighty effort of the mightiest century, we fell under the leadership of those who would compromise with truth in the past in order to make peace in the present and guide policy in the future.

One reads the truer deeper facts of Reconstruction with a great despair. It is at once so simple and human, and yet so futile. There is no villain, no idiot, no saint. There are just men; men who crave ease and power, men who know want and hunger, men who have crawled. They all dream and strive with ecstasy of fear and strain of effort, balked of hope and hate. Yet the rich world is wide enough for all, wants all, needs all. So slight a gesture, a word, might set the strife in order, not with full content, but with growing dawn of fulfillment. Instead roars the crash of hell; and after its whirlwind a teacher sits in academic halls, learned in the tradition of its elms and its elders. He looks into the upturned face of youth and in him youth sees the gowned shape of wisdom and hears the voice of God. Cynically he sneers at "chinks" and "niggers." He says that the nation "has changed its views in regard to the political relation of races and has at last virtually accepted the ideas of the South upon that subject. The white men of the South need now have no further fear that the Republican party, or Republican Administrations, will ever again give themselves over to the vain imagination of the political equality of man." [11]

Immediately in Africa, a black back runs red with the blood of the lash; in India, a brown girl is raped; in China, a coolie starves; in Alabama, seven darkies are more than lynched; while in London, the white limbs of a prostitute are hung with jewels and silk. Flames of jealous murder sweep the earth, while brains of little children smear the hills.

This is education in the Nineteen Hundred and Thirty-fifth year of the Christ; this is modern and exact social science; this is the university course in "History 12" set down by the Senatus academicus; ad quos hae literae pervenerint: Salutem in Domino, sempeternam!

In Babylon, dark Babylon
  Who take the wage of Shame?
The scribe and singer, one by one,
  That toil for gold and fame.
They grovel to their masters' mood;
  The blood upon the pen
Assigns their souls to servitude—
  Yea! and the souls of men.

GEORGE STERLING

"In the Market Place" from *Selected Poems.* Used by permission of Harry Robertson, Redwood City, California.

1. "Racial Attitudes in American History Textbooks," *Journal of Negro History*, XIX, p. 257.
1a. W. E. Woodward, *Meet General Grant*, p. 372.
2. Will Herberg, *The Heritage of the Civil War*, p. 3.
3. Rhodes, *History of the United States*, VII, pp. 232-233.
4. Burgess, *Reconstruction and the Constitution*, pp. viii, ix.
5. Burgess, *Reconstruction and the Constitution*, p. 218.
6. Burgess, *Reconstruction and the Constitution*, pp. 244-245.
7. Burgess, *Reconstruction and the Constitution*, p. 218.
7a. Dunning, *Reconstruction, Political and Economic*, pp. 212, 213.
8. Hamilton, "Southern Legislation in Respect to Freedmen" in *Studies in Southern History and Politics*, p. 156.
9. Interesting exceptions are Moore's and Ambler's monographs.
10. *The Economic History of the South* by E. Q. Hawk is merely a compilation of census reports and conventionalities.
11. Burgess, *Reconstruction and the Constitution*, p. 298.

BIBLIOGRAPHY

STANDARD—ANTI-NEGRO

(These authors believe the Negro to be sub-human and congenitally unfitted for citizenship and the suffrage.)

Burgess, John W., Reconstruction and the Constitution, 1866-1876.

Coulter, E. Merton, Civil War and Reconstruction in Kentucky.

Davis, William W., The Civil War and Reconstruction in Florida.

Dunning, William A., Reconstruction, Political and Economic.

Eckenrode, F. Hamilton, Political History of Virginia During Reconstruction.

Fertig, James Walter, The Secession and Reconstruction of Tennessee.

Ficklen, John R., History of Reconstruction in Louisiana.

Fleming, Walter F., Civil War and Reconstruction in Alabama.

——, Documentary History of Reconstruction, 1906, 1907.

Hamilton, Joseph G. de R., Reconstruction in North Carolina.

Hollis, John Porter, The Early Period of Reconstruction in South Carolina.

Lonn, Ella, Reconstruction in Louisiana after 1868.

Ramsdell, Charles W., Reconstruction in Texas.

Rhodes, James F., History of United States from the Compromise of 1850.

Scott, Eben G., Reconstruction During the Civil War.

Staples, Thomas S., Reconstruction in Arkansas.

Studies in Southern History and Politics. Inscribed to William Archibald Dunning.

    Carpet-Baggers in the United States Senate. By C. Mildred Thompson.

    The Literary Movement for Secession. By Ulrich B. Phillips.

    Negro Suffrage in the South. By W. Roy Smith.

    Some Phases of Educational History in the South Since 1865. By William K. Boyd.

    Southern Legislation in Respect to Freedmen, 1865-1866. By J. G. de Roulhac Hamilton.

    The Federal Enforcement Acts. By William Watson Davis.

    The New South, Economic and Social. By Holland Thompson.

    Grant's Southern Policy. By Edwin C. Woolley.

Taylor, Richard, Destruction and Reconstruction.

Thompson, Clara M., Reconstruction in Georgia, Economic, Social, Political, 1805-1872.

Wooley, Edwin C., The Reconstruction of Georgia.

PROPAGANDA

(These authors select and use facts and opinions in order to prove that the South was right in Reconstruction, the North vengeful or deceived, and the Negro stupid.)

Avery, Mrs. Myrta, Dixie After the War.
Bowers, G. Claude, Tragic Era; The Revolution After Lincoln.
Carpenter, Jesse T., The South as a Conscious Minority.
Craven, Avery, Edmund Ruffin, Southerner.
Herbert, Hilary A., The Abolition Crusade and Its Consequences. Four Periods of American History.
——, Why the Solid South, or Reconstruction and Its Results.
Morton, Richard L., The Negro in Virginia Politics, 1865-1902.
Phillips, Ulrich Bonnell, American Negro Slavery.
Pike, James, The Prostrate State. South Carolina Under Negro Government.
Pollard, Edward A., The Lost Cause Regained.
Reynolds, John S., Reconstruction in South Carolina, 1865-1877.
Van Evrie, J. H., Negroes and Negro Slavery, New York, 1863.

HISTORIANS

(Fair to Indifferent on the Negro.)

Beale, H. K., The Critical Year.
Blaine, James G., Twenty Years of Congress.
Brown, Junius H., Four Years in Secessia, 1865.
Cable, George W., The Silent South, 1885.
Campbell, Sir George, White and Black. The Outcome of a Visit to the United States, London, 1879.
Clemenceau, Georges, History of American Reconstruction. Letters to Le Temps, New York, 1928.
Commons, John R. and Associates, A Documentary History of American Industrial Society.
——, History of Labour in the United States.
Haworth, Paul L., Reconstruction and Union, 1865-1912.
Jordan and Pratt, Europe and the American Civil War.
Leigh, Frances Butler, Ten Years on a Georgia Plantation.
McClure, Colonel Alexander K., Recollections of a Half Century.
McPherson, Edward, A Political History of the United States During Reconstruction.
Nicolay, John G., and Hay, John, Abraham Lincoln.
Nordhoff, Charles, The Cotton States in the Spring and Summer of 1875.
Oberholtzer, Ellis Parson, A History of the United States Since the Civil War.
Olmsted, Frederick L., A Journey in the Seaboard Slave States, 1856.
Owen, Robert D., Political Results from Varioloid, Atlantic Monthly, XXXV, 1875.

The Results of Emancipation in the United States of America by a Committee of the American Freedmen's Union Commission.

Schlüter, Herman, Lincoln, Labor and Slavery, 1913.

Schurz, Carl, Reminiscences.

Sherman, John, Recollections.

Simkins, Francis B., and Woody, Robert H., South Carolina During Reconstruction.

Smedes, Susan Dabney, Memoirs of a Southern Planter.

Somers, Robert, The Southern States Since the War.

HISTORIANS

(These historians have studied the history of Negroes and write sympathetically about them.)

Bancroft, Frederic, Slave-Trading in the Old South.

Beard, Augustus F., A Crusade of Brotherhood.

Birmingham, T. M. C., Representative Government.

Bothune, Elizabeth H., First Days Among the Contrabands.

Brewster, James, Sketches of Southern Mystery, Treason and Murder.

Eaton, John, Grant, Lincoln and the Freedman, New York.

Lewinson, Paul, Race, Class and Party.

Reid, Whitelaw, After the War: A Southern Tour, May 1, 1865 to May 1, 1866.

Russell, Charles Edward, Blaine of Maine.

Skaggs, W. H., Southern Oligarchy.

Stewart, Lucy Shelton, The Reward of Patriotism.

Tinker, Edward L., Les Cenelles (In the *Colophon;* Sept., 1930).

Wilson, Henry, History of the Rise and Fall of the Slave Power in America.

MONOGRAPHS

(These authors seek the facts in certain narrow definite fields and in most cases do not ignore the truth as to Negroes.)

Ambler, G. H., Sectionalism in Virginia.

Ames, Herman V., Proposed Amendments to the Constitution of the United States During the First Century of Its History (In the Annual Report of the American Historical Association for the year, 1896).

Bancroft, Frederic A., A Sketch of the Negro in Politics, Especially in South Carolina and Mississippi, New York, 1885.

Banks, Enoch M., Economics of Land Tenure in Georgia.

Brooks, Robert P., The Agrarian Revolution in Georgia in 1865-1912.

Flack, Horace E., Adoption of the 14th Amendment.

Fleming, Walter F., Deportation and Colonization: An Attempted Solution of the Race Problem.

——, The Freedmen's Saving Bank.

Haworth, Paul Leland, The Hayes-Tilden Disputed Presidential Election.

Hickok, Charles T., The Negro in Ohio.
Kendrick, Benjamin Burks, The Journal of the Joint Committee of Fifteen on Reconstruction, 39th Congress, 1865-1867.
Knight, Edgar Wallace, The Influence of Reconstruction on Education in the South.
Moore, A. B., Conscription and Conflict in the Confederacy.
Pierce, Paul Skeels, The Freedmen's Bureau, a chapter in the history of Reconstruction.
Schlüter, Herman, Lincoln, Labor and Slavery.

ANSWERS

(These are the answers of certain carpetbaggers and scalawags to their traducers.)

Allen W., Governor Chamberlain's Administration in South Carolina. A chapter of Reconstruction in the Southern States.
Clayton, Powell, The Aftermath of the Civil War in Arkansas.
Holden, William Woods, 1818, 1892, Memoirs.
Tourgée, A. W., A Fool's Errand.
——, Bricks Without Straw.
Warmoth, Henry C., War, Politics and Reconstruction.

LIVES

(These are lives of leaders who took part in Reconstruction and whose acts and thoughts influenced Negro development.)

Callendar, Edward B., Thaddeus Stevens, Commoner.
Cox, Samuel S., Three Decades of Federal Legislation, 1855-1885.
Fuess, Claude Moore, Carl Schurz, Reformer.
Hall, Clifton R., Andrew Johnson, Military Governor of Tennessee.
Julian, George Washington, Political Recollections, 1840 to 1872.
Lawson, John, The Memoirs of W. W. Holden.
McCall, Samuel W., Thaddeus Stevens.
McClure, Colonel Alexander K., Recollections of a Half Century.
Nicolay, John G., and Hay, John, Abraham Lincoln.
Pierce, Edward L., Memoirs and Letters of Charles Sumner.
Schurz, Carl, The Reminiscences of Carl Schurz.
Seward, Frederick W., Story of the Life of William H. Seward.
Sherman, John, Recollections of 40 Years in the House, Senate and Cabinet.
Story, Moorfield, Charles Sumner.
Stovall, Pleasant A., Robert Toombs.
The Education of Henry Adams, An Autobiography.
The Trial of William W. Holden.
Winston, Robert Watson, Andrew Johnson, Plebeian and Patriot.

NEGRO HISTORIANS

(These are the standard works of Negro historians, some judicial, some eager and even bitter in defense.)

Cromwell, John W., The Negro in American History.

Delaney, Martin R., Life and Public Services of Sub-Assistant Commissioner Bureau Relief of Refugees, Freedmen and Abandoned Lands. By Frank A. Rollin.

Desdunes, R. L., Nos Hommes et Notre Histoire.

Du Bois, The Freedmen's Bureau, *Atlantic Monthly,* Vol. 87.

Emilio, Lois F., History of the Fifty-Fourth Regiment of Massachusetts Volunteer Infantry, 1863-1865.

Father Henson's Story of His Own Life, with an introduction by Mrs. H. B. Stowe.

Greene and Woodson, The Negro Wage Earner.

Gibbs, N. W., Shadow and Light.

Hill, J. J., A Sketch of the 29th Regiment of Connecticut Colored Troops.

Keckley, Elizabeth, Behind the Scenes.

Lynch, John Roy, Facts of Reconstruction.

——, Some Historical Errors of James Rhodes, Journal of Negro History, II.

Minutes of the Colored State Convention convened in the city of Indianapolis, 1865.

Mitchell, George W., The Question Before Congress.

Proceedings of the National Convention of Colored Men Held in the City of Syracuse, New York, October 4, 5, 6 and 7, 1864.

Shuften, John T., A Colored Man's Exposition of the Acts and Doings of the Radical Party, South, 1865-1876.

Slavery in the United States, A Narrative of the Life and Adventures of Charles Ball, a black man.

Taylor, Alrutheus A., The Negro in the Reconstruction of Virginia.

——, The Negro in South Carolina During Reconstruction.

The Journal of Negro History, 1916-1933, 17 volumes.

Wallace, John, Carpetbag Rule in Florida.

Wesley, Charles E., Negro Labor in the United States.

Williams, George Washington, History of the Negro Race in America from 1619 to 1880.

——, A History of the Negro Troops in the War of the Rebellion, 1861-1865.

Wilson, Joseph T., The Black Phalanx.

Woodson, Carter G., Negro Orators and Their Orations.

——, The Negro in Our History.

Wright, R. R., Negro Education in Georgia.

UNPUBLISHED THESES

(These are researches by young Negro scholars.)

Cade, John B., Out of the Mouths of Ex-slaves, Prairie View State, N. & I. College, 1932.

Christler, Ethel Maud, Participation of Negroes in the Government of Georgia, 1867-1870. Atlanta University, 1933.

Clement, Rufus B., History of Negro Education in North Carolina. Northwestern University, 1931.

Horne, Frank R., The Present Status of Negro Education in Certain of the Southern States, Particularly Georgia. University of Southern California.

Lanier, O'Hara R., The History of Negro Education of Florida. Leland Stanford Junior University.

Williams, Richard Thomas, A History of Public Education and Charitable Institutions in South Carolina During the Reconstruction Period. Atlanta University, 1933.

GOVERNMENT REPORTS

Alvord, J. W., Semi-Annual Reports on Schools for Freedmen (First to tenth) January, 1866-July, 1870. Made to the Commissioner of the United States Bureau of Refugees, Freedmen and Abandoned Lands (Washington, 1866-1870).

Annual Report of the Adjutant General, on the operations of the Freedmen's Branch of his office, for the year 1875-78, 6 volumes, Washington.

Annual Report of the United States Commissioner of Education, 1870-1880, Washington.

Ex. Doc. No. 2, First Session of the Thirty-ninth Congress, December 19, 1865.

Ku-Klux Conspiracy, Report of the Joint Select Committees to inquire into the condition of affairs in the late insurrectionary states, Vol. I of Ku-Klux Conspiracy. Senate Report, 42nd Cong., 2nd Sess., No. 41, Washington, 1872.

Ku-Klux Conspiracy, The testimony taken by the Joint Select Committee to inquire into the condition of affairs in the late insurrectionary states, Washington, 1872, 13 volumes.

Messages of the Presidents of the United States.

South Carolina in 1876. Testimony as to the denial of the elective Franchise in South Carolina at the elections of 1875 and 1876, 3 Vols., Senate Misc. Doc., No. 48, 44th Cong., 2nd Sess., Washington, 1877.

Reports of the Commissioner of the Bureau of Refugees, Freedmen and Abandoned Lands (Washington, 1865-1880).

Report of the Joint Committee on Reconstruction at the First Session of the Thirty-Ninth Congress, Washington, 1866.

Report of the Joint Investigating Committee of Public Frauds and Election of Hon. J. J. Patterson to the United States Senate made to the General Assembly of South Carolina at the regular session of 1877-1878, Columbia, 1878. Cited as Reports and Reconstructions, 1877-1878. Fraud Report.

Report of the Select Committee to Investigate the Freedmen's Savings and Trust Company, United States Senate, Washington, 1880.

The Congressional Globe, 1865-1872.

Reports of Committee of the House of Representatives, 42nd Congress, 2nd Session, Volume 2, No. 22.

OTHER REPORTS

American (Called from 1876 Appleton's) Annual Cyclopedia.

Annual Reports of the American Baptist Home Mission Society.

Annual Reports of the Freedman's Aid Society of the Methodist Episcopal Church, Cincinnati, Ohio, 1868-1879.

Annual Reports of the American Missionary Association and the Proceedings at the Annual Meetings, New York, 1864-1891.

Reports of the Freedmen's Union Commission.

ALABAMA—Alabama Constitutional Convention, 1867, Montgomery, 1868.

ARKANSAS—Arkansas Constitutional Convention, Little Rock, 1868.

FLORIDA—Florida Constitutional Convention, Tallahassee, 1868.

GEORGIA—Georgia Constitutional Convention, 1867-1868, Augusta, 1868.

MISSISSIPPI—Mississippi Constitutional Convention, 1868, Jackson, 1871.

NORTH CAROLINA—North Carolina Constitutional Convention, 1868, Raleigh, 1868.

SOUTH CAROLINA—South Carolina Constitutional Convention, 1868, Charleston, 1868.

TEXAS—Texas Reconstruction Convention Journal, Austin, 1870.

VIRGINIA—Virginia Constitutional Convention Debates, 1867-1868, Richmond, 1868.

INDEX

WILLIAM EDWARD BURGHARDT DU BOIS was born in Great Barrington, Massachusetts, on February 23, 1868. He received a bachelor's degree from Fisk University in 1888, another from Harvard University in 1890, and a Ph.D. from Harvard in 1895. Dr. Du Bois also studied at the University of Berlin. He held honorary degrees from Howard (LL.D., 1930), Atlanta (LL.D., 1938), Fisk (Litt.D., 1938), and Wilberforce (L.H.D., 1940) universities. Dr. Du Bois taught Greek and Latin at Wilberforce from 1894 to 1896 and at the University of Pennsylvania in 1896 and 1897. From 1897 to 1910 he was professor of economics and history at Atlanta University.

One of the founders of the National Association for the Advancement of Colored People, he was a member of its staff as director of publications and editor of *Crisis* from 1910 to 1932. In 1933, Dr. Du Bois returned to Atlanta as chairman of the University's sociology department, where he remained until 1944, when he rejoined the NAACP as head of its special research department, a position he held until 1948. In succeeding years, he was vice chairman of the Council on African Affairs and chairman of the Peace Information Bureau. At various times during his life, Dr. Du Bois was also editor of *Atlanta University Studies* and *Phylon Quarterly Review*, founder and organizer of numerous Pan-African congresses, and editor-in-chief of the *Encyclopedia of the Negro*. In 1961, he and his wife, Shirley Graham, emigrated to Ghana, where he served as editor-in-chief of *Encyclopedia Africana*.

Dr. Du Bois was the author of numerous books, among which are *The Suppression of the Slave Trade* (1896), *The Philadelphia Negro* (1899), *The Souls of Black Folk* (1903), *John Brown* (1909), *Quest of the Silver Fleece* (1911), *The Negro* (1915), *Darkwater* (1920), *The Gift of Black Folk* (1924), *Dark Princess* (1928), *Black Folk: Then and Now* (1939), *Dusk of Dawn* (1940), *Color and Democracy* (1945), *The World and Africa* (1947), *In Battle for Peace* (1952), and the trilogy, *The Black Flame* (1957-1961).

Dr. Du Bois died in Accra, Ghana, on August 27, 1963, at the age of ninety-five.